Daniel B. Grimes
1255 N. 53rd Street
Philadelphia, PA  19131

S0-FGA-049

# Public Policymaking in America

## Difficult Choices, Limited Solutions

Carl P. Chelf
*Western Kentucky University*

**Scott, Foresman and Company**
Glenview, Illinois
Dallas, TX   Oakland, NJ   Palo Alto, CA   Tucker, GA   London, England

Library of Congress Cataloging in Publication Data

Chelf, Carl P.
   Public policymaking in America.

  1. Unites States—Politics and government—1945—
2. Policy sciences.  I. Title.
JK274.C48    320.973    80-21510
ISBN 0-673-16276-1

Copyright © 1981 Scott, Foresman and Company.
All Rights Reserved.
Printed in the United States of America.

ISBN 0-673-16276-1

2 3 4 5 6-HAD-86 85 84 83 82 81

Book design: Mike Yazzolino

# Contents

Introduction vi

**Part One** The Setting 1

**Chapter 1** Some Theories and Concepts for the Study of Policymaking 2

    Who Makes Policy 5
    How Policy Is Made 9
    Types of Policies 13
    Tools and Techniques of Policy 15
    Conclusion / Points to Ponder / Notes / Suggestions for Further Reading 18

**Chapter 2** The Policymaking Environment 20

    Constitutional/Structural Factors 22
    Official Participants 26
    Unofficial Participants 37
    Social and Cultural Factors 43
    Conclusion / Points to Ponder / Notes / Suggestions for Further Reading 45

**Part Two** Management Policy 47

**Chapter 3** Government as Budget Maker 50

    The Executive Budget 54
    The Appropriations Process 59
    Budget Execution and Oversight 68
    Budget Reform 73
    Conclusion / Points to Ponder / Notes / Suggestions for Further Reading 75

iv   *Contents*

**Chapter 4**   Government as Fiscal Manager   79
    Monetary Policy   86
    Fiscal Policy   88
    Conclusion / Points to Ponder / Notes / Suggestions for Further Reading   97

**Chapter 5**   The Making of U.S. Foreign Policy   102
    The Machinery of Foreign Policymaking   105
    The Politics of Foreign Policymaking   119
    Current Issues   124
    Conclusion/Points to Ponder/Notes/Suggestions for Further Reading   128

**Chapter 6**   Providing for the Common Defense   131
    The Defense Policy Machinery   132
    Defense Policy Problems   138
    The Issues of Defense Policymaking   143
    Budgeting for Defense   150
    Arms Sales   154
    Conclusion/Points to Ponder/Notes/Suggestions for Further Reading   155

## *Part Three*   Subsidy Policy

**Chapter 7**   Spanning the Continent:
                   National Transportation Policy   163
    Early Federal Role   165
    The Politics of Transport Policy   180
    Conclusion/Points to Ponder/Notes/Suggestions for Further Reading   184

**Chapter 8**   To Educate a Nation: What Federal Role?   187
    Early Federal Aid Efforts   188
    Obstacles to Federal Aid   191
    Passage of General Aid Legislation   201
    The Politics of Education   203
    Conclusion/Points to Ponder/Notes/Suggestions for Further Reading   207

**Chapter 9**   Parity or Free Market? Federal Agricultural Policy   212
    Early Federal Involvement   213
    New Directions   216
    Other Federal Farm Programs   225
    The Politics of Agricultural Policy   227
    Conclusion/Points to Ponder/Notes/Suggestions for Further Reading   231

## *Part Four*   Regulatory Policy   239

**Chapter 10**   Competition, Consumerism, Co-optation?
                    Government and Business   250
    Early Federal Regulation   252
    The Politics of Business Regulation   258

Conflicting Views on Regulation  261
  Deregulation  263
  The Urge to Merge  265
  New Directions in Regulation  269
  Conclusion/Points to Ponder/Notes/Suggestions for Further Reading  271

**Chapter 11**  Government and Labor-Management Policy  275
  Early Federal Action  278
  The Politics of Labor-Management Policy  287
  Conclusion/Points to Ponder/Notes/Suggestions for Further Reading  290

**Chapter 12**  Governing the Environment and Natural Resources  293
  Land Management and Preservation  296
  Managing Water Resources  299
  The Management and Regulation of Energy Resources  303
  Regulating the Environment  315
  Conclusion/Points to Ponder/Notes/Suggestions for Further Reading  322

## *Part Five*  Redistributive Policy  327

**Chapter 13**  Equal Rights for All:
             Affirmative Action or Reverse Discrimination?  330
  Black Civil Rights  331
  Desegregating the Schools  339
  Economic and Political Discrimination  348
  Changing Trends in Civil Rights  351
  Conclusion/Points to Ponder/Notes/Suggestions for Further Reading  355

**Chapter 14**  Government and Human Services  360
  Social Security  362
  Medical and Health Programs  368
  Hunger and Nutrition  373
  Poverty  374
  Reforming the Welfare System  378
  Conclusion/Points to Ponder/Notes/Suggestions for Further Reading  380

## *Conclusion*  The Role of Policy Analysis
             and Evaluation in Policymaking  383

**Chapter 15**  Policy Analysis and
             the Utility of Evaluation in Policymaking  385
  Social Scientists and Policymaking  385
  Future Directions in Policy Analysis  397
  Points to Ponder/Notes/Suggestions for Further Reading  400

## *Index*  403

# Introduction

Plagued by a host of apparently unsolvable problems, including racial tension, urban decay, poverty, hunger, crime, drugs, economic instability, environmental decline, energy shortages, and political corruption, American society in recent decades has been extremely volatile. In the face of all the change and an endless parade of persistent and stubborn social problems, the national government has assumed more and more responsibility for an ever-growing variety of issues. The decades of the 1960s and '70s in particular produced a multitude of governmental efforts to solve a variety of social ills, but with only mixed results at best.

This lack of governmental success in coping with society's problems, coupled with such experiences as the Vietnam war, Watergate, the Wilbur Mills and Wayne Hays episodes, the Tongsun Park or Koreagate question, and the FBI's Abscam operation, have caused many Americans to harbor some serious doubts about some of their most cherished political ideas. They have suddenly awakened to the fact that for years they have been misled, if not lied to outright by their government — by Eisenhower about U.S. spy planes, by Kennedy about the Bay of Pigs, by Johnson about Vietnam, by Nixon about Cambodia and Watergate, and by Ford about the Nixon pardon. As a consequence, public confidence in government has suffered a serious decline. American faith in the ability of the government to solve our growing problems has eroded substantially. The feeling that governments, especially the national government, are less and less capable of providing ready solutions for the difficult problems we face is growing.

This growing lack of confidence in the ability of the government to cope with the problems faced has serious implications for the policymaking process. Is the current system no longer capable of meeting our needs? Must we junk the system that has served so well thus far and start all over? Can adjustments be made in the system that will make it function more effectively? Or has our government's performance really been all that ineffective and have expectations simply gone beyond its ability to deliver?

In his book *Policy Analysis,* Thomas Dye says,

> The smoke-filled room where patronage and pork were dispensed has been replaced with the talk-filled room, where rhetoric and image are dispensed. What governments *say* is as important as what governments *do.* Television has made the image of public policy as important as the policy itself.[1]

Has our political rhetoric become so inflated, promising so much, that unrealistic expectations are generated? Reflecting in a TV interview on his first year as president, Jimmy Carter noted, "I think my biggest mistake has been inadvertently building up expectations too high. I underestimated the difficulty and the time required for Congress to take action on controversial measures." Is this unrealistic, brash promising of governmental solutions for any and all problems a major contributing factor to the erosion of confidence in political and governmental institutions?

These are some of the questions we will try to bring into perspective as we pursue the study of the national policymaking process in this volume. This is no simple undertaking since the national policy process is huge and it is complex. The national government has its fingers in so many dikes that just finding out all the things it does is a formidable task; trying to explain and understand how and why it does what it does is a far greater undertaking.

## Blending the Traditional Focus and the Policy Focus

Until recently, policy was not generally the focus of political studies, as earlier efforts tended to deal more with institutions, structures, political behavior, and political processes. This volume blends the traditional focus with the policy focus, dealing with the history, the process and the content of policymaking. The term *policy* is applied quite loosely and is generally used to refer to a great variety of governmental activities and decisions. In Chapter 1 more detailed definitions will be presented, but in general the term *policy* will be used here to refer to what the government does, and *policymaking* will refer to the processes through which the government decides the content of its policies. Thus the policymaking process refers to all those myriad decisions and events that go into the formulation and proposal of a policy, its consideration, and finally its enactment and implementation, or its rejection.

As public policy has become the focus for more and more study, considerable disagreement has developed over the "best" way to study and analyze the process. On the whole, political scientists have displayed a much stronger penchant for debating methodologies and philosophizing about policy than for actually studying and explaining the process cogently and coherently. Consequently, a substantial gap exists between introductory texts and the process itself. Because decisions about what the government should do and how it should do it are reached not through the application of some abstract scientific principles but through a dynamic and highly political process, the real system is considerably more complex than its theoretical outlines.

In this volume an effort is made to blend the theoretical and the practical in a manner that will enable the undergraduate to devolop both a better understanding of the policy process and a desire to learn more about it.

## The Aim of This Text

The ideas and approaches in this text are the outgrowth of more than a decade's experience in teaching undergraduate policy courses. The aim of the text is to provide a perspective and analytical framework in which the student will be able to analyze and evaluate the process for himself. The book is designed primarily for students in introductory or intermediate-level policy courses rather than for those planning to become professionals or researchers in the field. An effort is made to blend a sound theoretical framework with the use of meaningful, practical examples of the process at work in a volume that has real substance but is not too "heavy" for the student just beginning the formal study of the subject. It is hoped that with the frame of reference provided here, students will be started on their way toward being able to think critically and to evaluate governmental activities on their own.

Considering the scope and complexity of the policymaking process, this is indeed an ambitious undertaking, and the result will assuredly be less than perfect. Let me make clear at the outset, I lay no claim to infallibility and I don't begin to have neat, precise answers for all the problems. This volume is written not so much to provide a full-blown, definitive explanation of the policy process, but rather to stimulate further reading, discussion, and exploration by the student. If some of the concepts presented and questions raised spark further interest and stimulate critical thinking and policy discussion, then the prime objective will be realized.

Just as there is no way for such a volume to be exhaustive in its coverage, neither can it be totally objective. In my opinion there is no such thing as scientific objectivity when dealing with such controversial or moral public issues as abortion, busing, the right of life, and many such questions. Therefore, I make no claim to totally unbiased presentation; however, the reader is not expected to blindly and unquestioningly accept everything as presented. While the aim is to be as open and above board as possible, readers are encouraged to challenge positions and conclusions and to think for themselves. It is my hope that those using this text will go beyond simply reading and understanding it to read and explore the process further and develop theories and ideas of their own.

## Why Study the National Policy Process?

Why should students be interested in studying the national policy process? Many basic courses in government or political science focus primarily on governmental structures and institutions; the study of policy is an important supplement to the traditional approach, focusing on problems and issues and what the government does or tries to do in response to them. In other words, the study of public policy focuses on what government is all about: in the words of Harold Lasswell, "Who gets what, when and how?"

People care about the government and its activities because it involves issues that affect *them*. Today's federal government consists of a massive array of agencies, boards, statutes, decisions, and regulations that make themselves felt in every home in the country. While the federal government and its policies may seem quite abstract and remote to many, in reality all Americans are profoundly affected by what it does. Consequently, the citizen who understands the process is in a much better position to be an effective participant and to seek those changes that will help achieve his personal goals. An understanding of the processes for the making of policy decisions is essential for an informed and effective citizenry. Watergate, the revelations of CIA and FBI excesses, and other flaws in the system are ample testimony to the importance of people keeping a watchful eye on the government.

Finally, studying the policy process is a real challenge for the student of our democratic system. The process is never static, but is dynamic and constantly changing. And, while the process is complicated and frequently confusing, it is never dull. For those who enjoy the interplay of politics, administration, and the full range of democratic political involvement, the policy process is "where it's at." The multifaceted policymaking process is not unlike a big three-ring circus. It has its clowns, its lions and tigers, even an occasional white elephant; but more than that, the process is characterized by various centers or "rings" of activity. To keep up with what is happening, one must constantly shift attention from ring to ring, as policy conflicts are found throughout the structure of government. Issues move from arena to arena, as a group losing on one front carries its battle to another in its efforts to swing the balance in its direction. Thus the two houses of Congress, the executive offices and agencies, and the courts are all the scenes of constant struggles among competing interest trying to sway decisions in their favor.

## The Framework of This Text

Since, as noted earlier, the study of the policy process is highly complex and involves vast amounts of material to be covered, a framework for organization and analysis is essential. I have tried to devise a format that will present the material in an orderly, understandable and meaningful context. While much of the focus is on particular areas of policy, each part also deals with the broader concepts of policymaking in general and seeks to make the student aware of the broader perspectives of the system.

Part One (Chapters 1 and 2) provides the theoretical and conceptual framework for the study of public policy. Part Two (Chapters 3-6) focuses on what I have elected to call "management policy." In this part the government's role as the agent with major responsibility for managing the nation's economic, foreign, and military affairs is explored. Part Three (Chapters 7-9) focuses on the government as subsidizer, covering agricultural, transportation, and educational policy. Part Four (Chapters 10-12) explores the government's role in the regulatory field, while Part Five (Chapters 13 and 14) deals with the complex and controversial area of redistributive policy by focusing on civil rights and social services policies. The concluding chapter discusses the role of policy analysis and evaluation in policymaking.

Each part will be introduced by a short essay defining and explaining the particular type of policy being considered in that part. Readers must keep in mind that any typology of public policies is somewhat arbitrary, and most policies will not fall neatly into any one category. This is certainly true of the typology used here. The categories are not mutually exclusive, but rather many policies will have characteristics of two or three or possibly even all the categories. The typology is useful, however, for organizational purposes and for developing some general concepts of policies and their applications. As long as the reader keeps in mind that many policies may possess certain aspects of different types of policy, this factor should pose no problem.

The study of public policymaking is an interesting and provocative undertaking with enough variety, complexity and unpredictability to challenge the strongest of intellects. It is hoped that this volume captures some of the excitement, conflict, and controversy that characterize the real process.

## Acknowledgements

I am indebted to many people for their cooperation and support which helped to bring this book to fruition. To the many authors and publishers without whose previous efforts my own work would have been impossible, I acknowledge my indebtedness; and to those who granted permission to use their previously published materials a special word of thanks. To my wife for willingly undertaking the thankless task of proofreading and to my children who, though they sometimes wondered how I could spend so much time sitting behind a desk shuffling little cards and writing, accepted my unavailability and took some pride in telling friends their dad was writing another book, thanks for your understanding and support. To my secretaries, Hazel Finley, Dorothy Share and Mary Riley, who typed what seemed to be endless rewrites, I express my gratitude. And finally to Jim Boyd and his assistants at Goodyear, a note of sincere thanks for their interest, encouragement, and support in getting the book to press.

### Note

1. Thomas Dye, *Policy Analysis: What Governments Do, Why They Do It and What Difference It Makes* (University, Alabama: University of Alabama Press, 1976), p. 20.

# Part One

# The Setting

In the United States governmental system, policymaking is an ongoing, many-faceted process involving action in many arenas with a constantly changing cast of participants. The vastness and complexity of the process make it essential to establish some points of reference for undertaking a study of the system.

In Chapter 1 an effort is made to provide the reader with a conceptual and theoretical framework for approaching the policy process. Entire volumes have been devoted to some of the theories presented, so they are not treated exhaustively here. However, the reader should get some understanding and appreciation of the many different ways in which policy decisions can be approached and some idea of the relative strengths and weaknesses of the different theories.

Chapter 2 discusses the structural, cultural, and political environment within which policymaking occurs in the United States. Again, while space precludes an exhaustive treatment of this aspect of the policy process, this chapter should point up to the reader the significance and impact of various environmental factors in the policymaking process.

Additional readings are suggested at the end of each chapter which will help the reader achieve a fuller understanding of the concepts and theories presented.

# 1
# Some Theories and Concepts for the Study of Policymaking

One of the first things essential to a study of public policy is a definition of the term. This is a term used daily, but in many cases quite loosely, to cover a wide range of activities. While for our purposes it is not necessary to have an all-encompassing definition that is set in concrete, it will be helpful to have a rather clear concept of what is or is not included when the term "public policy" is used.

Public policies are a result of governmental responses to public problems. Such public problems are an outgrowth of perceived needs on the part of the people or those who make decisions on their behalf. Not all societal problems are necessarily "public." Whether the soda you buy comes in a glass bottle, a can, or a plastic container is not necessarily an issue of public policy. However, should enough people or the right people become so concerned about the impact of such containers on our environment that governmental action is taken, then this matter does become an issue in public policy. Thus, though they may be affected by outside factors, "public policies" are those policies developed by governmental bodies and officials.

The literature in the field abounds with definitions of public policy, some more appropriate for our purposes than others. Robert Eyestone says that broadly speaking, public policy is "the relationship of a government unit to its environment."[1] This definition is too broad to be of much use in the effort to identify specific characteristics of public policy. Another rather general definition is Thomas Dye's observation that "public policy is whatever governments choose to do or not to do."[2] Dye's definition does include the concept that policy may be either positive or negative; that is, it may involve either governmental action or inaction. Non-decision may constitute a government policy as well as positive action on a matter. In somewhat the same vein, policy should be viewed as what government actually does, rather than what it proposes to do. As we will note in later analysis of the process, there may be considerable difference between a proposed or even an adopted course of action and what actually occurs. The formal enactment of a statute or regulation does not necessarily mean it is automatically an effective part of public policy. Adoption of a number of coal mine safety regulations has not resulted in a dedicated and vigorous enforcement by the government to ensure miner safety.

Another characteristic usually attributed to public policies is that they represent purposive and goal-oriented courses of action as opposed to random decision-making. This concept is expressed by H. Hugh Heclo, who writes, "At its core, policy is a course of action intended to accomplish some end."[3] While governmental intent and objectives may not always be clearly expressed and easily discernible, policies are generally designed with the intention of achieving some predetermined objectives. Thus, Anderson says policy is "a purposive course of action followed by an actor or set of actors in dealing with a problem or matter of concern."[4] This concept of policy as a purposive course of action needs to be qualified somewhat, however. While the policymakers may have certain objectives in mind as policy decisions are made, many governmental policies are the result of a rather haphazard, piecemeal approach to decision-making, with little effort at overall coordination and long-range planning or goal setting. This approach frequently produces results that were quite unanticipated by the policymakers. The so-called white flight from the urban school system as a result of desegregation policy is an example. Some policies adopted are really more symbolic than goal oriented. The fair housing provisions of the 1968 Civil Rights Act may be largely unenforceable from a practical standpoint, but symbolically they are a reassurance that the government does not condone discrimination. The Equal Rights Amendment, should it be ratified, really won't add a lot to the statutes and executive orders already on the books providing protection for women's rights, but the ERA is a largely symbolic issue. These types of policies serve as symbols for what society aspires to be, and they are different from certain policies such as coal mine safety, which are adopted and then simply ignored and not enforced.

Just as policies are purposive and deliberate, they also represent patterns or courses of action rather than isolated decisions. Policymaking extends over time and usually involves a series of several decisions on the part of various actors, as opposed to a single decision by one institution or agency of government. Along these lines, Richard Rose has suggested that public policies be considered as "a long series of more-or-less related activities" rather than discrete decisions;[5] and Heclo observes, "A policy may usefully be considered as a course of action or inaction rather than specific decisions or actions, and such a course has to be perceived and identified by the analyst in question."[6] This characteristic contributes to the complexity of the process, because it is rare that a single decision by the president, Congress, the Supreme Court, or any agency of government will constitute the whole of any governmental policy. Much more likely is that all branches of government, plus other actors as well, will be involved in a multitude of decisions involving a single policy. In recent years, non-governmental groups such as large multi-national corporations, private foundations, and research institutions and "think tanks" such as Rand, Brookings, and the American Enterprise Institute have come to play a growing role in policymaking. Advisory groups and special commissions or panels of experts also have come to play a greater role in the process, especially at the formulation and evaluation stages.

It should be apparent by this point that policy is a highly dynamic and somewhat ambiguous term that is applied in constantly changing situations. As Eulau and Prewitt point out, "What the observer sees when he identifies policy at any one point in time is at most a stage or phase in a sequence of events that constitute policy development."[7] Policymaking is a constantly evolving process that must adapt to the changing expectations and demands generated by a highly pluralistic system characterized by conflict, compromise, and confusion.

What is public policy? For our purposes, public policy is a course of governmental action, usually involving several different branches and agencies, in dealing with an issue or problem that is the object of public concern. Such public policies may be directed toward an infinite variety of issues such as inflation, unemployment, housing, welfare, crime, drug traffic, economic monopoly, television advertising, external activities of Cuba, China or the Soviet Union, and on and on, *ad infinitum*.

How do such issues get on the public policy agenda? Governmental action on such issues results from *policy demands*. Policy demands may emanate from a variety of sources in our society, both formal and informal, such as citizens, interest groups, the Congress, the president, or other agencies of government. The policies themselves are largely framed in executive and administrative, judicial, and legislative chambers; however, the policies are the result of a complex process of interaction of interests and ideas with governmental and political institutions. The American Enterprise Institute for Public Policy Research says that policymakers themselves rarely originate the concepts that go into the rules and regulations by which people are governed, but choose among various options in formulating laws, orders, regulations, and programs. These policy concepts come from the interplay and competition of ideas and perceived needs of the varied interests that make up our highly pluralistic society. Thus the *demands* or *inputs* into the system are varied and they are numerous.

While it is possible to identify various steps in the policymaking process—agenda setting, formulation, adoption or enactment, implementation, evaluation, and adjustment—there is no identifiable pattern applying to all policies as far as the procedures that will be involved in each stage of their development. Some policies such as foreign policies will be developed largely within the governmental structure itself, while other policies such as labor-management relations may be developed with extensive involvement of groups outside of government. Some policies may evolve through a highly democratic process involving a wide range of participants, while others may be developed through a rather exclusive process involving a select elite. This lack of consistent patterns makes the study of the policymaking process at the same time both frustrating and challenging.

Though it is difficult to identify consistent patterns in the process, this has not dampened the efforts of observers to develop theories explaining policy and governmental decision-making. Since entire volumes have been devoted to a number of these theories, it is not possible to give them an in-depth treatment here; however, several concepts will be presented briefly to acquaint the student with some of the various approaches that are sometimes applied. Most theories tend to emphasize a particular phase of the policy process—e.g., policy formulation, implementation, or evaluation—and they tend to focus on either *who* makes policy or *how* policy is made. While no single "grand theory" explains the complex policy process in its entirety, each theory has applications that can contribute to the understanding of the process. Some of the most prominent theories and their relative strengths and weaknesses are presented here in the framework of *who makes policy* and *how policy is made*.

## WHO MAKES POLICY

A question that has intrigued political scientists from their beginning has been "who governs?" The theories that deal with who wields governmental power tend to focus heavily on the agenda setting and formulation stages of policymaking. They are primarily concerned with who determines what issues are addressed and what goes into governmental policies. Their focus is on inputs into the process. Most of these theories are also spinoffs or refined versions of the group theory of policymaking. According to the group theorists, public policy is the product of the interaction and competition among the various group alignments in our society. A nation of joiners, more and more Americans have turned to organized group activity as a means of securing their political objectives. These organized interest groups have become the primary instruments through which inputs are funnelled into the system and policy decisions made.

### The Pluralist Theory

In recent years one of the most widely embraced and discussed adaptations of the group theory of governmental decision-making has been the pluralist concept. The pluralist approach gained wide acceptance among social scientists because it fits in well with the extremely heterogeneous nature of American society, and its anti-class, anti-Marxist orientation accommodates the democratic concepts of broad-based mass participation and competition as key elements in policymaking.

Pluralism places heavy emphasis on political participation, electoral processes, group interaction, and party competition, playing down any link between economics and politics. The pluralists view the political system as having multiple centers of power with influence widely dispersed among a variety of shifting coalitions. These frequently changing power alignments are in constant competition, necessitating compromise and negotiation among the various segments of society. According to pluralists, this broad-based competition tends toward political equilibrium, and for the pluralist, equilibrium among the competing groups produces the public interest. The pluralist model, thus, is based on an idealized concept of the group and the assumption that interaction and competition among the multiple sources of power within society will produce the public interest or ideal policies. The pluralist concept operates on the assumption that a governmental system built primarily upon intergroup competition, bargaining, and compromise is self-corrective, and we have nothing to fear from government as long as many different interests are vying for its favors. Under the pluralist concept the competition and give-and-take among the competing interests in the system constitute sufficient due process to provide democratic government, and pluralism's defenders contend that inequalities in the distribution of power and resources within society do not warrant the conclusion that there is a ruling class.

While the pluralists' emphasis on multiple power centers, changing interest alignments, and competition and compromise are all important elements in the policy process, the approach does not provide a complete theory of the determinants of policy outcomes. The pluralist approach tends to emphasize policy formation and process while largely disregarding policy substance and administration.

The pluralists' assumption that group competition will produce policy decisions in the public interest poses several problems. Access to the decision-making process is probably not nearly so easy as the pluralists seem to assume, particularly not for certain segments of society. Some elements in our system such as the poor, blacks, Chicanos, Indians, slum residents, migrant workers, and others in similar circumstances operate under almost insurmountable handicaps when trying to influence the political process. Add to this the fact that large numbers of citizens simply are not by nature political activists and you have large numbers for whom this system is not very responsive. The pluralist concept would appear to work best for those who already have access to the system and have a power base from which to operate.

Beyond this, the pluralist approach would seem to build into the system a participation bias by eliminating from the process those masses of citizens who are not organized around values pertinent to a particular policy or issue. Rather than a system of countervailing powers where competing groups may serve as a check on one another, a system of accommodation can develop wherein policy is shaped largely by those most interested and directly affected by the decisions, as is often the case with regulatory and subsidy policies. With this delegation of policymaking power to those most interested, an element of responsibility is lost and accountability is to the immediate interest rather than to the general public.

With its strong group orientation, the pluralist approach tends to reduce policymaking to nothing more than a series of different sets of competing interest groups. While interest groups do play a vital role, government is something more and any complete theory must also take into account such additional elements as economic, social, cultural, historical, and similar factors. In recent years pluralist concepts have been questioned more and more as several social scientists have come to feel that economic resources may be more significant in determining policy outcomes than such pluralist values as competition, participation, or malapportionment.

## Elite Theory

At the other end of the spectrum from the pluralists are the elitists. According to the elitist concept, governmental policy reflects the values and preferences of a governing elite. It is the few who have political and economic power, not the masses, who determine policy. For all practical purposes, governmental power rests in the hands of a select few who occupy leading positions in the nation's military, industrial, and corporate structure and in the executive branch of government. Probably the best known proponent of the elite concept is C. Wright Mills, who wrote in the *The Power Elite*, "It is the professional politician who has lost the most, so much that in examining the events and decisions, one is tempted to speak of a political vacuum in which the corporate rich and the high warlord, in the coinciding interests, rule."[8] According to Mills, the members of this governing elite share a common social background, a common ideology, and an interrelated set of interests. Because of their interests and background, those few who control governmental power are not typical of those who are governed. Through fear and manipulation, the power elite control and influence the masses much more than they in turn are influenced by the masses.

While the elite theory does focus attention on the important role of leadership in policymaking, it, like many other theories, is probably an oversimplification of the intricate policy process. Though select groups with wealth, social status, and "access" to the political process may exert an inordinate amount of influence in governmental decision-making, they do not always prevail. In such areas as desegregation and environmental policies, for example, decisions have not been controlled by the power elite. Policy decisions in many areas result from inputs from a variety of sources, and the coalitions that develop around various issues change constantly. Thus, while policy in certain areas may be dominated by an elite, no one group or social class is in a position to dominate the whole process.

Like the pluralists, the elitists tend to focus primarily on the agenda-setting and policy-formulation stages of the process. They also tend to emphasize the economic and social class aspects of political power and their influence on policy decisions to the exclusion of such other elements as public opinion, political parties and elections, and other such factors. Nonetheless, for many, Mills's hypothesis regarding elite power remains the most logical explanation for understanding the policymaking process.

## The Sub-Government Theory

Bridging the gap between the pluralist and elite theories and combining some of the elements of both is the sub-government concept of policymaking. Because these sub-governments bring together a coalition of members of Congress, officials from executive departments and agencies, and group representatives, all of whom share interests in a particular policy area, such alignments are also sometimes described as "iron triangles" or "triangles of interests."

As noted earlier, different policies are developed in different ways; the system that produces defense or foreign policy may be considerably different from that which produces transportation policy, energy policy, or education policy. Viewed as a whole, the policy process is fragmented and diverse. One reason for this is that different power centers and alignments of participants develop around different areas of policy. Ernest Griffith described these centers of activity revolving around particular policy issues as "whirlpools." Such sub-governments tend to develop around specialized areas of policy in which not everyone is interested. As a consequence of this lack of widespread interest and involvement, these sub-governments may come to wield considerable power and influence in the formation and implementation of policy in their respective fields.

Such sub-governments commonly ally some key congressional committee or subcommittee members, an administrative agency or two, and those groups with a particular interest in the specific policy area. The committees, agencies, and interest groups develop a continuing relationship based on their mutual concern with the particular policy area and, because of a virtual monopoly, become the experts in the field. These sub-governments or triangular alliances develop a pronounced capacity for self-preservation and strongly resist the emergence of competing systems. One example of such sub-government is the alliance of the members of the House Agriculture Subcommittee, the officials in the Department of Agriculture, and the sugar importers on legislation setting sugar import quotas; another example is the system that centers around rivers and harbors bills, involving the House and Senate Committees on Public Works, the National Rivers and Harbors Congress (several members of Congress belong), and the Army Corps of Engineers.

Displaying characteristics of both the pluralist and elite concepts, the sub-government theory has several weaknesses. Like the pluralist theory, this approach assigns policymaking in specific areas to those interests and participants most interested and directly involved. Since sub-government operations frequently occur in almost total obscurity from the view of the general public, decisions become insulated against public responsibility. Sub-government control of policymaking also makes reform and redirection difficult because of limited access to outside interests and a strong inclination to maintain the status quo.

Like the elite concept, the sub-government approach to policymaking is somewhat limited in its application to the total process. While the tendency to defer to such sub-groups as the recognized experts in their particular areas of policy interest gives them an inflated amount of influence on particular issues, this theory does not apply throughout the system. Such sub-systems are not free of all control, and their actions are usually subject to review somewhere along the way. In other areas of policy, the broader interest and the competition among a variety of participants in the process will prevent such lasting alliances from developing. So, while the sub-government theory may be quite appropriate for some areas of policy, it cannot be offered as a viable explanation for the whole process.

## HOW POLICY IS MADE

The theories presented thus far have tended to focus heavily on the policy formation stage and on *who* makes policy. We will now focus on some theories dealing with *how* policy is made, and while they still include the policy formation stage, these theories also give more emphasis to the implementation and evaluation aspects of policymaking.

### The Rational-Comprehensive Theory

One of the more idealistic concepts of decision-making, the rational-comprehensive theory has considerable appeal to those looking for a more logical, planned approach to policymaking. Under this concept, issues are approached in a well-ordered sequence: the problem is identified and isolated; goals, values, and objectives are then identified and ranked; various alternative solutions are formulated and weighed; and, finally, that alternative is chosen that will maximize the attainment of the identified goals and objectives.

The neatness and logic of this approach have considerable appeal; however, various difficulties arise when the rational-comprehensive approach is applied to the real world of policymaking. First, many of the complex problems facing the government are not concrete and clearly identifiable. For example, if the chronic problem of the economy over the last several years was simply a problem of inflation alone, or of unemployment alone, it might be isolated and attacked with some degree of success; but the problem has been a complicated one of inflation, unemployment, stagnating business, and reduced industrial growth all at the same time. Suggested solutions have been about as numerous and divergent as the economists available to offer them. In other words, identifying and defining the problem may in itself be the most formidable task faced by the policymakers.

Application of this approach is further complicated by other factors as well. The rational-comprehensive theory hinges upon the decision-maker having at his disposal the facts and information necessary for an informed, rational decision. In reality, policymakers usually consider only a few alternatives and the information on each is usually quite limited. Along with this, the theory further assumes the ability of the policymakers to predict with some degree of accuracy the consequences of various policy alternatives. Neither of these goals is readily attainable in the real world of policy decisions on highly complex issues. Take, for example, the area of defense policy. Decisions in this realm frequently involve choices on weapons systems so scientific and technical that the decision-makers could not really understand them even when information is available. And, they certainly cannot predict with any degree of accuracy what will happen should we not build the B-1 bomber or the Trident submarine. The same is true, though possibly to a lesser degree, in other areas. For example, when President Ford launched his campaign for the swine flu vaccine, medical experts lined up on both sides of the issue. What it boils down to in most cases is which group of "experts" and what set of "facts" do the decision-makers decide to go with? In many instances there is no clear-cut choice between black and white, good and bad.

Finally, application of the rational-comprehensive approach can be severely hampered when prior commitments limit the alternatives available. Once millions or even billions of dollars have been put into a particular project or program, it becomes extremely difficult to pull out and start all over. Programs, once implemented, generate considerable momentum of their own, and once set in motion, it is hard to retreat and start in another direction even though this is what a rational assessment of the facts indicates is needed. Once the decision has been made, on whatever basis, to build a facility in the desert in Arizona and it is built, it is difficult to move it elsewhere. As desirable as it might be to carefully plan policy decisions and base them on a careful, rational assessment of the facts, this is not the way most decisions are arrived at. For example, it is quite clear that if we want to reduce the inequities in per-pupil expenditures among the schools in districts throughout the nation, the way to do this is to concentrate federal expenditures in the poorer districts to bring them up to par with the wealthier districts. The harsh reality of the policy process is that in order to muster the necessary votes in Congress to pass an aid-to-education bill, the spending has to be spread over all congressional districts and the impact of federal funds in reducing inequities is thus blunted. So much for rational, objective policymaking when it collides head-on with the practicality of electoral politics.

Very rarely are policy decisions unilateral and clear-cut; they are more often a matter of bargaining and trade-offs, making political feasibility an essential consideration in the process. To be effective, rational-comprehensive decision-making requires identification of the whole range of possible alternatives, recognition and setting of goals and objectives, prioritizing of various alternatives, and selection of programs on the basis of an analysis of all relevant information. Very real limitations of time, intelligence, availability and reliability of information, and politics tend to make this approach unrealistic.

### The Incremental Theory

In his book *The Policy-Making Process*, Charles E. Lindblom defines incrementalism as "decision making through small or incremental moves on particular problems rather than through a comprehensive reform program. It is also endless; it takes the form of an indefinite sequence of policy moves. Moreover, it is exploratory in that the goals of policy-making continue to change as new experience with policy throws new light on what is possible and desirable.[9] Under the incremental approach the emphasis is on addressing immediate problems and finding "something that will work" rather than efforts at long-range planning and promotion of future policy goals. In other words, incrementalism is present-oriented and frequently remedial in nature; rather than considering a policy as a whole, incrementalism focuses on making necessary changes and adaptations in the already existing base. Incrementalism is a very practical approach to policymaking, recognizing that comprehensive analysis of policy issues is not always possible. As under the pluralist concept, decisions and policies are viewed as the product of considerable bargaining and compromise among the various participants in the process. Since incremental rather than major changes are usually involved, this concept suits a pluralist society well because diverse interests can compete without posing a major threat to one another.

Considered from a very pragmatic point of view, incrementalism has a number of strengths, and all policymaking is to a certain extent incremental in that it usually involves a series of decisions over time. Building on an existing base makes subsequent policy decisions considerably easier. The validity and applicability of new ideas and new approaches do not have to be proven and old arguments rehashed again. Rather, new decisions simply build on the established base, adding a bit here and there, thus limiting any disputes to mere changes in a program rather than reopening policy issues of considerable magnitude and passion.

While it probably comes closer to describing the true nature of our system than most other theories of policymaking, the incremental concept does have its shortcomings. Where the rational-comprehensive approach is probably too idealistic, the incremental approach is probably too pragmatic. It tends to place too much emphasis on what is possible, to the neglect of what is most desirable in the way of policy. Also, incrementalism works well if the base upon which it builds is sound, but what if the base itself is flawed? Does the concept allow for sufficient change at the base to correct such a defect? While incrementalism does tend to reduce the risks of cost and uncertainty by building on existing bases, it produces only limited and politically acceptable decisions. New needs result in expansions of existing programs rather than carefully planned and prioritized responses. With past actions as a major constraint, incrementalism may result in a failure to consider all alternatives available. Also, by building on past programs, effective reform or substantial changes in policy direction are frequently rendered difficult by the opposition of substantial vested interests built up in existing programs. In an area such as budgetary/fiscal policy, the incremental approach can make it difficult for the policymakers to achieve the necessary reductions in expenditures and tax reforms necessary to curb inflation and promote economic stability.

## The Institutional Theory

One of the oldest approaches to the study of governmental decision-making is institutionalism, which focuses on the relationship of the various governmental institutions with one another. The institutional approach to the study of politics concentrates more on the formal constitutional and legal aspects of the various governmental institutions and their functions. The institutional approach is particularly suited for studying the enactment and implementation stages of policymaking. A major drawback to the institutional approach is that it tends to fragment the study of policymaking by focusing on the various institutional participants in isolation, making it somewhat difficult to draw all the different elements together in a meaningful and coherent picture. While institutional structures, roles, and procedures play an important role in public policymaking and their significance must not be overlooked, the analysis of institutional functions alone gives only a partial picture. A more comprehensive concept is needed to grasp the full range of the process.

## The Systems Theory

As we have noted in discussing the foregoing theories, each tends to emphasize certain aspects of the process, and while each has certain strengths, their applicability is somewhat limited by their failure to cover all aspects of the policymaking process. An effort to overcome this shortcoming has been made by those social scientists who embrace the systems theory.

The systems theory has gained rather wide support in recent political research and writing. The main thrust of the systems approach is that in analyzing governmental action the focus must be broad and take in the interaction of all the elements of the entire system. The legislature, the executive, the bureaucracy, the judiciary, and the citizens cannot be viewed as operating in isolation from one another or from other participants in the system. All actors are an integral part of the system and their functions must be viewed in light of their relationship to the whole. While the systems approach does alert the student to the significant interrelationships of the various participants in the policy process, its usefulness is somewhat limited by its highly generalized nature. It fails to contribute a great deal in the way of insight into and explanation of how decisions are arrived at and policies made within the decision-making structures themselves.

## Summary

As was noted in introducing this discussion of the various theories of policymaking, no one approach or theory can be pronounced "best." Some are more applicable in one situation and others in other settings. Each of the theories has certain strengths and weaknesses and these should be kept in mind as the various concepts are applied to the policy process. There are some common threads running through all the theories, however, which emphasize certain characteristics of the policy process. Most of the theories view government as a process of struggle and accommodation among competing pluralist interests and regard policymaking as a matter of give and take. Within this framework each also assumes that ultimately decisions will be made and differences among competing interests resolved by an authoritative body.

In seeking to apply the various theories to policymaking in our system, it is best to maintain a flexible, eclectic approach. The process is so broad in scope, so fragmented and unstructured, that it necessitates an approach with fewer preconceptions than several of the current theories tend to allow. Over-generalization and efforts to force the process into the confines of a particular theoretical mould may tend to obscure important variations in the process. Therefore, it is important that the student of the policy process employ a variety of insights and avoid any inclination to represent all policy decisions in a single theory.

## TYPES OF POLICIES

Public policies come in more different varieties than Heinz has canned goods. Consequently, trying to analyze and discuss policies without some classification scheme or typology can be both confusing and misleading. Policies can be classed by subject or field; that is, labor policy, foreign policy, energy policy, antitrust policy, etc. But the range of governmental activity is so broad that this approach fails to narrow the categories sufficiently to be manageable. In this volume, I have chosen to use an adaptation of Theodore Lowi's typology, adding a category of my own, to classify policies according to their societal impact.[10] Four general categories of policy have been identified, each of which will be briefly described here and elaborated on later in the book.

### Management Policy

In certain areas of policy, a preeminent role has been assigned to the federal government both inherently and constitutionally. Though its powers in these areas are not totally exclusive, the federal government has the primary responsibility for *managing* or directing the nation's affairs in these realms. In this category the important areas of foreign, defense, and budgetary/fiscal policy are explored.

### Subsidy Policy

Quite early in our history, the federal government embraced the concept of promoting private endeavor in certain fields through governmental actions. Governmental programs providing tangible benefits to certain individuals and groups such as canal and turnpike builders, railroads, and homesteaders were early examples of such action. Subsidy was thus accepted early as a legitimate undertaking on the part of the federal government. Over the years numerous techniques, both direct and indirect, have been developed for increasing the rewards or benefits provided by the government to certain sectors of society. Subsidy policies represent the federal "pork barrel" in its truest form, as various sectors make their special cases for some form of federal reward in support of their role in our society.

## Regulatory Policy

Governmental actions extending control over certain types of activity on the part of private individuals, corporations, or particular segments of society constitute regulatory policy. Extensive governmental activity in the regulatory field dates from the post-Civil War era. The emergence of the corporation and the accompanying limits imposed on individual opportunity and freedom of action brought demands that eventually led to governmental action. Over the years governmental regulatory activity has grown from its roots in the Interstate Commerce Act and the Sherman Act to become one of the most extensive and most controversial areas of federal activity.

## Redistributive Policy

Much governmental activity involves the allocation of available resources, and over the long run almost all policies are to a certain extent redistributive. Redistributive policies are governmental actions consciously designed to bring about a transfer of resources in the form of wealth, property, individual rights, or something else of value among large groups or classes in society. Because such policies create "winners" and "losers" in terms of who gets what at the expense of whom, these are among the most controversial of governmental programs. Decisions in this area of policymaking are often further complicated by the presence of strong ideological arguments. Redistribution policies such as the income tax, welfare programs, etc., frequently run counter to strong beliefs in individual freedom, private property rights, and free enterprise. In the final analysis, the real issue in redistributive policy is who benefits how much and at the expense of whom.

Having explained the policy typology employed in this volume, let me now extend a word of caution to the reader. Most governmental policies will not fit neatly into one or the other of the categories outlined on the preceding pages, but rather will possess characteristics of one or more of the categories. As Raymond A. Bauer and Kenneth Gergen have noted:

> One disconcerting characteristic of policy problems is that they do not exist as units. The student of policy tends to think of "the problem" such as urban mass transportation as a unitary problem. In fact, there is no unity with respect to the problems people actually have, the way in which they perceive the problem or, as has been pointed out, of their interests and their values. Furthermore, since the policy process has a time dimension, each of these elements changes over time.[11]

Therefore, while it is helpful to break policy into types, thereby facilitating a more effective appraisal of the government's social and economic goals, the reader must keep in mind that this is an oversimplification of the complex nature of most governmental policies. Most policies are multifaceted and involve a variety of goals and objectives; thus the same policy may involve an element of subsidy, some regulation, and some redistribution. A good example of this is federal aid to education, which provides financial support for state and local school systems but has also been used as leverage to bring about desegregation of these systems as well. The placing of certain areas of policy in the various categories, therefore, has been somewhat arbitrary, but I trust this will not distort the overall picture unduly.

## TOOLS AND TECHNIQUES OF POLICY

In the realm of policymaking, resolution of the difficult questions of what to do are only a part of the total picture. Since there are numerous techniques and a variety of agencies that can be used in implementing and carrying forward policy decisions, disputes over *how* something is done and *who* does it may be as serious as the question of whether anything should be done at all.

For example, the debate over farm support legislation that has gone on since the late 1930s is a disagreement as to technique. As another example, when President Carter proposed the creation of a National Development Bank as a part of his urban program, this touched off a struggle between two cabinet departments, Commerce and Housing and Urban Development, over who should administer the bank. The Commerce Department contended it had more credibility than HUD among the business community and people with whom the bank would be working. HUD, supported by several black leaders and big city mayors, maintained it possessed greater expertise and interest in urban affairs and was more attuned to the employment needs of blacks and the poor. On the other hand, while James McIntyre, director of the Office of Management and Budget, and Stuart Eizenstat, President Carter's advisor on domestic policy, favored Commerce, they felt such a move would constitute a "visible defeat" for then HUD Secretary Patricia Harris, the administration's leading urban expert and only cabinet-level minority appointee. So, McIntyre and Eizenstat recommended that the bank be placed under the joint direction of the Departments of Commerce, Treasury, and HUD. Carter followed their advice.

As we explore the different areas of public policy, we will encounter applications of the various techniques available to the government. Several of these are identified and explained briefly in the paragraphs that follow.

### Government Ownership and Operation

From its very outset, the federal government has had the responsibility to provide certain types of services such as military and police protection and mail delivery. Over the years the extent of "socialized" governmental activities has grown to include the federal highway system, federal hospitals, the various academies for training certain federal employees, dams, and a variety of other public facilities. While there is still considerable controversy surrounding governmental provision of certain types of services, especially when similar services can be provided by private enterprise, laissez-faire is no longer the automatic starting point.

### Imposition of Legal Sanctions

Through governmental action, certain types of activities may be defined as socially unacceptable; i.e., illegal. Those guilty of violations are then subject to punishment under the law. Such sanctions may be either *criminal* or *civil* in nature.

In the case of criminal sanctions, the government seeks out and prosecutes those charged with violations. For example, anyone hijacking an airplane, transporting drugs into the United States, or threatening the life of the president would be subject to criminal prosecution under the federal laws.

In the case of civil sanctions, the government lays down certain rules governing various areas of human relations and provides the courts for adjudicating disputes that arise; but the government does not seek out and prosecute the violators. It is the responsibility of the aggrieved persons or parties to avail themselves of the legal procedures available for defending their rights. Examples would be the provisions in consumer protection and antitrust legislation that provide for those suffering injuries through violations of these laws to seek redress through civil proceedings. Under the antitrust laws, a party who suffers injury as the result of a competitive practice defined as unfair by the government may sue in a civil suit for treble damages. This provision has probably put more teeth into the antitrust laws than have the provisions for criminal sanctions. Legal sanctions have been employed quite extensively in federal regulatory policies.

### Taxation

Governmental taxing power can be employed in a number of ways to achieve a variety of objectives. It is an effective tool for controlling the economy; it can be used to redistribute wealth in the society; it can be used to encourage and stimulate action as a form of subsidy; and it can be used to discourage certain activities by making them difficult or unprofitable. During the New Deal, Treasury Secretary Henry Morgenthau, Jr. and others in the administration consciously planned the use of a variety of taxing techniques in pursuit of a number of specific manipulative ends, and in the 1960s Kennedy and his economic advisors used the taxing powers to stimulate economic recovery.

### Expenditures

Governmental expenditures can be used in much the same fashion as taxes. Government funds in the form of grants, loans, and contracts can be used to promote policy goals in a variety of ways. They can be used to stimulate a sagging economy; to subsidize a new and struggling industry to help it get off the ground or an old and floundering industry to help it survive; or to provide more revenues for state and local governments to help them carry on their functions. On the other hand, federal funds may be withheld from certain school districts to encourage them to comply with other federal policies prohibiting discrimination. The use of expenditures in the policymaking process affords the decision-makers a vast range of alternatives for attaining varied objectives.

### Contracts

The federal government is a user of a vast array of goods and services that are procured through government contracts. Over the years federal contracts have been used as instruments for carrying out a variety of policy objectives. While contracts can be used as instruments for all categories of policy, they have proved particularly useful in implementing various subsidy and regulatory policies, ranging from contracts to carry the mails in support of transport carriers to requirements that those holding federal contracts meet certain minimum requirements regarding wages and hours and hiring of minorities. Contracts and grants have also been widely used by the government as a major support of research and development activities.

### Certificates, Licenses, and Franchises

Many types of activity engaged in by private individuals or businesses require governmental approval. Such approval is frequently granted in the form of a certificate, license, or franchise. These constitute a permit from the government to engage in the particular activity and usually establish certain guidelines that must be met. These techniques are used more widely by state and local governments, but certain types of operations such as radio and TV stations, interstate motor carriers, and firearms dealers must have federal certificates or licenses to operate. This technique is a useful instrument of regulatory policy.

### Self-regulation

While its direct involvement in the regulatory field is extensive, the government also promotes self-regulation in many businesses and professions. The Federal Trade Commission holds "industry conferences" at which those engaged in certain types of businesses are encouraged to adopt certain rules and regulations governing their activities. The National Association of Broadcasters adopts its own code governing acceptable practices in the industry. Various professions such as medicine and law have adopted codes of ethics and their professional associations license members to practice. Educational institutions have established their own accrediting agencies to ensure that certain standards of quality are met. Were it not for all these efforts at self-regulation, many of which are sanctioned either directly or indirectly by the government, federal regulation would be even more extensive than it is.

### Inspection and Testing

One of the oldest of policy techniques, inspection has been most widely used by state and local governments, but is being used more and more by the federal government as it undertakes policies of consumer, employee, and environmental protection. Testing and inspection are vital instruments for agencies such as the Food and Drug Administration, the Environmental Protection Agency, and the Occupational Safety and Health Administration as they seek to protect the public from unsafe food and drugs, environmental pollution, and health and safety hazards.

### Publicity and Investigations

Employed by both congressional committees and administrative agencies, this technique has become more widely used and much more effective as an instrument of policy with recent developments in the mass media, especially the growth of television. Able to reach a vast audience, the governmental committee or agency is in a position to generate considerable adverse publicity for those they find guilty of misbehavior or illegal practices. Today, simply the threat to launch an investigation may be sufficient to bring about compliance. It should also be pointed out that this technique is subject to abuse by the users, and this has led to growing demands for some safeguards for those on the other end. This becomes a particularly difficult issue because once adverse publicity is incurred it is extremely difficult to undo its effects.

## CONCLUSION

In this chapter the reader is provided a rather basic and understandable but sound theoretical and conceptual framework for an effective study of the policy process. The process is so vast and so dynamic and it covers such a variety of activities that it is impossible to commit it to the confines of a textbook. However, this chapter and the chapter to follow should capture enough of its essence to provide the reader with some concept of what our democratic government is all about. In Chapter 2 we will complete our overview of the process by analyzing the significance of the environmental setting in which policymaking occurs.

## Points to Ponder

What is public policy?

Who makes public policy in the U.S.?

Is the American policy process democratic?

Does a democratic-pluralist system produce "better" policies than an elite system?

Are such factors as competition, broad-based participation, equality of access, and equal representation necessary for a system to produce policies in the public interest?

## Notes

1. Robert Eyestone, *The Threads of Public Policy: A Study in Policy Leadership* (Indianapolis: Bobbs-Merrill, 1971), p. 18.
2. Thomas Dye, *Understanding Public Policy*, 3rd ed. (Englewood Cliffs, N.J.: Prentice-Hall, 1978), p. 3.
3. H. Hugh Heclo, "Review Article: Policy Analysis," *British Journal of Political Science*, vol. 2 (January 1972), pp. 84–85.
4. James Anderson, *Public Policy-Making* (New York: Praeger, 1975), p. 3.
5. Richard Rose, ed., *Policy Making In Great Britain* (London: Macmillan, 1969), p. x.
6. Heclo, *op. cit.*, p. 85.
7. Heinz Eulau and Kenneth Prewitt, *Labyrinths of Democracy* (Indianapolis: Bobbs-Merrill, 1973), p. 481.
8. C. Wright Mills, *The Power Elite* (New York: Oxford University Press, 1956), pp. 276–77.
9. Charles E. Lindblom, *The Policy-Making Process* (Englewood Cliffs, N.J.: Prentice-Hall, 1968), p. 13.

10. See Theodore Lowi, "Distribution, Regulation, Redistribution: The Functions of Government," in Randall Ripley, *Public Policies and Their Politics* (New York: Norton, 1966), pp. 27–40.
11. Raymond A. Bauer and Kenneth Gergen, *The Study of Policy Formation* (New York: Free Press, 1968), p. 15.

## Suggestions for Further Reading

ANDERSON, JAMES E. *Public Policy-Making*. New York: Praeger, 1975.
CAPUTO, DAVID, ed. *The Politics of Policy Making in America*. San Francisco: Freeman, 1977.
DOMHOFF, WILLIAM. *Who Rules America?* Englewood Cliffs, N.J.: Prentice-Hall, 1967.
DOOLEY, MICHAEL, et al. *Political Economy of Policy-Making*. Beverly Hills: Sage, 1979.
DROR, YEHEZKEL. *Public Policy-Making Re-Examined*. San Francisco: Chandler, 1968.
DYE, THOMAS. *Understanding Public Policy*, 3rd ed. Englewood Cliffs, N.J.: Prentice-Hall, 1968.
EYESTONE, ROBERT. *The Threads of Public Policy: A Study in Policy Leadership*. Indianapolis: Bobbs-Merrill, 1971.
HOLDEN, MATTHEW, JR. and DRESANG, DENNIS, eds. *What Government Does*. Beverly Hills: Sage, 1979.
HUNTER, FLOYD. *Top Leadership, USA*. Chapel Hill, N.C.: University of North Carolina Press, 1959.
JONES, CHARLES O. *An Introduction to the Study of Public Policy*. North Scituate, Mass.: Duxbury Press, 1977.
JONES, CHARLES O. and THOMAS, ROBERT, eds. *Public Policy Making in a Federal System*. Beverly Hills: Sage, 1976.
LOWI, THEODORE. *The End of Liberalism: The Second Republic of the United States*, 2nd ed. New York: Norton, 1979.
LOWI, THEODORE and STONE, ALAN, eds. *Nationalizing Government: Public Policies In America*. Beverly Hills: Sage, 1978.
LINEBERRY, ROBERT. *American Public Policy: What Government Does and What Difference It Makes*. New York: Harper & Row, 1977.
LOCKARD, DUANE. *The Perverted Priorities of American Politics*, 2nd ed. New York: Macmillan, 1976.
MAY, JUDITH and WILDAVSKY, AARON, eds. *The Policy Cycle*. Beverly Hills: Sage, 1978.
MILLS, C. WRIGHT. *The Power Elite*. New York: Oxford University Press, 1956.
MILLS, C. WRIGHT. "The Structure of Power in American Society," *The British Journal of Sociology* 9 (March 1958), pp. 29-41.
ORNSTEIN, NORMAN. *Interest Groups, Lobbying and Policymaking*. Washington, D.C.: Congressional Quarterly, 1978.
PASSELL, PETER and ROSS, LEONARD. *State Policies and Federal Programs*. New York: Praeger, 1978.
RAE, DOUGLAS and EISMER, THEODORE. *Public Policy and Public Choice*. Beverly Hills: Sage, 1979.

# 2

# The Policymaking Environment

For a complete picture of the policymaking process we must view it in the environment in which the action occurs. The policy environment is the total matrix of cultural, political, and ecological factors within which policy decisions are reached. This complex network includes such factors as the governmental structure, political institutions, natural resources, topography, demographic variables, political and social culture, and the economic system. Environmental factors may either help or hinder policymakers in their endeavors by creating opportunities for leadership or by imposing substantial constraints within which decisions must be made. At times the environment is a neutral factor, at other times it produces competing demands that may be difficult for policymakers to resolve.

To fully understand how policy decisions are made, we must take into account a variety of factors. The environment cannot be ignored, because it generates demands and imposes constraints as to what policymakers can or cannot do. Available resources are a major constraint factor in the policy process, for example. The level of economic development in a society will be a prime determinant as to what the government can do in providing goods and services. Even a nation with the unequalled wealth of the United States does not have the resources necessary for meeting all the demands of society. In their study of public welfare policy, Dawson and Robinson concluded that environmental factors were of greater impact on decisions than party competition.[1]

The social environment within which the government operates is another important factor in policymaking. Changes in the social environment can hold significant implications for policymaking; for example, the shift from a largely rural, agrarian society to an industrial, urban society ushered in a whole new set of issues and problems for public policymakers. Such things as the massive relocation of blacks from the rural South to the urban North, the exodus from the central city to the suburbs, the development of a highly mobile society, and changes in social attitudes and values can have dramatic implications for the policymaking process. Such social changes can bring conflict and demands for governmental action such as civil rights legislation, the Equal Rights Amendment, legalization of marijuana, or the extension of voting rights to 18-year-olds. Furthermore, such changes can occur with relative quickness, making adjustment rather difficult.

Take, for example, the change in our nation's demographic profile over the last two decades. (See figure 2.1) In the 1960s we heard a lot about "youth

**FIGURE 2.1 Percent of U.S. Population Age 65 or Over**

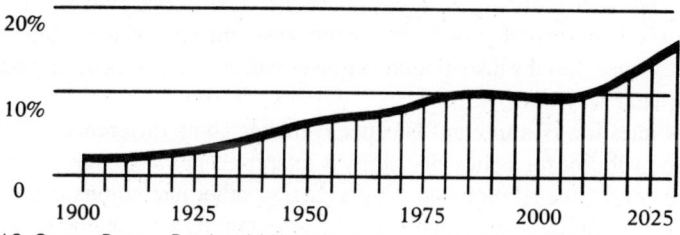

Source: U.S. Census Bureau. Reprinted with permission from The Wilson Quarterly.

power," and the average age of our population was under twenty-five. The 1970s was the decade of the emergence of "gray power," with one out of ten Americans reaching 65 years of age or older, and the median age of our population at the end of the seventies was 29.4 and rising. This "graying of America" is projected to continue, and by the year 2000 the median age is estimated at 32.5. Currently there are 22 million Americans age sixty-five or older; in thirty years the number will be 60 million. What are the implications of this for policymaking? These older Americans are a growing political and economic force who are increasingly well-organized and assertive in their demands, some of them founding a group in 1970 called the "Gray Panthers." They register and vote in larger proportionate numbers than any other age group in our society, further enhancing their political significance. As their influence continues to grow, the impact on policy priorities will become more apparent. They are inclined to oppose increased taxes and expenditures for things such as education and child support, and their influence has already been felt on social security, mandatory retirement, and age-based property tax relief legislation. This change in social composition will no doubt bring some accompanying changes in priorities for the policymakers. In a January 1979 report following a thirteen-month study, the House Select Committee on Population suggested that in the light of population changes, government agencies should seek more and better data on such trends so that policy could better reflect demographic change. Johns Hopkins economist Frank Cappiello says the "graying of America" will have greater impact over the next decade than either inflation or energy supplies. Massachusetts State Representative Barney Frank has said, "If socialism ever comes to America, it will come in a wheelchair."

The decade of the 1970s has brought other environmental changes also. Vietnam, the Cambodian incursion, Watergate, the Wilbur Mills and Wayne Havs episodes, the FBI and CIA investigations, and revelations of widespread corporate corruption have all contributed to a growing uneasiness about our governmental and political institutions. It would appear that Americans' faith in institutions and ideals, once deeply fixed and unshakeable, has been loosened by dramatic social changes. New laws governing campaign financing, new congressional ethics codes, congressional reforms and procedural changes, revisions in political party rules, modifications in presidential powers, reorganization of the intelligence agencies, and other actions have already been taken. However, the major question is, have these changes really modified the processes through which public policy is made? In essence, has the distribution of power within the system been modified in any significant way?

This question is important because it makes some difference whether the major responsibility for policy decisions is exercised in the Congress, the presidency, the courts, the administrative agencies, or other institutions. Each institution has its own unique constituency, value orientation, and method of operation that shapes its policy outputs; therefore, policies will differ depending upon which institution or institutions have the greatest role in their formulation and implementation.

Because of the fragmentation and substantial diffusion of power within our political system, the policy process is usually characterized by considerable interaction among a number of institutional participants. Citizens, legislators, judges, and bureaucrats do not operate in isolation from one another. Literally hundreds of power centers function within the political system and policies emanate from many sources as a result of constant interaction among different combinations of these various power clusters. Few of the complex problems of today fall completely within the responsibility of a single department or branch of government. Most issues, whether they deal with the economy, the environment, natural resources, or some other matter, will have impact on various segments of society and will therefore generate a multitude of viewpoints and interests that must be considered. Consequently, a national policy is likely to involve actions at a variety of levels and the participants in the process are drawn from various governmental and non-governmental institutions. Substantial institutional interaction is a hallmark of the policy process.

## CONSTITUTIONAL/STRUCTURAL FACTORS

This institutional interaction is both provided for and necessitated by the governmental structure created by the framers of our Constitution. With its concepts of federalism, separation of powers and checks and balances, the Constitution fragments governmental power and establishes all kinds of roadblocks to prevent any one branch from dominating the policy process. The only way really effective governmental action can occur is for the various levels and branches of government to cooperate and act in concert with one another. This, of course, is much easier to prescribe than it is to accomplish.

This fragmentation and careful hedging-in of governmental power by the framers was no accident. In *The Federalist* No. 51, James Madison observed, "A dependence on the people is, no doubt, the primary control on the government; but experience has taught mankind the necessity of auxiliary precautions."[2] Reflecting this suspicion and fear of unencumbered governmental power, the framers put together a constitutional framework that has lent itself much more to the curbing of powers, prevention of action, and delay of programs than it has to vigorous and bold initiatives to deal with critical problems. Because of our constitutional structure, the deck tends to be stacked in favor of those who seek to prevent action, since the complex system affords numerous points along the way where veto powers can be wielded effectively. This is why it becomes quite important for the student of the policy process to develop an understanding of the governmental structure involved. While, as Dye points out, social and economic factors may have a more direct impact on public policy than the structure or form of governmental institutions or political processes, machinery cannot be ignored.[3] In the final analysis, the machinery is the instrumentality through which public desires are translated into policies. Therefore, congressional structures and procedures, judicial review, bureaucratic organization and structure, and relations between the various branches and levels of government are all an integral part of the process for policy resolution and cannot be overlooked.

### Federalism

Largely as a result of necessity, the framers of the Constitution created a federal system in which authority was shared by two levels of government, each deriving its authority directly from the people. While the Constitution left no question as to which level of government was responsible for some areas such as foreign policy and the coining of money, in other areas it was not nearly so explicit. Consequently, in many areas of public policy both the state and federal governments have power and responsibility. Through the years, as the scope of federal activity has expanded, much of what the federal government does has become intertwined with state actions. Today officials at one level of government cannot operate very long without coming into contact with those at other levels. Because the federal system lends itself so readily to overlapping of efforts and possible conflict, cooperation between the levels of government to better coordinate their policymaking efforts becomes more and more the hallmark of this relationship, rather than conflict. Revenue sharing is a prime example of intergovernmental cooperation.

The relationships between the citizen and the different levels of government has also been altered by changes with the passage of time. In earlier days when people rode horses and wagons to the county seat, local governments were "closer to the people" and in a better position to respond to their needs and desires. Changes in communications, transportation, and political institutions have altered this relationship and in some respects the federal government in Washington may today be more closely attuned to the voters than state and local governments. Many citizens today seek solutions to their problems in Washington rather than the state capitals.

### Separation of Powers

An outgrowth of the framers' fear of uncontrolled power, this concept divides governmental authority among three branches of government—the legislative, the executive, and the judicial. In theory, each branch has distinct powers and functions: the legislature enacts the laws; the executive administers the laws; and the judiciary, when necessary, interprets the laws. In the realities of routine governmental activity, all is not so nice and neat. Quite frequently the president or the federal courts exercise legislative powers; the federal administrative agencies regularly engage in judicial functions. So, in its application to day-to-day governmental operations, the concept of separation of powers becomes somewhat less than pure. Such overlapping of functions does cause considerable jealousy among the branches and frequent conflicts over "turf" arise from this arrangement. Sometimes the friction generated may produce a stalemate, making effective action difficult or impossible. Such a division of basic governmental functions among different branches makes cooperation an important and necessary ingredient for effective policymaking.

### Checks and Balances

Closely related to the separation of powers arrangement is the concept of checks and balances. Here again the framers felt that certain safeguards were needed against the unchecked exercise of power by any one branch of government. So they built into the arrangement of separated governmental functions a system of checks by each branch over the others. Congress controls the purse, but the president possesses the veto. The courts can declare acts of either Congress or the president unconstitutional. Separation of powers and checks and balances are more than mere textbook cliches; they are realities of the politics of policymaking. They are part of an almost constant struggle among the branches of government for institutional preeminence in the governmental process. The different branches all leave their imprint on the policy process.

Again we have built into the system a tremendous potential for stalemate and inaction. This is particularly true when we bring into the picture a couple of elements the framers did not include in their constitutional structure—political parties and pressure groups. Because of the structural arrangement provided in the

Constitution, we have had three instances over the last three decades of divided party control of the machinery of government. Democratic President Harry Truman faced a Republican-controlled Congress for part of his term, and Republican Presidents Eisenhower, Nixon, and Ford had to deal with Democratic-controlled Congresses. While some cooperation develops of necessity, the phenomenon tends to complicate the policymaking endeavor and makes governmental solution of pressing policy issues more difficult. What Gerald Ford proposed, a Democrat-dominated Congress refused to enact into law; and what the Congress passed, Ford vetoed. Pressing social problems such as the economy, energy, and unemployment went largely unattended. While such inaction cannot be attributed solely to this structural arrangement, it is certainly a contributing factor.

### Congressional Committee Structure

To this point we have been considering formal or constitutional factors and their influence. The congressional committees are an informal element in the system, provided for only in the rules of each house. In fact, for many years Congress operated without committees, but over the years the legislative process has come to be dominated more and more by the committees and subcommittees. By the time Woodrow Wilson wrote his classic book, *Congressional Government*, in 1885, committees had risen to such a prominent role in the legislative process that Wilson denounced them along with the powerful speaker of the house for making it difficult for the voters to place the blame for poor performances and to bring a redress of their grievances through the ballot.[4]

No doubt the committee system does lend an element of obscurity to the policymaking process, and even with recent reforms and more committee sessions open to the public it is impossible for the average citizen to follow what goes on at the committee level. Another effect of the committee system on the policy process is to concentrate a disproportionate amount of power over particular policy areas in the hands of a relatively small number of legislators. Because of the tremendous demands on their time, members of Congress simply cannot be informed on all measures on which they must vote. The committee and subcommittee systems enable members to specialize and become "experts" in particular policy areas. Consequently, their colleagues come to rely upon them for information and defer to their judgment as the "experts" in their particular areas of policy responsibility. The result is that for all practical purposes, policy decisions of major significance are made by a handful of legislators and ratified by the remainder of their colleagues in Congress. A vast majority of the measures adopted in Congress are approved in the form reported from committee. Furthermore, the committees effectively control what comes to the floor for consideration; a major portion of all bills introduced die a quiet death in committee.

The committee structure also tends to fragment policy decisions in the Congress. Though the congressional committees are set up along subject matter lines, because of the fragmentation and diffusion of power in Congress, few policies fall into the exclusive domain of one committee. One factor complicating the development of an effective energy policy has been the fact that about sixteen different committees normally handle energy matters in Congress. The Senate recently reorganized and created a new committee on energy; but in the House, when President Carter sent his energy proposals to Congress, Speaker O'Neill elected to create a special ad hoc committee to attempt to coordinate the actions of all the other committees considering portions of the proposal. A similar situation prevails in many other policy areas.

Another impact of the committee system is the fragmentation of power among a large number of committee and subcommittee chairmen, making effective party and presidential leadership difficult. At the same time, the arrangement tends to give chairmen, who are often atypical of both their parties and their houses as a whole, disporportionate power in the policymaking process. Recent rules changes and reforms have tended to make the committee chairmen less arbitrary in their leadership and have reduced their powers somewhat, but they still exercise great power and influence and remain key figures in deciding what emerges from Congress in terms of substantive policies. It is impossible to talk about Congress's role in the policymaking process without talking about the role of congressional committees and their chairmen.

### Bicameralism

The two-house structure of Congress is another factor in the policymaking process with a number of implications. It contributes to the fragmentation of power in the system and makes effective leadership and control more difficult. The innate jealousies and competition between the House and Senate sometimes complicate the decision-making process on legislative matters. This friction is particularly apparent on appropriations and revenue legislation, where the House has jealously guarded its prerogative for taking first action on such measures, relegating the Senate Appropriations and Finance Committees to "courts of appeal" roles. The Senate, on the other hand, has held the upper hand in foreign policy because of its treaty ratification and appointee confirmation powers. The bicameral structure has also provided more "access" points for those seeking to influence policy decisions. If efforts at achieving one's policy objectives fail in one house, there's always the possibility the other may respond more favorably. Groups with only slight influence in one body may have considerable influence in the other and may be able to influence policy outcomes as a result. Thus bicameralism has come to be more in the policymaking process than just another compromise of the framers of our Constitution.

## OFFICIAL PARTICIPANTS

As we observed earlier, the policymaking process is characterized by the interaction of a variety of participants. These participants may be classified according to the basis for their involvement in the process. The *official* policymakers are those who have the constitutional or legal authority to engage in the formation, enactment, and implementation of public policy—Congress, the president, the courts. The *unofficial* participants are those who have a legitimate role in the process but do not have a constitutionally or statutorily defined role in the process—political parties, interest groups. Each of these participants, as we shall see, plays a unique role in the system.

### Congress

As we observed when talking of the concepts of separation of powers and checks and balances, the respective roles of the various branches in policymaking do not always exactly fit the textbook concepts. In theory and probably in the minds of the Constitution's framers, the Congress was to have been the principal policymaking agency of the government, at least in the realm of the formulation and enactment of legislation. Through the nineteenth century this was substantially the case as policymaking was generally dominated by Congress, a situation lamented by Woodrow Wilson as a graduate student when he wrote *Congressional Government* in the mid 1880s. Since the turn of the century, however, and especially in the years since the Great Depression, there has been a dramatic shift in the balance of power in the policymaking process. The twentieth century has seen a marked decline in the policy-initiating role of Congress relative to that of the presidency, so much so that frequent references are made to the "imperial presidency."

While much of the initiative in policymaking has shifted from the legislative to the executive branch, this does not mean that Congress has become a mere rubber stamp. Senator Alan Cranston (D-Calif.), majority whip in the Senate, says, "All decisions shouldn't be made in the White House. Congress has a constitutional responsibility to slow down and rethink executive decisions." Thus, in many areas such as foreign and defense and social welfare policies Congress has become more of a sounding board and review agency for proposals that are initiated outside its halls: reviewing, questioning, and amending proposals, but in many respects lacking the inclination, the expertise, or the time for taking the initiative. In other areas such as tax policy, subsidy policies, and some areas of regulatory policy, Congress plays a dominant role.

Involvement of the federal government in an ever-growing number of problems, the increasing complexity of issues faced, the creation of more and more departments and agencies of government, and the fact that each member represents a constantly growing number of constituents have all contributed to the changing role of the member of Congress. Because of these factors, today's congressman has become more of an ombudsman helping his constituents in their dealings with the vast federal bureaucracy than a policymaker. Even the most conscientious member finds that he simply lacks the time to be a policymaker in the fullest sense of the word. In a recent report on the typical day of a member of Congress, the House Commission on Administrative Review stated, "Rarely do members have sufficient blocks of time when they are free from the frenetic pace of the Washington 'treadmill.'" The upthrust of this is that the member of Congress, when he has attended to all his other representative duties, has only a few minutes each day to devote to policymaking in the sense that he has time to sit back and reflect on problems and their solutions, do extensive reading or research, and arrive at carefully thought out decisions.

Other factors also tend to impose constraints on Congress's policymaking role. The Congresses of the twentieth century have not been very susceptible to effective party or presidential leadership. This characteristic has become even more apparent in recent Congresses. Congressional campaigns tend to be on the whole highly personal endeavors and consequently those elected owe very little to the party. (In the 96th Congress, 72 percent of the Democrats elected ran stronger than their party's presidential candidate in their states and districts). Congressmen view themselves as being more closely attuned to their constituents than the president or their party leadership. Furthermore, they represent a variety of special and unique constituencies with widely differing interests. Finally, within the Congress power is widely dispersed among a number of highly individualistic committee and subcommittee chairmen. Add to this the fact that, as one House leadership source lamented, "sanctions are almost non-existent," and it all boils down to a system that means that the party leadership faces a tremendous task in trying to deliver a bloc vote in support of almost any measure.

The leadership's role is further complicated by recent rather large-scale changes in the membership in Congress. Seventy percent of all House members have served less than ten years, with just under one-half of them having been elected since 1972. This takes on added significance because this new generation of senators and representatives is a different breed. They are better educated, better informed, and much more independent in their behavior than were many of their predecessors. To paraphrase the late Hubert Humphrey, members of Congress are politically independent; they don't march to the drum beat of the president or the party leaders. This is particularly true of Congress currently. The decline in the traditional power centers—the committee chairmen and the party leadership—coupled with the growing influence of special interest groups and the personal independence of the younger members, has made effective leadership and direction of Congress almost impossible. As Representative Morris Udall (D-Ariz.) has observed, it is hard enough anytime to get members to sacrifice their parochial concerns, but it becomes all the more difficult when power is widely dispersed.

The fragmentation of congressional interests is attested to by the variety of special groups developing within the body itself. Joining some of the older groups such as the Black Caucus are the Senate and House Steel Caucuses, the Mushroom Caucus (seventy-six members), the Roller and Ball Bearing Coalition (thirty-five members), the Shipyard Coalition (forty-five members), and the High Altitude Coalition (to promote clean air and mass transit). These internal groups reflect the growing impact on Congress of special interests, which makes presidential and party leadership more and more difficult. Effective leadership is also complicated by a growing spirit of independence in the Congress as it becomes more determined to compete with the executive on an equal footing. This determination has been manifested in Congress's enactment since January 1976 of over sixty provisions that provide for legislative vetoes of executive action or require advance notification of action to be taken, as well as Congress's efforts to improve its status relative to the executive in terms of support staff, research capacity, and independent sources of information. Such efforts should help Congress establish more independence in the policy process, but at the same time current trends toward decentralization of power and excessive fragmentation of interests frequently make effective congressional action difficult if not impossible. It is Congress's apparent inability to arrive at any consensus on pressing issues of the day that has contributed to its poor standing in public confidence. At the same time it is asserting its independence in policymaking, the Congress must also develop means for overcoming the growing fragmentation of power and intense parochialism that have come to characterize the legislative branch. This may prove more difficult than reasserting itself relative to the executive.

## President

The very nature of our constitutional system builds into the policymaking process an innate antagonism between the president and Congress. Governing the country requires the support of two different constituencies which are frequently in conflict —a presidential constituency and a congressional constituency. The presidential constituency is a national constituency, broad-based and much less specific in terms of narrowly defined interests. The congressional constituency by contrast is much narrower, consisting of the various regional and rather parochial interests throughout the country. It is characterized by a highly acquisitive instinct (pork barrel) and an even stronger inclination for self-protection and self-preservation.[5] It is most adept at defending the status quo. An example of how their different constituencies often bring presidents and members of Congress into conflict is the current issue of energy policy. Senator J. Bennett Johnston, Jr. of Louisiana is the chairman of the Senate subcommittee dealing with energy conservation and regulation. A fellow southerner and member of the same party as President Carter, the two would be expected to view issues in much the same way. However, Louisiana has large supplies of intrastate natural gas, and should the president, looking out for his national constituency, have proposed a plan to allocate Louisiana's intrastate gas to other regions, this would quickly have brought Carter and Johnston on a collision course. In this sort of arrangement, horse-trading, bargaining, and compromise become the essence of the policymaking process.

The system really functions most effectively in times of emergency or national crisis. It is in such situations that the regional constituent interests tend to be subordinated more to overriding national interests and the situation lends itself more to effective policy leadership. It is such periods of crisis and turmoil that have produced most of our "great" presidents.

Much of the president's problem in dealing effectively with Congress on policy matters arises from the very fact that Congress has become so accustomed to government by "crisis management" that when no crisis exists it becomes difficult to generate the consensus necessary for action. In the wake of these pressing emergency situations, the various vested interests that were suppressed or pushed to the rear by the crisis reassert themselves with renewed vigor, and effective leadership again becomes difficult. These are times that Woodrow Wilson described as "congressional government." Under such circumstances, Congress is largely unresponsive to pleas to "come let us reason together."

Another factor complicating effective presidential leadership in recent years is that the skills currently required for getting elected to the presidency are of little use in attaining his goals once elected. What motivates the electorate—appearing well on television, projecting decency, integrity, maturity, intelligence, and authority, and not being an "insider"—may be of little value in getting the necessary action once in the government. Once in office, a whole different set of talents is necessary—horse-trading, bullying, cajoling, patronage management, the setting of priorities, and the act of give-and-take.

The first year of President Carter's administration was a prime example of this phenomenon at work. Much of Carter's appeal to the electorate stemmed from his image as an "outsider" and his projection of the "down home" qualities of honesty and decency. While these were advantages in his campaign, they were of little value, maybe even handicaps because he assumed he could continue the same approach, once elected. The White House is, as Teddy Roosevelt observed, a "bully pulpit," and the temptation is strong to misconstrue rhetoric for action. If not already aware of the fact, presidents learn quickly that the Constitution does not provide them with unlimited power. The White House is not a command post from which orders are accepted and carried out unquestioningly. The president must use his position to bargain and develop support for his programs.

The president, if he is going to bridge the gap between presidential and congressional constituencies, must be an effective political "bargainer." He must employ all the various tools available to him in the form of patronage, favors, invitations to the White House, phone calls, and support for pet projects to build up support and obligations. The relationship between the president and Congress in the policymaking process is not so much a "reasoning" process as it is one of bargaining, mutual accommodation, and give-and-take. It was the early refusal to make this type of accommodation that handicapped the Carter presidency in its early efforts. On the water projects cancellations, matters of considerable concern to the constituents of several members of Congress, Carter went for principle rather than accommodation. He ultimately dropped only nine of eighteen proposed projects, but in the process stepped on a number of congressional toes. Also, by opposing the price levels in the 1977 farm bill and the level of the appropriation for HEW, Carter alienated the farmers and urban Democrats. These types of actions tend to stiffen congressional resolve and make future compromise more difficult.

A couple of additional key elements in the president's handling of policy issues are timing and the determination of priorities. To be most effective in getting his programs approved, a president needs to develop some momentum. Each victory he achieves makes the next contest a bit easier; on the other hand, if he develops an early image as a lightweight, his task will be all the more difficult. Reflecting on the first year of the Carter administration, Vice President Walter Mondale said he feared the president might have overloaded Congress with too many issues and as a consequence many got pushed to the back burner. Some

Carter aides indicated a feeling that he had "dissipated the moral force of the presidency" on too many different fights rather than zeroing in on a more limited number of top priority items. This "shotgun" approach may make it difficult to generate the needed momentum to get major issues moving through the process, and because the president's power is limited it should not be dissipated on fights that are not really all that important.

Though much of the leadership in the policy process has shifted to the president in this century, he remains one of a number of power centers, and he must be particularly cognizant of the role of Congress. He ignores the Congress and its leaders only with considerable risk to his programs. Many members of Congress have extremely sensitive egos, and if they feel ignored by a president this can be sufficient cause for foot-dragging on key proposals. It is a good practice for the president to confer with the party leaders and key members as frequently as time will allow. Otherwise he runs a risk of alienating those who can smooth the way for the enactment of his policy proposals into law.

The president's role in the policy process also depends upon his own individual style, ego, expectations, and concepts of his office and its responsibilities. Some presidents are much more vigorous in their leadership than others. Contrasting the Carter and Johnson styles, James Reston, columnist for the *New York Times*, wrote that Johnson said, "come let us reason together" and then skulled with a two-by-four those who didn't go along. Carter, Reston said, really believes reason will work. Several members of Congress, including the house speaker, advised President Carter that he needed to make his presence felt more on Capitol Hill.

The president has a number of advantages in policymaking: the visibility and symbolic status of the office; his position and status as spokesman and leader of the entire country; his access to the latest and most complete information available; the unity of his office; and the great variety of resources at his disposal. Nonetheless, the system necessitates a certain degree of cooperation and interaction if anything is to be accomplished. While the president can usually place items on the agenda without too much difficulty, he lacks the power and authority to dictate their substance.

In his book *The Presidency*, Aaron Wildavsky says there are really "two presidencies," one for domestic policy and one for foreign policy. In an article in the *Presidential Studies Quarterly*, Robert Spitzer expands on this concept by identifying four "presidencies." These "presidencies" are related to the executive role and type of policy involved. They are the "Special Interest Presidency" dealing with subsidy policies, the "Presidential Broker" dealing with regulatory policies, the "Public Servant Presidency" dealing with policies of redistribution, and the "Administrative Presidency" dealing with management policies.[6] Regardless of the policy type, presidents engage in three policy-related functions—policy formation and initiation, policy advocacy or support building, and policy application and execution. The president's role in the policy process has become more and more complicated as a result of some significant changes in the political system over the last three decades. The legacies of Watergate and Vietnam have eroded presidential authority, and with the political parties' decline in influence, his party no longer provides a president much leverage. Reforms in Congress have fragmented power and dispersed it widely, and the rise of myriad single issue groups has greatly intensified the problems of compromise and consensus building. In this type of political environment it became easier for President Carter to get an Arab-Israeli accord at Camp David than to get an energy policy through Congress. Effective leadership has become difficult if not impossible.

### Courts

Writing about the United States in the nineteenth century, French nobleman Alexis de Tocqueville took note of the special esteem Americans displayed for their courts. Twentieth century U. S., if anything, has become even more judicially oriented. In no other country in the world do the courts play a more significant role in the policymaking process than in the United States. Sooner or later virtually every major policy issue finds its way into the courtroom for resolution, redress, or at least a hearing. Through their exercise of judicial review and statutory interpretation, the courts have played a key role in determining the nature and content of public policy. In fact, the mere existence of the power of judicial review has frequently affected policy decisions in other branches such as Congress, the presidency, or the regulatory agencies.

Quite frequently the provisions of the statutes are rather generally stated as in the case of the Interstate Commerce Act, the Sherman Antitrust Act, the Natural Gas Act of 1938, and many others; therefore, it falls the lot of the courts to flesh out such laws by interpreting key words and phrases. Key provisions of the Constitution such as the Commerce Clause, the Necessary and Proper Clause, or the Fourteenth Amendment have also been interpreted by the courts in such a way that the thrust of policy in such areas as the regulation of business, civil rights, legislative apportionment, and individual rights have been substantially affected.

Traditionally the courts, through their applications of common law and equity, played a significant role in the formation of economic policy. But in recent years they have become a much more positive force in the policy process as they have ventured into more and more areas previously considered off-limits to the judiciary: such volatile areas as apportionment, welfare, the environment, abortion, etc. Also, the courts have made their weight felt more by specifying in their decisions not only what government cannot do, but spelling out, quite specifically in some cases, what it must do to meet its legal or constitutional responsibilities. Thus, while the courts have always been a rather potent instrument at the disposal of those who sought to block the effective implementation of policy decisions, they now lend themselves as well to those elements seeking positive governmental action for a redress of grievances. Some view such action on the part of the courts as a violation of the constitutional concept of separation of powers. Others point out that such judicial lawmaking has been the only means for bringing about positive governmental action on such difficult issues as civil rights and apportionment. Regardless of how one views judicial activism, it has made the courts a more potent participant in the policy process.

## Bureaucracy

Not provided for in the Constitution but created by Congress and the president, the vast federal bureaucracy has become at the same time one of the most important and most criticized participants in the policymaking process. No doubt Norman

*Reprinted with the permission of Jeff MacNelly.*

Thomas is correct when he says, "It is doubtful that any modern industrial society could manage the daily operation of its public affairs without bureaucratic organizations in which officials play a major policy-making role."[7] Its necessity does not, however, make the bureaucracy a lot more palatable to its constituents. In the Declaration of Independence our forefathers complained that George III had "erected a multitude of new offices, and sent hither swarms of officers to harass our people and eat out their substance." And what did they know of bureaucracies?

When we speak of the bureaucracy, we make reference to those political appointees in executive branch organizations, all civil servants, part of the military establishment, portions of the congressional operation, and probably should include those state and local employees whose positions are funded largely with federal revenues. This vast network is made up of almost 2,000 agencies and employs close to 3 million persons, of which only a small portion actually work in the nation's capital. About 84 percent are scattered across the nation in a vast network of regional and local field offices and another 6 percent work in foreign countries. An example of the federal bureaucratic structure is the United States Department of Commerce. It is composed of thirteen bureaus, sixty-three field offices, and eleven overseas trade offices, and has its own naval and air fleets, research laboratories, and vast statistical resources. Its annual budget is in excess of $2 billion and its staff fluctuates between 38,000 and 40,000 employees. Neither the largest nor smallest of federal departments, Commerce is larger than some national governments. Created for good purpose and in the belief that sound administrative effort was essential for effective policymaking, the federal bureaucracy has been allowed to grow like topsy. (See figure 2.2) While growth in the

**FIGURE 2.2  Government Employment**

| Year | Federal (1000s) | State and Local (1000s) | All Governmental Units (1000s) | Federal as % of Total |
|---|---|---|---|---|
| 1942 | 2272 | 3310 | 5582 | 40.7 |
| 1947 | 2082 | 3568 | 5650 | 36.8 |
| 1952 | 2574 | 4134 | 6708 | 38.4 |
| 1957 | 2391 | 5380 | 7771 | 30.8 |
| 1962 | 2485 | 6533 | 9018 | 27.6 |
| 1967 | 2877 | 8898 | 11775 | 24.4 |
| 1972 | 2795 | 10964 | 13759 | 20.3 |
| 1975 | 2890 | 12097 | 14628 | 19.3 |

Source: U.S. Census Data and Statistical Abstract of the United States.

federal bureaucracy has been substantial, it has not matched the growth in state and local bureaucracies over the last two decades. (See figure 2.3)

As both the volume and technicality of the governmental workload has grown, more and more responsibility has been delegated to the bureaucracy. These factors, coupled with the legislators' lack of time and information and limited enthusiasm for wrestling with highly controversial political issues, have resulted in many matters being referred to the bureaucrats for action.

As more and more policymaking responsibility has been delegated to administrative agencies, their role and influence have dramatically increased. Today agencies in the federal bureaucracy regularly make decisions that have far-reaching political and policy implications. Administrative interpretation and application can make or break a statute or program enacted elsewhere. Many a policy's impact has been blunted by heel-dragging and non-enforcement by administrative agencies. One of the reasons President Johnson set up the OEO (Office of Economic Opportunity) as a separate agency reporting directly to the White House when launching his War on Poverty was to try to avoid some of the bureaucratic inertia and status quo orientation of the established departments and agencies. The personnel who develop and administer governmental programs are just as important in determining a policy's final impact as is the statutory content of the program.

Not only do they play a key role in policy administration, the bureaucrats also make a sizable amount of public policy without any direct input from other sources in government. While some legislation delegating authority to the agencies is tightly and specifically drawn, the trend has been toward broad, unrestrictive grants of authority. The 1964 Economic Opportunity Act, for example, left to OEO the interpretation of the meaning of "maximum feasible participation." In interpreting and applying such broad, general terminology, the agencies engage in extensive policymaking themselves. A steadily increasing proportion of the laws

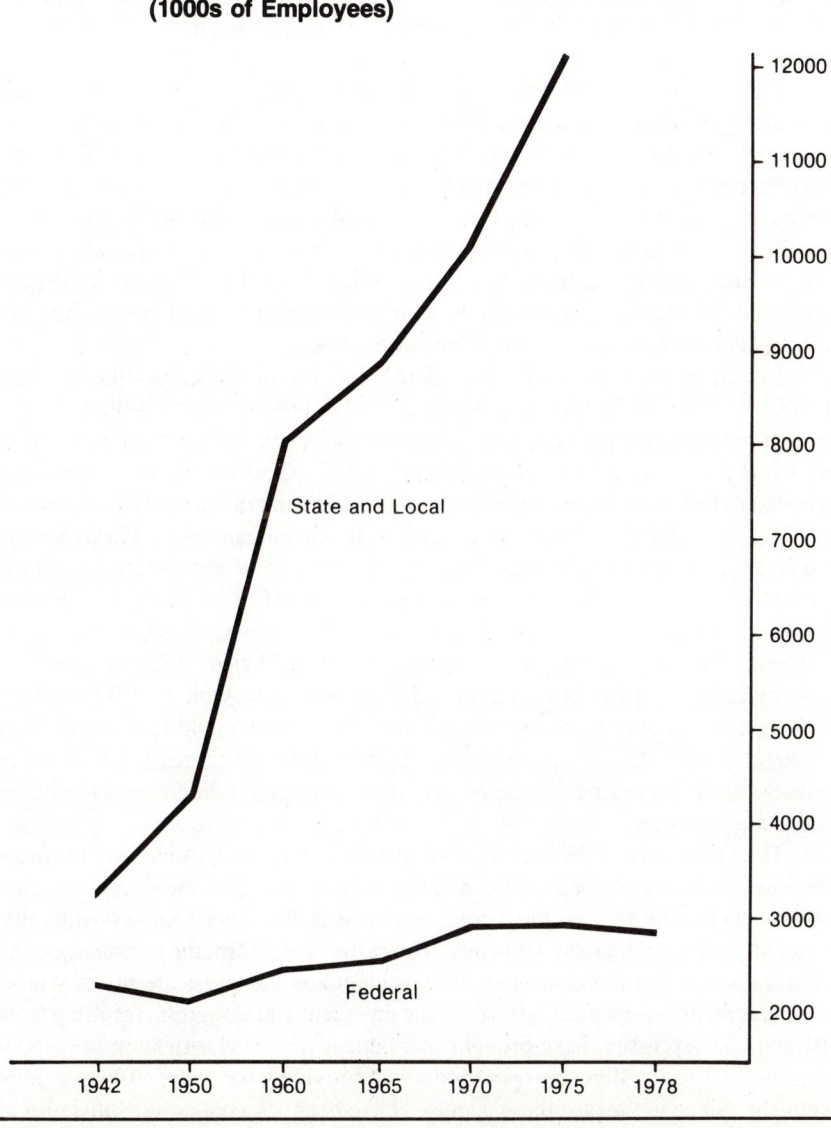

**FIGURE 2.3 Growth in Governmental Employment 1942–1978 (1000s of Employees)**

under which we operate are not really "laws" but rules and regulations formulated and implemented by unelected bureaucrats in the agencies created by Congress.

The role of the bureaucracy in the policy process is not confined to interpreting and implementing policies once enacted; it is also an active, sometimes dominant, participant in the initiation and formulation of policy proposals. Since they are directly involved with the day-to-day administration of policies and programs, the bureaucrats are in a better position than others to see whether policies are having the desired impact. Consequently there is extensive interaction among the bureaucracy, the president, and Congress in the formulation of policies. Not only do the agencies suggest needed action, they also lobby vigorously on behalf of particular programs.

The role, power, and influence of this vast bureaucratic network pose some areas of concern in policymaking. How do we keep such a behemoth composed of unelected officials responsive and responsible to the public's needs and desires? The perspectives of the departments, agencies, and bureaus composing the bureaucracy are inherently narrower than those of the president; and because of the way they are organized, they cultivate and in turn are cultivated by special interests and develop special constituencies. These alliances of the agencies and departments and their special constituencies then become powerful lobbies pushing for dollars, recognition, prestige, and special treatment.

Effective oversight of what President Carter has described as "the horrible, bloated bureaucracy" becomes a highly desirable but most formidable task. We have already noted that on the whole the bureaucracy proceeds about its business without much meaningful direction from Congress. Occasionally an agency may be called to task in its budget hearing or an investigation threatened by an irritated member, but ordinarily Congress is willing to let the bureaucracy go its own way. Thus, it falls the lot of the president to provide most of the direction, and the bureaucracy is so vast that it makes impossible any effective direct relationships with the bureaucrats. And even in those instances when he undertakes some effort at reform, the president may find his hands are tied. President Carter decided a good place to start his bureaucratic reforms would be with the 1175 federal advisory boards, only to discover that a mere 16 of them could be terminated by unilateral presidential action, with the others requiring congressional action as well. So there is nothing simple or easy about bringing a huge and entrenched bureaucracy to heel.

The imperative of the bureaucratic agency is self-preservation; and the more activities, the more personnel it has and the larger its budgets, the stronger its case for existence. The bureaucrat whose existence is threatened knows wiles that would make Svengali green with envy. Thus efforts to reform the bureaucracy and bring it more under the control of the president and Congress are no easy task. However, recent cooperative efforts by the president and Congress, resulting from FBI and CIA excesses, have brought reorganization and clarification of responsibilities in the intelligence operations and provided for more effective joint oversight. Since in the past these agencies have been "sacred cows," this turn of events indicates the case is not hopeless.

## UNOFFICIAL PARTICIPANTS

In addition to the official participants already discussed, there are a number of unofficial participants who play important roles in the policymaking process. These participants are classified as unofficial, not because they are any less significant or lack influence, but because they do not usually possess any constitutional or statutory authority to make legally binding policy decisions. Their involvement is usually less direct than that of the official policymakers. These unofficial participants play a particularly important role in the expression and advocacy of policy demands, the presentation of alternatives, and the pulling together of competing elements into working coalitions on particular policy issues.

### Political Parties

While the Constitution makes no provision for the participation of parties in the governmental process, they have become an integral and important part of the American political system. Currently our parties are held in rather low esteem, with some observers even predicting their imminent demise. Over the years they have proved to be resilient institutions and they will likely continue to be a viable part of the political process, though their role may change. Regardless of their future, any current evaluation of the policy process without a consideration of parties would be incomplete.

In the United States we have traditionally had what is referred to as a "weak party system." This has no reference to the role or importance of parties, but rather refers to their organizational structure and the lines of authority within that structure. American party organization is characterized by a high degree of decentralization, with power flowing from the grass roots level toward the top rather than from the top down. The national party organizations have traditionally exercised little control over state and local party organizations or their rank-and-file membership. Few instruments exist for imposing any degree of discipline from the top down.

On the whole, American parties have been more electorally oriented, concerning themselves more with getting their nominees elected to office than with policy. To a marked degree this may be attributed to a similar lack of policy orientation on the part of the electorate. This is not to say that there are no differences in the policy orientations of our two major parties. In fact, some policy issues are highly partisan while others tend to divide policymakers along other lines. Party alignments may be quite pronounced on such policy items as welfare, labor, business regulation, public power, public housing, and farm price supports. Other issues, such as foreign policy, may be highly bipartisan.

A significant contribution of parties to the policy process has been their role in the organization of and leadership selection in Congress. The parties have been effective instruments in staffing the machinery of Congress and have provided the motive power that makes the legislative wheels turn. Beyond this, however, the role of the parties as policymaking instruments has been less effective. Both parties have "policy" committees in the two houses of Congress, but as instruments for determining party positions on policy issues and then bringing the party's members in line with these positions, they have been ineffective. Unlike the British member of Parliament who feels his first obligation is to his party, the U. S. congressman feels his primary loyalty is to his personal constituency. This parochialism of the Congress makes effective party leadership on controversial policy issues extremely difficult. Thus the policy commitees in Congress serve as forums for debate where issues can be discussed and party views presented, but individual members remain relatively free to vote their own convictions or constituencies. Because of the nature of our system and the congressman's concept of his representative role, the influence of the parties as policy leaders is blunted in the legislature.

Since their primary focus is on gaining political power through election to public office, parties have not been prolific sources of initiative and creativity in developing and promoting policy issues. Probably their major contribution to the process has been the pulling together of divergent interests into workable coalitions so that policy action has been possible in the institutions of government.

### Interest Groups

Another most significant unofficial participant whose influence was noted by Madison in *Federalist* No. 10, but whose role has grown significantly since that time, is interest groups or pressure groups. The impact of these groups in the policy process is enhanced by the weak party system. Though their power and influence derives from no formally defined role in the government, interest groups have been co-opted into the policymaking process itself and their impact is substantial.

When visiting in the mid-nineteenth century, de Tocqueville noted Americans' penchant for "joining." Organizing for the purpose of attaining political objectives has become more and more common in recent decades as the number and variety of special interest groups have grown substantially. In the early 1940s there were still only about 1900 trade and professional associations and labor unions; today there are more than 6300 such groups. Not only have the numbers grown, but the types of groups engaging in political activity have changed also. Traditional lobby groups such as the AFL-CIO, National Association of Manufacturers (NAM), American Medical Association (AMA), American Farm Bureau Federation, Chamber of Commerce, and Americans for Democratic Action have been joined by a vast array of public interest and single-issue groups. Since the 1960s public interest groups such as Common Cause, Consumers Union, Consumer Federation of America, Ralph Nader's Congress Watch, the Sierra Club, and others have had considerable impact on legislative action in such areas as auto safety, campaign finance, and environmental protection. Because they tend to attract as members local opinion leaders, these groups frequently wield influence beyond their numbers alone. Their strength is also enhanced by their ability to focus on single issues and to frequently combine efforts in ad hoc coalitions. Operating with less visibility but also with increasing influence on public policymaking are a number of private or semi-private agencies. Foundations such as Ford, Rockefeller, Carnegie, Brookings, and the American Enterprise Institute have come to have a substantial impact on public policy. Through such structures as the huge multi-national corporations, the private sector has also come to have more and more impact on public-policy decisions. Many economists are coming to the conclusion that one reason governmental efforts to control the economy haven't been more successful is because their impact has been negated or substantially blunted by private actions and decisions. In whose interest are such decisions made, and how do public policy decisions accommodate such outside influences?

As more and more citizens have turned to organized groups for promoting their special political interests, the society has become more fragmented and conflict resolution has become more difficult. We have movements for black power, gray power, gay power; we have the sunbelt versus the frostbelt, the environmentalists versus the developers, the hardhats versus the hippies — all equally dedicated to protecting their rights. In the words of Harvard President Derek Bok, "When so many groups organize to protect their special interests, the politics of activism can become a politics of immobility, and we find ourselves unable to reach effective solutions for inflation, energy shortages, environmental issues or other national problems."[8]

This politics of confrontation, in which interest groups seem less and less inclined to exercise the political talent for accommodation and compromise, makes policy decisions extremely difficult. The policymakers feel trapped in a series of special-group confrontations, and decisions, if possible at all, satisfy no one. Thus, interest groups when they function in this manner tend to complicate policymaking by emphasizing confrontation and conflict rather than pulling competing interests together and helping with consensus formation.

Because they usually act on behalf of rather narrow, specialized interests, groups are viewed by many as being high-pressure, anti-democratic spokesmen for narrow segments of society. On the whole, however, group involvement in the policy process is usually based on mutual consultation and long-term interaction with other governmental institutions rather than high-pressure, hard-sell tactics. The touchstone as far as organized interest groups are concerned is "access." They work long and hard to develop relationships with the official policymakers that will enable them to get a hearing when matters in which they have a direct interest come before the decision-makers. Administrators, congressmen, and interest-group representatives frequently work together on a long-term basis. It is really not unusual for the representatives of certain interest groups and administrators and congressmen to consult and work together on an issue of mutual concern. Sometimes such collaboration may extend over a period of years. In this regard, the balance between cooperation and mutual assistance and collusion probably depends on one's point of view.

Regardless of how one views interest groups, they do make some worthwhile contributions to the policy process. They provide an element of functional representation in the process that is lacking in our formal system of representation based on geographical districts. Because they are many in number and quite broad in their interests, they provide a voice for certain elements in our diverse society that would not otherwise be heard. They supply our official policymakers with useful information and data, frequently of a highly specialized and technical nature. In this way they contribute to the relevance and validity of policies enacted. They also serve as a source of initiative and creativity in generating policy demands and even in helping to formulate programs and alternatives. In this way they help to broaden the base for inputs into the system and make active participants of elements in society who otherwise would not be involved. Finally, these groups, like parties, may help facilitate decision-making by generating consensus among their members and among other groups through coalition building, although more recently groups seem to have been more of a divisive factor in our society than promoters of compromise and consensus building.

Because victory in our system most frequently goes to the group able to enlist the support of the largest number of public officials, there is some possibility for abuse and unequal treatment inherent in this process. The power and influence of organized groups depends on a number of factors such as size, cohesiveness, political skills, social status, presence or absence of competing groups, attitudes of public officials, locus of the decision-making, and financial resources. Since the possession of these skills and resources can be decisive factors in a group's campaign for a particular policy and since they are not possessed equally by all groups, the system does not respond equally for all participants. Those interests that have the money, organizational skills, and other political resources can get their cases heard and in many instances achieve their policy goals. It is those groups who lack the necessary resources who may have considerable difficulty even getting their interests on the policy agenda. Thus, while groups play a vital role in bringing issues to the attention of the official policymakers, certain significant social issues may remain overlooked.

### Citizens

Though in theory all authority for policymaking ultimately rests with the people, the individual citizen is often almost totally ignored in discussions of policymaking. Some citizens such as Rachel Carson or Ralph Nader may engage in activities that have impact on public policy, but on the whole the individual citizen makes his weight felt only by joining with others to take collective action on matters of mutual concern. It is the normal pattern for public officials to define public policies, and public debate and involvement may occur after the formal decisions are made.

Because the people do, in a sense, have a constitutional role in the process, the author had some difficulty in deciding whether to place them with the official or unofficial policymakers. Since their role is more indirect than direct, however, I felt they would fit most logically in the unofficial category. Under the concept of republican government, policy demands on the part of the citizen should be expressed primarily through contacts between constituents and their representatives and through voting for elective policymakers on the basis of issues presented in election campaigns. The republican theory loses quite a bit in its translation into the realities of electoral politics in the United States. Neither our political parties, the candidates, nor the electorate are very policy oriented. Most people are not particularly concerned about problems unless they affect them directly, and survey research shows the majority of voters to be neither well-informed nor deeply interested in political issues. Add to this widespread lack of interest the lack of detailed and accurate information, the highly complex nature of many policy issues, the tremendous diversity of views on any given issue, and in some cases a need to act expediently and with some degree of secrecy, and extensive public involvement in the process becomes rather impractical. Solutions to most complex issues of public policy ultimately have to be hammered out by a relatively small number of public officials and policy experts rather than by a heterogeneous public pulled in a variety of directions by the issues, candidate personalities, and smooth campaign rhetoric. Even if campaigns do involve a serious discussion of policy issues, an election at two-, four-, or six-year intervals can seldom be interpreted as a clear-cut mandate on policy because of the variety and number of issues normally involved. Very rarely do election campaigns define policy issues clearly and completely for the voters. Add to this the fact that the policymaking task is shared by many participants and institutions not directly responsible to the voters and the effectiveness of elections as instruments for citizen expressions of their policy wishes is further blunted.

While all these factors combine to reduce the direct involvement of citizens in the process, it should not lead to the conclusion that their role is meaningless. Since large numbers of the policymakers *are* popularly elected, they are not immune to public pressure and the vote is not a meaningless exercise in futility. Likewise, letters, telegrams, phone calls, and direct personal contacts are not without their impact. When other means fail, acts of civil disobedience, mass demonstrations, and political violence make their weight felt in policy decisions. Thus, while the citizen's direct involvement in the process is rather limited, there are numerous devices for influencing policy outcomes.

## Public Opinion

An integral part of citizen participation and influence in the policymaking process is public opinion. While the impact of public opinion on policy decisions will vary from issue to issue and situation to situation, it is a vital element in the linkage between the rank-and-file citizens and their policymakers. Because of their elective status, the president and members of Congress are more subject to the influence of public opinion; but unelected policymakers—the judges and bureaucrats—are not immune to its pressures. As an element in the policymaking process, public opinion is highly volatile. On many issues public sentiment may lie dormant for some time, only to be sparked to groundswell proportions over a relatively short period. The impact of public opinion on the policymaking process depends on a number of factors—the depth and intensity of opinions expressed, the type of policy involved and its impact on constituents, and the inclination of the policymakers to consider public sentiment on a particular issue. Sometimes policy issues may bring a quick groundswell of public debate and reaction but these may dissipate rather quickly. The reaction to President Carter's request for the reinstating of registration for the draft is an example. On other issues, such as the busing of schoolchildren to achieve integration, opinions may form more slowly but persist over long periods of time. Public opinion is likely to be more intense and more persistent on issues that affect the voters most directly and intimately—issues such as taxes, social security, and inflation, for example. Policymakers respond to public opinion in different ways depending on the issues involved and the individual. Some elected officials are much more receptive to public pressures than others. Congressmen are usually more responsive to public pressure at election time, and members from closely competitive districts are likely to be more responsive than those from safe districts. Legislators may also feel more inclined to respect public sentiment on some issues than on others. On an issue such as the Panama Canal Treaty or the SALT II treaty a member might feel that national interest as he views it should take precedence over opinions of a less-informed public. Thus, in the final analysis, while public opinion plays a vital linkage role between citizens and policymakers, its impact on policy outcomes will vary greatly from issue to issue and situation to situation.

## The Media

Closely tied to public opinion and its role in policymaking in American society today is the media. The emergence of modern media technologies and their greatly expanded role in society have had far-reaching effects on American political institutions and the policymaking process. The media serve as a two-way channel through which policymakers and constituents can communicate, thus performing a vital linkage function in the system. More importantly, however, the media have resulted in changes in the political process itself. Using modern media technologies and techniques, the candidate for public office can now form a direct relationship with the electorate and get elected. This has been a contributing factor in the decline of political parties and their role in the system. With television providing an instant audience of millions, presidents are more and more inclined to seek to govern by circumventing the system and going directly to the people. And though the media may work well in helping candidates get elected, it is not a substitute for the hard give-and-take bargaining and compromise that are an integral part of policymaking. Our elected policymakers cannot afford to think that media politics is a substitute for effective governing.

Because they are both selective and interpretive in what they present, the media also have a tremendous impact on the perceptions and opinions formed by their audiences. Thus, public opinion on significant public issues may be the result not of public analysis of the facts of the situation, but rather of the interpretations and selective presentations of the media. What the media choose as newsworthy and the emphasis they place on these events are most important in determining public perceptions and responses. Pictures of police dogs attacking demonstrators in Alabama can have significant effect on the civil rights movement, or the picture of a South Vietnamese official brutally executing a Viet Cong prisoner can help shape attitudes on U. S. involvement in Southeast Asia.

Some observers are inclined to view the overall effect of the media as being even more pervasive than its immediate impact on public perceptions and opinion. In an article in the *Washington Monthly*, Curtis Gans says the decline in participation in elections and in community political and social institutions was simultaneous with the advent of television as a central factor in the lives of millions of Americans. He feels the rise of the "media candidate," with the accompanying decline of party role and influence, accounts for this.[9] American correspondent for the *Times* of London, Henry Fairlie, writes:

... America is now becoming politically illiterate. Largely as a result of television and of the distortions in the political system for which it is responsible, a whole generation now exists which has very little understanding of what politics is and so despises its methods even while cursing the politicians.[10]

The media can be an effective tool in governing when skillfully used, as demonstrated by FDR with the radio and Charles de Gaulle with television. Use of the media should not be confused, however, as a substitute for effective leadership and skillful political bargaining, which are essential to governmental decision-making. Roosevelt and de Gaulle were successful not because of the "fireside chats" and television appeals, but because of their consummate political skills.

## SOCIAL AND CULTURAL FACTORS

Though their application to the policymaking process may be quite difficult and, for those who prefer a more scientific approach, rather imprecise, political, social, and cultural factors must be considered as significant elements in the policymaking environment. The values, beliefs, and attitudes prevalent within the society serve as both guidelines and constraints for those making policy decisions for the system. In the United States the overriding concern for individual freedom has fostered a rather widespread and persistent opposition to governmental involvement in certain realms of activity. In Great Britain, governmental ownership and operation of key industries has been rather widely accepted for decades; yet, in the United States, governmental ownership is rather generally opposed. The strong American aversion to socialism is a major reason for the adoption of a system of extensive governmental regulation rather than governmental ownership and operation. Though the welfare rolls have grown persistently over the last few decades, deeply felt beliefs that a really good citizen should refuse public assistance and take care of himself are still persistent both among citizens and policymakers in the U.S.

Thus, what a people feel and what they think, especially about government and its role in their lives, has considerable significance for policymaking. A substantial part of political activity is influenced not so much by rules or by governmental structures, but by the expectations, the attitudes, and those other intangibles that people understand to have a bearing on governmental decision-making. Such factors as the existence of various subcultures and regions within the society, each having its own set of values, ideologies, and traditions, have implications for policymaking. Is the society more future oriented or past oriented? This may determine whether it invests more heavily in space programs and the environment or puts its dollars in social security, hospitals, and subsidies to failing businesses.

Recent decades have brought considerable change to American society. What have been the implications as far as citizen attitudes on government and related political matters? It appears that skepticism about the efficacy of federal programs has been growing and there is an increasing reluctance to have the government undertake more responsibilities than it already has. At the same time there has been an erosion of confidence in political institutions and the ability of the average citizen to have much influence on governmental and political processes. A 1970 national survey showed that half those responding agreed with the statement, "The government is pretty much run by a few big interests looking out for themselves." Only 14 percent of those questioned agreed that the government was "run for the benefit of all the people."[11] In 1964, 60 percent of the respondents surveyed expressed confidence in elections as a means of influencing government; by 1972 fewer than 50 percent retained that confidence. A Harris poll in 1978 showed some improvement as 54 percent said voting made a difference, while 38 percent felt it did not. In 1964, 20 percent of those questioned had confidence in political parties; in 1972, fewer than 10 percent continued to hold that view. This declining confidence in parties and elections has been reflected in lower rates of voter participation over the last decade. In 1960, 63.8 percent of the eligible voters voted for president. In 1976, only 54.4 percent voted. In the November 1978 elections only 37.9 percent of those eligible participated, the lowest rate since 1942; 59 million voted while 96 million who were eligible did not. In some elections for the House, participation was under 35 percent. This seems to indicate that a growing number of voters feel their vote simply does not matter. Since democratic government depends upon substantial constituent participation, this growing voter pessimism and sense of futility is cause for concern.

While a number of complex reasons probably account for these voter attitudes, a contributing factor has no doubt been the creation of unrealistic expectations of the government through overselling on the part of candidates for public office. Ben Wattenberg, author of *The Real Majority*, has observed that overblown rhetoric dispensed by ambitious politicans "destroys our feeling of self-worth as a nation, distorts our policy judgments, and turns people to six-packs rather than political involvement." He concludes that much of the disillusionment results from overexpectation. The government, he says, is expected to come up with solutions that not even religions can provide. Thus, to stem this tide of rising expectations and to place governmental ability to solve difficult public issues in proper perspective, the public must learn to expect and accept less than is promised by charismatic politicians. And, candidates for public office need to assess problems more carefully and exercise some caution about creating expectations that the government cannot hope to meet. There is a mutual responsibility on the part of both the electorate and the politicians to see the government for what it is, an imperfect instrument, at best, for attacking tough social problems, not the easy answer to all our social ills.

## CONCLUSION

Students must keep in mind that reality in the policymaking process is never quite so simple and clear-cut as analysts and authors might wish. Policymaking is an ambiguous, complex, frequently confusing process on which even the experts have difficulty agreeing. On most issues, there are a variety of positions, and choosing among the available alternatives often becomes a difficult decision. For most problems there are no clear-cut answers, only partial solutions. In our heterogeneous society with its pluralistic political institutions, political power is shared among many centers, and the coalitions and balances among these various power centers shifts constantly. Thus the system functions differently at different times and on different issues. Sometimes the system benefits one group or alliance of interests, at other times another. The same interests do not prevail on all issues as the coalitions and power structure are constantly changing. Sometimes the system responds to leadership, at other times leadership is next to impossible. At times the system seems to function quite rationally, and at other times totally irrationally. There is no overall pattern and consistency cannot be expected.

In this chapter we have been able to hit only the high points in the complex process of interaction between the policymakers and the environment in which they operate. As we move on to explore some specific areas of policymaking, however, this kaleidoscopic view of the process should help the student to understand better the interplay of all the various elements that go into the formulation, adoption, and implementation of a public policy.

## Points to Ponder

Considering the nature of many issues now facing the country, is a federal system still viable?

Has the constitutional system of checks and balances become more of an obstacle to effective policymaking than a necessary safeguard?

Can a Congress based on local-interest, geographical districts make policy in the national interest?

What is the policy role of the media in a democratic republic?

Have the effects of the rise of special interest groups and the mass media made effective government of our system impossible?

## Notes

1. Richard Dawson and James Robinson, "The Relation Between Public Policy and Some Structural and Environmental Variables in the American States," *Journal of Politics* XXV (May 1963), pp. 265–89.
2. *The Federalist*, No. 51 (New York: Modern Library, 1937), p. 337.
3. Thomas Dye, *Policy Analysis*, p. 1.
4. Woodrow Wilson, *Congressional Government* (New York: Meridian Books, 1956), pp. 82–90.
5. "Pork barrel" is a term applied to the projects, funds, and benefits congressmen are expected to acquire for their home states and districts as agents in Washington.
6. See Aaron Wildavsky, ed., *The Presidency* (Boston: Little, Brown & Co., 1969), and Robert J. Spitzer, "The Presidency and Public Policy: A Preliminary Inquiry," *Presidential Studies Quarterly* IX (Fall 1979), pp. 441–56.
7. Norman Thomas, *Rule 9: Politics, Administration, and Civil Rights* (New York: Random House, 1966), p. 6.
8. Derek Bok, Address to Harvard Alumni Exercises, Cambridge, Mass. June 1978.

9. Curtis Gans, "The Cause: The Empty Voting Booths," *The Washington Monthly* (October 1978), p. 29.
10. Henry Fairlie, "Seeking a leader in a democracy," special to the *Washington Post*, reprinted in *The Courier-Journal*, Louisville, Ky. (September 23, 1979), ©1979 Washington Post Co.
11. Arthur Miller, "Political Issues and Trust in Government: 1964–1970," *American Political Science Review* vol. 68 (September 1974), table I, p. 973.

## Suggestions for Further Reading

BARBER, JAMES D. *The Presidential Character*. Englewood Cliffs, N.J.: Prentice-Hall, 1972.
BECKER, THEODORE and MALCOLM FEELEY, eds. *The Impact of Supreme Court Decisions*, 2nd ed. New York: Oxford University Press, 1973.
BOLLING, RICHARD. *Power in the House*. New York: Capricorn Books (G. P. Putnam & Sons), 1974.
BRODER, DAVID. *The Party's Over: The Failure of Politics in America*. New York: Harper & Row, 1971.
CHELF, CARL P. *Congress in the American System*. Chicago: Nelson-Hall, 1977.
CLAUSSEN, AAGE. *How Congressmen Decide: A Policy Focus*. New York: St. Martin's Press, 1973.
COBB, ROGER and CHARLES ELDER. *Participation in American Politics*. Boston: Allyn & Bacon, 1972.
CRONIN, THOMAS. *The State of the Presidency*. Boston: Little, Brown & Co., 1975.
DEVINE, DONALD. *The Political Culture of the United States*. Boston: Little, Brown & Co., 1973.
DOWNS, ANTHONY. *Inside Bureaucracy*. Boston: Little, Brown and Co., 1967.
FENNO, RICHARD. *Congressmen in Committees*. Boston: Little, Brown and Co., 1973.
GUTOWSKI, MICHAEL and FIELD, TRACEY. *The Graying of Suburbia*. Washington, D.C.: Urban Institute, 1979.
HINCKLEY, BARBARA. *The Seniority System in Congress*. Bloomington, Ind.: University of Indiana Press, 1971.
JOHNSON, LYNDON B. *The Vantage Point: Perspectives on the Presidency 1963-1969*. New York: Holt, Rinehart & Winston, 1971.
KLEYMAN, PAUL. *Senior Power: Growing Old Rebelliously*. San Francisco: Glide, 1974.
LASSWELL, HAROLD. *Politics: Who Gets What, When, How?* Cleveland: World, 1958.
MCFARLAND, ANDREW S. *Public Interest Lobbies: Decision Making on Energy*. Washington, D. C.: American Enterprise Institute, 1977.
MURPHY, THOMAS. *The New Politics Congress*. Lexington, Mass: Lexington Books, 1974.
NADEL, MARK V. *Corporations and Public Accountability*. Lexington, Mass.: Heath, 1976.
NEUSTADT, RICHARD. *Presidential Power*. New York: Wiley, 1960.
OPPENHEIMER, BRUCE. *Oil in Congress*. Lexington, Mass.: Lexington Books, 1974.
PIOUS, RICHARD M. *The American Presidency*. New York: Basic Books, 1979.
PRATT, HENRY J. *The Gray Lobby*. Chicago: University of Chicago Press, 1976.
REDMAN, ERIC. *The Dance of Legislation*. New York: Simon & Schuster, 1973.
REEDY, GEORGE. *The Twilight of the Presidency*. New York: New American Library (Mentor Books), 1970.
ROSENBAUM, WALTER A. *Political Culture*. New York: Praeger, 1975.
SCHUMAN, DAVID. *Bureaucracies, Organization and Administration: A Political Primer*. New York: Macmillan, 1976.
SIMON, HERBERT. *Administrative Behavior*. New York: Macmillan, 1961.
WILSON, WOODROW. *Congressional Government*. New York: Meridian Books, 1956.

# Part Two

# Management Policy

Since the publication of Professor Theodore Lowi's original article describing three basic policy typologies—distributive, redistributive, and regulatory—some observers have added a fourth category, which they have usually designated as *constituent* policies, to cover a number of "housekeeping" functions carried out by the government. In Part Two we will explore policymaking in some of these areas; however, because of the scope and significance of these policies, I have chosen to designate them as *management* rather than constituent policies. *Webster's New Collegiate Dictionary* defines management as "the judicious use of means to accomplish an end," and a manager as one "who conducts business . . . affairs with economy." Though some might question the judiciousness and economy of some governmental actions, the role of the federal government in the areas of foreign, defense, and budgetary-fiscal matters is substantially managerial in nature. That is my reason for designating these policies as management rather than the more routine-type constituent policies.

These major policy areas explored in Part Two are areas in which the federal government has both inherent, constitutional, and statutorily defined roles. American experience with a weak central government under the Articles of Confederation (1781-1788) illustrated the desirability of strong central leadership in such policy areas as foreign relations, national defense, and monetary-fiscal matters. When the constitution framers concluded their work at Philadelphia, they had put together a document that assigned to the federal government a paramount role in these significant policy areas.

While Alexander Hamilton, George Washington's designee for the nation's first secretary of the treasury, was the nation's first fiscal planner and advocated active involvement of the government in the country's economic development, his views were not widely embraced by early policymakers. Beyond efforts to provide a sound monetary and banking system, early leaders sought little direct involvement of the government in economic affairs. Early American policymakers, influenced by the concepts of such authors as Adam Smith, Herbert Spencer, and William Graham Summer, were strongly laissez-faire on economic matters.[1] Active governmental involvement was sporadic, usually resulting from cyclical depressions, and was regarded as only a temporary departure from the normal laissez-faire approach. The Great Depression of the 1930s ushered in new concepts of the role of government in the nation's economy. The classical economic concepts of the past were superceded by those of the British economist, John M. Keynes, and the federal government became an active participant in economic affairs. Today the question is not so much one of whether the government should be involved, but rather questions of how governmental powers can best be used to manage and regulate economic affairs in the desired directions. Since such decisions have significant impact on different sectors of society, they are politically volatile. Decisions on taxes and federal expenditures affect the economic lives of many citizens, and such decisions are approached cautiously by elected officials.

In the realm of foreign and defense policy, the role of the federal government has never been seriously questioned, but is considered by most to be an inherent responsibility of the central government. Beyond this, however, there is little agreement as to what course of governmental action will best achieve the desired objectives. Because of the scope of the decisions, their significance for national, even world survival, and the volatility of the decision-making environment, defense and foreign policymaking are among the most complex policy areas. Pressures on the policymakers when considering decisions in those areas are often intense. Policymaking in these areas also involves a great variety of participants and a complex array of agencies.

By their nature, management policies affect broad groups of voters, and their impact, compared to subsidy or regulatory policies, is relatively diffuse. In spite of their widespread impact, however, management policies may attract only limited public attention and involvement. Such policies frequently involve the interaction of relatively limited elites engaged in low visibility political decision-making. While taxes are a politically sensitive issue of concern to most voters, federal tax policy is rather firmly controlled by an elite of a few White House and Treasury Department officials and the House Ways and Means and Senate Finance Committees. Foreign policy decisions also are dominated by a relatively small inner circle of governmental, military, and eastern establishment intellectuals. Thus, while public opinion and involvement may on occasion be factors, as a general rule management policy decisions are made with only limited public involvement.

Management policymaking is also influenced considerably by constitutional provisions and the structure of our government. The system of separation of powers and checks and balances is very much in evidence in policymaking and implementation in this particular realm. While foreign, defense, and budgetary policies are areas of great presidential initiative and influence, appropriations and revenue policies are largely the domain of Congress. Nevertheless, each must share its position of dominance or risk the possibility of having its initiatives thwarted by the other. The president must have the necessary funds appropriated for his foreign policy initiatives or his treaties ratified, and Congress may see its appropriations and revenue measures vetoed by a disapproving president. Management policies dramatically illustrate the interactions of all the many different elements that go into making and implementing public policies.

## Note

1. Adam Smith was the political economist and author of *The Wealth of Nations* who espoused the concept of a free-market economy regulated by the "invisible hand" of supply and demand. Herbert Spencer was a British philosopher whose applications of Darwinian theories to social and economic affairs gave rise to the concept of "Social Darwinism." William Graham Summer was an American sociologist and economist, probably the leading advocate and defender of Social Darwinism in the United States, who vigorously opposed governmental involvement in economic affairs.

# 3

# Government as Budget-Maker

It is most appropriate to start our look at substantive policy areas with budgetary policy because governmental decisions on budget-making are the heart of the policymaking process. Governmental expenditures for defense, education, highways, welfare, law enforcement, and a multitude of other goods and public services are our best available yardstick for measuring governmental activity and impact on our society. Since virtually every policy adopted will sooner or later involve the expenditure of funds, all citizens feel the impact and pay the costs of governmental decisions. Because the benefits of governmental taxing and spending policies are not distributed evenly among all citizens, these decisions become highly political and frequently controversial. Since the essence of politics is, in the words of Harold Lasswell, "who gets what, when and how," governmental budget decisions are what it's all about.

For this reason budget decisions frequently reflect a vast amount of competition and are influenced by the interaction of a variety of institutions and factors. According to Redford, the role of the government in the economy is determined by a combination of ecological, political, and ideological factors: such things as the existing social and economic conditions in society; prevailing economic philosophies and values; group demands and pressures; ideas of the public as to what is appropriate, necessary, and desirable in the way of public services and levels of support; the level of resources available; and the powers and constraints within which public officials and political institutions must function.[1]

Relative to the latter, a number of political and institutional relationships affecting budgetary decision-making are written into the Constitution. Decisions on taxing and spending were made an integral part of the constitutional system of

## Major Legislative Acts

**Budget and Accounting Act of 1921.** Established a national budget system and created the Bureau of the Budget (BOB), now the Office of Management and Budget, to assist the president in preparing a national budget.

**Legislative Reorganization Act of 1946.** Included provisions for a legislative budget system that was used for a couple of years and then allowed to lapse into disuse.

**Budget and Accounting Procedures Act of 1950.** Provided for the performance principle in federal budget planning based on the activities, services, and functions performed rather than on items purchased and salaries paid within departments and agencies.

**Congressional Budget and Impoundment Control Act of 1974.** Created budget committees in both houses of Congress, established the Congressional Budget Office (CBO), changed the fiscal year from July 1–June 30 to October 1–September 30, and established a timetable for congressional action on the budget.

---

separation of powers and checks and balances. Article I, Section 9 of the Constitution states, "No money shall be drawn from the Treasury, but in Consequence of Appropriations made by Law; . . . ." This is Congress's much talked about check on the other branches of government through its "power of the purse." Since virtually every program of government involves some expenditure of public funds, this provision means that Congress has a check on everything government does. About nine-tenths of Congress's time is spent on matters involving the expenditure of funds, making this probably the single most important function of the legislative branch.

Article I, Section 7 of the Constitution requires that "all bills for raising revenue shall originate in the House of Representatives; but the Senate may propose or concur with Admendments as on other bills." This then gives the legislative branch control of both aspects of governmental fiscal policy — the raising of revenue and the expenditure of public funds. Even with these provisions, however, the role of the executive in this realm of policy, as in other areas, has grown substantially over the years and has been the source of considerable tension and disagreement between the legislative and executive branches. Congress has created numerous agencies with substantial powers in the realm of economic policy, such as the Treasury Department, the Office of Management and Budget, the Federal Reserve Board, and the Council of Economic Advisors, so that governmental policy in the area of fiscal affairs has become more and more the result of complex interactions of a multitude of agencies and economic and political interests.

## Principal Departments and Agencies

**Office of Management and Budget (OMB).** Part of the Executive Office of the President, OMB has primary responsibility for budget preparation and administration in the executive branch.

**Congressional Budget Office (CBO).** Created under the Congressional Budget and Impoundment Control Act of 1974, this office assists Congress in analyzing and developing an overview of the federal budget.

**General Accounting Office (GAO).** An independent agency headed by the comptroller general that controls and audits federal expenditures as the agent of Congress.

**Council of Economic Advisers (CEA).** A staff agency in the Executive Office of the President composed of three economists who advise the president on policies for maintaining economic vigor and stability.

As a measure of governmental involvement in the nation's development, the federal budget reflects the tremendous growth that has occurred in governmental activity. Today the range of public policy is virtually overwhelming as the government has expanded its activity into many areas once private. This expansion has been accompanied by tremendous growth in the budget, as well as some dramatic shifts in what the government spends its money for. Until the start of the present century, federal budgets were relatively small, with per capita expenditures under $100; in 1900, for example, expenditures by all governments amounted to about $80 per person or about 2 percent of the gross national product. In 1835 Andrew Jackson had a budget of less than $50 million, only the tariff as a revenue source, and a surplus in the treasury. The budget grew gradually in the early decades of the twentieth century, reaching 5 percent of the GNP in 1931. Over the past decade alone federal expenditures have doubled, with the budget going over a half billion dollars and 20 percent of the GNP. Federal spending as a proportion of the gross national product now averages about 10 percent more than in the 1960s. (See figure 3.1) In 1980, in his efforts toward balancing the budget, Carter wanted to bring federal spending levels under 20 percent of the GNP in the next couple of years.

While the federal budget has been growing at a considerable rate, there have also been significant shifts within the budget as far as what money is spent for. Always a topic for considerable debate, spending for national defense as a proportion of the total budget has declined rather significantly over the last twenty-five years. In 1951 defense spending was $25 billion but accounted for 48 percent of the budget; by 1977 defense expenditures were up to more than $200 billion but constituted only about 25 percent of the total budget. By contrast, expanded federal involvement in social service and income maintenance programs has produced tremendous growth in these budget areas. In the three-year span

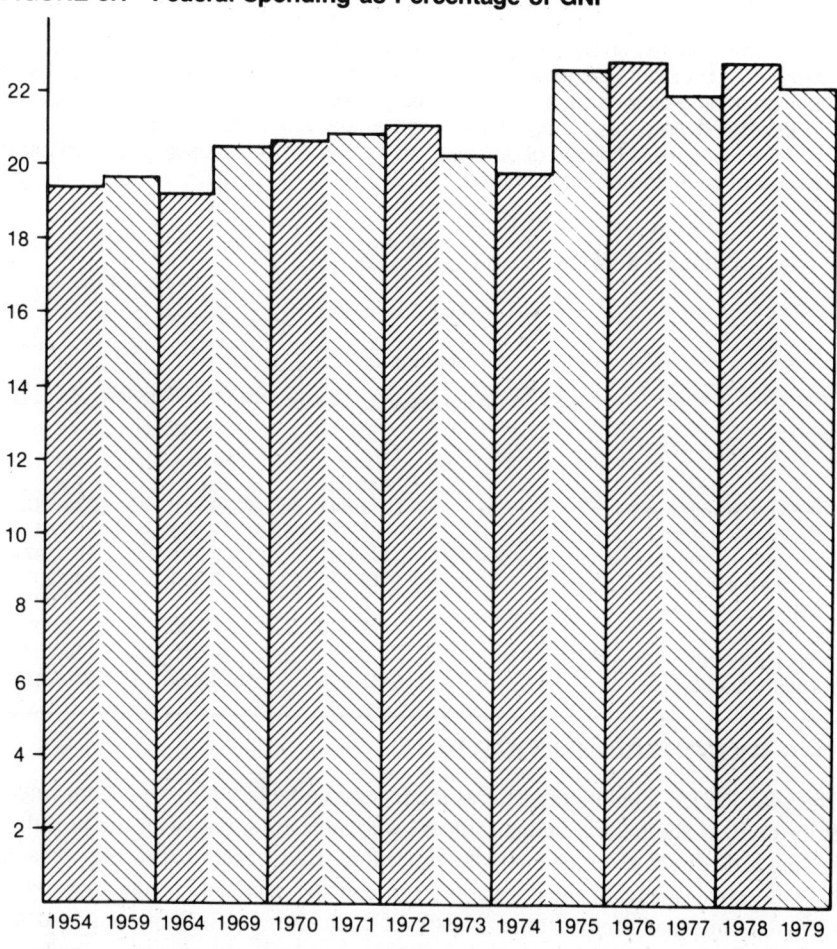

**FIGURE 3.1  Federal Spending as Percentage of GNP**

*Source:* National Journal, *January 28, 1978, p. 125. Reprinted with permission.*

between 1969 and 1972 alone, spending in the social services area increased by 600 percent. The Department of Health, Education and Welfare (changed to Health and Human Services in 1979) now administers the largest budget in the federal government. Income maintenance programs have made income redistribution a significant policy element in the federal budget. Such shifts in spending priorities have been accompanied by considerable philosophical and political controversy. (See figures 3.2 and 3.3 for a picture of where budget dollars come from and where they are spent.)

## FIGURE 3.2

The following tables show receipts by source and the outlays by function as estimated in President Carter's recommended federal government budget for fiscal 1981, beginning October 1, 1980 and ending September 30, 1981. It is compared with estimated amounts for fiscal 1980 and actual amounts for fiscal 1979.

Numbers are in billions of dollars. Columns may not necessarily add to totals because of rounding of the numbers involved.

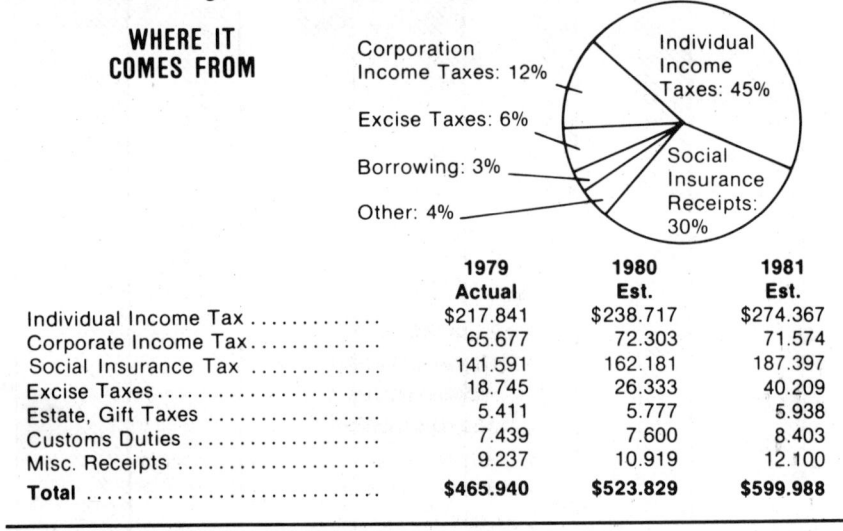

**WHERE IT COMES FROM**

Corporation Income Taxes: 12%
Excise Taxes: 6%
Borrowing: 3%
Other: 4%
Individual Income Taxes: 45%
Social Insurance Receipts: 30%

|  | 1979 Actual | 1980 Est. | 1981 Est. |
|---|---|---|---|
| Individual Income Tax | $217.841 | $238.717 | $274.367 |
| Corporate Income Tax | 65.677 | 72.303 | 71.574 |
| Social Insurance Tax | 141.591 | 162.181 | 187.397 |
| Excise Taxes | 18.745 | 26.333 | 40.209 |
| Estate, Gift Taxes | 5.411 | 5.777 | 5.938 |
| Customs Duties | 7.439 | 7.600 | 8.403 |
| Misc. Receipts | 9.237 | 10.919 | 12.100 |
| **Total** | **$465.940** | **$523.829** | **$599.988** |

## THE EXECUTIVE BUDGET

The year 1921 is a hallmark as far as the federal budgetary process is concerned. Prior to 1921 the federal budget process was quite informal, with the president having little direct involvement in the procedure. Budget estimates were prepared by individual agencies and forwarded through the secretary of the treasury to Congress in what was called a "Book of Estimates." The president and the secretary of the treasury were largely passive bystanders in the process. Gradually the need for a more formalized and more centralized process for handling budgetary matters became apparent and Congress responded with the Budgeting and Accounting Act of 1921. This act is a landmark as far as the role of the president in federal spending. It called for the president to develop and submit to the Congress his proposed budget for each new fiscal year; from this beginning, presidents have greatly expanded their power and influence in the planning and spending of federal funds.

The executive budget submitted early in each congressional session along with the president's budget message is the culmination of many months of planning and analysis. It is the principal means of federal fiscal planning and as such is the single most important reflection of the president's priorities; it is his

*Government as Budget-Maker* 55

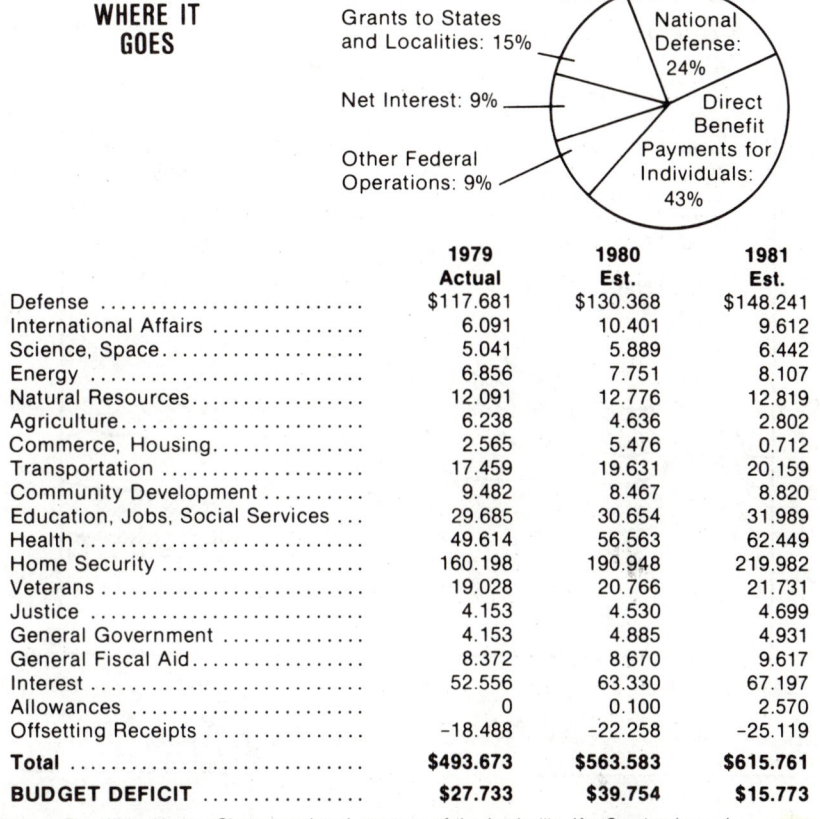

**WHERE IT GOES**

Grants to States and Localities: 15%
Net Interest: 9%
Other Federal Operations: 9%
National Defense: 24%
Direct Benefit Payments for Individuals: 43%

|  | 1979 Actual | 1980 Est. | 1981 Est. |
|---|---|---|---|
| Defense | $117.681 | $130.368 | $148.241 |
| International Affairs | 6.091 | 10.401 | 9.612 |
| Science, Space | 5.041 | 5.889 | 6.442 |
| Energy | 6.856 | 7.751 | 8.107 |
| Natural Resources | 12.091 | 12.776 | 12.819 |
| Agriculture | 6.238 | 4.636 | 2.802 |
| Commerce, Housing | 2.565 | 5.476 | 0.712 |
| Transportation | 17.459 | 19.631 | 20.159 |
| Community Development | 9.482 | 8.467 | 8.820 |
| Education, Jobs, Social Services | 29.685 | 30.654 | 31.989 |
| Health | 49.614 | 56.563 | 62.449 |
| Home Security | 160.198 | 190.948 | 219.982 |
| Veterans | 19.028 | 20.766 | 21.731 |
| Justice | 4.153 | 4.530 | 4.699 |
| General Government | 4.153 | 4.885 | 4.931 |
| General Fiscal Aid | 8.372 | 8.670 | 9.617 |
| Interest | 52.556 | 63.330 | 67.197 |
| Allowances | 0 | 0.100 | 2.570 |
| Offsetting Receipts | -18.488 | -22.258 | -25.119 |
| **Total** | **$493.673** | **$563.583** | **$615.761** |
| **BUDGET DEFICIT** | **$27.733** | **$39.754** | **$15.773** |

Source: The White House. Charts reprinted courtesy of the Louisville, Ky. Courier-Journal.

blueprint for meeting national needs. Because they involve the translation of financial resources into national objectives, budget decisions involve a high degree of controversy and competition. The budget, more than any other policy device, compels the decision-makers to establish program priorities. When this is done, considerable problems can arise. In his 1964 State of the Union message Lyndon Johnson proposed to give Americans a war on poverty, a reduction in taxes, and economy in government—all in the same budget. Such objectives did not prove realistic nor attainable, especially when the nation became more deeply involved in an undeclared war in Vietnam that was not part of the budgetary planning.

As an instrument of policy and a statement of executive goals, the budget serves the following purposes:

1. It is a tool of economic policy, outlining the proposed taxing and spending policies of the administration.

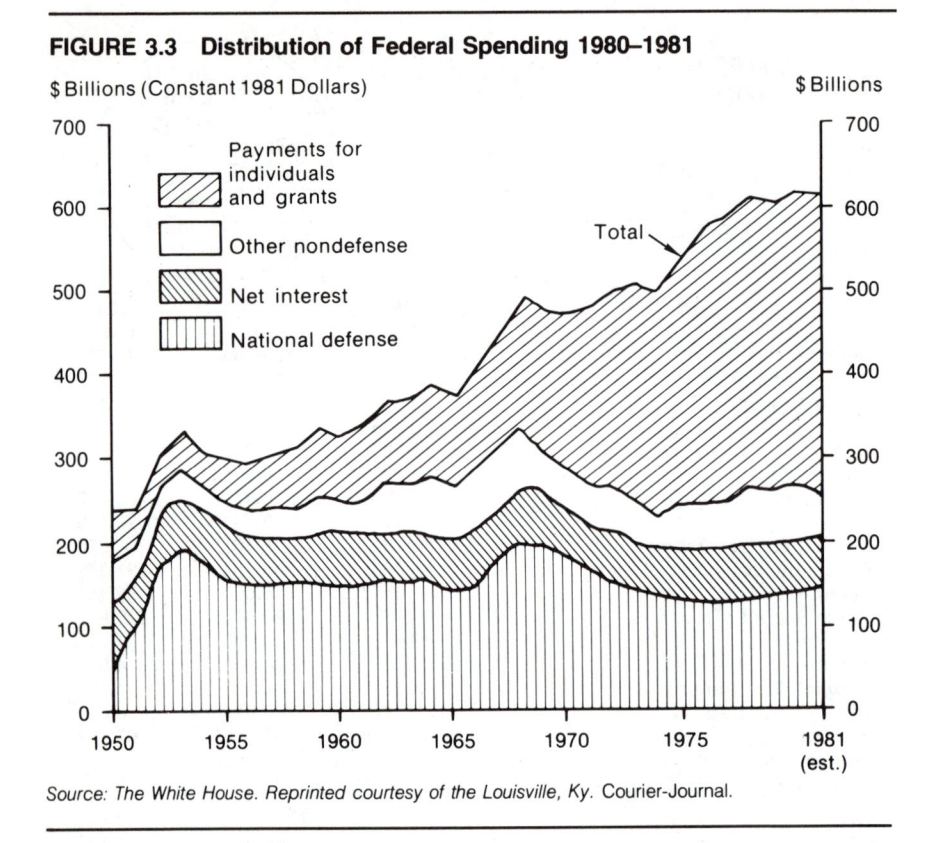

**FIGURE 3.3  Distribution of Federal Spending 1980–1981**

Legend:
- Payments for individuals and grants
- Other nondefense
- Net interest
- National defense

Source: The White House. Reprinted courtesy of the Louisville, Ky. Courier-Journal.

2. It is a request for legislative action calling for support of new and existing programs.
3. It is the president's financial report to the nation, outlining how funds have been spent in the past and proposals for future spending.
4. It is an appraisal of national needs and priorities, with proposals for allocation of available resources to meet these needs.

In all of its detail and complexity, however, the budget document itself fails to present a complete picture of governmental financial activity. This was especially true prior to 1968, when the *administrative budget* included only annual federal fund transactions, a figure much lower than total federal financial transactions. Since 1968 a *unified budget* encompassing all federal programs including trust funds has been used. This is one reason for the big increase in the total federal budget figure in the late 1960s. Trust fund activities alone have increased tenfold over the last twenty years, accounting for much of the federal budget growth. While the unified budget provides a much more complete picture of federal finances, it also leaves out numerous transactions of federal agencies.

Much more than a simple accounting of federal income and expenditures, the budget-making process is awesome in both its magnitude and complexity. Chairman and veteran of many years service on the House Appropriations Committee, George Mahon (D-Tex.) was asked by a colleague if he understood the budget. "Not too well," was his response. The federal budget cycle spans more than thirty months, and at any point in time three budgets are actually involved—one in the planning stages, one in the authorization/appropriations stage, and one being spent. New budget preparation actually begins eighteen to twenty months in advance of the fiscal year in which it will apply. Jimmy Carter started in mid-May 1979 planning his budget for fiscal year 1981. Another factor contributing to the complexity is the large cast of characters involved. No president could hope to formulate a budget without the assistance of a substantial bureaucracy.

### Office of Management and Budget

Paramount in the federal budgetary bureaucracy is the Office of Management and Budget. Created by Congress in the 1921 Budgeting and Accounting Act as the Bureau of the Budget, OMB has become the key agency in the Executive Office of the President. While its principal tasks are budget preparation and financial administration, OMB has other significant functions as well. It is a translation and communications center between the president and the other agencies of the executive branch, and its Office of Legislative Reference serves as the clearinghouse for executive legislative proposals. Further, once proposals are enacted, OMB recommends presidential approval or veto. Thus, among executive agencies, OMB enjoys a special status in the policymaking process. In spite of its significant policy role, OMB operates with considerable anonymity and had been considered such an intimate part of the presidency that prior to 1970 appointments of the director and deputy director were not even confirmed by the Senate.

In 1970, President Nixon proposed to change the name of the agency from the Bureau of the Budget to the Office of Management and Budget. Nixon said such a change meant the agency would go beyond simple preparation of the budget to "assessing the extent to which programs are actually achieving their intended results, and delivering the intended services to the intended recipients."[2] Following the adoption of the Nixon proposal expanding the OMB's role, reactions began to develop in Congress. In 1973 the Senate Government Operations Committee reported a measure to require that the director and deputy director of OMB be confirmed by the Senate. In recommending this measure, the committee declared that OMB had developed into a "super department with enormous authority over all activities of the Federal Government. Its Director has become, in effect, a Deputy President who exercises vital Presidential powers."[3] The measure was adopted, giving testimony to the significance Congress attaches to the role of the OMB.

A primary function of OMB remains the central role it plays in the budgetary process. Departments and agencies are prohibited from making requests for funds directly to Congress without clearance through OMB. Since 1921 the routine for the formulation and approval of the budget has become well established and a rather formal and essentially uniform set of procedures is faithfully followed. About eighteen months prior to the next fiscal year, ceilings are set for the various agencies and OMB sends out its budget requests. This is followed by about three months of intensive work as the agencies try to assess presidential priorities and prepare to engage in efforts to influence budget decisions. The agencies that tend to play to their special constituencies when planning their budgets typically propose program expansion, while the OMB, as presidential budget agent, usually acts with a budget-cutting bias. Each department in the executive branch has its own budget office that acts as its mediary in dealings with both the OMB and Congress. Following the submission of their estimates, each agency has a hearing or budget review by OMB. Next comes review by the president and the director of OMB; agencies not satisfied with their treatment at the hands of OMB can appeal to the president. While the pressures of other duties prevent the president's playing a continuing role in the formulation process, he may exert considerable influence on the budgets of particular agencies.

Agencies vary considerably in their assertiveness in the budgetary process, with some employing a great variety of tactics to promote their particular causes. In 1978 Housing and Urban Development Secretary Patricia Harris and OMB went to battle over HUD's 1979 budget. In the spring and summer OMB and HEW had looked at the housing budget as a potential source of funds to fill a gap in the welfare budget. This convinced HUD officials that OMB was anti-housing. Responding to OMB's request for budget estimates, HUD submitted a budget proposal including various options, some of which would have pushed the budget to $54 billion, an increase of almost 40 percent over the current year. OMB immediately bounced the request back, directing the department to develop more realistic projections and suggesting a total under $30 billion or a cut of about 25 percent from current spending levels. With this, HUD tempers really flared and a series of attacks and counterattacks was launched by HUD and OMB. HUD turned to its outside constituencies of housing and urban interest groups who launched a campaign of letters to the president, news conferences, and other expressions of support for the department's position. Ultimately, OMB trimmed the HUD budget, but Secretary Harris managed to emerge with the support of her interest group constituency intact and ready to lobby Congress to get the reduced funds restored.

Another favored agency tactic in budgetary policies is to get the president's support through the use of some well-known person or organization. When OMB made a substantial cut in HEW's proposed 1979 budget for mental health, Dr. Thomas Bryant, executive director of the President's Commission on Mental Health, set out to reverse OMB's decision. Following the president's review, the budget still remained low. So Bryant arranged a hearing with OMB Director James McIntyre and took along with him Rosalynn Carter, honorary chairperson of the Commission on Mental Health. Shortly after this hearing, the budget for alcoholism, drug abuse, and mental health research was increased from the $11 million HEW had requested to $40 million. Even such political ploys as this do not always prove successful as both Congress and interest groups are inclined to allow OMB to operate as an isolated power center in budget matters. As a general rule, the OMB is respected for its thoroughness and fairness in its decisions.

Because cabinet secretaries and agency heads may want to go off in their own directions, it frequently falls the lot of OMB to bring them in line with presidential objectives. In this respect OMB is able to overrule both career and cabinet officers. It is OMB that has the difficult task of molding all the agency budget proposals into a coherent statement of administration policy. It is inevitable that in this process OMB personnel make vital budgetary decisions. Because of the magnitude of the budget and the tremendous pressures of time, sometimes neither the president nor OMB is sure exactly where and how a budget decision is made. One congressional aide, commenting on the process, observed, "It's hard to believe, but there are GS 14s and 16s at OMB who are more powerful than elected officials." The president has little choice but to rely on the OMB and its professional staff of about 200 as his final arbiters on budgetary matters.

While much of OMB's substantial influence derives from the fact that it speaks for the president in controlling the purse strings, its powers extend considerably beyond simple budget preparation. It also oversees spending after the budget is approved by parceling out spending allowances among the executive agencies. In making its "apportionments" (OMB divides an agency's appropriation into quarterly allotments referred to as apportionments), OMB can in effect reduce an agency's appropriation by simply not apportioning the total amount. This authority can be used to hold spending below authorized levels for economic impact or when spending on a particular program simply appears less urgent than originally anticipated.

### Budget Timetable

Under the Congressional Budget and Impoundment Control Act of 1974 the budget timetable was altered somewhat. (See figures 3.4 and 3.5 for the timetable on budget action.) The president is required to submit his "current services" budget to Congress by November 10 of the year preceding the fiscal year for which the budget is being prepared. This is an estimate of the level of revenues and expenditures required to maintain governmental functions at the same level as in the current fiscal year. No later than fifteen days after Congress convenes in January, the president must submit his complete budget for the next fiscal year, which will begin October 1. All of this extensive preparation sets the stage for the next phase, which occurs in the Congress.

## THE APPROPRIATIONS PROCESS

Once submitted to Congress, the budget is literally torn apart and parcelled out among the various subcommittees of the House and Senate Appropriations Committees. Like Humpty Dumpty the budget is never really put back together again as appropriations decisions flow intermittently through the congressional mill with only minimal interaction and coordination among the various appropriations subcommittees. Thus it becomes difficult for Congress to really assess the overall

# FIGURE 3.4 Formulation of President's Budget

| APPROXIMATE TIMING | AGENCY | OFFICE OF MANAGEMENT AND BUDGET | THE PRESIDENT |
|---|---|---|---|
| **BUDGET POLICY DEVELOPMENT** | | | |
| MARCH (or earlier in some agencies) | Reviews current operations, program objectives, issues, and future plans in relation to upcoming annual budget. Submits projections of requirements that reflect current operations and future plans, supporting memoranda and related analytic studies that identify major issues, alternatives for resolving issues, and comparisons of costs and effectiveness. | **Develops economic assumptions. Obtains forecasts of international and domestic situations. Prepares fiscal projections.\*** | |
| APRIL MAY | | Issues policy guidance on material to be developed for Spring planning review. | Discusses budgetary outlook and policies with the Director of the Office of Management and Budget, and with the Cabinet as appropriate. |
| MAY | | Discusses program developments and management issues, and resulting budgetary effects, with agencies. Compiles total outlay estimates for comparison with revenue estimates. Develops recommendations for President on fiscal policy,\* program issues, and budget levels. | Discusses with the Director of the Office of Management and Budget and others as necessary, general budget policy, major program issues, budgetary planning targets, and projections. Establishes general guidelines and agency planning targets for annual budget. |
| JUNE | Issues internal instructions on preparation of annual budget estimates. | Issues technical instructions for preparation of annual budget estimates. | |

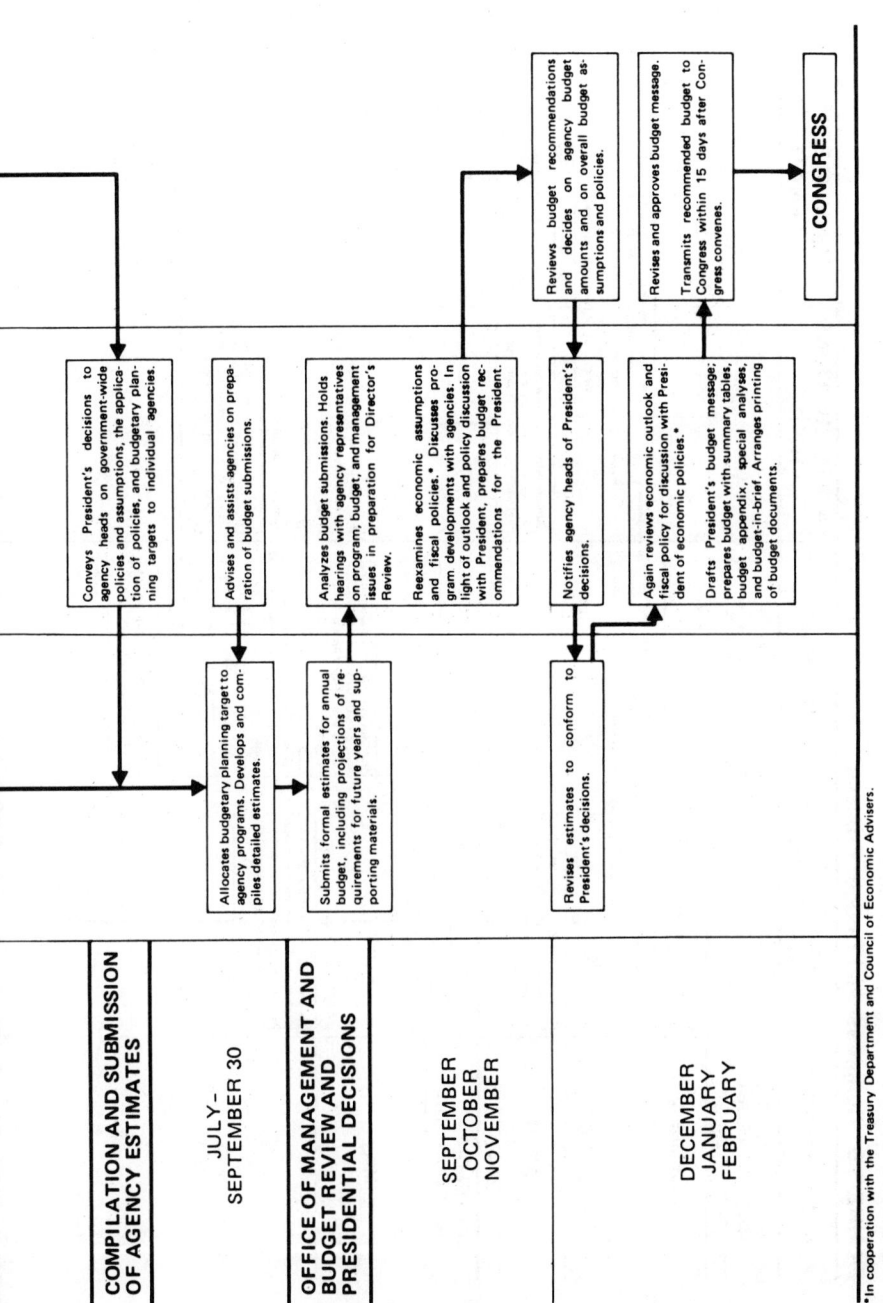

# COMPILATION AND SUBMISSION OF AGENCY ESTIMATES

**JULY–SEPTEMBER 30**

Conveys President's decisions to agency heads on government-wide policies and assumptions, the application of policies, and budgetary planning targets to individual agencies.

Advises and assists agencies on preparation of budget submissions.

Allocates budgetary planning target to agency programs. Develops and compiles detailed estimates.

# OFFICE OF MANAGEMENT AND BUDGET REVIEW AND PRESIDENTIAL DECISIONS

**SEPTEMBER OCTOBER NOVEMBER**

Submits formal estimates for annual budget, including projections of requirements for future years and supporting materials.

Analyzes budget submissions. Holds hearings with agency representatives on program, budget, and management issues in preparation for Director's Review.

Reexamines economic assumptions and fiscal policies. Discusses program developments with agencies. In light of outlook and policy discussion with President, prepares budget recommendations for the President.

Reviews budget recommendations and decides on agency budget amounts and on overall budget assumptions and policies.

Notifies agency heads of President's decisions.

Revises estimates to conform to President's decisions.

**DECEMBER JANUARY FEBRUARY**

Again reviews economic outlook and fiscal policy for discussion with President of economic policies.\*

Drafts President's budget message; prepares budget with summary tables, budget appendix, special analyses, and budget-in-brief. Arranges printing of budget documents.

Revises and approves budget message.

Transmits recommended budget to Congress within 15 days after Congress convenes.

→ **CONGRESS**

---

\*In cooperation with the Treasury Department and Council of Economic Advisers.

# FIGURE 3.5 Congressional Budget Process

| APPROXIMATE TIMING | BUDGET COMMITTEES | CONGRESS | APPROPRIATIONS HOUSE | COMMITTEES SENATE |
|---|---|---|---|---|
| **DEVELOPMENT OF BUDGET TARGETS** | | | | |
| NOVEMBER | | Receives current services estimates from the President. (Nov. 10) | | |
| DECEMBER | Receive Joint Economic Committee analysis of current services estimates. (Dec. 31) | | | |
| JANUARY | Hold hearings in preparation for drafting 1st concurrent resolution on the budget. | Receives President's budget within fifteen days after Congress convenes. | Hold special hearings on budget overview with Director of Office of Management and Budget, Secretary of the Treasury, and Chairman of the Council of Economic Advisers. | |
| FEBRUARY | Receive views and estimates of all committees (March 15) and begin drafting 1st concurrent resolution on the budget. | | Subcommittees hold hearings, review justifications from each agency, and draft appropriation bills and reports. | Subcommittees hold hearings and review justifications from each agency. |
| MARCH | | Receives first Presidential update of the budget estimates. (April 10) | | |
| APRIL | Report 1st concurrent resolution, which sets spending, revenue, and other budget targets for the upcoming fiscal year. | Adopts 1st concurrent resolution on the budget. (May 15) | Full Committee reviews actions of subcommittees and adopts or revises bills and reports. | |
| **ACTION ON INDIVIDUAL BILLS** | | | | |
| MAY | | Shall not consider any bill authorizing new budget authority for the upcoming year unless bills are reported by May 15. | Completes committee action on all regular appropriation bills, to the extent practicable, and submits a summary report of its actions to House Budget Committee, before reporting the first appropriation bill. | |
| JUNE– AUGUST | Review and evaluate the effect of Congressional action on the budget targets, in preparation for drafting the 2nd concurrent resolution on the budget. | House debates and passes appropriation bills, with or without amendments. Senate receives House-passed version of appropriation bills and refers to Senate Appropriations Committee. Receives mid-year Presidential update of the budget estimates. (July 15) | | Subcommittees draft revisions to House bills and reports. |

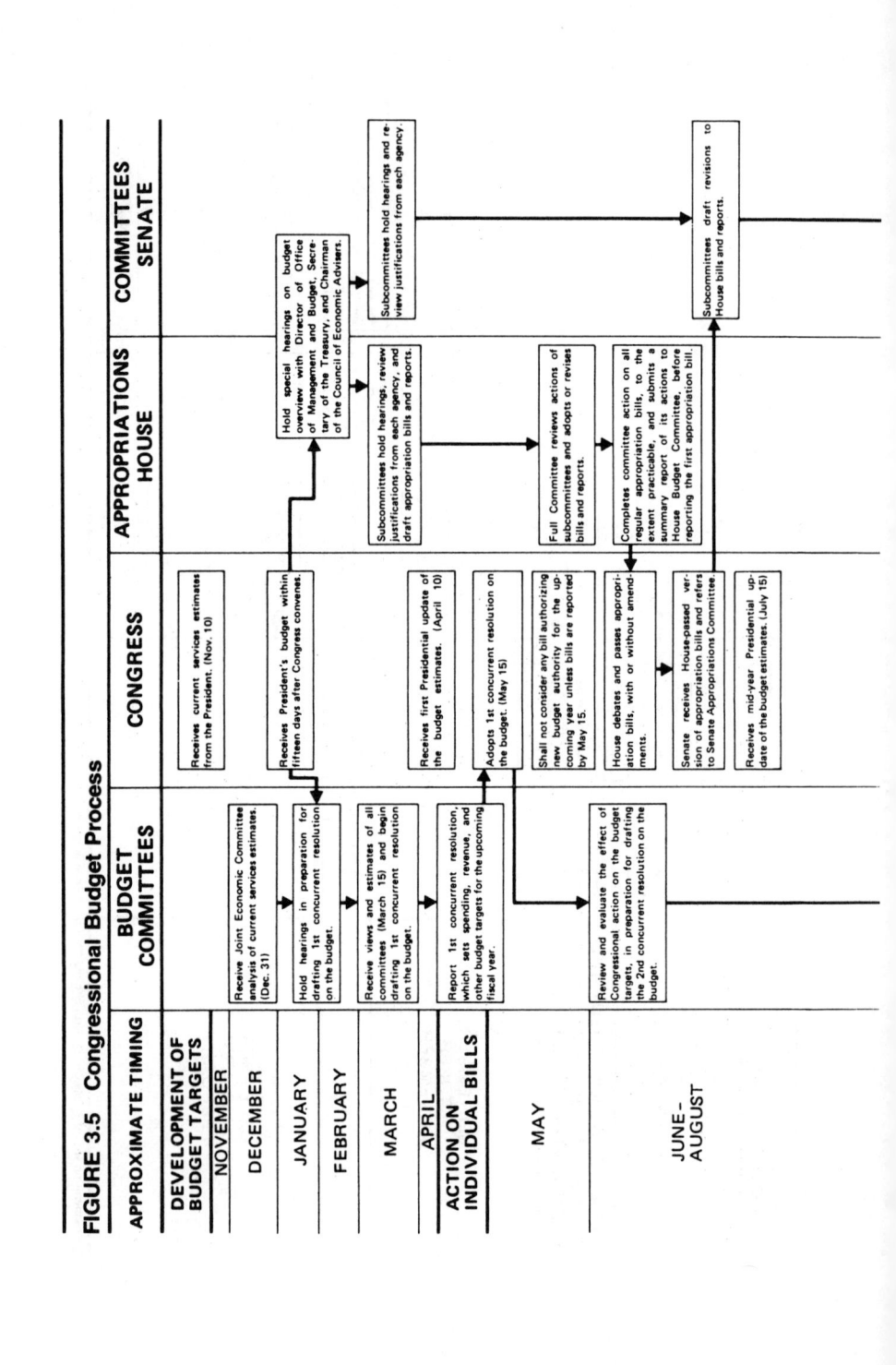

Full Committee reviews actions of subcommittees and adopts or revises bills and reports.

Conference committee(s) considers items of disagreement between the two Houses and makes recommendations for resolution of differences in conference reports, which are submitted to each body for action.

Senate debates and passes appropriation bills with or without amendments. If Senate bills differ from House versions, bills are sent to conference. If House and Senate versions are identical, bills are sent directly to the President.

House considers and passes appropriation bills, as amended by conference committees. After House approval, Senate considers and passes the appropriation bills, as amended.

Sends appropriation bills to the President for his approval or veto. If appropriation action is not completed by September 30 or if a Presidential veto is not overridden by Congress, then the affected programs are covered in a continuing resolution until an appropriation bill(s) is approved by Congress and the President.

By the 7th day after Labor Day, completes action on all bills and resolutions providing new budget authority for the fiscal year beginning Oct. 1.

Adopts 2nd concurrent resolution on the budget. (Sept. 15)

By Sept. 25, completes action on any reconciliation bill or resolution so that budget totals for enacted legislation conform with ceilings established in the 2nd concurrent resolution on the budget.

Prepare and report 2nd concurrent resolution on the budget, which sets spending, revenue and other budget ceilings for the upcoming fiscal year.

**RECONCILIATION**

**SEPTEMBER**

**OCTOBER**

NEW FISCAL YEAR BEGINS
OCTOBER 1

**GENERAL NOTES**

Action represented in the column labeled "Congress" reflects action of one or both bodies of Congress (House and Senate), as specified. Information is also included on reports sent to Congress as a whole.

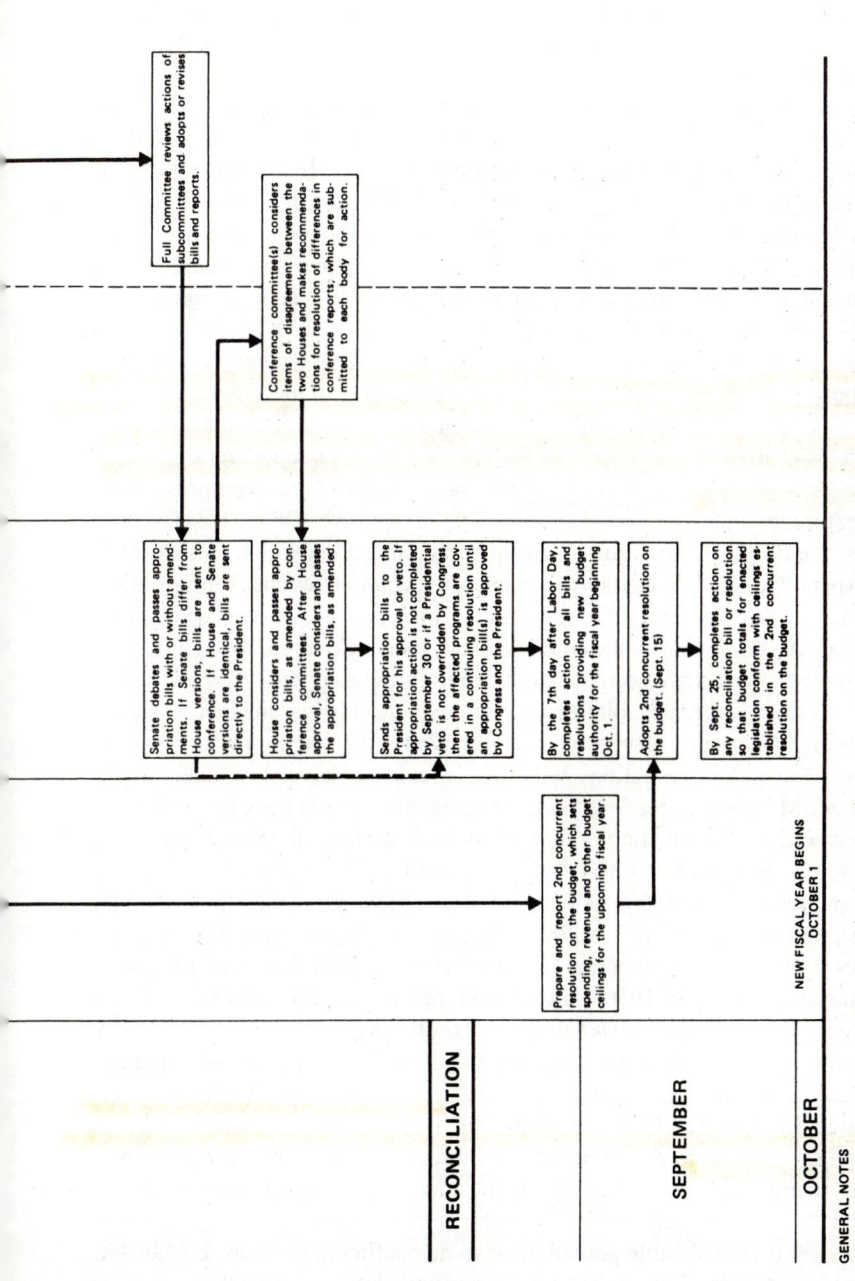

Action on revenue measures follows the same general procedure as action on appropriation bills, except that revenue measures are reported by the Ways and Means Committee in the House and by the Finance Committee in the Senate.

policy impact of the budget. In a July 1972 message to Congress, President Nixon criticized the "hoary and traditional procedure of the Congress, which now permits action on the various spending programs as if they were unrelated and independent actions."

Concern with its performance on budgetary matters prompted Congress to appoint a Joint Study Committee on Budget Control. This committee's findings led to the adoption in 1974 of the Congressional Budget and Impoundment Control Act. This legislation changed the government's fiscal year from July 1–June 30 to October 1–September 30, created budget committees in both houses of Congress, created a Congressional Budget Office, established guidelines on impoundment of funds and backdoor spending, and established a timetable for congressional action on the budget. (See figure 3.5)

As soon as the president submits his current services budget, no later than November 10, the Joint Economic Committee (members of the Ways and Means and Appropriations Committees of the House and the Appropriations and Finance Committees of the Senate, meeting jointly) analyzes this budget and submits its own recommendations. By March 15 the various legislative committees must submit estimates on the cost of programs they will approve. On the basis of these analyses, the Budget Committees draw up a first budget resolution, which establishes expenditure guidelines for the authorization committees and Appropriations Committees. The committees thus have not only the president's proposed budget, but also target amounts set by the congressional Budget Committees to guide them in their deliberations. In September as the appropriations process is drawing to a close, a second concurrent resolution is submitted, and whereas the first resolution was advisory, the second resolution is a directive for the committees to reconcile their previous budgetary actions with the levels that have now been finally established. Measures exceeding the target amounts are sent back to committees for reconciliation. A final congressional budget, including all appropriations and tax measures and a debt ceiling, is to be passed prior to October 1.

How well the new system works depends to a great extent on how determined Congress is to make it work. In '78, '79, and '80 Congress failed to meet the deadlines set for completing action on appropriations and had to resort to provisional financing.[4] Only in 1976 has Congress met the deadline. When fiscal year 1980 began, Congress had enacted only three of its thirteen regular appropriations bills. Seven cabinet departments and various other agencies had to be authorized provisional financing. One point is obvious; with its own Budget Office and the new Budget Committees, Congress should be more independent of the executive in the budgetary process. At the same time, the new system could generate some problems internally. Since the new Budget Committees have authority that places them in a "watchdog" relationship with the legislative and appropriations committees, there is considerable potential for some conflict to develop. Ed Muskie, while chairman of the Senate Budget Committee, ruffled the feathers of some colleagues by insisting that other committees keep spending in line with Budget Committee resolutions. The system has considerable potential for improving Congress's budgetary performance, but in the words of a former assistant director of OMB, "To make it work, Congress and its individual members will have to act a hell of a lot differently than they do now."[5] While many observers feel the new congressional budget process has brought more order to legislative decisions on budget matters and has made Congress a more equal partner by making it less dependent on executive agencies for information and analysis, the new process also has its critics. There is growing evidence that several members of the appropriating and tax-writing committees are unhappy with some provisions in the 1974 act. Thus far this has not produced a movement for repeal. Many members share the sentiments expressed by majority whip in the House, John Brademas (D-Ind.), who said, "I am concerned about the way the budget process is used for purposes for which it was not intended. But I would strongly oppose any effort to do away with it. If we gave it up, we would again give the executive branch complete control over the budget."[6]

### Appropriations Committees

In Congress the budget is acted on in the form of appropriations bills, which are reported for action by the House and Senate Appropriations Committees. These committees are among the elite of Congress, and seats on these panels are eagerly sought. Because of the power and influence they wield in the legislative process and the deference with which they are treated by their colleagues, members of the Appropriations Committees play a significant role in the policymaking process. The House committee, with fifty-five members, is the largest committee in either chamber; the Senate committee has only twenty-six members. Both committees are divided into a number of subcommittees, which do most of the real work on appropriation measures. Because the House has insisted that the constitutional provision that all revenue bills must originate in the House also applies to appropriations bills, the House committee gets first shot at the budget proposals. This position has resulted in considerable jealousy and rivalry among the House and Senate Appropriations Committees over the years and has made their roles in the appropriations process somewhat different. In the House, where members represent smaller and relatively more homogeneous constituencies, economy may take precedence over the development of various costly programs. The Senate committee tends to be a court of appeals for restoring cuts imposed by the House. Senate committee members are inclined to feel the House committee frequently tends to cut programs unrealistically simply to bolster their image as the "guardians of the treasury." In his study of the appropriations process, Richard Fenno found that in 56 percent of their decisions the Senate committee increased House figures, while in only 10 percent of the cases did they recommend a lower figure than the House.[7] In addition to functioning as a court of appeals for reviewing House cuts, the Senate committee also seems to be somewhat more open and accessible to other members. Until the adoption of rules opening up many committee sessions, the House Appropriations Committee was largely a closed operation even to other members of the chamber.

The real workhorses of the appropriations process and the principal instruments of congressional budget analysis are the standing subcommittees, each of which has the responsibility of reviewing the budgets for certain administrative units. Because their membership tends to be relatively stable and they review the same agency budgets year after year, the subcommittee members become the "experts" in their respective budgetary areas. Other members tend to listen to them and defer to their judgment on matters involving programs within their purview. Thus powerful subcommittee chairmen such as William Natcher or Jamie Whitten may exert tremendous influence over particular policy areas. Because of repeated exposure, the subcommittees develop considerable familiarity with the departments and agencies under their purview, their programs, monetary needs, and past performance records. As a consequence, the tendency is to focus primarily on the changes in budget requests year to year, questioning only unusually large increases.

Subcommittee influence is enhanced even further by the traditional patterns of congressional attitudes on budgetary matters. On the Appropriations Committees, "partisanship" is downplayed and "professionalism" is emphasized. Coupled with the congressional tendency to go along with the "experts" on particular issues this gives added weight to subcommittee recommendations. The normal pattern is for the full Appropriations Committees to accept the subcommittees' recommendations with little discussion and no change. Since the House and Senate usually accept recommendations of the Appropriations Committees with little or no change on the floor, this means that the fate of an agency's programs really rests in the hands of three to five members of an appropriation subcommittee.

### The Politics of Budget Decisions

How an agency or department fares in the appropriations process depends on many factors. The nature of the programs administered by different agencies makes some much more acceptable than others. Members are much more inclined to support a program of aid to disabled American veterans than one for assisting unwed mothers. An agency's reputation in Congress or even the relationship of its director with committee members may affect its budget treatment. When Sam Brown, a leader in the 1960s in the anti-Vietnam War movement, was appointed to head the federal volunteer agency, ACTION, House Minority Whip Robert Michel and some Republican colleagues launched a drive to kill funding for ACTION's urban program because of their strong dislike for Brown. For decades the FBI, because of J. Edgar Hoover's and the agency's image as the nation's number-one crime fighters, had no problem getting budgets approved.

Various strategies are employed by agencies to try to insure favorable treatment for their budgets: determined efforts to spend all their funds for the previous fiscal year; never requesting less than for the previous year; requesting increases but making them appear small; and asking for more than is needed, thereby giving the reviewers something they can cut without inflicting severe damage. Several agencies in the Department of Interior have, for example, regularly requested budget increases considerably above average and have had their requests cut rather severely by the economy-conscious House committee. Over the long run, however, their programs have not suffered substantially. One of the first things the clever bureaucrat does when threatened with a reduction in his budget is to translate it into bad news for some congressmen in a position to come to his rescue. While this ploy does not always work, it can go a long way toward producing the desired action.

Another interesting aspect of the federal expenditure process is that it normally requires enactment of two measures by Congress for spending to occur. Under the rules of both houses of Congress the Appropriations Committees are prohibited from reporting legislative measures and the legislative committees cannot report measures appropriating funds. Therefore, an *authorization* bill that establishes the statutory basis for a program must be reported by the appropriate legislative committee and approved by Congress. This then must be followed by an *appropriations* bill from the Appropriations Committees to provide the funds for the actual expenditure. This creates some interesting possibilities in budgetary decision-making. While these two channels obviously are associated, they also are quite distinct. Membership and policy orientation of the legislative and appropriations committees may be considerably different. Members of the Appropriations Committees are predominantly members with long tenure from relatively safe districts and as noted earlier are likely to be more economy oriented than program oriented. Members of the legislative committees, on the other hand, are frequently assigned to committees handling legislation of particular interest to their constituencies and are therefore likely to be very program oriented. This causes frequent differences of opinion between legislative committees, which authorize programs at one spending level, and the Appropriations Committees, which may provide funding at a different level.

As Leonard Freedman notes in his study on public housing, authorization is one thing, appropriation is another.[8] The mere fact that the legislative committees have authorized a particular program does not mean its funding by the Appropriations Committees is a foregone conclusion, at least not funding at the level provided in the authorization. Strange things sometimes happen on the way through the authorization/appropriation process. A congressman may vote for a measure authorizing a particular program, especially if there is a recorded vote and the program is one of interest to his constituents, and then may vote against the appropriation of funds for the program where a recorded vote is unlikely. Whereas the president does not have an item veto, the Appropriations Committees can be very selective in their funding, appropriating for some programs in an authorization measure and not for others and raising some funding levels while lowering others. Their discretion in the handling of funding measures is substantial. The whole authorization/appropriation process makes policy outcomes quite uncertain. Those who prevail at the authorization stage may still lose out because the tables may be turned and other interests may emerge victorious at the appropriations stage. The authorization/appropriations process is one of the most political, complex and uncertain in the policymaking process.

## BUDGET EXECUTION AND OVERSIGHT

While Congress, especially the House, prides its image as "guardian of the treasury" and "holder of the purse strings," its actual record does little to support this image. On the whole, Congress usually changes only about 5 percent of the budget as submitted by the president. In the minds of the framers of our Constitution, the power of the purse was clearly the prerogative of the Congress and would be an effective check on the other branches of government. In *Federalist* No. 48 Madison assured the people, "The legislative department alone has access to the pockets of the people."[9] On more careful analysis, Madison's concept is much too rosy and simplified. Many factors have come together to make legislative control of the appropriations process considerably less meaningful as a check on governmental actions than the framers anticipated.

In fact, Congress's power of the purse may well have become one of the major difficulties in controlling budgets. Frequently it is not the executive that raids the treasury but alliances of special interests and their congressional friends. Every special interest group lobbies its select group of members and committees to promote its particular legislative programs. It is in Congress that the deals and compromises are made that attempt to satisfy the many competing interests that make up our society. Frequently these bargains struck in legislative horse-trading cost the taxpayers. The president has more insulation against these special pleaders than members of Congress, and as the defender of national interest must take a broader view on issues. In this vein, Carter warned Congress in 1978 that he would veto inflationary legislation providing for farm subsidies, tuition tax credits, and similar measures. Congress is much less likely to risk offending such powerful voting blocs, thus making them susceptible to vast outside pressures opposed to reduced expenditures in various programs.

The nature of the congressman's job and the expectations of his constituents tend to make objectivity on spending decisions difficult. The elected representative is expected to look out for the economic welfare of his district or state. Thus every representative is for economy in the federal budget and reductions in spending, but only so long as they come in someone else's state or district. As Senator Dale Bumpers (D-Ark.) observes, "The job becomes an end in itself—public relations, cosmetics, how much pork you can take home, how many grants you can get for your state. We are all trying to make a record to run on." The result is a lot of sacred cows in the budget, which make reductions in federal expenditures extremely difficult. The Impacted Aid program is a prime example. This legislation provides federal aid to schools in districts where federal installations have removed large amounts of property from local tax rolls while at the same time contributing to the school-age population in the districts. Nixon, Ford and Carter have all proposed reductions in this program as our military operations have been cut back. But because this program benefits schools in so many congressional districts, the funds are always restored by Congress.

Frequently, executive efforts at economy run head-on into the congressman's need to look out for the economic welfare of his state and district. No sooner does the Veteran's Administration announce the closing of VA hospitals or the Pentagon the closing of military bases than the cries begin. In 1978 when the Pentagon announced 107 closings and combinations of bases in 31 states to save $337 million annually but eliminating 23,200 jobs, congressional cries of "betrayed," "irreparable damage," "appalled," were common. As testimony to the clout of congressmen in such matters, the Pentagon announced thirteen years ago the closing of the Portsmouth Naval Shipyard. It is still open.

In all fairness, it should be noted that in many cases Congress's discretion in approving expenditures has been substantially reduced once the appropriations stage is reached. In many cases executive commitments may virtually tie their hands. Jefferson had already negotiated the Louisiana Purchase when Congress was asked to provide funds. If a president or secretary of state has already made commitments to foreign nations, then for Congress to refuse could reduce the effectiveness of our foreign policy efforts. Also, once Congress has approved substantial spending for a program, it may not then be feasible to drop it completely. Already Congress has appropriated close to $500 million for construction of the Tennessee-Tombigbee Waterway. Do they drop it after such an investment?

### The General Accounting Office

While the president has the principal responsibility for administering the budget, Congress shares in the role. The Budget and Accounting Act, which created the principal agent of presidential supervision, the OMB(BOB), also established the General Accounting Office (GAO) as an agency of the Congress. Congress relies heavily on the GAO in seeking to fulfill its oversight function. Senator William Proxmire (D-Wis.), one of the most frequent users of the GAO's services, says of the agency, "Without it and its powers to audit and investigate, the Congress would be almost powerless in its watchdog and oversight functions." As the official auditor and debt collector of the federal government, the GAO has the responsibility of determining for the Congress how effectively its appropriations are being spent. With a budget of about $200 million annually and a staff of 5200 employees, the GAO produces about 1000 reports a year on federal agency activities.

As the official auditor of federal agency accounts, the GAO determines the legality of federal expenditures. As head of the agency, the comptroller general, appointed by the president for a term of fifteen years, exercises the important "power of disallowance." If he determines that an expenditure has not been authorized by Congress, he can deny the agency's expenditure. The only recourse is for the agency to request congressional approval for expenditures for the purpose denied. Through these procedures, the GAO recovers substantial amounts annually that would otherwise be spent for unauthorized purposes.

### Congressional Oversight

Outside the GAO's auditing and investigative functions, congressional efforts at oversight are sporadic and unsystematic, frequently growing out of abuses that have already occurred rather than any organized effort at effective control. Effective legislative oversight does encounter a number of substantial problems, some stemming from external factors and some from internal lack of determination and clarity of purpose. For a number of years the Pentagon has exercised the authority to modify defense contracts to take care of increases in costs of production. In recent years "cost over-runs" have become substantial and have committed Congress to sizeable increases in defense expenditures, thus reducing their budgetary discretion. From 1959–1970 the Pentagon exercised its authority to modify defense contracts 3407 times, increasing procurement costs by $69,916,000. Finally, after huge cost over-runs on the C-5A transport plane and the AH-56A Cheyenne helicopters, Congress in 1973 imposed a ceiling on such modifications.

A reverse of the contract modification problem, but nonetheless a challenge to congressional control and direction of federal expenditures, is presidential impoundment—or executive decisions not to spend funds. Traditionally, presidents were inclined to view appropriations as permissive rather than mandatory and impoundment as a tool they could use for economic management purposes. Presidents from Thomas Jefferson's time had occasionally used impoundment, but during Richard Nixon's administration the question of impoundment developed into a constitutional confrontation between president and Congress. The scope and severity of Nixon's impoundments were unprecedented, and where earlier impoundments had been largely management efforts, Nixon's were more far-reaching policy decisions that actually altered and challenged congressional priorities and decisions in policy matters. In the words of then House Appropriations Committee Chairman George Mahon, "Economy is one thing, ... the abandonment of a policy and program of the Congress another thing."

As a consequence of this experience, a major thrust of the 1974 Budget and Impoundment Control Act was to strengthen Congress's control over budget priorities. Included were provisions dealing with presidential "deferral" and "rescission" of funds appropriated by Congress. Under the act, deferral meant a presidential decision to delay or spread out the spending in a program, while rescission meant the actual cancellation of an expenditure. Both actions are to be reported to Congress and deferral requires the concurrence of one house, while rescission requires concurrence by both. Interestingly, this act did not discourage impoundments. During Gerald Ford's administration attempted impoundments actually increased. This was probably the result of a lack of clarity in the 1974 act as it was adopted. What Ford did was to send back to Congress in the form of deferrals or rescissions much of what Congress added to his proposed budget, thus requiring Congress to act again on these items. What Congress had done unintentionally was to provide the president with a sort of "item veto." What impoundment ultimately boils down to is whether the president or the Congress determines how and when funds are spent.

Yet another obstacle to effective congressional oversight is the practice of hiding certain expenditures by placing them in budgets that cloak their real purpose. Committee hearings revealed that since its adoption in 1954, the Food for

Peace Program had been a vehicle through which $1.6 billion in military aid had been channeled to various countries. Hearings in 1972 confirmed that the Agency for International Development, the agency set up to administer the nation's non-military assistance programs, had provided funds for supplying food, medical care, and supplies to the Lao military and paramilitary forces. It has been a standard practice to inflate certain appropriation accounts and then allow the excess funds to be transferred to the CIA, NSA, and other intelligence operations. Few members of Congress were aware of these practices, but few have been concerned enough to even raise questions until recently.

A subcommittee of the Senate Appropriations Committee shares responsibility for oversight of CIA activities. At the time the CIA was supporting military operations in Laos with huge amounts, Senator Allen Ellender (D-Miss.), chairman of the Appropriations Committee, said he "did not know anything about it." Elaborating further, he said, "It never dawned on me to ask" about CIA funds being used in Laos. The situation was similar in the House, where Representative Lucien Nedzi (D-Mich.), chairman of the subcommittee handling CIA oversight, observed that probably only the BOB (Bureau of the Budget, now OMB) and the Kremlin had a full understanding of U. S. intelligence operations. In 1971, in an effort to gain somewhat more control, Congress did place some restrictions in the Foreign Assistance Act on the use of funds provided. Provisions in 1974 legislation restricted the CIA to spending funds for operations in foreign countries only for those purposes "intended solely for obtaining necessary intelligence." In 1975 Senator William Proxmire (D-Wis.) introduced a bill that would authorize GAO audits and analyses of intelligence agency expenditures. While there have been some questions, concern is not widespread, as was indicated when the House voted 323 to 43 to approve the 1979 funding for intelligence agencies even though most members had no idea how much money was involved. Representative James P. Johnson (R-Colo.) called the measure a "blank check for the expenditure of a lot of money to those who in the past have not warranted that trust." Members of Congress cannot make intelligent decisions and provide effective oversight on the budget when they are denied basic data and information. In some areas it will take a more determined effort on their part to obtain this.

While a number of Congress's oversight problems stem from external forces, they contribute to the difficulty with some of their own practices. In the 1950s and 60s Congress resorted to "backdoor" spending in committing substantial expenditures. This is a procedure whereby programs are financed through the authorization bill, thus bypassing the normal appropriations procedures. Most common practices are to provide for the agencies' administering programs to implement them by contracting for services for which they are billed later or to borrow money that will be repaid as income is produced. In an effort to curb this bypassing of normal spending channels, the 1974 Budget and Impoundment Control Act included provisions against "backdoor" financing. In recent years another method of financing has become more and more popular with members of Congress — the "tax expenditure" method. This method finances programs through the tax code rather than through the appropriations process. This approach has become popular with many members of Congress because it can be used to fund programs without adding directly to federal expenditures. In a way this is self-delusion, because while it does not expand expenditures, it does add to the national debt by reducing revenues. According to the Congressional Budget Office, such tax expenditures are now costing about $150 billion annually in lost revenues, or the equivalent of about one-fourth of federal expenditures. In addition to being a misleading means of spending, tax expenditures are not subject to the same review and checks as are other spending proposals. Tax measures follow a different route in Congress than appropriations measures, and the tax code, unlike the budget, is not subject to built-in annual review. Under the 1974 budget reform act, provision is made for prioritizing spending among sixteen categories such as health, defense, income security, etc. Tax expenditures are not subject to this review and priority setting. The congressional Budget Committees have noted their inability to fit these expenditures into their review of federal spending priorities. Like backdoor spending, tax expenditures are a means of bypassing the normal spending process, thereby reducing Congress's control of the purse strings.

One of Congress's difficulties in its oversight efforts has been the absence of any real clarity of purpose. Over the years Congress has used a highly fragmented, departmental approach in acting on appropriations and has had no real budgetary philosophy of its own to guide its actions. Once it reaches Congress and is parcelled out among the subcommittees, the president's proposed budget is almost never reviewed again as a total package. Consequently there is little coordination in the Congress between the tax programs recommended by the revenue committees, the spending programs recommended by the authorizing committees, and the appropriations approved by the Appropriations Committees. There is a virtual absence of consideration of the relative merits and benefits of various programs in determining their levels of funding because the different subcommittees confine their deliberations to their own relatively small segment of the total budget package. In an effort to impose some degree of program review, Senator Edmund Muskie (D-Maine) urged adoption of a "sunset bill," a proposal that won the support of such groups as Common Cause, the Chamber of Commerce, the Business Roundtable, and the NAM. If adopted, this legislation would require every federal program to be reviewed and reauthorized by Congress once every six years or it would be automatically terminated. This proposal stems from the philosophy that old, ineffective programs that are eating up available dollars must be weeded out to free money for new efforts and also to reduce the budget. President Carter endorsed the measure, but did little to push it in Congress, where it has encountered stiff opposition from a number of committee chairmen supported by an alliance of the executive agencies and interest groups who do not want their spending programs subjected to mandatory review. Any program that has been in existence for a while has developed its own bureaucratic and interest group support systems that staunchly oppose any efforts to change the status quo. Reform becomes extremely difficult. With Muskie having left the Senate for the State Department, the legislation will have to await a new champion in Congress.

If Congress is going to fulfill its role as controller of the purse, it must assert itself more effectively. To play a positive role in policy decisions, Congress must avoid situations locking them into commitments and decisions ahead of time and over which they have little or no control. This means they must have access to information and data in advance, enabling them to make informed decisions. Much data on federal expenditures are already available, but Congress must use it more effectively. They need to make more effective use of the GAO. Possibly the Congressional Budget Office also can bring improvement in this respect. As Louis Fisher notes, "Unless Congress strengthens its control over budget execution, it cannot legislate back to reality its vaunted 'power of the purse.' "[10]

## BUDGET REFORM

The budget is a highly political matter and there is considerable disagreement as to how it should be managed. The so-called "new economists" and the classical economists or traditionalists are inclined to view budgets quite differently. For the new economists the budget is an instrument for governmental financial control and management, while the traditionalists are more inclined to view the government's budget on the same terms as a family budget, that is, an instrument of financial discipline. While the new economists are much more willing to accept deficit financing, the traditionalists believe strongly in balanced budgets. While the U. S. has experienced a surplus only once during the last two decades and the national debt has doubled since 1969, presidents still are inclined to promise balanced budgets because of their strong political appeal. However, attaining a balanced budget is an extremely difficult task, because it usually means either raising taxes to increase revenues or cutting program spending to reduce outlays — both decisions that can be very unpopular politically. Furthermore, close analysis of the budget reveals that there really are not a whole lot of things the president can cut. About 75 or 80 percent of federal spending is, in a sense, "uncontrollable." It involves fixed costs such as interest on the national debt, pensions, etc.; long-term contracts and obligations such as for weapons, federal buildings, and facilities; and entitlement programs such as social security, veterans benefits, and medicare. Out of a total fiscal year 1979 budget of $531 billion, $404 billion or about 76 percent represented such "fixed" costs. These could be reduced only with great difficulty. This leaves the president only 20–25 percent of the budget with which to maneuver, and even this is subject to strong pressures from supporters of existing programs. OMB Director James McIntyre observed, "I've yet to see a group come in and argue for less money."

Jimmy Carter's 1979 budget was the first ever to go over a half trillion dollars, yet it included very little in the way of new spending initiatives. The increases in spending were lower than for Ford's two budget proposals, and Carter's budget marked the first time in this century that a newly elected Democratic president failed to request funds for a single significant new welfare program. In spite of this determined effort to hold the line, the budget produced a $50.9 billion deficit. Projections for 1980 and 1981 indicated that the increases in real spending might be only about 1 percent, but unless the revenue picture changed considerably these budgets would still produce deficits in spite of President Carter's determined efforts to produce a balanced budget.

In efforts to gain more effective control over the process and to reduce the "politics" in budgetary decision-making, various techniques have been tried from time to time. Zero-based budgeting (ZBB), a gimmick of the Carter administration, is only the latest of a number of other "reforms" attempted without much long-lasting effect on the process. Like Ole Man River, the budgetary process just keeps rolling along with only an occasional ripple on the surface.

In the 1960s, Secretary of Defense Robert McNamara decided he would make Pentagon decision-making more rational by introducing a system of planning, programming, and budgeting (PPBS). PPBS attempts to link budget decisions to a rational assessment of alternative means for attaining policy objectives. Decision-makers are to consider a variety of factors and alternatives when choosing goals and the policies to meet them. PPBS is a cost-benefit approach to policy decisions; goals and priorities are defined, various alternatives for achieving these are identified, and each program is evaluated in terms of current and proposed costs. In 1965 President Johnson ordered that PPBS be adopted by all major executive agencies. Six years later the system was dropped, having experienced only limited acceptance and success.

Zero-based budgeting, the latest method undertaken to reform the federal budgetary process, was brought by President Carter from Georgia. The theory of zero-based budgeting is to force department heads to examine all their expenditures annually from the ground up and, as in PPBS, to set priorities for spending and weigh various programs against each other. In President Carter's words, ZBB would "require every program that spends the taxpayer's money to rejustify itself annually." In a way, calling the 1978 effort of the Carter administration zero-based budgeting is a misnomer, because they did not wipe the slate clean and start from ground zero. Each department was ordered to determine the minimum level, something less than the current level, at which useful programs could be maintained. This was zero base and from this the agency was to project a budget based on increments of 90, 100, and 110 percent. The ZBB system is built around program assessments, and the first step is to identify the programs on which the budget will be built. These programs are then to be assigned priorities in the agency's budget.

While the White House declared the first year of ZBB a success, most observers questioned how much ZBB had changed the overall process. OMB said there had been "subtle but real improvements." Writing in the *Public Administration Review*, Allen Schick said the new system "did not really change the rules by which budgetary decisions are made. It changed the terminology of budgeting, but little more."[11] Robert W. Hartman of the Brookings Institution said the new technique "seems to have led to little restructuring of the budget base." Even with the new guidelines, most departments, as usual, requested more than their ceilings provided, and many observers felt that many agencies simply played the old game by the new rules. Very few departments and agencies seriously considered alternatives to what they had been doing; and even though called upon to prioritize their programs, most ended up ranking only their requested add-ons, not all their programs. Commerce begged off on this task, saying it had such a diversity of programs that comparisons among them would be meaningless. Some agencies felt that even OMB did not follow the game plan by not ranking programs of the various agencies on a government-wide basis. With only a few modifications, review of the budget proposals by OMB and the president were about the same as in previous administrations.

Thus ZBB in its first year apparently did not bring any revolutionary changes in the budgetary process. Agency reponses varied and the approach did make some agencies examine the potential impact of a reduced budget. A few agencies made some shifts in personnel and funds: the Environmental Protection Agency decided to transfer 12 percent of its personnel in its pesticide program to other areas, and the Department of Labor eliminated thirty-two low-priority positions. Many agencies, feeling they were expected to recommend some reductions, proposed cuts in programs they were sure would not be accepted anyway. At this stage about the only point of agreement on ZBB is that in 1978 it substantially increased the amount of paperwork involved in budget preparations without significantly affecting the final outcome.

While Ford's projected budget for 1979 would have attempted to eliminate or reduce over one hundred programs, Carter's budget using ZBB asked Congress to reduce only a handful of programs. From this shakedown cruise, it would appear ZBB was not the panacea providing the degree of control necessary for Carter to achieve his twin goals of a balanced budget and all the nation's program needs by 1981. While agencies took ranking of their programs somewhat more seriously in '79 and '80 and played fewer games with ZBB, OMB became less enamored of the process itself. When it embarked on its own efforts at priority ranking for budget items, it found itself faced with determining the relative merits of more than 3000 separate programs and activities. How does one prioritize the relative merits of the National Weather Service and the School Lunch Program? OMB found itself facing an impossible task.

## CONCLUSION

Though cloaked disarmingly in apparently endless pages and columns of sterile figures, the budget is a deceptively political document. Efforts at reforming the budgetary process such as PPBS and ZBB have failed to a substantial degree because such approaches run head-on into some basic American political values. Budget-making in the American system is not a very scientific and objective accounting process that lends itself to centralized leadership and direction. It is a system, rather, that invites the give and take of competing economic and political interests, thriving on compromise, bargaining, trade-offs, and horse-trading that would be largely precluded if such policy decisions were turned over to the technical analysis of PPBS or ZBB. A host of bureau chiefs, department heads, and organized interests have their projected needs and pet projects they want accommodated; consequently, the budgetary process is permeated throughout by established loyalties, commitments, and political considerations. Thus, for a new approach such as PPBS or ZBB to succeed, the policymakers have to be convinced that such an approach simply modifies rather than replaces the existing political process. Otherwise, these approaches are seen as threats to the democratic processes of compromise and negotiated settlements and are doomed to failure.

Approaches such as PPBS and ZBB encounter other negative elements in the present system as well. They are based on a programmatic approach, and this runs counter to the traditional approach in federal budgeting. Traditionally, program decisions and appropriations have been made on the basis of agencies rather than for particular programs, and most agencies administer programs in several functional areas with a considerable amount of overlap resulting. In the area of environmental and natural resources, for example, at least a dozen different agencies are involved in administering programs. Therefore, if money is budgeted by program, what agency administers it? To further cloud the issue, many programs are hidden in such broad budget categories as "personnel services," "travel," "capital expenditures," "supplies," etc. All of this tends to make the programmatic concept difficult to apply. Also, it is much easier to agree to appropriate so many dollars to particular agencies than it is to make a choice in terms of basic differences on specific programs. Finally, many agencies feel extremely uncomfortable having to tell precisely what they plan to do and what it will cost and will go to great extremes to avoid having to do so.

Since most governmental programs and expenditures are of a continuing nature, ongoing programs become a powerful inertial force in the budget-making process. Consequently, as Wildavsky noted in his study of the process, traditionally the "largest determining factor of the size and content of this year's budget is last year's budget."[12] Because it is considered a waste of time to wipe the slate clean and review every program anew each year, much of the budget is a product of previous decisions. It would be next to impossible to consider all possible alternatives when considering the budget, and since each new fiscal year is begun with substantial programmatic commitments already established, the current base of expenditures has generally been regarded as the most practical starting point. Most budget decisions then revolve around proposed increases in existing programs.

This makes the federal budget process a rather classic example of the incremental process of decision-making. As Sharkansky describes it, incrementalism is an approach to decision-making that deals with complex issues by narrowing and simplifying the scope of the decisions to be made. Thus, instead of trying to make decisions on the whole of the federal budget, the incrementalist focuses on a manageable portion of the whole. He does not start anew each time, but accepts as given those policies already in effect.[13] The incremental approach has a number of advantages for budgetary decision-making. It makes the decisions much more manageable by focusing on increases or decreases in individual programs rather than trying to compare the merit of various programs. By starting from the base of existing programs, it may eliminate considerable wasted time and effort to justify accepted programs. From a political standpoint it limits new political conflict by accepting past decisions rather than refighting old battles again. Approaches such as PPBS and ZBB threaten to open up a whole range of established programs to new questions and controversies, whereas the incremental approach does not hold the potential for undoing all those compromises and accommodations hammered out in previous decisions. On the other hand, incrementalism does favor the status quo, making it difficult to weed out and eliminate old, ineffective programs. It also contributes to the fragmented approach in budget-making and appropriations, making it difficult for Congress to view the overall policy impact of the budget. As testimony to the persistence of incrementalism in the federal budget process, Jerome Miles of the Agriculture Department commented after the 1978 preparations for fiscal year 1979, "When you're through with zero-based budgeting, you have the best incremental budgeting system I've ever seen." Chances are the process won't change a lot the next time around.

## Points to Ponder

Technically, no federal money can be spent without Congress's approval; in reality, how effective is Congress's control of the federal purse strings?

To date, what have been the major results of the 1974 Congressional Budget and Impoundment Control Act?

Once Congress has appropriated funds, is the president obligated as the executor of federal laws to spend the money?

What is the impact of "fixed costs" on federal budget-making?

## Notes

1. Emmette S. Redford, *The Role of Government in the American Economy* (New York: Macmillan, 1966) p. 1.
2. *Public Papers of the Presidents,* 1970, pp. 260–61.
3. Senate Report No. 7, 93rd Congress, 1st Session (1973), p. 3.
4. When necessary appropriations have not been approved, both houses adopt resolutions authorizing affected agencies to continue spending at currently authorized levels until action on current appropriations can be completed.
5. As quoted in *Congressional Quarterly Weekly Report* (September 7, 1974), p. 2415.
6. John Brademas as quoted by Richard E. Cohen in "The Congressional Budget Process — Is It Worth All the Headaches?" *National Journal* (September 29, 1979), p. 1605.
7. Richard Fenno, *The Power of the Purse* (Boston: Little, Brown & Co., 1966) p. 575.
8. Leonard Freedman, *Public Housing: The Politics of Poverty* (New York: Holt, Rinehart & Winston, 1969), pp. 20–21.
9. James Madison, *The Federalist,* No. 48 (New York: Random House [Modern Library Edition], 1937), p. 323.

10. Louis Fisher, *Presidential Spending Power* (Princeton: Princeton University Press, 1975), p. 260.
11. Allen Schick, "Road from 2BB," *Public Administration Review,* 38 (March 1978), pp. 177–80.
12. Aaron Wildavsky, *The Politics of the Budgetary Process* (Boston: Little, Brown & Co., 1964), p. 13.
13. Ira Sharkansky, *The Politics of Taxing and Spending* (Indianapolis: Bobbs-Merrill, 1969), pp. 49–52.

## Suggestions for Further Reading

BERMAN, LARRY. *The Office of Management and Budget and the Presidency, 1921–1979.* Princeton, N.J.: Princeton University Press, 1979.

BROWN, RICHARD E. *The GAO: Untapped Sources of Congressional Power.* Knoxville, Tenn: University of Tennessee Press, 1970.

COHEN, RICHARD. "The Congressional Budget Process—Is It Worth All the Headaches?" *National Journal* (September 29, 1979) pp. 1605–07.

DANZIGER, JAMES N. *Making Budgets: Public Resource Allocation.* Beverly Hills: Sage, 1979.

FENNO, RICHARD. *The Power of the Purse.* Boston: Little, Brown & Co., 1966.

FISHER, LOUIS. *Presidential Spending Power.* Princeton, N.J.: Princeton University Press, 1975.

General Accounting Office. *Tax Expenditures: A Primer.* Washington, D.C.: Government Printing Office, 1979.

HAVEMANN, JOEL. *Congress and the Budget.* Bloomington, Ind.: Indiana University Press, 1978.

HORN, STEPHEN. *Unused Power: The Work of the Senate Committee on Appropriations.* Washington, D.C.: The Brookings Institution, 1970.

IPPOLITO, DENNIS. *The Budget and National Politics.* San Francisco: Freeman, 1978.

KLOMAN, ERASMUS, ed. *Cases in Accountability: The Work of the GAO.* Boulder, Colo.: Westview Press, 1979.

LELOUP, LANCE. *Budgetary Politics: Dollars, Deficits, Decisions.* Brunswick, Ohio: Kings Court Communications, 1977.

LYNCH, THOMAS D. *Public Budgeting in America.* Englewood Cliffs, N.J.: Prentice-Hall, 1979.

MCALLISTER, EUGENE J. "Congress and the Budget: Evaluating the Process," *Commonsense,* vol. 2 no. 2 (Summer 1979), p. 62.

PECHMAN, JOSEPH, ed. *Setting National Priorities: The 1980 Budget.* Washington, D.C.: The Brookings Institution, 1979.

PFIFFNES, JAMES. *The President, the Budget, and Congress: Impoundment and the 1974 Budget Act.* New York: Westview Press, 1979.

PRESSMAN, JEFFREY. *House vs Senate: Conflict in the Appropriations Process.* New Haven, Conn.: Yale University Press, 1966.

PHYRR, PETER. *Zero-Base Budgeting: A Practical Management Tool for Evaluating Expenses.* New York: Wiley & Sons, 1973.

SHARKANSKY, IRA. *The Politics of Taxing and Spending.* Indianapolis: Bobbs-Merrill, 1964.

WILDAVSKY, AARON. *Budgeting: A Comparative Theory of Budgeting Processes.* Boston: Little, Brown & Co., 1975.

WILDAVSKY, AARON. *The Politics of the Budgetary Process.* Boston: Little, Brown & Co., 1964.

# 4

# Government as Fiscal Manager

As was noted earlier, the budget is a significant instrument of governmental fiscal policy that may have considerable impact on the national economy. Thus, the task of the national budget-makers is not merely one of determining what programs will be funded at what levels and the taxes necessary to generate the needed revenues, but must include a careful assessment of the impact these policies will have on the overall state of the economy. The taxing, borrowing, and spending activities of the federal government have become important factors in the growth and stability of the nation's economy; therefore, one of the constraints imposed on national policymakers is the need to take into consideration the potential economic impact of their decisions that are directed primarily at other goals.

Earlier policymakers did not have to operate under such a constraint since government expenditures were small and the tariff produced all the revenue needed for federal operations. In fact, prior to 1930 the United States economy was dominated by the private sector and the federal budget was not really large enough to be a significant factor. Excluding war-time budgets, federal expenditures didn't reach 5 percent of the GNP until 1931. Prior to 1930, the federal budget was not seen as a tool for managing the economy. When an economic recession reduced federal revenues, the president and Congress simply cut expenditures enough to maintain fiscal balance. Thus, through the Hoover administration federal spending and taxing policies *reflected* the economic cycles rather than attempting to control them.

This pattern of governmental fiscal policy was in keeping with the dominant classical economic concepts of the period. Influenced by such authors as Smith, Edgeworth, and Say, the classical economists held that a decentralized, laissez-

> **Major Monetary and Financial Legislation**
>
> **Treasury Department Act of 1789.** Created the U. S. Treasury Department, to be headed by a presidentially appointed secretary.
>
> **Federal Reserve Act of 1913.** Created the Federal Reserve System to regulate monetary and banking policies through its influences on the amount of credit available and the currency in circulation.
>
> **Sixteenth Amendment to the Constitution.** This amendment, adopted in 1913, authorized Congress to levy taxes on incomes, thus paving the way for individual and corporate income taxes, which provide approximately three-fourths of federal revenues.
>
> **Employment Act of 1946.** For the first time, established a responsibility for the national government to maintain a stable national economy and created the Council of Economic Advisors (CEA) to advise the president on economic matters.

faire economy guided by individual self-interest and supply and demand would allocate resources more efficiently than any alternative, governmentally "controlled" system.[1] Under this approach, extreme economic fluctuations were accepted, in fact expected, as the business cycle moved through its various natural phases of prosperity, recession, depression, and recovery. It was the rather general feeling that there was little that government could or should do to alter the natural ups and downs of the business cycle. These were not seen as matters of concern to political decision-makers. Reflecting this philosophy, President Warren Harding told a 1921 conference on unemployment, "There has been vast unemployment before and there will be again. There will be depression and inflation just as surely as the tides ebb and flow. I would have little enthusiasm for any proposed remedy which seeks palliation or tonic from the Public Treasury."

The Great Depression and the New Deal brought sweeping changes in thinking on the government's role in economic matters. As John M. Gaus once observed, certain changes in our society "coerce us into the use of government."[2] The Depression and World War II brought rather dramatic changes in both attitudes toward the government's role and the scope of governmental activity. As the objectives Americans sought to obtain through government grew, government involvement in the economy expanded. Depression in the 1930s, inflation in the 1940s, and fears of widespread unemployment following World War II prompted greater acceptance, even expectations, of active governmental involvement in the national economy. Thus the years following World War II witnessed changes making the national economy heavily dependent on governmental spending. In the words of Emmette S. Redford,

## Principal Departments and Agencies

**Department of the Treasury.** Established in 1789 as one of the original cabinet departments, Treasury has responsibility for federal fiscal management including tax collection, debt management, and the coining and printing of money.

**Council of Economic Advisors.** This is a three-member advisory group created by the Full Employment Act of 1946 to counsel the president on economic policy matters.

**Federal Reserve Board of Governors.** The seven-member board oversees the operations of the Federal Reserve System and determines general monetary and credit policies by controlling interest rates and monetary supplies.

**Internal Revenue Service (IRS).** This is the unit within the Department of the Treasury with responsibility for the collection of taxes and customs duties.

---

Public expenditures for defense, social welfare, public works and foreign rehabilitation and relief have become so large a part of the total income of society that they may at times be the largest single influence on economic operations. Their rate, timing and direction, and their effect on government's fiscal operations are significant.[3]

To accommodate this new role of government in economic affairs, the laissez-faire orthodoxy of the classicists was replaced by the "new economics" of John M. Keynes. In his *General Theory of Employment, Interest and Money* (1936), Keynes espoused a much more activist role for government in the economy than accepted by the classicists. He felt that the government should consciously use its taxing and spending powers to regulate the ups and downs of the economic cycles, reducing taxes and increasing expenditures in times of recession and employing reverse policies when faced with inflation.

It was Keynes's contention that through the manipulation of government taxing and spending policies the public sector could stimulate or depress economic activity. According to Keynes, depression and unemployment resulted from inadequate total demand, thus as the economy slowed down, government should compensate for the decline in private investment by increasing its own spending to maintain high levels of investment, employment, and national income. On the other hand, when inflation threatens, taxes can be raised, expenditures reduced, and interest rates raised to put a brake on the economy. From the 1930s to the 1950s, the Keynesian concept that governmental fiscal and monetary policies should be adjusted to the ebb and flow of economic tides was widely embraced.

The Employment Act of 1946 established the statutory responsibility of the government as an active participant in the nation's economy. This law made it the responsibility of the federal government, under the leadership of the president, to pursue economic policies designed to maintain a stable and prosperous economy. Section 2 states:

> The Congress hereby declares that it is the continuing policy and responsibility of the Federal Government to use all practicable means consistent with its needs and obligations and other essential considerations of national policy, with the assistance and cooperation of industry, agriculture, labor and state and local governments, to coordinate and utilize all its plans, functions and resources for the purpose of creating and maintaining, in a manner calculated to foster and promote free competitive enterprise and the general welfare, conditions under which there will be afforded useful employment opportunities, including self-employment, for those able, willing, and seeking to work, and to promote maximum employment, production, and purchasing power.

This act made it clear that no longer was the government to be a passive bystander in economic matters. Even the more fiscally conservative Republicans soon came to accept a more active role for the government in economic matters. In his 1953 message accompanying his economic report to Congress, President Eisenhower noted:

> The demands of modern life and the unsettled status of the world require a more important role for government than it played in earlier and quieter times.... Government must use its vast power to help maintain employment and purchasing power as well as to maintain reasonably stable prices. Government must be alert and sensitive to economic developments, including its own myriad activities. It must be prepared to take preventive as well as remedial action; and it must be ready to cope with new situations that may arise. This is not a start-and-stop responsibility, but a continuous one.

Through the 1960s many economists felt the answers had been found for controlling the nation's economy. The major economic problems of recession, depression, and inflation would be eliminated through the "fine tuning" of the economy with adjustments in taxes, interest rates, money supply, and spending. In 1965 *Time* magazine wrote, "We are all Keynesians now."

Regulating the economy is not, however, simply a "technical" matter undertaken in a highly rational environment, and in the 1970s the Keynesian bubble burst. A basic element in Keynesian theory is the trade-off between unemployment and inflation. Anti-Keynesians contend that there is a natural rate of unemployment and that trying to use fiscal and monetary policies to reduce beyond this point only breeds inflation without reducing unemployment. Experience in the 1970s indicated that at times the inflation/unemployment trade-off indeed becomes highly complicated and traditional fiscal policies may have limited application. During 1973–74 both inflation and unemployment rose sharply—inflation going from 8.8 to 12.2 percent and unemployment from 4.9 to 5.6 percent. Economists coined a new word to describe this phenomenon—

**FIGURE 4.1  Inflation's Effect on the Consumer Price Index Month by Month**

**Consumer prices in the past 12 months**
percent change from previous month

Source: Dept. of Labor

| 1978 Mar. | Apr. | May | June | July | Aug. | Sept. | Oct. | Nov. | Dec. | Jan. | Feb. 1979 |
|---|---|---|---|---|---|---|---|---|---|---|---|
| .8 | .8 | .8 | .9 | .6 | .6 | .9 | .8 | .6 | .6 | .9 | 1.2 |

Source: U.S. Department of Labor. Reprinted courtesy of the Louisville, Ky. Courier-Journal.

"stagflation." Stagflation is a combination of inflation, rising unemployment, and slowed rates of economic growth.

Stagflation raised a number of difficult questions for economic policymakers, many of them as yet unanswered. Faced with stagflation, what action takes priority? Do you seek a tax cut to encourage consumer spending, thus promoting production and employment but at the same time risking more inflation? Or, do you raise taxes and interest rates to curb inflation and chance touching off a recession? Are today's prices in reality a product of supply and demand in the market place or are they controlled by other factors? In our highly complex economy, is full employment still a realistic goal? Regardless of how these questions are answered, it is apparent that the government must inevitably play a major role in the nation's economy. In 1902 the GNP was about $21.6 billion and government expenditures accounted for about 7.7 percent of that. In 1976 the GNP

**FIGURE 4.2  The Effect of Inflation**

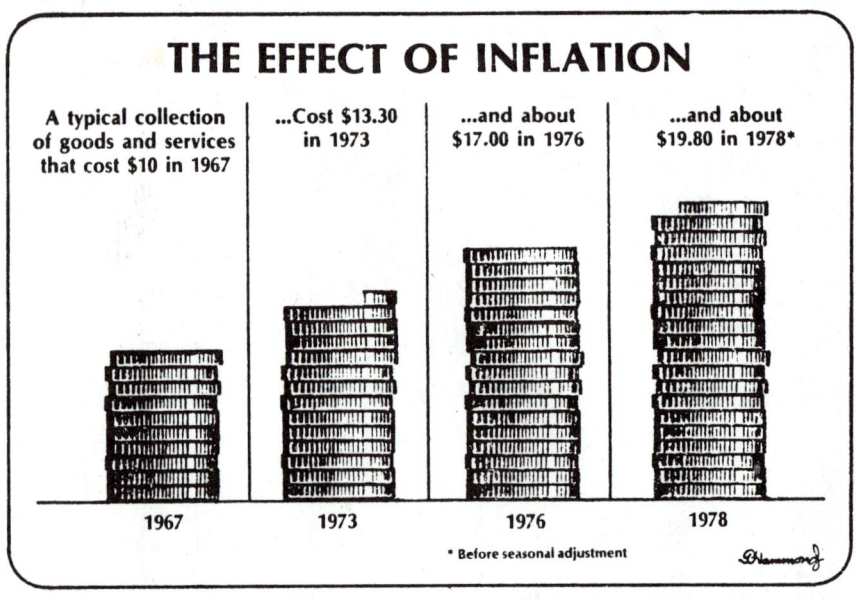

## THE EFFECT OF INFLATION

| A typical collection of goods and services that cost $10 in 1967 | ...Cost $13.30 in 1973 | ...and about $17.00 in 1976 | ...and about $19.80 in 1978* |
|---|---|---|---|
| 1967 | 1973 | 1976 | 1978 |

* Before seasonal adjustment

Source: Labor Department, Bureau Labor Statistics. From Congressional Quarterly. Reprinted with permission of Congressional Quarterly, Inc.

was $1.8 trillion and government expenditures accounted for approximately 30 percent of it. Government activity now accounts for about one-third of all economic activity in the country. Under these circumstances it is no longer a question of should the government be involved, but a question of how it can best use its position to achieve the desired objectives.

### The Politics of Economic Management

As the older laissez-faire approach has given way to active governmental participation in economic affairs, the issue is no longer government control of the economy, but to whose advantage should such control work. Governmental intervention in economic matters is not neutral; some segments of society benefit more than others from various policy choices. Consequently, such policy decisions are not purely technical choices based on economic theory, but are a unique blending of economics and politics. Because different decisions affect different citizens in different ways, taxing and spending policies generate considerable conflict among the many different interests composing our pluralistic society. Far from being made in a political vacuum, these decisions are at the very heart of the political process, and only one thing is certain in governmental economic policy—whatever the ultimate decision, it will be shaped by both economic and political considerations. The determination of who benefits the most and who pays the disproportionate share of the costs is a matter of prime concern for politicians as they shape policies in the midst of competing interests.

### The Mechanics of Economic Management

Another factor complicating the process is the multitude of participants that become involved. There is no lack of advisors when it comes to government economic policies as their formulation involves the president, Congress, a host of administrative agencies, interest groups, the media, and public opinion. The Employment Act of 1946 created the Council of Economic Advisors to counsel the president on economic matters, and while different presidents will use the council differently, theirs is only one of a number of voices the president hears on economic issues. Because the federal government has broad powers to alter the economic system, these are decisions upon which there is frequent disagreement, even among policymakers within the government. Thus, presidential calls for action don't necessarily result in immediate responses.

Because the variety of tools available to government for influencing the economy is so great, this may further complicate decision-making by providing a number of alternative approaches. Included in the possibilities are credit controls administered by the Federal Reserve System, debt-management policies controlled by the Treasury Department, the president's authority to vary the terms of mortgages carrying federal insurance and his flexibility in administering the federal budget, agricultural price supports, modifications of the tax structure, and governmental expenditures on public works, social security, unemployment insurance, etc. While this arsenal is substantial, it has led to considerable disagreement as to what approach is best for producing the desired economic objectives.

### Fiscal vs. Monetary Controls

Much of this disagreement has centered around *fiscal* versus *monetary* policies for economic regulation. The fiscal approach involves the deliberate use of governmental taxing and spending to regulate income levels, employment, and economic growth rates. Those inclined to favor a vigorous and active federal government are most likely to favor the fiscal approach. It appeals largely to Democrats. The monetary approach emphasizes economic regulation through the manipulation of the monetary supply, interest rates, and management of the debt. Because monetary controls are somewhat more indirect and impersonal than fiscal controls, many feel that this approach involves less governmental interference in private economic activity. This approach is generally more favored by Republicans.

While economic policy involves considerable economic and philosophical disagreement, its formulation and implementation are further complicated by the great diffusion of responsibility among governmental branches and agencies. While the president has been assigned considerable authority in the economic realm, his control of virtually every instrument is shared with other agencies who may be influenced by perspectives and responsibilities completely different from his. Therefore, in spite of efforts by the president, it is not at all uncommon for different agencies to act independently and even in contradiction to the president and to one another. While the Treasury Department pursues an inflationary borrowing policy, the Federal Reserve Board may well be employing a deflationary policy on interest rates. Consistency throughout is not necessarily a hallmark of governmental economic policy. As the old saying goes, too many cooks spoil the broth.

## MONETARY POLICY

Because the primary responsibility for different parts of governmental economic policy rests with different and largely autonomous agencies, effective control and coordination are quite difficult. Monetary policy, for example, is controlled primarily by the Treasury Department and the Federal Reserve System. The Treasury Department, headed by a secretary who is a political appointee, usually reflects presidential priorities in economic matters. However, its influence on monetary policy is rather limited, being exercised through its management of the national debt. And, though the debt has reached substantial proportions, its use in economic regulation is rather restricted.

By far the most prominent actor in the field of monetary policy is the Federal Reserve System and its board of governors (the Federal Reserve Board or the FRB). Created by Congress in 1913 with the objective of reducing the vulnerability of the nation's banking system to financial panics, the "Fed" has come to exercise considerable influence over governmental economic policy. Headed by a seven-member board of governors appointed by the president and confirmed by the Senate, the Federal Reserve System has several controls it can use in regulating economic activity. The Fed's powers are exercised primarily through the influence it has over the nation's banking system. Since the supply of money is a prime factor in economic activity, regulation of the rate at which money is lent and borrowed becomes a major factor. This is what the Fed determines through its controls and influence on the nation's banking community.

Banks belonging to the Federal Reserve System are required to keep a certain portion of their assets on deposit with a Federal Reserve Bank—this is the *reserve*

*Government as Fiscal Manager* **87**

"There! This tourniquet should prevent your dying from acute inflationitis... if it doesn't kill you."

Reprinted courtesy of Hugh Haynie and the Louisville, Ky. Courier Journal.

*requirement*. By manipulating up or down the portion of the banks' assets that must be "held in reserve," the Fed can control the amounts banks are able to lend. Because changes in reserve requirements are rather cumbersome to administer, this control is used rather sparingly. Another instrument is the Fed's control of the interest rate it charges when its banks loan money to member banks—the *discount rate*. By raising or lowering the discount rate, the Fed determines the interest rates of commercial banks, thus influencing the volume of loans issued. Probably the most effective tool of the Fed is its buying and selling of government securities on the open market. This buying and selling of U.S. Treasury securities is carried out through the New York Federal Reserve Bank acting on instructions from the Federal Open Market Committee. The Federal Open Market Committee, composed of the seven members of the board of governors plus five of the twelve presidents of the Federal Reserve Banks, sets monthly interest-rate and money-supply targets and bases open market transactions on these goals. When securities are bought, payments for them are deposited in the accounts of member banks, thus increasing their reserves and expanding the money supply. If the committee wants to contract the supply of money, it sells securities, thus reducing available reserves. The Fed also influences economic activity through its control of the *margin requirement*, the portion of a stock purchase that can be bought on credit, and through what might be termed its moral suasion over the banking community and to a lesser degree, the public. Recent chairmen of the Federal Reserve Board have been respected and influential policymakers, commanding considerable media and public attention. The "Olympus-like" pronouncements of an outspoken chairman like Arthur Burns can have considerable impact on attitudes about economic health and stability.

The Fed, on the other hand, is not immune to public and political pressures, and in times of economic disagreement comes in for its share of criticism. In its earlier years, the rather extensive powers given the Fed were exercised only gradually and cautiously. Even today, many criticize the Fed as being "timid" in exercising its powers. Some observers also question the adequacy of monetary controls alone to accomplish the objective of a stable, healthy economy. They point out that during the Great Depression these were not sufficient. In recent years, under the leadership of more vigorous chairmen such as William McChesney Martin and Arthur F. Burns, the Fed has been much more assertive and has frequently challenged the president on economic policies. In 1965–66 Lyndon Johnson was incensed when the Fed raised interest rates in a move counter to his efforts to stimulate economic growth. Arthur Burns, Martin's successor, took issue with the policies of both Nixon and Carter, claiming they were flirting dangerously with inflation. President Carter's selection of G. William Miller to replace Burns as Federal Reserve Board chairman was seen as a move to eliminate or at least reduce challenges to White House authority and economic policies. Miller's successor, Paul Volcker, showed signs, however, of a return to the independence of earlier chairmen.

The Fed's role in policymaking may well face a more formidable threat than presidential domination, however. Since 1950 the proportion of the nation's banks belonging to the Federal Reserve System has been declining steadily, in recent years at the rate of almost one per week. In 1950 about one-half of the country's banks belonged to the Federal Reserve System and they controlled about 86 percent of the total banking assets. By the end of 1976 this had dropped to 39 percent membership controlling 74 percent of bank assets as banks increasingly preferred state regulations to Federal Reserve requirements. In 1976 Federal reserve requirements varied from 7 percent to 16.25 percent depending on size of deposits and these reserves earned no interest. State regulations usually require no reserve, thus allowing banks to draw interest on larger portions of their assets. In an effort to curb the tide of banks leaving the Fed, Congress in 1980 adopted legislation that would allow the Fed to pay interest on reserve deposits. Should the current decline in Federal Reserve participation continue, the Fed could see its ability to regulate the monetary supply severely hampered.

## FISCAL POLICY

Whereas decisions on monetary policy can be made largely by administrative agencies, major fiscal policy decisions usually require congressional action. This necessity has two significant implications for decision-making on fiscal policy—fiscal policy decisions may be highly partisan and action may encounter considerable delay. Since the timing of an action may determine its economic impact, the latter point may have considerable importance for a policy's effectiveness.

### Tax Policy

Since we have already discussed federal budgetary and spending policy earlier, our focus here will be on the other side of the coin; i.e., federal taxing or revenue policy. Again, the cast of characters and the political inputs that go into the decision-making on tax policies are substantial. A variety of executive agencies including the Council of Economic Advisors, OMB, and the Treasury Department provide advise on tax policies. In Congress, several committees such as the Joint Economic Committee and its specialized subcommittees, the Congressional Budget Committees, the House Committee on Ways and Means, and the Senate Finance Committee participate in tax policy decisions. These participants are joined by a whole host of specialized interest groups in proposing policies on taxation. In the end, however, the two prime actors are the executive and the Congress, whose different responsibilities, economic interests, and policy perspectives lead to frequent clashes.

Although the Constitution states that all revenue bills must originate in the House of Representatives, as in so many areas of policymaking, the initiative has gradually shifted to the executive branch. Today most revenue and tax policies are largely formulated in the Treasury Department's Office of Tax Policy and forwarded by the president to the House Committee on Ways and Means and the Senate Finance Committee. This shift in initiative, however, has really done very little to diminish the prestige and importance of these two committees in their respective bodies. Because of the power and influence of these committees, the Congress remains a powerful influence in determining the nation's taxation and financial policies.

Because their legislative role includes not only tax policy but a number of the most significant areas with which Congress deals—medicare, social welfare, trade and tariff controls—Ways and Means and Finance are among the elite of the congressional committees. They probably handle more nationally significant legislation than any other committees in Congress, and as a consequence their prestige and influence are substantial. Because of this, members of these committees enjoy substantial bargaining advantages with their colleagues. Members of Ways and Means and Finance usually have long tenure with years of congressional experience, and their "expertise" on tax measures enhances their influence. The chairmen of these two powerful committees are particularly influential policymakers and on occasion have been troublesome thorns in the sides of presidents trying to implement economic programs.

The House Ways and Means Committee has jealously guarded its prerogative of getting first shot at all revenue measures, and as a result tends to exert a disproportionate amount of influence on tax bills. House Ways and Means members develop considerable special expertise, and as a consequence tax measures are accorded special treatment on the floor of the House. Once Ways and Means members reach a decision on tax policy, it is generally accepted in the House that the "specialists" have spoken and that the full membership could do little to improve upon the product. Amendments offered by other members would be considered inadequately prepared; therefore, tax measures are almost always taken up under "closed"[4] rules in the House. Few if any changes are made in a bill once reported by Ways and Means.

The Senate Finance Committee functions as a sort of court of appeals on measures reported by Ways and Means. It is somewhat less rigid in its procedures and more accessible. In fact the *Washington Post* contrasted the two committees in this way:

> The Ways and Means Committee is a serious operation, genuinely devoted to a decent standard of fairness. The Senate Finance Committee, in contrast, is a kind of hospitality center for special interests, a safe haven for every kind of artfully drafted tax dodge, costly preference, protectionist ruse and fiscal outrage.

While tax bills are not handled under as many constraints in the Senate, where they can be amended on the floor, the Finance Committee and its chairman retain considerable influence. The Finance Committee controls the selection of conference committee members from the Senate and thus exerts considerable influence over what goes into the final version of a bill. (A conference committee is appointed each time the House and Senate pass different versions of a bill. This special committee irons out a compromise version for both houses to approve.)

Since taxes are compulsory contributions made from private sources for the support of public goals and objectives and because those who contribute most usually do not benefit most, tax decisions are not overly popular with either citizens or their elected representatives. Probably very few taxpayers feel as Justice Holmes, who said, "When I pay taxes, I buy civilization." The desire of both the public and their elected policymakers to avoid the unpleasant makes tax policy a complicated and politically volatile issue.

In theory taxes are a simple enough matter; the basic goal of taxation is to finance governmental expenditures for public services. Were taxes used solely for this purpose, tax policy and tax decisions would remain relatively uncomplicated. However, as the government begins to use its taxing powers to achieve various economic and social objectives, then the tax laws and their application become much more complicated and politically controversial.

### The Income Tax

The primary instrument of federal revenue policy since the adoption of the Sixteenth Amendment in 1913 has been the income tax. In fact, with the exception of the social security tax, no new taxes of major proportions have been added since 1913. Created for revenue purposes, the income tax was quite simple in concept; it was to be a progressive tax with those having larger incomes paying taxes at a higher rate. While it remains the principal source of federal revenue, the income tax has also been made impossibly complex by its use as an instrument for attempting a multitude of social and political objectives. Using the tax laws for social purposes has not only made the code complex, but has made the income tax the object of considerable political conflict. In every Congress since 1952 a resolution has been introduced to repeal the income tax.

While repeal of the amendment providing approximately three-fourths of the government's revenue is not realistic, policymakers do need to take a careful look at the purpose of taxation policies and determine whether the present system measures up to sound democratic precepts. Congress has never undertaken any comprehensive revision of federal tax laws and the current Internal Revenue Code filling hundreds of pages was described by President Carter as "a disgrace to the human race." Though he promised reform when elected, as have presidents and congressmen regularly, nothing happened. One member of Congress has observed that tax reform hearings are as much an annual rite of spring in Washington as the Cherry Blossom Festival.

Though the federal income tax started out as a relatively simple and equitable tax, it has over the years become less and less progressive and more and more an instrument of special privileges for selected groups and interests. Because of changes made since its inception, the income tax is progressive up to the middle income levels and not much beyond that. Because of various exemptions and tax breaks for special groups, the effective rate (rate actually paid) is even less progressive than is generally believed. Recent "reforms" have not improved this aspect of the tax laws. The Revenue Act of 1954, with its numerous special exemptions and rules for the treatment of capital gains, actually made it more possible that those with large incomes could pay taxes at a lower rate than many with lower incomes. The so-called Tax Reform Act of 1969 actually brought little reform. The oil depletion allowance was reduced from 27.5 percent to 22 percent, the capital gains tax rate was increased from 25 percent to 35 percent, and the personal exemption was increased from $600 to $750. The overall impact of this act was to make the tax structure *less* progressive.

The middle class is the base for the current tax system. In 1975, families with incomes between $12,000 and $30,000 paid more than half the individual income taxes collected. At the same time, almost half of the total personal income in the country is not taxed because of all the exemptions and deductions written into the tax laws. Because of these special considerations, each year 100–200 persons with incomes in excess of $200,000 pay no income taxes and over 3000 individuals making $50,000 to $200,000 pay no taxes. On the other hand, taxpayers making $10,000 or less make up 52 percent of the taxpaying public but get only 12 percent of the benefits from tax breaks because most of the breaks go to the upper-middle class and the very wealthy, those making $30,000 or more per year. An equitable tax is one that distributes the costs of public service in a fair manner among economic groups. It is clear the current income tax structure falls short of this mark.

The solution to the taxing problem is not a "soak the rich" approach. As Professor Thomas Dye has pointed out, taxing the rich is not going to provide a great deal more revenue because the bulk of taxable income rests in the middle class.[5] Those earning $25,000 and up (top 25 percent of earners) currently pay 72 percent of the taxes collected. The top 1 percent of taxpayers pay 19 percent of the total taxes. Put another way, 93 percent of all taxes collected come from the top 50 percent of the taxpayers. The problem arises from all the special privileges that have been written into the tax code, which make the tax burden of different groups of taxpayers highly inequitable. Tax benefits, often euphemistically referred to as "tax expenditures" serve a variety of purposes.[6] The investment tax credit extended to businesses is a tax break designed to encourage economic growth through federal subsidization of business investment. The oil depletion allowance was aimed at encouraging exploration and development of new sources of petroleum. Many tax breaks or incentives were designed to encourage economic growth and development by reducing corporate operating costs, encouraging investment and capital growth, and helping cover losses. On the other hand, many are the result of effective lobbying efforts by various groups for special treatment under the federal tax laws.

Ultimately, the question boils down to one of how and for what purposes federal taxing power should be used. In a symposium discussing tax reform, Daniel Holland, professor of finance at MIT, said, "One of our great discoveries may be that a tax system is useful when it raises revenue, and that it is not useful when it tries to accomplish other social goals." He went on to note:

> If we were to use taxes only to raise revenue, and use other non-taxing mechanisms to accomplish all the things we want to accomplish to improve the conditions of man, those other mechanisms would probably be more efficient, less costly to the community, and result in a better distribution of the sacrifices needed to reach our objectives.[7]

Others feel that tax incentives or tax expenditures are a most appropriate means for achieving certain goals. Syndicated columnist George Will feels "Government is better at providing incentives than services and should rely more on tax incentives and less on bureaucratic programs to achieve social goals." From a practical standpoint a tax break may in many instances be more acceptable than a direct governmental expenditure for both political and economic reasons. Several problems arise from using the tax code in this way. Many tax preferences have been enacted not to achieve some particular goal that has been promoted in the policy arena, but rather in response to the insistent demands for tax relief by a select group. As a result, our effective tax base has been considerably eroded by the removal of whole categories of wealth and income from the tax structure. Many feel that if governmental subsidies are really needed in certain areas, there are more appropriate means for accomplishing them than by further complicating the tax code. Using the tax code for such a variety of purposes has made it so complex that former Secretary of the Treasury William Simon suggested scrapping the whole thing and starting over. Even more significant, the Brookings Institution estimates that by eliminating special exemptions and deductions from the tax code, tax rates, now ranging from 14 to 70 percent, could be reduced to a range of 10 to 44 percent and still generate the same level of revenue.

There is growing evidence that the voters are becoming more and more dissatisfied with their lot as taxpayers. In 1974, when a Lou Harris poll asked taxpayers if they had "reached the breaking point" on taxes, 57 percent responded yes. A survey by the Associated Press in 1978 showed property tax reform to be an issue in thirty-nine of the fifty states, and the Advisory Committee on Intergovernmental Relations reports that between fifteen and twenty states have enacted restrictions on property taxes since 1970. In a referendum in the 1978 election, California voters approved the Jarvis-Gann Amendment (Proposition 13) reducing property taxes by about 50 percent, and the ballot in California's next election contained a proposal to reduce income taxes by a similar amount (that measure, however, was rejected). A major reason for such voter responses is the dramatic growth in taxes over the last two decades. The Tax Foundation, a non-profit, public-interest organization, reports that taxes have risen 350 percent since 1960. In spite of federal tax cuts three of the last four years, taxes as a percentage of personal income have still increased as a result of inflation. Taxes now take more of the taxpayer's income than any other item in the family budget: 14 percent for federal taxes and another 9 percent for state and local. It now takes two hours and forty-five minutes of each eight-hour working day for the taxpayer to pay his taxes, and one hour and forty-six minutes to pay his federal taxes. While all of this may not add up to the making of a "taxpayers rebellion," it is a situation of which policymakers must take note.

In a democratic society, the quality of the tax structure is a key index to how well or how poorly the system is functioning. There are indications that Americans all across the land are dissatisfied with the quality of government for which they are paying. In California a citizen wrote the San Francisco *Chronicle*, saying, "We are not anarchists, we are not radicals and we do not think we are irresponsible. We are simply full sick and tired of having our pockets picked at every level of government...." In Wisconsin a constituent stopped Representative Henry Reuss in the airport terminal and told him, "When you go back to Washington, don't do anything for me. I can't afford it." Such widespread feeling that taxes are unfair can contribute to noncompliance with the law or to meat-ax approaches to reform such as Jarvis-Gann in California

Why has reform of the tax code been so slow and hard to come by? One reason is that the elected policymakers feel that taxes are a matter on which they can't win. Benefits from changes in the tax laws are perceived by different taxpayers in relative terms; therefore, even a reduction in tax rates may turn out a loser because some sectors will benefit less than others. Congress has come to feel that action on any major tax proposal generates as much grief as it does gratitude, and thus has developed a reluctance to act, especially in election years.

The policymakers are further confused by the general lack of agreement by both the public and governmental institutions as to what policy is desirable. Different agencies within government develop alliances with certain committees in Congress and with constituent groups and these loyalties frequently come into conflict with the loyalties of other similar alliances when it comes to taxing and spending decisions. Those shaping the policies are then faced with the difficult task of deciding among a variety of competing interests. The public also is characterized by considerable unfamiliarity and confusion when it comes to tax policy and therefore provides little real guidance for the policymakers. The tax structure has become so technical and highly complex that it is largely removed from public debate. Even in Congress, debate tends to center largely in the committees handling revenue measures and the other members tend to defer to the "experts" on these committees. Thus the lack of information and general inability of people to understand the tax system helps to insure that the system in the end is less democratic. The result is that those having a direct pecuniary interest are the most active and influential while those not directly affected or unaware of the effect remain largely inactive and silent. Consequently, while there is widespread dissatisfaction and discussion of taxes, there is not any clearly formed public opinion on the issue sufficient to bring the desired reform.

In the absence of clear public and executive directives, the tax system has evolved through a framework that has provided substantial access to an increasing variety of special economic interests. Every interest group that feels entitled to special treatment beats a path to the tax committees to plead its case. The whole political balance of power has shifted away from the middle class, which bears most of the tax burden, to a combination of the wealthy and organized special interests, who wield disproportionate influence with the congressional elite who determine tax policy. Thus, at the heart of the issue of tax reform is the fact that tax policy is almost exclusively the domain of the tax experts in the Treasury Department, the members of the tax committees in Congress and the special interests whose wealth and political contributions provide them access. Talking about tax reform, Martin Huff, executive officer to the Franchise Tax Board in California said, "Until one recent death and one political retirement, the federal tax system was in the hands of three people: Russell Long, Larry Woodworth, and Wilbur Mills."[8] The elite that dominates taxing policy has from time to time made slight concessions, but has yet to relinquish its power or alter its priorities to any substantial degree. This is not likely to occur as long as wealth continues to wield its current level of influence in Congress. Public disclosure requirements revealed that in 1978, twenty-two senators listed assets of more than $1 million and another nineteen were possibly millionaires. Russell Long, chairman of the Senate Finance

Committee, estimates his oil royalties at $1.1 million. In the absence of public financing of congressional elections, many members are forced to rely heavily on large campaign contributions from wealthy supporters and organized interests. These interests frequently are opposed to tax reform.

Another factor complicating tax reform is the ambivalence of both the public and Congress. While there has been considerable evidence of voter dissatisfaction with rising taxes during the last few years, there is little indication of any inclination on their part to accept as an alternative a reduction in governmental services. As Senate Majority Leader Robert Byrd (D-W.V.) noted in a weekly news conference, "Big government is the result of big demand," but few voters want to see their special benefits reduced or eliminated. Business, labor, farmers, citizens generally all denounce the government for its growing interference in their lives, yet each year they seek more and more from government. When a president approaches Congress with a proposal for reducing expenditures or changing tax rates, members immediately fly to the defense of those policies that benefit their particular constituents. Most members are very economy-minded, but only as long as changes are at the expense of someone else's constituents.

Still another obstacle to full-scale reform is the highly incremental nature of decision-making on tax policy. Over the years there has been a sort of tacit understanding among the members of Congress that they would not undertake to build a wholly new tax structure. Thus, when changes are considered, the tendency is to avoid any full examination of the current exemptions, deductions, and other special considerations in the law. The tendency is to simply build on the existing base, thus making any efforts at wholesale reform quite difficult.

Finally, in the shaping of tax policies, they must be weighed as to their impact on the economy. Under the concepts of the new economics, taxes have become a basic instrument of governmental economic control. Different taxes may have different effects on the economy. The income tax can be altered with considerable precision to affect certain sectors of the economy. Even in the 1920s, Treasury Secretary Andrew Mellon recognized the value of the income tax as a tool for stabilizing the economy. When the Kennedy administration was faced with a recession in 1962, the Council of Economic Advisors, headed by Walter Heller, devised a sophisticated package of economic management devices including an accelerated depreciation program and investment tax credits for industry. Enacted by Congress, these programs encouraged investment, reduced unemployment, and pulled the economy out of recession. Such uses of the tax system can be targeted rather specifically to attain certain desired results. President Carter proposed a tax program aimed at reducing unemployment among youth between the ages of 18 and 24: presently businesses are granted a tax saving of $1806 for each new job created, and Carter proposed to raise the tax break to $2000 for each new job provided in the targeted age group.

Because economics is far from being an exact science, policymakers frequently get conflicting advice on taxing policy. Economists, like the policymakers themselves, are not immune to ideological and political biases. Since economic growth is dependent on the investment rather than the consumption of resources, use of the taxing power to encourage investment becomes a major issue in economic management. Because different taxes affect different sets of taxpayers differently, tax policy decisions come to involve a considerable amount of politics. While many observers feel taxes should as a general rule be progressive, some maintain that some regressive taxes are desirable since they leave more resources in the hands of the wealthy, who are much more likely to invest and thus promote economic growth.

A major issue in the management of tax policies is the effect different levels of taxation will have on revenues and economic growth. Professor Arthur B. Laffer of the University of Southern California, father of the "Laffer Curve," proposes that two different tax rates will produce the same revenues. A high tax rate will reduce investment and lower production, thus generating lower revenues, while a lower tax rate will encourage investment and production, thereby increasing government receipts. He further maintains that a lower tax rate, while generating the same level of revenue, will actually cost the government less because with high tax rates reducing production, the government has to spend more to support those who become unemployed. The question is at what level does this trade-off produce the maximum benefits.

Much of the debate over the use of taxes for controlling the economy centers around the timing and the conditions under which rates should be raised or lowered. Faced with an economic slowdown, President Kennedy and his economic advisers set out on a campaign to sell Congress on the idea of a tax reduction to stimulate economic growth. Finally, in March 1964 Johnson was successful in getting Congress to pass the Revenue Act of 1964, reducing personal income taxes by almost 20 percent. This act demonstrated that under the right conditions, a reduction in taxes could actually produce an increase in revenues. The 1964 tax cut produced the highest real investment growth in modern history, the most rapid growth in disposable income, the biggest advance in industrial output, and at the same time, the lowest inflation rate in recent years. Where the treasury had anticipated revenue losses for 1963–68 of $89 billion, they actually realized an increase of $54 billion. Since this experience, tax cuts were used in 1965, 1971, and 1977 to stimulate the economy, and in 1968 an increase was passed to slow inflation.

Even the more fiscally conservative Republicans, who opposed the tax cuts of the 1960s, are now embracing the concept of using the tax structure to regulate the economy. In 1978 many Republicans expressed support for a proposal by Representative Jack Kemp (R-N.Y.) and Senator William Roth (R-Del.) that would have reduced personal income taxes 10 percent per year over a three-year period. Democrats who supported the Kennedy-Johnson tax reductions contended that a big reduction under 1978 economic conditions would fuel inflation and create a large budget deficit. Charles Schultze, chairman of Carter's Council of Economic Advisors, called the Kemp-Roth proposal "a sure-fire recipe for inflation," and Representative Robert Giaimo (D-Conn.), chairman of the House Budget Committee, said the proposal would feed inflation, generate record deficits, and boost interest rates. President Carter, who started the year in 1978 proposing a rather large tax reduction, decided that curbing inflation and reducing deficit spending took higher priority and reduced his proposed cuts from about $24 billion to $15 billion. Congress eventually adopted cuts of approximately $19 billion.

Experiences in recent years have demonstrated that taxes can be used as an instrument to manipulate the economy, but because taxes are such a politically volatile issue, the national tax system remains more a product of political considerations and the processes through which tax policies are formulated than a carefully analytical approach to using taxes for purposes of economic regulation. Until citizen attitudes on tax increases change, it will remain very difficult to convince Congress to raise taxes in an election year, whether it appears economically desirable or not.

## CONCLUSION

Though its involvement is still marked by considerable controversy as to techniques used, the federal government is now committed to efforts at economic management designed to maintain maximum employment and sustained economic growth while at the same time contain inflation. In trying to use governmental taxing and spending powers to maintain the right equilibrium, the policymakers tread an economic tightrope. If fiscal policy is not used wisely, then the economy may stagnate resulting in unemployment, declining investment, reduced purchasing power, and growing budget deficits. On the other hand, too much governmental spending and large federal deficits may lead to inflation and an overstimulated economy.

Through the 1950s and 60s the advocates of Keynesian economics felt they had found the keys to fine-tuning the economy, thus eliminating any extreme fluctuations. Since the 1950s Keynesian theories, which stressed the demand side of the supply-and-demand equation, have been quite severely challenged by the "Chicago School" of economists led by Milton Friedman, who tend to emphasize "market" solutions to economic problems. These economists feel that Keynesian emphasis on fiscal policies leads to large deficits and inflation, and they favor a heavier reliance on monetary devices such as the open market operations of the Federal Reserve Board and changes in interest rates to regulate the economy. A look at the economy's performance over the last decade gives ample evidence of sufficient grounds for differences of opinion, even among professional economists.

Differences of opinion occur and problems arise because regulation ultimately becomes a question of trade-offs—governmental spending, deficit financing, and high employment versus inflation and unemployment; higher interest rates, lower inflation, balanced budgets versus lower investment, unemployment,

**98  MANAGEMENT POLICY**

bankruptcies, and shrinking home construction. Former member of the Council of Economic Advisors Arthur Okun observed in 1978, "It's a tragedy of the political situation that the only way to stop inflation is to put people out of work, stop building houses, stop production." These decisions become highly political because different policies will affect different citizens differently. Some persons (wage earners whose wages are tied to cost-of-living increases, property owners) benefit from some inflation while others (those on fixed incomes) are hard hit by inflation. Because our economic and political systems are so closely linked, economic stability becomes an important governmental concern. Economic instability can lead to considerable political tension and conflict in our system.

Since most revenue and spending bills now originate with the president, he must shoulder much of the political responsibility for the state of the economy. This frequently leads to a conflict between the president's desires to manipulate taxing and spending policies in keeping with Keynesian concepts and congressional objectives of a smaller deficit or support for spending programs to benefit their various constituents. Congressmen are much less likely to subscribe to Keynesian economics than are presidents. Before Johnson could get the votes he needed for the 1964 tax cut, he had to promise to reduce federal spending. Of course, these congressmen demanding this expected the president and his advisers

"Now that you mention it . . . I did hear sumpthin' go 'THUNK! SPLAT!' back at that grade crossing."

Reprinted courtesy of Hugh Haynie and the Louisville, Ky. Courier Journal.

Government as Fiscal Manager   99

to be judicious enough to make all the reductions in programs that benefitted someone else's constituents. Regardless of the economic indicators, members of Congress frequently find it easier to reduce the size of a tax cut than to reduce or eliminate spending programs benefitting their constituents or interest group supporters. The "new" economics runs head on into "practical" politics.

Another factor that also tends at times to blunt the impact of governmental efforts to control the economy is the response of the private sector. While spending on defense and welfare programs has greatly expanded government's role in the economy, private expenditures still exceed public expenditures about two-to-one. The power of private businesses to administer prices may serve to reduce the effectiveness of governmental efforts to regulate the economy. For example, governmental spending or tax breaks aimed at producing more jobs and employment may be diverted to other uses. In 1978, while President Carter was urging cooperation in his fight to curb inflation, U. S. Steel raised prices by $10.50 per ton, blaming the increase on the coal strike. Chairman of the President's Council of Economic Advisors Charles L. Schultze said that in reality only $4.50 of the increase could be traced to the coal settlement. Realizing the importance of public and private cooperation, Carter in June 1978 urged Congress and business leaders to join his administration in a "common sacrifice" to control inflation. He admonished private enterprise not to "mount intense lobbying efforts to control some privilege they have in setting unnecessarily high prices." The erratic ups and downs in the economic cycle prior to adoption of the Employment Act in 1946 illustrate the importance of public and private cooperation in regulating economic activity.

Not only does the government seek to manage the economy for economic stability and prosperity, it also affects the economy through the transfer of money from one group to another. In fiscal year 1977, 69 percent of the total federal tax receipts went for "income transfer" programs; i.e., social security, medicare, medicaid, food stamps, etc. In other words, over half the budget went for income redistribution, since those who pay federal income taxes are seldom the ones who benefit in any direct fashion. Yet, despite the income tax and other devices that are supposed to redistribute income, the concentration of wealth in the United States has changed very little since the report of the Temporary National Economic Committee in 1938. The United States remains a society of both extreme wealth and severe poverty. The 1975 Census Bureau figures indicated that 5 percent of the citizens, those earning $34,000 or more per year, had 15.5 percent of all income in the country. The top 20 percent of the populace accounted for 41.1 percent of all income, while the poorest 20 percent, those with incomes of $6900 or less, had only 5.4 percent of all income. Much of the wealth in the U. S. is concentrated among very few persons. About 50 families are worth $100 million or more; several hundred families are worth $10 million or more, and about 100,000 persons are in the billionaire category. At the other end of the scale, millions of Americans live in comparative poverty. Twelve percent, or 26 million, have incomes below the poverty level. Raise the poverty level by only $1000 and the figure below the poverty line becomes 40 million.

Poverty persists in the United States not because of lack of production but because of inequities in distribution of available resources. The American economy is unequalled in the history of the world; by 1975 the nation's GNP was almost $6000 per person as compared to $3000 in Western Europe and $100 to $500 in Africa, Asia, and Latin America. Despite their faster economic growth rates, the U. S. GNP is still three times that of Japan and four times that of West Germany. Thus, what is needed in the U. S. is not more GNP, but a more equitable distribution of what is already being produced.

By what principles are the goods and services produced by the economy to be distributed among the nation's citizens? If the elimination of poverty and more equitable distribution of available resources are among the objectives of governmental management of the economy, then the policymakers need to re-evaluate current policies in light of these objectives. This will not be an easy task, because while the government has at its disposal unequalled resources, it is faced with an enormous range of demands from a highly pluralistic society. The tremendous political pressures and conflicting viewpoints will make the policymakers' choices difficult. But, that is really what policymaking is all about.

## Points to Ponder

Why is it frequently difficult politically for the government to manage the economy effectively?

What role and powers does the Federal Reserve System have for regulating the national economy?

Is the income tax an equitable means for financing the operations of the federal government?

Does the Keynesian economic model provide sufficiently for the trade-off between unemployment and inflation?

Are tax "expenditures" a good way of financing federal policy objectives?

## Notes

1. Adam Smith was author of *The Wealth of Nations* and a proponent of laissez-faire economics. Francis Edgeworth, "the father of mathematical economics," is known for his theories on contract in the free market. Jean-Baptiste Say, French economist, is father of the *loi des debouche's* or "law of markets," the concept of market equilibrium.
2. John M. Gaus, *Reflections on Public Administration* (University of Alabama: University of Alabama Press, 1947), p. 5.
3. Emmette S. Redford, *Administration of National Economic Control* (New York: Macmillan, 1952), p. 131.
4. Rules issued by the House Rules Committee that limit both debate and amendments during consideration of a bill on the House floor.
5. Thomas Dye, *Understanding Public Policy* (Englewood Cliffs, N.J.: Prentice-Hall, 1978), p. 232.

6. Tax expenditures are a technique used by Congress to promote and finance certain policy objectives. Rather than collect taxes and then appropriate funds directly for the support of these objectives, Congress writes a "tax break" into the revenue code providing a federal subsidy to promote its objectives. The recently adopted provision allowing a deduction on federal income taxes for a portion of the costs of home insulation is an example.
7. Daniel Holland in "Taxation and Human Values," *The Center Magazine* (May/June 1978), p. 43.
8. Martin Huff in "Taxation and Human Values," p. 47. Woodruff was an expert on taxation, employed in the Treasury Department.

## Suggestions for Further Reading

BALZ, DANIEL. "Why the Bright New Congressman Couldn't Deliver on Tax Reform," *The Washington Monthly* (July/August 1976).

BEST, MICHAEL and CONNOLLY, WILLIAM. *The Politicized Economy*. Lexington, Mass.: Heath, 1976.

BREAK, GEORGE and PECHMAN, JOSEPH. *Federal Tax Reform: The Impossible Dream*. Washington, D. C.: The Brookings Institution.

CONGRESSIONAL QUARTERLY. *Taxes, Jobs and Inflation*. Washington, D. C.: Congressional Quarterly, 1978.

EYESTONE, ROBERT. *Political Economy: Politics and Policy Analysis*. Chicago: Markham, 1972.

FRY, BRYAN and WINTERS, RICHARD. "The Politics of Redistribution," *American Political Science Review*, vol. 64 (June 1970).

HARRIS, SEYMOUR, ed. *The New Economics: Keynes' Influence on Theory and Public Policy*. New York: Knopf, 1947.

HEILBRONER, ROBERT L. "Modern Economics as a Chapter in the History of Economic Thought," *History of Political Economy* (Summer 1979).

KOSTERS, MARVIN H. *Controls and Inflation: The Economic Stabilization Program in Retrospect*. Washington, D. C.: American Enterprise Institute, 1975.

MANLEY, JOHN. *The Politics of Finance: The House Committee on Ways and Means*. Boston: Little, Brown & Co., 1970.

PATINKIN, DON. *Keynes' Monetary Thought*. Durham, N. C.: Duke University Press, 1976.

PECHMAN, JOSEPH and OKNER, BENJAMIN. *Who Bears the Tax Burden*. Washington, D. C.: The Brookings Institution, 1974.

PIERCE, LAWRENCE. *The Politics of Fiscal Policy Formation*. Pacific Palisades, Calif.: Goodyear, 1971.

REGAN, MICHAEL. "The Political Structure of the Federal Reserve System," *American Political Science Review*, vol. 55 (March 1961), pp. 65ff.

ROBERTS, PAUL C. "The Breakdown of the Keynesian Model," *The Public Interest*, no. 52 (Summer 1978), pp. 20-33.

ROLL, ERIC. *The World After Keynes: An Examination of the Economic Order*. New York: Praeger, 1968.

RUSKAY, JOSEPH and OSSERMAN, RICHARD. *Halfway to Tax Reform*. Bloomington, Ind.: Indiana University Press, 1970.

SHUCK, PETER. "National Economic Planning: A Slogan Without Substance," *The Public Interest* (Fall 1976).

SICHEL, WERNER. *Economic Advice and Executive Policy*. New York: Praeger, 1978.

SURREY, STANLEY. *Pathways to Tax Reform*. Cambridge, Mass.: Harvard University Press, 1971.

# 5

# The Making of U.S. Foreign Policy

In 1968, when Los Angeles Mayor Sam Yorty was speaking out as a potential candidate for the Democratic Party's presidential nomination, someone remarked that Los Angeles was the only city in the country with its own foreign policy. While there has been considerable debate as to just what direction U. S. foreign policy should take, there has been rather general agreement that policymaking in this realm is the domain of the federal government. The delegates to the Philadelphia convention that drew up the Constitution felt that successful foreign relations must be the function of a central spokesman, and therefore they assigned exclusive responsibility for this area of policymaking to the national government.

A nation's foreign policy consists of the way in which it goes about promoting and defending its interests that involve other nations. Over the years the major objective of U. S. foreign policy has been the preservation and strengthening of national security. Because foreign policy proceeds from the leaders' perceptions of how this objective may best be attained, there is no uniform pattern to policies that have been followed. Our foreign policy, possibly more than other policies, depends to a marked degree on who makes the decisions. From whose perceptions of national interest and the realities of the world situation do foreign policy decisions stem?

Traditionally, Americans and their leaders have tended toward isolationism in their foreign relations. Geographically isolated and with its leaders primarily concerned with internal growth and development, the United States for decades shied away from "entangling alliances" and involvement in European wars. Benefitting from a favorable balance of power internationally and left largely to pursue their own course, Americans developed an aversion to "power politics" and international involvement that was not easily abandoned.

Only with the disappearance of the American frontier and involvement in the Spanish-American War did the U. S. begin to move away from its strong isolationist tradition. In 1901 Theodore Roosevelt, a leading spokesman for those advocating a more internationalist position, urged his countrymen to accept the fact that, "We stand supreme in a continent, in a hemisphere. East and West we look across two great oceans toward the larger life in which, whether we will or not, we must take an ever-increasing share."[1] Isolationism did not die easily, however, and when World War I broke out in Europe, the U. S. insisted on remaining neutral. When President Wilson, after repeated German submarine attacks on U. S. shipping, sought authority to arm U. S. merchant vessels, he encountered a determined filibuster in the Senate, which incensed him. Finally, when public opinion was aroused by the indiscriminate submarine warfare of the Germans, the U. S. entered the war in a crusade to "make the world safe for democracy."

The United States emerged from World War I as a power — politically, economically, militarily. Refusing to accept the position into which it had been thrust, America reverted to a policy of resurgent isolationism. U. S. membership in the League of Nations was rejected, and the U. S. refused to assume a meaningful leadership role in international affairs. One observer said that when Europeans looked across the Atlantic for a glimpse of the American Eagle, all they saw was the rear end of an ostrich. This posture on the part of one of the most powerful nations in the world contributed to the rise of Hitler, Mussolini, and Tojo and eventually helped lead to another World War.

World War II went a long way toward eroding U. S. isolationism as Americans finally began to accept the idea that what happened in other parts of the world was of considerable significance for the security and economic survival of the United States. Emerging from the war physically untouched and in sole possession of the atomic bomb, the United States was the dominant power internationally. Changes in the international situation came so rapidly after 1945, however, that it became almost impossible for them to be effectively integrated into the decision-making processes.

The Soviet Union acquired the atomic bomb, quickly developed a potential delivery system, established its dominance in Eastern Europe, and challenged the U. S. position as the dominant force in international politics. For the next two decades the confrontation between the world's two superpowers was the dominant factor shaping U. S. foreign policy decisions. During this period American foreign policy ranged from the "brinksmanship" of John Foster Dulles to the détente of Richard Nixon and Henry Kissinger as American policymakers attempted to adjust to an ever-changing international environment.

The decades of the sixties and seventies brought additional changes with far-reaching implications for U. S. foreign policy making. Many of the factors currently most influential in foreign policy decisions didn't even exist prior to 1945 or were largely insignificant. Technological changes in communications and weaponry have brought revolutionary changes in statecraft and warfare. National boundaries, oceans, and other geographical factors are no longer the barriers they once were. Foreign policy making is extremely volatile. Writing in the *Wall Street Journal*, Irving Kristol notes, "To a very large degree, makers of foreign policy are constantly being made captive to unexpected events, . . . even the most sophisticated analyses collapse before the onrush of events over which *no one* has any control."[2]

Though the United States remains the single most dominant factor in international relations, it has seen its relative position undergo considerable change and learned in Vietnam that there are limits to even its vast economic, political, and military power. In 1945 the U. S. produced 45 percent of the world's goods and claimed over 20 percent of the world market, yet had only 6 percent of the world population. By the early 1970s the United States' share of international production had declined to 30 percent and its share of the world trade was 14 percent. At the same time, American dependence on outside sources for the raw materials it needs has been increasing. These are factors that will increasingly influence American foreign policy in the next decade.

While U. S.–Soviet relations still dominate the international scene, some of the most pressing problems now involve countries that weren't even on the international scene twenty-five years ago. A growing factor in world politics is the Third World—the emerging nations of Asia, Africa, and Latin America. As more and more of these nations emerge, the East-West struggle frequently is manifested in competition for their allegiance and support. In 1961 there were only 25 nations in the so-called non-aligned nation movement; currently there are 111 members and the group grows regularly. As the non-aligned bloc grows, the intricate network of international dependencies and alliances becomes more and more complex. The whole world, including the U. S., Russia, and China, is drawn into conflicts that have gone on for years and have roots going much deeper than communism versus non-communism. For many of these Third World nations, economic issues may be of primary concern. Of the 3.5 billion people in the world today, one-third are classified as "very poor" (annual per capita income less than $100 per year), another one-third are "poor" (per capita income of $100 to $250 per year). For these people poverty may be the major concern, and since it is frequently linked to volatile political and racial overtones, this gap between the "haves" and "have nots" of the world becomes a major challenge to those shaping our foreign policy. Within the next decade, concerns with such economic issues as hunger, poverty, world inflation, access to raw materials, maintenance of world markets, and the international monetary system may come to overshadow even the threat of international communism as the prime consideration shaping U. S. foreign policy.

This brief synopsis of U. S. foreign policy illustrates the dynamic and multifaceted nature that makes it both complex and challenging. Foreign policy making is made even more complex in that so many factors influence the final outcomes — national values, public opinion, mass media, interest groups, economics, political parties, cultural differences, history, and tradition. Also, though we usually think of foreign and domestic policies separately, it has become increasingly less possible to separate the two completely because decisions in one area inevitably have implications for the other. We cannot discuss the energy crisis at home without considering foreign oil and its implications for our foreign policy. And, since American foreign policy is the product of many individuals and agencies making and implementing decisions, the human element cannot be overlooked. We need look no further than Henry Kissinger to see the impact of individual personalities on foreign policy.

## THE MACHINERY OF FOREIGN POLICY MAKING

As was noted earlier, the framers of the Constitution generally agreed that foreign policy should rest exclusively under the direction of the national government, but as a safeguard they divided responsibility between the executive and legislative branches. This constitutionally imposed separation of powers has, in the words of Professor Edward S. Corwin, been "an invitation to struggle for the privilege of directing American foreign policy."[3] The reality of this arrangement has been an atmosphere of frequent conflict and suspicion between the Congress and the president. The president, because he is in a position frequently to generate public support for his moves and because he harbors misgivings about congressional competence and objectives, may try to exercise his powers unilaterally. Congress, on the other side, is distrustful of the president and frequently seeks to impose tighter controls over presidential operations.

In the aftermath of Vietnam, Cambodia, and Watergate, Congress has been more assertive than in several decades, causing recent presidents to complain frequently. Gerald Ford protested that Congress was infringing on executive authority in foreign affairs when legislation was adopted placing a ceiling on U.S. arms sales in any one fiscal year, prohibiting aid to countries violating human rights, lifting the trade embargo against Vietnam, and assuming the right of Congress to halt foreign military sales by concurrent resolution of both houses. More recently President Carter complained that such constraints as the Clark Amendment, which barred aid to forces fighting in Angola, tend to tie the executive's hands in conducting foreign policy.

The Constitution is really quite brief and, especially in the case of the president, rather vague on the assignment of powers in foreign policy making. In Article I, Section 8, Congress is charged with providing for the common defense, regulating commerce, declaring war, and raising and supporting the militia. Article II, Sections 1, 2, and 3 make the president commander-in-chief of the army and navy and give him the authority to negotiate treaties and to send and receive ambassadors. Since it has become increasingly difficult to separate domestic and

## Major Foreign Policy Statutes

**State Department Act of 1789.** Created the State Department, headed by the secretary of state, which has primary responsibility for implementing and carrying out American foreign policy.

**Rogers Act of 1924.** Created the professional Foreign Service corps, which is instrumental in implementing U.S. foreign policy abroad.

**National Security Act of 1947.** Created the position of national security adviser, the National Security Council, and the Central Intelligence Agency to provide information and advice on foreign policy making.

**Peace Corps Act of 1962.** Provided a statutory basis for the Peace Corps volunteer program, which President Kennedy had started with contingency funds. The Peace Corps program brings Americans into face-to-face contact with citizens of Third World nations.

---

foreign policy, other powers of each branch also take on significance for foreign policy. On the whole, however, it becomes clear that the president has the primary responsibility for proposing and the Congress for responding.

### Presidential Role

While his powers are largely implied, assumed, and strengthened through tradition, court interpretation, and congressional acquiescence, the president has become the central figure in American foreign policy. Although the constitutional basis for his role may appear rather meager, a combination of factors has built a tradition of presidential initiative, if not total dominance, in both the formation and execution of foreign policy. Frenchman Joseph Barthélemy, writing in 1917 of President Wilson's foreign policy, observed, "Mr. Wilson exercises a virtual dictatorship over foreign policy. There are few sovereigns of authoritarian countries who have as much power over the international destinies of their kingdom as that temporary monarch."[4] Because international crises tend to cause the public to rally to the support of their leaders, the almost constant crisis atmosphere existing since the end of World War II has strengthened the role of the American president. The atmosphere in which our foreign policy is made and conducted today encourages the dominance of a "leader" rather than the calm, leisurely debate of a deliberative government.

From the standpoint of constitutional prerogative, nature of his constituency, organization of his office, and his access to information, the president is in a much stronger position than anyone else in government to be the dominant fiture in foreign policy making.

In its relations with the nations of the world, the United States must have a spokesman, and the president is the only elected representative who speaks for the

## Principal Departments and Agencies

**Department of State.** One of the original cabinet-level departments created in 1789, the department is primarily responsible for initiating and executing American foreign policy.

**National Security Council (NSC).** The National Security Act of 1947 created the NSC as the primary policy adviser to the president on domestic and foreign matters relating to national security.

**Central Intelligence Agency (CIA).** Created by the National Security Act of 1947, the CIA functions under the National Security Council to coordinate information gathering and intelligence activities in the interest of national security.

**National Security Agency (NSA).** The largest and most secretive of the agencies comprising the intelligence community, the NSA is involved primarily in electronic surveillance and code breaking.

**The Foreign Service.** The professional Foreign Service organization is the instrument for implementing U.S. foreign policy abroad.

**Agency for International Development (AID).** AID is a semi-autonomous agency within the State Department that directs economic and technical assistance programs to foreign nations.

**Peace Corps.** The Peace Corps is a program providing economic and technical assistance to underdeveloped nations through a people-to-people approach. Americans with special skills and expertise serve as volunteers in countries needing assistance.

**International Communication Agency (ICA).** Successor to the United States Information Agency (USIA), the ICA is a U.S. propaganda agency with responsibility for the conduct of international communications, educational, cultural, and exchange programs promoting understanding of the U.S. abroad.

---

entire country. In the area of foreign policy he becomes the focus of attention both at home and abroad. Any time the president speaks about foreign affairs—in press conferences, in college commencement addresses, in public statements of any type—his words are transmitted around the world and carefully weighed by other governments and world leaders. Internally, since the president is our highest authority figure, he is in a position to exert considerable influence and leadership on foreign policy matters. In the words of Woodrow Wilson,

> His is the only national voice in affairs. Let him once win the admiration and confidence of the country, and no other single force can withstand him, no combination of forces will easily overpower him. His position takes the imagination of the country. He is the representative of no

constituency, but of the whole people. When he speaks in his true character, he speaks for no special interest.⁵

In the realm of foreign policy making, the president also enjoys other advantages. The organization and unity of his office make it possible for him to act with both speed and secrecy, elements often necessary in effective foreign policy making and elements that place the 535-member Congress at a considerable disadvantage. A further advantage of the president is his ready access to vast sources of information and intelligence so vital to effective foreign policy decisions. Of all the branches of government, the executive alone has the worldwide network of intelligence and information sources for sound, well-informed judgments on foreign policy. Lacking similar sources of information and analysis, Congress is forced to rely heavily on executive agencies for its information.

Because of the more positive nature of his role—commander-in-chief, treaty negotiator, concluder of executive agreements, recognizer of governments—the president is usually the initiator who shapes the alternatives in foreign policy making. Presidents quickly discover, however, that they are not the only participants in the process and that despite substantial constitutional and traditional powers, they must share the foreign policy making role with other participants.

### Congressional Role

While the powers of the executive in foreign policy making are largely positive, those of Congress tend to be more negative in nature. The Senate must ratify treaties and confirm presidential appointments for them to become effective, and both houses of Congress must approve appropriations measures providing funds for foreign policy programs. Thus, while Congress's powers in foreign policy making are ample, they are of a different nature than those of the executive. The congressional role in the realm of foreign policy tends to be largely one of reacting to presidential initiatives.

While the executive, as we noted earlier, has certain characteristics of office that tend to enhance performance in foreign policy making, Congress on the other hand is sometimes handicapped by the nature of its organization and normal procedures. In his book *Congress and Foreign Policy*, Robert A. Dahl gives several reasons why Congress "is remarkably ill-suited to exercise a wise control over the nation's foreign policy."⁶ By its very nature, foreign policy sometimes necessitates speedy and secret action. Implicit in the legislative process is the idea of debate and consideration of various alternatives and decisions arrived at through a carefully deliberative process. Effective decision-making on foreign policy may preclude the methodical and deliberate process of compromise and give-and-take bargaining that usually characterizes the legislative process. Also, the fact that foreign policy is a day-to-day process tends to preclude continuous involvement by Congress, thus making it an intermittent participant. While some members develop a high degree of expertise in the foreign policy field, Congress as a whole

*The Making of U.S. Foreign Policy* 109

lacks the superior sources of information and expert analysis. This places Congress at a further disadvantage.

All of this is not to say that the Congress is not an effective partner in the foreign policy process. Though most of the initiative in establishing the parameters

"Well, everything seems t'be shipshape and ready t'take 'er through the canal..."

"...except the crew...."

Reprinted courtesy of Hugh Haynie and the Louisville, Ky. Courier Journal.

of our foreign policy has shifted to the executive, the president ignores the Congress only at the risk of having his efforts short-circuited. Congress's power of the purse and the Senate's treaty ratifying authority have helped Congress to retain a vital role in the process. And although the president tends to attract the most attention and wield the greatest influence, the Congress can through committee investigations and hearings have considerable impact on public opinion. The Senate Committee on Foreign Relations in particular provides a forum through which foreign policy alternatives can be brought to public attention. A powerful chairman of this committee such as former Senator William Fulbright may be in a position to exert considerable influence. The televised hearings of Senator Fulbright's committee on the Vietnam conflict are a prime example of the impact the committee can have on public opinion.

The point is that the president, though he is the star on the foreign policy stage, must move with a certain degree of caution because the Congress, if it comes to feel it is being deceived or manipulated, may strike back and effectively counter his efforts. While collaboration and consultation with the Congress can be irksome, time-consuming, and tiring, our system of separation of powers and checks and balances makes a certain degree of cooperation between the White House and Congress absolutely essential for effective foreign policy making.

The first two decades after World War II saw an erosion of Congress's role in foreign policy making and the emergence of an almost totally dominant executive branch. In the fifties and sixties the notion of foreign policy as being the rather exclusive domain of the "experts" was rather widely embraced. Since the executive had a virtual monopoly of information sources and experts, the president's role was enhanced by this attitude. Prior to Vietnam, American foreign policy really wasn't debated all that much in Congress, as its members pretty much accepted foreign policy objectives as defined by the executive and confined their discussion to the means for achieving these objectives.

Events in the sixties and seventies, however, such as the Bay of Pigs, Vietnam, and Watergate, all combined to strip the executive of the aura of infallibility, and the president has been much more vulnerable to congressional challenges. While Congress is still no "equal partner," its post-Vietnam resurgence has resulted in a much stronger foreign policy role. By the 1970s a congressional revolt was in full swing. The Gulf of Tonkin resolution was retracted, funds for bombing strikes in Cambodia were cut off, and the War Powers Act was adopted limiting the president's authority to commit troops without congressional concurrence. These actions marked the beginning of a trend as Congress has added additional limits in various pieces of legislation adopted since. A provision in the Arms Export Control Act of 1976 prohibits assistance of any kind to promote military or paramilitary operations in Angola and a section in the 1976 foreign aid bill requires the president to vouch for any covert operation undertaken and to report it to Congress. Congress also has included in several pieces of legislation provisions for "legislative vetoes," devices built into the laws that enable Congress to disapprove certain presidential proposals that he must submit for their scrutiny.

A victim of this post-Vietnam congressional independence, President Carter warned Congress that he did not consider legislative vetoes as legal and binding. Carter also criticized the Congress for restricting presidential abilities to take decisive action abroad. In a nationally broadcast news conference in May 1978, the president said, "There's a trend in Congress that is building up that puts too much restraint on a president to deal with rapidly changing circumstances."

The current resurgence of Congress in the foreign policy field has raised an old question. How far should the Congress encroach upon the executive's daily decision-making authority in carrying out foreign policy? Is Congress's role to provide broad guidelines for policy and leave the specific details to the executive? Will this approach provide sufficient oversight? Some curbs, framed in reponse to particular crises, could prove unnecessarily restrictive under different circumstances. How do we balance sufficient control and oversight with effective policymaking and implementation? The relationship between the executive and legislative branches in foreign policy making is at best an uneasy balance between cooperation and confrontation.

## The Bureaucratic Role

In today's complex and fast-moving world, American foreign policy can be made and implemented only through a vast bureaucratic structure. Since World War II the number of agencies and people involved in foreign policy has grown immensely, making direction and control of our foreign policy substantially more difficult. Effective foreign policy making in a democracy depends on the skills of the elected officials to manage and direct a vast bureaucratic network. Much of this responsibility, of course, falls upon the president as the head of this huge bureaucracy. This is a most difficult task, since most presidents have little or no education or background in foreign policy and come to the job relatively unprepared to cope with a well-entrenched and powerful bureaucracy committed to previous policies and patterns. The newly elected president quickly encounters an array of foreign policy and security agencies resistant to change, committed to preserving their programs and prerogatives.

In earlier days the primary instruments of foreign policy were the diplomatic corps and the military. In the post-World War II era these traditional elements have been supplemented by new instruments of intelligence, propaganda, cultural exchange, and economic and military assistance. Because it tends to outlive the elected decision-makers, thus making it difficult for them to direct and control it, the vast foreign policy bureaucracy has come to exert considerable influence of its own on policy decisions and their implementation. As former Secretary of State Henry Kissinger pointed out, the purpose of the bureaucracy is to handle the day-to-day routine of policymaking. Problems arise when the bureaucracy widens its role in the policy process by defining as "routine" highly significant issues that should be resolved at another level of government, or when it follows a "prescribed mode of action" that is irrelevant to the immediate problem.[7] The likelihood of these problems occurring is increased by the presence of certain characteristics in the foreign policy bureaucracy. Foreign policy making for the last several decades has been characterized by a high degree of "in-breeding." Regardless of who the elected officials are, the senior foreign policy officialdom is almost always drawn from the same New York–Washington–Boston foreign affairs establishment. The pervasiveness of this inclination is well-illustrated by the Carter administration. President Carter, running as an "outsider" who would bring new blood to the government, appointed to top foreign policy positions many principals from the years of Johnson policy, which he had severely criticized when he was a candidate.

To a certain extent, this appointment pattern also stems from the undying faith of Americans in "experts." The overall effect of this has been to perpetuate past policies and mistakes. While our foreign policy has not been a captive of history, it reveals that past successes sometimes tend to become traditions — Washington's farewell address and isolationism, the Monroe Doctrine and nonintervention, the Cold War and containment. The bureaucrats have a strong tendency to approach new problems and new issues in much the same way as in handling past problems. Thus the bureaucracy has a tendency to become routinized and cautious, making changes in foreign policy slow and difficult. Institutional policies tend to become entrenched, reducing the flexibility needed to adapt policies to different situations. Because of its tendency to go with the established routine, the bureaucracy may oppose changes in policy and may even go so far as to subvert the implementation of programs of which it does not approve. It is not unusual for something to be lost in the translation of a policy statement into an applied policy in the field.

It is this aspect of the bureaucracy's operation that makes effective oversight and supervision by elected officials of extreme importance. While a select group of foreign policy opinion-makers may have some access to the foreign policy bureaucracy, it is largely immune to public opinion. As a general rule the career bureaucrat concerns himself very little with satisfying the public or any sizeable segment of it. It, therefore, falls the lot of the president and Congress to provide effective oversight of this vast bureaucratic structure to keep it responsive and responsible. The bureaucrats tend to limit alternatives by basing decisions on past practices and thus limit executive initiative and flexibility in policy decisions, and while the president's White House staff can help guard against this tendency, the bureaucratic influence on foreign policy directions is difficult to overcome completely. The almost irreversible momentum of these bureaucratic pressures is evident in President Carter's experiences. In spite of his campaign promises to change the process, the system once again prevailed and foreign policy under Carter became pretty much the same as under his predecessors.

### Department of State

At the top of the foreign policy bureaucratic structure is one of the oldest cabinet-level departments—the Department of State. While the primary responsibility for foreign policy rests with the president, he physically cannot make every decision and attend to all the myriad details affecting our international affairs. A principal advisor and right-hand man in handling the day-to-day routine of conducting U.S. foreign policy is the secretary of state. In his memoirs, Franklin Roosevelt's first secretary of state, Cordell Hull, wrote, "With the present immense network and mass of details involved in conducting our foreign relations, the President finds it impossible to keep familiar with more than the principal acts of the State Department. The Secretary of State must do the rest."[8] Hull was writing of the comparatively uncomplicated days before World War II and the complex international relations of the Cold War era. In Thomas Jefferson's days as president, he personally read all dispatches and frequently inserted personal comments in the

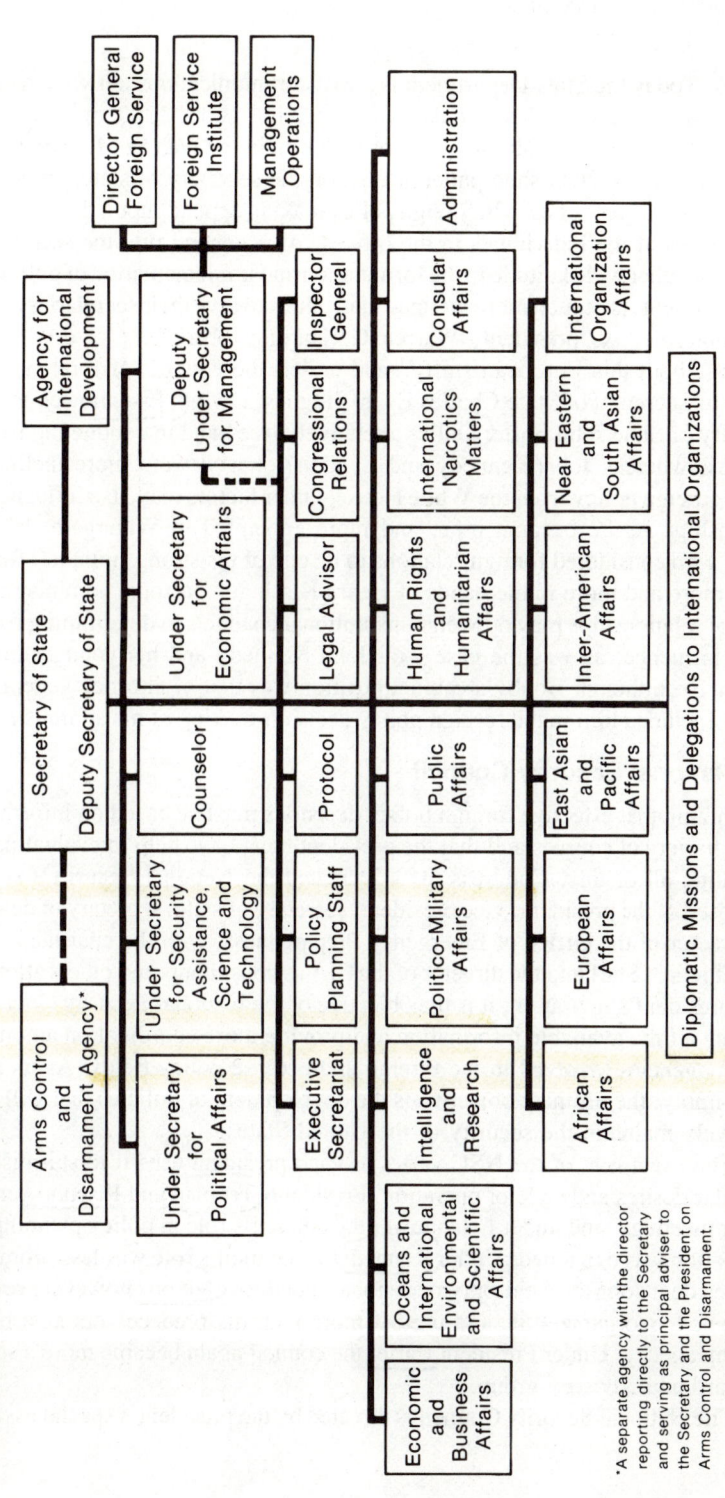

**FIGURE 5.1 Department of State**

*A separate agency with the director reporting directly to the Secretary and serving as principal adviser to the Secretary and the President on Arms Control and Disarmament.

Source: *1978-1979 United States Government Manual, Office of the Federal Register*, Washington, D.C., Government Printing Office.

margins. Today the State Department is a vast communications network, sending approximately 1000 cables per day and receiving about 1300 in return. The president has to rely heavily on others to help him in the realm of foreign policy.

Because no established patterns exist on the secretary of state/presidential relationship, the role of each in foreign policy making depends upon the talents and personalities of the individuals in the offices. As a general rule the secretary of state has a rather wide latitude in the formulation and implementation of policy, but some presidents are much more inclined than others to give their secretaries of state a leading role. As president, Warren G. Harding observed, "I don't know anything about this European stuff," and he left the conduct of foreign affairs largely to Secretary of State Charles Evans Hughes. Dwight Eisenhower gave his Secretary of State John Foster Dulles a relatively free hand in conducting foreign relations, whereas John Kennedy and Lyndon Johnson were more inclined to control foreign policy from the White House. Other factors may also influence the relationship. As he became more and more entangled in Watergate, Richard Nixon, who considered foreign relations to be one of his strong suits, left foreign affairs more and more in the hands of Henry Kissinger. In some administrations personal relationships may outweigh institutional channels in determining foreign policy influence, as was the case with John Kennedy and his younger brother Robert. Even though Bobby's cabinet position was that of attorney general, his brother included him in the foreign policy decision-making of his administration.

### National Security Council

Recognizing that effective foreign policy decisions must be based on information from a variety of sources and that the president must have help in evaluating and integrating all of this, Congress in 1947 created the National Security Council. Composed of the president, vice president, secretary of state, secretary of defense, and director of the Office of Emergency Preparedness, with the chairman of the Joint Chiefs of Staff and the director of the CIA as consultants and others attending at the president's invitation, it is the objective of the National Security Council to integrate all the available information and provide more coordination among the various agencies involved in the foreign and defense policy fields. As its name would imply, the ultimate objective is the development of policies that will most effectively maintain the security of the United States.

The exact role of the NSC varies as each president uses it to suit his own particular desires and style of operation. Presidents Truman and Eisenhower held regular meetings, and under Eisenhower the council's role in policy planning and formulation was expanded. Under Kennedy the council's role was less prominent and President Johnson held only occasional meetings. Nixon, however, revived the council, reorganized it, and used it more than his predecessors as a policy planning agency. Under President Carter the council again became more a sounding board and advisory group.

The National Security Council is directed by the president's special assistant for national security affairs, who in recent years has come to rival the secretary of state as the president's right-hand man in foreign affairs. As Nixon's national security advisor, Henry Kissinger tended to overshadow Secretary of State William Rogers and at one point Kissinger filled both positions, leading Congress to adopt legislation requiring that the two positions not be filled by the same person. During Carter's administration, before Cyrus Vance resigned as secretary of state, there was often considerable speculation as to whether the president's position was most influenced by his National Security Advisor Zbigniew Brzezinski or by Secretary of State Vance. While Vance was inclined to avoid tones of polarization and Cold War rhetoric, Brzezinski tended to take a harder line, feeling the U. S. should be "responsibly tough." Because of his proximity (White House office) and access (usually briefs the president daily), the national security advisor is in a position to wield considerable influence in foreign policy making. The tendency in the Carter administration for Secretary of State Vance and National Security Advisor Brzezinski to speak in different tones and for the president to swing back and forth between the two bred some confusion both internally and abroad regarding U. S. foreign policy.

## The Intelligence Community

Military strategists have long appreciated the value of sound intelligence. One of George Washington's first official acts as commander of the colonial forces was to hire Nathan Hale, who was later hanged by the British for spying. Just as sound intelligence is a key to the military commander, the political decision-maker also must have accurate and detailed data to effectively formulate policy. Realizing the importance of information gathering to effective foreign policy making in an increasingly complex world, the United States has developed an elaborate intelligence community since World War II.

Prior to and during World War II, intelligence was considered primarily a function of the military. The massive intelligence structure currently in operation is a product of the Cold War. Up until the 1950s and the Korean conflict, the American intelligence community grew rather slowly; after 1950 the rate increased and by the 1970s the operation had reached massive proportions. Nine different agencies currently make up the United States "intelligence community." They are the CIA (Central Intelligence Agency), the DIA (Defense Intelligence Agency), the NSA (National Security Agency), the FBI (Federal Bureau of Investigation), the Division of Intelligence of the Nuclear Regulatory Commission, the Bureau of Intelligence and Research of the State Department, and the intelligence units of the air force, army, and navy.

The CIA, created by the National Security Act of 1947 and headed by the director of central intelligence, has the overall responsibility for coordinating the intelligence operations of the federal government. The director also heads the United States Intelligence Board (USIB), which functions as a coordinating committee for intelligence operations. The Watch Committee, whose role is to observe events throughout the world and keep the appropriate decision-makers informed of those events considered vital, is under USIB direction. Though less publicized and well-known than the CIA, the largest, wealthiest, and most secretive of the intelligence agencies is the NSA, established in 1952. With about 15,000 employees and a budget at least twice the size of the CIA's, NSA's primary involvement is in electronic surveillance and code studying/breaking. The chief competitor of the CIA is the DIA and some friction between the two surfaces on occasion. Opposed by the three service branches, DIA became operational in 1961 and has contributed to the enlarged role of the secretary of defense in foreign policy

"Well, that explains why ol' Fang didn't warn us about the Iranian and Russian intruders."

Reprinted courtesy of Hugh Haynie and the Louisville, Ky. Courier-Journal.

making by providing him his own source of strategic intelligence. All together the intelligence agencies spend about $3 billion annually and generate an overwhelming amount of information. Some feel that the volume of their output may have become so great that policymakers are unable to select that information that is most vital for sound decision-making.

Another problem, as recent revelations have shown, is the secrecy with which these agencies operate and the accompanying potential for irresponsible behavior on their part. Though the Foreign Intelligence Advisory Board was created in 1955 as a sort of executive watchdog committee, no really effective oversight was provided by either the executive or legislative branches in the 1950s and 1960s. Finally, after numerous public revelations of CIA wrongdoings, the first congressional restraints were imposed in 1972, and the Hughes-Ryan Amendment to the 1974 Foreign Aid Act required that eight different congressional committees be notified when the CIA planned to engage in clandestine operations. In spite of such expressions of concern, on the whole Congress has neither the time and staff nor the inclination to keep close check on intelligence agency activities. Most members of Congress still have no idea of how much they approve each year for intelligence operations. These expenditures are carefully hidden throughout the budget, and few members of Congress are strongly motivated to try to find out what is really going on. If they raise embarrassing questions, they might appear unpatriotic.

While an intelligence operation is vital to national security in providing information that facilitates sound decision-making, and while secrecy is a necessary element in its functions, experience of the last decade illustrates the need for effective oversight. President Carter expressed considerable displeasure with his intelligence sources in 1978 after American policymakers were caught unprepared and poorly informed on the Iranian situation when demonstrations and open revolt broke out against the Shah and his government. Carter immediately took steps to make the CIA more responsible and accountable to his national security adviser in its operations. Recent tensions in the Middle East and Afghanistan have resulted in a push to relax the controls imposed earlier on the CIA. Congress has adopted legislation that will relax the Hughes-Ryan controls and will restore to the CIA some of its freedom of operation without removing all congressional control and oversight.

### The Foreign Service

The instrument for implementing U. S. foreign policy in the field is the Foreign Service. The Foreign Service personnel are a vital link in a worldwide communications network; they are the State Department's eyes and ears abroad. This network generates some 10,000 reports, messages, policy decisions, and instructions daily. Of these, about 2,000 are telegrams that usually require some action or immediate attention. Though sometimes referred to by its critics as the "striped-pants cookie-pushers," the Foreign Service is an elite guild in the foreign policy apparatus.

The Foreign Service staffs almost 300 embassies, legations, consulates, and special missions in over 100 foreign nations. The embassies are made up of political, economic, administrative, military, aid, and information divisions. The U. S. embassy in London, for example, is staffed by about 700 persons employed by 32 different agencies. Each embassy is headed by an ambassador who is the personal representative of the president in his assigned country and who has full responsibility for implementation of American foreign policy in that country. Though he heads the "country team," the ambassador's control may be quite limited because so many members of his mission are employees of other governmental agencies and feel little obligation to follow his leadership. This frequently results in the U. S. speaking with many voices in foreign countries and makes effective coordination of policy quite difficult. Efforts to bring about more coordination and centralized direction have met with only limited success.

Over the years the Foreign Service has been criticized on other grounds also. For many years the appointments in foreign countries were used as political patronage, and those who were large contributors to a president's campaign were rewarded with choice assignments. While many of the top ambassadorial positions are still filled politically, about 70 percent are now filled with professional career personnel. As for its career professionals, the Foreign Service has been criticized for recruiting too narrowly. A special committee reviewing the Foreign Service in 1954 said it relied too heavily on the Ivy League axis for its recruits. Some efforts have been made to broaden its base, but the Foreign Service remains a rather exclusive club among the government bureaucracy.

### Agency for International Development

A semi-autonomous agency operating out of the State Department, the Agency for International Development is responsible for administering U. S. economic assistance programs abroad. In the post-World War II era economic assistance became an important instrument of U. S. policy in the effort to contain communist expansion. Frequently this economic assistance has had less than the desired impact because its application, like our overall foreign policy of the period, has lacked a clearly defined purpose and identification of the objectives to be obtained. In theory, the purpose of our economic assistance has been the economic development of other nations to make them less vulnerable targets for communist expansion. Because the impoverished and hungry are more vulnerable to tyrants, it is assumed that the world becomes less dangerous when needy countries become self-sufficient. In its application, our aid policy has fallen short of these goals because it has been used more as an instrument of support for governments whose continued existence our own government has viewed with favor. In other words, we have used economic aid to attempt to buy friends around the world, sometimes in a fashion working against the national interests of the recipients. As a consequence of its misapplication, the U. S. aid program has had less than the desired impact. It has done little in closing the gap between the rich and poor nations of the world, and this gap remains a major problem of international relations.

While many continue to feel that economic assistance must remain an important part of U. S. policy, others question whether we are getting our dollars worth from these programs. In light of the tendency for Congress to reduce our foreign aid for the past several years, the Louisville *Courier-Journal* warned, "In short, foreign aid is far more than a humanitarian gesture. It is a cost-effective way to benefit our own economy and increase national security. . . . If we falter, the cost will be paid first by the world's poor. The ultimate price could well be the world's security."[9] Though the U. S. continues to give more economic aid than anyone else in terms of dollar amounts, eleven of the world's seventeen industrial democracies now devote a proportionately larger share of their GNP to foreign aid. In 1978 about one-fourth of 1 percent of the U. S. GNP went for economic assistance. At the same time, Congress has been more inclined to limit AID's discretion in distributing economic assistance by attaching certain directives to the aid bills. In 1978, for example, a three-year ban on aid to Turkey was included in the $2.8 billion aid package. This is another reflection of Congress's growing tendency to limit the discretion of the executive in the conduct of foreign policy.

### Other Agencies

A host of other federal agencies are also involved in activities affecting foreign policy. Because a goal of our foreign policy is national prestige, information and propaganda programs are an instrument of foreign policy. These are administered by the ICA (International Communications Agency). The Peace Corps, NASA, and many other agencies conduct policies that are important to our international relations. In fact, domestic and foreign policies have become so interwoven that virtually every agency of government today has foreign policy implications. This multitude of actors simply adds to the complexity of the process and makes effective coordination and direction all the more difficult.

## THE POLITICS OF FOREIGN POLICYMAKING

While tomes could be written about the agencies in the foreign policy process and while the bureaucratic structure itself has considerable impact on the outcomes, in the final analysis American foreign policy is the result of people making decisions. The human element is a most important factor that must not be overlooked. It was the force of individual leadership that gave us the Marshall Plan, the Truman Doctrine, the brinksmanship of John Foster Dulles, and the personal diplomacy of Henry Kissinger. From whom do the people shaping our foreign policy take their cues? What shapes their perceptions of international realities? Are they influenced by public opinion, interest groups, political parties, the media? What is the politics of foreign policy making? In his book on Congress and foreign policy, Robert Dahl states:

> Mass democracy has a twofold meaning for foreign policy. First, an extraordinarily broad range of groups and strata in society insist upon a consideration of their claims and interests in the making of public policy. Second, and as a result, policy makers must reckon on the possible effects of a policy decision on all or nearly all strata in the society.[10]

Just how much influence do these various elements have on the final outcome of foreign policy? Let's take a look at some of these factors.

## Public Opinion

As the French nobleman Alexis de Tocqueville noted when writing about America, democracies are really not well-suited to the effective conduct of foreign policy.[11] The theories of democratic government with mass participation and open discussion do not fit in well with the frequent necessity for speed and secrecy in foreign policy decision-making. To a great extent, foreign policy must be made by the federal government and beyond that by a relative elite within the government. These requirements make compliance with democratic principles extremely difficult at times.

On the whole, the American public is not well-equipped to participate effectively in foreign policy making. Many issues involved in foreign policy are not within the immediate and direct experience of most citizens, making them largely unconcerned and poorly informed. Add to this the extraordinary complexity of many foreign policy issues and the average citizen is not in a position to participate very effectively. As a rule, the general public possesses only limited information about foreign affairs and tends to be rather pessimistic about its ability to influence the outcome of world problems. In his study of public attitudes on foreign policy, Thomas Molnar reported that only 19 percent felt that public opinion played an important role in shaping foreign policy.[12] In their study of public opinion and world affairs, Leonard Cottrell, Jr. and Sylvia Eberhart reported, "It would appear that a third of the people live in a world that psychologically does not include foreign affairs. As for the other two-thirds, it must be said that at best . . . only a minority of the people can be considered actively conversant with contemporary world problems."[13] Various studies would seem to indicate that about 25 to 30 percent of the electorate have some information and knowledge about foreign policy issues. Those able to articulate their opinions and exert some influence, however, constitute an even smaller portion. Gene Rainey categorizes the public in three groups based on their influence on decision-makers: the *influentials* composing about 3 to 5 percent of the public; the *knowledgeables* accounting for another 20 to 30 percent, and the *general public* making up the remaining 65 to 75 percent of the population.[14]

While the remoteness and complexity of the issues of foreign policy have contributed to the lack of involvement of the average citizen, other factors have added further to his isolation and exclusion from foreign policy decisions. American candidates and political campaigns contribute very little in the direction of informing the public and providing clear-cut choices on foreign policy. Most campaign treatment of foreign policy issues is far too superficial to provide the voters a worthwhile examination of existing policies, and any alternatives offered are frequently so vague and ambiguous as to simply add further confusion. Elections are usually a choice between leaders whose foreign policies are unclear and rarely a clear-cut referendum on foreign policy. Frequently the citizen's access to information is limited because the government feels that revealing certain facts would jeopardize national security. A basic dilemma of our democratic system in the making of foreign policy in a tense international environment is the issue of the public's "right to know" versus the government's need for some security of information. How can we reconcile the conduct of a foreign policy that will insure national security with the need in an open society to guarantee free dissemination of information to insure its continued existence as a democracy? Thomas A. Bailey, in *The Man in the Street*, writes:

> A president who cannot entrust the people with the truth betrays a certain lack of faith in the basic tenets of democracy. But because the masses are notoriously shortsighted, and generally cannot see danger until it is at their throats, our statesmen are forced to deceive them into an awareness of their long-run interests.[15]

This raises another aspect relative to public opinion and foreign policy making. Since the government controls most foreign policy information, to what extent does public opinion reflect conversion to governmental positions? Does public involvement on this basis satisfy the principles of republican government by providing our elected representatives with the necessary direction and oversight?

While some leaders are more inclined to hear the public than others — Speaker Joe Cannon said President McKinley kept his ear so close to the ground that it was "full of grasshoppers" — as a general rule public opinion is more a factor in Congress than in the executive branch. Even in the Congress, however, members get less direction on foreign policy issues from their constituents than they do on domestic policies. As a consequence, they come to rely more on other sources for their decisions. While the president, as Cannon's remark on McKinley indicates, may be influenced by public opinion, he is in a position where he can, if he chooses, go a long way toward generating public support for his policies. In the long run, the public is probably much more susceptible to being led by the president on most foreign policy issues than he is likely to be their pawn. The area where public opinion has the least impact on policy is in the vast foreign policy bureaucracy. Though the State Department maintains a Public Opinion Studies Staff, the foreign policy bureaucracy is largely insulated from public opinion. Molnar says that because of the growth of the bureaucracy, the influence of the individual on foreign affairs is approaching zero.[16] While this may be somewhat of an overstatement, public opinion on most foreign policy issues probably is not an overriding factor. Because of the institutional structure, complexity of issues, limited information, and general lack of concern, the public-at-large does little more than demonstrate moods that may establish some outside parameters beyond which foreign policy initiatives should not stray. Beyond this, the impact of public opinion on foreign policy making is sporadic and only on rare occasions of major significance.

### Political Parties

As we noted in an earlier chapter, American political parties are not very policy oriented; and even though foreign policy has been a subject of partisan squabbles and debate through most of U. S. history, the parties have not been the source of much initiative and creativity in foreign policy making. Neither party campaign rhetoric nor party platforms have served as vehicles for the parties in developing effective foreign policy initiatives, and in Congress the lack of party discipline and control has prevented that body from developing effective foreign policy leadership.

Some observers feel that foreign policy should be removed from the arena of partisanism and that we should have *bipartisan* foreign policy. Their contention is that in the conduct of foreign relations, unity is a great advantage and disagreement a large liability. Senator Arthur Vandenburg (R-Mich.) promoted this concept following World War II, urging that we needed to present a united front in opposing communist expansion. He said we would remain Republicans and Democrats on domestic issues but on foreign policy we were Americans.

While bipartisanism does bolster the appearance of unity and agreement—Vietnam clearly illustrated how appearances of internal disagreement and disunity may be interpreted by our foes as signs of weakness and lack of commitment—it also has a number of disadvantages. As already noted, foreign policy decisions may require speedy action and limit the sharing of information; these constraints tend to handicap effective bipartisanism. Today, domestic policy and foreign policy have become so interwoven it is all but impossible to separate the two. Thus we can hardly have partisan debate on one but not on the other. It is hard to be partisan at home and bipartisan abroad. Another shortcoming of the bipartisan approach is that it may limit the consideration of alternatives. The best decisions cannot be made unless the various alternatives are presented and intelligently weighed; bipartisanism may sometimes result in a tendency to suppress the discussion of alternative approaches in the interest of an appearance of unanimity. Finally, the bipartisan approach may make it difficult for the electorate to place responsibility for policy failures.

While there are differences between Republicans and Democrats on foreign policy issues, the tendency in recent years has been more toward *nonpartisan* foreign policy as individual party members have relied on their own judgments in reaching foreign policy decisions. During Lyndon Johnsons's administration, one of his staunchest supporters on Vietnam was Senate Minority Leader Everett Dirksen (R-Ill.), while some of his harshest critics were in his own party. During President Carter's term this was also the case on such issues as the Panama Canal treaties and the Arab-Israeli plane sales. On the decision to sell planes to both the Arabs and Israelis, Senate Minority Leader Howard Baker (R-Tenn.) said a vote against the president would have been "a highly political decision." He said he believed that "in the long run, the right decision is the best politics." On this particular issue, Republicans voted with Carter 26 to 11 while Democrats voted 33 to 28 against him. On specific issues, differences may be greater between individuals within the parties than between the parties.

The parties may influence foreign policy in a couple of other respects. The party may serve as a source of personnel for policymaking, but primarily only at the top levels. The largest bloc in the foreign policy bureaucracy is recruited through channels other than the parties. For many citizens the parties may serve as a point of reference on foreign policy issues. As noted earlier, because of limited access to information and only limited interest in foreign policy in general, many citizens are poorly informed. They may turn to the leaders of their parties to interpret world events and provide them some cues as to what position to take. As noted before, however, even in this respect the parties may provide very limited leadership.

## Interest Groups

Though the list of groups with an interest in foreign policies is quite numerous, they are probably less influential in the foreign policy realm than in the domestic policy arena. Since foreign policy tends to be controlled more by the executive and the foreign policy bureaucracy has not developed a large domestic constituency, interest-group access to the policymaking process is more limited than on domestic policy. To some extent the president and the State Department can formulate policy without extensive pressures from specialized interests.

On the other hand, this is not to say that interest groups are without influence in the foreign policy arena. The China Lobby was a key factor in the rigidity of U.S. policy on China for over two decades, and the very active Zionists groups have influenced U. S. policy toward Israel beginning with recognition almost before it was a nation. In general it is those groups organized around economic, religious, and ethnic interests that are most active and influential on foreign policy issues. During the 1978 debate over President Carter's proposal to sell warplanes to both Saudi Arabia and Israel, there was a feeling in the White House that the president's control of foreign policy was being challenged by the Israeli's through their lobbying efforts focused on members of Congress. In recent years foreign lobbyists have become much more active in the foreign policy field. In 1938 Congress passed the Foreign Agents Registration Act, requiring lobbyists representing foreign interests to register. Today about 500 agents register under this act annually, including such persons as the wife of Senator Jacob Javits of New York, and President Carter's brother Billy. Other groups such as the American Legion, the Veterans of Foreign Wars, and other veterans organizations may take a particular interest in foreign policy. In recent years groups representing the business community have become among the most active in the foreign policy field. The large corporations such as IBM, IT&T, GM, and others, as they expand their international operations, become very interested in U. S. foreign policy. As the great multinational corporations, most of them American, come to exert more and more economic and financial power across national boundaries, they will become more a factor in international relations. This has already become apparent in the petroleum industry and will also occur in other areas.

The primary function of a number of groups that focus directly on foreign policy has been education of both the public and the policymakers. Such groups as the Committee on the Present Danger, the American Security Council, and the American Committee on East-West Accord would fit into this category. These groups hope to gain both public attention and access to those in positions of power by including among their members prominent Americans whose names are widely recognized. One of the most prestigious groups of this type is the Council on Foreign Relations, whose membership has provided policymakers for both Republican and Democratic administrations. The council also publishes the journal *Foreign Affairs*, which is widely read among the foreign policy elite, and numerous books on foreign policy issues. Such groups as these tend to focus on the broader aspects of foreign policy in general, and their influence on particular issues may be rather limited. Other groups may zero in on particular issues and wage vigorous campaigns in efforts to influence a particular decision. The campaigns of the American Conservative Union and the Conservative Caucus against the Panama Canal treaties are examples. The ACU mailed over 2.4 million letters, purchased large amounts of radio and television time, and spent about $1.4 million in its efforts. The Conservative Caucus mailed over 2 million letters and spent an equally large amount in its efforts to block ratification. President Carter threw the full power and prestige of his office into this battle and the treaties were ratified.

Some observers, such as distinguished author and journalist David Halberstam, see the public and interest groups as somewhat supplanting the foreign policy elite as a result of reactions to Vietnam.[17] However, the public and interest groups have their greatest success with those who are responsible to internal constituencies, and many of those shaping U.S. foreign policy have never run for public office nor been politically accountable and are responsible to no active and well-defined internal constituency. While the president usually will not ignore interest groups on foreign policy issues, he may not feel nearly as inclined to follow them as might be the case on a domestic issue. Thus, on the whole, interest groups, with the exception of certain isolated issues, tend to be less a factor in foreign policy than in domestic policy.

## CURRENT ISSUES

The setting in which foreign policy decisions must be made has changed dramatically in the decades since World War II. The United Nations has grown from 51 members in 1946 to over 150 currently and about half of these members are nations born since the end of World War II. Developments in transportation and communication have had a significant impact on international relations to the extent that today national problems can quickly become global problems. National boundaries and the oceans are no longer the barriers they once were. These rapid, far-reaching changes in the international setting have brought an accompanying revolution in statecraft and the conduct of international relations. American policymakers must grasp and understand the rapid changes that are taking place in the world, and in light of these changes, must reconsider their traditional methods of diplomatic behavior and in many cases adopt new approaches for new problems.

In the 1950s and 60s American foreign policy was based largely on two factors that have changed substantially in the last two decades: (1) the characterization of the world communist movement as monolithic, and (2) the assumption of unlimited U. S. power and its applicability to all problems. In 1947 an article appeared in *Foreign Affairs* that would shape U. S. foreign policy for the next three decades because it planted the seeds of the policy of *containment*. The thesis of the article was this:

> The Soviet pressure against the free institutions of the Western world is something that can be contained by the adroit and vigilant application of counterforce at a series of constantly shifting geographical and political points, corresponding to the shifts and maneuvers of Soviet policy.[18]

Signed by "Mr. X," the article was the work of George Kennan, the foremost expert on the Soviet Union in the U. S. State Department, and was instrumental in lauching the U. S. on a policy of "long-term, patient, but firm and vigilant containment." For a time, the policy of containment served U. S. needs quite well. By the 1950s the post-World War II situation was rather clearly one in which two rival coalitions, each headed by a superpower, dominated world politics. In this setting, American policy decisions throughout the world were made with an eye on the Soviets and the Soviets' own policy moves. Our policy decisions were shaped almost exclusively by considerations of economic, political, and military competition with the communists—at this stage, primarily the Soviets.

Though recent years have changed the foreign policy setting, American policy has frequently lagged in reflecting these changes. As George Kennan, the father of containment, has pointed out, in the 1970s the world communist movement became widely fragmented with only a portion retaining ties with Moscow.[19] The traditional view of two cohesive blocs, each dominated by a superpower, which shaped our policy decisions for so long, is no longer totally applicable. Neither the U. S. nor the Soviet Union effectively controls the international actions of their allies; and beyond that, China has emerged as a third power center. While the East versus West alignment and communist imperialism remain important challenges to American policymakers, careful consideration of other relevant factors should not be excluded. Forcing all decisions into the East-West, communist-noncommunist mold tends to ignore significant developments in the current international scene. Colonialism has died in Asia and Africa and has been replaced by strong sentiments of nationalism. A North-South international alignment is emerging in which the differences are largely economic, but with strong racial and political overtones. Over the next few decades this developing confrontation between the "haves" and the "have-nots," the developed and underdeveloped nations of the world, may have far greater implications for our foreign policy than the threat of international communism. Yet all too often our policy decisions tend to be based largely on the concepts of containment and the competition between East and West. In Vietnam and Africa our policymakers have tended to ignore strong nationalistic movements; and we insist on viewing the Middle East, with roots of conflict going back for centuries, as a confrontation of communism and the free world.

Another element that American policymakers have had difficulty in accepting is the fact that not all international problems are susceptible to solution by the application of unlimited amounts of American power. The United States emerged from World War II physically untouched and with a monopoly of nuclear power. For three decades U. S. military and economic power was overwhelming and the U. S. dominated international politics. Through prolonged involvement in Vietnam, however, the U. S. was rather rudely awakened to the fact that there are political problems for which its overwhelming manpower and unequalled technology do not provide a solution. It was a shock to discover that in guerrilla warfare, Asian peasants were a match for the vast American military might. Consequently, Vietnam had a chastening effect and many Americans emerged with a more modest view of what the U. S. and its power could do. Writing in the *New York Times*, Henry Brandon, American correspondent of the *Sunday Times* of London, observed, "The era of American omnipresence, the willingness to exercise power alone and the idea that the United States can control events are passing into history."[20] Noted political writer Theodore White was somewhat less certain of the effects of Vietnam's lessons when he commented, "What we should have learned is clear: the reach of American power is not the reach of our bombers, our helicopters, our fleet, our logistics. The reach of American power extends only as far as the reach of American political understanding."[21]

While America's relative decline in power in an increasingly complex world may be apparent to many, there are indications that those shaping our foreign policies may be slower to accept these realities. Both Ford and Kissinger criticized Congress for "losing its nerve" and not supporting more U. S. involvement in Angola. Recent experience, such as the Iranian holding of American hostages, seems to indicate quite clearly that the United States' two biggest assets — its military might and its economic power—do not guarantee either quick or successful solutions to international problems.

On the other hand, in accepting the realities of the limits to American power, our policymakers should not revert to our earlier tradition of isolationism and non-involvement. The U. S. remains a principal on the international scene and must assume its role as a leader in world affairs. As former Vice President Nelson Rockefeller observed, "Now that we have realized that we cannot solve all the world's problems, we are in danger of convincing ourselves that we cannot solve any of them."[22] This also would be a mistake, because while we have been made painfully aware of the limits to our power, the U. S. remains the single most important actor on the international scene. A return to political isolationism could possibly lead all too quickly to economic and social isolation as well.

American foreign policy makers are faced with the task of grasping the current realities of the international scene, adopting new approaches based on fresh assumptions, and prescribing new alternatives. They must accept the reality of the limits to U. S. economic and military power, face the prospect of nuclear parity for the USSR, recognize the emergence of the Third World and strong nationalist movements, and search for alternatives to the impotency of the United Nations and the absence of any viable machinery for resolving international disputes. In other words, to be effective, U. S. foreign policy must be made more responsive to the changing international setting and commitments to traditional policies of the past need careful review.

A strong dose of realism might help to overcome some of the moralistic overtones that have complicated an objective analysis of our policies in the past. No nation has a monopoly on justice and virtue, yet our policymakers have tended to follow an overly simplified "good guys versus bad guys" concept in making policy. This has resulted in gross inconsistencies, with the U. S. espousing democracy while supporting some of the world's worst dictators. The ten countries cited most frequently for human rights abuses received over $500 million in military aid from the U. S. in 1978. Despite President Carter's rhetoric on human rights, there has been no appreciable decline in U. S. support for some of the world's most repressive regimes. At the same time Nixon went to China to make overtures to her communist leaders, he was authorizing the CIA to undertake efforts to undermine a Chilean regime leaning leftist. Such contradictions in policy give the impression the policymakers don't know where they are going and undermine confidence in the government.

While commitment to certain basic human values is desirable, most issues of foreign policy cannot be decided on the basis of purely moralistic considerations. Diplomacy frequently involves the compromise of clashing principles, and the majority of foreign policy decisions become questions of judgment and maneuver rather than questions of good versus evil. For the greatest portion of foreign policy efforts, moral considerations cannot be decisive. As Arthur Schlesinger, Jr. points out, "Saints can be pure, but statesmen must be responsible. As trustees for others, they must defend interests and compromise principles." Whether Jimmy Carter, whom Fred Warner Neal has described as "a Woodrow Wilson reincarnated as a born-again Southern Baptist," could embrace a more realistic approach for American foreign policy still remained to be seen after nearly four years of his presidency.

Though Richard Nixon and Henry Kissinger were able to revise the traditional Cold War concept of communism as a monolithic movement, thus opening the way for overtures to China and the promotion of the concept of détente, our overall foreign policy has not changed all that much. Kissinger's style of highly personalized diplomacy would have fit the world of the nineteenth century much better than the late twentieth century world of nuclear powers, the Third World, and multinational corporations. Much of the analysis, style, and goals of the

Nixon-Kissinger foreign policy was made obsolete by the international setting of the 1970s. Likewise, in 1980, much of the rhetoric and action of the Carter administration seemed to indicate little in the way of a fresh new approach to foreign policy making. Both Nixon's and Carter's policies seem to be based largely on standards of performance and evaluation valid thirty years ago. By 1980, not much had emerged in the way of clear and consistent policy as Carter vascillated from "peacemaker" to "cold warrior."

## CONCLUSION

Foreign policy making has become overwhelmingly complicated in the latter half of the twentieth century, possibly to the point of defying effective management. George Washington had only three departments of government to run, and he and his early successors communicated only infrequently with ministers in a few foreign capitals in their conduct of foreign policy. Today the Department of State alone is a sprawling bureaucratic network that virtually defies effective oversight and direction, and it is only a part of the total foreign policy operation. Foreign policy has been further complicated by the fact that more and more it has become an extension of domestic policy. While democratic policymaking cannot be judged in terms of efficiency alone, the complexity of today's foreign policy raises some serious issues for democratic government. Is it possible to be democratic in some areas of policymaking and not in others? Constructive criticism being an important element in the democratic process, can we reconcile open dissent and discussion of alternatives with national security needs? Is our society informed enough and organized to promote effective foreign policy? And finally, can our government conduct effective foreign policy and at the same time preserve the democratic values on which it is based? Can our system withstand the challenges from outside, and not in the process destroy those very values and principles we seek to preserve? This is the challenge facing those who shape American foreign policy.

### Points to Ponder

Can a democracy make foreign policy effectively?

Does our system of checks and balances impose too many restraints upon the president in the conduct of foreign policy?

In the conduct of U.S. international relations, who determines what constitutes the "national interest"?

In the interest of national security, should agencies such as the FBI and CIA be permitted to spy on American citizens within the United States?

Do American citizens have sufficient access to information to be effective participants in foreign policy making?

### Notes

1. Quoted by Donald Brandon in *American Foreign Policy* (New York: Appleton-Century-Crofts, 1966), p. 33.

2. Irving Kristol, "Our Foreign Policy Illusions," *The Wall Street Journal* (February 4, 1980).
3. Edward S. Corwin, *The President, Office and Powers*, 4th ed. (New York: New York University Press, 1957), p. 171.
4. Joseph Barthélemy, *Democratic et politique etrangere* (Paris, 1917), p. 141.
5. As quoted by Clinton Rossiter in *The American Presidency* (New York: New American Library, 1956), p. 22.
6. Robert A. Dahl, *Congress and Foreign Policy* (New York: Norton, 1964), p. 3.
7. Henry A. Kissinger, "Domestic Structures and Foreign Policy," *Daedalus* 95 (Spring 1966), reprinted in *American Foreign Policy* (New York: Norton, 1969), p. 18.
8. Cordell Hull, *The Memoirs of Cordell Hull*, vol. 1 (New York: Macmillan, 1948), p. 194.
9. "Aid cuts imperil U.S. interests," Louisville, Ky. *Courier-Journal* (July 9, 1978).
10. Dahl, *op. cit.*, p. 261.
11. Alexis de Tocqueville, *Democracy in America*, VI (New York: Schocken Books, 1961), pp. 272-75.
12. Thomas Molnar, *The Two Faces of American Foreign Policy* (Indianapolis: Bobbs-Merril, 1962), p. 101.
13. Leonard Cottrell, Jr. and Sylvia Eberhart, *American Opinion on World Affairs in the Atomic Age* (Princeton: Princeton University Press, 1948), p. 14.
14. Gene Rainey, *Patterns of American Foreign Policy* (Boston: Allyn & Bacon, 1975), pp. 83–85.
15. Thomas A. Bailey, *The Man in the Street* (New York: Macmillan, 1948), p. 13.
16. Molnar, *op. cit.*, p. 101.
17. David Halberstam is author of *The Best and the Brightest* and *The Making of a Quagmire*. See Ron Ridenour, "Interview with David Halberstam," *Skeptic* magazine, Special Issue No. 8. (July/August 1975), pp. 4–11.
18. Mr. X, "The Sources of Soviet Conduct," *Foreign Affairs*, v. 25 (July 1947), p. 576.
19. George F. Kennan, "Reappraising Our Vital Interests," *Skeptic* (July/August 1975), pp. 38–41.
20. Henry Brandon, "Is Our Power Still Intact?" *New York Times* (April 13, 1975).
21. Theodore White, "Putting Down the White Man's Burden," *Skeptic* (July/August 1975), p. 28.
22. Nelson Rockefeller, "On U.S. Foreign Policy," *Center Report* (October 1974), p. 14.

## Suggestions for Further Reading

ABSHIRE, DAVID. *Foreign Policy Makers: President vs Congress*. Georgetown University Center for Strategic and International Studies. Beverly Hills: Sage, 1979.

BLANKE, WENDELL. *The Foreign Service of the United States*. New York: Praeger, 1969.

BROWN, SEYOM. *The Crises of Power: Foreign Policy in the Kissinger Years*. New York: Columbia University Press, 1979.

CARROLL, HOLBERT. *The House of Representatives and Foreign Affairs*. Pittsburgh: University of Pittsburgh Press, 1958.

CHEEVER, DANIEL and HAVILAND, H.F., JR., *American Foreign Policy and the Separation of Powers*. Cambridge, Mass.: Harvard University Press, 1952.

COHEN, BERNARD. *The Influence of Non-Governmental Groups on Foreign Policy-Making*. Boston: World Peace Foundation, 1959.

COOPER, C. L. "The CIA and Decision-Making," *Foreign Affairs* 50 (January 1972), pp. 223–36.
CRABB, CECIL, JR. and HOLT, PAT M. *Invitation to Struggle: Congress, the President and Foreign Policy*. Washington, D.C.: Congressional Quarterly, 1980.
CRONIN, THOMAS and GREENBERG, S.D. *The Presidential Advisory System*. New York: Harper & Row, 1969.
DAVIS, DAVID H. *How the Bureaucracy Makes Foreign Policy*. Lexington, Mass.: Heath, 1972.
DESTLER, I.M. *Presidents, Bureaucrats, and Foreign Policy*. Princeton, N.J.: Princeton University Press, 1972.
ELDER ROBERT. *The Policy Machines: The Department of State and American Foreign Policy*. Syracuse, N.Y.: Syracuse University Press, 1960.
ELDER, ROBERT E. *The Information Machine: The United States Information Agency and American Foreign Policy*. Syracuse, N.Y.: Syracuse University Press, 1968.
FALK, STANLEY. *The National Security Council Under Truman, Eisenhower, and Kennedy*. Beverly Hills: Glencoe Press, 1968.
FARNSWORTH, DAVID N. *The Senate Committee on Foreign Relations*. Urbana, Il.: University of Illinois Press, 1961.
FRANCK, THOMAS and WEISBRAND, EDWARD. *Foreign Policy by Congress*. New York: Oxford University Press, 1979.
FULBRIGHT, WILLIAM. *The Crippled Giant: American Foreign Policy and Its Domestic Consequences*. New York: Vintage Books, 1972.
GILPIN, ROBERT G, JR. *U. S. Power and the Multinational Corporation*. New York: Basic Books, 1975.
HALPERIN, MORTON. *Bureaucratic Politics in Foreign Policy*. Washington, D.C.: The Brookings Institution, 1974.
HUMPHREY, HUBERT H. "The Senate in Foreign Policy," *Foreign Affairs*, Volume XXXVII (1959), pp. 525-36.
JACKSON HENRY M., ed. *The Secretary of State and the Ambassador*. New York: Praeger, 1964.
KEGLEY, CHARLES, JR and MCGOWAN, PATRICK J. *Challenge to America: United States Foreign Policy in the 1980s*. Beverly Hills: Sage, 1979.
LEHMAN, JOHN. *The Executive, Congress and Foreign Policy*. New York: Praeger, 1976.
MANSFIELD, HARVEY, SR. *Congress Against the President*. New York: Praeger, 1975.
MORGAN, JOHN H. *The Foreign Service of the United States: Origins, Development, and Functions*. Washington, D.C.: Government Printing Office, 1961.
PLISCHKE, ELMER, ed. *Modern Diplomacy: The Art and the Artesans*. Washington, D.C.: American Enterprise Institute, 1979.
RANSOM, HARRY HOWE. *The Intelligence Establishment*. Cambridge, Mass.: Harvard University Press, 1970.
ROSENAU, JAMES N. *Public Opinion and Foreign Policy*. New York: Random House, 1961.
ROURKE, FRANCIS E. *Bureaucracy and Foreign Policy*. Baltimore: Johns Hopkins University Press, 1972.
SPIRO, HERBERT J. *A New Foreign Policy Consensus*. Beverly Hills: Sage, 1979.
STOESSINGER, JOHN G. *Crusaders and Pragmatists: Movers of Modern American Foreign Policy*. New York: Norton, 1979.
WORSLEY, PETER. *The Third World*. Chicago: University of Chicago Press, 1970.
X. "The Sources of Soviet Conduct," *Foreign Affairs* 25 (July 1947), p. 576.

# 6

# Providing for the Common Defense

The Cold War era of the 1950s and '60s brought substantial changes in the United States' traditional military policies. Traditionally the military was used primarily as an instrument of U. S. policy in crisis situations and these were viewed as only temporary aberrations from the normal course of conducting foreign policy. Little more than a couple of decades prior to World War II, President Woodrow Wilson ordered his secretary of war to cease all war planning because it was not in keeping with the U. S. image as a peace-loving nation. In this setting it was a boast that the U. S. was never prepared for a war. The nation had always had time to mobilize when such an effort did become necessary; therefore, large standing armies were not felt to be desirable or necessary.

Emerging from World War II, the United States was the world's premier military power, sole possessor of the atomic bomb. The country was all set to follow its normal course of action following a war — demobilize its armies, mothball its military machines, and get back as quickly as possible to peacetime endeavors. The 15-million-member U. S. military force was reduced to 1 million and the defense budget was cut back to $12 billion. The East-West confrontation in the Cold War era changed this normal course of action dramatically, however. The Soviets quickly acquired the capacity to build the atomic bomb, and the launching of Sputnik in 1957 jolted Americans from their complacency with the harsh realization that the Russians not only had nuclear weapons but the means of delivering a direct strike on the United States.

These changes in the international power structure forced American policymakers to completely re-evaluate U. S. defense policy. In the event of an all-out war, the United States would likely be an immediate target and we would no longer have the time to mobilize our forces as in the past. An immediate implication was the need to maintain a large standing army in a constant state of readiness, something the country traditionally had not done. Thus, in this century, the United States has changed from a country with only a small armed force to one with a global military establishment and all the problems accompanying such a vast operation — a huge defense budget, proper civilian supervision and control, appropriate strategy, etc.

## THE DEFENSE POLICY MACHINERY

Because of their great concern with the possibility for the establishment of a military dictatorship, the framers of the Constitution divided the powers for defending the country between the executive and legislative branches and wrote in several checks and balances and other safeguards. As is the case in foreign policy, much of the initiative in defense policy rests with the president, but many of his actions are subject to approval by one or both houses of Congress.

### The President

Experience under the Articles of Confederation indicated the need for centralized direction and authority in the realm of defending the nation, and defense could best be directed by someone with ready access to information and who could act with some dispatch. Thus, in Article II, Section 2, the framers declared that the "President shall be the Commander-in-Chief of the Army and Navy of the United States." There was some discussion in the convention as to whether a president should actually be allowed to take the field to command, but in the end this grant of power to the president was left quite broad.

The president's role as commander-in-chief has become one of his most significant responsibilities and has made him the paramount figure in the shaping of U. S. foreign and defense policies. While his actions may ultimately require the approval or acquiescence of Congress, he is frequently in a position as commander-in-chief to create an atmosphere in which the Congress may feel obligated to support his actions. The Tonkin Gulf Resolution of 1964 authorizing the president to take necessary action for defending U. S. security in Southeast Asia is a prime example. Though several members of Congress suffered doubts later, at the time it was presented, the resolution passed 82 to 2 in the Senate and 416 to 0 in the House. There is even some evidence that the Tonkin Gulf Resolution was actually prepared sometime in advance of the alleged incident and President Johnson merely awaited an opportune time to seek Congress's approval. With this kind of discretion, the executive is in a position to virtually put the legislature in a straight-jacket when it comes to approving or disapproving his actions.

As an outgrowth of the president's authority as commander-in-chief to commit troops in the absence of a formally declared war, Congress in November 1973 approved legislation directed toward limiting the president's war powers.

Under the War Powers Resolution a president is required to report within forty-eight hours any commitment of U. S. troops abroad. Congress must then approve such commitment within sixty days or the president must cease such action. Congress may extend the deadline another thirty days if necessary for the withdrawal. The act also provides that both houses may, if they are so inclined, adopt a concurrent resolution calling for immediate withdrawal. This would appear to give the Congress considerable control over the President's use of troops in unauthorized situations. Again, however, the president may, by creating the impression of more urgency than really exists, sway the Congress to accept considerable discretion in his exercise of his role as commander-in-chief. Gerald Ford ruffled hardly a feather in Congress when he used U. S. Marines in the Mayaguez incident, and this came on the heels of Vietnam and the adoption of the War Powers Resolution. The president is in a position, through the judicious use of his broad powers in foreign and defense matters, to determine to a great extent the directions these policies take.

### Congress

While the president's role is paramount and he retains most of the initiative, the Constitution reserves a substantial role for the Congress in defense policy. Only Congress can declare war; and while the president directs the sword, only Congress can raise and maintain the army and navy. The president takes the initiative in treaty making, but final approval rests with two-thirds of the Senate. All appropriations for defense purposes must be approved by Congress, and these cannot be for longer than two years at a time. The president appoints the top-ranking civilian and military officials responsible for administering defense policy, but they must be confirmed by the Senate. Thus, though the president is clearly the leader in formulating our defense policy, he must in most areas secure the blessings of Congress to carry his policies forward effectively.

Crisis situations have usually enhanced the powers of the executive, and Congress has been inclined to delegate more authority to the president under such circumstances. The almost constant crisis situation of the post-World War II years brought incredible growth to presidential powers in the area of foreign and defense policy. Vigorous presidential initiative, coupled with growing congressional tendencies to delegate broad responsibility to the executive, has reduced the effectiveness of some congressional checks on defense policy. While American presidents have committed U. S. troops on more than a hundred different occasions, Congress has been called upon to formally declare war only five times. The changed setting of the Cold War has caused some to feel that the president should have an even freer rein in his conduct of foreign and defense policy. Near the end of the Johnson administration, Under-Secretary-of-State Nicholas Katzenbach maintained that Congress's power to declare war had been rendered obsolete by the nuclear age. Even Congress's venerable power of the purse may be a less effective check when dealing with "sacred cow" defense budgets than in some other areas.

## Major Defense Policy Statutes

**War Department Act of 1789.** Created the cabinet-level Department of War.

**Selective Service Act of 1917.** Provided for the drafting of persons to staff the military for World War I.

**Selective Training and Service Act of 1940.** Was the first peacetime selective service program ever adopted by Congress.

**National Security Act of 1947.** Provided for a national military establishment with Departments of Army, Navy, and Air Force and created the National Security Council and the Central Intelligence Agency.

**National Security Act Amendments of 1949.** Made changes in the 1947 structure by creating a Department of Defense headed by a civilian secretary and including the Departments of Army, Navy, and Air Force; also established the Joint Chiefs of Staff with a chairman.

**Defense Department Reorganization Act of 1958.** Strengthened the role of the secretary of defense in the military establishment by authorizing the consolidation of a number of functions to bring them under the control of the secretary.

**Gulf of Tonkin Resolution of 1964.** Authorized the president, as commander-in-chief, to take all necessary measures to repel armed attacks and further aggression against the forces of the U. S. in Southeast Asia.

**Draft Lottery Act of 1971.** Modified the selective service system, providing for a national lottery to select personnel for military service.

**War Powers Act of 1973.** Enacted to limit presidential troop commitments without congressional approval. Commitments beyond sixty days without a declaration of war must be approved by Congress.

The large fixed costs in the budget plus the uncertain choice between, as one congressman expressed it, "economic ruination or atomic devastation" makes any substantial reduction in the defense budget difficult.

Even with the growing pressures for more presidential freedom in conducting foreign and defense policy, the post-Vietnam/post-Watergate era has brought some resurgence in Congress as an active partner in the process. The War Powers Resolution has been accompanied by a number of other legislative provisions aimed at giving Congress more voice in foreign and defense policy decisions. The president and secretary of defense no longer have a completely free hand on arms sales abroad, only one manifestation of a growing tendency for Congress to write legislative veto provisions into economic and military aid bills. In considering the 1978 military authorization bill, which Carter eventually vetoed as unacceptable,

## Principal Departments and Agencies

**Department of Defense** (DOD). Created by the National Security Act Amendments of 1949, the DOD is the successor to the former separate Departments of War and Navy. It includes the military departments of the Army, Navy, and Air Force.

**Armed Forces Policy Council.** A sort of inner cabinet within the Department of Defense, this council advises the secretary on defense and security matters.

**Joint Chiefs of Staff.** Each of the military departments—Army, Navy, Air Force—is headed by a military chief of staff. These combined form the Joint Chiefs of Staff, headed by a chairman appointed by the president.

**Defense Intelligence Agency.** Created in 1961 as an intelligence and information gathering agency within the Department of Defense, the DIA provides the secretary of defense an independent source of intelligence in foreign and defense policy.

**National Aeronautics and Space Administration** (NASA). This agency is responsible for coordinating America's space programs, including satellites for intelligence gathering and other defense-related programs.

**Nuclear Regulatory Commission** (NRC). Formerly the Atomic Energy Commission, the NRC has responsibility for fostering research and development of atomic energy and regulating private development efforts in the field.

**U.S. Arms Control and Disarmament Agency.** Created in 1961, the agency conducts studies and provides advice on arms control and disarmament to those shaping U. S. defense and security policies.

**Federal Bureau of Investigation** (FBI). A division of the Department of Justice, the FBI has the responsibility for seeking out and apprehending violators of the internal security statutes, including foreign agents operating within the United States.

Congress not only gave the president an aircraft carrier he didn't want, they took out of the measure some of what the president had requested. All of these are indications the Congress is no longer willing to play the passive rubber stamp to executive initiatives on defense policy matters. Just how far Congress will go with its new assertiveness remains to be seen. Already both Presidents Ford and Carter have warned Congress against "tying the president's hands" on defense matters.

### The Defense Department

At the heart of the vast bureaucratic complex administering U. S. defense policy is the Department of Defense, which occupies the Pentagon, the world's largest office complex. A vast information and communications network, the DOD would make General Motors or IT&T look like small town businesses. Today, the Defense Department is the largest single gatherer and provider of information in the foreign and defense policy formulation process. Since 1945 the Pentagon and the intelligence community have experienced spectacular growth as their role in policymaking has taken on greater and greater significance. Five of nine agencies composing the intelligence community are a part of the military establishment. Headed by the civilian secretary of defense, the Defense Department is a major source of information for the president on defense policy and handles the day-to-day responsibilities of administering defense policy around the world.

American experience in World War II illustrated the need for more effective coordination of civil-military policies. At that time, American forces were under two separate departments—the War Department and the Department of Navy. In 1947, after lengthy debate, Congress passed the National Security Act reorganizing the armed services and creating a unified National Security Establishment, which was very shortly changed to the Department of Defense. Under the reorganization, three separate branches of the military were retained—army, air force and navy, with each branch headed by a civilian secretary under the overall supervision of the civilian secretary of defense. Each military branch also has a military chief-of-staff who is under the civilian secretary. Collectively these chiefs-of-staff make up the Joint Chiefs of Staff, headed by a chairman appointed by the president. The chairman of the joint chiefs is the top-ranking military man in government, and the joint chiefs are the principal military advisors to the president and the secretary of defense. (See Figure 6.1 for an organizational chart of the Defense Department.)

### Other Agencies

In addition to the unified Defense Department, the 1947 National Security Act also created two other agencies that play a vital role in defense policy—the National Security Council and the CIA, both discussed in the preceding chapter. Many other agencies also deal with matters having considerable significance for defense policy decisions—such agencies as the Nuclear Regulatory Commission (NRC), the Agency for International Development (AID), the International Communication Agency (ICA), and the Arms Control and Disarmament Agency (ACDA). Today, domestic and foreign policies have become so intertwined that the actions of almost any agency of the federal government may have defense-policy implications. The involvement of such a vast bureaucratic network and such a variety of agencies make overall control and direction of defense policy a next-to-impossible task.

By creating the unified armed forces under a single Department of Defense, the National Security Council to formuate and review basic policies relating to national security, and the CIA to coordinate intelligence activities, Congress tried through the National Security Act to bring some degree of centralized direction and

**FIGURE 6.1 Department of Defense**

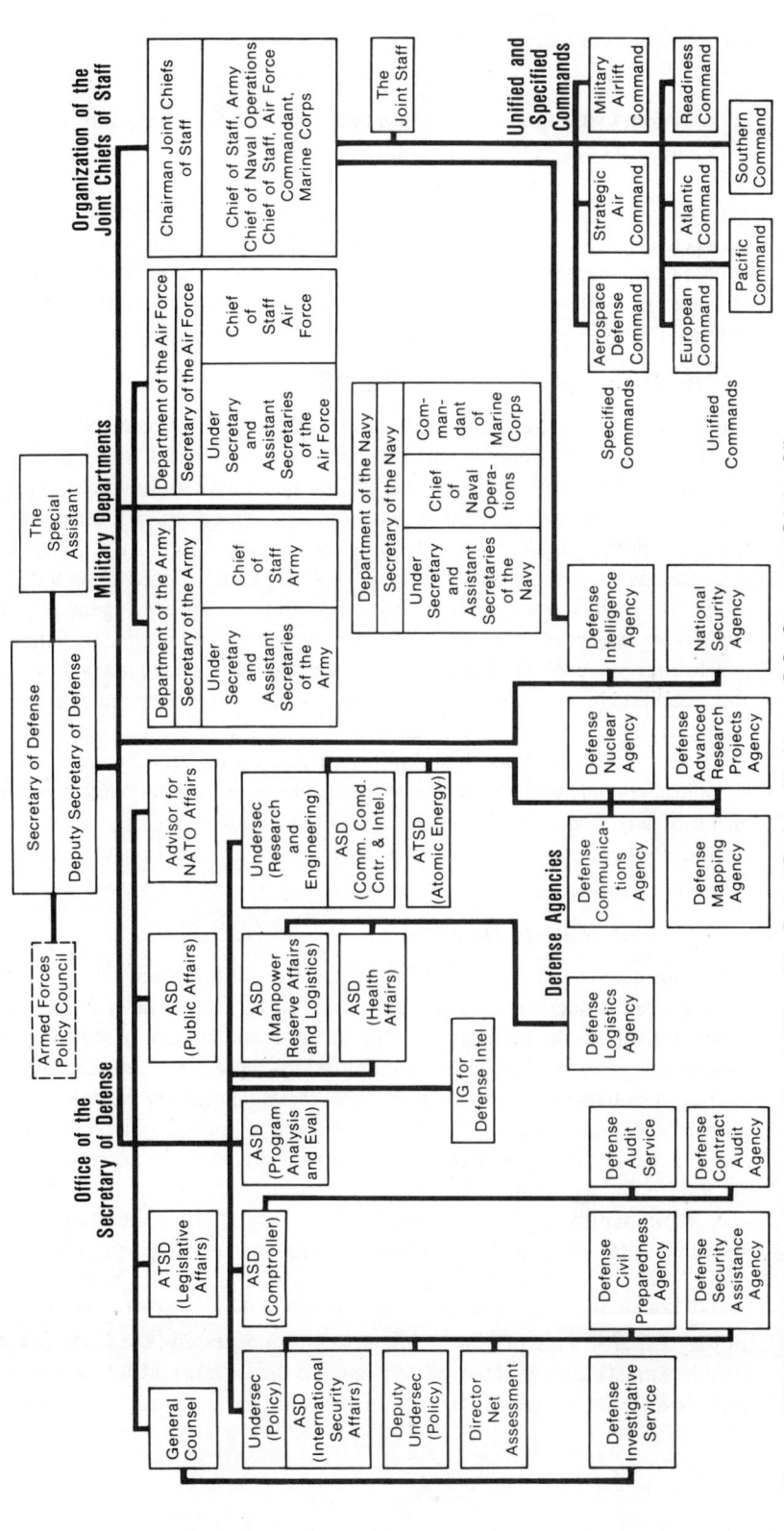

*Source: 1978–1979 United States Government Manual, Office of the Federal Register, Washington, D.C., Government Printing Office.*

coordination to the sprawling defense policy structure. These efforts have brought only partial success, and it is doubtful that any institutional reforms alone will be sufficient to overcome the internal competition, overlapping of functions, and general disjointedness that characterize the overall defense efforts. Differences between civilian and military officials within the defense structure cannot be overcome by mere institutional changes, and any policy area involving the myriad of agencies involved in defense policy will inevitably experience problems of duplication, conflict, and dis-coordination.

## DEFENSE POLICY PROBLEMS

Until recent decades, military or defense policy had never received all that much attention, but was simply a sort of adjunct to our overall foreign policy. The explosion of the atomic bombs on Hiroshima and Nagasaki, however, changed the meaning of war and brought a revolution in American defense policy. The necessity of maintaining a large standing army and developing a military structure and strategy to protect America from a direct attack posed new and difficult problems for U. S. policymakers. Prior to World War II, it was generally felt that the military was primarily an arm of policy execution and needed to be heard only in wartime. Since World War II, military considerations have become so inextricably bound up in our foreign policy decisions that military personnel have become vital participants in the formulation as well as the execution of policy. Since decisions can be no better than the information on which they are based, it has become absolutely essential to include the professional military and their expertise in the highest councils of foreign and defense policy making. This is accomplished, however, at the risk of undermining civilian direction and control of the military.

### Civilian-Military Balance

It was no accident that the framers of the Constitution made the president, a civilian, commander-in-chief of the army and navy. Traditionally Americans have adhered firmly to the belief in civilian direction and control of the military, and until recent years civilian-military relationships were not a cause for much concern. In the changed world situation where strategic military considerations have become such an important factor in all aspects of public policy, however, the possibility of the emergence of a strong military organization not readily susceptible to effective civilian control must be considered.

A fundamental problem faced by the president and secretary of defense is that of making certain that the military remains an effective participant in shaping our defense policy but does not come to dominate the process. In an international setting, where military confrontation is a constant threat and effective inclusion of military experts in the policymaking process is a necessity, the Congress and the president must ensure that the military remains the servant and not the master in the decision-making process. Changes in our military structure over the last few decades make this an extremely difficult task. Our traditionally skeletal standing army has become a huge, complex fighting machine with international capabilities. With this large standing army and the elimination of the draft, the traditional citizen soldier was replaced by the volunteer professional soldier. New highly technical weapons systems and a revival of guerrilla warfare have made military strategy and policy much more complicated. With five of the nine agencies composing the intelligence community a part of the military establishment, the Pentagon has become the single largest source of information in the foreign and defense policy process. In light of these developments, can the president and Congress provide effective control and oversight?

While Congress has gained in expertise on defense matters and some lawmakers are now convinced that their judgment is superior to that of the executive branch, Congress faces substantial problems as an effective oversight agency. It has no counterpart to the National Security Council and must rely on the executive and outside "experts" for most of its counsel and information. The House and Senate Armed Services Committees have been largely co-opted by the military and do not function effectively as oversight agencies or as internal sources of information on defense policy. Because access to information is a key element in policymaking and oversight, members of Congress face numerous problems in this area with regard to defense policy. Much information is classified and since much of it comes through the executive branch, Congress is largely at the executive's mercy as far as what is provided. When it comes to the analysis of complex technical data, Congress must rely heavily on interpretations by not always unbiased experts. Thus, the congressman is thrust into the difficult position of working frequently with incomplete, sometimes suspect data that he himself has little or no expertise to analyze, and upon which he must base a decision that could in a decade or so waste millions of dollars or millions of lives. His position is further complicated by the necessity of reconciling his decision with his personal preferences and those of his constituents.

The secrecy and lack of information surrounding many defense policy decisions make congressional debate and effective weighing of alternatives difficult. Consequently, decisions for acquiring new weapons systems are frequently made in Congress with only limited debate and very little analysis of the implications of the issues involved. Lamenting the lack of effective debate in the Senate on the proposed neutron bomb, Senator Mark Hatfield (R-Ore.) noted that classification of the weapon had hampered congressional debate and a thorough review of its need. He said he had to learn about the bomb through the press rather than through congressional sources. Speaking of the Senate subcommittee of the Appropriations Committee that approved funds for the bomb, Hatfield said, "Very few members of the committee even knew such a weapon was included in the budget request until recently."

In the final analysis, however, it is probably through its power of the purse that Congress exerts most of its control. Even this congressional control and

140  MANAGEMENT POLICY

direction can be debated as to its ultimate effectiveness. George Mahon, retired chairman of the House Appropriations Committee and its subcommittee on military appropriations, maintains that since all military expenditures must be approved by Congress, they retain effective control. While technically this is true, many observers feel that a variety of factors work to reduce Congress's discretion and make the purse strings quite elastic when it comes to defense appropriations. Congressional decisions on defense appropriations are not based on a coolly detached and rational analysis of the facts and clearly defined priorities. Members are frequently subjected to a wide range of emotional, economic, and political pressures when faced with difficult defense policy decisions. Appropriations time brings to Capitol Hill a rather steady stream of scare stories about alleged Soviet weapons developments, and the Pentagon has been quite effective in selling the idea of Russian superiority. The Pentagon is one of the Capitol's most effective lobbyists, and its legislative liaison budget is over $3.5 million a year as compared to the $300,000 reported by the United Federation of Postal Clerks, the top spender among lobbying groups required to register under the law. The Pentagon, in alliance with the nation's major defense suppliers, is a most potent force in the defense policy making process. It was not without cause that Dwight Eisenhower, an ex-general, felt compelled as president to speak to this matter in these words:

> The conjunction of an immense military establishment and a large arms industry is new in the American experience. The total influence — economic, political, even spiritual — is felt in every city, every State house, every office of the Federal Government.... We must not fail to comprehend its grave implications. Our toil, resources, and livelihood are all involved; so is the very structure of our society. In the councils of government we must guard against the unwarranted influence, whether sought or unsought, by the military-industrial complex. The potential for the disastrous rise of misplaced power exists and will persist.[1]

On weapons system procurements Congress is often the target of high pressure lobbying campaigns from both the Pentagon and large defense contractors who stand to benefit. Rockwell International carried on an intensive campaign for the B-1 bomber, pointing out to individual members of Congress how many jobs B-1 production would mean for their districts. The jobs element of the Rockwell campaign points up that for many in Congress, defense contracts have become a big item of "pork," further reducing congressional objectivity on defense appropriations. Charles Peters, editor of the *Washington Monthly*, says defense appropriations have less to do with real defense than with having something for everyone — a military base in one district, an airplane contract in another. These considerations, along with such other factors as prior commitments and the lack of expertise necessary to make really informed judgments on frequently complex technical issues, many times place members in a position where they feel they have little choice other than to approve appropriations requests. To do otherwise could undermine national security.

Former Budget Director Charles L. Schultze says that Congress can, if proper information is available and the proper institutional framework created, critically and responsibly examine and debate the defense budget. And it can do so, he says, in the context of comparing priorities. To date, Congress has neither the framework, the access to information, nor the necessary expertise to perform this function effectively. Consequently, rather than an effective overseer, the Congress may on occasion be a friendly court of last resort for military men whose budgets have been cut by their civilian chiefs.

## Executive Control and Oversight

In the light of the many obstacles to effective congressional oversight, executive direction and control become even more important. Executive direction and control involve two principal aspects: development of a structure within the executive branch to ensure civilian control, and procedures to ensure that military training and involvement in policymaking sustain traditional democratic values.

A number of structural safeguards against military control and domination have been written into the Constitution and statutes adopted by Congress. As noted earlier in this chapter, the president, a civilian, is the constitutional commander-in-chief of the army and navy; and the Constitution includes a further safeguard by prohibiting members of the military from holding public office. The 1949 amendment to the National Security Act of 1947 created the Defense Department headed by a civilian secretary and provided for a civilian secretary to head each of the branches of the armed services. The 1949 amendments also replaced the chiefs-of-staff on the National Security Council with the civilian vice president, a move to increase civilian involvement in NSC deliberations.

While the structure for civil-military relationships has been rather clearly defined constitutionally and statutorily, the substance of this relationship remains much less clearly defined. Even the constitutional provisions are open to interpretation and are the source of dispute. In reviewing President Truman's actions in the steel seizure case of 1952, Justice Jackson of the U. S. Supreme Court said the commander-in-chief clause implies "something more than an empty title. But just what authority goes with the name has plagued presidential advisers who would not waive or narrow it by nonassertion yet cannot say where it begins or ends."[2] Several members of Congress are members of the national guard or military reserves, including several members of the armed services committees. General Alexander Haig served as Nixon's White House chief-of-staff. Are these violations of the constitutional provision against military personnel in public office?

Even more difficult to define is the appropriate relationship between military leaders and their civilian superiors. In 1951 President Truman relieved General Douglas MacArthur of his command in Korea because the general had challenged the president's authority as commander-in-chief. More than two decades later, when Major General John Singlaub publicly questioned the wisdom of President Carter's decision to withdraw ground troops from Korea, he was immediately recalled from his command. Where is the line of distinction between White House "muzzling" of the military and the unnecessary "politicization" of the military leadership? Once policy decisions have been reached, should the military leaders still have the right to question such decisions publicly or in Congress? In testimony before the Senate Armed Services Committee in 1978, the chairman of the Joint Chiefs of Staff, General David C. Jones, said senior officers should not make "end runs" around the White House to win support in Congress for programs they favor. Just where is the fine line between military insubordination and the necessary open discussion of alternatives in the interest of sounder policy?

In what way is too much military influence a threat to sound defense policy? This is not really an issue of black versus white or right versus wrong, but rather a question of the appropriate blending of participants, philosophies, and values to produce the soundest overall policy decisions. Most Americans feel as did French Prime Minister Clemenceau that war is much too serious a business to be turned over exclusively to the military. "The military," says Louis J. Halle, "are always disposed to make their estimates in terms of theoretical military capacity. . . ." He then adds, "It is simply not true that the military know best when it comes to matters which can be denominated military-strategic. The vision to which they are trained is too narrow, too technical, too crude."[3]

The "military mind," say Snyder and Furniss, may be characterized by certain predispositions that are inappropriate in formulating public policy. Because of certain rigidity in its thought processes, the military mind can produce distortions that result in misjudgments. Since effective defense policy involves continual reevaluation, the traditional conservatism of the military may make necessary adaptation difficult. Professional military personnel display a frequent tendency to act on present events as if they were repetitions of earlier experiences. Their strong tendencies to stick with proven strategies and weapons make them slow to change.[4] In 1912, when Rudolf Nebel asked the German Army for assistance in building an airplane, their response was that "aircraft can never have military significance because flying an airplane requires acrobatic agility." So much for the Luftwaffe!

The principal danger to democratic policymaking stemming from the "military mind" is that if such an approach to policymaking becomes too widespread then there is the possibility of the development of of what Harold Lasswell has termed the "garrison state." This is a state in which all other values and considerations have been subordinated to the requirements of military security. Lasswell describes the state in these terms:

> Continuing fear of external attack sustains an atmosphere of distrust that finds expression in spy hunts directed against fellow officials and fellow citizens. Outspoken criticism of official measures launched for national defense is more and more resented as unpatriotic and sub-

versive of the common good. The community at large, therefore, acquiesces in denials of freedom that go beyond the technical requirements of military security.⁵

The "garrison state" and those characterized by the "military mind" fail to take into consideration that there is more to security than mere military defense of our physical territory; security involves the preservation of democratic values as well as territory. Since military personnel have become indispensable in formulating sound defense policy, an important element in their control and direction must be the assurance through efforts of both the legislative and executive branches that the military establishment is not isolated from the traditional values of American democracy.

At stake in this question of civilian-military control is the broader question of the future direction of the American democratic system. To ignore military considerations in policy decisions is to risk national security, while to ignore effective control over the military may be to risk the continuance of democratic institutions. The ultimate question facing the policymakers is how to attain the appropriate balance between individual freedom and national security—a balance that will preserve American democracy in a dangerous world.

## THE ISSUES OF DEFENSE POLICY MAKING

In his first annual address to both houses of Congress, President George Washington observed, "To be prepared for war is one of the most effectual means of preserving peace." Almost two centuries later, Defense Secretary James R. Schlesinger, in an interview with *U. S. News & World Report*, said, "Military strength and peace go together. The abandonment of one will ultimately result in the loss of the other." Though the intervening years and the introduction of mass-destruction nuclear weapons have revolutionized military doctrine and strategy, American policymakers, like many athletic coaches, feel that the best defense is a good offense.

Post-World War II U. S. defense policy has been based on the concept of *deterrence*. Deterrence is the proposition that an enemy will never launch a nuclear attack on the U. S. as long as it knows that this country could absorb such an attack and in turn still be able to destroy the attacker with a counterstrike. Each side holds the other's populace as nuclear hostages in a tenuous "balance of terror." In the words of peace advocate Bertrand Russell, it is a shaky balance between "brinksmanship and surrender." This philosophy of deterrence has produced the frightening situation that writer Walter Pincus describes in these terms: "It is a functional truth of the nuclear arms competition that both the Soviet Union and the United States spend billions each year to produce and develop holocaustal weapons whose chief value to mankind is that they never be used."⁶

Two elements are essential if deterrence is to function effectively: one is the real capabilities of the contestants, and the other is the perception of those capabilities that makes a preemptive "first strike" for the other unthinkable—

neither side can ever be allowed to believe it can destroy the weapons the other side needs to retaliate. It logically follows as well that it is in no one's interest to take steps to reduce the other's confidence in his own retaliatory capacity. It becomes extremely important in this scenario for each side to have an accurate perception of the opposition's capabilities so that neither side will act precipitously because of miscalculation. Thus it becomes our own self-interest for the other side to have certain information about our capabilities, otherwise deterrrence won't work.

### Strategy

The big question facing American defense policy makers is what strategy will best achieve deterrence and maintain our national security. Choices must be made among weapons and strategies, and relative costs and effectiveness must be carefully weighed. The whole process becomes a sort of international chess game because each major power must shape its own policies not just in terms of its own objectives but also in anticipation of what others will do. Thus far, American and Soviet policies have followed somewhat different paths. U. S. policy has been based primarily on making war unthinkable by developing a capability for massive retaliation. It has been much cheaper to develop a good offense than to develop a strong defensive system. Soviet policy includes a strong civil defense system designed for survival and quick recovery from a nuclear attack. A study by the Boeing Corporation entitled "Industrial Survival and Recovery After a Nuclear Attack" claimed that 98 percent of the Soviet productive capacity could survive a nuclear attack, whereas in the U. S. it would take twelve years for productive capacity to be restored after a similar attack. This immediately led, of course, to demands from some for more U. S. emphasis on civil defense programs, and the Carter administration included more for civil defense in the 1979–80 defense budget. Representative Les Aspin (D.-Wis.) contends the effectiveness of Soviet civil defense has been greatly exaggerated. He maintains a U. S. nuclear strike could kill as many as 40 million Soviets and destroy as much as 60 percent of their industrial capacity.

Debates on appropriate military strategy for best ensuring American security have been as heated as they have been complex. During the Eisenhower years the doctrine was one of "massive retaliation" with emphasis on technological superiority and air-atomic power. It soon became apparent that this concept had only limited application and was not practical for fighting smaller scale, brushfire wars. Under Kennedy there was a return to the concept of "balanced" military forces, including special forces trained for guerrilla-type warfare. However, American military superiority still was based largely on technology rather than on conventional forces, and Vietnam revealed the vulnerability of this approach in a limited guerrilla-type war. The result of the Vietnam experience was not, however, a beefing-up of conventional forces, but rather a sort of withdrawal under the Nixon doctrine, with the pronouncement to nations threatened by aggression that they must assume primary responsibility for their own security. In the future, U. S.

aid would be limited to economic assistance and military supplies, and under some circumstances the provision of sea and air support. This approach is an outgrowth of two factors: one is the strong reluctance since the Vietnam experience to commit American troops abroad; and the other is the fact that for the U. S., manpower is a very costly item in the defense budget.

Since the maintenance of both conventional and nuclear forces is quite expensive and because of increasing emphasis on "more bang for the buck," American defense strategists are constantly looking for ways to use U. S. technological and nuclear capabilities on a limited scale. We cannot compete with the Soviets or the Chinese on a conventional basis, but in technology we hold an edge. The question is how to use this technology to its fullest advantage. Can nuclear weapons be used tactically to fight a "limited" war? Secretary of Defense Harold Brown told the House Defense Appropriations Subcommittee, "My own judgment is that once one starts to use nuclear weapons, even in a tactical way, it is quite likely that it will escalate." Arguments in support of the neutron bomb are that it could be used as a tactical weapon, but again the chances are that once nuclear weapons of any type are used, a confrontation would quickly escalate into an all-out nuclear war. Still, American policymakers continue to explore the possibilities of "tactical" uses of nuclear weapons on a limited basis.

World tensions growing out of the Iranian seizure of American hostages and the Soviet invasion of Afghanistan have brought a new look at American military posture. Current world tension and a revival of the Cold War have emphasized the need for stronger, more mobile conventional forces, according to many. Defense Secretary Harold Brown told Congress that the U. S. must improve its "ability to move with great power and speed on a world-wide basis." Brown cited a need for the ability to reinforce friends and allies with air and ground forces, but told the House Armed Services Committee, "We have never fully acquired the agility and the mobility required by such a reinforcement strategy." President Carter called for the development of a 100,000-man rapid deployment force that could quickly be moved anywhere in the world. Currently, however, the aircraft, ships, and support equipment for deploying such a force are either insufficient or still in the planning and development stages. President Carter also requested a 12 percent increase in the fiscal year 1981 defense budget, and that budget concentrated on improving U. S. ability to deploy troops worldwide.

### Arms Technology

The tenuous balance of deterrence is kept highly unstable by the constant state of flux in the weapons technology field. Currently, the second-strike capability of both of the major powers is sufficient to deter the other from attacking. However, when one side gains a weapon system it feels is dominant, the possibility of an attack is increased. With the current state of technology, each weapon system is replaced by a new one about every seven years. The almost constant state of international tension has touched off a spiraling weapons technology contest

146  MANAGEMENT POLICY

'...And It Only Kills People, Leaving All The Buildings, Museums And Churches Intact'

Engelhardt in the St. Louis Post-Dispatch.

between the superpowers. Because of the delicate balance of nuclear capabilities, each side feels it must match the other weapon for weapon. Thus Soviet Deputy Foreign Minister Kornienko told American visitor Fred Warner Neal, "If the United States insists on having a cruise missile, we will have it also. We don't want it, but if you have it we will follow suit. This would accelerate the arms race dangerously; we hope you will not force it on us."[7]

The cruise missile is a prime example of the state of advancement in weapons technology. It was not even discussed at negotiations leading to the 1974 Vladivostok agreement. Critics said the cruise missile was not needed by the U. S. and felt its development would only spur Soviet development, thus making the U. S. more vulnerable since our defense against such weapons is not as good as that of the Soviets. President Carter chose to go with the development of the cruise missile rather than the B-1 bomber, however.

Though leaders on both sides have for some time expressed grave concern with the proliferation of weapons, the arms race seems to have developed, as Secretary of Defense McNamara termed it, a "mad momentum" that leads us "hopelessly on to no sensible purpose on either side." Likewise, Soviet Politburo member Boris Ponomarev said of the arms build-up, "It is dangerous, stupid and terrible. We both have enough weapons to destroy each other and the rest of the world, no matter what."[8] While Secretary of State, Henry Kissinger observed:

> What in the name of God is strategic superiority? What is the significance of it, politically, militarily, operationally, at these levels of numbers? What do you do of it?
>
> Throughout history, increases in military power—however slight—could be turned into specific political advantage. With the overwhelming arsenals of the nuclear age, however, the pursuit of marginal advantage is both pointless and potentially suicidal. Once sufficiency is reached, additional increments of power do not translate into usable political strength.[9]

In December 1978, in a talk with students at Western Kentucky University, Vladimir Mikoyan, third secretary of the Soviet Embassy in Washington, told his audience, "It is high time for our people to realize that in this age of nuclear weapons there is no other alternative but to cooperate where we can ... to find answers to our mutual problems. We need to build bridges across the rivers, not alongside them."

This type of rhetoric, however, is balanced by statements from spokesmen on both sides who make equally clear the determination of each not to allow the other to gain the slightest advantage in weaponry. "We are the number-one nation," said LBJ, "and we are going to stay the number-one nation." George McGovern, a frequent advocate of cuts in defense spending, in his acceptance speech at the Democratic National Convention in 1972 stated, "America must never become a second-rate nation.... I give you my sacred pledge that if I become President of the United States, America will keep its defenses alert and fully sufficient to meet any danger." Addressing a joint session of Congress in 1972, President Nixon said, "No power on earth is stronger than the United States of America today. None will be stronger than the United States of America in the future." Paving the way for recommended increases in defense spending, President Carter in 1978 observed, "For more than a decade, the military power of the Soviet Union has steadily expanded, and it has grown consistently more sophisticated. In significant areas, the military lead we once enjoyed has been reduced."

On the other side the Soviets echo similar sentiments. In the annual review of the military in Red Square in Moscow, Soviet Defense Minister Dmitry F. Ustinov said the international situation was aggravated as the result of the striving by "aggressive imperialist circles to return the world to the cold war. They are whipping up the arms race, trying to achieve military superiority over the socialist countries and interfere in their internal affairs," he charged.

## 148  MANAGEMENT POLICY

What does being "number one" mean? Is it really necessary to be "number one" to be secure? Is numerical superiority essential in the maintenance of an effective deterrent force? Where does the steady build-up of arms finally end? While still secretary of defense, James Schlesinger admitted that "the capabilities at the levels...already reached are perhaps unnecessarily high." In 1974 the U. S. already had thirty-six nuclear warheads for every Russian city of 100,000 population or more. The USSR had eleven warheads for each American city of that size. In 1968 the U. S. and USSR combined had about 2600 nuclear warheads. Today the Soviets alone have more than that and together the two nations have 12,000 warheads plus thousands more so-called tactical nuclear weapons and bombs. Even with the signing of SALT I (Strategic Arms Limitation Treaty) in 1972, both the U. S. and USSR experienced increased military spending and new weapons have been developed, leading to efforts for a SALT II agreement imposing further limits. After months of negotiations a SALT II agreement was finally concluded in 1979, but was greeted by considerable questioning in the Senate where it would have to be ratified. While President Carter was trying to line up sufficient support to launch a ratification effort, the Russians occupied Afghanistan, reviving the Cold War and delaying any possibility of immediate ratification. In the absence of the SALT II agreement, both U. S. and Soviet defense spending will increase drastically. (Figure 6.2 shows a breakdown of U. S. and Soviet weapons revealed in the course of SALT II negotiations.)

Though the talk in recent years has shifted in some circles from "superiority" to "sufficiency" and "rough equivalency," the military is still quite successful in selling policymakers on the need for newer and more sophisticated weapons. The rapid technological change in the weapons field, combined with constantly perceived threats to our national security, provide a sort of built-in momentum for

### FIGURE 6.2  Breakdown of U.S.-Soviet Weapons

The United States and the Soviet Union attached to their strategic arms limitations agreement figures on the number of strategic offensive weapons they claimed they had. The figures, unverified by intelligence experts, were:

|  | U.S. | U.S.S.R. |
|---|---|---|
| Launchers of ICBMs | 1,054 | 1,398 |
| Fixed launchers of ICBMs | 1,054 | 1,398 |
| Launchers of ICBMs equipped with MIRVs | 550 | 608 |
| Launchers of SLBMs | 656 | 950 |
| Launchers of SLBMs equipped with MIRVs | 496 | 144 |
| Heavy bombers | 573 | 156 |
| Heavy bombers equipped for cruise missiles capable of a range in excess of 600 kilometers (372 miles) | 3 | 0 |
| Heavy bombers equipped only for ASBMs | 0 | 0 |
| ASBMs | 0 | 0 |
| ASBMs equipped with MIRVs | 0 | 0 |

(ICBMs are intercontinental ballistic missiles. MIRVs are multiple independently targeted re-entry vehicles, or multiple warheads on a single missile. SLBM refers to submarine-launched ballistic missiles. ASBM refers to air-to-surface ballistic missiles, a category that includes the American cruise missile.)

*Reprinted with permission of the Associated Press.*

the arms build-up, and in spite of considerable evidence that the U. S. still holds the edge, military alarmists are quite effective in playing on the constant fear of falling behind.

The London-based International Institute for Strategic Studies reported in 1976 that while Soviet warheads had greater destructive power, the U. S. held about a two-to-one edge in deliverable warheads. The U. S. also holds the edge in warhead technology and accuracy. A decade ago, U. S. missiles might come within a half-mile of their targets, while today they can hit within 200 yards of a target. Many U. S. missiles are armed with ten to fourteen warheads with each set for a different target. While both the USSR and the U. S. rely on the triad of land-based missiles, missile-firing submarines, and manned bombers, Russia's missile system is probably more vulnerable to "silo-busting" attack. Whereas land-based missiles provide only 25 percent of the U. S. capability, they represent about 75 percent of the Soviet capability, and because of its advanced warheads and their accuracy, the U. S. has the capability to destroy most of Russia's land-based missiles. Because survivability is an essential ingredient in a deterrent strike force and since the Soviets will not have comparable "silo-busting" capability until the mid-eighties, the U. S. currently holds an edge in this regard. The U. S. is already seeking to counter the Soviet missile-busting capability by developing the M-X ICBM system, which would provide the U. S. its own version of "Russian roulette." The U. S. would develop a system of multiple silos connected by tracks, and real and dummy missiles would be shuttled from silo to silo to confuse the targeting of any potential attacker. While some feel such an edge is absolutely essential to U. S. security, other observers fear that if the U. S. gains a substantial edge in weapons it could encourage rather than discourage a Soviet attack. Paul Warnke, former head of the U. S. Arms Control and Disarmament Agency, points out, "There is the temptation to strike first because you fear you won't be able to strike second."

Currently the official view is that the U. S. is in a position of rough parity with the Soviet Union in nuclear capability. Secretary of Defense Harold Brown told the House Armed Services Committee in February 1978 that "although both are heavyweights, I am confident that we remain the more agile of the two." He said the administration's objective was "deterrence and stability, not overbearing military power." Brown noted that projections to 1985 showed the U. S. keeping the lead in nuclear warheads. Nonetheless, some observers are concerned with the growth in Soviet arms and military expenditures and contend that the trend is against the U. S. They fear that unless the U. S. spends more and develops more weapons, the Soviets will gain superiority and use it as a form of blackmail.

The bottom line in the debate over defense policy then becomes a question of which is the best way to ensure our national security. Do we follow the more militant concept that the way to peace is through the expansion and diversification of our arsenal in the hope that no one will dare attack? Or is the road to peace through arms limitations and controls on the deployment of additional weapons? In other words, can peace best be ensured through ever-increasing armaments or through reductions in armaments? Some observers feel that current trends toward more and more armaments inevitably increase the likelihood of a nuclear war. Paul Warnke has said, "Unless we are able to control strategic nuclear arms, technological developments may decrease stability, increase the risk and bring us closer to nuclear war." Carl Friedrich von Weizacker, resident scholar at the Center for the Study of Democratic Institutions in Santa Barbara, predicts that "with continuing technical progress and the current world-political constellation, it is highly probable that there will be an atomic world war before the end of this century."[10] Such prospects lead many to emphasize the need to move quickly in the direction of arms limitations and efforts to prevent a nuclear war. Vice President Walter Mondale said, "There is an alarming danger that the number of nuclear powers will increase to the point that the possibility of nuclear war changes from *whether* to *when*." He went on to add, "We believe that arms control programs, in the long run, are just as important to our military security as our weapons programs."[11] A former military commander himself, Dwight Eisenhower observed:

> No matter how much we spend for arms, there is no safety in arms alone.... I have had a varied experience over a lifetime, and if I have learned anything, it is that there is no way in which a country can satisfy the craving for absolute security—but it can bankrupt itself, morally and economically, in attempting to reach that illusory goal through arms alone.[12]

Harvard political economist Thomas C. Schelling predicts that by the 1990s few if any countries will lack the technology and trained personnel to make nuclear weapons out of indigenously produced fissionable materials.[13] It is the prospect of such widespread nuclear proliferation that causes many policymakers to feel that the emphasis must be on policies and strategies to curb both the production and incentives to use such weapons.

## BUDGETING FOR DEFENSE

Eisenhower's statement touches on several other problems growing out of an arms race with which policymakers must come to grips. Huge military budgets can have a very negative effect on the nation's economy, and at best, military expenditures are a costly trade-off on domestic programs. Currently about 5 percent of the U. S. GNP goes for defense; 10 percent of our work force is employed in defense production; and about 25 percent of the national budget is spent for defense. While the Soviet Union and the U. S. rank one and two in defense expenditures, the U. S. is fourth in the world in terms of per capita expenditures on education and tenth in per capita expenditures on health. Stated another way, the cost of one heavy bomber is a modern brick schoolhouse in thirty cities, a single fighter plane equals the cost of a half million bushels of wheat, and a single destroyer compares to new homes for more than 8000 persons. These heavy defense expenditures prompted Eisenhower to observe, "This is not a way of life, it is humanity hanging from a cross of iron."

There are those on the other hand who feel that recent trends in U. S. defense spending have allowed the Soviets to put us at a disadvantage, especially in the area of weapons procurement. In May 1975 Defense Secretary James Schlesinger said, "What we cannot accept—what we cannot live with—is the trend of recent years in which the Soviets continue to increase strength while the United States continues to shrink."[14]

In 1945 defense expenditures accounted for 85 percent of the U. S. budget, in 1960 the figure was 59 percent, and currently the figure is about 25 percent. In the mid-1950s defense spending took about 13 percent of the GNP, by the 1960s it had declined to about 8 to 9 percent, and in the early 1970s was running about 6 percent. Currently defense spending takes about 5 percent of the GNP, the lowest since Pearl Harbor. Whereas in 1971–72 the U. S. defense budget, according to the International Institute for Strategic Studies, was larger than the combined defense budgets of all the communist countries, today U. S. and Soviet defense expenditures are about the same. For 1980 President Carter proposed a defense budget of $124 billion, an increase of 3 percent. The CIA estimates the Soviets spent about $130 billion on defense in 1979, and their defense spending has been growing at a rate of 4 to 5 percent annually. Our defense spending, on the other hand, in inflation-adjusted dollars has increased only about 5 percent over the last eighteen years. (See figure 6.3) What further concerns many observers is that a much smaller proportion of the U. S. defense budget goes for weapons than that of the Soviet budget. Because so much of the U. S. defense budget goes for personnel, the Soviets actually spend about 75 percent more on weapons than the U. S. Though U. S. defense budgets have steadily increased, outlays for weapons have actually declined by 24 percent over the last eighteen years.

Two major elements account for the large expenditures in the defense budget for personnel—the move to the all-volunteer army and the retirement system. In 1972 the draft was ended and the concept of a well-paid, all-volunteer army was adopted. The volunteer approach resulted in numerous problems and was much more costly than was anticipated. Personnel costs under the volunteer army soared. In 1966 the Selective Service System spent less than $300 per inductee while in the 1970s the volunteer army was costing about $1200 per enlistee. While the army has had trouble keeping enlistments at the desired level, costs have gone up. Annually the volunteer army has cost about $3 billion per year more than its draft-era counterpart, with costs for the first six years totalling $18.4 billion more than for the draft army. Besides the additional costs, other problems developed with the volunteer approach. Since many of those volunteering are doing so because they "couldn't find no other job" and only about one-half are high-school graduates, the army has had to change its training. Both volunteer rates and morale are low as well. In a 1978 documentary on the volunteer army, ABC television painted a rather gloomy picture of the army's state of readiness. This concern apparently is shared by many in the army as well, since in 1978 the Joint Chiefs of Staff, saying they felt the nation's system for mobilization was weak, recommended the revival of draft registration. President Carter did not act at that time,

**152** MANAGEMENT POLICY

**FIGURE 6.3   Relative Expenditures for Manpower and Weapons as Part of Total Defense Budget**

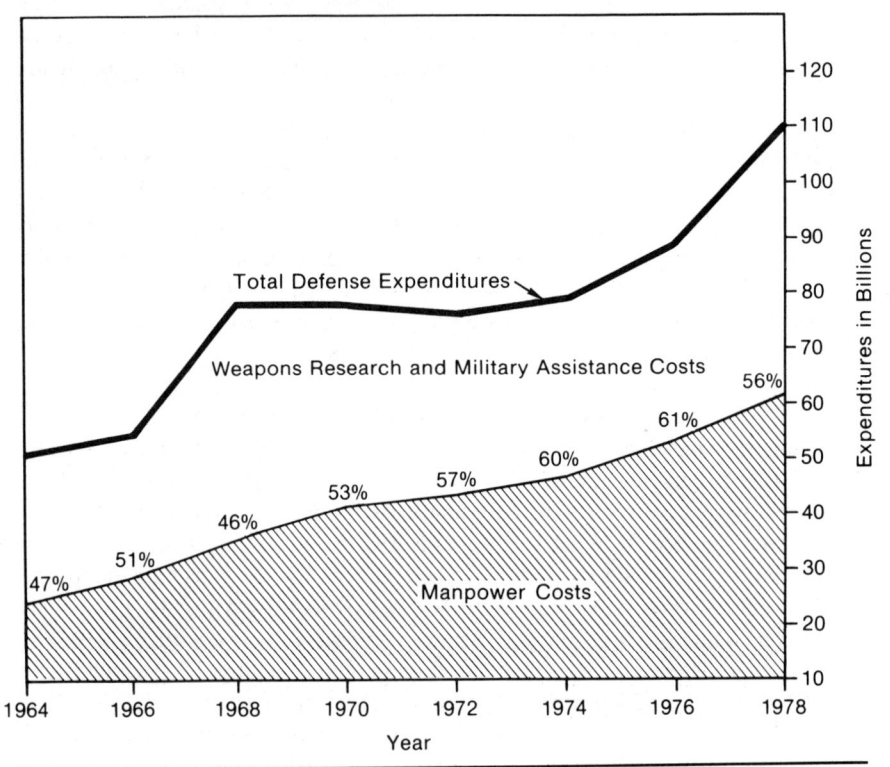

*[Graph showing Total Defense Expenditures rising from about $50 billion in 1964 to about $110 billion in 1978, with Manpower Costs as percentage of total: 47% (1964), 51% (1966), 46% (1968), 53% (1970), 57% (1972), 60% (1974), 61% (1976), 56% (1978). Weapons Research and Military Assistance Costs make up the remainder. Y-axis: Expenditures in Billions.]*

but when enlistments remained below the desired levels and tensions mounted in Iran and Afghanistan, the president called in his 1980 State of the Union Address for a revival of registration for the draft. In June 1980 Congress, after overcoming a filibuster in the Senate, passed a $13.3 million appropriation measure to finance revival of registration for the draft. Nineteen- and twenty-year-old males were required to register in 1980 and regular registration of eighteen year olds was to begin in 1981. Thus, if dissatisfaction with the volunteer approach continued to grow, costs to rise, and international tensions persist, the machinery was now in place for the reinstitution of the draft.

In 1965 a General Accounting Office study reported the nation had 462,000 military retirees drawing $1.4 billion annually in pensions. By 1977 these figures had grown to 1.2 million retirees drawing $9 billion in pensions. By 1982 the costs will be almost $14 billion and by the end of the century will have reached $35–38 billion. Senator Thomas Eagleton (D-Mo.) commented, "That kind of expense could sink the Pentagon." Under current provisions, officers are retiring at the average age of forty-six after twenty-four years of service and enlisted men at an average of forty-one after twenty-one years of service; however, some twenty-year retirees are leaving as early as age thirty-seven at one-half their basic pay for life. Many of these military retirees move into government jobs and become "double-dippers," drawing two salaries from the government. In 1975, 141,000 military retirees drawing pensions amounting to $958 million annually held civilian jobs as well. These figures included 78,124 retirees employed in the Department of Defense and thirty-two members of Congress drawing military pensions ranging from $41 to $1109 per month. In 1978 Charles J. Zwick was appointed to chair a Commission on Military Compensation. In its 207-page report, the commission proposed overhauling the military pension system, which it described as "expensive, inefficient" and "inequitable." The commission said $10 billion per year could be saved.

As noted earlier, the heavy expenditures in the U. S. defense budget on personnel make it difficult for the U. S. to compete with the Soviets on weapons procurement. Noting that manpower is an expensive item for the U. S., William Lind, an aide to Senator Gary Hart (D-Colo.), says the U. S. cannot compete with the Soviets and Chinese in terms of manpower. He says the U. S. must take advantage of the inherent strengths of our system by investing and depending more on technology.

These factors, coupled with a number of others, frequently result in decisions on defense spending being made on bases other than objective analysis of strategic considerations and cost benefits. Defense budget decisions are subject to intensive lobbying efforts both internally and externally. Each military service has its own bureaucracy with its particular objectives and each lobbies vigorously for its particular programs. Former Missouri Senator Stuart Symington, one-time secretary of the air force, said that part of the game at the Pentagon was vying for funds with the other branches of the military. "Everybody fights for their own team," he said; "you can't blame them for trying." In addition to the internal lobbying, Congress is also the object of tremendous pressures from competing defense contractors trying to sell them on the superiority of their particular product. The picture is further clouded by the fact that defense contracts are quite beneficial to the member of Congress's home state and district. A *Congressional Quarterly* study of fiscal year 1971 showed that on the Senate Armed Service Committee, eleven of sixteen members (69 percent) represented states in which Department of Defense outlays were the number-one source of federal expenditures, while on the House committee, twenty-five of the thirty-nine members (64 percent) represented districts in which DOD expenditures were the top source of federal spending.[15] The question asked may not be which alternative weapons systems will provide the most for the least money, but whose states and districts will benefit most; or not whether a particular system is really vital for national security, but what will be its benefits to local economies.

Technological change and Congress's lack of expertise in the weapons field may result in decisions which later prove to be costly misdirections. The U. S. spent billions on hardened silos for our ICBMs, only to decide that they are still vulnerable. The MIRV system was sold to Congress on the basis that it was needed to penetrate the thick Soviet ABM system, which ultimately failed to materialize.

## 154   MANAGEMENT POLICY

Currently being tested before going into production is the XM-1, 59-ton tank, costing over a million dollars per copy while at the same time weapons now in development may make the tank obsolete.

All of these factors come together to make decision-making in the defense realm a less than totally rational and scientific process. While the Congress is now more inclined to subject defense programs to more scrutiny and debate than in the past, the Pentagon can still count usually on their support and approval for its most important programs. A major reason for this is that many feel it is better to err in the direction of too much security rather than too little. In the words of former Chairman of the House Armed Services Committee Edward Hebert (D-Miss.), "In war they don't pay off for second place.... There's one bet and you've got to have the winner.... Money is no question. The yardstick should be necessity, not money."[16] Representative Les Aspin (D-Wis.), a frequent critic of defense spending, expressed the feelings of many members when he observed, "The weapons systems are complicated, people don't like to vote against defense measures, and there's always that lurking fear that there's some secret classified document which shows that this thing is really necessary and not just the pet project of some general."[17]

## ARMS SALES

Another element of U. S. defense policy that causes considerable concern for those who feel peace lies in the direction of limitations on the spread of arms, is the U. S. role as the principal source of armaments for the rest of the world. In the past, the U. S. referred to itself with considerable pride as the "arsenal of democracy." Today this is more a statement of fact than a boast and is cause for considerable concern to those who view the worldwide growth in arms with misgiving. Former Secretary of Defense Robert S. McNamara launched the U. S. as a world arms supplier when he set up an office of International Logistics Negotiations, the DOD's sales division, in 1961 and started a policy of aggressive marketing. Since then the DOD has used imaginative and aggressive salesmanship to sell our arms abroad and the U. S. has become the major supplier of arms to other countries. In 1968 the U. S. arms sales were $1.4 billion; in 1977 sales reached $11.3 billion and in 1978, $13.2 billion. For the last several years the U. S. has accounted for 30 to 40 percent of world arms sales. U. S. arms sales have several objectives. Like foreign economic assistance, arms sales have been a substantial element in support of U. S. foreign policy and national security objectives. In May 1977 President Carter announced that, "The United States will henceforth view arms transfers as an exceptional foreign policy implement, to be used only in instances where it can be clearly demonstrated that the transfer contributes to our national security interests."

In spite of Carter's pronouncement, other objectives seem to have come to play more of a role in U. S. arms sales. One of these of course is the profit motive; by selling arms abroad, the U. S. can help to pay the ever-increasing costs of its own weapons production. In this respect, the more sold abroad the more we can afford at home. Along somewhat the same line, this increased demand also helps the arms manufacturers stay geared up for production and therefore in better position to respond to emergencies. And finally there is the contention that if we don't provide the arms someone else will, and that by providing them we are in a better position to control the arms market. President Carter announced a ceiling of $8.43 billion on foreign arms sales for 1979. This did not include, however, sales to NATO countries, Japan, Australia, and New Zealand. The comparable ceiling for 1978 was $8.55 billion and total sales exceeded $13 billion. One Pentagon official estimates there are about $30 billion worth of arms in the sales pipeline at any one time. Carter made it clear that the U. S. will continue to use arms transfers to promote our security and that of our close allies. This means the U. S., which supplied about 39 percent of the world's arms in 1978, will continue to be a major supplier.

## CONCLUSION

The uncertain environment of tense international confrontations has assured United States commitment to defense, and the preservation of our national security has become an everyday, continuing task of American policymakers—a task of which they are well aware and to which they are strongly committed. President Carter has observed, "There is no way that I can cut down the ability of our nation to defend itself." While there is no lack of commitment to the task of preserving national security, there frequently is considerable disagreement among those shaping the policies as to how best to insure that objective. In recent years the preservation of national security has been one of the most perplexing and crucial problems with which the federal government has had to deal.

Adding to the complexity of decisions in this realm is the fact that national security is really much broader than mere physical defense of the country. It involves the implications of policy decisions for such things as the overall health of the economy and society, the morale of the populace, the state of technological development, and the industrial and agricultural productive capacities of the nation. There is also considerable potential in our system for conflicts between constitutional values of individual freedom and values associated with national defense and national security. How far do we go in the interest of security in placing limits on such First Amendment freedoms as speech, assembly, and press? How far do we go in accepting limits on "the public's right to know"? Who decides what information is kept secret? What criteria should be applied? What is national security? The potential for abuse is substantial. The Pentagon alone already has more than 1 million cubic feet of classified documents, the oldest being a 1912 contingency plan. In 1976 the executive branch classified 4.5 million documents. It is estimated that government files may contain possibly 100 million classified documents. During World War II, papers on the bow and arrow as a "silent, flashless weapon" were classified. What are the implications of such limits on access to information for effective public oversight and control? Ultimately, the question becomes what we have gained if in the interest of national security we sacrifice the basic concepts and values of our democratic system. Where is the proper balance between individual freedom and national security?

A further key to maintaining our national security is a high degree of correlation between our military policies and the realities of the international situation. The worldwide growth in military armaments is basically a reflection of international tensions. These tensions must somehow be reduced if arms are to be controlled. It becomes extremely difficult to reduce such tensions, however, when two countries are separated by such deep historical, ideological, and political differences as are the U. S. and the USSR. Senator Abraham Ribicoff (D-Conn.) noted these perplexing differences while touring the Soviet Union with a group of Senate colleagues in 1978. He observed of their meeting with Premier Kosygin:

> Out of it came the realization of how deeply people can feel about the same circumstances and facts and still reach opposite conclusions.
> The overriding tragedy is that there is such basic suspicion between the United States and the Soviet Union that it clouds the clarity that should exist between two great powers.[18]

This mutual suspicion and lack of understanding tends to undermine such policy efforts as detente and the SALT negotiations aimed at reducing international tensions and arms. Russian activities such as their involvement in Africa, the strengthening of Warsaw Pact forces, and their military occupation of Afghanistan tend to be viewed with alarm, as expressed by Senator Lloyd Bentsen, Jr., (D-Tex.) when he said, "There is a nagging feeling—and substantial evidence to support that feeling—that our partner in detente has taken us for a ride." The Russians, on the other hand, have difficulty understanding our undisciplined party system and a Congress not controlled by the president and his party. They fail to appreciate that for U. S. senators the SALT II treaty cannot be separated from such other issues as human rights, emigration, trade, Russian and Cuban involvement in Africa, and the Middle East. Soviet Premier Kosygin told a delegation of U. S. Senators visiting Moscow in 1978, "Don't tell me about the U. S. Senate. I know all about the U. S. Senate. A vote against SALT is a vote for war. And if you vote against it, the voters will turn you out of your office."[19] Yet President Carter, in efforts to gain support among senators for the SALT II treaty, had to take a harder line, announcing he would not cut the defense budget and would accelerate the development of two new missiles and neutron warheads. When the Soviets moved troops into Afghanistan in early 1980, the president had little choice but to withdraw SALT II from further consideration. This inability of each side to really understand the other makes it difficult to bridge the differences and to communicate effectively on mutual objectives.

Thus, the difficult task facing America's policymakers becomes that of devising policies that will indicate to the other side our resolve to deal effectively with their build-up, while at the same time demonstrating restraint on getting involved in a costly weapons race that would hamper further efforts toward arms control. This is a difficult policy tightrope to tread, but the future of the country and the world are in the balance. In the words of President John F. Kennedy,

> Peace takes more than words. It takes hard work and large-scale efforts. Above all, it takes a government which is organized for the

pursuit of peace as well as for the possibility of war, a government which has a program for disarmament as well as a program for arms.[20]

## Points to Ponder

Are current defense expenditures sufficient for maintaining our military security?

How do we include the military in the decision-making process yet insure civilian control over policymaking?

Is Congress an effective participant in defense policy making?

What is the appropriate role for the public in defense policy making?

Can a democracy withstand the threats to security from non-democratic sources and retain its democratic character?

## Notes

1. As quoted by Malcom Moos in "Clearly World Order Is One of the Four Pillars on Which the Center Is Founded," *Center Report* (October 1974), p. 6.
2. *Youngstown v Sawyer*, 343 U. S. 579.641 (1952).
3. Louis J. Halle, "Lessons of the Cuban Blunder," *New Republic*, CXLIV (June 5, 1961), pp. 13–17.
4. See Richard Snyder and Edgar Furniss, *American Foreign Policy: Formulation, Principles, and Programs* (New York: Holt, Rinehart & Winston, 1954).
5. Harold Lasswell, "Does the Garrison State Threaten Civil Rights?" *The Annals*, 275 (May 1951), p. 111.
6. Walter Pincus, "Man, the endangering species," Louisville, Ky. *Courier-Journal* (November 26, 1978), © *Washington Post*.
7. As quoted by Fred Warner Neal in "Report From the Kremlin," *World Issues*, (October/November 1976), p. 12.
8. *Ibid.*, p. 12.
9. Henry Kissinger, address at *Pacem in Terris III*, Washington, D. C. (October 1973), p. 5.
10. Carl Friedrich von Weizacker, "On the Avoidance of Atomic War," *World Issues* (Dec. 1976/Jan. 1977), p. 3.
11. Walter Mondale, "Excessive U. S. Arms Sales Must Stop," *World Issues* (Dec. 1976/Jan. 1977) pp. 22, 28.
12. Dwight Eisenhower as quoted by Congressional Quarterly in *The Power of the Pentagon* (Washington, D. C.: Congressional Quarterly Service, 1972), p. 2.
13. Thomas C. Schelling, "Who Will Have the Bomb?" *International Security* (Summer 1976).
14. James Schlesinger, interview, *U. S. News and World Report* (May 26, 1975).
15. Congressional Quarterly Service, *The Power of the Pentagon* (Washington, D. C.: Congressional Quarterly, 1972), p. 5.
16. *Ibid.*, pp. 5, 3.
17. *Ibid.*, p. 5.
18. Dan Fisher, "Senators leave Soviet Union with clearer view of differences," Louisville, Ky. *Courier-Journal*, (November 26, 1978), © 1978, Los Angeles Times. Reprinted by permission.
19. *Ibid.*

20. John F. Kennedy as quoted by Walter Mondale in "Excessive U. S. Arms Sales Must Stop," *World Issues* (Dec. 1976/Jan. 1977), p. 28.

## Suggestions for Further Reading

ALEXANDER, GEORGE and SMOKE, RICHARD. *Deterrence in American Foreign Policy: Theory and Practice.* New York: Columbia University Press, 1974.
BOSTON STUDY GROUP. *The Price of Defense: A New Strategy for Military Spending.* New York: Times Books, 1979.
CONGRESSIONAL QUARTERLY. *U.S. Defense Policy: Weapons, Strategy and Commitments.* Washington, D. C.: Congressional Quarterly, 1978.
COOPER, RICHARD, ed. *Defense Manpower Policy.* Santa Monica: Rand Corporation, 1980.
COOPER, RICHARD. *Military Manpower and the All-Volunteer Force.* Santa Monica: Rand Corporation, September 1977.
DAVIS, VINCENT. *The Admiral's Lobby.* Chapel Hill, N.C.: University of North Carolina Press, 1967.
DUNN, LEWIS and KAHN, HERMAN. *Trends in Nuclear Proliferation, 1975-1995.* New York: Hudson Institute, 1975.
HAUSER, WILLIAM. *America's Army in Crisis: A Study in Civil-Military Relations.* Baltimore: Johns Hopkins University, 1973.
HOXIE, GORDON. *Command Decision and the Presidency: A Study in National Security Policy.* New York: Readers Digest Press, 1977.
HUZAR, ELIAS. *The Purse and the Sword: Control of the Army by Congress Through Military Appropriations.* Ithaca, N.Y.: Cornell University Press, 1950.
IKLE, FRED, et al. "The All-Volunteer Force: Problem of Solution," *Commonsense* (Fall 1979), pp. 1–26.
KANTER, ARNOLD. *Defense Politics: A Budgetary Perspective.* Chicago: University of Chicago Press, 1979.
KNORR, KLAUS and TRAGER, FRANK, eds. *Economic Issues and National Security.* Lawrence, Kans.: Regents Press of Kansas, 1977.
KOISTINEN, PAUL. *The Military Industrial Complex.* New York: Praeger, 1979.
LASSWELL, HAROLD. "Does the Garrison State Threaten Civil Rights?" *Annals of the American Academy of Political and Social Sciences* 275 (May 1951), p. 111.
LONG, F. A. and RATHGENS, R. W. eds. *Arms, Defense Policy and Arms Control.* New York: Norton, 1976.
MORGAN, PATRICK. *Deterrence: A Conceptual Analysis.* Beverly Hills: Sage, 1979.
MOULTON, HARLAND. *From Superiority to Purity.* Westport, Conn.: Greenwood Press, 1973.
NEWHOUSE, JOHN. *Cold Dawn: The Story of SALT.* New York: Holt, Rinehart & Winston, 1973.
PERLMUTTER, AMOS and BENNETT, VALERIE. *The Political Influence of the Military.* New Haven, Conn.: Yale University Press, 1977.
RASKIN, MARCUS. *The Politics of National Security.* Boulder, Colo.: Westview Press, 1979.
ROHERTY, JAMES M. *Robert S. McNamara: A Study of the Security of Defense.* Miami, Fla.: University of Miami Press, 1970.
SARKESIAN, SAM. *The Military-Industrial Complex: A Reassessment.* Beverly Hills: Sage, 1979.
WOLFE, THOMAS. *The SALT Experience.* A Rand Corporation Research Study. Cambridge, Mass.: Ballinger, 1979.

# Part Three

# Subsidy Policies

In the preceding part we focused on policies on which there is rather general agreement that the federal government should exercise primary responsibility. In this part we move to a category of policy where there is considerable disagreement as to whether involvement of the federal government is desirable, and even more disagreement as to where, to what extent, and in what fashion the government should be involved. Federal subsidy policies frequently collide with strongly held traditional concepts of private enterprise and individual freedom of decision-making.

*Webster's New Collegiate Dictionary* defines *subsidy* generally as "any gift made by way of financial aid" and more specifically "a government grant to assist a private enterprise deemed advantageous to the public." That volume also defines the related term *subsidize* in this way: "To aid or promote as a private enterprise, with public money."

In spite of persistent and rather widespread philosophical opposition, the federal government has engaged in various subsidy programs almost from its inception. Early support was provided for education, canals, turnpikes, and other "internal improvements." While the Constitution does not grant specific powers in many areas where subsidies have been provided, it does charge the federal government with the responsibility for defense and promoting the "general welfare." As the nation has grown and diversified economically, federal involvement has increased as various enterprises have been deemed essential to continued economic growth and development, the security of the nation, and/or the health and stability of society and government generally. This federal involvement has grown to the point where syndicated columnist George Will writes of "today's subsidy society" in which "organized interests compete at bending public power for private purposes."

Because direct federal subsidization is much more rare than the relatively hidden indirect subsidies, the average citizen is little aware of the extent to which various sectors of the economy reap substantial benefits from special privileges granted through federal policies. A subsidy is rarely called that but is couched in such camouflaging language as "mail pay," "operating differential," or "construction grant." Consumers, upset with the high prices of foodstuffs, may complain about the government's price support program for farmers; but few are aware that their first-class postage rates help to subsidize publishers and bulk advertisers who use the U. S. mail at less than cost. Indirect subsidies may take a variety of forms: low interest loans, contracts, tax breaks, depreciation allowances. Mail contracts were used to subsidize the railroads, steamship lines, and later the airlines industry. The federal tax code allows businesses to depreciate equipment 20 to 30 percent faster than its "useful" life. The idea is that this subsidy will encourage investment and prompt manufacturers to keep plants up to date. For years petroleum companies were allowed a tax subsidy in the form of the 27 percent "depletion allowance," which enabled them to avoid paying taxes on this portion of their production, again on the pretext that this would encourage exploration and development of new petroleum resources. This allowance was reduced after the fuel crisis in the 1970s.

Tax subsidies to business and industry are quite common. Two prime examples are timber and paper companies and small petroleum refiners. The powerful timber lobby has been successful in having concessions enjoyed by few other industries written into the tax codes. Special tax exemptions on the sale of timber and logs have been on the books since 1944. Currently these provisions cost the federal government about $400 million annually in lost tax revenues. The contention is that these special tax provisions encourage better management and conservation of our timber resources. Because of these special considerations, the small handful of paper companies realize profits well above the average for corporations. A major special consideration is that while the corporate tax rate for most companies is about 48 percent, most paper companies have a much lower effective tax rate. By taking special deductions provided by Congress on their capital gains from timber sales, credits for foreign tax payments, investment tax credits, and accelerated depreciation allowances on machinery and equipment, the paper companies are able to reduce their tax liability substantially. In 1977 the Weyerhaeuser Corporation earned about $412 million and had taxable income of about $80 million. For the same year the Scott Paper Company reported worldwide profits of $109 million, but claimed on its tax return that the government owed it $12 million. Other large paper companies realize similar benefits.

Reaping similar subsidies are corporations benefitting from the government's "small refiner bias," which is aimed at helping small petroleum refiners compete with the larger petroleum companies. Critics contend that subsidizing such small operations, which could not compete otherwise, encourages inefficiency. Another questionable aspect of such subsidy programs is that the benefits may sometimes be misdirected. Realizing benefits under the small refiner bias are such familiar corporate names as Burlington Northern, Dow Chemical, Monsanto, and Tenneco. Because they have subsidiary small-refinery operations, these firms have received governmental subsidies of several million dollars. The airlines industry, which already benefits from investment tax credits and accelerated depreciation benefits, is currently seeking legislation that will levy a tax on airfares to provide a subsidy for modernization of the industry's equipment. Titled the Noisy Aircraft Revenue and Credit Act, the measure is being pushed on the grounds that the airlines need help to meet the 1985 deadline set by the FAA for complying with noise reduction standards. Chances for adoption have been reduced somewhat by a new round of fare increases by most airlines.

Business and industry are not the only beneficiaries of governmental subsidies. A 1970 law provides for payments to beekeepers whose bees are killed by federally registered pesticides. Since its inception, over $30 million has been disbursed to beekeepers, mostly in Washington, California, and Arizona, with one keeper alone getting $225,000 in 1974. When the OMB proposed to drop this program from the 1980 budget, it touched off a flurry of lobbying by the American Honey Producers Association and its friends in Congress. Among those friends is Representative Jamie Whitten, chairman of the House Appropriations Committee and its Agricultural Appropriations Subcommittee. Whitten responded to OMB's proposal with this ringing defense:

> Bees are so essential to our food supply and our standard of living. We have a very deep interest in seeing that beekeepers keep bees so that pollination of our crops can occur.
>
> It's hard for me to think of anything more important than bees, so we can eat and export our agricultural commodities.[1]

Funds for reimbursing beekeepers remained in the budget.

Since they provide special financial benefits, governmental subsidy policies involve some of the most heated controversies and intense political pressures in policymaking. The politics of subsidy policies is usually not partisan but is characterized by political accommodation, noninterference, and logrolling. A good example of the accommodation principle has been the use of the Food for Peace program to subsidize tobacco farmers for the past decade. When the program came up for renewal in 1978, Representative James Johnson (R-Colo.), proposed an amendment to drop tobacco and tobacco products from the program. Congressmen from Kentucky, North Carolina, Virginia, and other tobacco states launched an immediate counterattack. In the ensuing debate, Representative William Natcher (D-Ky.) reminded Johnson that as a member of the powerful House Appropriations Committee Natcher had pushed for emergency aid for drought-stricken Colorado and also pointed out that the sixteen tobacco states congressmen had "marched down the line" to assist sugar beet growers. Johnson's amendment was defeated 189 to 126.

Decisions on subsidy policies are characteristically made by small groups of policymakers, usually including congressional committees or subcommittees, administrative agencies, and interest groups directly affected. Because of the nature of the policies and the process, a rather intimate relationship frequently develops between the policymakers and those who seek such policies. Since it is the essence of subsidy policies to try to provide something for everyone, and because individual benefits themselves are almost always quite narrowly defined, direct confrontation among the benefit groups or between them and those who do not benefit from the policy is rather rare. Because of the close relationships that develop between the policymakers and the subsidy recipients, the beneficiaries have access lacked by the average citizen; therefore, subsidy policies are less subject than regulatory or redistributive policies to direct influence by ordinary citizens. In fact, most subsidy policies go largely unnoticed by the rank-and-file citizens.

In Part Three we will look at three areas where the government has been involved extensively as a subsidizer — in transportation, in agriculture, and in education. In considering these policy areas, the student should always be aware, as was pointed out earlier, that policy in any one area does not fit neatly into any particular category. Governmental policy in all the areas discussed in this part involves regulatory and redistributive aspects as well as subsidization. While this should be kept in mind by the reader, the material presented in Chapters 7–9 will emphasize the subsidy aspect of policy in these areas. Chapters in this part also illustrate other aspects of the policymaking process. Policies in the transportation and agricultural fields are good examples of policymaking by sub-governments, although in recent years, especially in agricultural policy, the sub-governments have had to share their dominant positions on occasion with consumer and public interest groups. Educational policy is a good example of interest group pluralism in policymaking, with a full range of groups from church and racial groups to professional education groups and general interest groups such as the AFL-CIO and Chamber of Commerce as active participants. Policies in all three areas, but particularly in transportation and education, illustrate the incremental approach to policymaking.

## Note

1. Jamie Whitten as quoted by Tim Clark in "Beekeepers and Tourists Alive and Well in Congress," *National Journal* (March 24, 1979), p. 490.

# 7

# Spanning the Continent: National Transportation Policy

Though the casual observer may tend to overlook the role of transportation, perhaps no other single economic function is more central to our nation's economic life and development. Accounting for almost 4 percent of the annual economic production, transportation is one of the country's major industries, whose activities touch the lives of virtually every citizen. Since they account for about 20 cents of every dollar spent, transportation costs are an important element in the prices of consumer goods purchased; a strike by the Teamsters Union or the longshoremen can virtually hamstring the national economy; and a shortage of rail cars can prevent the farmers' grain from reaching the market or the miners' coal from reaching the powerplants. Thus national transportation policy becomes a vital element in the nation's economic growth and development.

The role of the federal government in transportation policy is one of the oldest issues in American politics, dating almost from the inception of the government itself. Though the Constitution provides that the federal government maintain a system of post roads (Article I, Section 8) and in general charges it with national defense and promoting the general welfare, there were early differences as to just what the federal role should be in the development of what was generally termed "internal improvements." While some early legislation aided the construction of turnpikes and canals, questions were frequently raised regarding the constitutionality of large-scale federal involvement in such endeavors. The issue became tied up in the sectional political differences of the early 1800s.

Following the War of 1812, with the British threat largely removed from the West, attention shifted to internal improvement and development. In the West in particular, where the farmers were spending one-half to two-thirds of their profits transporting their goods to market, demands for better transportation began to grow. As a spokesman for western interests, Henry Clay in his "American System" called for a national program of internal improvements as a means of expanding the domestic market and reducing the United States' dependence upon overseas sources.

It was John C. Calhoun of South Carolina, however, who took the initiative to involve the federal government in a large-scale internal improvement program. Urging Congress to "bind the Republic together with a perfect system of roads and canals," Calhoun introduced a measure to create a permanent fund for internal improvements by setting aside $1.5 million of the bonus paid by the Bank of the United States and all future dividends from bank stock held by the federal government. In proposing this measure, Calhoun said the authority for such action could be drawn from the "general welfare" clause and the provision empowering Congress to establish post roads. Calhoun's bill passed the Congress, but in his last official act as president, Madison, who failed to buy Calhoun's broad interpretation of the "general welfare" clause, vetoed the measure. In his earlier annual message to Congress, Madison had recommended a federally subsidized network of roads and canals, but he felt a constitutional amendment was needed to provide the proper federal authority. His veto of the Calhoun bill was a heavy blow to the South and West and a damper on their economic growth and expansion.

In 1818 the House took action, declaring that Congress had the authority to appropriate money for building military roads and other land routes, canals, and improved natural waterways. Nevertheless, in 1822 President James Monroe vetoed a measure to fund the Cumberland Road, holding that Congress did not have the authority for construction. His veto was sustained by both houses. Again, Monroe recommended a national system of internal improvements based upon an appropriate amendment to the Constitution. Led by western interests, the demand for more and better internal transportation continued to grow, and in 1824 the General Survey Bill was passed, directing the president to make "surveys, plans and estimates of the routes of such roads and canals as he may deem of national importance." Though this measure did not call for the actual construction, it authorized the president to initiate surveys and estimates for roads and canals required for national military, commercial, or postal purposes. While the demand for more federal support grew, the constitutional issue persisted.

In the landmark case of *Gibbons* v *Ogden* in 1824 the Supreme Court did not directly address the issue of federal financing of roads and canals, but Chief Justice John Marshall, speaking for the Court, did include some pertinent views on the nature of federal authority. Speaking of the commerce clause Justice Marshall observed:

> The power over commerce, including navigation, was one of the primary objects for which the people of America adopted their government, and must have been contemplated in forming it. The convention

must have used the word in that sense (including intercourse among the states); because all have understood it in that sense, and the attempt to restrict it comes too late. . . .

The genius and character of the whole government seems to be that its action is to be applied to all the external concerns of the nation, and to those internal concerns which affect the States generally; but not to those which are completely within a particular State, which do not affect other States, and with which it is not necessary to interfere, for the purpose of executing some of the general powers of the government.[1]

While Marshall's broad constructionist views would eventually prevail, they did not immediately allay the constitutional concerns regarding internal improvements financed from the national treasury.

In his first annual message to Congress in December 1829, Andrew Jackson referred to the constitutional issues relative to federal financing of internal improvements. When a bill was introduced and passed authorizing a government subscription in stock of up to $150,000 in the Maysville, Washington, Paris and Lexington Turnpike Road Company to build a 60-mile turnpike in Kentucky, Jackson vetoed the measure on constitutional grounds. If federally subsidized roads and canals were felt desirable, he said, they should be sanctioned by a constitutional amendment. As president, however, Jackson generally supported internal improvements, and although he terminated sizeable federal expenditures on roads and canals, he allowed improvements of rivers and harbors.

Gradually the barriers of constitutional opposition were worn down and with the physical and economic growth of the South and West the demands for more and better transportation became overwhelming. Also, as the population continued to expand westward, more and more interest began to develop in a transcontinental railroad. The eastern merchants and manufacturers began to see the market potential of the growing western population, thus enhancing their interest in a better system of transportation and broadening the base of support for federal involvement.

## EARLY FEDERAL ROLE

As the national economy developed and as the nation's population increasingly moved westward, pressures for more and better means of transportation mounted. The turnpike movement was strong from the 1790s through the 1820s, and in spite of some constitutional questions, Congress started with legislation in 1806 providing funds for construction of highways leading westward. Notable among those aided was the Cumberland or Old National Road, which became a major artery in westward expansion. Though several internal improvement measures suffered presidential vetoes, the precedent was set quite early for federal subsidies to various segments of the transportation industry. Legislation adopted in 1824 provided funds for improvements of rivers and harbors, and assistance for canal construction was also provided by the federal government.

## Railroads

The coming of the railroad era brought a marked expansion of federal involvement in the transportation industry. For the last half of the nineteenth century railroads dominated the transport field. No other single industry has been more closely linked with the economic development of the nation than the railroads were during this period. They experienced a rise and decline of tragic proportions. Governmental policies relative to the railroads have also come complete circle—from heavy subsidization and encouragement, through stringent regulation, and back to heavy subsidization.

The first railroads were chartered in the United States in 1830, and early development was rather slow. Through the 1830s and 1840s the states provided support for railroads and canals, but federal support was limited. By 1840 the

---

**Major Transportation Measures**

**General Survey Act of 1824.** Provided for federal surveys for roads and canals.

**Act to Regulate Commerce of 1887.** Created the Interstate Commerce Commission and assigned it rate-making authority.

**Hepburn Act of 1906.** Amended the Interstate Commerce Act and expanded the ICC's rate-making authority.

**Mann-Elkins Act of 1910.** Expanded ICC's rate authority to include rate suspension authority.

**Federal Road Act of 1916.** This act and subsequent amendments provided federal assistance for highway construction.

**Shipping Act of 1916.** Provided federal assistance for an extensive domestic shipbuilding program.

**Transportation Act of 1920.** Introduced the concept of rates that would provide a "fair return" in ICC regulation of the railroads.

**Air Mail Act of 1925.** Authorized the Post Office Department to contract with private air carriers to deliver the mail.

**Jones-White Act of 1928.** Provided for loans to ship builders and mail contracts to subsidize maritime operators.

**Motor Carrier Act of 1935.** Provided for ICC authority over interstate motor carriers.

**Merchant Marine Act of 1936.** Provided federal assistance for the development of a domestic merchant fleet.

**Civil Aeronautics Act of 1938.** Established the Civil Aeronautics Board, with responsibility for the airlines industry.

country still had only 3328 miles of rail lines, mostly in the East. Early federal assistance to the railroads was in the form of indirect subsidies such as grants for rights-of-way, the use of timber and other materials from federal lands for construction, and refunds of the tariff levied on imported rails. As interest in the railroads grew, the federal government stepped up its efforts to encourage their expansion, especially in the West.

The 1840s marked the beginning of the land grant era in the federal government–railroad relationship, a period of heavy federal subsidy to encourage railroad construction and expansion. Starting rather modestly, the policy of land grants to rail corporations reached full swing in the 1850s and 1860s when millions of acres of federally owned lands were given to the railroads to help finance construction. For example, the Pacific Railroad Act of 1862 authorized the Union Pacific Railroad land grants of ten alternate sections per mile on both sides of its

---

**Major Transportation Measures (Cont.)**

**Transportation Act of 1940.** Included provisions aimed at eliminating "destructive" competition among the railroads.

**Federal Aid Highway Act of 1944.** This act and subsequent amendments greatly expanded federal financial support for highway construction.

**Federal Airport Act of 1946.** Provided federal matching funds for airport construction projects.

**Reed-Bullwinkle Act of 1948.** Exempted rate agreements among common carriers from antitrust provisions.

**Federal Aid Highway Act of 1956.** Authorized the biggest road-building program in U. S. history, including the beginning of the vast interstate highway system. Also established the federal Highway Trust Fund.

**Transportation Act of 1958.** Provided federal guarantees for extensive loans to railroads.

**Urban Mass Transportation Act of 1964.** Provided for increased federal assistance to urban mass transportation systems.

**Department of Transportation Act of 1966.** Created a cabinet-level Department of Transportation and consolidated a variety of federal transportation programs under its direction.

**Rail Passenger Service Act of 1970.** Created the National Railroad Passenger Corporation, or Amtrak.

**Federal Aid Highway Act of 1973.** Provided for the first time for highway trust funds to be used for mass transit projects as well as highway construction and maintenance.

entire road. Many similar grants were authorized for other lines, and by the end of the land grant era in the early 1870s, grants totalling 155,504,994 acres, almost the area of Texas, had been approved. In the end, only 131,350,534 acres were actually transferred; and while estimates vary, railroad land grants were probably worth at least $500 million. In addition to the land grants, federal assistance was also granted through long-term loans provided for railroad construction in 1866 legislation. Under provisions of this act, $64,623,512 was advanced to six companies building Pacific routes. These loans eventually were repaid with interest, some after federal suits.

As the railroads began to encounter heavy criticism in the 1870s and 1880s, especially from disgruntled farmers who felt rates were too high, federal subsidy policies began to be questioned. Under such public pressures, most direct subsidies were ended by the 1870s and the federal government began to move toward a policy of regulation rather than subsidy. Federal land grants to the railroads did no doubt turn choice lands over to the railroads, making them unavailable to homesteaders, and such policy probably in some instances encouraged the construction of rail lines in areas where profitable operation was not possible. On the other

---

### Important Departments and Agencies

**Department of Transportation (DOT).** Created as a cabinet-level department in 1966, the DOT has responsibility for a variety of programs that promote and regulate the transport industry.

**Interstate Commerce Commission (ICC).** Created in 1887, the ICC is the oldest of the independent regulatory commissions. It has responsibilities relating to the rail and trucking industries.

**Civil Aeronautics Board (CAB).** Established in 1938, the CAB is responsible for regulating the commercial airlines industry.

**Federal Maritime Commission (FMC).** The Maritime Commission has jurisdiction over the operations of commercial ocean-going shiplines.

**Federal Highway Administration.** The Federal Highway Administration is a division within the Department of Transportation whose most important function is the administration of the Highway Trust Fund.

**Urban Mass Transit Administration.** This administration is a division within DOT with responsibility over urban mass transit programs.

**National Railway Passenger Corporation.** Better known as Amtrak, this agency operates the rail passenger service of railroads in the U. S.

**Consolidated Rail Corporation.** Better known simply as ConRail, this agency was created in 1975 to operate a number of railroads that were experiencing severe financial difficulties.

hand, it is questionable whether in the absence of federal support, enough capital could have been attracted to construct the western roads at such an early date, and this would have meant a much slower rate of settlement and economic expansion of the West.

In the latter decades of the nineteenth century, federal policy toward the railroads came to focus almost exclusively on regulation and protection of the users. The adoption of the Interstate Commerce Act (1887), creating the Interstate Commerce Commission, the first of the so-called independent regulatory agencies, was largely in response to the public cry for federal regulation of the railroads. The Hepburn Act (1906) and the Mann-Elkins Act (1910) strengthened the regulatory role of the ICC. By the time of United States' involvement in World War I, the era of railroad expansion had ended. Facing the pressures of wartime transportation demands, President Woodrow Wilson issued a proclamation nationalizing the railroads, and during the war they were administered by the government. With the end of the war and the return of the railroads to their private owners, the industry was faced with numerous problems. Earlier financial excesses and over-building began to plague many of the railroads as they found themselves burdened with heavy investments in obsolete and worn-out equipment and unprofitable routes. Heavy fixed costs coupled with ICC regulations holding down rates and preventing the dropping of unprofitable routes made it difficult for the railroads to compete with the emerging trucking and airlines industries.

By the 1920s and 1930s the railroads were no longer the financial giants they had once been, able to dominate whole sections of the country with their financial power. Federal policy of the period began to reflect the changing structure in the transportation industry. While the Transportation Act of 1920 retained regulatory objectives, it also reflected a new attitude that the railroads themselves had to be protected from too severe competition. The ICC would still seek to protect shippers, but it would also have as objectives the protection of the railroads against rate wars among themselves and provision through ICC rate regulations of a "fair return" (5.5 percent) on their capital investment. Even this was not enough to remedy the sagging finances of the railroads, and the government moved back toward its earlier policy of subsidies to the rail industry. Legislation creating the Reconstruction Finance Corporation in 1932 provided for loans to aid temporary financing of the railroads. Between 1932 and 1954 loans of over $1 billion were approved.

Faced with growing competition from other carriers, rising operating costs, miles and miles of unprofitable routes, and deteriorating equipment, the railroads saw their share of national income and traffic continue to decline. (See figures 7.1 through 7.4) Increasing their rates in an effort to offset operating costs only made it more difficult for the railroads to compete with other carriers. From 1946 to 1952 rail rates increased 78.9 percent, and for the same period the motor carriers' share of traffic rose from 7.28 percent to 16.21 percent. As the financial decline of the railroads continued to make them the "sick man" of the transport industry, the

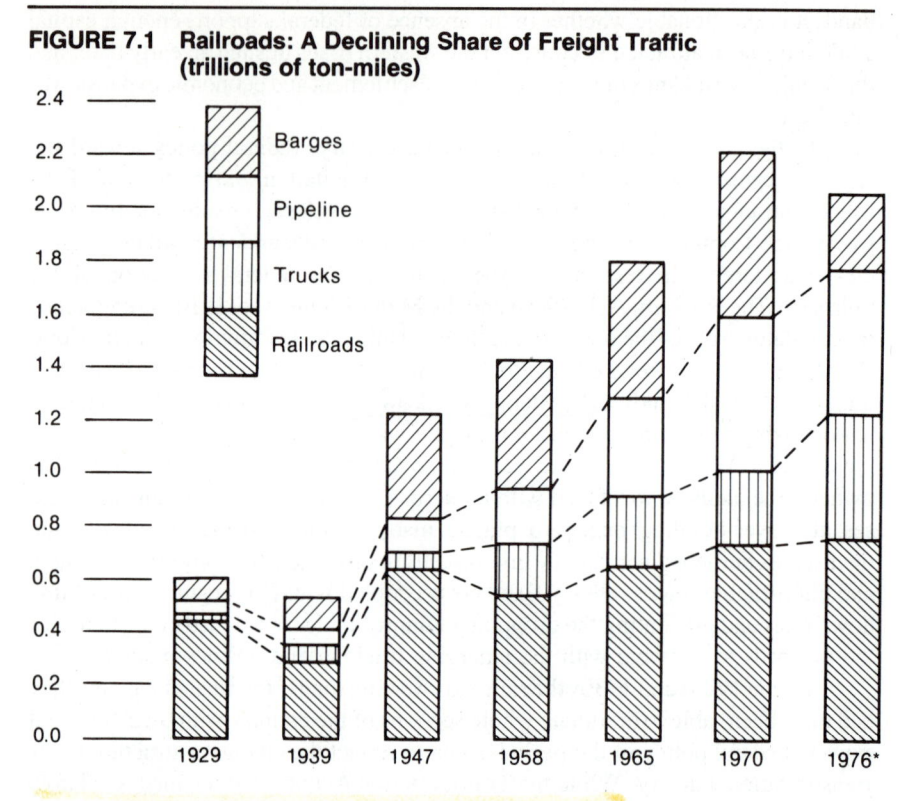

**FIGURE 7.1  Railroads: A Declining Share of Freight Traffic**
(trillions of ton-miles)

Source: Association of American Railroads.                    *Preliminary Estimates

federal government looked for ways to help them become more competitive with other carriers. The Transportation Act of 1958 included provisions for loan guarantees to the railroads to enable them to modernize their equipment, which in many cases was literally falling apart. Nationally the railroads were experiencing 7000 to 8000 derailments annually because of poor roadbeds and defective equipment.

Saddled with governmental regulations making effective competition difficult, too much track, too many workers, and severe management problems, the railroads' future continued to look bleak.[2] In 1970 the rail industry experienced its lowest point, earning its lowest income in twenty-five years, and several railroads were on the verge of economic collapse. Eastern railroads had deficits of over $200 million and the Penn Central Transportation Company, the nation's largest railroad serving sixteen states and seventy-two cities and providing 70 percent of the passenger and 20 percent of the freight service provided by rail, became the country's largest bankruptcy. With $3 billion in debts, the Penn was placed in receivership and the federal government advanced $100 million in loans to prop up the line. In 1973 the Penn Central trustees requested an additional $600 million in federal funds over four years, saying that with this help they could save the line by reducing the 80,000 workforce by 57,000 and abandoning unprofitable tracks. Only 11,000 of 19,864 miles were estimated to be profitable. The Penn trustees' appeal was rejected and with nationalization of the rail industry appearing as a distinct possibility, Congress appointed an independent agency to plan a general

**FIGURE 7.2   Intercity Freight Traffic in the United States[1]**
**(millions of ton-miles)**

| Year | Railroads[2] | Motor Trucks[3] | Great Lakes[4] | Rivers and Canals | Oil Pipelines | Air Carriers[5] | Total |
|---|---|---|---|---|---|---|---|
| 1929 | 454,800 | 19,689 | 97,322 | 8,661 | 26,900 | 3 | 607,375 |
| 1939 | 338,850 | 52,821 | 76,312 | 19,937 | 55,602 | 12 | 543,534 |
| 1950 | 596,940 | 172,860 | 111,687 | 51,657 | 129,175 | 318 | 1,062,637 |
| 1960 | 579,130 | 285,483 | 99,468 | 120,785 | 228,626 | 778 | 1,314,270 |
| 1965 | 708,700 | 359,218 | 109,609 | 152,812 | 306,393 | 1,910 | 1,638,642 |
| 1970 | 771,168 | 412,000 | 114,475 | 204,085 | 431,000 | 3,295 | 1,936,023 |
| 1975[6] | 759,000 | 454,000 | 99,171 | 243,039 | 507,300 | 3,731 | 2,066,241 |
| 1978[6] | 872,000 | 609,000 | 98,000 | 291,000 | 583,000 | 5,000 | 2,458,000 |

[1]Includes intercity freight traffic of private as well as contract and common carriers, except deep-sea coastwise and intercoastal traffic outside U. S. domestic waters.
[2]Freight ton-miles of line-haul railroads and electric railways—estimated allowance for mail and express excluded for years subsequent to 1969.
[3]Highway ton-miles, for both regulated and non-regulated trucks, include movements between cities and between rural areas and urban areas—rural to rural movements and city deliveries are omitted.
[4]Includes Canadian and overseas traffic on the Great Lakes.
[5]Domestic revenue service including freight, express, mail and excess baggage.
[6]These are preliminary estimates and are subject to frequent adjustments.
*Sources: ICC Annual Reports to Congress and Annual Reports of railroads (R-1) and Corps of Engineers, except that rail figures for 1977 and 1978 are partially estimated by AAR and air carrier data for 1974-1976 are from CAB reports. Data for 1977, except rail, Great Lakes and rivers and canals, and all 1978 figures, except rail, are estimated by Transport Association of America. Data provided by Association of American Railroads.*

**FIGURE 7.3   Rail Income: 1929-1977 (in thousands of dollars)**

| Year | United States | Eastern District | Southern District | Western District |
|---|---|---|---|---|
| 1929 | $896,807 | $486,978 | $ 73,059 | $336,769 |
| 1939 | 93,182 | 110,405 | 11,668 | ( 28,892) |
| 1951 | 693,176 | 234,970 | 110,703 | 347,503 |
| 1960 | 444,640 | 81,013 | 81,650 | 281,977 |
| 1965 | 814,629 | 243,767 | 124,175 | 446,687 |
| 1970 | 226,583 | ( 276,291) | 159,508 | 343,366 |
| 1975* | 144,362 | ( 345,291) | 189,278 | 300,375 |
| 1977* | 283,532 | ( 442,326) | 240,269 | 485,589 |

(Parentheses indicate deficit.)
*Includes provision for deferred taxes beginning in 1971 and equity in undistributed earnings of affiliated companies beginning in 1974.
*Source: Association of American Railroads*

reorganization of all freight service in the Northeast and Midwest.

A semi-nationalization of rail passenger service had already been implemented with the creation by Congress in 1970 of the National Railroad Passenger Corporation (Amtrak). Under the provisions of the Rail Passenger Service Act of 1970, Amtrak was set up as a for-profit corporation to take over the rail passenger service of those lines that wanted to get out of the passenger business. Many in the rail industry had maintained for some time that being required by the government to maintain unprofitable passenger service was a factor contributing to the economic hardships of the railroads. In spite of the fact that rail passenger service had declined dramatically, with the number of passenger trains dwindling from 20,000 per day in 1930 to 400 per day in 1970, some still viewed the rehabilitation of rail passenger service as a solution to several transportation problems, including the provision of an alternative to the energy-consuming automobile and a slowing of highway expansion, thus saving the environment. Under provisions of the 1970 act, the railroads technically continue to own and operate their trains and tracks, but to be relieved of their passenger responsibilities they pay Amtrak a fixed amount over a three-year period and bill Amtrak for the costs of running their passenger trains.

Amtrak started operations in 1971 with a $40 million federal grant and $100 million in federally guaranteed loans, plus any fees collected from participating railroads. Inheriting passenger lines whose roadbeds were in terrible state of disrepair, and rolling stock that was old and in many cases dangerously decrepit, inefficient to operate, and uncomfortable to travel on, Amtrak faced a tremendous task making income even match operating costs, much less show a profit. By October 1971, Amtrak had run out of money and Congress approved an additional $225 million for operating costs and another $100 million in loan guarantees. Although rail passenger traffic increased by over 10 percent during Amtrak's first year of operations, mounting operating costs continued to cause deficits. In 1972 the deficit was $152.3 million and for 1973, $124 million. While Amtrak's revenue improved steadily, growing from $137 million in 1972 to $311 million in 1977, operating costs increased at such a rate that passenger revenues still covered

**FIGURE 7.4  The Railroad Industry**

|  | 1929 | 1955 | 1977 |
|---|---|---|---|
| Employment | 1,660,850 | 1,058,216 | 501,390 |
| Rail lines (miles) | 249,433 | 220,670 | 191,205 |
| Freight |  |  |  |
| (thousands of tons) | 1,339,091 | 1,396,339 | 1,393,562 |
| (millions of ton miles) | 447,322 | 623,615 | 826,291 |
| Revenue (billions) | $4.8 | $8.5 | $18.9 |
| Profits (millions) | $896.8 | $927.1 | $283.5 |
| Net investment (billions) | $23.9 | $26.9 | $27.6 |
| Average annual |  |  |  |
| employee earnings | $1,743 | $4,719 | $18,396 |

Source: Association of American Railroads

only 37 percent of costs. Amtrak had gained a certain political popularity in Congress, however, that prevented executive cuts and vetoes of subsidy measures. Congress approved $154.3 million in 1974 and $200 million in 1975, plus an additional $25 million for the restoration of dilapidated terminals.

Continued operating deficits have increased the pressures to eliminate some of the less profitable of Amtrak's routes. Since 1971, federal subsidies to Amtrak have totalled more than $3 billion and federally guaranteed loans more than $1 billion. To reduce operating expenses, Secretary of Transportation Brock Adams proposed in 1978 to eliminate several of the less profitable routes. However, he made the mistake of including in the proposed cuts a line through Keysey, West Virginia, hometown of Harley O. Staggers, chairman of the House Committee on Interstate and Foreign Commerce. Chairman Staggers introduced legislation to postpone the cancellations and rallied other members who were not inclined to sit still for cancellations affecting their districts, even in the name of economy. The cancellations were postponed. In his budget message in January 1979, however, President Carter indicated the issue was still alive, asking for a 25 percent reduction in subsidies and declaring, "The nation can no longer afford the luxury of maintaining rail passenger trains that, on many routes, are little used." Shortly afterward, Secretary Brock Adams announced a plan to eliminate more than one-third of Amtrak's national system. He said such cutbacks were necessary to forestall deficits of up to $1 billion by 1984. The 1979 deficit was projected at about $600 million.

The administration's proposal to further reduce Amtrak routes touched off a widespread debate over rail passenger service. The government spokespersons pointed out that the sixteen trains and 12,000 miles of track to be eliminated served only 9 percent of Amtrak passengers and could save $1.4 billion in operating costs over the next five years. They pointed out that taxpayers were currently paying two-thirds of the average Amtrak passenger's ticket and contended that most Amtrak routes were served by other more popular and less costly modes of transportation. Opponents contended that Amtrak should be supported because it was an energy-efficient means of transportation. Ross Capon, executive director of the National Association of Railroad Passengers, said the proposed cutbacks would drive people to the most energy wasting forms of transportion, the plane and the automobile. When the gasoline shortages in 1979 caused people to flock to Amtrak, this bolstered the opponents' arguments. In May 1979, Amtrak turned away 756,000 passengers and in June over 1 million could not be accommodated. Congress decided the proposed cuts were too drastic and agreed to only about one-half (5000 miles) of them.

With this action both Congress and the administration still failed to come to grips with the real issue of what to do about rail passenger service. While Amtrak was given a partial reprieve, it continues to operate under impossible conditions. It has about 1200 passenger cars, more than half of which are over thirty years old, its roadbeds are in such sad state of disrepair that high-speed travel is risky, and the system is poorly managed. A decade of limited governmental effort and a generation or more of neglect by private owners have created a situation that will be quite costly to remedy. Thinking about Amtrak is colored by a widely held theory that rail travel is an expensive luxury that the federal government cannot afford to subsidize and that it has declined because there is no demand for it. Some feel that with our overdependence on the auto and the heavily subsidized federal highway system increasing our dependence on foreign oil, now is the time to consider other alternatives. Writing in the *Washington Monthly,* Deborah Baldwin says that nationwide rail passenger service is never going to be profitable and we should simply face that fact and keep it going anyway. She contends, "The government now subsidizes all major forms of transportation in one way or another, and rail travel is subsidized less than the other kinds, although its potential benefits are greater."[3]

Thus far payments to Amtrak have been small compared to appropriations from the Highway Trust Fund to support the federal highway system. (See figure 7.5) Consequently, if payments to support Amtrak are viewed as investments in a system of transportation that is less dependent on foreign oil, pollutes the environment less, and helps to unclog the nation's streets and highways, such expenditures may appear more justified. The question the policymakers ultimately have to face is whether there is a place in federal transportation policy for a system of rail passenger service.

Following the Amtrak pattern, the United States Railway Association, set up in 1973 to devise a plan for salvaging the operations of seven northeastern railroads, proposed in 1975 the creation of a privately operated government subsidized rail corporation. This corporation would take over the operation of the Penn Central, Ann Arbor, Boston and Maine, Central of New Jersey, Erie Lackawanna, Lehigh Valley, and Reading railroads. These roads served a region with 42 percent of the country's population and accounting for 50 percent of the country's industrial output. Congress, acting on the association's recommendation, adopted legislation creating the Consolidated Rail Corporation (ConRail). Representing the largest corporate reorganization in United States history, the federally subsidized ConRail took over the operation of 15,000 miles of track in seventeen states. Beginning operations in April 1976, ConRail was to become independent and operate at a profit by 1979, an objective not achieved. The legislation implementing ConRail provided for over $2 billion in start up costs for the new system. The bill included $1.5 billion in loan guarantees, $43.5 million to design the new system, $85 million to keep the existing roads running until the new system was operational, $250 million to pay benefits to employees who lost their jobs or salary in the reorganization, and $180 million for operating subsidies. Another $2 billion was provided for the improvement of track and facilities and to subsidize rail service on lines not included in the reorganization.

With the creation of Amtrak and ConRail, federal rail policy has returned to a program of heavy federal subsidies. The objective is to place the rail industry on a footing where it can compete effectively and function as a vital component of a national transportation system. Whether a policy of heavy subsidization alone will achieve this or not remains to be seen.

Considerable time and space have been devoted here to the railroads because for more than half a century the railroads were synonymous with transportation, and federal policy with regards to other segments of the transport industry has pretty closely followed the pattern established relative to the railroads. Each new mode of transportation as it has developed has faced certain unique problems, and the federal government in the interest of promoting national economic growth and development has responded with federal aid. While the aid may not have been distributed equitably, all segments of the transport industry have received aid in

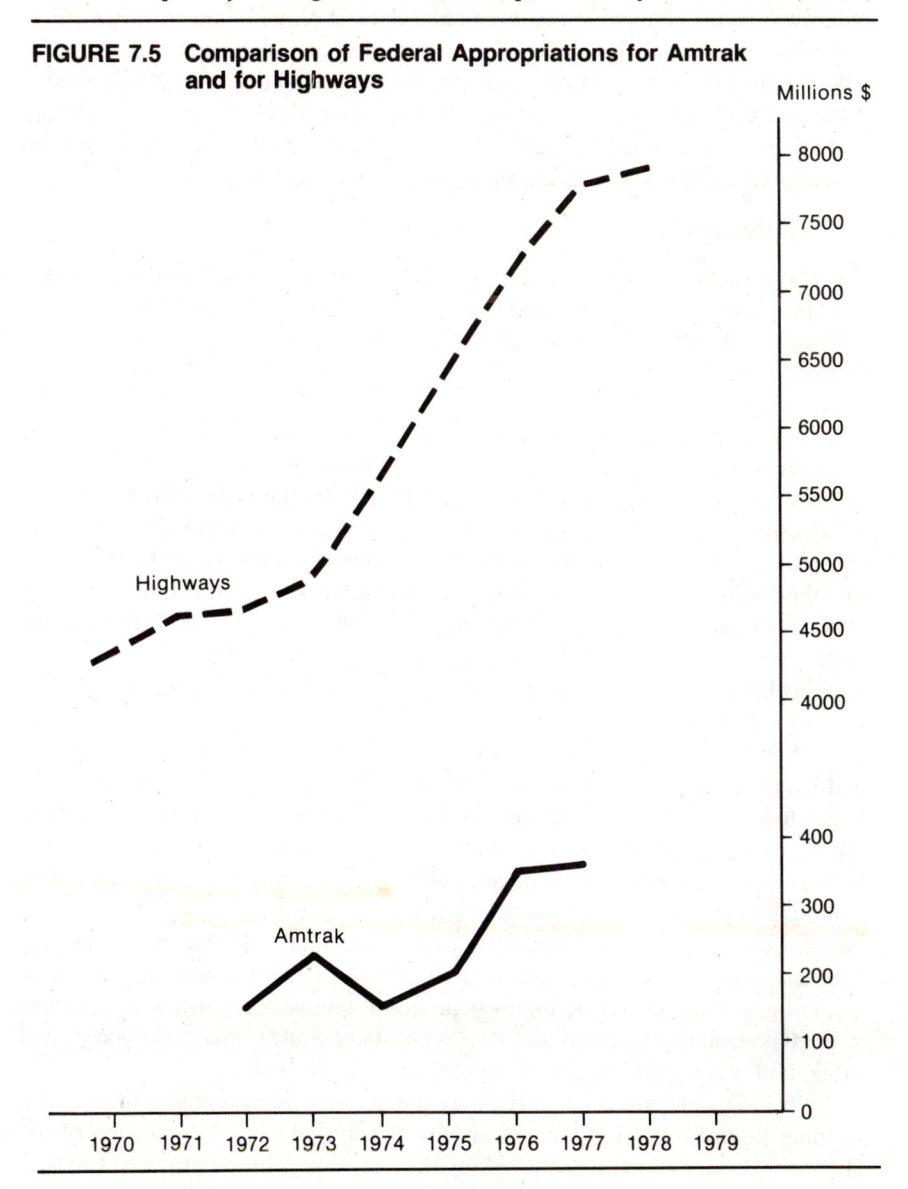

**FIGURE 7.5  Comparison of Federal Appropriations for Amtrak and for Highways**

one form or another. Railroads and highways benefited from rights-of-way and roadbed provision; airlines and ships from maps and charts, weather service, radio-navigational aids, airport construction, and the dredging of rivers and harbors; and motor carriers from highways built with federal tax dollars. While some subsidies go back to the nation's beginnings, technological developments of the twentieth century brought a sharp upsurge in federal subsidies as the government sought to promote a more diversified national transportation system. Governmental promotion of the various sectors of the transport industry was an outgrowth of the conviction that the public interest required the development or expansion of a particular mode of transportation at a particular period in our national development. As a consequence, the American taxpayers have invested billions of dollars in support of transportation, only to discover that the patchwork system that has emerged frequently does not provide the most desirable or most economical transportation in the right place at the right time.

## Highways

Highways were the first system of transportation to receive federal aid when funds were provided for the Cumberland Road in 1806. No great surge of roadbuilding followed, however, and it remained for the automobile at the turn of the century to dramatize the primitive nature of the country's roads and city streets. By 1900 various interest groups had begun to promote better highways, and in 1916 the federal government launched what would develop into one of its major grant-in-aid programs with the adoption of the Federal Road Act, authorizing $75 million for highway construction. This was followed in 1921 by the Federal Highway Act, which established the basic pattern for highway aid followed until 1956. Under this legislation, aid was distributed to the states one-third on the basis of population, one-third on the basis of area, and one-third on the basis of rural postal routes. Each state was required to match federal funds to qualify for the aid. Reflecting the dominance of rural interests in Congress, federal aid prior to 1934 was limited to a system of primary rural post roads. Only in 1934 was federal aid extended to cover urban roads as well.

As a national system of highways became a vital element in national defense and industrial and economic growth and development, support for expanded aid began to grow. In 1944 legislation was approved authorizing the development of the National System of Interstate and Defense Highways. This system was not fully launched, however, until passage of the Federal Aid Highway Act of 1956 authorized the largest roadbuilding program in American history. The 1956 act established the Federal Highway Trust Fund through taxes levied on gasoline and tires and authorized the expenditure of $31.5 billion over the next thirteen years. Under the current federal aid highway program, interstate highways are financed with 90 percent federal funds and 10 percent state, while primary, secondary and urban highways (ABC roads) are funded on a 50-50 basis.

In 1958 Congress adopted legislation to provide bonus funds to those states banning billboards along interstate rights-of-way, and in 1965 passage of the Highway Beautification Act pushed by Mrs. Lyndon Johnson provided funds to improve highway appearance. In 1976, the Highway Trust Fund provided over $7 billion in federal aid for highway construction, but the potent highway lobby was somewhat stunned when for the first time Congress adopted provisions setting a ceiling of $7.2 billion on the amount of funds that could be spent from the fund in any one year. Such federal subsidies have enabled the states to build a massive network of highways linking all parts of the country and have had substantial impact on population patterns and national transportation priorities.

Through the grant-in-aid highway program, Washington left the nation's cities and states no real alternatives to highway and expressway construction programs. Comparable funding for rail, subway, bus, or other transit systems simply was not available. It was either build highways and expressways or lose out on federal funding, so our vast network of highways was built. This system has made our cities not only more accessible to each other but to the vast suburbs surrounding them. The system of expressways and beltlines has devitalized the old inner cities by accelerating the move to the suburbs of the middle class and business, contributing to a declining urban tax base and the problems of urban sprawl. This vast highway system has also made America a nation of automobile addicts with 80 percent of all households owning one or more cars and with private autos accounting for one-third of the oil consumed. The emphasis on highway building contributed to the neglect of public transportation systems that are much more energy efficient, pollute less, and create fewer traffic problems. Recent concern for energy conservation has focused much more attention on mass transit systems.

## Urban Mass Transit

As is true with most subsidy policies, all this building of federal highways has not occurred without disagreements and political pulling and tugging. With the establishment of the Highway Trust Fund in 1956, an ongoing battle developed between the highway and mass transit proponents over the use of highway trust funds. From its inception, urban legislators sought either to kill the Highway Trust Fund or open it up for tapping by mass transit programs. In 1964 mass transit proponents were able to secure passage of the Urban Mass Transportation Act authorizing $375 million in grants and loans for construction and improvement of the services, equipment, and facilities for mass transportation. Mass transit supporters still had their eyes on the trust fund, however, and their growing numbers in Congress, coupled with increasing concern for energy conservation, helped them get provisions adopted in 1973 and 1976 legislation that opened up the Highway Trust Fund to provide some support for urban mass transit. Until passage of the 1973 legislation, the sanctity of the Highway Trust Fund had been carefully and successfully guarded by the highway interests. The 1973 act made trust fund monies available for urban bus and rail projects, and for the first time this increase provided funding to urban areas equal to that allotted rural areas. Both the 1973 and 1976 measures shifted funds from support for rural roads to urban roads. With the energy crisis strengthening their case, the mass transit supporters were also able to persuade Congress to pass 1974 legislation authorizing $11.9 billion over six years to help mass transit systems meet increasing operating and capital expenses. This marked the federal government's biggest commitment to mass transit compared to the highway program and was the first time federal funds had been authorized for operating subsidies rather than capital outlay. Mass transit proponents were also encouraged by President Carter's indication that a portion of the funds from the windfall profits tax on petroleum would go for mass transit.

Continuing concern with reducing U. S. dependence on foreign oil imports led Congress to increase the amounts authorized for mass transit systems in the 1980 budget as well. Spending for construction was increased about 50 percent while operating costs were increased by about 6 percent per year for the next five years.

### Airlines

Like other segments of the transportation industry, the airlines faced substantial financial difficulty in their early stages. In fact, in the period following World War I commercial aviation showed little likelihood of succeeding without outside assistance. The federal government first provided assistance under the Air Mail Act of 1925, through which it subsidized the airlines by overpayments on mail contracts. After 1934, airmail payments were progressively reduced but other subsidies were provided in their place. The 1938 Civil Aeronautics Act created the Civil Aeronautics Board with broad responsibility for the "encouragement and development" of civil aviation. Through the Federal Airport Act of 1946, which provides federal matching grants to states and municipalities for airport construction, the federal government has aided the development of a nationwide system of public airports. Even beyond construction, airports are heavily subsidized through the charts, weather reports, radio-navigational aids, and other related services provided by public agencies.

In spite of heavy federal subsidies amounting to approximately $1 billion for airport construction since 1947 and $1.5 billion in payments to assure a "fair return on investments" since 1939, some airlines, like the railroads, were experiencing financial difficulties in the early 1970s. Even though passenger airmiles had doubled between 1955 and 1963, rising fuel costs, declining foreign travel by Americans, and stiff competition from subsidized foreign airlines had placed some American lines in financial difficulty. Pan Am requested federal assistance to the tune of $10.2 million a month to make it competitive. Congress turned them down, but passed legislation aimed at putting U. S. airlines operating internationally on an equal financial footing with their foreign competitors. Congress also increased its appropriations from the Airport and Airway Trust Fund supported by taxes on airlines tickets and other aviation revenues. In 1973 Congress authorized $310 million in airport development grants and raised from 50 percent to 75 percent the federal share of airport construction costs. In 1976 Congress further increased federal aid to airports and for the first time approved the use of trust fund monies for airport maintenance and operating costs. With the deregulation of the airlines and increases in passenger use, many airlines showed substantial gains in profits in 1978 and 1979. If this trend continues, heavy subsidies to the airlines may come under closer scrutiny, especially such proposals as one to help the airlines meet noise abatement requirements through large tax incentives.

Current regulations require that the airlines meet federal standards on noise pollution by 1985. This would require either installing noise-reducing equipment on many jets currently in use or replacing them. Claiming unique hardships, the airlines industry asked Congress to divert funds from the Airport and Airway Trust Fund to help them meet the noise standards. Legislation was introduced in the 96th Congress that would have provided about $3.3 billion in subsidies to help the airlines bring their jets into compliance with federal noise standards. However, with the airlines enjoying a banner year as a result of deregulation and increased passenger traffic—profits of $800 million for 1978—many began to question the need for the proposed subsidy. Ralph Nader's group, Public Citizen, Inc., charged that the airlines were using the noise abatement issue as a "subterfuge to underwrite a new jet fleet at taxpayer expense." Many opponents saw this proposal as a dangerous precedent that could bring a whole line of industries to Congress pleading for help to comply with federal environmental standards. Congress adjourned without acting on the subsidy bill.

### Water Carriers

The vast majority of facilities used by the water transport industry have been developed or improved through governmental efforts. The dredging and improvement of rivers and harbors, construction of canals and port facilities, and provision of various navigational aids at the taxpayers' expense have been a great benefit to water carriers. Barge operators in particular have long benefited from free use of the inland waterways system built and maintained by the U. S. Army Corps of Engineers with public funds. Like the airlines and railroads, maritime shippers have also been subsidized through U. S. mail contracts. The Jones-White Act of 1928 provided both loans for shipbuilding and mail subsidies. By 1937, $176 million had been paid the industry in mail subsidies. The Merchant Marine Act of 1936 provided assistance for construction and operating expenses through low-interest construction loans and subsidy payments to offset the advantages of low-cost foreign competitors. Between 1936 and 1963 over $2.2 billion in such subsidies had been distributed among various commercial shipping operations. In recent years construction subsidies have run about $100 million annually, providing about 55 percent of ship construction costs, and the government has provided another $200 million annually in operating subsidies.

In more recent years some sources have begun to question the effect of federal subsidies on the industry. Critics charge that the heavy subsidies have resulted in governmental interference in operating decisions and have contributed to poor management generally. They contend there is little incentive to cut operating costs and increase profits because such efforts will reduce federal subsidies received. The critics view the subsidies as a damper on innovation and more efficient management. In a 1960 study the National Academy of Sciences concluded that "the subsidy system as it now stands, is actually hindering maritime progress."[4]

Both Presidents Kennedy and Johnson called for reductions in the subsidies to maritime operators but met with little success. President Johnson's appointee to head the Maritime Administration, Nicholas Johnson, called for reforms in the industry, urging more automation, more competition, and the construction of more ships in foreign shipyards. Both maritime management and the powerful maritime unions were threatened by Johnson's proposals and screamed for his scalp. The maritime unions have numerous supporters in Congress and the subsidized shiplines belong to the powerful and well-financed Committee of American Steamship Lines ("Castle"). Encountering vigorous opposition, Johnson was transferred by the president in 1966 to membership on the Federal Communications Commission, testimony to the political influence of the maritime lobby.

In the past, Congress had routinely approved annual renewal of programs benefiting water carriers. By the mid-1970s questions began to arise as to whether such subsidies resulted in unfair advantages for some segments of the transport industry. For decades, barges, which are the least expensive of the major freight carriers, had used the federally maintained inland waterways free. In 1975 the Department of Transportation proposed that they be charged a users fee to be collected either in the form of taxes or a toll. In 1976 such a provision was dropped from a bill reported to the floor by the Senate Public Works Committee, but support for such fees continued to grow. Finally, after a heated congressional debate, Senator Russell Long (D-La.) forged a compromise on the users fee in the 96th Congress. While the original proposal called for users fees to cover all inland waterway maintenance costs and half of any new construction costs, Long's compromise provides for a phased-in fuel tax, starting at 4 cents per gallon in 1980 and rising to a maximum of 10 cents in 1985. The revenue goes into a trust fund for new construction. Also in 1976, subsidies to maritime carriers came under the close scrutiny of the Anti-trust Division of the Justice Department, which felt such subsidies might be impeding competition in the transport industry. More and more when transport subsidies are being considered, a critical issue raised is how much of the cost of facilities and operation should be borne by the particular industry group. As the federal government moves more toward a system in which the various segments of the industry compete among themselves and with one another on their own, subsidies may come under much closer scrutiny than in the past.

## THE POLITICS OF TRANSPORT POLICY

Since the transportation industry is really not a single industry but several industries with substantially different and often conflicting interests, federal policymakers often face a confusing variety of policy demands. The railroads, truck lines, bus companies, airlines, and barge and shipping lines have different interests and frequently seek very different responses from government. As is often true with policies of subsidy, economic considerations are usually the essence of transportation politics. Transportation policy is a prime example of incremental policymaking, as new policies have simply been added on with the emergence of new technologies and new modes of transportation. Little effort has been made to look at the overall industry picture and develop a coordinated policy incorporating all the different modes of transportation. One of the reasons for this is that transportation policy has been largely shaped by a series of sub-governments developing around each mode of transportation. These coalitions of congressional committees, federal agencies, and transport groups have tended to focus on that segment of the industry of immediate concern to them and direct little or no attention to the rest. The result has been a highly specialized and fragmented approach to policymaking.

Also, because of the variety of transport carriers and the far-ranging effects of the industry, transportation policy involves a wide range of interest groups. Each major carrier is represented by various organizations and these are joined by a host of satellite groups with special interest in transport policy. Principal spokesman for the railroads is the Association of American Railroads (AAR), founded in 1934 and including in its membership railroads accounting for 97 percent of the rail business in North America. On the political scene the AAR *is* the railroad industry. Organized in 1933 and speaking for the interstate trucking lines is the American Trucking Association, Inc. Representing the scheduled airlines is the Air Transport Association; and water carriers are heard through the American Waterways Operators. This only begins to scratch the surface of those groups seeking to influence transport policy, however. Add to the list other such groups as the American Automobile Association, the American Road Builders Association, the Highway Users Federation for Safety and Mobility, the American Association of State Highway and Transportation Officials, the Transport Association of America, the Committee of American Steamship Lines, the Teamsters Union, the railroad brotherhoods, the maritime unions, and a whole list of shipper and supplier groups as well as consumer and environmental groups. The policymakers don't have to look far for advice and the pressures are frequently intense and confusing. Some of the major groups such as the AAR, the ATA, and the Transport Association of America report annual lobbying expenditures in excess of $50,000 each, which represents only a portion of their total expenditures to influence public policy decisions.

The issues of transportation politics reflect the highly fragmented nature of the transport industry and heavy dependence of the various segments upon governmental policies for their economic well-being. In any discussion of transportation policy, one of the first issues to arise is that of public assistance to carriers for their roadbeds and facilities. In pressing their case, the railroads have complained that many of their financial problems stem from having to compete with other carriers who are subsidized by the government—truckers who use federal highways and airlines who use airports built largely with federal funds. Because many fear that heavy truck usage causes more rapid deterioration of the highways, the feeling is growing that trucks should pay more in taxes. Currently, auto drivers provide about 57 percent of the revenues that go into the Highway Trust Fund, and trucks and buses provide the remainder. In 1974 truck weight limits were increased from 73,000 pounds to 80,000 pounds, and an Illinois Highway Department Study says the increased truck weights further reduce highway life. In opposing higher taxes, the ATA points out that trucks represent only 18 percent of all registered vehicles and that evidence that increased truck weights speed highway wear is inconclusive. With the imposition of users fees on barge lines and hearings on increased tax levies for truckers, it appears that Congress is moving gradually toward making carriers pay a larger share of the cost of their roadbeds and operating facilities.

While the primary focus in this chapter has been on subsidy policy, it is virtually impossible to talk about transportation politics without discussing federal regulation. Often in the transport field, federal regulatory policies have had substantial bearing on subsidy policies as well. Many observers feel that the current necessity for large subsidies to the rail industry to try to revive it was brought about at least in part by federal regulatory policies. The railroads were not allowed to charge rates that enabled them to adequately maintain their equipment and were prevented from dropping routes that were unprofitable. Speaking to the Midwest Governor's Conference in 1978, Robert Gallamore, deputy administrator of the Federal Railroad Administration, said that one problem with the railroads was that "the government requires railroads to provide service whether it is profitable or not, while the other carriers choose only the most profitable business." Explaining his department's concern with excessive rail regulations, Secretary of Transportation Brock Adams said, "Many government policies were developed when the railroads were the dominant mode—a circumstance which is no longer the case." On another occasion he observed of the nation's railroads, "That industry is sinking rapidly and we've got to free it from a lot of that regulation and let it try to adapt to the modern economics of the country. If they cannot adjust into the marketplace, then the federal government is going to have to spend more and more money just supporting essential rail services."

Many observers feel that past ICC policies regulated the railroads, motor carriers, and water carriers in a manner calculated to prevent competition among them that could benefit shippers and consumers and save millions of dollars in transport costs. Under current ICC regulations new entries into the interstate trucking or rail industries are virtually nonexistent and the ICC prescribes the routes carriers travel and the commodities they carry. Regulations of the trucking industry in particular have come under fire for discouraging competition, sanctioning price-fixing by trucking "rate bureaus," and forcing carriers to follow less-direct, fuel-wasting routes, often with empty trucks. The ICC itself estimates that trucks are empty 20 percent of the time under current regulations. Brock Adams's successor as secretary of transportation, Neil Goldschmidt, pushed for regulatory reforms that would reduce antitrust immunity and allow more price responsiveness, allow abandonment of unprofitable lines and ease access for new companies, speed merger procedures and ease the expansion of existing companies. He pushed regulatory policies that will foster more competition than do arbitrarily fixed rates.

In March 1979 President Carter proposed a plan for deregulation of the rail industry, noting that the railroads were "caught in the squeeze between tight regulation . . . and increased competition." The president said deregulation was the only viable option to either massive increases in subsidies or increased governmental involvement in railroad operations. Carter's proposal would allow the railroads to drop up to 20 percent of their current lines as unprofitable and to substantially increase rates on the profitable ones. Such proposals generate opposition from farmers, mine operators, unions, local officials, and many members of Congress whose constituents would pay higher rates. The AAR endorsed part of the Carter proposal. Fear of further increases in subsidies to the industry may generate support for deregulation.

Senator Ted Kennedy and the Carter administration proposed legislation to deregulate the trucking industry also. Provisions of the 1948 Reed-Bullwinkle Act exempt the trucking industry from anti-trust laws and allow them to meet and set freight rates. Charging that this "legalized price-fixing in the regulated trucking industry has cost shippers and consumers billions of dollars in higher prices over the last thirty years," Kennedy said deregulation could save consumers as much as $2 billion per year and President Carter said savings could reach $5 billion annually. Currently about 44 percent of the trucking industry, 16,000 firms, are regulated. In 1978 the nation's eight largest trucking firms reported earnings averaging better than 20 percent return on their investment. Already the battle lines are being drawn on deregulation: the currently unregulated carriers favor deregulation, while the American Trucking Association, Inc. and the Teamsters Union have indicated their opposition. Two Chicago trucking attorneys have formed a lobby (ACT) specifically to oppose deregulation. Supporters of deregulation contend it will foster lower prices and better service for freight shippers. Because deregulation involves uncertainties for those in the industry, many who are comfortable with current competition prefer the status quo. Many transport executives contend that current anticompetitive rules are essential to stability in the transport industry. They contend that removal of the regulations will lead to cutthroat competition, bankruptcies, and concentration of the industry in a few companies. They also contend that deregulation will leave many smaller communities without service as operators will seek the more profitable larger volume routes. Industry interests are now counting on the congressional committees, where they have numerous friends, to produce modest deregulation legislation that will head off more radical moves by the ICC. The ICC shows a growing inclination to deregulate significantly by itself, a move the industry wants to prevent if possible.

From the time of its creation in 1956 with the primary objective of funding construction of the 42,500-mile interstate system, the Highway Trust Fund has been a bone of political contention between urban and rural interests. Considered by the highway lobby to be its exclusive domain, the trust fund for years was used almost completely for funding highway construction in spite of repeated efforts on the part of urban interests to open the fund to urban mass transit uses. Finally, with the interstate system fast approaching completion and the numbers of urban representatives substantially increased, Congress did act to make the distribution of highway trust funds more equitable between rural and urban roads with changes in the law in 1973 and again in 1976. However, the proponents of urban mass transit rather quickly discovered that their victory was somewhat hollow. Even though the new legislation permitted the use of money from the urban highway allocations for public transit in urban areas, most of the funds still went for highways rather than mass transit. Of approximately $800 million annually allotted to the urban program, less than $50 million went to public transit. Representative James J. Howard (D-N.J.), chairman of the House Public Works and Transportation Subcommittee on Surface Transportation, explains that there simply isn't enough money to meet all the urban transportation needs. Faced with all the needs and the sad state of repair of many city streets, the mayors feel they have little choice but to use available funds for street construction and repair. Consequently the public transit lobby has given up on the Highway Trust Fund as a source for its needs and has now decided to work for a separate fund of its own, a move which not only will take it out of competition with the highway lobby but may gain the lobby as an ally.

## CONCLUSION

Normally no one worries much about how the nation's passengers and freight move and what this means to the American economy. The whole operation is taken pretty much for granted. Policy for an industry that constitutes the very backbone of our national defense and economic welfare is almost totally ignored by the general public. On the whole, policy decisions have been shaped largely by the spokespersons for the various segments of the industry itself.

The rise of a variety of competing forms of transportation has profoundly affected public policy in this field. Because of the fragmented nature of the industry, the government has developed its policy over the years on a carrier-by-carrier basis, resulting in a disjointed and patchwork approach to federal transport policy. The national network of highways, waterways, railways, and airways Americans take for granted is the product of 150 years of uncoordinated, incremental political decision-making. The Bureau of Public Roads believes in highways, the Army Corps of Engineers believes in waterways, and each plans and carries out its projects largely without regard to other modes of transportation. The various programs and agencies have been mandated legislatively with the task of promoting their segments of the industry, and each newly created bureaucracy has developed a constituency and become its own best lobbyist. The uncoordinated planning approach serves the interest of the variety of sub-governments that have developed around the different sectors of the transport industry. These diverse transportation bureaucracies and their supporting constituencies do not lend themselves readily to a well-coordinated approach to policymaking. Consequently, a preeminent problem in this area has been the absence of any unified and overall approach to national transportation policy. In 1950, President Harry Truman created the position of undersecretary of commerce for transportation, with the purpose of giving central leadership to "the development of over-all transportation policy." The success in obtaining this objective is pretty well reflected by President Kennedy's 1962 description of federal transportation policy as "a chaotic patchwork of inconsistent and often obsolete legislation and regulation."

The disjointed approach is further reflected in the governmental structure dealing with transportation policy. Over the years a variety of agencies has been created to administer narrowly focused programs involving a single mode of transportation and with no consideration of what other agencies were doing for other modes. In an effort to achieve a more coordinated approach, a cabinet-level Department of Transportation was created in 1966 and agencies from various other departments reassigned to this new department. Transportation has remained largely a department in name only, and its separate agencies continue to function as independent fiefdoms. Even with the 1966 reorganization, responsibility and authority remained scattered. Thirty-two different agencies still administer transportation programs, only eight of which are in the Department of Transportation. The picture is much the same in Congress, where more than thirty House and Senate subcommittees have jurisdiction over various major transportation programs.

In a 1975 report the General Accounting Office said that federal transportation programs had been created haphazardly to meet specific crises, with little or no consideration of their effect on the transportation system as a whole. In spite of growing criticism and repeated calls for a more coordinated approach, Congress has continued to extend existing programs on a mode-by-mode basis. It is very doubtful that a truly national and coordinated transportation system can be developed through such a policy approach. And, until the policymakers approach transportation policy with a broader perspective, seeking to blend all the different modes into a unified plan that best serves national needs, the likelihood that various segments of the industry will need federal subsidies persists. The ultimate question facing the policymakers is whether to continue heavy subsidies to an uncoordinated and inefficient system or to seek the development of a plan for integrating the various modes of transportation into a more coordinated national transportation network.

Transportation policy is a good example of two aspects of the policymaking process—the frequently unanticipated consequences of policy decisions and the linkages between policy decisions in various fields. Decisions on transportation policy have far-reaching implications for policies in other areas such as energy, defense and foreign policy, agricultural policy, and others. The heavy emphasis over the last three decades on highway building has tied our nation to a system heavily dependent on petroleum, much of which must be imported at steadily rising costs. These largely unanticipated consequences of past policies contributed to the Department of Transportation's observation in a 1971 report that, "There is a need to rethink the way this nation should go about developing a transportation system." In the light of developing trends, the report concluded, "The practices and policies of the past will almost certainly be inadequate for the future."[5] With world petroleum supplies dwindling, fuel costs rising rapidly, and America's transportation needs growing, the development of a plan for the future becomes more critical than ever.

## Points to Ponder

Since automobiles and trucks are high energy consumers, should federal policy continue to heavily subsidize highway construction?

Are federal subsidies to Amtrak a losing proposition or should more funds be committed to make it a viable transportation alternative?

Can deregulation and competition among different sectors of the transport industry bring about a more efficient and less costly transportation system?

Should trucklines and waterway users help to pay more of the construction and maintenance costs of facilities (highways, canals, harbors, etc.) they use?

## Notes

1. *Gibbons* v *Ogden*, 9 Wheat. 1 (1824).
2. For example, when the Southern Railway sought to enhance its competitive position by introducing its jumbo hopper car, the Big John, the ICC blocked it. Southern had to appeal to the federal courts before eventually being allowed to use this innovation.
3. Deborah Baldwin, "Amtrak: The Wreck We Have To Fix," *The Washington Monthly* (May 1979), p. 47.
4. National Academy of Sciences, *Proposed Program for Maritime Administration Research*, vol. 1 (Washington, D.C.: National Academy of Sciences, 1960), p. 143.
5. *Congress and the Nation*, vol. III (Washington, D.C.: Congressional Quarterly, 1973), p. 147.

## Suggestions for Further Reading

ALTSCHULER, ALAN. *Current Issues in Transportation Policy*. Lexington, Mass.: Lexington Books, 1979.

BURKE, CATHERINE G. *Innovation and Public Policy: The Case of Personal Rapid Transit*. Lexington, Mass.: Lexington Books, 1979.

FISHLER, STANLEY. *Moving Millions: An Inside Look at Mass Transit*. New York: Harper & Row, 1979.

GLICKMAN, NORMAN, ed. *The Urban Impacts of Federal Policies*. Baltimore: Johns-Hopkins Press, 1979.

HACKER ANDREW. "Pressure Politics in Pennsylvania: The Truckers vs the Railroads" in Alan Westin, ed., *The Uses of Power*. New York: Harcourt, Brace & World, 1962.

LOCKLIN, PHILIP. *Economics of Transportation*, 7th ed. Homewood, Il.: Richard D. Irwin, 1972.

NELSON, JAMES C. *Railroad Transportation and Public Policy*. Washington, D.C.: The Brookings Institution, 1959.

NORTON, HUGH. *Modern Transportation Economics*, 2nd ed. Columbus, Ohio: Charles Merrill, 1970.

PEGRUM, DUDLEY F. *Transportation: Economics and Public Policy*, 3rd ed. Homewood, Ill.: Richard D. Irwin, 1973.

RUPPENTHAL, KARL, ed. *Transportation Subsidies: Nature and Extent*. University of British Columbia, 1974.

SAMPSON, ROY and FARRIS, MARTIN. *Domestic Transportation: Practice, Theory and Policy*, 2nd ed. Boston: Houghton-Mifflin, 1971.

SAUNDERS, RICHARD. *The Railroad Mergers and the Coming of Conrail*. Westport, Conn.: Greenwood Press, 1978.

SCHREIBER, ARTHUR F. "Providing Incentives in Urban Transportation: Prices v Subsidies," *Business/Economics News* (March 1976).

STONE, T. R. *Beyond the Automobile: Reshaping the Transportation Environment*. Englewood Cliffs, N.J.: Prentice-Hall, 1971.

STOVER, JOHN F. *The Life and Decline of the American Railroad*. New York: Oxford University Press, 1970.

WILLIAMS, ERNEST. *The Future of American Transportation*. Englewood Cliffs, N.J.: Prentice-Hall, 1971.

# 8

# To Educate a Nation: What Federal Role?

Though American educators have persistently promoted the myth that education is nonpolitical, social philosophers have long recognized the intimate relationship between government and education. Beginning with Plato, many philosophers have viewed education as the means for attaining the ideal state. A leading exponent of education among our own founding fathers was Thomas Jefferson, who maintained that, "Any nation that expects to be ignorant and free, in a state of civilization, expects what never was and never will be." Principal author of the Declaration of Independence, president, inventor, and statesman, Jefferson regarded as his crowning achievement the founding of the University of Virginia. Under the Jeffersonian concept, public education was to develop citizens in our democratic society who would know what their rights were and be capable of defending them against those who would encroach upon them. If citizens were to participate and maintain a democratic system, they must be educated to the task.

Jefferson's belief in education was shared by many of the early colonial leaders, as is reflected by early governmental actions. The Survey Ordinance of 1785 reserved one section of land in every township in the Western Territory for the endowment of schools within that township. The Northwest Ordinance of 1787, providing for the organization of the Northwest Territory, stated, "Religion, morality, and knowledge being necessary to good government and the happiness of mankind, schools and the means of education shall forever be encouraged." The Constitution, however, drafted in the same year, makes no specific reference to education, charging the federal government only with promoting the "general welfare." Consequently, schools and public education came to be viewed as primarily state and local responsibilities and federal aid became yet another issue in the long-standing debate over the nature of our federal system. With "local control" as the watchword, the nation developed a highly diversified and unequally supported system of education state to state.

The movements for publicly supported education and compulsory school attendance reflect this patchwork development. Debates on educational policy in the early and middle nineteenth century centered on these two issues. The movement for publicly supported systems of education began in the East in the 1830s and spread slowly westward, reaching the states along the Mississippi River in the 1850s. Compulsory education started in Massachusetts in 1852 and was finally adopted in Mississippi in 1918.

The issue of public education also got caught up in the egalitarian politics of Jacksonian democracy. If voting and office holding were to be open to all citizens, then it became more important that they be educated. As public education expanded in response to egalitarian impulses, it also became an instrument of economic and social mobility. Education was, in the words of noted educator Horace Mann, "the great equalizer of the conditions of men." Using the schools to broaden the base of social equality and to expand the opportunities for social advancement was in keeping with American egalitarian goals. While the schools remained primarily a state and local responsibility, it was their development as instruments of social and economic advancement that led to demands for federal support. The rural, agrarian elements in particular felt that the traditional system was not meeting the needs of their offspring, especially at the higher education level.

## EARLY FEDERAL AID EFFORTS

In response to pressure for federal assistance, Congress in 1862 passed the Morrill or Land-Grant College Act. This legislation awarded each state a grant of 30,000 acres for each representative and senator in Congress in 1860 to be used for the establishment and support of a college to provide training in the agricultural and mechanical arts. With the assistance provided under this act, sixty-seven land-grant colleges were established in fifty states and Puerto Rico, revolutionizing the American system of higher education. Giving further evidence of growing national interest in education, President James A. Garfield persuaded an indifferent Congress to create a Department of Education in 1867 as a part of the Department of the Interior. This new department was aimed at advancing recognition and financing of education.

Following the adoption of the Morrill Act and creation of the Department of Education, federal activity in the education field was quite sporadic. In 1890 the second Morrill Act was adopted, creating a system of Negro land-grant colleges. The Smith-Hughes Act of 1917 provided for federal grants in support of vocational education, but support of education was still viewed as primarily a responsibility of state and local governments. In 1938 a national Advisory Committee on Education

## Major Education Measures

**Survey Ordinance of 1785.** Provided for one section of land in each township in the Northwest Territory to be used for the support of education.

**Morrill Act of 1862.** Provided grants of public lands to the states and territories for the support of "land grant" colleges to provide training in agricultural and mechanical arts.

**Department of Education Act of 1867.** Created a national agency to collect and disseminate information on education.

**Second Morrill Act of 1890.** Expanded federal funding for land-grant institutions and created a system of land-grant colleges for blacks.

**Smith-Hughes Act of 1917.** Provided federal grants to the states for agricultural, industrial, and trade-related education below the college level.

**Vocational Rehabilitation Act of 1918.** Provided grants for job training for World War I veterans.

**Lanham Act of 1940.** Provided for federal aid to schools in districts "impacted" by federal operations.

**Serviceman's Readjustment Act of 1944.** Also called the GI Bill, provided federal aid for World War II veterans to continue their education.

**George-Barden Act of 1946.** Also called the Vocational Education Act, provided expanded federal support for vocational education.

**School Construction in Areas Affected by Federal Activities Act of 1950.** Provided assistance for school construction in localities where federal activities resulted in increased school enrollments.

**National Defense Education Act of 1958.** Provided federal funds for education programs in science, mathematics, foreign languages, and other subjects to help meet national defense needs.

**Higher Education Facilities Act of 1963.** Authorized assistance for classrooms, libraries, and laboratories in colleges, universities, and technical schools.

**Elementary and Secondary Education Act of 1965.** Provided financial assistance for the education of children from low-income families.

**Higher Education Act of 1965.** Provided funds to colleges and universities for community service, continuing education, cooperative education, and libraries.

**Comprehensive Employment and Training Act of 1973.** Established a system of programs for educating and training economically disadvantaged and unemployed persons.

**Department of Education Organization Act of 1979.** Created a cabinet-level Department of Education and consolidated 152 programs from HEW and other agencies.

reported it had found substantial inequality of educational opportunity among the states. However, though hearings were held on an aid bill, legislation never reached the floor. The federal government continued to provide support only in limited areas. In the Lanham Act of 1940 Congress provided support for schools impacted by federal installations and in 1944 provided educational assistance for veterans under the first of the so-called "GI Bills." Legislation in 1946 provided school aid through the National School Lunch and Milk programs. The tide was beginning to build.

The World War I draft had revealed a high rate of illiteracy among American soldiers, especially those from the poorer states. The World War II draft showed that this problem still persisted. Demands for general federal aid to help alleviate this situation began to gain support. In 1946 Robert H. Taft, conservative Republican senator from Ohio, explained his support for federal aid by saying:

> Education is primarily a state function—but in the field of education the Federal Government, ... has a secondary interest or obligation to see that there is a basic floor under those essential services for all adults and children in the United States.[1]

In the 1940s and '50s problems in the education system began to approach crisis proportions. Substantially increased birthrates began to be reflected in school enrollments. From 1946 to 1951 public school enrollments grew by more than half million per year and from 1951 to 1959 by more than 1 million per year.

---

### Important Departments and Agencies

**Department of Education.** This newest cabinet-level department was approved by Congress in 1979, removing education from HEW as well as consolidating a number of other programs under the new department.

**U.S. Department of Agriculture.** The USDA has a role in the school lunch programs and the Extension Service works closely with the Land Grant College and County Extension Agent systems.

**National Science Foundation (NSF).** The NSF is a prime source of funds for research in the nation's colleges and universities and has funded programs for training in math and the sciences.

**Veterans Administration (VA).** Many veterans and military personnel have had their education funded through programs administered by the VA.

**National Endowment for the Humanities (NEH).** This agency provides support for research and programs in the humanities.

**National Endowment for the Arts.** Like NEH, the National Endowment for the Arts promotes research and programs in the arts through grant and fellowship programs.

By 1947 both educators and lawmakers were warning of a school crisis unless help was forthcoming. Because salaries were so low, teachers were leaving the profession in unprecedented numbers while enrollments were growing steadily. Both classroom and teacher shortages were becoming major problems. In 1948 both the Republican and Democratic party platforms called for federal aid to the troubled schools. President Truman in his 1948 State of the Union Message charged, "We are not yet assuring all children of our nation the opportunity of receiving the basic education which is necessary to a strong democracy."

The decade of the 1950s brought increased discussion of federal aid to education and congressional action on a variety of special education programs, but produced no general aid bills. In 1950 the Federal Impacted Areas Aid Program was expanded to provide funds for the construction, operation, and maintenance of schools in districts with extraordinary costs due to the pressure of nearby federal bases or installations. Also in 1950 Congress established the National Science Foundation (NSF) to provide federal support for scientific research and the education of future scientists. The act was amended in 1952, 1953, 1958, and 1959 to broaden the NSF's educational functions. The NSF budget has grown from $500,000 in 1950 to over $400 million today. In 1952 the GI Bill included educational benefits to help veterans readjust to civilian life. Under provisions of this legislation 7.8 million World War II veterans and 2.4 million Korean conflict veterans received educational benefits totalling $19 billion. In 1953 Congress created the new cabinet-level Department of Health, Education and Welfare, and the Department of Education was transferred to this new agency.

The rapid advances by the Russians in the field of rocketry and their launching of the first Sputnik in 1957 made Americans quickly and uncomfortably aware that education and national defense were closely related. Recognition that the Russians were gaining on the U. S. technologically touched off an extended debate on the needs of the U. S. educational system. Congress responded with the passage of the National Defense Education Act (NDEA) in 1958, providing funds for the improvement of the teaching of science, mathematics, and foreign languages at all school levels. First presented as a "temporary" measure to improve schools and instructional programs, NDEA became a permanent part of federal aid programs.

## OBSTACLES TO FEDERAL AID

Throughout the 1950s and '60s federal aid to education was one of the most controversial domestic political issues. Though Congress had acknowledged a limited federal role by providing grants for vocational education, authorizing the buying of school lunches, helping to build college dormitories, educating veterans, aiding in school construction, and providing aid to impacted areas, it refused to make a total commitment to federal responsibility for the general level of U. S. education and rejected all proposals for general aid to elementary and secondary schools. Despite widespread public support and strong campaigns by proponents who contended that current educational support was inadequate and that a major federal effort was necessary to improve the quality of the schools, broaden educational opportunities, and provide classrooms and teachers for an expanding school population, general aid bills were repeatedly defeated. For two decades opponents were able to block action on aid bills by invoking the three R's: Race, Religion, and Reds (federal control).

### Federal Control Issue

One of the major issues hindering passage of a general aid to education bill was the age-old debate over the nature of the federal system. Traditionally in America, education was viewed as a state and local responsibility and federal aid was seen as a step in the direction of federal control and domination. For some reason local control by some 27,000 locally-elected school boards is seen as nonpolitical while federal aid and involvement in educational policy is highly political. Thus, as a matter of principle, conservative states' rights elements have opposed federal aid to education because it would expand the federal role and the federal budget. In 1949, while president of Columbia University, Dwight Eisenhower wrote a house education and labor subcommittee this warning: "Unless we are careful, even the great and necessary educational processes in our country will become yet another vehicle by which the believers in paternalism, if not outright socialism, will gain still additional power for the central Government."[2] Five years later, as president of the U. S., Eisenhower told the Congress in his budget message:

> I do not underestimate the difficulties facing states and communities in attempting to solve the problems created by the great increase in the number of children of school age, the shortage of qualified teachers, and the overcrowding of classrooms.... At the same time, I do not accept the simple remedy of federal intervention.

While Eisenhower did come to accept federal support for classroom construction, he continued, as did many other conservatives, to question general federal aid. On the question of federal aid for teachers salaries, Eisenhower went back to the traditional states' rights position, saying:

> I do not believe the Federal Government ought to be in the business of paying a local official. If we're going into that, we'll have to find out every councilman and every teacher and every other person that's a public official of any kind... and try to figure out what his right salary is.... I can't imagine anything worse for the Federal Government to get into.[3]

The conservative elements opposing federal aid as a matter of principle frequently joined forces with elements who opposed aid for religious or racial reasons, thus creating a formidable block against passage of general aid measures.

In the last decade the debate over school finance and federalism has taken a somewhat different direction. As differences in levels of school support from district to district and state to state have attracted more attention, reformers have raised the question whether the federal government should not seek a more equitable level of educational opportunity among the states. Because educational policy has been shaped largely at the state and local level, the states differ substantially in educational expenditures per pupil, average teachers' salaries, teacher-pupil ratios, retention rates, and other education measures. In New York, expenditures per pupil are about two times the per pupil expenditure in Mississippi. California's teacher salaries are double those of South Dakota, and teacher-pupil ratios range from 15 to 1 on the low end to 30 to 1 on the high end. In 1975-76 Arkansas had the lowest per pupil expenditure among the states at $1045 per pupil and Alaska was highest at $2705 per student; the national average was $1581 per pupil.

Levels of financial support also vary substantially among districts within the same state. While most states require a minimum level of local support, the distribution of state and local support varies greatly from state to state. In 1975-76, 93 percent of school support in Hawaii came from the state and none from local governments, while in New Hampshire the state provided 10 percent and local units 85 percent. On the whole, school consolidation programs and "minimum foundation" programs have tended to make the state's role more significant over the last decade. These state efforts have failed, however, to correct the unequal levels of support provided by different school districts. Usually districts with some industry, commercial development, or high-class residential neighborhoods generate more revenue, are able to pay higher salaries to attract better teachers, have better facilities, and offer more varied educational programs. With property taxes providing the bulk of local revenues used for school financing, substantial differences in expenditures developed between wealthy and poorer districts within the states, and economic and population shifts frequently rendered old formulas of financing inadequate. In Los Angeles, for example, the Baldwin Park district expenditure per pupil was $577 compared to $1232 per pupil in the wealthy Beverly Hills district. In Bexler County, Texas, expenditures in the Edgewood district were $356 per pupil and in Alamo Heights $594 per pupil, yet the poor district was taxing at a higher rate than the more affluent district. This means that many poorer school districts with low property values cannot generate the revenues to support their schools at an equitable level because tax rates would have to be raised to exorbitant levels.

For ten years forces seeking a system of more equitable support sought federal aid bills to provide equalization funds. Their efforts produced relatively little at this level and in the 1970s they shifted their focus to the state level. In a case filed in the California courts, the plaintiffs challenged the school financing system based on local property taxes, contending such taxes could not provide equal education because taxable wealth in the various districts was unequal. Basing its decision on the state's equal protection statutes, the California Supreme Court ruled in *Serrano* v *Priest* (1971) that children in poor school districts could not get as good an education as youngsters in rich districts, a violation of their civil rights. In its decision the court noted, "So long as assessed valuation within a district's boundaries is a major determinant of how much it can spend for its schools, only a district with a large tax base will be truly able to decide how much it really cares about education."[4]

The concept expressed in the *Serrano* decision resulted in a number of victories for the school finance reformers in the lower federal and state courts. In 1973 the U. S. Supreme Court entered the picture also and the school finance issue became a mixed bag. In the case of *San Antonio Independent School District* v *Rodriquez*, the Supreme Court ruled in a 5-4 decision that disparities in property taxes to finance education did not violate the equal protection clause of the Fourteenth Amendment and that a child's right to public education is not a "fundamental right" under the Fourteenth Amendment.[5] Thus the *Rodriquez* decision ruled out the use of the federal constitution as an instrument in the effort to equalize educational revenues. The reformers had to turn back to state constitutions and statutes.

Though a blow to the finance reform efforts, the *Rodriquez* decision did not halt the move toward more equitable financing. In fact, by the time of the Court's decision, more than a dozen states had already adopted new formulas for financing education. Between 1970 and 1977, state courts in California, Kansas, New Jersey, Connecticut, Washington, and Ohio ruled that either their state constitutions or statutes prohibited unequal educational expenditures resulting from reliance on the property tax for revenues. The reformers, using computer simulations and the courts, have been able to give considerable impetus to the move toward equalizing school expenditures. The overall effect, however, has not been a great equalization up to this point.

Federal aid generally is designed to help equalize school resources by concentrating larger contributions in the poorer districts. The overall impact has been blunted, however, as a result of two factors. One, to get the necessary votes in Congress for passage, aid bills must benefit large numbers of congressional districts. This practical political consideration results in formulas for aid allocation that make it difficult to concentrate federal funds where they would do the most good. Second, the impact of federal funds is further reduced because in most states they constitute only a small portion of total expenditures on education. Thus the federal portion is usually not large enough to have much overall impact on the total expenditure picture.

Despite both federal and state efforts toward equalization, great differences still persist. Possibly the most significant impact thus far has not been greater equalization, but the increased role of the states in school financing. Those who have sought to keep the federal role limited may ultimately see the cherished "local control" of the schools largely replaced by control at the state level as a result of changed patterns of school financing.

### The Religious Issue

Another issue that has cropped up periodically to block aid-to-education measures is the church-state dispute. The First Amendment to the Constitution states, "Congress shall make no law respecting an establishment of religion or prohibiting the free exercise thereof." Disagreement as to just what this clause means has been persistent and emotional. Does this provision constitute a "wall of separation" between church and state, or is it something less? In 1801 Thomas Jefferson wrote the Danbury Baptist Association that the First Amendment built a "wall of separation" between church and state. Since then the controversy has waxed and waned, with the public schools and federal aid frequently at the center of the conflict.

Actually religion is a twofold issue in federal education policy—does the Constitution allow for religious instruction in the public schools, and can the federal government provide financial aid to sectarian schools? As with many policy issues, the courts have been called upon to clarify these issues. In 1930 in *Cochran* v *The Board of Education*, the Supreme Court upheld state legislation providing free textbooks for children in both public and parochial schools on the grounds that such aid benefited the *children* rather than the church.[6] Again in 1947, reviewing a New Jersey law authorizing the payment of transportation costs for children attending nonprofit schools, the Court held that the act was primarily for the children's safety and upheld it. However, in this case, *Everson* v *Board of Education*, the Court included some statements that tended to cloud rather than clarify the separation issue. In its opinion, the Court stated:

> Neither a state nor the federal government can set up a church. Neither can pass laws which aid one religion, aid all religions, or prefer one religion over another. Neither can force nor influence a person to go to or to remain away from church against his will, or force him to profess a belief or disbelief in any religion. No person can be punished for entertaining or professing religious beliefs or disbeliefs, for church attendance or nonattendance. No tax in any amount, large or small, can be levied to support any religious activities or institutions, whatever they may be called, or whatever form they may adopt to teach or practice religion. Neither a state nor the federal government can, openly or secretly, participate in the affairs of any religious organizations or groups, and vice versa.[7]

After *Everson* the question of how much aid and in what form could go to the public school remained unresolved.

The following year, the Court addressed the issue of religious instruction in the public schools. In Champaign, Illinois, children were released from class to receive religious instruction that was held in classrooms of the school. In *McCollum* v *Board of Education* the Supreme Court held that such a plan for religious instruction violated the provisions of the First Amendment.[8] Four years later in *Zorach* v *Clauson* the Court held that a New York City plan under which students were released to attend religious instruction held on private property did not violate provisions of the First Amendment. In its opinion the Court stated, "We are a religious people whose institutions presuppose a supreme being" and the First Amendment does not include "a philosophy of hostility to religion."[9] Thus the instruction issue remained clouded. The early 1960s brought a series of suits challenging prayers and Bible reading in the public schools. In 1962 in the case *Engle* v *Vitale* the Court in a 6-1 decision ruled that official state sanctioning of religious utterances in the schools amounted to an unconstitutional tendency to "establish religion."[10] Overall in its 1960s decisions the Court seemed more inclined to view First Amendment provisions as rigid barriers between church and state.

In 1971, when Pennsylvania legislation providing for state payment of teachers' salaries and costs of instructional materials in parochial schools came before the Court, it declared the legislation unconstitutional because it represented an "excessive entanglement between government and religion." The Court contended that state payments to parochial schools would require excessive governmental controls and surveillance to insure that such funds were not used for religious instruction.[11] Five years later in *Roemer v Maryland* (1976) the Court upheld general public grants of money to church-related colleges, declaring that "Religious institutions need not be quarantined from public benefits which are neutrally available to all."[12] However, in a 1979 decision the Court ruled that New Jersey could not provide a special income-tax deduction to parents sending their children to nonpublic schools because such a deduction "advanced religion." Thus the Court has failed to establish any clearcut guidelines as to exactly what the First Amendment does and does not allow regarding the relationship between government, the schools, and religion.

The church-state question has also been a major issue in Congress on aid-to-education matters. In the 1940s a major hurdle in the way of general aid bills was the question of aid to parochial schools. In 1949 Francis Cardinal Spellman of New York attacked Graham Barden (D-N.C.), chairman of the House Education and Labor Committee, as a "new apostle of bigotry." Barden in turn charged that the Catholic Church had injected the religious issue and blocked school aid in Congress. Ranks began to form over the issue of aid to private schools and the National Education Association, though favoring federal aid, opposed funds for private church-related schools. Joining in the opposition to any aid to parochial scohols was the National Council of Churches and other protestant denominations. On the other side, the National Catholic Welfare Conference refused to support any aid-to-education bills that did not include aid to parochial schools. Leading spokesman for the Catholic cause, Cardinal Spellman maintained:

> We feel that it is un-American that any federal law be passed disposing of federal monies for auxillary services, and depriving American children of these public facilities. Now they are attempting to keep American children off public transportation facilities. Tomorrow they will try to keep us out of the public libraries, the public gardens and perhaps off the sidewalks....[13]

Pointing out that there were over 5 million children, about 13 percent of the total school population, enrolled in Catholic elementary and secondary schools, the National Catholic Welfare Conference in a 1961 brief said, "There is no constitutional bar to aid the education in church-related schools in a degree proportionate to the value of the public function it performs." The supporters of public aid for parochial schools also pointed out that numerous pieces of legislation already on the books provided funds to private schools, including the National Defense Education Act, College Housing acts, the GI Bill, the National School Lunch Act, and the Hill-Burton Act.

In 1960 John Kennedy became the first Catholic ever elected president, and he was a strong supporter of general aid to education. In 1961 Kennedy sent his education bill to Congress, describing it as "probably the most important piece of domestic legislation" for the year. The Rules Committee, frequently a bottleneck for liberal legislation, had been enlarged and the administration felt the time for general federal aid had at last arrived. Kennedy, however, very sensitive over the Catholic issue, refused to include aid to parochial schools in his education proposal. Consequently two Catholic members of the Rules Committee from heavily Catholic districts refused to support the measure and it remained bottled up in the Rules Committee. In 1962 Kennedy was again unsuccessful with his education proposal. In 1963 Kennedy sent Congress a huge omnibus education proposal which they proceeded to take apart, eventually enacting several parts separately and providing $2 billion in various aid programs and $1.2 billion for facilities. In 1964 action followed the 1963 pattern as Congress passed several education measures but still refused to approve general aid to elementary and secondary schools. The aid to parochial schools was still a big issue with many members.

### The Race Issue

The third major issue complicating the passage of federal aid-to-education measures was that of race. The roots of this issue extend back to the late nineteenth century when the Supreme Court in its decision in *Plessy* v *Ferguson* established the basis for the "separate but equal" doctrine.[14] Under this concept the states established separate school systems for blacks.

Following the "separate but equal" doctrine of *Plessy*, dual school systems were established throughout the country; but in reality while they were separate, they were far from equal. In the 1930s the NAACP (National Association for the Advancement of Colored People) began to challenge this approach with limited success, but primarily at the graduate and professional school level. As late as 1954, twenty-one states and the District of Columbia either tolerated or required segregation in their public school systems. In a landmark case in 1954 the NAACP's Legal Defense Fund filed suit asking that the policy of segregation in the public schools be held unconstitutional.

Speaking for the majority of the Court in *Brown* v *Topeka Board of Education*, Chief Justice Earl Warren stated, "We conclude that in the field of public education the doctrine of 'separate but equal' has no place. Separate educational facilities are inherently unequal."[15]

While this part of the decision was clear enough, it left many questions unanswered, and for the next quarter century school desegregation became one of the most controversial issues facing public policymakers. The Court did not specify how much desegregation would be required nor how soon it was to be achieved. Furthermore, the decision was not self-implementing, but was left up to the lower federal courts for implementation. Consequently, for the next decade the government was quite passive in enforcing desegregation, and in the South in particular, where opposition was strongest, the lower courts were particularly slow in requiring compliance. Five years after the *Brown* decision, only five southern states had even begun desegregating their schools and 98.8 percent of all black students in the South were still in all-black schools. Ten years after *Brown*, Mississippi's schools were still as segregated as they were half a century earlier; even in Texas, the most desegregated of the confederacy states, 92 percent of the black pupils were still attending segregated schools.

In Congress the issue of desegregation had become yet another stumbling block in the way of passage of general aid-to-education bills. While support for aid-to-education bills had grown to the point where the necessary votes appeared forthcoming, passage of such legislation was complicated by the racial issue. Through the 1950s, Harlem Representative Adam Clayton Powell persistently proposed amendments to aid-to-education bills that would bar any federal aid to segregated schools. Liberal representatives from northern urban districts felt compelled to support Powell's nondiscrimination riders, which with their support passed. With the nondiscrimination amendment attached, the aid measure then became unacceptable to southern congressmen who feared federal efforts to compel desegregation, and they joined forces with conservative members who opposed federal aid as a matter of principle and defeated such measures. This combination of philosophical and desegregation opponents blocked general federal aid until the passage of the Civil Rights Act of 1964 helped to reduce segregation as an issue in aid bills.

Finally, in 1964, ten years after the *Brown* decision, Congress took some action to facilitate desegregation in the schools. The Civil Rights Act of 1964 directed the commissioner of education to conduct a study "concerning the lack of availability of equal educational opportunities for individuals by reason of race, color, religion, or national origin in public educational institutions at all levels in the United States...." The act called for more involvement of federal authorities in the desegregation of schools by bringing the Justice Department in on the side of blacks who were being discriminated against, and Title VI provided for federal funds to be withheld from schools found guilty of segregation. The Civil Rights Act of 1965 went one step further, barring the use of federal funds in *any* segregated program or activity. With the passage of the general-aid Elementary and Secondary Education Act of 1965, the threat of cutting off federal funds provided even greater leverage in federal efforts to promote desegregation of the nation's schools.

With the stepped-up federal effort, HEW began to assign investigators to determine whether discrimination existed in school systems, and in 1966 the department promulgated new guidelines. The new guidelines moved away from the "freedom of choice" concept, whereby black parents and students chose whether to enroll in white schools, to the prescription of the minimal proportions of blacks who were to be enrolled in white schools. The stiffer guidelines, coupled with the cutting off of funds to several school districts, resulted in substantial desegregation efforts, especially in a number of southern school systems. Yet, even the tough 1966 guidelines and the threat of funds cut-offs failed to bring compliance on the part of some systems in the Black Belt of the deep South. In 1968 new guidelines were adopted stating, "Compliance with the law requires integration of faculties and activities as well as students so that there are no Negro or other minority group schools and no white schools—just schools."

As a result of HEW's stricter guidelines and enforcement efforts, 203 school systems in the South eventually lost federal funds; but even then only 51 of the systems submitted plans acceptable for restoration of federal funding. Finally the Justice Department moved to enjoin state funding as well as federal, and faced with this additional loss of funding, the districts were finally forced to capitulate. As a result of insistent federal pressures, by the fall of 1970 southern school systems had become the least segregated in the country.

With the substantial progress toward desegregation of the southern school systems, federal attention shifted from *de jure* segregation to *de facto* segregation, a potentially much tougher issue to resolve. *De jure* segregation results when official state or local school district actions, such as the drawing of school district boundaries, create segregated schools, while *de facto* segregation results from social and economic factors such as housing patterns, income distribution, etc., which are much more difficult to alter. Furthermore, efforts to alter such patterns run head-on into such strong fundamental beliefs as freedom of choice, community schools, and local control of educational policy. With the shift in focus to *de facto* segregation, the racial challenges have shifted largely to the urban school districts, many of them in the North. The battles over school integration have now moved from Little Rock and Birmingham to Pontiac and Boston. Chicago's school system illustrates the racial problems faced in many large urban systems. Chicago's 500,000-pupil system is largely black, and like many other systems it tiptoed around the issue of desegregation for two decades. As more and more whites have left the central city, the system's schools have progressively become more black. In 1977 the city's white student population declined by 8 percent and in 1978 by 10 percent. As a result of such declines, only 21 percent of the students remaining in the system are white. Many other urban school systems are facing the same pattern of population change. Under the stricter federal guidelines, northern schools have been ordered to desegregate when it can be shown that they were located or enlarged, their attendance zones were shifted, or their students were allowed to change schools in a manner that promotes racial isolation.

It was this sort of racial maldistribution in many school systems that gave birth to the issue of "busing" in the 1970s. In 1971 the U. S. Supreme Court in its decision in *Swann* v *Charlotte-Mecklenburg Board of Education* supported crosstown busing to achieve racial integration under certain conditions.[16] The *Swann* decision set in motion busing efforts in many parts of the country and touched off a prolonged and sometimes violent debate over the shifting of pupils from one school to another to achieve integration. In 1973 the Supreme Court held in *Keyes* v *School District Number 1 of Denver* that if a system had ever acted to facilitate segregation, then it was obligated to take whatever steps are necessary to correct its misdeeds.[17] With public sentiment against busing growing among both blacks and whites, Congress got into the act in 1974. In the Education Act of 1974, Congress endorsed the concept of the "neighborhood school" and specified seven alternative approaches to desegregation that were to be tried before resorting to busing. This act also directed school districts to bus students no further than the second-closest school to their homes.

Under the direction of President Richard Nixon and Attorney General John Mitchell, the Office of Civil Rights began to ease off on school desegregation and ceased the use of fund cut-offs. No southern school district has lost federal aid since 1970 and only the Ferndale, Michigan district has in the North. Congress also enacted a program to try to make desegregation more attractive by providing extra funds to help school systems defray the costs attributable to their efforts to desegregate. Thus far, the federal courts have largely ignored Congress's efforts to restrict busing and have continued their efforts to promote more racial balance in the schools. In Louisville, Kentucky a lower federal court judge ordered consolidation of the city-county school systems in which the 49,000-pupil city system was 51 percent black and the 96,000-pupil county system was only 4 percent black. Because of this imbalance, the judge's order required busing and the Supreme Court accepted the lower court ruling in the case. Under President Carter and HEW Secretary Joseph Califano there has been a return to the use of federal funding as a lever to encourage integration in the schools. In 1978 Califano directed HEW to defer consideration of funds for North Carolina universities "if those new federal funds would contribute to continuing segregation in the University of North Carolina system." North Carolina quickly worked out an agreement with HEW, since this move could have cost the state's universities some $10 million in federal funds.

While it no longer blocks the passage of aid-to-education bills in Congress, the racial problem is far from being resolved as an issue in the nation's schools. Debate over the impact of such issues as "busing" and "white flight" continues as both sides march out their "experts" and the policymakers try to resolve the difficult issue. Professor James S. Coleman, University of Chicago sociologist whose 1966 report is cited by many judges in their decisions on court-ordered busing and desegregation, has now changed position, saying that most segregation is the result of residential patterns and cannot be successfully remedied by court order.[18] Coleman now urges more incentives toward "voluntary cooperation" to achieve integration, and feels that school integration has failed to produce the achievement gains predicted for black students, one of the main arguments for forced integration. He has also indicated that court decisions produced white "flight to the suburbs," a thesis supported by the findings of David Armor. Armor, a sociologist with the Rand Corporation, a Santa Monica, California think-tank, found in a study of fifty-four school districts that busing was causing white flight.[19] Coleman has been criticized by other "experts" for abandoning his earlier position and they contend that racial mixture in the schools has improved black student achievement. While this issue remains to be resolved, one fact is becoming apparent to the policymakers. With the flight of residents from the inner city to the suburbs, the tax base is shrinking even further and the financing of inner-city schools becomes more and more a problem. This means the level of support for inner-city schools, often heavily black, and the level of support for suburban schools, usually predominantly white, begins to widen. Though it stems from different reasons, we find ourselves back to a system of "separate but unequal" schools again in spite of all the federal government's efforts.

## PASSAGE OF GENERAL AID LEGISLATION

With the adoption of the Civil Rights Act of 1964, race discrimination was largely eliminated as an issue in aid-to-education legislation. Coupled with increased public support for aid to education and the fact that President Lyndon Johnson had made education the keystone in his Great Society program, it appeared the time had finally come for approval of a general aid-to-education bill. In the 1960s the log jam in Congress on federal aid to education began to break. In 1963, the 90th Congress, which Lyndon Johnson called the "education Congress," passed the Higher Education Facilities Act, aid to vocational education, and extensions of the National Defense Education Act. In 1964 the Library Services and Construction Act was adopted. Then came the major breakthrough in federal aid programs in 1965 with the passage of the Elementary and Secondary Education Act. With the adoption of this act, Congress had, within the short span of two years, adopted five major aid-to-education bills, which catapulted the federal government into the American educational system to a degree never before matched. Prior to the adoption of ESEA, Congress had been very selective in providing aid through highly specialized programs and most of the assistance for local schools had come through impacted-areas aid. Providing the first general aid to elementary and secondary schools, ESEA substantially increased federal involvement and has reached most of the nation's 16,000 school districts.

The 1965 Elementary and Secondary Education Act was a masterfully drawn measure that skillfully skirted some of the major political roadblocks to previous education aid bills. By emphasizing that his proposed bill provided aid to students rather than to schools, President Johnson rather effectively undercut many of the arguments raised by both sides on the church-state issue. The act also allowed church-related schools to receive federal funds for specific nonreligious educational services and facilities. While neither Protestant nor Catholic groups were overly enthusiastic in their support, they accepted the bill, thus removing a major roadblock to its passage. In another clever ploy, Johnson tied educational aid under ESEA to the matter of poverty and broadened the concept of "impacted" school districts to include those with large numbers of low-income families. The aid to schools thus became a part of the broader "war on poverty." One other key aspect of ESEA was the fact that grants are made to the states and state educational agencies have the responsibility for making allocations. Again in a clever political move, Johnson emphasized the creation of a federal-state educational partnership in which the federal government only "suggests guidelines." This was a move to allay the fears of those who saw this legislation as a step in the direction of federal control of the nation's schools.

On signing the Elementary and Secondary Education Act, President Johnson proclaimed, "No law I have signed or will ever sign means more to the future of America." Taking into account the practical politics of the votes needed for passage, ESEA provided some benefits for about 95 percent of the nation's school districts and most congressional districts; however, funds were concentrated in poorer districts. Over $1 billion of the $1.3 billion approved in 1965 went to school districts with large numbers of children from families on relief or with incomes under $2000 per year. Because the distribution formula was based on the states' per-pupil expenditures, however, the wealthier states tended to benefit more from ESEA funds than the poorer states.

In recent years considerable debate has centered around the formula to be used for the distribution of funds. Some critics have focused on the categoric grants-in-aid, favoring general block grants which would give states more discretion over the use of funds. Nixon pushed the block grant approach but the categoric approach was retained. Former Representative Albert Quie (R-Minn.) proposed that funds be distributed on the basis of low school achievement rather than poverty. Critics contended that this approach would take money from poorer school districts and give it to middle-class districts needing it less. Economic changes and shifts in population bring alterations in the distribution of funds. Traditionally the South had benefited most from federal aid programs, but as it has become more prosperous and the inner cities have declined, the Northeast has begun to get more funds. A key issue still is how to allocate the funds available. Who should get federal dollars and for what? Traditionally an objective of federal aid has been to use federal funds to ensure a uniform and minimum level of education nationally. However, the practical necessity of benefiting as many congressional districts as possible has tended to spread federal dollars widely and reduce the impact in those districts needing help most. This remains one of the most difficult problems in devising the formula for funds allocation.

With its emphasis on benefits to students from poorer families, ESEA was expected to reduce the differences in spending between rich and poor school districts by channeling more resources into those districts with more poor children. Since passage of the act, Congress has remodeled the allocation with varying results. In 1967 the act was amended to allow states to use either their average per-pupil expenditure or the national average per-pupil expenditure, whichever was higher, in determining their share of federal funds. This formula would provide more funds for the poorer states with low per-pupil expenditures. In 1974 Congress again altered the distribution formula, adopting a more complex system for determining the number of poor children in a district and changing the guidelines on per-pupil expenditures. Under the new formula, the wealthier states cannot exceed 120 percent of the national average per-pupil expenditure in qualifying for funds, and states having per-pupil expenditures below the national average now are entitled to only 80 percent of the national average. The impact of the 1974 changes is to make both the top per-pupil spenders and the lower per-pupil spenders eligible for less aid. However, for those qualifying for less aid under the new formula, there would be a gradual reduction. No one would get less than 85 percent of the previous year's allocation. In the initial stages, much of the ESEA money was being used by school districts for general support. But as the Office of Education has tightened its oversight—in 1976 OE held up payment of over $150 million in Title I funds to California—it appears that funds are increasingly being used to upgrade the educational opportunities of low-income students and less of the money is being directed into other educational areas. Thus, while its impact has fallen somewhat short of the ultimate objective, ESEA and its amendments have promoted the equalization of expenditures among both the rich and the poor states and the rich and poor districts within states.

Assessment of the impact of expenditures on educational quality is mixed. A Rand Corporation study of the Elementary and Secondary Education Act of 1965 concluded it had improved education very little if at all. The report said many projects were undertaken simply because federal funds were available and that "seed" money was not very successful in improving education. The 1972 Jencks Harvard Study reported little or no correlation between resource allocation and improvement in test scores for disadvantaged children. The Stanford Research Institute, on the other hand, reported that a five-year study of 3 million pupils from forty states who were in ESEA Title I reading programs showed an average increase of one month's reading skills for each month in the program. These pupils' rate of improvement was on a par with that of typical students nationwide. Thus, currently available evidence does not prove conclusively whether federal dollars improve educational quality or not, but with ESEA opening the door for general aid, federal funds are not likely to be withdrawn completely.

## THE POLITICS OF EDUCATION

While public testimony on the value of education to society is widespread, there is little agreement on the appropriate direction for educational policy. Though educators have persisted in promoting the myth that education is nonpolitical, educational policy has been an area of pronounced social debate and expert disagreement. Because America's schools have been expected to accomplish many things in society, their role has been vigorously debated by a variety of interests. Educational policy has been further complicated by the frequent involvement of peripheral issues—race, religion, and campus unrest, among others.

Because of the benefits bestowed through federal programs, educational policy has stimulated a great deal of interest-group activity. Professional education groups with headquarters in Washington, D.C. are numerous and many individual institutions of higher education maintain their own Washington offices. Principal spokesmen for the nation's more than 2 million elementary and secondary teachers as well as many college and university teachers are the National Education Association (NEA) and the American Federation of Teachers (AFT). NEA alone has a membership approaching 2 million and in 1976 contributed more than $600,000 to Democratic congressional candidates. For years the NEA has pushed federal aid measures in Congress. Smaller in membership, but concentrated in the larger urban areas where it has considerable influence, is the AFT, an affiliate of the powerful AFL-CIO. Promoting the interests of the higher-education sector are a host of associations including the American Council on Education, the American

Association of Higher Education, the American Association of State Colleges and Universities, the National Association of State Universities and Land Grant Colleges, the Association of American Universities, the American Association of University Professors, and a whole host of more specialized groups. On certain issues a variety of other groups also get involved in the educational policy process. For several decades both racial and religious groups have frequently mobilized to lobby on educational policy — such groups as the NAACP, CORE, National Catholic Education Association, American Jewish Congress, and various Protestant groups. Among those pushing for general federal-aid legislation were the NEA, AFL-CIO, AAUP, AAUW, Americans for Democratic Action, Friends Committee on National Legislation, National Congress of Parents and Teachers, American Parents Committee, National Farmers Union, American Veterans Committee, International Brotherhood of Teamsters, American Association of School Administrators, American Library Association, and National Council of Jewish Women. Usually lined up in opposition were the Chamber of Commerce, National Association of Manufacturers, National Economic Council, American Farm Bureau Federation, Daughters of the American Revolution, Southern States Industrial Council, National Conference of State Taxpayers Association, and various other business and conservative organizations.

The political impact of the vast array of professional education groups has been reduced by their frequent internal differences. Prior to 1965 the coalition supporting federal aid programs was constantly split over differences involving assistance for parochial schools, segregation, and funding formulas. In the 1960s, with the racial and religious issues either sublimated or taking a different form, Congress became largely pro-education. In this era education policy was usually dominated by a progressive Democratic–moderate Republican coalition operating from a "more is better" philosophy. As the 1980s began, with President Carter emphasizing a balanced budget and inflation curbs and the taxpayers in protest, it appeared this philosophy might be moderated. Despite rather widespread endorsement of education programs, some feel that compared to other policy areas, educational politics is relatively "small potatoes."

Another characteristic of the politics of educational policy has been the wide diffusion of responsibility within the government structure. Until Congress created a new cabinet-level Department of Education in 1979, there were some 400 different federal education programs administered by more than 40 different departments and agencies. The sprawling Department of Health, Education and Welfare, created in 1953, had primary responsibility for managing over 130 different programs and administering $19.6 billion in aid; but other programs were assigned to the Veterans Administration, the Department of Agriculture, the Department of Labor, and the Department of Defense, among others. The practice had been to parcel programs out among the agencies depending upon particular program goals and objectives.

In Congress, though both the House and Senate have standing committees with education as a primary assignment, educational legislation is formulated by almost a hundred different subcommittees, depending on a measure's particular nature and objectives. The implication of this approach is that educational policy is never viewed as a whole, but is enacted on a piecemeal basis which makes assessment of overall impact and objectives difficult. It also means that a system of alliances is developed among certain interest groups, agencies, congressional committees, and constituencies, which makes any changes in the established pattern extremely difficult.

In an effort to consolidate responsibility for educational policy and promote somewhat more visibility within the cabinet, President Carter proposed that Congress establish a cabinet-level Department of Education. Carter's proposal quickly exposed the nature of the politics of educational policymaking. The president's initial proposal was to consolidate responsibility for 164 programs scattered through several federal agencies in a single Department of Education. Agencies whose programs were to be transferred immediately mounted a counterattack, including HEW Secretary Joseph Califano, from whose department education would be removed. Lining up their supporters among interest groups and congressional committees whose members would lose jurisdiction if programs were transferred, the agencies applied pressure on the president. Deciding some concessions would be necessary to secure approval of the proposal, Carter modified his initial proposal to placate some of the special interests. The GI benefits program was left with the Veteran's Administration and the National Endowment for Arts and Humanities remained independent, for example. Carter also applied some pressure, as indicated by Secretary Califano's reversal of his earlier position to endorsement of the revised proposal. Education groups were split over the proposal for a separate department. The NEA felt a separate department would enhance the standing of education within the federal bureaucracy, while the smaller AFT opposed a separate department. Several higher-education groups tended to oppose a separate department because they feared it would be dominated even more than the existing Office of Education was by the elementary and secondary interests. Some conservatives feared creation of such a department would lead to more federal control over education. These elements were joined by the AFL-CIO, whose spokesman testified against the proposal, maintaining that a separate department would result in a breakup of the labor, welfare, civil rights coalition and would subsequently divert funds away from education programs for the poor and the cities. Thus, the position of most groups both inside and outside government tended to be shaped largely on the basis of their vested interests rather than any ideological considerations.

After considerable discussion in Congress, the measure passed the Senate 69 to 22 and the House 215 to 201. While the final version of the bill did not consolidate all education programs under the new department, President Carter hailed the measure as "a significant milestone in my effort to make the federal government more efficient." He said the legislation would streamline the administration of more than 150 federal education programs, save tax dollars, and reduce red tape. The new department, with 17,400 employees and a $14.1 billion budget, was given responsibility for 152 federal education programs—131 from HEW and 21 from various other agencies, but some, such as veterans education (VA), Indian schools (Interior), and Headstart (HEW) remained with the prior administering agencies. Patricia Roberts Harris, Califano's successor as secretary at HEW (changed to Department of Health and Human Services) responded to losing the education programs by saying, "Sure education . . . should be given recognition and priority as great as that of national defense—for it is every bit as essential to our survival and success as a nation."[20]

Named to head the new cabinet department was California judge Shirley Hufstedler. The new secretary pledged that the department's primary role would be to help state and local governments with problems that are beyond their scope and resources: "To help them help themselves and to try to create a climate in which people can begin to think in cooperation terms instead of confrontation terms."[21] The new Department of Education, she said, would seek to promote the quality rather than the amount of federal involvement in education.

Another recent issue that further illustrates the fragmentation of interests in educational politics is the tuition tax-credit proposal. This proposal to provide federal assistance on educational expenses by allowing a credit on federal tax returns touched off an extensive debate over the merits of the tax-credit approach versus the traditional student-aid approach. As is frequently the case on educational aid bills, some peripheral issues were also drawn into the discussion. Both HEW Secretary Califano and Treasury Secretary Michael Blumenthal warned Congress that the proposed tax-credit approach would create an "inflationary and uncontrollable" drain on the U. S. Treasury, yet would not meet the needs of persons facing the rising costs of education. The public-school lobby groups opposed the measure, dusting off the old issue of church-state separation. When the House acted favorably on the proposal, Senator Daniel Moynihan applauded, "The House of Representatives has overturned the religious bigotry of the nineteenth century, and I am sure that the Senate will now do the same." Professor James Coleman endorsed tax credits as a way of increasing integration in the schools. He said such credits would "increase the range of choice of low-income black parents."

In supporting the tax-credit measure, Representative Clarence Brown, Jr. (R-Ohio) said the proposal would determine the success or failure of colleges facing enrollment difficulties. He said, "We need this tax-credit approach for the future determination of the survival of those institutions." Opponents, however, contended that the tax-credit approach would not provide the type of assistance needed. Representative Charles Rangel (D-N.Y.) asserted that the tax-credit bill would help only the "privileged few" who were able to send their children to college anyway. W. Glenn Terrell, Jr., president of the National Association of State Colleges and Land Grant Universities, typified the reaction of the professional education groups when he told House Education and Labor Committee members that the proposed bill "would be a regrettable error in public policy." It "spreads minimal funds over such a broad population," he said, "that it will have little impact on the relief sought by middle-income families."[22] President Carter's alternative middle-income student aid bill on the other hand, he said, would provide "meaningful assistance." Also joining in support of the president's plan were the NEA, AFT, American Association of State Colleges and Universities, Association of American Universities, and American Association of University Professors.

In spite of the rather extensive debate, little real consideration was given to alternative approaches, especially any serious discussion of expanded institutional support to reduce educational costs. In reality, the debate over tax credits boiled down to a question of political power and control of educational funds. In its March 1978 *PER Report*, Postsecondary Educational Resources, Inc. described the debate this way:

> The great national debate which should be taking place on this issue has degenerated into a struggle for power between tax committees in Congress and Congressional educational committees and federal student-aid bureaucrats to maintain their control over the allocation of billions of dollars in federal funds.[23]

Adoption of the tax-credit approach would take control over several billions of dollars from the education committees and give it to the tax-writing committees. The alliance of education committees, the educational bureaucracy, and the educational lobbies would have to share their domination of student aid programs with other centers of power under a new approach. On the other hand, expanding the existing student aid program would leave the coalition in control and pose no challenge to its domination of student aid policy. The tax-credit proposal got caught in a power play, and fearing an almost certain Carter veto, aid supporters decided to go with the president's proposed expansion of the traditional aid program. With all the concern over reducing taxes, however, the tax-credit proposal will be a recurring issue in educational politics.

## CONCLUSION

Though education has traditionally been regarded as primarily a state and local function, the federal government's role is a longstanding one. Historically federal involvement has focused on specific needs in particular segments of the school populace. Virtually every federal program, at least until 1965, was designed to achieve certain objectives—vocational training, veterans adjustment, equal opportunity, scientific training, or research. Most early federal programs were quite narrow and specific in their focus. The first major breakthrough in federal aid came in 1958 with the passage of the National Defense Education Act, which authorized a variety of categorical aid programs. Even the NDEA was still short of a massive general aid-to-education program, placing special emphasis on education related to national defense and security. Congress eventually took the final step to a general aid program with the passage of the Elementary and Secondary Education Act in 1965. With the adoption of ESEA there was considerable hope on some fronts that federal aid would continue to expand. This failed to develop, however, as federal aid has remained fairly stable.

Primary responsibility for financing education, especially at the elementary and secondary levels, has remained with the states. The states now spend about $200 billion annually on education and provide about 40 percent of the funds, while the federal share is still less than 10 percent. While federal expenditures have grown from $14.4 billion in 1958-59 to $64 billion in 1977, the federal share of education funding remains relatively small. (See figures 8.1 and 8.2) The federal role is still one of supplementing the states. While there has been fear of loss of local control to the federal government, most of the centralization in educational financing and administration has occurred at the state level. While federal aid has brought some changes in staffing of state educational agencies, the dominant force in educational policymaking in the 1970s has been the state legislature.

Substantial questions remain regarding federal policy, however. With the federal government now committed to extensive general aid, how can its policies best be refined to achieve the maximum desired impact? With some states still having illiteracy rates among those over fourteen years old of more than 5 percent, and with gross disparities among school districts in their ability to generate needed revenues and equalize per-pupil expenditures, what role must the federal government play? A central issue still facing educational policymakers is that of allocating the costs and benefits of education in an equitable fashion.

## Points to Ponder

Is the substantial inequality in the level of educational support provided from state to state and district to district anti-democratic? Is it a matter appropriate for federal policy efforts?

Are the schools instruments for social and economic equality?

Are racially integrated schools essential to equality of education?

Is busing a viable instrument for achieving racial integration in the nation's schools?

Is the property tax a sound mechanism upon which to base local educational funding?

Do federal dollars bring burdensome and unnecessary federal controls on education?

Should parochial schools receive federal aid?

Is there any relationship between level of funding and quality of education in the schools?

## Notes

1. Robert Taft as quoted in *Congress and the Nation* 1945-1964 (Washington, D.C.: Congressional Quarterly, 1965), p. 1202.
2. Dwight Eisenhower, Budget Message, January 21, 1954, as quoted in *Congress and the Nation*, op. cit., p. 1206.
3. Eisenhower as quoted in *Congress and the Nation*, p. 1209.
4. *Serrano* v *Priest*, 487 p. 2d 1241 (1971).
5. *San Antonio Independent School District* v *Rodriquez*, 411 U.S. 1 (1973).
6. *Cochran* v *The Board of Education*, 281 U.S. 370 (1930).
7. *Everson* v *Board of Education of Ewing Township*, 330 U.S. 1 (1947).
8. *McCollum* v *Board of Education*, 333 U.S. 203 (1948).
9. *Zorach* v *Clauson*, 343 U.S. 306 (1948).

**FIGURE 8.1  Federal Outlays for Education, Related Activities: 1960-1976
(figures in millions of dollars, totals rounded)**

| Type of support, program area | 1960 | 1964 | 1968 | 1972 | 1973 | 1974 | 1975 | 1976 (estimated) | Transition quarter (estimated) |
|---|---|---|---|---|---|---|---|---|---|
| Federal Funds Supporting Education in Educational Institutions* | | | | | | | | | |
| Grants, total | $1,474 | $2,312 | $7,178 | $11,422 | $12,344 | $12,727 | $17,110 | $19,670 | $4,213 |
| Elementary and secondary education | 490 | 667 | 2,967 | 3,857 | 4,085 | 4,207 | 4,998 | 5,079 | 1,181 |
| Higher education | 830 | 1,457 | 3,240 | 5,172 | 5,965 | 6,064 | 7,995 | 9,700 | 1,762 |
| Vocation-technical and continuing education | 154 | 189 | 971 | 2,393 | 2,294 | 2,456 | 4,116 | 4,891 | 1,271 |
| Loans, total (higher education) | 240 | 465 | 603 | 349 | 346 | 352 | 480 | 467 | 51 |
| Other Federal Funds for Education and Related Activities** | | | | | | | | | |
| Total | 2,286 | 3,217 | 3,620 | 4,527 | 4,712 | 4,859 | 5,784 | 6,489 | 1,341 |
| GRAND TOTAL | $4,000 | $5,994 | $11,401 | $16,298 | $17,402 | $17,938 | $23,374 | $26,626 | $5,605 |

*Includes education funds from all 11 cabinet departments and 15 agencies, as well as funds for research and development in colleges and universities.
**Includes such programs as military service academies, school lunch and milk, library services, international education, agricultural extension service.
Source: National Center for Education Statistics, Department of Health, Education and Welfare. Reprinted with permission of Congressional Quarterly, Inc.

**FIGURE 8.2  Federal Funds for Education 1940-1978**

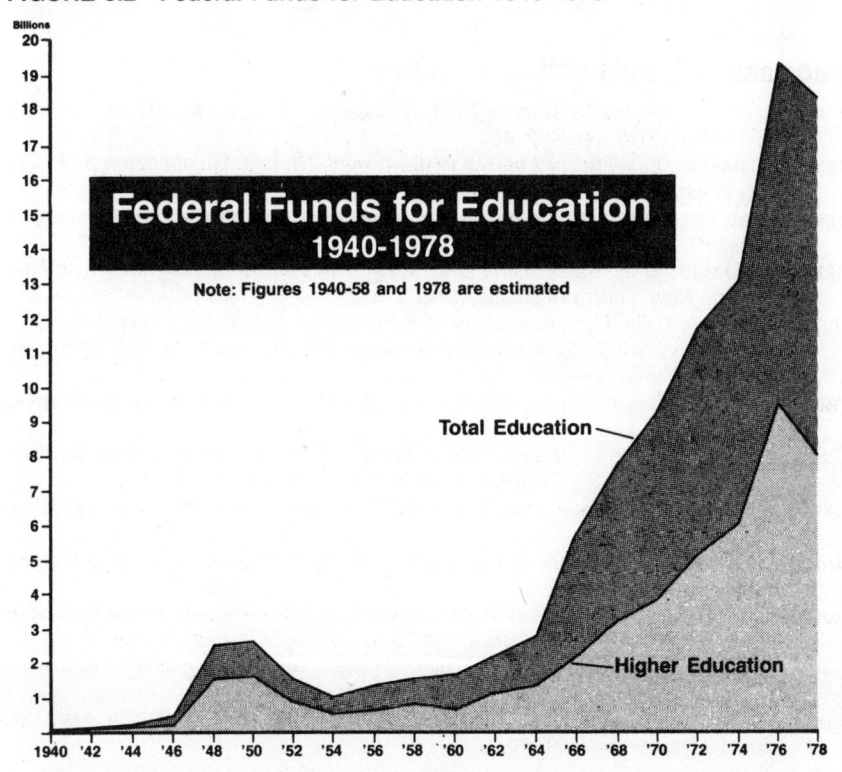

Source: National Center for Education Statistics. Reprinted courtesy of The Chronicle of Higher Education.

10. *Engle* v *Vitale*, 370 U.S. 421 (1962).
11. *Lemon* v *Kurtzman*, 403 U.S. 602 (1971).
12. *Roemer* v *Maryland*, 415 U.S. 382 (1976).
13. Francis Cardinal Spellman as quoted in *Congress and the Nation*, p. 1203.
14. *Plessy* v *Ferguson*, 163 U.S. 537 (1896).
15. *Brown* v *Board of Education of Topeka*, 347 U.S. 483 (1954).
16. *Swann* v *Charlotte-Mecklenburg Board of Education*, 402 U.S. 1 (1971).
17. *Keyes* v *School District #1 of Denver*, 413 U.S. 189 (1973).
18. See James S. Coleman, et al., *Equality of Educational Opportunity* (Washington, D.C.: Government Printing Office, 1966).
19. David Armor, "The Evidence on Busing," *The Public Interest*, No. 28 (Summer 1972), pp. 90-126.
20. Patricia Roberts Harris in speech to Washington Press Club as quoted in *National Journal* (Sept. 8, 1979), p. 1502.
21. Shirley Hufstedler as quoted in Fred Hechinger, "A class struggle? . . . Education chief to fight some program cuts," Louisville, Ky. *Courier-Journal* (January 13, 1980), © 1980 New York Times Company. Reprinted by permission.
22. Glenn Terrell, Jr. as quoted in *Higher Education and National Affairs*, v. 27, no. 16 (April 21, 1978), p. 1.
23. *PER Report*, vol. II, no. 8 (March 1978), p. 2.

## Suggestions for Further Reading

AMOSIKE, BENJI. "The Jencks: Harvard Study Revisited," *The Educational Forum*, vol. 3, no. 4 (May 1975), pp. 435–46.

BENSON, CHARLES. *Educational Finance in the Coming Decade*. Bloomington, Ind.: Phi Delta Kappa, 1975.

BERKE, JOEL and KIRST, M. *Federal Aid to Education*. Lexington, Mass.: Lexington Books, 1972.

BRESNICK, DAVID, et al. *Black/White/Green/Red: The Politics of Education in Ethnic America*. New York: Longmans, 1979.

DUGAN, THOMAS. "The Constitutionality of School Finance Systems Under State Law: New York's Twin," *Syracuse Law Review*, vol. 27, no. 2 (Spring 1976), pp. 573–610.

FRIEDMAN, MURRAY, et al. *New Perspectives on School Integration*. Philadelphia: Fortress Press, 1979.

GRAGLIA, L.A. *Disaster by Decree: The Supreme Court Decisions on Race and the Schools*. Ithaca, N.Y.: Cornell University Press, 1976.

GRUBB, W.N. *New Programs of State School Aid*. Washington, D.C.: National Legislative Conference, 1974.

HALPERIN, SAMUEL. "Politicians and Educators: Two World Views," *Phi Delta Kappan* (November 1974).

JENCKS, CHRISTOPHER. *Inequality: A Reassessment of the Effect of Family and Schooling in America*. New York: Basic Books, 1972.

JOHNS, ROE and MORPHET, EDGAR. *The Economics and Financing of Education: A Systems Approach*. Englewood Cliffs, N.J.: Prentice-Hall, 1975.

KELLY, GEORGE, ed. *Government Aid to Nonpublic Schools: Yes or No?* New York: St. Johns University Press, 1972.

KERR, DONNA. *Educational Policy: Analysis, Structure and Justification.* New York: David McKay, 1976.
KIRP, DAVID. "School Desegregation and the Limits of Legalism," *The Public Interest*, vol. 47 (Spring 1977), pp. 101–128.
LEHNE, RICHARD. *The Quest for Justice: The Politics of School Finance Reform.* New York: Longmans, 1978.
LEVIN, BETSY, ed. "Future Direction for School Finance Reform," a symposium in *Law and Contemporary Problems*, vol. 38 (Winter/Spring 1974), pp. 293–581.
LINDQUIST, ROBERT and WISE, ARTHUR. "Developments in Educational Litigation: Equal Protection," *Journal of Law and Education* (January 1976).
McLAUGHLIN, MILBREY. *Education and Reform.* Lexington, Mass.: Heath, 1974.
MORGAN, RICHARD E. *The Politics of Religious Conflict.* New York: Pegasus, 1970.
MURPHY, JEROME. "The Politics of Implementing Title I," *Harvard Educational Review* (1970).
PORTER, D.D. *The Politics of Budgeting Federal Aid.* Beverly Hills, Sage, 1973.
REISCHAUER, R.D. and HARTMAN, R.W. *Reforming School Finance.* Washington, D.C.: The Brookings Institution, 1973.
ROSSELL, CHRISTINE. "School Desegregation and White Flight," *Political Science Quarterly* 90 (Winter 1975–76), pp. 675–95.
SORAUF, FRANK J. *The Wall of Separation.* Princeton, N.J.: Princeton University Press, 1975.
SOWELL, THOMAS. "Tuition Tax Credits: A Social Revolution," *Policy Review*, no. 4 (Spring 1978), pp. 79–83.
THOMAS, NORMAN. *Education in National Politics.* New York: David McKay, 1975.
WEST, E.G. "Tuition Tax Credit Proposals: An Economic Analysis of the 1978 Packwood/Moynihan Bill," *Policy Review* no. 3 (Winter 1978), pp. 61–75.
WILKINSON, J. HARVIE III. *From Brown to Bakke: The Supreme Court and School Integration, 1954-1978.* New York: Oxford University Press, 1979.
WILLIAMS, MARY F. *Government in the Classroom: Dollars and Power in Education.* New York: Praeger, 1979.
WILLIAMS, WALTER E. "Tuition Tax Credits: Other Benefits," *Policy Review* no. 4 (Spring 1978), pp. 85–89.
WIRT, FREDERICK and KIRST, M. *The Political Web of American Schools.* Boston: Little, Brown & Company, 1972.
WISE, ARTHUR. *Rich Schools, Poor Schools: The Promise of Equal Educational Opportunity.* Chicago: University of Chicago Press, 1972.
ZEIGLER, HARMON and JENNINGS, KENT. *Governing American Schools.* Boston: Duxbury Press, 1974.

# 9

# Parity or Free Market? Federal Agricultural Policy

Back in the 1950s Marryin' Sam in the Broadway musical hit, *Lil Abner*, appeared on stage 693 times singing about the farm bill and "parity." In 1978 and 1979 members of the American Agricultural Movement marched on state capitals and Washington, D.C. demanding federal guarantees of 90 percent parity. About all the average American knows about parity is that it somehow has a relationship to the government's farm price support program and probably means higher prices at the grocery counter. For four decades now debate over parity levels has been at the heart of federal agricultural policy.[1]

Agriculture and farmers traditionally have been held in high esteem by Americans. One of the staunchest defenders of the agricultural way of life was Thomas Jefferson. Jefferson, an advocate of scientific farming, invented an early plow himself, little realizing that the new technologies of agriculture would eventually make it possible for a small farm population to feed an urban, industrial nation, a development that Jefferson, who opposed cities as "sores on the body politic," would have found disturbing.

In Jefferson's day American agriculture was largely subsistence farming with most of the produce being consumed by the farmer's own family. Over 90 percent of the country's population lived on farms. Half a century later in 1850, one farmer still supplied only five people with his produce. During the next half-century American agriculture underwent a dramatic change as mechanization revolutionized farming methods and farm production. Cyrus McCormick, born three days after Abraham Lincoln, was a prime figure in the nation's agricultural revolution. At age twenty-three, McCormick invented a mechanical reaper, and before his death in 1884 he had pioneered many of the mass-production techniques that contributed to the mechanization of American agriculture.

Mechanization, coupled with the market stimulation of the Civil War, brought a rather quick transition from subsistence to cash or commercial farming. The change to commercial farming brought many advantages to the farmers, but it brought problems as well. The new style of farming made farmers highly dependent on markets for their products, and transportation to get their crops to market became a necessity. As farming more and more became a business highly dependent upon the market, farmers quickly discovered they did not control the market so much as the market controlled them. Traditionally farmers have been plagued by boom and bust cycles characterized by dramatic price fluctuations and highly unstable income. It has been characteristic of the agricultural market for a small increase in the supply of a particular commodity to produce a relatively large decline in price.

An interesting outgrowth of this market vulnerability is that American farmers, among the most independent of the nation's rugged individualists, have frequently turned to the federal government to protect them from or at least to alleviate the impact of highly unstable markets. Thus, American political history is spotted with periodic outbreaks of farmer protest and demands for governmental action to improve their economic lot—the Greenbackers (1870s), the Populists (1890s), the Farm Bloc (1920s), the American Agriculture Movement (1970s). Consequently, through the years agriculture has come to be shaped more by governmental policy than probably any other industry. Federal undertakings from early land policies aimed at encouraging expansion, through rural electrification and price support programs, made agriculture, in part, a governmental enterprise. Some critics of federal agricultural policy charge that the alliance of government and farmers has become so close that no clear demarcation can be discerned between the public and private sectors. In his discussion of federal agricultural policy, Professor Theodore Lowi says the distinction between public and private has come close to being obliterated. This has come about, he says, not as many charge, by government takeover of agriculture, but rather by private agriculture expropriating public authority.[2]

## EARLY FEDERAL INVOLVEMENT

As long as American agriculture was largely of the subsistence type, there was little governmental involvement. It was only after the transition to commercial farming that demands began to grow for federal assistance to the agricultural sector. Early efforts to assist agriculture were indirect efforts through such policies as the sale of public lands at cheap prices and the assistance and encouragement of transportation developments. The year 1862 marks the beginning of significant efforts by the federal government to promote agriculture. The Homestead Act encouraged farm expansion by providing public lands virtually free; the Department of Agriculture was created to promote agriculture and to coordinate federal

## Major Agricultural Legislation

**Homestead Act of 1862.** Provided for grants of 160 acres from the public domain to persons paying a filing fee and occupying the land for five years.

**Morrill Act of 1862.** Provided for grants of land to the states for support of colleges to teach agriculture, engineering, and home economics. Basis for the nationwide system of land-grant colleges and universities.

**Smith-Lever Act of 1914.** Provided for the extension agents working with the land-grant colleges to provide information and assistance to farmers.

**Farm Relief Act of 1933.** Major portions of this act were held unconstitutional, but the Commodity Credit Corporation survived.

**Soil Conservation Act of 1935.** Created the Soil Conservation Service.

**Bankhead-Jones Farm Tenant Act of 1937.** Provided federal assistance to farm tenants through easy credit terms to purchase their own farms.

**Agricultural Marketing Agreement Act of 1937.** Provided a program to boost the income of producers of perishable commodities, milk, fruits, and vegetables.

**Water Facilities Act of 1937.** Provided federal loans for construction of farm water storage facilities.

**Agricultural Adjustment Act of 1938.** Provided for the federal program of price supports/production controls for various storable farm commodities.

**Agricultural Trade Development and Assistance Act of 1954.** Provided for the purchase of surplus farm commodities for resale overseas.

**Agricultural Act of 1956.** Created the Soil Bank program providing payments for retiring farmland from production in an effort to reduce surpluses.

**Agriculture and Consumer Protection Act of 1973.** Marked the movement away from the price support/production control programs of three decades toward a free-market agricultural policy. A "target price" approach was adopted for supports and a subsidy limit of $20,000 per year was established for any one farmer.

---

agricultural policies; and the Morrill Act was passed, creating the agricultural and mechanical colleges to educate the sons and daughters of rural America. These actions were followed by the Hatch Act in 1887, which provided matching federal funds for support of state agricultural experiment stations. The agricultural extension agents provided under the Smith-Lever Act (1914), working closely with the land-grant colleges and the agricultural experiment stations, promoted the scientific and technological changes that revolutionized American agriculture and made it a major economic enterprise.

With the government promoting the agricultural sector through the creation of educational and service agencies that contributed to improved farming methods, increased productivity, and larger profits, farming made considerable strides in the

## Principal Departments and Agencies

**United States Department of Agriculture (USDA).** A major cabinet-level department which provides numerous services for farmers and regulates various aspects of agriculture. Included under the Department of Agriculture are the following agencies:

*Agricultural Research Service.* This division conducts research in crop and livestock production and marketing helpful to farmers.

*Extension Service.* Through this service the county extension agents and land-grant colleges provide useful information and research to farmers.

*Forest Service.* This division administers the national forest lands under the jurisdiction of the federal government.

*Soil Conservation Service.* This agency promotes programs and conducts research for erosion and flood control and soil conservation.

*Commodity Exchange Authority.* This agency supervises trading on commodity exchanges where agricultural products are bought and sold.

*Commodity Credit Corporation.* The CCC makes loans to and purchases from farmers to stabilize agricultural prices.

*Federal Crop Insurance Corporation.* This agency insures farmers against loss or damage to their crops.

*Farmers Home Administration (FmHA).* This agency makes low interest loans to low income farmers for crops and farm facilities.

*Rural Electrification Administration (REA).* REA provides loans to finance the extension of electric power to rural areas.

**Farm Credit Administration.** The Farm Credit Administration, an independent agency, is responsible for the supervision, examination, and coordination of the banks and associations that comprise the borrower-owned cooperative Farm Credit System.

**Bureau of Land Management.** A division of the Department of Interior, the BLM has responsibility for grazing on federally controlled lands and other programs related to the conservation and use of natural resources.

---

last decades of the nineteenth and early years of the twentieth century. The 1909–1914 period is frequently referred to as the "golden years" of American agriculture. With war stimulating the market for farm products, farmers continued to prosper through World War I. Contributing to the wartime boom, the government in 1916 adopted the system of Federal Farm Loan Banks to aid farmers with their purchases of land, machinery, and fertilizer. Encouraged by wartime prices and governmental loan policies, many farmers invested heavily in land and machinery. Then the war ended, the bubble burst, and many farmers found themselves over-extended.

With the war over and governmental supports removed, farm prices dropped precipitously. While the rest of the economy prospered in the 1920s, farmers experienced a severe depression. Led by groups such as the Farm Bureau and the Grange, midwestern and southern congressmen formed the "farm bloc" in Congress, which sought the passage of legislation to aid the stricken farmers. The government first tried to raise farm prices by increasing the tariff on imported farm products, but such efforts in both 1921 and 1922 had only slight impact because production continued to exceed demand. When the War Finance Corporation tried to stimulate domestic prices by dumping millions of dollars of surplus commodities abroad, it brought foreign retaliation. The next effort was the so-called "two-price plan" of the McNary-Haugen bills, which proposed to stimulate domestic prices through the purchase of surplus production which would then be sold abroad. Strongly supported by the Farm Bureau and the Grange, McNary-Haugen bills were defeated in Congress in 1924 and 1926. Following a slight but temporary improvement in 1924-1925, agricultural prices continued their decline. In 1927 and again in 1929 Congress passed the McNary-Haugen proposal but President Coolidge vetoed both measures. Congress then looked for other means to bolster farm prices and in 1929 created the Federal Farm Board and provided it with a revolving fund of $500 million to purchase commodities and thereby stimulate farm prices. The board created the Grain Stabilization Corporation, which over the next year bought and stored 257 million bushels of wheat. Another commodity agency, the Cotton Stabilization Board, acquired 1.3 million bales of cotton. Still, with increased farm production and no production controls imposed, prices continued to drop. Wheat dropped to 25 cents per bushel and cotton declined to 5 cents per pound. After one year the Federal Farm Board had spent $400 million with no appreciable effect on farm prices.

President Herbert Hoover began to advocate the use of production controls, but no action was taken during his administration. The arrival of the Great Depression brought even deeper distress to the already economically hard-hit farmers. Corn in 1930 was bringing only one-fifth of what it had brought in 1900. By 1931, three-fifths of all Iowa farms were mortgaged and one-seventh had already suffered foreclosure. On one day in 1932, sheriffs in Mississippi sold a quarter of the land in the entire state to satisfy mortgage and tax claims. When the distraught farmers turned to strikes and demonstrations, Vice President Charles Curtis told them they were "too damn dumb" to understand the issues.

## NEW DIRECTIONS

The coming of the New Deal marked some major changes in direction for federal farm policy. Experience with the Federal Farm Board and other efforts of the 1920s to improve farm prices had illustrated that a basic problem was overproduction. The normal tendency for farmers when faced with lower prices has been to increase production in an effort to generate more income. The result has usually been to drive prices to even lower levels. Appeals to reason and pleas for the farmers to voluntarily reduce production have usually proved futile. The approach embraced by the New Deal aimed at both curbing production and providing some cash to economically strapped farmers. The Farm Relief Act of 1933 proposed to pay farmers for limiting their production of certain commodities. The act provided for the levying of a tax on processors of certain commodities to finance payments to farmers. In January 1936 the Supreme Court declared the Farm Relief Act unconstitutional because it levied a tax on one group for the benefit of another.[3] Undaunted, the Roosevelt administration continued to propose legislative measures designed to benefit farmers. In 1934 the Frazier-Lemke Act was adopted, placing a five-year moratorium on farm mortgage foreclosures. This act was also struck down by the Court in 1936 as a violation of property rights under due process of law. The administration followed the Farm Relief Act with the Soil Conservation and Domestic Allotment Act of 1935, which provided payments to farmers for reducing their production of "soil depleting" crops and using other conservation measures. It just happened that most crops identified as "soil depleting" were those for which overproduction was a problem. The act also created the Soil Conservation Service to provide farmers with aid and technical assistance in soil conservation programs and authorized payments to cover part of the costs of projects. This was followed by the Agricultural Marketing Agreement Act of 1937, which empowered the secretary of agriculture to set minimum prices for fruits, vegetables, and milk.

In 1938 the administration returned with legislation embodying the dual concept of production controls coupled with a system of price supports on various nonperishable farm commodities.[4] The Agricultural Adjustment Act (AAA) of 1938 set the pattern for federal agricultural policy for the next three decades. Under this legislation, the secretary of agriculture could, with the approval of two-thirds of the producers of a particular crop, impose mandatory production controls. This act was quickly challenged in the courts, but was upheld by the Supreme Court in decisions in 1939 and 1942.[5] A primary objective of the 1938 AAA was to increase farm income by stimulating the prices of farm commodities. The legislation sought to accomplish this through production controls to be implemented through a system of flexible price supports, acreage allotments, and marketing quotas. A basic assumption underlying the system is that low support levels will result in reduced production, an assumption that has not always proven valid. Since acreage allotments have not always proved sufficient to curb production, marketing quotas have been necessary for certain crops such as rice and tobacco. Acreage allotments were voluntary, but to qualify for federal price supports on his crops, the farmer had to comply. Marketing quotas on the other hand were mandatory, but to be implemented required the approval of two-thirds of the producers of a particular crop. The alternative to such production curbs is a sharp reduction or in some cases complete removal of governmental price supports. With the exception of rice and tobacco farmers, production controls were never very popular, and a major objective of farm policy critics has been to get the government out of the production control business.

A basic concept incorporated in the 1938 AAA is that of parity for the farmer. Parity is a sort of catchword for economic justice for farmers. The idea of parity actually originated in the 1920s and was adopted as a part of federal farm policy in 1938. In calculating parity, the Department of Agriculture (USDA) uses a list of 350 items—goods, wages, interests, and taxes—and compares these to

218   SUBSIDY POLICIES

prices of the 1910-1914 base period. One hundred percent parity would mean the farmer's produce should have the same purchasing power today as in the 1910-1914 period. Critics contend that the concept of parity is misleading and that parity prices don't necessarily assure farmers a profit. They maintain that because the parity formula doesn't accurately reflect the differences in production costs for different types of farmers, even with parity prices some farmers may go broke while others reap windfall profits. Because agriculture has changed so much since 1910-1914, the critics argue, using that period as a base for calculating parity is not realistic. Whether the parity formula is or is not valid or equitable, a basic issue of agricultural policy for four decades has been at what level farm prices should be supported. Legislation usually has not called for price supports at 100 percent of parity. The 1938 AAA provided for supports ranging from 52 to 75 percent of parity. From 1942 to 1954 the government supported prices at 90 percent of parity. In 1954 the Eisenhower administration got a flexible system reinstated and since then parity levels have ranged between 62.5 percent and 90 percent. Current farm legislation authorizes levels up to 90 percent, but current support levels are about 75 percent. The Democrats have been inclined to endorse higher and more rigid price supports while the Republicans have favored lower, more flexible scales of support.

As new technologies, improved farming methods, and more mechanization continued to increase farm production, the federal price support program began to face surplus problems. Since no farmer need sell for less than the support price guaranteed by the government, if the market price failed to reach the support level, then the government acquired the farmer's crop, thus accumulating and storing large supplies of supported commodities. As the price support programs resulted in the accumulation of growing surpluses, this posed two problems. The stored surpluses tended to have a damper effect on the market price of these commodities, and the government was faced with skyrocketing storage costs. In the 1950s storage costs were reaching $1 million annually and by 1960 the government had spent $156 million for the storage of surplus agricultural products. This led to the search for surplus disposal programs such as PL480, the Food for Peace program, and the School Lunch program. All such efforts, however, made only a small dent in the accumulated surpluses.

By the mid-1950s surpluses had become a major agricultural problem and their persistence began to erode some of the support for high levels of governmental support. Eisenhower, while searching desperately for new markets for farm products, pushed for lower levels of support and a move toward a free market in agriculture. In the Agriculture Act of 1954, Congress adopted a flexible scale of supports pegging prices at from 82.5 to 90 percent of parity and the following year at 75 to 90 percent. Eisenhower and his secretary of agriculture, Ezra Taft Benson, were able to secure legislation reducing supports on rice, cotton, and corn even further, to 65 percent of parity over a period of years. In a further effort to curb surpluses, the Eisenhower administration submitted the Soil Bank program adopted by Congress in 1956. Under this program farmers were paid to retire a part of their acreage. Sometimes under this plan whole farms were taken out of production; however, farmers were retiring their least productive land and several hundred millions were spent with little apparent effect toward surplus reduction. Though the Soil Bank was allowed to lapse in 1960, a variation has been continued through the *diversion payments* program, under which farmers agree to reduce their alloted acreage for a particular crop to qualify for federal payments or in some cases full price supports.

The 1960s saw the government placing more emphasis on direct payments to farmers to curb production and maintain farm income. Kennedy espoused a "supply management" approach to farm policy, but was only partially successful in his efforts. His moves for stricter production controls were defeated in both a referendum among wheat farmers and in Congress. He did secure approval of price supports at a level near world prices and income supplements in the form of cash payments to farmers who voluntarily reduced their crop acreage.

The Republican administrations of Nixon and Ford had as their goals the reduction of governmental controls and a return to free-market agriculture. The trend of the 1970s in U. S. agricultural policy was toward a gradual reduction in governmental controls and a move away from support payments to reimbursement for removing land from production in times of oversupply. This trend is reflected in the Agricultural Act of 1970, which eliminated several of the traditional commodity-by-commodity supply management controls and replaced them with "set-aside" provisions. Under the new approach, once the farmer met the minimum acreage set-aside requirement, he was then free to plant the rest of his farm as he desired. However, to retain their traditional crop bases, farmers were required to plant minimal amounts of certain crops. The 1970 act also for the first time set a ceiling of $55,000 on subsidy payments under any one commodity program. Up to this time subsidy payments of several hundred thousand dollars were not uncommon and some farms received payments of over $1 million.

Plagued with surpluses through the 1950s and 1960s, farm policy began to be influenced by different forces in the 1970s. Worldwide demand eliminated U. S. farm surpluses, and by 1970 one was hearing more and more around Washington that "we should be paying people to grow rather than not grow food." In the early 1970s the U. S. was exporting nearly 60 million tons of grain annually. With the huge grain sales to the Soviets in 1972, the U. S. bins were finally emptied. This placed agricultural policy in a completely different setting. For two decades surpluses had suppressed farm prices and shaped federal farm policy and finally these were gone.

It was this setting that produced the Agriculture and Consumer Protection Act of 1973, which moved farm policy another step away from production controls and price supports and in the free-market direction. In 1973 U. S. storage bins were empty, prices of farm products were rising, and the world demand for U. S. farm produce seemed unabating. The Nixon administration saw the 1973 world market situation as the opportunity for achieving the long-time Republican goal of a free-market agricultural policy. As an alternative to a free market, the Democratically-controlled Senate proposed a system of "target prices." Under the 1973 legislation, "target prices" are substituted for traditional price supports for wheat, cotton, corn, and feed grains. Only tobacco and extra-long staple cotton retain the traditional production control and price support program. Under the target price system, farmers are guaranteed a particular price for their commodity and if market prices do not equal the target price, then producers are paid deficiency payments equal to the difference. A major difference in this approach is that subsidy payments are tied to market prices. When market prices remain above target prices, farmers will receive no payments. Target prices are to be adjusted to reflect changes in the cost-price index. Whereas, in the past, subsidy payments had been tied to the amount of voluntary set-asides a farmer made, under the 1973 act, setting aside acres simply qualifies the farmer for target price guarantees. If market prices stay above the target prices, the farmer gets nothing for his diverted acreage. In the event surpluses should again become a problem, the secretary of agriculture can reintroduce much stronger set-aside requirements, and the act retains standby authority for paying farmers to retire land from production. The act does retain provisions for disaster payments, price support loans, and resource adjustment payments to help farmers with unique problems. The act further reduces the ceiling on subsidy payments to $20,000 and applies the limit to all commodity programs, not to each separate program.

Developments in the farm market situation quickly made the target price approach a hot political issue. Following the huge sale of wheat to the Soviets, the U. S. Department of Agriculture lowered wheat support prices and stopped paying farmers to set aside their land. With the limits removed, farmers planted fencerow to fencerow. Faced with rising inflation, Ford, when he took over the presidency, halted U. S. grain shipments to Russia and Poland. His action was followed by a bumper crop year in 1974, and with foreign markets closed down, the American market was glutted, resulting in sharply tumbling prices. Thus, although their production had increased, the farmers found inflation and rising production costs eating into their profits. In 1975 when Congress passed a bill to raise target prices, Ford vetoed the measure, saying it called for "increased non-essential spending" that could lead to "an escalation of farm program subsidies in succeeding years."

The next year, 1976, saw another bumper crop, and as prices dropped sharply and grain stocks began to mount substantially, some farmers and legislators began to question the free-market approach of the 1973 farm act. Over the vigorous protests of the growers and their congressional supporters, Congress in 1976 replaced the traditional price support and production control program for rice with a target price system that permits both increased production and new producers to enter the market. When the target price program came up for renewal in 1977, President Carter and Congress, under severe pressures from farm interests, clashed over the level for target prices. Opposing congressional efforts to increase subsidy levels, Carter said such a farm bill would be "intolerably inflationary" and threatened a veto. The Senate passed a measure for higher target prices but it was defeated in the House.

As the farmers continued to expand their production, surpluses began to accumulate and prices began to decline. In 1977 farm prices dipped to about 60 percent of parity, their lowest level since the depression year of 1933. In an effort to stem the tide of growing surpluses and declining prices, President Carter resorted again to subsidies and set-asides. The 1977 farm bill, for example, set wheat prices at $2.90 per bushel and required a 20 percent set-aside. Legislation in 1978 reduced target prices on wheat to $2.10 per bushel and continued the set-aside requirements. When farmers produced a bumper corn crop of 6.8 billion bushels in 1978, Carter called for greater acreage set-asides for corn also. Continued high production could bring renewed demands for more production controls.

Although in 1978 net farm income was the third highest on record, climbing from $21 billion in 1977 to $26 billion in 1978, farmers were not particularly happy with the performance of the Carter administration. With the law of supply and demand pushing down the prices of what they had to sell and inflation increasing the prices of everything they had to buy, the farmers once again found themselves in a cost-price squeeze. With farm prices averaging about 75 percent of parity, many farmers began to demand that the secretary of agriculture exercise his authority to raise target prices to the 90 percent parity level. Secretary of Agriculture Bob Bergland and President Carter opposed raising crop support prices to the full legal limits, contending this would feed inflation and would dry up the export market for U. S. grain. Seeking consumer support for the administration's position, Bergland said farmers' demands for 90 percent of parity could add some $50 billion to the nation's food bill.

Feeling that Washington was not responding to their demands, numbers of farmers associated with the American Agriculture Movement decided to press their case directly by marching on the Capitol in a "tractorcade." With their rallying cry of "We've raised enough corn, but not enough hell," about 5000 farmers massed at points around Washington and in February 1979 converged on the Capitol in 2000 farm vehicles, snarling traffic and riling tempers. Secretary Bergland told the farmers that 1978 had been a good year and they were better off than a year before. He said, "Farm income is up . . . prices are at levels where farmers are now able to pay off their bills and keep producing, and we are not going to throw this away and come up with some new scheme." Terming the farmers' demonstration an "unmitigated disaster," Bergland said the display tended "to discredit all of agriculture and does not reflect the majority." The secretary really incurred the wrath of the farmers when he suggested that some of the demonstrators were motivated by greed. Representative Marvin Leath (D-Tex.) even went so far as to call for Bergland's resignation. Other members of Congress were less positive in their responses to the farmer's protests. Representative Peter Peyser (D-N.Y.) said, "I can think of few demonstrations as inappropriate and as counterproductive as the game currently being played on the streets of our nation's capital." Congressman John T. Meyers (R-Ind.) declared, "I'm for farmers, but not that kind. They've lost my support." Even the elements seemed against the farmers as the capital experienced one of its worst snow storms in years, adding to the discomfort of the participants and contributing to the rapid decline in both their numbers and spirit. While Secretary Bergland was quite willing to meet with the farmers and discuss their problems, he refused to accede to their demands for higher price supports.

While 1979 was generally a good year for U. S. farmers with prices improving and good crop yields, many felt the administration was pursuing a "cheap food policy." Then came the Soviet invasion of Afghanistan and the president's embargo on grain sales to Russia, which sent grain prices plunging. With the USDA predicting that 1980 farm income would decline by 20 percent and costs continuing to rise, the farmers again began to press for higher supports.

In 1980, as production costs continued to rise, surpluses continued to build, and farm income continued to decline relatively, it remained to be seen if the administration and Congress would continue to adhere to the target price–set-aside approach embraced in the 1973 legislation, or if they would be tempted to return to a system of the more rigid production controls and price supports of an earlier era. A basic question is what has been the real objective of federal price support programs over the years. An obvious objective, of course, has been to try to insulate farmers and their income against the extreme fluctuations of a market system that tends to react dramatically to even slight variations in supply and demand. Has such protection against drastic price and market fluctuations had as a further objective the protection of the family farm and the perpetuation of a traditional system of agricultural production? If a primary objective of governmental farm policies has been to save the family farm and eliminate farm poverty, then some vehicle other than subsidized commodity prices will be necessary.

D. Gale Johnson in a study titled *Farm Commodity Programs* says net farm income has probably been one to two billion dollars higher annually as a result of governmental price supports.[6] He says this has probably cost consumers another three to four billion in higher prices. Leo Meyer, Earl Heady, and Howard Madsen in a 1968 study estimated that net farm income for 1970 would be $15.6 billion with governmental supports, $11.3 billion in a free market.[7] These studies would seem to indicate that federal programs have bolstered farm income. But have they achieved their primary objectives in doing this? Such programs were said to be on behalf of the poorer farmers, those who could not survive the free-market competition. In reality most of the benefits from the price support programs went to those needing it least. For years Republican opponents argued that federal subsidy payments rewarded too many marginal farmers who went on contributing to the growing surpluses which held down farm prices. Actually, price support operations enlarged the disparities between higher and lower income groups by directing most of the benefits to larger, more economically well-off commercial farms. In 1970 about 75 percent of all payments went to only 35 percent of the farmers, most of whom were among the upper-income group. Over the years 80 to 90 percent of the subsidy payments have gone to the larger farmers whose incomes were already above average; low-income farmers have benefited comparatively little from federal price-support programs.

In a study for the Southern Regional Council, Ray Marshall and Allen Thompson reported that U. S. Department of Agriculture programs had shown little concern for small farmers. In fact they noted a definite USDA bias in favor of the larger-scale farm operations owned and operated by corporate interests. While advancing the "big is better" concept through its programs, the USDA had virtually ignored the small family farms.[8] Thus, while purporting to advance the cause of the small, family-operated farm, federal policies frequently were working toward the opposite effect.

One result of the growing emphasis on cost-efficient, energy, chemical, and capital-intensive farming has been a steady decline in farm population and numbers of farms with an accompanying growth in farm size. (See figures 9.1, 9.2, and 9.3) Starting in 1936, farm population has declined steadily, with average annual declines of 3.1 percent since 1970; 1976 and 1977 were big years for people leaving the farm, with declines of 6.9 percent and 5.4 percent respectively. While the total amount of land under cultivation has remained about the same for the last three decades, the number of farms and farmers has been declining. In their study Marshall and Thompson state:

> One of the greatest tragedies in the past several decades was the large-scale displacement from agriculture of people ill-prepared by education, training or experience for non-farm jobs. Clearly this has resulted in increased urban congestion, with all its associated problems and costs, as well as widespread poverty and unemployment in rural areas.[9]

Should federal agricultural policy be directed more toward stemming this flow of population and maintaining the family farm as a viable element in the agricultural production system? This question is usually sufficient to touch off a heated and prolonged debate as to the appropriate objectives of federal farm policy. Many observers feel that many family farm operations are expensive and inefficient and should not be propped up by federal subsidies. Republican opponents of high price supports pushed by congressional Democrats argued that such policies supported inefficient farm operations that should not be maintained at taxpayer expense. Various sources have come to view the family farm as an expensive luxury paid for by the consumer. They contend that the government should not continue to subsidize the family farm. While many consumers probably share the feeling that taxpayers subsidize farmers heavily, the farmers have their defenders. Pointing out that Americans spend about 17 percent of their income on food, the lowest of any country in the world, Senator Gaylord Nelson (D-Wis.) says that farmers actually subsidize the consumer. Representative Charles Grassley (D-Iowa) says the family farm has proved more efficient than the corporate farm; and Marshall and Thompson in their study of farm policy observed that while the USDA had favored economies of scale, recent developments seem to indicate that size is not necessarily a major determinant of farming efficiency. They further noted that the mass production techniques of the corporate farms have contributed to environmental problems and land exhaustion.[10] Shannon says the small, family farm is doomed, but he notes "When the family-sized farm is gone and factory methods of production replace it, something vital to the American

## FIGURE 9.1 Changes in Number of Farms and Farm Population

| Year | No. of Farms | Population on Farms | Farm Population as % of Total |
|---|---|---|---|
| 1935 | 6,814,000 | 32,161,000 | 25.3 |
| 1940 | 6,350,000 | 30,547,000 | 23.1 |
| 1945 | 5,967,000 | 24,420,000 | 17.5 |
| 1950 | 5,648,000 | 23,048,000 | 15.2 |
| 1955 | 4,654,000 | 19,078,000 | 11.5 |
| 1960 | 3,962,000 | 15,635,000 | 8.7 |
| 1965 | 3,340,000 | 12,363,000 | 6.4 |
| 1976 | 2,924,000 | 9,712,000 | 4.8 |

Source: U.S. Census Reports, Statistical Abstract of the United States.

## FIGURE 9.2 Size of Farms and Value of Production Assets, 1940-1979

| Year | Avg. Farm Acres | Assets (billions) |
|---|---|---|
| 1940 | 174 | 34 |
| 1945 | 195 | N/A |
| 1950 | 215 | 94 |
| 1955 | 243 | 118 |
| 1960 | 302 | 157 |
| 1965 | 340 | 188 |
| 1970 | 373 | 249 |
| 1975 | 387 | 411 |
| 1977 | 393 | 533 |
| 1979 | 400 | N/A |

Sources: Statistical Abstract of the United States and U.S. Department of Agriculture Statistical Report Service

## FIGURE 9.3 Federal Outlays to Stabilize Farm Income (in billions of dollars)

| Year | Agricultural Outlays (billions) | Portion for Stabilizing Farm Income |
|---|---|---|
| 1959 | 5.365 | 4.057 |
| 1964 | 5.186 | 3.803 |
| 1965 | 4.807 | 3.234 |
| 1966 | 3.679 | 1.932 |
| 1967 | 4.376 | 2.536 |
| 1968 | 5.944 | 3.934 |
| 1969 | 5.448 | 4.509 |

Source: Congress and the Nation. Reprinted with permission of Congressional Quarterly, Inc.

scene will also be lost."[11] Former member of Congress and chairman of the House Agriculture Committee, Bob Poage, (D-Tex.) on the other hand maintains "I am convinced that the family farming system—which has survived the technological and social changes of the past forty years—will continue because it is the most efficient instrument we have for agricultural production."[12]

If governmental policies are aimed at saving the small farmers, then they must be reassessed, because in the decades of heaviest federal expenditures of farm subsidies farm closures were high. In the past quarter century more than half the country's farms were forced out of production. While the small farmers were being forced to close their operations, larger farmers were increasing production and often reaping large federal subsidies. Until urban and consumer interests included limits in 1970 and 1973 farm legislation that imposed ceilings on subsidy payments to any one grower, some of the nation's largest farms were receiving huge subsidies. In 1967, for example, five farms got payments of $1 million or more; fifteen farms received payments ranging from $500,000 to $999,000; and 1285 farms were paid $50,000 to $99,000 in federal subsidies. So federal subsidies could hardly be said to be going to the smaller farmers. If anything, during this period federal policy contributed to the growth of the large corporate farms rather than helping to save the smaller farms. Don Paarlberg, a former employee in the Department of Agriculture, notes

> When government undertakes to assist some special group, the chief beneficiaries will turn out to be those in the upper ranges of eligibility. Leadership of the program tends to be captured by those who are more aware, more aggressive, and more politically sophisticated. These are also the ones who are more affluent.[13]

This has definitely been the pattern as far as federal price support programs have been concerned.

## OTHER FEDERAL FARM PROGRAMS

While the production control–price support programs have been the most widely debated and have attracted the most attention, they are only a portion of the federal subsidy program related either directly or indirectly to agriculture. Farmers have reaped substantial benefits from a whole variety of programs, all of which we cannot cover here, but some of the more significant ones will be described. As is often true with governmental subsidy policies, many of the benefits to farmers are provided indirectly. Agricultural cooperatives are exempt from the antitrust laws, farm trucks are exempt from federal motor carrier regulations, farm workers are not included under the unemployment compensation or workmen's compensation regulations, and until 1966 were not even covered by minimum wage provisions, and farmers benefit from a whole host of federal tax write-offs. The USDA carries out extensive research in marketing, crops, chemicals, etc., and government-sponsored research has been a major factor in agricultural change. Many governmental programs are aimed at increasing farm productivity and operating efficiency. In 1976 the federal government provided $645 million for agricultural research. Over the years farmers have benefited substantially from such federal programs as the Rural Electrification Act, the Soil Conservation Service, the Federal Crop Insurance Corporation, the Water Facilities Act, and other programs that helped to develop resources vital to farming.

An area of early and rather extensive federal involvement is farm credit. The Federal Farm Loan Act of 1916 created a system of twelve federal land banks to provide long-term loans to farmers for purchases of land, buildings, and other property. This has been followed by numerous other pieces of legislation that now comprise the Farm Credit System. A key agency in these programs is the Farmers Home Administration (FmHA), sometimes confused with the Federal Housing Administration (FHA). The FmHA is an arm of the U. S. Department of Agriculture and administers a variety of assistance programs for farmers needing economic aid. FmHA makes "economic emergency loans" and loans to "limited resource farmers." Loans are provided to low-income farmers at 3 percent interest for the first three years, 5 percent for the next two years, and not less than 5 percent thereafter, depending upon ability to pay. Some critics suggest that FmHA makes subsidized loans to those who don't really qualify. The agency insists it makes loans only to applicants who don't seem to qualify elsewhere. FmHA defenders point out that as farming becomes more sophisticated and more costly, regular lending institutions become more cautious, tending to make loans only to farmers already well-established. Therefore, to many farmers, FmHA represents the best, maybe only, hope of gaining or holding on to a place in the farming world. When protesting farmers pointed out their economic difficulties, FmHA's role was expanded in 1978 and the agency loaned about $12.5 billion to rural families and communities that year. Farmers suffering from the results of natural disasters may also receive special assistance. The Consolidated Farm and Rural Development Act (1961) provides for loans at low interest rates to farmers and rural homeowners in areas affected by natural disasters. Also in 1976 the legislation providing for the small business disaster loan program was amended to make farmers eligible. Because borrowing from the Small Business Administration is much less involved than borrowing from FmHA, many farmers have turned to this program. In 1977 the interest on these SBA loans was reduced to 3 percent and since the program was opened to farmers, loans have increased from $370 million per year to $2.6 billion per year. In 1977, 11 percent of $460 million loaned went to farmers; the following year 75 percent of $2.26 billion went for farm loans. In 1978, in a move to save money and curb inflation, President Carter vetoed a bill that would have continued the 3 percent interest rate on disaster loans. After October 1, 1978 the interest on such loans rose to 7⅜ percent. In 1979 an amendment to the Small Business Administration reauthorization bill provided for loans of up to $250,000 to farmers at 5 percent interest if credit was not available elsewhere. Carter accepted the new proposal.

It should be pointed out that farmers are not the only ones to benefit from these programs. The benefits from many programs spill over to a variety of citizens and generate a much broader base of support than just among farm interests. A major assumption underlying most of these types of programs, of course, is that agriculture is such a vital function in our welfare and economy that the government must do what it can to keep the nation's farms healthy and productive. As in most areas of public policy, the questions are how this can best be accomplished, and who should pay the bill.

## THE POLITICS OF AGRICULTURAL POLICY

While among the most independent-minded of the country's citizens, farmers have not hesitated to turn to government for redress of their grievances. American history has been punctuated by periodic outbursts of agrarian unrest and political activism, and over the years farmers have organized a variety of interest groups, third parties, and political movements. As observed by noted political scholar, V. O. Key, Jr., such agrarian discontent and political agitation have tended to ebb and flow with the rise and decline of the economic fortunes of the farmers.[14] America's farmers have frequently combined agriculture and politics to their advantage.

Among the most effective manifestations of farm political interests have been the various interest groups developed over the years. However, because the farm population is so heterogeneous, there is no single farm interest. Farmers differ so greatly in terms of farm size, crops, investment, operating efficiency, income, educational level, and political loyalty that their interests and needs frequently bring them into conflict. Many of these differences within the agricultural sector are reflected in farm interest groups and their policy positions. While commodity and specialized groups are numerous, we will discuss here only the larger general interest groups. The largest and probably best known of these is the American Farm Bureau Federation organized in 1919. Claiming 1.8 million "farm family" members, the Farm Bureau has its largest membership in the Midwest and South among the corn, hog, and cotton farmers. The most conservative of the major farm groups, the Farm Bureau usually aligns with the Republican party and business interests in promoting "free market agriculture."

Chief rival of the Farm Bureau is the National Farmers Union (NFU) founded in 1902. With about 225,000 "farm families" as members, the NFU draws its members primarily in the wheat-growing states of the Great Plains and Wisconsin, Minnesota, and Montana. Most liberal of the major farm groups, the Farmers Union usually aligns with the Democratic party and stresses an active role for government in agricultural policy. Their guiding philosophy is, "Farm prices are made in Washington," and they have favored high price-support levels. A staunch defender of the family farm system, the Union is often a political ally of organized labor.

Oldest of the general farm organizations is the National Grange, dating from 1867. Once powerful in the Midwest, the Grange now has most of its 750,000 individual members in New England, New York, Pennsylvania, Ohio, and Washington and Oregon. It is strongest among fruit and vegetable growers, poultrymen, and dairymen. Once rivaling the Farm Bureau in its conservatism, Grange policies have shifted since the 1940s and the Grange is now closer to the Farmers Union in its politics than the Farm Bureau. Like the Farmers Union, it is a

### FIGURE 9.4 Farm Commodity Organizations

| | |
|---|---|
| American National Cattlemen's Association | National Wood Growers Association |
| American Meat Institute | National Wheat Growers Association |
| American Poultry and Hatchery Federation | National Canners Association |
| American Sugar Cane League of the United States | National Association of Frozen Food Packers |
| | National Rural Electric Cooperatives Association |
| Association of Sugar Producers of Puerto Rico | National Turkey Federation |
| Institute of American Poultry Industries | United Fruit and Vegetable Association |
| Industrial Sugar Users Group | United States Beet Sugar Association |
| Hawaiian Sugar Planners Association | United States Cane Sugar Refiners Association |
| National Council of Farmer Cooperatives | |
| National Milk Producers Federation | Vegetable Growers Asociation of America |
| National Cotton Council of America | Western Growers Association (Fruit and Vegetable) |
| National Livestock Feeders Association | |

defender of the family farm and now supports governmental controls and high price supports.

Among the newcomers is the National Farmers Organization (NFO), which emerged in Iowa in the mid-fifties and attracted considerable attention with its early militancy. Representing primarily small and medium-sized farms, the NFO has most of its 200,000 members in the Midwest. An early advocate of direct action to apply pressures to the buyers of farm produce, the NFO attracted attention with its withholding actions and stockyard "stall-ins" in the 1960s, but achieved little success with this approach. The NFO has now become more conventional in its activities.

The new militant among farm groups is the American Agriculture Movement (AAM) formed in the 1970s and drawing its heaviest support among the grain and cotton farmers of the West and South. The AAM has staged massive "tractor-cades" in many state capitals and in Washington, D.C. to call the attention of policymakers to AAM demands for higher price-support levels to offset the farmer's rising production costs. The group has called upon the nation's farmers to strike if their demands are not met.

Joining the general farm groups in the agricultural policy arena are a whole host of commodity organizations too numerous to describe individually (figure 9.4 lists some of these groups). Because Congress has traditionally formulated policy on a commodity-by-commodity basis, and because they are usually more united, better organized, and can zero in on specific legislative provisions, the commodity organizations are frequently more effective politically than the larger general-farm organizations.

Through the years the interests and policy objectives of the farm groups have changed, of course. Since World War II the most politically sensitive programs have been those involving the questions of price supports and production controls. The overall political effectiveness of farmers on such issues has been reduced by their own lack of unity and frequently conflicting policy interests. Higher price-support levels for the grain farmers mean higher feed and production costs for beef, hog, and poultry farmers. While tobacco and rice farmers may welcome production controls and marketing quotas to maintain higher prices, wheat and corn farmers may abhor such governmental interference with their planting practices. Farm groups also are divided substantially by different ideological and political orientations which, according to Graham Wilson, may do more to direct the lobby demands of farm interest groups than the pragmatic, material interests of producers.[15] In 1973 the farm bill was adopted in Congress while the two major farm lobbies, the American Farm Bureau and the Farmers Union, were locked in a philosophical confrontation over what direction governmental support should take. In spite of the declines in farm population and political power, farm groups have not directed much effort toward lining up outside support. Former House Agriculture Committee Chairman Bob Poage says that too many farmers simply assume that since people cannot survive without food and fiber, everyone in society sees the necessity for helping farmers survive. Rather than cultivating such support, some groups such as the NFO and AAM have been ineffective in building alliances with other groups and in some instances actually alienated potential supporters with some of their militant tactics. In spite of the multitude of groups representing farm interests, a majority of American farmers remain unorganized. The farm sector that has been most neglected in the policy process—the small, marginal farmers and the farm laborers—is largely unorganized and its interests largely unarticulated. For the most part, its concerns do not reach the political agenda.

The diversity and fragmentation among farm interest groups is also characteristic of the governmental machinery for making and implementing agricultural policy. A General Accounting Office study a few years ago found that thirty congressional committees and twenty-six executive departments and agencies had a hand in food and agricultural policy. While, as in many policy areas, much of the initiative in agricultural policymaking is now exercised by the executive branch, Congress has retained a substantial role in the shaping of farm programs. The division of responsibility sometimes results in stalemate as in the 1955-1960 period or in open confrontation as in 1975 when Congress seized the initiative only to have President Carter veto the result of its efforts.

Heading up the executive bureaucracy in the agricultural field is the United States Department of Agriculture with about 80,000 employees and an annual budget of about $15 billion. The difficulties of administering federal farm policy are attested to by the fact that no secretary of agriculture since Henry Wallace in the 1930s has remained popular for long. Many of the more specialized agencies have identified very closely with their clientele groups, and many charge that for all practical purposes the USDA is a captive of the agribusiness interests. Marshall and Thompson concluded that, "The present agricultural system is dominated by certain actors who attempt to maintain control primarily for their benefit." This includes large farmers and their organizations, the USDA, the land-grant college system, food processors, agricultural equipment dealers, and key members of Congress.[16]

In Congress, agricultural policy has been dominated by key members on the House and Senate Agriculture Committees. Operations of these committees have been characterized by a system of influential subcommittees organized along commodity lines. Because of the practice of appointing members to committees on the basis of their district and personal interests, these subcommittees have usually been dominated by representatives from districts producing the particular commodity under committee purview. This highly specialized committee approach has contributed to the decline in general application farm legislation and the adoption of a series of commodity programs acceptable to representatives and groups from the commodity areas. Another set of subcommittees also influencing farm policy is the Agricultural Subcommittees of the Appropriations Committees, especially the House subcommittee chaired by Representative Jamie Whitten (D-Miss.). Because of his subcommitee's oversight of the USDA budget, Whitten, a forty-year member of Congress, has had his impact on agricultural policy. A staunch conservative, Whitten expresses his sentiments this way: "It always pays to follow what's tested, tried and true. It pays to put money where you can expect returns." Through his control of the purse strings, Whitten has frequently been a thorn in the side of secretaries of agriculture. Carter administration Secretary of Agriculture Bob Bergland complained that Whitten was "seriously impairing" his right to run his department. Although Whitten took over as chairman of the full House Appropriations Committee in 1979, he retained his chairmanship of the Agricultural Subcommittee and if anything his influence is likely to be even greater.

For many years, agricultural policy was shaped largely in a tightly-knit governmental sub-system dominated by the USDA, the Agricultural Committees of Congress, and farm and farm-related interest groups. From the 1930s to 1960 farm policies were usually arrived at by negotiation and compromise among various sub-government participants with very limited input from such outside interests as "consumer" or "public" groups. A classic example of this process was milk policy, which was determined by a sub-government comprised of the National Milk Producers Federation, other dairy and farmer groups, the House and Senate Agriculture Committees, and the USDA marketing authorities. The 1960s brought changes that began to erode the political power and control of this agricultural sub-government. Farmers declined in both numbers and relative economic influence, reapportionment and population change brought losses in representation and changes in leadership in Congress, and the emergence of other interests brought increased competition for the available budgetary resources. Farm population now accounts for less than 4 percent of the nation's total and continues to decline. This trend, coupled with the Supreme Court's decisions requiring congressional districts to reflect population more accurately, has brought appreciable changes in farm representation in Congress. There are fewer than 20 farmers in Congress, and since 1965 the number of House districts in which 20 percent or more of the population live on farms dropped from 154 to only 12 in 1973. These changes have also been reflected in the congressional committees shaping agricultural policy. Traditionally, southern Democrats had dominated the Agriculture Committees. In 1973, half the Democrats on the House Agriculture Committee were from thirteen southern states; in 1977, only ten of thirty-one Democrats were southerners. The major significance of these changes has been that though the Agriculture Committees are still controlled by farm-oriented members, the decline in rural membership overall has meant that the farm-oriented members must now seek the support of urban congressmen to get their legislation passed. In other words, farm politics is not what it once was.

Some observers feel that these recent developments have broken the hold of the agricultural sub-system on farm policy and that the change in emphasis from "farm" policy to "food" policy has marked the dawn of a new day in agricultural politics. Don Paarlberg, a USDA official during the Eisenhower-Nixon years, says, "The agricultural establishment has, in large measure, lost control of the farm policy agenda." A look at some recent programs would seem to indicate that, indeed, farm groups are no longer able to control the agricultural policy agenda as successfully as they once did. As Congress has become a more urban institution, more rural-urban accommodation has become a necessity for getting farm legislation approved. The 1965 Food and Agriculture Act received urban votes in exchange for rural votes in support of the repeal of Section 14-b of Taft-Hartley. The 1970 Agricultural Act also was a rural-urban package, combining price supports and the food stamp program. By the 1970s consumer groups were also getting into the picture more with the activities of such groups as the Consumer Federation of America, National Consumers Congress, and Congress Watch. The $20,000 limit on subsidy payments included in the 1973 farm bill was passed by the urban and consumer interests over the opposition of farm interests. While these developments have prompted predictions that the farmers were losing their grip on agricultural policy, such conclusions may be premature. There is no doubt but what the process has been opened up somewhat to new participants and that urban votes are now a necessity for passage of farm bills, but with farm-state members such as Jamie Whitten and William Natcher heading key appropriations committees in Congress, accommodation is still the name of the game. An old hand at the game of political log-rolling, former Representative Bob Poage advised farmers in these words:

> If any group makes up less than 5 percent of the population in a democracy, the friends of that group must work out an accommodation with the 95 percent and—in many cases—must make more concessions than they want to....
>
> The surest way of serving the farmers' interest in the long run, is to try to combine farm and consumer interests in running the Department of Agriculture and designing our farm and food programs.[17]

Though the farm sector has seen its political base severely eroded and its almost total control of the farm policy agenda reduced somewhat, the nature of the governmental and political institutions that make farm policy insure a substantial role for farm interests and their representatives for some time to come.

## CONCLUSION

Agricultural policy in the 1970s has been in a state of flux, in part as a result of the tremendous changes taking place in agriculture since 1930. From its early subsistence beginnings, American agriculture has evolved into the nation's largest single industry, now accounting for almost 3 percent of the nation's total economic production and employing nearly 17 million people in its various phases. Technological and managerial changes in the last half-century have made modern agriculture a highly scientific, capital-intensive operation. Today's farmer makes extensive use of electricity and machinery; he relies heavily on chemical fertilizers, pesticides, herbicides, and scientifically developed new plant varieties, methods of disease control, and treatment and breeding; and he employs the latest cost-accounting methods. Today's farmer is better educated and much more sophisticated in his operation than his predecessor of a few decades ago; he is also much more dependent upon governmental and private research and extension programs. Take for example Marlowe Park III, a fourth-generation planter in the Mississippi Delta. He manages 1500 acres and has a bachelor's degree in agronomy and a master's degree in horticulture with a minor in weeds from Mississippi State University. Luther Alexander, associate county extension agent in Washington County, Mississippi observes, "The farmer today has to be a market analyst, a weatherman, a soil scientist. Everything is mechanized, six and eight-row equipment, insecticides, fertilizers, but it's expensive."[18]

The technological revolution in agriculture has expanded the scale of almost everything connected with farming. While the number of farms has steadily declined, their average size has grown, doubling since 1940. Fewer farmers produce more and more on less land. The modern farmer faces high day-to-day

**FIGURE 9.5  Farm Prices and Farm Costs February 1970–February 1979**

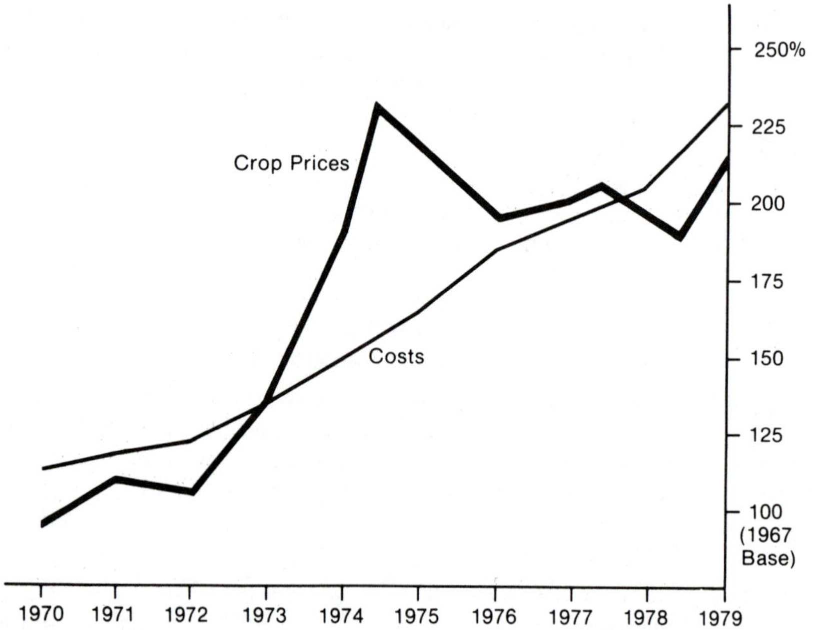

Source: U.S. Department of Agriculture

operating costs and enormous financial investments in land and equipment. The average capital investment for farmers in the Ohio River Valley in Kentucky doubled between 1973 and 1978. Some land is now valued as high as $3000 per acre. This is not an unusual situation in prime farming regions. Many young farmers have gone deeply in debt trying to operate on a scale that will make farming profitable. Joe Neal Ballance, a twenty-eight-year-old Warren County, Kentucky farmer, owns 1000 acres and leases another 1000 acres. He owns two $55,000 combines and a $52,000 tractor and pays $90,000 interest annually. Ballance's is not a unique pattern among farmers. As production costs and inflation have eaten up their margin, farmers have had to expand production to make a profit. Many have gone deeply in debt, piling up hundreds of thousands of dollars in investments, and interest payments alone of $60,000 per year are not unusual.

With its big investments, long hard workdays, big problems, and numerous uncertainties, farming has become an extremely high-pressure profession, now ranking among the top ten in stress. This is little wonder when such factors largely beyond their control as unpredictable weather, market fluctuations, or bumper crop yields can dramatically affect the farmer's economic well-being. Regardless

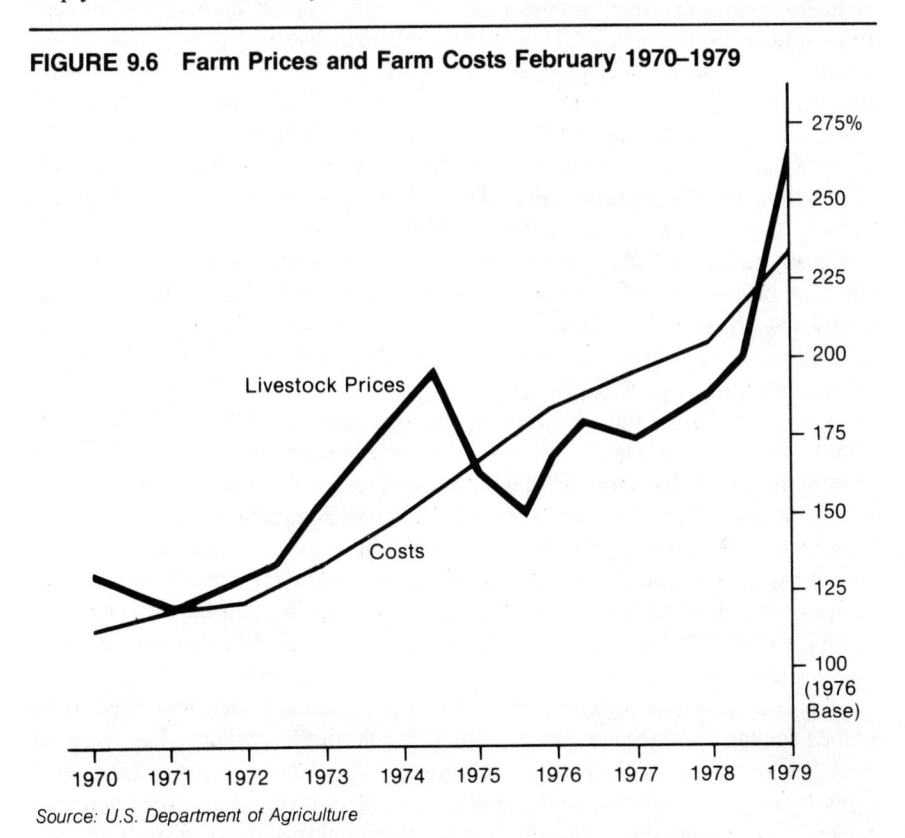

**FIGURE 9.6  Farm Prices and Farm Costs February 1970–1979**

Source: U.S. Department of Agriculture

of what either they or the government does, farmers always seem in the words of Charles Dickens to face "the best of times and the worst of times" economically. The problem has usually been diagnosed as one of prices and income, as farmers have frequently found themselves caught in a cost-price squeeze. (See figures 9.5 and 9.6) Since the emergence of commercial farming, farmers have found themselves at the almost absolute mercy of the marketplace. Because of the nature of their operations and their produce, most farmers have few options when it comes to marketing their crops, either as to time, place, or price. Traditionally farm prices have been substantially affected by commodity supplies, and the very productivity achieved through improved mechanization and technology has often compounded the problem of securing adequate prices for the farmers. Furthermore, farmers have not been very successful in their own efforts to voluntarily reduce supplies and increase prices.

Consequently, even when other sectors of the economy have been faring quite well, the farm sector has frequently been plagued with cost-price problems. While, as noted earlier, farmers remain a major producer in the American economy, as the economy continues to expand, the farm sector accounts for a smaller and smaller proportion of the national income. Over the last few decades, virtually every other major industry has grown more rapidly than agriculture, and to complicate the farmer's lot even further, he usually doesn't even benefit as much as others from increases in prices of what he produces. From 1963 to 1977 the cost of food increased by $107 billion. Of this increased cost, however, only 31.5 percent went to the farmer while the other 68.5 percent went to labor/middleman costs. Since 1963 food advertising expenditures have increased by 100 percent to $2.6 billion in 1977 and profits in the food advertising industry have grown by 240 percent to $8 billion annually. Still in 1977 farmers got only 32 cents of the nation's food dollar, a share that has remained relatively stable since 1974, while the share of the middleman has grown by more than $30 billion during the same period. (See figure 9.7) Statistically, 1978 was a good year for farmers as national farm income rose by 40 percent to $28 billion. This picture is deceiving, however, because the farmers gained little, if any, in purchasing power. The prices for most everything the farmer buys continue to increase more rapidly than the prices of what he produces, or at least, the share he receives for what he produces. The cost of farm machinery has increased about twice as fast as farm income and a tractor may now cost more than a Mercedes. In 1977 farmers paid $3 billion in state and local taxes, a 53 percent increase since 1967. Under current conditions a farmer with a paper worth of $2 million may earn about $18,000 annually, and many farmers work dawn to dark for less than the minimum wage. Many others don't make it; in 1977 four times as many farmers left the land in Wisconsin as in 1974. This has been the pattern in many other farm states as well.

It is against this backdrop that federal agricultural policy will have to be shaped for the next decade. As agriculture's role in the economy has emerged through the years and farmers have become more interdependent with other groups economically, agricultural and food policy have taken on considerable importance for national economic stability, human health and nutrition, social welfare, and

*Parity or Free Market? Federal Agricultural Policy* 235

"Why, yes, we're called 'middlemen'... how'd you guess?"

Reprinted courtesy of Hugh Haynie and the Louisville, Ky. Courier-Journal.

international relations. More than 40 percent of food aid goes to countries that are important to the U. S. for military and political reasons. Also having implications for our foreign policy is the fact that foreign markets have increasingly become an important outlet for U. S. farm products, especially grain and soybeans. In recent years about 62 percent of U. S. wheat, 24 percent of U. S. corn, and 35 percent of the soybeans have been exported. For many nations of the world the U. S. has become a major supplier of agricultural products. In 1975 the U. S. supplied 48 percent of the wheat, 56 percent of the feed grains, 50 percent of the oil seeds, and 27 percent of the rice sold internationally. Currently, producers of wheat and feed grains are experiencing their biggest cost-price squeeze since the Great Depression of the 1930s. A drastic reduction in production in these areas could have serious implications both at home and abroad.

As the economically pinched farmers march on Washington to press their case for parity, the sixty-four-dollar question facing agricultural policymakers is essentially the same as that faced for the last four decades. Can farmers be provided a fair share of the national income and enabled to produce effectively without governmental regulation of their production and market prices? In a 1978 speech to the Mid-Continent Farmers Association in Columbia, Missouri, President Carter told his audience that he wanted to do everything possible "to get the government out of the farm business." He said, "The person most competent to make a farmer's decisions is not a bureaucrat in Washington or anywhere else; it is the man

**FIGURE 9.7**

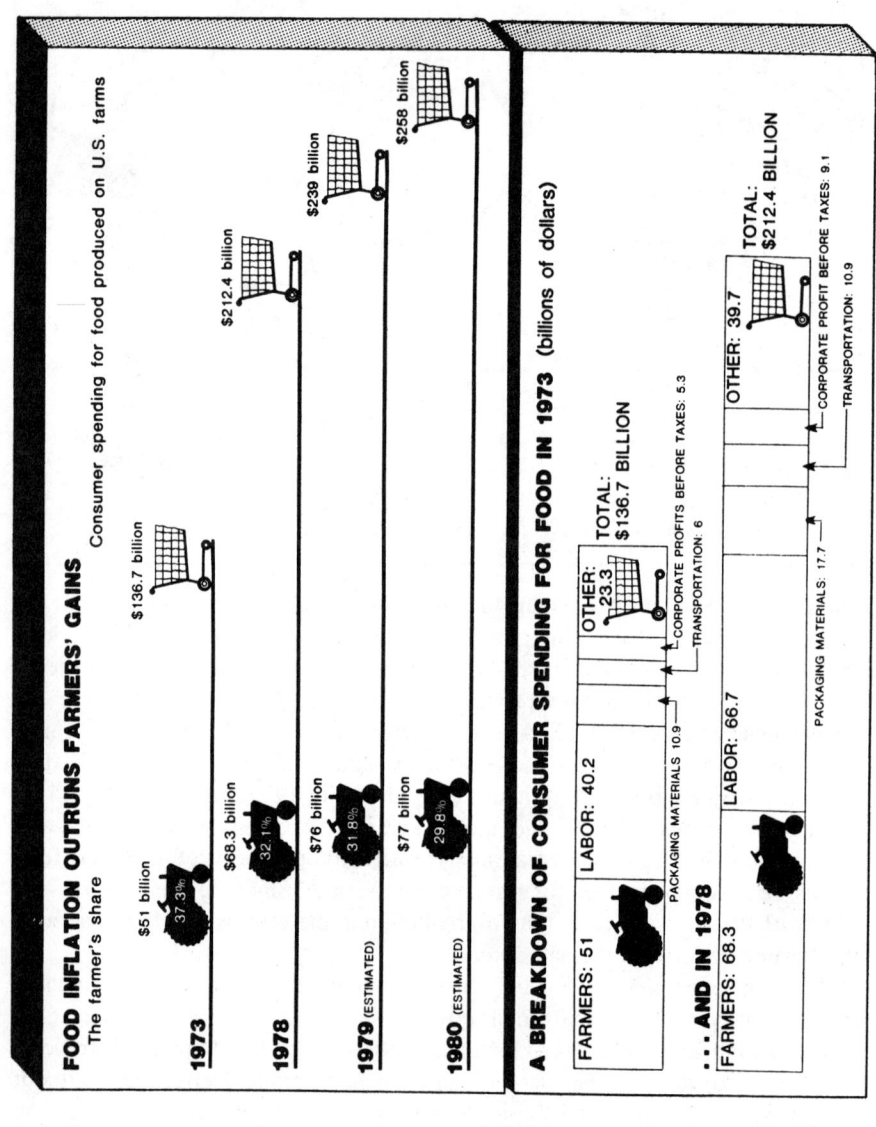

## FOOD INFLATION OUTRUNS FARMERS' GAINS
The farmer's share — Consumer spending for food produced on U.S. farms

**1973** — $51 billion / 37.3% — $136.7 billion
**1978** — $68.3 billion / 32.1% — $212.4 billion
**1979** (ESTIMATED) — $76 billion / 31.8% — $239 billion
**1980** (ESTIMATED) — $77 billion / 29.8% — $258 billion

## A BREAKDOWN OF CONSUMER SPENDING FOR FOOD IN 1973 (billions of dollars)

FARMERS: 51 | LABOR: 40.2 | PACKAGING MATERIALS 10.9 | OTHER: 23.3 | TOTAL: $136.7 BILLION
— CORPORATE PROFITS BEFORE TAXES: 5.3
— TRANSPORTATION: 6

### ...AND IN 1978

FARMERS: 68.3 | LABOR: 66.7 | PACKAGING MATERIALS: 17.7 | OTHER: 39.7 | TOTAL: $212.4 BILLION
— CORPORATE PROFIT BEFORE TAXES: 9.1
— TRANSPORTATION: 10.9

Source: U.S. Department of Agriculture. Reprinted courtesy of the Louisville, Ky. Courier-Journal.

or woman on the farm."[19] Does this mean governmental abandonment of production controls and set-asides and adoption of the free-market approach in agriculture? If so, are the days of the family farm numbered and are we on the way to huge corporate farms that like so much else in America will one day be owned by the giant conglomerates? Though farm politics seem to have changed considerably, the basic issues remain much the same.

## Points to Ponder

Are organized farm groups such as the American Farm Bureau Federation and the National Farmers Union very representative of the smaller, rank-and-file farmers?

Is a free-market system possible in agriculture?

Would elimination of small family farms and a move to large corporate farm operations reduce production costs and bring lower consumer prices?

Do governmental price support programs cause overproduction and contribute to the instability of agricultural markets?

If the smaller-scale family farms are less cost efficient, should governmental policy try to save them?

## Notes

1. Today parity involves complex formulae used by the Department of Agriculture to determine farm price support levels. Simply stated, parity is the relationship between the prices farmers receive for their produce and the prices they pay for things they buy. With 100 percent parity, a farmer's bushel of wheat should have the same buying power today as in the base period used.
2. Theodore Lowi, *The End of Liberalism*, 2nd ed. (New York: Norton, 1979), p. 68.
3. *U.S.* v *Butler*, 297 U.S. 1 (1936).
4. Actually most farm commodities have not come under price support programs. Only about 20 of some 300 farm commodities have been covered. They include wheat, cotton, corn, peanuts, rice, tobacco, milk, wool, mohair, tung nuts, barley, oats, rye, soybeans, grain sorghum, honey, flaxseed, dry edible beans, and gum naval stores.
5. *Mulford* v *Smith*, 307 U.S. 38 (1939), and *Wickard* v *Filburn*, 317 U.S. 111 (1942).
6. D. Gale Johnson, *Farm Commodity Programs* (Washington, D.C.: American Enterprise Institute for Policy Research, 1973), p. 3.
7. Leo V. Meyer, Earl O. Heady, and Howard C. Madsen, *Farm Programs for the 1970s* (Ames, Iowa: Iowa State University Center for Agricultural and Economic Development, 1968), pp. 34, 51.
8. Ray Marshall and Allen Thompson, *Status and Prospects of Small Farmers in the South* (Atlanta: Southern Regional Council, 1976), pp. 61–68.
9. *Ibid.*
10. *Ibid.*, pp. 1–2.
11. Fred Shannon, *American Farmers' Movements* (Princeton: D. Van Nostrand, 1957), p. 96.
12. W. R. (Bob) Poage, "How Can Farmers Live in An Urban Society?" *Progressive Farmer* (February 1979), p. 19.
13. Don Paarlberg, "A New Agenda for Agriculture," *Policy Studies Journal* (Summer 1978), p. 506.
14. V.O. Key, *Politics, Parties, and Pressure Groups*, 4th ed. (New York: Crowell, 1958), pp. 27–36.

15. Graham K. Wilson, "Special Interest, Interest Groups Misguided Interventionism: Explaining Agricultural Subsidies in the U.S.," *Politics* (November 1976), pp. 123–139.
16. Marshall and Thompson, *op. cit.*, pp. 13–14.
17. W. R. Poage, *op. cit.*, p. 18.
18. Wayne King, "Winds of Change Blowing Through Cotton's Kingdom," Louisville, Ky. *Courier-Journal* (November 1978), © 1978 New York Times Company. Reprinted by permission.
19. James Gerstenzang, "Carter wants bureaucrats off the farm," Louisville, Ky. *Courier-Journal* (August 15, 1978), Associated Press News Story. Reprinted by permission.

## Suggestions for Further Reading

COCHRANE, WILLARD and RYAN, MARY E. *American Farm Policy, 1948-1973*. Minneapolis: University of Minnesota Press, 1976.

CRAMPTON, A.J. *The National Farmers Union: The Ideology of A Pressure Group*. Lincoln, Nebr.: University of Nebraska Press, 1965.

EBELING, WALTER. *The Fruited Plain: The Story of American Agriculture*. Berkeley: University of California Press, 1979.

FRAENKEL, RICHARD, et al., eds. *The Role of U.S. Agriculture in Foreign Policy*. New York: Praeger, 1979.

GARDNER, BRUCE and RICHARDSON, JAMES, eds. *Economic Problems of U.S. Agriculture: Papers and Proceedings of the National Farm Summit*. College Station, Tex.: Texas A & M Press, 1979.

HADWIGER, DON F. and FRAENKEL, RICHARD. "The Agricultural Policy Process," *Policy Studies Journal* (Autumn 1975), p. 20.

HADWIGER, DON and BROWNE, WILLIAM. *The New Politics of Food*. Lexington, Mass.: Lexington Books, 1978.

JOHNSON, D. GALE. *Farm Commodity Programs*, Washington, D.C.: American Enterprise Institute for Public Policy Research, 1973.

JONES, CHARLES O. "Representation in Congress: The Case of the House Agriculture Committee," *American Political Science Review* (June 1961), pp. 358–72.

LEWIS-BECK, MICHAEL. "Agrarian Political Behavior in the United States," *American Journal of Political Science*, vol., no. 1 (Summer 1978), p. 79.

MORGAN, DAN. *Merchants of Grain*. New York: Viking Press, 1979.

O'ROURKE, DESMOND. *The Changing Dimensions of U.S. Agricultural Policy*. Englewood Cliffs, N.J.: Prentice-Hall, 1978.

PAARLBERG, DON. "A New Agenda for Agriculture," *Policy Studies Journal* (Summer 1978), p. 504.

PAARLBERG, DON. *Farm and Food Policy: Issues of the Nineteen Eighties*. Lincoln, Nebr.: University of Nebraska Press, 1979.

TALBOT, ROSS and HADWIGER, DON. *The Policy Process in American Agriculture*. San Francisco: Chandler, 1968.

TWEETEN, LUTHER. *Foundations of Farm Policy*, 2nd ed. Lincoln, Nebr.: University of Nebraska Press, 1979.

WILCOX, WALTER, et al. *Economics of American Agriculture*. Englewood Cliffs, N.J.: Prentice-Hall, 1974.

YOUNGBERG, GARTH. "U.S. Agriculture in the 1970s: Policy and Politics," in Anderson's *Economic Regulatory Policies*, pp. 51–68. Lexington, Mass.: Heath, 1976.

YOUNGBERG, GARTH. "U.S. Agriculture Policy in the 1970s: Continuity and Change in an Uncertain World," *Policy Studies Journal* 4 (Autumn 1975), p. 25.

# Part Four

# Regulatory Policy

Governmental regulation and its discussion are not new phenomena; Adam Smith's *Wealth of Nations*, appearing at the time of the American Revolution, was a protest against the extensive regulation of the English mercantilist system, and the debate has continued in the United States through the 200-year history of our republic. However, the greatly expanded role of the government in regulating individual, institutional, and corporate activity in the latter half of the twentieth century has greatly intensified the discussion of this realm of federal policy.

Until the latter part of the nineteenth century, federal regulation was largely confined to the enactment of tariff legislation and the creation of a national banking system designed to maintain a uniform and sound money supply. Through the years, as our population grew and became 75 percent urban, the country changed from rural-agrarian to urban-industrial, and technological change brought new problems. The federal regulatory role grew until today virtually every aspect of people's lives—the food they eat, the air they breathe, the prices they pay, their working conditions, what they hear on the radio or see on television—is touched by federal regulation. Almost every facet of business activity is subject to scrutiny by one or more governmental agencies that have the power to inspect, review, modify, or reject the actions of private enterprises. This growth in the federal regulatory role has become cause for concern among both liberals and conservatives. Syndicated columnist James J. Kilpatrick complains, "One of the most depressing aspects of our supposedly free society is the government's itch to regulate the lives of the people." Again he writes, "We are cosseted half to death by a government that excessively loves our safety, our health, our diets and our dear children's delicate little psyches. Aaarghh!"[1]

While governmental regulations and agencies have grown steadily through the years, the decade of the 1970s brought an unprecedented expansion in the scope and pervasiveness of federal regulatory activity, exceeding even the New Deal era. (See figure A) The period 1970-79 saw the creation of twenty new regulatory agencies, compared to only eleven produced by the New Deal era. In the 1970s regulation became the "growth industry" of the decade, with the leading growth areas being in the fields of social regulation such as job safety, energy, environment, consumer safety, and health. Current staffing of federal regulatory agencies is three times the 1970 level, and current regulatory expenditures are approximately six times larger than for 1970. Forty-one regulatory agencies had 1979 budgets of $4.82 billion, double their budgets only four years earlier. Agencies start small but grow quickly; in 1979 the Environmental Protection Agency had a $522 million budget compared to $232 million four years earlier. During the 1970s Congress passed more than thirty laws making substantial changes in the regulatory framework. The agencies also substantially expanded the regulatory field through the issuance of regulations and amendments frequently carrying the weight of law. In 1974 Congress enacted forty laws, while that same year administrative agencies cranked out 7496 new or amended regulations. For 1978, the *Federal Register* carried announcements of 7031 final regulations, many of them carrying fines and other sanctions just as acts of Congress do.

Not only has the magnitude of federal regulatory activity grown, but it has also shifted significantly in its scope and purpose. Early governmental regulatory efforts were part of a much broader development in American social history— outgrowths of the Populist and Progressive impulses to create an economic system

**FIGURE A  Federal Regulation Growth in the '70s**

| | Major Regulatory Agencies | | Agency Spending (millions) | | Pages in Federal Register | Pages in Code of Federal Regulations |
|---|---|---|---|---|---|---|
| | Economic | Social | Economic | Social | | |
| 1970 | 8 | 12 | $166.1 | $1,449.3 | 20,036 | 54,105 |
| 1971 | 8 | 15 | 196.8 | 1,882.2 | 25,447 | 54,487 |
| 1972 | 8 | 15 | 246.3 | 2,247.5 | 28,924 | 61,035 |
| 1973 | 8 | 18 | 198.7 | 2,773.7 | 35,592 | 64,852 |
| 1974 | 9 | 18 | 304.3 | 3,860.1 | 42,422 | 69,270 |
| 1975 | 10 | 18 | 427.6 | 4,251.4 | 60,221 | 72,200 |
| 1976 | 10 | 18 | 489.8 | 5,028.3 | 57,072 | 73,149 |
| 1977 | 10 | 18 | 544.8 | 6,383.7 | 65,603 | 83,700 |
| 1978 | 10 | 18 | 512.5 | 7,225.4 | 61,261 | 88,562 |
| 1979 | 10 | 18 | 608.6 | 7,576.1 | 77,497 | 93,000* |
| Percent increase (1970-79) | 25% | 50% | 266% | 423% | 287% | 72% |

*estimate

Source: American Enterprise Institute for Public Policy Research. Reprinted with permission from The National Journal.

that would distribute economic and other social benefits of the capitalistic system more equitably without sacrificing the benefits of the traditional system. As the economic power of the railroads and other large business concentrations began to emerge in the 1870s and 1880s, the public began to look more and more to the federal government as the legitimate instrument to counter the economic and political power of big business. From 1870 to 1886 more than 150 bills and resolutions were introduced in Congress proposing federal regulation of the railroads. With Supreme Court decisions in cases such as *Munn* v *Illinois* and *Wabash, St. Louis and Pacific Railroad Co.* v *Illinois* providing impetus for the adoption of legislation such as the Interstate Commerce Act (1887) and the Sherman Act (1890), regulation gradually came to be more widely accepted as a legitimate federal endeavor.[2]

Initially regulation was conceived of as a governmental undertaking that could be done outside of politics, and with the adoption of the Interstate Commerce Act creating the Interstate Commerce Commission (1887), Congress embraced the concept of the "independent" regulatory commission, an expert, nonpartisan agency. Elaborating on the independent commission concept, the Supreme Court said the agencies were "created with the avowed purpose of lodging functions in a body specifically competent to deal with them by reason of information, experience, and careful study of the business and economic conditions of the industry affected."[3] Responding to perceived public needs and desires, Congress created a series of regulatory agencies to develop and administer policies pointing in several directions.

While many of the earlier regulatory agencies were created primarily to break up excessive concentrations of economic power and to restore ideal market conditions by replacing market processes with political and administrative ones, more recent regulatory efforts have embraced much broader social goals. By the mid-1960s the federal government had developed and used a wide range of regulatory techniques affecting virtually every segment of the American economy and society. As the focus of regulatory activity began to shift, the nature and role of the regulatory agencies also began to change. In a 1952 dissenting opinion, Justice Robert N. Jackson observed that the rise of agencies for consumer protection was "probably the most significant legal trend of the last century."[4] As the federal government has moved more into the realm of *social* as opposed to *economic* regulation, significant changes have emerged in both the statutes and the agencies that would appear to support Justice Jackson's prediction.

Many of the earlier statutes creating the older regulatory agencies were quite general, failing to set forth any specific public objectives to be pursued. Several aimed in rather general terms at preserving competition and free enterprise. In the Natural Gas Act of 1938 the Federal Power Commission is directed to set rates for natural gas that are "just and reasonable." Other statutes charge their agencies with regulating "in the public interest," without any attempt at defining the phrase. Newer regulatory statutes, on the other hand, typically go into much more detail and are much more likely to be quite lengthy and specific. The Environmental Protection Agency (EPA), for example, administers statutes filling hundreds of pages in the Federal Code of Regulations, and the Clean Air Act is so specific that it spells out precise pollution-reduction standards and timetables that leave the EPA only limited discretion. Many of the newer regulations reach down into the most minute details of production, and there is more of a tendency for the newer agencies actually to prescribe internal procedures for private operators. The Food and Drug Administration, for example, has required drug manufacturers to set up quality-control units and has spelled out their powers and responsibilities in substantial detail. In 1973 Bell companies were directed to establish compliance procedures in the hiring, firing, and advancement of women and minorities and the duties of company compliance officers were spelled out quite explicitly. Thus, the newer agencies such as the EPA, OSHA (Occupational Safety and Health Administration), CPSC (Consumer Product Safety Commission), and EEOC (Equal Employment Opportunity Commission) are likely to get into more detailed requirements than the older agencies such as ICC (Interstate Commerce Commission), CAB (Civil Aeronautics Board), or FCC (Federal Communications Commission). While the older agencies deal more with licenses to operate, markets to be served, and rate approval, the new-style regulation is directed more toward the conditions under which goods and services are generated and the physical characteristics of the products produced. Whereas many of the older agencies were assigned the somewhat contradictory roles of regulation and promotion of the economic well-being of an industry, most of the newer agencies are more purely regulatory in nature and have been delegated considerably more regulatory authoority than their predecessors. Because the newer agencies are more purely regulatory and are organized more along functional lines with their jurisdiction cutting across various industries, they are less subject to industry cooptation than their older counterparts. On the other hand, since they are frequently staffed by persons dedicated to the regulatory concept who are motivated by concerns for health, safety, and the environment, they are probably more subject to domination by safety and environment-oriented groups.

The considerable expansion in agencies and regulatory activity has also enhanced the leverage of the president in the governmental process. While many of the regulatory agencies have a degree of insulation from presidential control, he sets the tone of their operations and his requests and suggestions can go a long way in charting the direction for agency activities. Presidential influence in the regulatory process has been further enhanced by the fact that in more recent regulatory legislation the distinction between the executive branch and independent agency regulations has become less distinct. Many of the newer agencies have closer ties with the executive branch, and at the same time the regulatory powers of several executive branch departments, such as Labor and HHS, have been expanded.

The tremendous growth in federal regulatory policy, coupled with the fact that the newer-style regulation extends to far more industries and affects far more citizens than were affected before, has created a sort of regulatory "backlash."

Conservatives and liberals alike have joined in criticizing federal regulatory policy and calling for reform. Demands to "get government out of our lives" are spreading to an ever-widening group of both citizens and public officials. While running for governor in Wisconsin, victorious candidate Lee Dreyfus said Washington had three responsibilities: "Deliver the mail, defend the shores, and get the hell out of my life." Citing review of regulatory policy as an objective of his administration, President Carter in his 1979 State of the Union Address said, "Let's reduce government interferences" and give our system a chance to work.

Two major considerations have contributed to the growing demand for regulatory reform: questions as to the effectiveness of regulatory policies in achieving their objectives, and concern with increasing costs resulting from federal regulatory requirements. Sort of lumping these two together, many critics have condemned governmental regulatory efforts as a "rip-off" with no "redeeming social value." Peter H. Schuck says the litany of regulatory shortcomings includes: inflating of costs to consumers, encouragement of inefficiency in critical sectors of the economy, stifling of innovation, corruption of the political and administrative processes by the regulated interests, and enervation of competitive forces in the economy.[5]

Some of the harsher critics have concluded that regulation is really the antithesis of proper public policy and is incapable of promoting the public interest. Those subscribing to this viewpoint are inclined to view regulatory policy as a contest between private and public interests, in which by the nature of this contest programs serving the one cannot serve the other. Contributing further to this concept is the fact that many of the older agencies in particular have tended to become as much the protectors as the regulators of the industries they oversee. Because in several areas regulatory policy is dominated by the "iron triangle," a coalition of the regulated interests, the regulatory agencies, and the congressional subcommittees overseeing the particular policy field, policies have worked to the advantage of those regulated, rather than the public generally. Many industries quickly realized it was to their advantage to cooperate with rather than fight the regulators; not only did this make regulations less onerous, but through the process of cooptation, the agencies actually became the benefactors of those they were to regulate.[6] Lewis A. Engman, former chairman of the Federal Trade Commission, described the situation as one in which many of the regulated industries had become "federal 'protectorates' living in an atmosphere of government protection which tended to discourage competition, efficiency, and innovation." John A. Jenkins, writing in the *Washington Monthly*, says it is fairly common in Washington for regulatory agencies to be beholden to the industries they regulate.[7]

One of the worst examples of this type of regulation is the oldest of the federal regulatory agencies, the Interstate Commerce Commission. Describing the ICC and its regulatory approach, Stephen Chapman writes, "It has held rates above their normal levels, inflated the costs of doing business, contrived to shut out newcomers, encouraged inefficiency, and made a thorough mess of surface transportation in the U. S."[8] Responsible for regulating railroads, motor carriers, and inland water carriers, the ICC has discharged this responsibility in a manner calculated to prevent intercarrier competition that could have benefited shippers and consumers. Until some recent changes, ICC regulations almost eliminated new entries into interstate trucking and rail industries, and the ICC's exercise of routing authority over truckers resulted in circuitous routes and increased costs and inefficiency.

Other agencies as well are accused of operating hand-in-glove with those they are supposed to be regulating. In the case of the SEC (Securities and Exchange Commission), for example, discipline is usually very mild and cooperation with the agency is usually good business. The agency processes about 300 cases a year and about 90 percent are settled by "consent decree" with no finding of guilt.[9] This kind of regulator/industry relationship is not confined to the older agencies. The Consumer Product Safety Commission, a relative newcomer among the regulatory agencies, has frequently appeared more concerned with the impact of its actions on corporate profits than on public safety and health. Thus far, the CPSC has been inclined to view manufacturers rather than consumers as its most important constituency, and commissioners have frequently voted to ban products only with considerable reluctance and under intense public pressure. In a survey of its own employees, 43 percent felt the agency wasn't doing a good job. The list could go on.

The FTC, on the other hand, sometimes referred to in the past as "the little old lady of Pennsylvania Avenue," has recently stirred the wrath of business and industry with its stepped-up consumer protection efforts and industry criticisms. Businesses large and small joined in an attack on the FTC, charging the agency with exceeding its mandate and attempting to regulate private-sector activitites that were not the proper object of governmental regulation. While their efforts to secure either executive or congressional vetoes of FTC regulations were not totally successful, these elements were able to get some limitations on FTC authority adopted in the 96th Congress.

Because of the growing dissatisfaction with regulatory policy, since 1974 there has been a rather concerted, broad-based movement to reform, and in some instances abolish, some of the older regulatory programs. Deregulation has become the largest element in efforts at bureaucratic reform, and it has attracted the support of a strange coalition including liberal Democrats and conservative Republicans. Within the executive branch, deregulation is pushed by the Council of Economic Advisors, the Anti-trust Division of the Justice Department, and the Office of Management and Budget, and the movement is supported by laissez-faire economists, conservatives, consumer interest groups, and liberals. Senator Ted Kennedy (D-Mass.) has proposed a cabinet-level Committee on Regulatory Evaluation that would present a bill to reform one regulatory agency per year. He also proposed funds to encourage more public participation in regulatory proceedings.

Adding impetus to the reform movement recently has been a growing

'He Says There Are Too Many Unfriendly Dogs
In The Neighborhood Already'

Engelhardt in the St. Louis Post-Dispatch.

concern that the costs of regulation may be prohibitively high and may be a contributing factor to the persistent problem of inflation. In the past, little or no attention was given to weighing the social or public benefits expected from regulation against the economic costs of such policies. More recently, many have come to feel that while the objectives of a policy are most desirable, the costs involved must also be taken into consideration. With the newer regulatory agencies becoming involved in much greater detail, their policies have become a much greater factor in determining production procedures, product quality, and consequent cost to the consumer. The increasing costs of regulation have led many to question whether the resulting benefits are sufficient to outweigh the costs. The difficulty is that no one knows exactly what the economic impact of regulation is. The Environmental Protection Agency estimated that its new water effluent guideline for the steel industry would result in $2.5 billion added capital costs and

$1.3 billion annually in operating and maintenance costs. The Council on Environmental Quality estimated that the regulations administered by the EPA alone would cost the economy an additional $40 billion per year by 1984.[10] A staff report of the National Commission on Water Quality estimated that meeting 1983 standards for water pollution will require industry to spend $59.2 billion for capital equipment and another $12.6 billion annually for operation and maintenance costs.[11] All of this, of course, is passed on to the consumer in the form of higher product costs. A 1978 study for the Joint Economic Committee by Professor Murray Weidenbaum of Washington University concluded that federal regulations added $666 to the cost of an automobile and $1500 to $2500 to the cost of a home. Weidenbaum put the cost of compliance plus government administrative costs at $102 billion for 1978. However, Mark Green of Ralph Nader's Congress Watch said Weidenbaum's estimates on regulatory costs were much too high. The cost of administering federal regulatory policies alone is estimated to run over $10 per person per year and the added cost of items purchased probably runs about $2000 per household.

While growing concern with double-digit inflation in the 1970s gave added weight to the issue of regulatory costs, there is no simple solution to the matter. In the final analysis, as Brookings Institution economist Arthur Okun said, trade-offs are "inescapable." This was illustrated by the debate within the administration in 1976 over OSHA (Occupational Safety and Health Administration) efforts to control cotton dust in the textile industry. Byssionosis (brown lung), caused by breathing cotton dust, had already disabled 35,000 workers and another 20,000 to 30,000 were suffering acute cases. Late in 1976 OSHA established tough new standards aimed at reducing the incidence of cotton dust. The industry quickly complained that the cost—$2.7 billion—was too high. Subsequently the standards got caught up in President Carter's anti-inflation efforts and differences developed between the "regulators" and the "inflation fighters." OSHA was forced to modify its standards because they lacked "cost-effectiveness." In other words, the standards would increase prices at a time when the president was trying to hold the line. Thus, desirable health and safety standards collided head-on with the desire to curb inflation. On the other hand, those who feel no value can be placed on human lives contend that the cost-benefit approach is not an appropriate yardstick. These persons hold that economic impact should not be a major consideration in shaping regulatory policy. Regardless of the approach, the policymakers face a difficult task because the results of their actions, especially a decision not to regulate, are intangible and nonquantifiable.

The ultimate question is not whether to regulate or not to regulate, but how to make regulation more effective both costwise and in achieving the real purposes for which it is undertaken. Most regulations begin as well-intended efforts to deal with real public problems. In the absence of some regulation, the consumers *are* endangered unnecessarily, and public health, safety, and ultimate survival may be placed in jeopardy. The major question facing policymakers in the regulatory arena, then, is how to attain the necessary protection of the public interest without experiencing what James Kilpatrick has labelled "well-intended bureaucratic overkill." Though in some cases the underlying legislation has been faulty, the big problem in regulatory policy to date has been the poor performance in its execution. In the words of Carter Harrison, urban-affairs manager for the Louisville, Kentucky, Area Chamber of Commerce, "Our dilemma may not be as much a problem of the basic regulatory system but rather malfunctions caused by people most able to influence it—elected legislators and career administrators."[12]

Regulation has not been the total washout that some critics would have one believe. Representative Charles Rose (D-N.C.) polled his constituents regarding their attitudes on regulation and received 9000 responses. While 55 to 68.5 percent of his respondents felt they were *worse off* because of regulations affecting how businesses are run, hiring, unemployment, and schools; 56.7 to 59.9 percent said they were *better off* as a result of federal regulation of food and drugs, water and air, advertising, packaging and labelling; and 37.7 percent felt better off as a result of federal regulations of working conditions.[13]

Regulation has produced some positive results: water quality has been improved substantially and air quality is up in several respects; auto emissions have been reduced; accidental deaths of children are down as a result of childproof caps for bottles; working conditions are less hazardous in many industries; and consumer mistrust has been eased by regulations curbing corporate irresponsibility. It would be most unfortunate if, in the backlash from over-regulation and the rush to reform, the public and their policymakers should lose sight of the positive aspects of federal regulatory efforts.

One of the reasons regulatory policy generates such widespread negative reaction is because it is fundamentally in conflict with several basic philosophical assumptions undergirding the American political system. It reduces the freedom and autonomy of individual citizens and increases the power of the state by extending governmental authority over private decisions. Charles L. Schultze, chairman of President Carter's Council of Economic Advisors, told his 1976 Godkin Lecture audience at Harvard, "Whenever we seek to achieve some social purposes, we now characteristically do not restructure things so that public goods become private incentives; we choose instead to remove the decision-making power from the private sector and turn it over to the public sector."[14]

The extensive authority of the federal government is nowhere more dramatically demonstrated than in the regulatory realm because the numbers affected by regulatory policy are usually much larger than the numbers affected by subsidy or redistribution policies. Adding to the potential for negative response is the fact that regulatory decisions frequently involve choices as to who will be benefited and who will be deprived, and usually there are more losers than winners.

Because it involves the exercise of governmental authority in deciding who benefits and who doesn't, regulation is inevitably a political process and the political costs associated with regulatory policies may be quite high. The politics of regulation is usually not so much partisan politics as it is the politics of patronage and privilege. The groups exerting the most influence are those with the most political access and clout, with the result that considerations of efficiency and equity may take a backseat in regulatory decisions. Since regulatory policies are frequently more specific and direct in their application, the decision-making process tends to be highly fragmented and policies are developed on a unit-by-unit basis. Consequently the coalitions that must be built to pass legislation and shape the various programs are frequently quite transient. Because regulatory policies cover such a range and variety of activities, relationships among the various elements within the arena are so unstable that no cohesive leadership elite can be identified. Different coalitions form around different areas of policy, and compromise and conciliation among a whole host of conflicting groups and interests are the hallmarks of regulatory policymaking; it is a good example of interest group pluralism. Reform and change in the regulatory process are made difficult because those most directly served, the economic and bureaucratic interests benefiting from the status quo, have greater political access and superior organization and tend to dominate the process. The public and consumer interests with the greatest stake in reform are largely diffused and unorganized, thus reducing their political impact.

In this part we will explore three areas of governmental regulatory policy. Chapter 10 will explore governmental regulation of business and the laying of the historical foundation for governmental regulatory policy, Chapter 11 will look at the government's role as a sort of referee in the area of labor/management relations, and Chapter 12 will deal more with the new style of regulatory policy in exploring the government's role in the realm of natural resources and the environment. Taken as a unit, these chapters should provide some grasp of the tremendous scope and variety of governmental activity in the regulatory area.

## Notes

1. James J. Kilpatrick, columns in Louisville, Ky. *Courier-Journal* issues for September 1, 1978 and March 27, 1979, © 1979 Universal Press Syndicate.
2. *Munn* v *Illinois*, 94 U.S. 113 (1876). A landmark decision in establishing the power of government to regulate businesses in the public interest. The Court held that privately owned businesses "affected with a public interest . . . must submit to be controlled by the public for the common good. . . ." *Wabash, St. Louis & Pacific Railroad Co.* v *Illinois*, 118 U.S. 557 (1886). This decision was significant because the court ruled Congress's authority over interstate commerce was exclusive, thus invalidating state regulations and leaving a void where no federal regulation existed. The decision gave added emphasis to growing demands for federal regulations, especially of the railroads.
3. *FTC* v *R.R. Keppel and Bros., Inc.*, 291 U.S. 304, (1934).
4. *FTC* v *Ruberoid Co.*, 343 U.S. 470 (1952) dissenting opinion, p. 488.
5. Peter H. Schuck, "Why Regulation Fails," *Harpers*, vol. 251 (September 1975), pp. 16ff.
6. Cooptation is the term used to describe the situation when regulatory agencies fall under the control of the interests they are supposed to be regulating.

7. John A. Jenkins, "Such Good Friends: The SEC and the Securities Lawyers," *The Washington Monthly* (February 1978), pp. 53–57.
8. Stephen Chapman, "Too Much: The ICC and the Truckers," *The Washington Monthly* (December 1977), p. 33.
9. A consent decree is a voluntary compliance procedure used by a number of federal regulatory agencies. Many corporations or industries against whom complaints are issued choose to settle through the consent decree because there is no finding of guilt and no formal records that might be used in civil court proceedings.
10. Council on Environmental Quality, *Environmental Quality: Seventh Annual Report*. (Washington, D.C.: Government Printing Office, 1976), p. 145.
11. National Commission on Water Quality, *Staff Report*, (Washington, D.C.: Government Printing Office, 1976), Section I, p. 34.
12. Carter Harrison, "In defense of airlines and their regulation," Louisville, Ky. *Courier-Journal* (April 2, 1978).
13. Constituent Survey, U.S. Representative Charles Rose.
14. Charles L. Schultze as quoted by Waldemar Nielsen in "The Crisis of the Nonprofits," *Change* (January 1980), p. 28.

## Suggestions for Further Reading

ANDERSON, JAMES E., ed. *Economic Regulatory Policies*. Carbondale, Ill.: Southern Illinois University Press, 1977.
FRIEDEN, BERNARD. "The new regulation comes to suburbia," *The Public Interest* no. 55 (Spring 1979), pp. 15ff.
FRIENDLY, HENRY J. *The Federal Administrative Agencies*. Cambridge, Mass.: Harvard University Press, 1962.
KAHN, ALFRED E. *The Economics of Regulation*. New York: Wiley, 1970.
KATZMANN, ROGER. *Regulatory Bureaucracy*. Cambridge, Mass.: MIT Press, 1979.
KAUS, ROBERT M. "The Dark Side of Deregulation," *The Washington Monthly* (May 1979), pp. 33–40.
KOHLMEIER, LOUIS M., Jr. *The Regulators*. New York: Harper & Row, 1969.
KRASNOW, ERWIN G. and LONGLEY, LAWRENCE D. *The Politics of Broadcast Regulation*, 2nd ed. New York: St. Martins Press, 1978.
LILLEY, WILLIAM and MILLER, JAMES. "The new 'social regulation'," *The Public Interest* no. 47 (Spring 1977), pp. 49ff.
MITNICK, BARRY. *The Political Economy of Regulation: Creating, Designing, and Removing Regulatory Forms*. New York: Columbia University Press, 1979.
MOOZE, JOHN E. "Recycling the Regulatory Agencies," *Public Administration Review*, vol. 31, no. 4 (July/August 1972).
NOLL, ROGER. *Reforming Regulation*. Washington, D.C.: The Brookings Institution, 1971.
REDFORD, EMMETTE S. *The Regulatory Process*. Austin, Tex.: University of Texas Press, 1969.
SEIGAN, BERNARD H., ed. *Regulation, Economics and the Law*. Lexington, Mass.: Lexington Books, 1979.
WEAVER, PAUL H. "Regulation, social policy and class conflict," *The Public Interest* no. 50 (Winter 1978).
*Regulation,* journal of the American Enterprise Institute, Washington, D.C.

# 10

# Competition, Consumerism, Co-optation?
# Government and Business

Though the earliest recorded legal codes include provisions against undue concentration of economic power, governmental regulations proscribing the free use of private property have usually encountered strong opposition. Concepts of freedom of the individual and free enterprise in economic activity have generally been widely and fervently embraced by Americans. The framers of the United States Constitution tried to balance the rights of private property with the demonstrated necessity for some governmental regulation of commerce and economic activity. The Fifth Amendment includes the provision that no person shall be deprived of private property without due process of law, nor shall any private property be taken for public use without just compensation. According to the classical free enterprise philosophy, governmental regulation, except in those cases where the free market fails as a result of natural monopolies, external forces, or other unnatural influences, always produces an inferior product to free, voluntary exchanges between individuals. Justice Hugo Black described the ideal of the American free enterprise system, saying it "rests on the premise that the unrestrained interaction of competitive forces will yield the best allocation of our economic resources, the lowest prices, the highest quality and the greatest material progress, while at the same time providing an environment conducive to the preservation of our democratic, political and social institutions."[1]

Strongly influenced by these free enterprise concepts, federal policymakers stayed largely out of the regulatory arena during the first century of development under the Constitution. Although Chief Justice Roger Taney, speaking for the Supreme Court in the landmark *Charles River Bridge* case, noted that property rights were to be "sacredly guarded," he went on to add that the "interest of the public must always be regarded as the main object."[2] The Court's concern with "public interest" notwithstanding, the major responsibility for regulating the prices and competitive practices of producers remained with the state legislatures as the federal government continued its laissez-faire approach.

The last half of the nineteenth century brought many technological and

## Major Antitrust Laws

**Sherman Act of 1890.** The cornerstone of federal antitrust policy, this act outlawed "monopolies" and "attempts to monopolize" interstate commerce.

**Clayton Act of 1914.** An amendment to the Sherman Act, this measure defined price discrimination, exclusive and tying contracts, interlocking directorates, and mergers that reduce competition and tend toward monopoly as violations of antitrust laws.

**Federal Trade Commission Act of 1914.** This act created the Federal Trade Commission (FTC) to enforce antitrust policy.

**Webb-Pomerene Act of 1918.** Exempted businesses engaged in export trade from the antitrust laws.

**Robinson-Patman Act of 1936.** Sometimes called the anti-chainstore act, this measure sought to protect small businesses from special discounts and rebates to large purchasers.

**Miller-Tydings Act of 1937.** Provided that manufacturers' contracts and agreements to maintain resale prices did not violate the Sherman Act and sanctioned state "fair trade" laws providing for such contracts.

**Celler-Kefauver Act of 1950.** An amendment to Section 7 of the Clayton Act, this measure enabled the FTC to act against mergers that would reduce competition and tend toward monopoly.

**McGuire Act of 1952.** Amended the Miller-Tydings Act to strengthen provisions for state "fair trade" laws.

**Antitrust Civil Process Act of 1962.** Empowered the Justice Department to require companies to turn over records for civil antitrust investigations.

**Antitrust Improvements Act of 1976.** Aimed at further strengthening Section 7 of the Clayton Act, this measure requires the filing of detailed information with the FTC by companies anticipating stock acquisitions involving companies above a certain size.

---

organizational changes in American business and industry, and such revolutions tend to produce accompanying changes in concepts of property and law. With the railroads showing the way, the United States entered the era of corporate enterprise and "big business" in the latter decades of the nineteenth century. As the market system was transformed, the economic balance of power underwent radical changes also and various elements began to call upon the government to intervene to maintain the desired balance. As the state efforts at regulating the new business and industrial enterprises proved less and less effective, demands for federal regulation increased. Federal regulatory efforts of the late nineteenth and early twentieth centuries took their substance largely from the Populist and Progressive

> **Principal Departments and Agencies**
>
> **Department of Justice.** The Antitrust Division of the Department of Justice, created in 1908, is one of two agencies primarily responsible for enforcement of the antitrust laws.
>
> **Federal Trade Commission (FTC).** Created by Congress in 1914, the FTC shares with the Antitrust Division responsibility for the enforcement of the antitrust laws.
>
> **Department of Commerce.** Functions of the Department of Commerce are generally more promotional than regulatory, but its responsibility includes a variety of programs important to business.
>
> **Consumer Product Safety Commission.** Created in 1972, this agency is primarily responsible for establishing product safety standards and policies to reduce the risk of injury to consumers from consumer products.
>
> Many other agencies also engage in regulatory actions affecting business such as the EPA, EEOC, OSHA, and NLRB. These are covered more fully in other chapters.

movements against trusts, monopolies, and big business. Farmers, small businessmen, reform elements, and others feeling their interests were being harmed by large business and industrial combines pushed vigorously for federal regulation.

The move toward a more active federal role in regulatory policy was hastened by a couple of key Supreme Court decisions. In a landmark decision in the 1877 case of *Munn* v *Illinois*, the Court ruled that business enterprises "affected with a public interest" were subject to governmental regulation.[3] This decision was a key element in the move toward federal regulation because it established the idea that public regulation of private enterprise is acceptable under the constitutional concept of due process when the private property concerned is clothed with a degree of public interest that affects society at large. The second case adding impetus to the movement for federal regulation was the *Wabash* decision in 1886.[4] In this decision involving interstate rail operations, the Supreme Court modified the "Cooley Doctrine" and held that the states could not regulate *interstate* commerce.[5] The significance of this decision was that in the absence of any federal controls and with the states no longer allowed to regulate, interstate commerce was unregulated. This increased pressures on Congress for some regulatory legislation.

# EARLY FEDERAL REGULATION

Response to the pressures for federal regulation came first in the form of the Interstate Commerce Act of 1887, directed toward the railroad industry. This legislation created the first of the independent regulatory agencies, the Interstate Commerce Commission. This was followed three years later by the Sherman Act (1890), the first federal effort to regulate business generally. Both of these acts, springing from waves of public protest against big business, marked significant departures from the traditional concept that federal regulation of private enterprise should be concerned primarily with the punishment of wrongful acts. These bills had as their objective the protection of the consumer by keeping prices as low as possible and the prevention of unfair acts or rates, and they introduced to government regulation the concept of day-to-day surveillance of private industry, not so much with the purpose of punishing wrongdoing as with the objective of preventing unfair, discriminatory, or unreasonable actions. Both the Interstate Commerce Act and the Sherman Act passed Congress with only token opposition. The business community had decided that public demand was so overwhelming that some sort of legislation was inevitable. Besides, it would probably be more effective in the long run to blunt the reform movement by accepting legislation and then focusing their efforts on insuring that its implementation and enforcement were as favorable as possible.

### The Sherman Act

A relatively brief and simple piece of legislation, the Sherman Act became the cornerstone for federal business regulatory policy. In Section 1, the act provides that:

> Every contract, combination in the form of trust or otherwise, or conspiracy, in restraint of trade or commerce among the several states or with foreign nations is hereby declared to be illegal....

Section 2 states:

> Every person who shall monopolize, or attempt to monopolize, or combine or conspire with any other person or persons, to monopolize any part of the trade or commerce among the several states, or with foreign nations, shall be deemed guilty of a misdemeanor....

While the act declared all "monopolies" and "restraints of trade" illegal, it avoided specific and precise language, leaving the meaning of various passages quite vague. As a result the act became a judicial football that has produced a pandora's box of often contradictory and inconsistent decisions. Some, however, such as Justice Charles Evans Hughes, have endorsed the flexibility of the act. In the *Appalachian Coals* case Hughes said:

> As a charter of freedom [it] has a generality and an adaptability comparable to that found to be desirable in constitutional provisions. It does not go into detailed definitions which might work either injury to legitimate enterprises or through particularization defeat its purposes by providing loopholes for escape.[6]

Commenting on the philosophy and purpose of the Sherman Act, the Supreme Court in the *Northern Pacific* case said the act was designed to be "a comprehensive charter of economic liberty aimed at preserving free and unfettered competition as the rule of trade."[7]

Maintaining a competitive free enterprise system through governmental regulation is an objective often much easier proclaimed than accomplished. A competitive free market involves a maximum amount of rivalry among producers, resulting in the best and most up-to-date goods and services at the lowest prices for consumers. Regulation is somewhat contradictory to this concept in that it involves some governmental direction of private economic endeavor with the objective of improved consumer benefits.

The Sherman Act provides for both criminal and civil actions against those engaged in attempts to eliminate competition or restrain trade. While "intent" to monopolize must be shown, the courts have in recent years tended to require less strict evidence. Even though 1955 amendments raised maximum fines to $50,000 and in 1961 some electric company officials were given jail sentences for price fixing, civil proceedings under the act are still probably more significant than the criminal sentences. Under the equity provisions of the act it is possible for an individual or competitor who proves injury as a result of illegal competitive practices to recover treble damages. This can run into substantial sums as in recent cases involving IBM and Kodak and suits brought by their competitors.

Since the adoption of the Sherman Act in 1890, governmental enforcement of antitrust policy has been sporadic and has followed no consistent pattern. Though Congress had intended that they be exempted from its provisions, the first application of the Sherman Act was to a labor union rather than a business trust. When a Supreme Court did apply the Sherman Act in the *E. C. Knight* case, it held that provisions of the act applied to *interstate commerce*, not *manufacturing*, thereby substantially weakening the law as an instrument for regulating large-scale manufacturing enterprises.[8] This situation was remedied somewhat by the decision in the *Addyston Pipe Company* case, in which the Court broadened the concept of interstate commerce to include manufactured products destined for interstate trade. It wasn't, however, until 1904 that the Court finally used the Sherman Act in the *Northern Securities* case to actually order the dissolution of a large holding company.[10] Though the Sherman Act technically outlawed trusts and monopolies, it failed to define these terms very specifically, thus leaving it to the courts to resolve the issue.

In an 1897 decision with Justice Peckham speaking for the majority, the Court held that the Sherman Act prohibited all monopolies; however, Justice White dissented, contending that the act was intended to prohibit only "unreasonable" trusts and monopolies.[11] Eventually Justice White's view would prevail when in 1911 in the *Standard Oil* case the Supreme Court embraced his "rule of reason."[12] Under this concept, monopolies or trusts were not bad per se, but their impact on the public interest must be weighed in determining their legality or illegality. This decision marked the beginning of a period of considerable uncertainty and confusion as to the application of the Sherman Act, and under this concept, some of the largest business combinations in the country were held not to be in violation of the law.

Under the Sherman Act, governmental regulation was carried out through suits brought by the Justice Department and decided by the courts. Because this procedure had not done much to stem the tide toward industrial concentration during the two decades following the act's adoption and because of confusion stemming from judicial actions, President Woodrow Wilson, many members of Congress, and much of the public felt the Sherman Act was not sufficient. Wilson proposed two pieces of new legislation to beef up federal antitrust statutes—the Clayton Act and the Federal Trade Commission Act.

### The Federal Trade Commission

Adopted by Congress in 1914, the Federal Trade Commission Act provided for the creation of another independent regulatory commission (the FTC) with the principal objectives of heading off greater business concentration and preventing unfair methods of competition. Section 5 of the act provides, "Unfair methods of competition in commerce and unfair or deceptive acts or practices in commerce are hereby declared illegal." Granted broad inquisitorial powers, the FTC was to use its investigatory and public hearing procedures to explore issues of industrial concentration, unfair competitive practices, and their impact on consumers and the economy. On the basis of its findings, the FTC was to advise the president and Congress on needed new legislation or file formal complaints against firms for such illegal practices as *price discrimination, false advertising, deceptive practices*, or efforts to *reduce competition*.

Unlike the Justice Department, the Federal Trade Commission does not have to wait until violations of the antitrust laws actually occur, but may move to prevent unfair competitive practices. It also possesses its own subpoena powers and its orders become final unless appealed to the federal courts within sixty days.

In actual operation the FTC has been a study in contrasts. As a law enforcement agency it has responsibility for policing various consumer-oriented statutes dealing with truth in advertising, false labeling of products, price discrimination, and other unfair practices. It is also charged with economic planning on a national scale through its role in seeking out and regulating economic concentration.

Since its actions frequently place it on a collision course with business and industry, the FTC has received its share of criticism among the federal regulatory agencies. It is frequently criticized for the slowness with which its cases are handled and for spending too much time on trivia and not enough on the real issues of mergers and economic concentration. Illustrative of its pace, the FTC filed a complaint against Kellogg's, General Foods, and General Mills for having a "shared monopoly" of ready-to-eat cereals. The complaint went to trial on April 26, 1976 and was unresolved three years later after 200 trial days and 28,000 pages of testimony. The defendants have already spent about $20 million. Should the case be appealed, another ten years could elapse before the issue is finally resolved.

### The Clayton Act

The Clayton Act, also adopted in 1914, was designed to plug some loopholes and extend provisions of the Sherman Act. Somewhat more explicit than its predecessor, the Clayton Act defined four types of practices as illegal when the "effect may be to substantially lessen competition or tend to create a monopoly." Prohibited under the act were price discrimination, exclusive dealing and tying contracts, acquisitions or mergers of competing companies, and interlocking directorates. Potentially the most significant provision of the Clayton Act was Section 7, dealing with stock acquisitions and mergers. This section stated:

> ...No corporation engaged in commerce shall acquire, directly or indirectly, the whole or any part of the stock or other share capital of another corporation engaged also in commerce, where the effect of such acquisition may be to substantially lessen competition between the corporation making the acquisition, or to restrain such commerce in any section or community, or tend to create a monopoly of any line of commerce.

Unlike the Sherman Act, the Clayton Act is not a criminal statute, but it may be used to head off mergers that might prove monopolistic. Under its provisions the government, through the Federal Trade Commission, may declare illegal, acquisitions where it can be shown that such would have the effect of reducing competition or would "tend" toward a monopoly. In spite of some loopholes, the Clayton Act became the government's most potent weapon in the post-World War II years. As a result of Court decisions in the 1930s, however, Section 7 was rendered much less effective in controlling stock acquisitions than was its original intent. In a 1934 decision, the Supreme Court held, "The statute does not forbid the acquirement of property, or the merger of corporations pursuant to state laws, nor does it provide any machinery for compelling a divestiture of assets acquired by purchase or otherwise or the distribution of physical property brought into a single ownership by merger."[13]

### Celler-Kefauver act

Numerous attempts were made to amend the Clayton Act, but prior to 1950 all such efforts failed. Finally in 1950 Congress adopted the Celler-Kefauver Act, amending the Clayton Act by changing the wording in Section 7. The new provision reads:

> No corporation engaged in commerce shall acquire, directly or indirectly, the whole or any part of the stock or other share capital and no corporation subject to the jurisdiction of the Federal Trade Commission

shall acquire the whole or any part of the assets of another corporation engaged also in commerce, where, in any line of commerce in any section of the country, the effect of such acquisition may be substantially to lessen competition or to tend to create a monopoly.

The Celler-Kefauver wording, designed to increase the FTC's control over stock acquisitions and mergers, was challenged in the federal courts. In a 1962 decision in *Brown Shoe Company* v *U.S.*, the Supreme Court upheld the new wording of Section 7, saying, "We cannot avoid the mandate of Congress that tendencies toward concentration in industry are to be curbed in their incipiency...."[14]

It soon became apparent that Celler-Kefauver also left a loophole making enforcement of Section 7 less than totally effective in policing undesirable mergers. While the legislation provided the FTC the necessary authority to prohibit mergers that might tend toward monopoly or reduce competition, it provided only for voluntary rather than compulsory pre-merger clearance procedures. Though the FTC had the authority to prevent illegal acquisitions, it was hobbled in its efforts by being denied the machinery necessary for learning of anticipated acquisitions and mergers before they actually occurred. Congress moved to correct this oversight in 1976, adopting the Antitrust Improvements Act, requiring major corporations considering mergers or stock purchases of a competing firm to notify the FTC and seek pre-merger clearance at least thirty days prior to completing the transaction. Even this requirement, however, may have its shortcomings since many of the current mergers and acquisitions involve conglomerates rather than competitors in the same business. More on this later.

A major difficulty with federal regulatory policy in the business field has been the widespread confusion and lack of clarity and consistency in procedures and objectives. While in theory the objective of governmental regulation has been to make private economic activity safer and more beneficial to the consumer by making necessary adjustments in the self-regulation of the free market, this has not always been so apparent in the actions taken. Policymakers have on occasion confused "protectionism" with "competition," as is illustrated in the Robinson-Patman, Miller-Tydings, and McGuire Acts. The Miller-Tydings and McGuire Acts, which sanction state "fair trade" laws, are aimed at protecting small businesses from the large chain-store operators.[15] This legislation aims at reducing rather than maintaining competition. The same is the case with Robinson-Patman, adopted in 1936 as an amendment to the Clayton Act. The Clayton Act made it illegal to "discriminate in price between different purchasers ... where the effect may be to substantially lessen competition or tend to create a monopoly." Robinson-Patman was an effort to use this clause of the Clayton Act to protect the small businessmen from higher prices charged by their wholesalers and suppliers than were charged to their larger competitors. The act has proved virtually impossible to apply and enforce effectively. While some governmental agencies become quite concerned over economic concentration, consumer protection and enforcement of the antitrust laws, others actually encourage mergers and contribute to small business failures and reductions in competition through their extensive and often misdirected regulations. This pattern has contributed to a growing feeling that federal regulation of business is not serving its real purpose; that many regulatory agencies do not control business, but are in reality controlled by it. Regulation, therefore, is not serving the public interest, but rather is promoting special interests at the expense of the public interest. A factor contributing to this impression is the politics of the regulatory process.

## THE POLITICS OF BUSINESS REGULATION

Traditionally business and government have been regarded as almost natural adversaries in the political arena, and frequently when the business community has spoken on governmental policies it has been with a note of hostility. In earlier years most business and trade groups regarded government as a negative influence on their operations and an instrument to be opposed, not used. Recent decades have brought considerable change in the realm of business politics. While businessmen generally may retain much of the rhetoric of hostility to "government control," a growing number now find reasons to support the expansion of agencies and programs relevant to their interests. Even the conservative United States Chamber of Commerce, for example, has endorsed the expansion of federal regulation to curb "truckers who engage in cutthroat competition, ignoring the regulations of the Interstate Commerce Commission."

Taking a cue from its political rival, organized labor, business in the last decade has become much more organized and systematic in its political efforts. Business interests had long been represented by such traditional lobby groups as the National Association of Manufacturers, the U. S. Chamber of Commerce, the Committee for Economic Development, the Federation of Independent Businessmen, and a variety of more specialized trade associations; but business groups had not been directly involved in political activities and campaigns on a scale comparable to organized labor. As early as the 1930s labor started the use of political action groups (PACs) through which to channel their campaign contributions and political activities; in the 1950s civil rights groups used similar action groups, and in the 1960s consumers and environmentalists promoted their causes with effective political groups.

Never much interested in political action groups earlier, the business community dramatically increased its political role in the 1970s. Columnists Martha Angle and Robert Walters say that probably the biggest "growth industry" in American politics currently is the political action committees established by corporations, trade associations, and other business groups to handle their campaign contributions and political activities. In the *Sun Oil* case the Federal Election Commission ruled that corporations could solicit both their stockholders and employees and set up payroll deductions to be used for political activities. This ruling gave corporations, which had been prohibited from contributing to political campaigns, a great boost in their political efforts. The Supreme Court followed the

FEC's ruling with a decision in 1978 upholding corporations' constitutional right to speak out and contribute to campaigns on political issues. Both of these decisions, coupled with recent changes in federal campaign finance laws, provided additional stimulus to the formulation of political action groups. In 1968 there were fewer than 60 corporate PACs and in 1974 there were only 89 corporate political action committees; within six months of the FEC's ruling in the Sun Oil case 150 new PACs were formed, and the adoption of legislation by Congress in 1976 restricting corporate solicitations for political purposes to stockholders and management personnel rather than all employees has failed to stem the tide. Under the 1976 legislation, corporations and labor unions can "cross over" twice a year in their solicitations; that is, management can solicit union members and unions can seek contributions from management. Labor was extended the right to use the check-off payroll deduction for political contributions if the employer used the same method. Even with these new legislative guidelines, corporate PACs continued to be chartered at a rate of six to ten per week. By March 1978 business PACs were up to 595, and by July 1978 the number had already reached 711. In addition to PACs the business community also has the Business Roundtable, an alliance of various business interests, and a multitude of trade associations that engage in political activities.

The dramatic increase in business PACs and the surge in business political activity has raised concern about campaign finance laws. The Supreme Court's 1978 decision allowing corporate involvement in campaigns on political issues raises the question of corporate contributions to individual candidates. Already the public financing of presidential elections coupled with the increase in PACs has resulted in significant increases in interest group contributions to congressional campaigns. Some feel that the PACs are the new "fat cats" of the electoral process and their dramatic increase has made a mockery of campaign finance laws. By July of 1978 business PACs alone had already raised $54 million for use in the 1978 congressional elections. Because of the growing influence of PACs there is now a movement in Congress to place limits on PAC contributions. With PAC contributions more than doubling for congressional elections between 1972 and 1978, several members of Congress have voiced concern. Representatives David Obey (D-Wis.) and Tom Railsback (R-Ill.), along with 110 co-sponsors have introduced legislation that would limit PAC contributions to a candidate for Congress to $5000 for all elections and total contributions from all PACs combined to $50,000 per candidate. In the 1978 elections, twenty-two House committee chairmen got 56 percent of their funds from PACs, and the House Democratic Study Group reported that 175 candidates received over $50,000 each from PACs. One hundred thirty of these were elected. DSG reported that thirty-two of seventy-seven freshmen members elected in 1978 got PAC contributions in excess of $50,000. While in theory those contributing to political campaigns are motivated by the high-minded desire to promote the democratic process, in reality many have as a prime motive the subtle advancement of their own special cause. As campaign costs continue to rise and specialized political interest groups experience unprecedented growth, elected policymakers find themselves with a "second constituency" — those organized interests who help to foot the bill for their costly campaigns. More and more we are, in the words of President Eisenhower, putting a "dollar sign on public service."

The impact of these business-oriented PACs and their contributions is already becoming apparent in the federal policy process. The 95th Congress, though heavily Democratic (Republicans are traditionally more pro-business in their attitudes) favored big business: labor reform legislation was defeated, capital gains taxes were reduced, and the deregulation of oil prices sought by the industry for twenty-five years was approved. The automotive industry lobby, the hospital-medical lobby, and business lobbies all fared well in the 95th Congress. As the business-oriented political groups have channeled their contributions to powerful committee and subcommittee chairmen and freshmen and sophomore members of Congress who frequently display a high degree of partisan independence, their influence has become substantial. These influences have tended to make effective party leadership in Congress extremely difficult, as alignments shift back and forth from issue to issue.

A prime example of the shifting coalitions faced by the congressional leadership is consumer legislation. Various groups jump back and forth from one side to the other depending on how a particular measure will affect their interests. Normally, for example, labor and consumer advocates will align against business and industry, but on tariff legislation labor lines up with industry to protect jobs. Also, the efforts of the business interests are benefiting from the election of a new breed of more conservative Democrat and from the growing feeling that the creation of yet another bureaucratic agency is not the solution to every problem. All of those elements were evident in the House vote on the Consumer Protection Agency proposal, which lost 227 to 189 in spite of White House support. The Chamber of Commerce had spearheaded a well-organized campaign by national and hometown business groups against the measure and they were aided in their efforts by growing antibureaucratic sentiment. House Speaker Tip O'Neill said he knew the votes weren't there because of commitments so many members had made at home, but the White House insisted the measure be brought up. Typifying the new, more conservative Democratic members of Congress, Carroll Hubbard (D-Ky.) said he felt the proposed consumer protection agency would have been "yet another unwieldy federal regulatory bureaucracy." O'Neill said general antigovernment sentiment contributed to the measure's defeat.

Currently, business groups seem to face a very favorable situation politically. In many respects they enjoy natural advantages over their political competitors: because of social status, educational background and other factors, they have ready access to governmental policymakers; because of the nature of their training and experience, they possess organizational and advertising skills that are useful politically; and they have substantial resources that can be used in political campaigns for a variety of purposes.

## CONFLICTING VIEWS ON REGULATION

In spite of business's currently favorable position politically, views on the need and nature of governmental regulation vary substantially. Though many still oppose federal regulation as a matter of philosophy, much of the current debate centers on approaches. Should federal regulatory agencies dictate actual procedures in implementing regulations, or should the government simply offer incentives but leave business and industry to develop their own devices for compliance? Jack Carlson, chief economist for the U. S. Chamber of Commerce, contends that policy goals and objectives would be achieved more efficiently and readily through government incentives. Eula Bingham, assistant secretary of labor for occupational safety and health, feels, however, that what business has considered most efficient often was inadequate. She points to 170,000 new cases of occupationally related diseases each year, 37,000 deaths annually, and possibly 10 percent of cancer caused by occupational exposure to carcinogens as indications of inadequate standards in industry. In a speech to a graduating class at Eastern Kentucky University in 1978 she lashed out at the critics of federal regulation, saying:

> Never before has there been such a broadly based, highly financed, tightly organized, and widely publicized attack on government regulations. To listen to the shrill war cries coming from the corporate boardrooms and the trade associations, you would think that effective regulations...[are] a two-pronged spear puncturing the profits and opening a gaping hole for the infection of socialism.[16]

Others have joined Dr. Bingham in chiding the business community for its frequently bitter complaints about over-zealous federal regulation while largely ignoring the corporate excesses that have led to such governmental involvement. In an address to the Economic Club of Detroit, Joan Claybrook, head of the National Highway Traffic Safety Administration, urged auto manufacturers to consider a less narrow concept of "freedom" for industry that would provide citizens who purchased their vehicles freedom from unnecessary casualties, excessive fuel consumption, auto repair frauds, and pollution-related diseases. She chided the industry for accepting government subsidies, protection from competition, tax write-offs, and other governmental services while attacking regulation.

Many point up the fact that growing governmental regulation stems from the inability or unwillingness of business and industry to develop their own standards to insure that the public interest is served. In a speech at the University of Chicago in April 1978, Henry Ford II told his audience:

> In recent decades we businessmen have neglected many genuine problems and turned a blind eye to conditions that should have caught our attention. Often we have simply been stupid.
> We have refused to confront some of the crucial issues of our time, and as a result we have played directly into the hands of our critics and helped to make matters worse.[17]

In a column in the Louisville, Kentucky *Courier-Journal*, syndicated columnist Ellen Goodman observes, "But the thing that continues to evade my understanding is how business people have the nerve to bellow against government when they won't address their own faults and hazards." Paul Harvey, a staunch free-enterprise advocate, notes, "Businessmen fuss and fret over the usurpation of their prerogatives by alphabetical agencies of government—yet if they don't discipline themselves, government has to move in and free enterprise becomes that much less free."[18] Another staunch free-enterpriser, James J. Kilpatrick, wades in with this observation:

> Yecch! I am, at the moment, fed up to the teeth with American business. I'm ordinarily regarded as a "pro-business" spokesman, a free-enterpriser to the core. But I would say to my friends in industry: "This is your Dutch uncle speaking. Shape up!"[19]

Ken Wessner, president of Servicemaster Corporation, has warned his business colleagues, "To the extent that we businessmen vacate our moral obligations to stewardship, to that extent our businesses will be taken out of our hands."

In spite of such warnings, the corporate sector has seemed to show more inclination to explain away or stonewall examples of corporate irresponsibility than to seek remedies. In the 1970s when leaks of PCBs turned up in the food chain and resulted in the deaths of hundreds of livestock, Monsanto, a St. Louis-based chemical manufacturer of PCBs, launched a $4.5 million publicity campaign to counter the negative public attitude toward chemicals. Monsanto officials claimed the company was the victim of "scare tactics, political charges and sensational headlines." Although one official did concede that "maybe we should have tracked the problem a little harder and a little faster," the board chairman and president complained of "strict regulatory interpretation" and "outbursts of emotionalism" in dealing with chemicals.[20]

When the National Highway Traffic Safety Administration announced that Firestone 500 tires were unsafe and posed a potential safety hazard, the company denied the tires were unsafe. Yet the Akron *Beacon-Journal* reported that Firestone knew as early as 1975 that some of its radial tires were defective, since more than half of forty-six tires tested from a warehouse in 1975 failed. NHTSA urged Firestone to recall the tires, but the company maintained recall was unnecessary. Finally, NHTSA ordered recall. NHTSA also found the Ford Pinto to be unsafe and sought recall. After months of pressure, Ford agreed to recall 1.9 million Pintos, but the company staunchly maintained "that no unreasonable risk to safety is involved in the design of those cars."

Recent evidence indicates that asbestos companies hid or ignored for three decades the dangers from asbestos fibers. Ron Motley, a South Carolina attorney handling several lawsuits now in the courts, says, "Now we know what they knew and did, and that was to try to put a lid on the whole thing and keep on making money."[21]

In other recent actions the government has ordered Safeway, one of the nation's largest grocery chains, to sell advertised bargains at advertised prices. McDonald's in Los Angeles was ordered by the court to stop advertising frozen orange juice as "fresh" orange juice and syrup as "maple" which wasn't. The Federal Trade Commission reported that 40 percent of all auto repairs paid for were either not needed or not actually performed. And in 1976 Lockheed reached new levels of international business notoriety when its bribes brought down a prime minister in Japan and almost toppled the royal throne in the Netherlands. By September 1976, fearing the possible repercussions of the Lockheed scandal, 200 firms had confessed to bribes or questionable contributions.

While the business community has complained loudly of governmental "interference" and "over-regulation" there is little evidence that Firestone was going to remove its tires from the market or that Ford was going to improve the safety of the Pinto in the absence of federal intervention. It is this sort of performance that causes many critics to feel that governmental regulation is essential for public safety and health. Although the number of private groups aimed at promoting corporate responsibility has increased, many observers feel they cannot establish the necessary standards for maintaining the public interest. Emmette Redford states, "It can be expected that standards of corporate conscience will continue to develop. Yet it may be doubted whether these will be adequate, or will be sufficiently respected, unless embodied in the law."[22] He goes on to observe that companies that do not act promptly to correct violations must know that the result will be costly enough to hurt. Otherwise they will be content to pay an occasional fine and continue to operate in violation of the law. This is unfair and makes competition difficult for scrupulous operators who do abide by the law.

## DEREGULATION

Because of concern with the growth in the federal bureaucracy, increasing federal involvement in the private sector, and the increased production costs as a result of regulations, strong sentiment has developed on many fronts for regulatory reform and in many cases "deregulation." However, presidents from Teddy Roosevelt in 1905 to Jimmy Carter have sought to reform the federal bureaucracy, with most achieving little or no success. John F. Kennedy sent a special message to Congress in which he charged that the federal agencies were shot through with "delays ... incompetence." Jimmy Carter made bureaucratic reform a high priority item in his administration, yet only limited progress has been made.

One factor complicating efforts at reforming the federal regulatory agencies is that the degree of competition existing among the firms in an industry is one of the most difficult subjects to discuss accurately and dispassionately. Add to this the frequent opposition of the industry itself and the innate tendency of bureaucratic organizations to defend the status quo and the obstacles to effective reform begin to become apparent. In a number of industries the firms have decided their interests are best served by using the federal agencies and regulatory processes to limit competition from newcomers. This situation has been most apparent in the transportation field, where for all intents and purposes the industry became a government-sanctioned cartel. Under the 1948 Reed-Bullwinkel Act, carriers under the jurisdiction of the ICC are exempt from federal antitrust laws, and many of the rail, truck, barge, steamship, and air lines have maintained rate-fixing conferences with ICC approval. The ICC became the instrument of those in the industry for limiting new entries into the field. Little wonder that proposals for deregulation have met strong opposition within the industry.

Typical of the deregulation debate was the case of the airlines. Critics charged that the Civil Aeronautics Board (CAB), created in 1938 to regulate the airlines industry, was unnecessarily protective of existing airlines and hampered competition that could benefit airlines users. Senator Ted Kennedy (D-Mass.) said, "It is now clear beyond doubt that the aviation regulatory scheme devised in the Depression to protect an infant industry, has resulted in higher fares, less service... and generally less competition than the public deserves."[23] Representative Millicent Fenwick (R-N.J.) said the CAB had "woven a cocoon around this industry that is absolutely hampering development." The Louisville Courier-Journal said there was "plenty of evidence to suggest that less federal regulation and freer competition would be a tonic for the airlines and a boon for the traveling public."[24] By the 1970s the CAB was routinely rejecting requests for new routes, approving fare increases, and allowing little or no reduction in fares that might stimulate competition.

Most airlines fought the deregulation proposals vigorously, with several companies and unions arguing that deregulation would bring the collapse of the domestic aviation system. Opponents also contended that the industry, freed of governmental regulations, would concentrate on high-profit routes, leaving smaller communities without service. Among the major airlines, only United supported deregulation. When Alfred E. Kahn, a Cornell University economics professor and former regulator of New York's public utilities, became chairman of the CAB, he started a campaign of deregulation and price competition by allowing discount fares and urging innovation. This was followed by Congress's adoption of a deregulation bill providing for competitive fares, reassignment of routes, and abolition of the CAB in 1985.

Following deregulation, the airlines, which had been experiencing financial problems and declining air travel, attracted record numbers of passengers and earned record profits. Many consumers benefited from reduced fares and expanded service. Fred Wertheimer of Common Cause, a citizens' lobby group, said the airlines deregulation bill was "the first major breakthrough in the fight to reform the existing system of government regulation." Frank Borman, president of Eastern Airlines, told Chairman Kahn, "We didn't want to get pushed into these low fares, but you did it. Now, Eastern has had its most profitable March in history, and April looks like another record—we bow to you, Dr. Kahn, and we hope it's not an apparition."

While the airlines are currently experiencing profitable operations under deregulation, it is not a total solution to the regulatory problem. Already the beginnings of a merger movement has appeared in the industry and deregulaton has resulted in a decline in service to some smaller towns and communities as the major airlines have dropped some routes. Also, several major airlines have raised fares and are talking of more substantial increases in the near future. As the reformers push for deregulation in other sectors, these are factors that must be weighed. Already President Carter has proposed to trim ICC regulations, especially for the trucking industry. Currently the ICC forbids underselling, controls the number of trucking firms that can operate between the same markets, and dictates the routes they can travel. Critics contend ICC regulations are costly and inefficient, while most transport executives maintain these anticompetitive rules are essential to the stability of the transport industry. The American Truckers Association, the Teamsters Union, and others in the industry contend that deregulation will result in rate wars, leading many firms to bankruptcies, and will ultimately reduce service to users, especially in smaller towns and cities. If deregulation should ultimately lead to more mergers and business combinations, then the question is raised whether in the long run the consumer is better served.

## THE URGE TO MERGE

A major issue running through federal antitrust policy has been the question of the implications of mergers, combinations, and large economic concentrations for the public interest. A. A. Berle, Jr. says that roughly 70 percent of American industry is what he calls "concentrates." He further concludes that legal controls over them are so limited that "the only real control which guides or limits their economic and social action is the real, though undefined and tacit, philosophy of the men who compose them."[25] The last, and possibly the only dedicated trust-buster in the federal government was Thurman Arnold, assistant attorney general in charge of the Justice Department's Antitrust Division from 1938 to 1943, whom the Chicago *Tribune* described as an "idiot in a powder mill." Under Arnold's leadership the Antitrust Division was more active than at any previous or current time in its history. From the time of the adoption of the Sherman Act in 1890 to Arnold's appointment, the federal government had brought 433 antitrust suits, an average of 9 per year. During Arnold's tenure at Justice, the division brought 347 suits, or an average of 69 per year. With Arnold's departure federal antitrust activity declined and mergers and acquisitions have grown rather steadily.

Between 1940 and 1954, an average of 246 firms disappeared annually through mergers and stock acquisitions. Between 1948 and 1967, the nation's 200 largest corporations acquired 476 other companies with aggregate assets of $22.5 billion. In the 1970s more than 2000 small businesses were taken over each year by larger firms. With inflation, corporations found it more profitable to purchase existing businesses than to reinvest in their own companies. Thomas Thompson, vice president for corporate affairs at Continental Group, a large conglomerate, told Business Roundtable colleagues, "You can now buy assets at 25 to 30 percent of replacement value. This is the best investment a company can make." The trend has been for more and more big, cash-rich conglomerates to buy smaller firms. In 1969 there were more than 6100 mergers, but even more significant in recent years has been the growth in numbers of mergers involving firms with assets of more than $100 million. (See figure 10.1) The impact of this trend is an increasing concentration of manufacturing assets in a smaller and smaller number of huge

**FIGURE 10.1 Number of Mergers Annually with Purchase Price of $100 Million or More**

| Year | Number |
|------|--------|
| 1973 | 28 |
| 1974 | 15 |
| 1975 | 14 |
| 1976 | 39 |
| 1977 | 41 |
| 1978 | 80 |

Source: Senate Judiciary Committee.

corporations. (See figure 10.2) In 1950 the top 200 manufacturing corporations owned 46.1 percent of all manufacturing assets; by 1977 their share had risen to over 60 percent. Presently about one-third of the nation's total manufacturing assets are controlled by the 50 largest corporations, and the 500 largest corporations account for more than two-thirds of the total manufacturing assets.

Governmental success at halting such trends toward economic concentration has been spotty. The Federal Trade Commission is a prime example of the contrast between legislative intent and the final product that emerges as governmental

**FIGURE 10.2 Growth in Number of Corporations with Assets of More Than $1 Billion**

| Year | 1 billion | 5 billion | 10 billion |
|------|-----------|-----------|------------|
| 1955 | 65 | 8 | 2 |
| 1970 | 152 | 22 | 10 |
| 1977 | 193 | 26 | 12 |

Source: Federal Trade Commission

policy. Each year the FTC gathers extensive data on industrial growth and economic concentration. The commission spent sixteen years, amassed a record of 15,000 pages, and issued a 267-page decision to get the "liver" out of Carter's Little Liver Pills. Each year the commission grinds out literally hundreds of orders and regulations on miniscule matters, while the tide of mergers and combinations goes largely unchecked. The commission did in the 1960s use its powers to halt the trend toward increased concentration in the cement and concrete industry. And in 1966 the commission blocked Procter and Gamble's proposed purchase of Clorox, ruling that Procter and Gamble could go into the bleach business on its own, but could not purchase Clorox because of the resulting reduction in competition. The decision was upheld by the Supreme Court in 1967. Such actions have been sporadic, however, and the FTC has failed to block numerous mergers or acquisitions of major corporations, such as General Electric's purchase of Utah International or Atlantic Richfield's purchase of Anaconda Copper for approximately $700 million, or the mergers of Occidental and Mead paper companies, United Technologies and Carrier Corporation in air conditioning, Avon and Tiffany Companies in cosmetics, and American Express and McGraw-Hill.

Another example of the national policymakers' hesitancy to stem the tide of concentration has been in the communications field. In many cities all the media outlets are under one ownership and the trend has been more and more toward ownership by a few large syndicates. The trend toward concentration has been particularly noticeable in the newspaper field. In 1930, newspaper chains controlled papers accounting for 43 percent of daily circulation. In 1960 the figure had reached 46 percent, but by 1977 the figure had mounted to 74 percent. By 1976 the twenty-five largest newspaper chains accounted for over half of all daily circulation, an increase from 38 percent in 1960. Sixty percent of the nation's daily newspapers accounting for 72 percent of total circulation are now controlled by 170 news syndicates. Most of the remaining independents have a circulation under 10,000 each, and virtually all of the local daily newspapers have no local competitors. In June 1978 the Supreme Court did rule that the Federal Communications Commission could bar single-party ownership of both newspapers and broadcast stations. The impact of this decision was blunted, however, by the inclusion of a "grandfather clause" allowing existing ownership situations to continue. Such concentration in the news media takes on double significance because of the influence the media have come to have on public opinion and political decision-making in our society. Commentator Paul Harvey cautions on the media's influence by noting, "As a fourth wheel we can help to stabilize government; but as a steering wheel we might mislead." With the exception of the 1978 case, the federal policymakers have demonstrated little concern for the concentration trends in the media industry.

### Conglomerate Mergers

While the responsible governmental agencies have failed to demonstrate much enthusiasm for vigorous enforcement of the antitrust laws, major shortcomings in the current statutes have also contributed to the current concentration trend.

Current antitrust laws are directed primarily at practices that reduce competition and tend toward monopoly, and as a consequence neither the FTC nor the Justice Department can touch most of the current mergers that involve conglomerates; currently 80 to 90 percent of all merger activity involves conglomerates. Since bigness, by itself, is not a valid reason for blocking a merger and since conglomerates usually involve companies operating in many different industries rather than direct competitors, it becomes extremely difficult to prove that such mergers of the diverse operations hurt the consumer and therefore are contrary to the public interest.

In its efforts to regulate conglomerates the government has developed three arguments: contention that the acquiring company would otherwise have entered the market of the acquired company and thereby have become a competitor (potential entrant argument); contention that the acquired company's competitors will be overwhelmed by the acquisition (entrenchment argument); or contention that the two merged companies will engage in reciprocal dealings that will disadvantage their competitors (reciprocity argument). Thus far, the courts have not proved too receptive to these arguments in reviewing antitrust cases. Some raise the question as to whether such mergers represent an inefficient combination of production facilities that increases consumer prices for goods and services. Opponents also feel that the formation of such huge conglomerates through mergers concentrates too much economic and political power in too few hands.

Since existing laws are felt inadequate to cope with the wave of conglomerate mergers, the Senate Antitrust Subcommittee and the Justice Department are preparing new legislation that would outlaw some of the larger mergers. The legislation being drafted would ban mergers in which the resulting company would have annual sales or assets of $2 billion or more, providing each of the companies involved has at least $100 million in sales or assets. When this measure reaches the floor of Congress, it is sure to touch off a major debate, as there is still considerable disagreement over the role of government in regulating business activity.

In opposing new merger legislation, business groups have contended that such governmental action could worsen inflation by driving up production costs and also make American products less competitive abroad. President Carter deleted anti-conglomerate merger legislation from his 1980 State of the Union Address and the White House has not endorsed any of the proposed measures.

According to Harvard economist John Kenneth Galbraith, federal antitrust is a "charade." He and some other liberal economists contend that antitrust law is outmoded because giant corporations and their technostructures are necessary for modern goals of economic stability, corporate security, and consumer protection. Reflecting Galbraith's position, Professor J. Fred Weston of the UCLA Graduate School of Management says that in some industries such as the auto, steel, petroleum, and aerospace fields, large firms are necessary. "No one has ever shown," he argues, "that aggregate concentration results in anything."[26] Opponents to the "big is better" concept contend it is the smaller businesses who deserve a break from federal regulations, and they point to some impressive statistics to support their case. Fourteen million small business firms in the U.S.

constitute about 97 percent of all business enterprises and account for 55 percent of all private employment and 43 percent of the gross national product (GNP). Over the last decade the nation's 1000 largest industries contributed only 2 percent of all new jobs, and small business output has grown at three times the rate of big business. While small firms get only about 3.4 percent of federal research and development funds (about half goes for military projects), they produce about one-half of all the technological innovations produced by U. S. industry. It was data such as this that prompted the late Senator Phillip Hart (D-Mich.) to promote legislation that would have broken many of the nation's largest conglomerates down into their various component industries. While Hart's approach never gained wide support, others have expressed desires for governmental policy to give more consideration to the nation's small businesses. Jimmy Carter stated early in his term, "It will be the goal of my administration to have the growth rate of small business exceed the growth rate of big business and government."

## NEW DIRECTIONS IN REGULATION

Many of the difficulties experienced with federal regulatory policy by small businesses stem from the new directions this policy has taken over the last two decades. While earlier regulation of business was directed primarily at preventing monopolies and other practices that reduced competition, the newer regulations are more concerned with promoting health, safety, a cleaner environment, and in general more social responsibility. A basic idea behind much of the new-style regulation is that of making business and industry more responsible for the safety and health of their employees and the consumers of their products.

Typical of the new direction in federal regulatory policy has been the activity relating to coal mining, probably the most hazardous of all American industries. Major changes in federal policy have usually followed mining disasters as the government has intensified its efforts to ensure less hazardous working conditions. Federal involvement started in 1910 with the creation of the Bureau of Mines. This action came only after 7000 miners had been killed, 361 of them in a single explosion in a mine near Monogah, West Virginia, in December of 1907. As mining tragedies continued, the bureau's regulatory powers were expanded gradually. Still, between 1900 and 1977, 100,833 miners lost their lives in coal mine accidents. In 1968 national television covered the disaster at Consolidated Coal Company's No. 9 mine in Farmington, West Virginia, where seventy-eight miners were killed in an underground explosion. This disaster was followed by the adoption in 1969 of the Coal Mine Health and Safety Act, the toughest and most comprehensive mining legislation to that time, which created the Mining Enforcement and Safety Administration (MESA) to carry out the provisions of the act. The coal companies immediately complained that the new regulations were too stringent and blocked early enforcement with a barrage of law suits. MESA's early enforcement of the mine safety laws was lax, with the agency collecting only about one-third of the fines originally assessed for violations. In 1970, deaths in coal mine accidents still numbered 260. Following a disaster in March 1976 in Letcher County, Kentucky, in which two explosions resulted in the deaths of twenty-three miners and three federal inspectors, major revisions were undertaken in mine safety regulation. MESA was shifted from the Interior Department to the Department of Labor and the Federal Mine Health and Safety Amendments Act was passed by Congress, another in a long line of mine safety measures adopted over the years. In 1977 there were 139 deaths in coal mine accidents. Such regulatory measures are costly, as the critics point out. A spokesman for the Western Kentucky Coal Operators Association estimates that MESA and EPA regulations have cost the coal industry more than $130 million. He says the added costs bring concentration in the industry by forcing small operators to sell out to the bigger corporations. Proponents of the new-style regulation contend that dollar costs are secondary to concern with saving human lives and reducing suffering and that the added cost of production is a relatively reasonable price to pay. They agree with Undersecretary of Labor Robert J. Brown, who says, "The necessity for stringent safety regulations is apparent by looking at the cost in human lives of mining coal in the United States."

But just how far does the government's responsibility extend when exercising its powers in the interest of public health and safety? Is the federal government encroaching on parental responsibility when it seeks to regulate television advertising directed toward children? In a nation in which a family is more likely to be without indoor plumbing than without television and where the average child between ages two and eleven watches almost four hours of television per day and 20,000 commercials a year, should a governmental agency exercise any control over what the children view? When the FTC set out to regulate television ads for foods aimed at children, a heated debate arose and battle lines were quickly drawn. The FTC, led by its chairman, Michael Pertshuk, said foods advertised for children were among the least nutritious and were more costly, and the ads were aimed at turning children into "naggers." The broadcast and cereal industries charged that the government was interfering with both freedom of speech and the parent-child relationship. Lining up in support of the FTC were Action for Children's Television (ACT), the Center for Science in the Public Interest, and the Consumer's Union. Leading the opposition to the FTC proposal were the National Association of Broadcasters (NAB) and the Cereal Institute. While there was no firm evidence that television advertising has had an adverse effect on child nutrition, proponents for curbs on ads directed toward children point to the massive and one-sided exposure. Robert Choate, president of the Council on Children, Media and Merchandising, reported that in the first nine months of 1975, the council found that a child watching weekend television on the three major networks could have seen 3832 ads for cereals and 1627 for candy and chewing gum. By contrast, only two ads for meat and poultry and one each for vegetables and cheese would have been seen. A child watching television for twenty-five hours per week would have been exposed to a barrage of between 8500 and 13,000 food and beverage ads in the course of a year.

Opponents to FTC regulation of ads directed toward children focus on the issue of the government as a substitute parent. An article in the Louisville *Courier-Journal* said the FTC's proposed curb "is a disturbing assumption that your friendly federal government can and should step in to protect children from unscrupulous advertisers and parental spinelessness."[27] Shawn Sheehan, a spokesman for the NAB, sounded the same note, saying, "What we are talking about here is who controls the media. The government is well-intentioned, but it is dictating to parents how they should conduct their family life. We think that is dangerous."

This case raises some key questions that extend beyond a mere proposal for a governmental agency to curb advertising aimed at children. Should the government intervene to protect individuals when their actions may jeopardize their health and safety? These are emotion-laden issues for which there are no simple solutions. As a result of this heated children's ad dispute, Representative Frederick W. Richmond (D-N.Y.) has introduced legislation that seeks a more balanced exposure to advertising by requiring television stations to carry messages on nutrition as well as the food ads. The Congress adopted a measure in 1980 to prevent the FTC from regulating ads on children's programs, by limiting the FTC to policing only "false" and "deceptive" advertising. Regardless of the outcome on this particular issue, many basic and unresolved questions remain regarding the degree to which the government can regulate individual and corporate activity in the interest of promoting public health, safety, and welfare.

## CONCLUSION

Governmental regulation of business has been an extremely mixed bag over the years. The federal statutes dealing with antitrust actually constitute only a small portion of the U. S. Code and as under the tax laws, numerous special exemptions have been granted through the years. As a result it has been estimated that only about one-fourth of the nation's commerce is now covered by antitrust provisions. Add to this the general decline in vigor of antitrust enforcement over the last two decades and loopholes opened by court decisions such as the 1976 Supreme Court ruling that only parties "directly" hurt by price rigging have a right to sue for treble damages, and one begins to wonder if federal antitrust efforts really serve their purpose. The late Senator Phillip Hart (D-Mich.), former chairman of the Senate antitrust subcommittee, once observed, "Antitrust is sick and nobody seems greatly concerned. What our corporate executives desire is not competition but security."

While the government has not completely abandoned antitrust efforts (it filed a suit against IBM in January 1969, and another against AT&T in November 1974, in the two biggest cases ever to be tried in U. S. history), a major concern with federal regulatory efforts in recent years has been the additional cost imposed on both business and the consumer.[28] With the increase in federal regulations aimed at maintaining health, safety, environmental, and other standards, more attention has been focused on the sometimes negative impacts of federal requirements. These new-style regulations, which frequently prescribe minimum standards that must be met by all producers, tend to limit entry, reduce diversity and consumer choice, and frequently increase the cost of operation. In effect they may reduce competition and there is little doubt but that they increase costs.

Because the increased production costs are passed on as higher prices, Louis M. Kohlmeier says that governmental regulation of business is clearly costing American consumers several billions of dollars annually.[29] The steel industry has to comply with some 5600 regulations administered by 26 different federal agencies. Pollution abatement alone cost industry about $32 billion in 1977 and polution control on automobiles cost about $7.5 billion, raising the price of a new car by $666. Business compliance with federal regulations accounts for about 10 cents of every dollar spent by the American consumer. This burden falls particularly hard on the smaller operators. Kenneth W. Chilton of the Center for the Study of American Business, Washington University, says, "The impact of the recent expansion of federal government regulation of business has been particularly severe on the smaller companies." The Commission on Federal Paperwork reported that 5 million small businesses now spend between $15 and $20 billion annually on paperwork. This is about $3000 per business and does not reflect the additional costs of lost time, additional staff, etc. In his battle to curb inflation, the costs of federal regulations became a major concern of President Carter.

While some have seized upon the cost factor as a basis for advocating a massive retrenchment in federal regulatory efforts, others feel such wholesale attacks are unjustified. Susan B. King, chairman of the Consumer Product Safety Commission says:

> I get very upset when I hear this mounting criticism of government regulation as the source of inflation and something that the public doesn't want.... What I see is a powerful segment of the business and industrial community trying to turn a general irritation with government into a specific attack on health and safety regulations.[30]

While a November 1978 survey by the Opinion Research Corporation showed that 70 percent of the members of Congress polled favored a reduction in regulations, results of the public survey were mixed. Forty-three percent of those surveyed favored less regulation of business, but 25 percent wanted more and 23 percent supported the current level. Ultimately the question of governmental regulation of business becomes a much broader issue of democratic government. Can big business and an economic system based on high technology and mass production be effectively managed for the benefit of the people in a constitutional democracy? The jury is still out.

## Points to Ponder

What are the purposes and objectives of federal antitrust policies?

Should corporations and political action committees (PACs) be permitted to make expenditures in political campaigns?

Should large conglomerate mergers be subject to federal antitrust regulations, or is corporate size alone not a cause for governmental concern?

Does governmental regulation of business and industry stifle initiative and discourage innovation, thus hampering economic growth and productivity?

In the absence of federal regulation, do business and industry demonstrate sufficient concern for consumer interests and engage in effective self-regulation?

Should regulatory agency decisions be subject to congressional veto?

Have regulatory costs made costs of production prohibitively high?

Does most regulation today benefit the public or the regulated business or industry?

## Notes

1. *Northern Pacific Railway Co.* v *U.S.*, 356 U.S. 1, 4 (1958).
2. *Charles River Bridge* v *Warren Bridge*, II Peters 420 (1837).
3. *Munn* v *Illinois*, 94 U.S. 183 (1877).
4. *Wabash, St. Louis and Pacific Railway Co.* v *Illinois*, 118 U.S. 557 (1886).
5. The so-called Cooley Doctrine proclaimed by the Supreme Court in *Cooley* v *Board of Wardens*, 12 Howard 299 (1851), allowed the states to regulate interstate commerce in the absence of any federal regulation. In the *Wabash* case the Court said the regulation of commerce crossing state lines was an *exclusive* responsibility of the federal government under the commerce clause.
6. *Appalachian Coals* v *U.S.*, 288 U.S. 344.
7. *Northern Pacific Railway Co.* v *U.S.*, 356 U.S. 1, 4 (1958).
8. *U.S.* v *E. C. Knight,* 156 U.S. 1 (1895).
9. *Addyston Pipe and Steel Company* v *U.S.*, 175 U.S. 211 (1899).
10. *Northern Securities Co.* v *U.S.*, 193 U.S. 197 (1904).
11. *U.S.* v *Trans-Missouri Freight Assoc.*, 166 U.S. 290 (1876).
12. *Standard Oil Company* v *U.S.*, 211 U.S. 1 (1911).
13. *Arrow-Hart & Hegeman Electric Company* v *FTC*, 291 U.S. 587 (1934).
14. *Brown Shoe Company* v *U.S.*, 370 U.S. 294 (1962).
15. The so-called state "fair trade" laws are designed to protect small businesses by prohibiting chain and discount stores from selling a name-brand manufacturer's product at less than the suggested retail price.
16. Eula Bingham, Commencement Address, Eastern Kentucky University, August 3, 1978.
17. Henry Ford II as quoted by John Cunniff, Associated Press feature writer, in "Neglect by business?," *Park City Daily News*, Bowling Green, Ky. (July 9, 1979).
18. Paul Harvey, "Self-government on trial," *Park City Daily News*, Bowling Green, Ky. (September 28, 1978), © 1978, Los Angeles Times Syndicate.
19. James J. Kilpatrick, "Why a free-enterpriser is fed up with American business attitude," Louisville, Ky. *Courier-Journal* (June 20, 1978), © 1979, Universal Press Syndicate.
20. Martha Angle and Robert Walters, "A chemical danger ignored," *Park City Daily News*, Bowling Green, Ky. (June 2, 1978), © 1978, NEA.
21. See Bill Richards, "Asbestos battles 'Pentagon Papers' hailed by critics," Louisville, Ky. *Courier-Journal* (November 19, 1978), © 1978 Washington Post Co.
22. Emmette Redford, *The Role of Government in the American Economy* (New York: MacMillan, 1966), p. 113.
23. Ted Kennedy as quoted in "Senate approves bill deregulating airlines," Louisville, Ky. *Courier-Journal* (April 20, 1978).
24. "Now it's up to the House to let the airlines compete," Louisville, Ky. *Courier-Journal* (April 27, 1978).

25. A. A. Berle, Jr., *The 20th Century Capitalist Revolution* (New York: Harcourt, Brace & World, 1954), p. 180.
26. As quoted by Lawrence Mosher in "Conglomerate Mergers — A threat or a Blessing?," *National Journal* (March 24, 1979), p. 481.
27. "FTC shouldn't try to supplant parents," Louisville, Ky. *Courier-Journal* (March 25, 1978).
28. The IBM and AT&T cases illustrate the scope, time, and expense that makes the prosecution of major antitrust cases such a difficult matter. The suit against IBM was filed in 1969 and finally came to trial in 1975 after volumes of pre-trial arguments and wrangling. IBM's legal staff was headed by former U.S. Attorney General Nicholas Katzenbach and they also retained the firm of Cravath, Swaine and Moore at about $10 million per year. Appeals of the case have lasted into the 1980s. The suit against AT&T, a firm with 3 million stockholders and 1977 income of $38.06 billion (three times the GNP of Egypt), was filed in 1974 and has been bogged down in legal maneuvers since. It is estimated this suit will generate 100 million pages in documents, will take at least eight to ten years, and will result in $1 billion in legal fees for AT&T. Over 2000 AT&T employees are working on documents for the suit.
29. Louis Kohlmeier, *The Regulators* (New York: Harper & Row, 1969), p. 128.
30. As quoted by Linda Demkovich, "King and Her Court at the Consumer Product Safety Commission," *National Journal* (October 28, 1978), p. 1732.

## Suggestions for Further Reading

BERLE, ADOLPH. *The Twentieth Century Capitalist Revolution*. New York: Harcourt, Brace & World, 1954.
BERNSTEIN, MARVER. *Regulating Business By Independent Commission*. Princeton, N.J.: Princeton University Press, 1955.
BLAKE, HARLAN M. "Beyond the ITT Case: The Politics of Antitrust Enforcement," *Harpers* (June 1972), pp. 74–78.
BROWN, COURTNEY C. *Beyond the Bottom Line*. New York: Macmillan, 1979.
GABLE, RICHARD. "NAM: Influential Lobby or Kiss of Death?" *Journal of Politics*, vol. 15 (May 1953), pp. 254–273.
HUGHES, JONATHAN. *The Governmental Habit*. New York: Basic Books, 1977.
KOONTZ, HAROLD and GABLE, RICHARD. *Public Control of Economic Enterprise*. New York: McGraw-Hill, 1956.
LANDIS, JAMES. *Report on Regulatory Agencies to the President Elect*. Washington, D.C.: Government Printing Office, 1960.
LINDBLOM, CHARLES E. *Politics and Markets*. New York: Basic Books, 1977.
MASON, EDWARD. *Economic Concentration and the Monopoly Problem*. Cambridge, Mass.: Harvard University Press, 1957.
REAGAN, MICHAEL. *The Managed Economy*. New York: Oxford University Press, 1963.
REID, SAMUEL R. *The New Industrial Order*. New York: McGraw-Hill, 1976.
SCHMALENSEE, RICHARD. *The Control of Natural Monopolies*. Lexington, Mass.: Lexington Books, 1979.
STONE, ALAN. *Economic Regulation and the Public Interest*. Ithaca, N.Y.: Cornell University Press, 1977.
WEAVER, SUZANNE. *Decision to Prosecute: Organization and Public Policy in the Antitrust Division*. Cambridge, Mass.: MIT Press, 1977.
WEIDENBAUM, MURRAY L. *The Future of Business Regulation*. New York: Amacom, 1979.

# 11

# Government and Labor-Management Policy

As was the case with business, early governmental policy toward labor was one of laissez-faire, a position promoted by both labor and governmental policymakers. Organized labor did not become a really potent political force in American policymaking until the 1930s, though the movement for organization had gone on for several decades. A major reason for this was the attitude of the early labor movement leaders that their main objective should be the right to organize and bargain collectively, and they did not view the government as an instrument for gaining that objective, at least not during the early years of the movement. Governmental action, when it did occur, tended to be to the benefit of management, as in the case of President Cleveland's use of federal troops to break up the Pullman strike in 1894, thus reinforcing labor's wariness toward governmental involvement.

Early efforts at labor organization started about the time of Washington's administration and were largely local efforts patterned after the guild system of Europe. These efforts were generally quite weak and usually withered when they encountered the opposition of employers. The forerunners of modern-day union organizations began around the middle of the nineteenth century. The first national union to maintain a continuous existence was the Typographical Union, founded in 1852; the Brotherhood of Locomotive Engineers started in 1863. The Knights of Labor, a loose national combination of diverse labor interests, enjoyed a flurry of growth in the 1870s and 1880s, but was eventually torn apart by internal differences. As the Knights were declining, a new federation of craft unions was founded in 1886, the American Federation of Labor (AFL).

As labor organizations began to grow, they encountered much stiffer opposition from employers, who resorted to economic pressures, the courts, and frequently even violence to block organizational activities. In several early cases the courts applied an English common-law concept, the conspiracy doctrine, to labor unions and held that they were conspiracies to deprive employers of their legal property rights. Employers also resorted to widespread use of the so-called "yellow dog contract." Before a worker would be hired, he had to sign a contract agreeing not to join a union or engage in efforts to organize one. When employees attempted to organize, the employer simply went to court and secured an injunction enforcing the contract signed by his employees. When unions attempted to use the strike to press their cause, employers resorted to hiring professional "strikebreakers" and bloody encounters frequently occurred between striking workers and these hired thugs. Faced with the combined opposition of employers and the courts, the union movement made slow headway in its early going. By 1900, the unions still had only 868,000 members, not many more than the Knights of Labor had attracted two decades earlier.

About all the laboring class had going for it was its numbers. The workers lacked the lobbying skills and economic and political power of the employers. The only way to really use their numbers effectively was through organization and collective bargaining. As long as workers had to bargain with employers individually, their power was severely limited; and as long as employers could use the courts to get injunctions, labor's most effective tool, the strike, was also ineffective. In light of their experiences, labor unions and their leaders began to turn more to political activity to seek their objectives; here they could also put their numbers to good use. The AFL and other unions gradually moved away from their traditional laissez-faire position and began to view government more as an instrument that could help in the attainment of their goals of organization and collective bargaining. Shortly after the turn of the century, the AFL adopted as its political philosophy the rule of thumb it still follows today, "Reward your friends and defeat your enemies." As union members became more active politically, their impact at the polls and in governmental policies became gradually more apparent. Labor's influence helped to put into office more pro-labor politicians such as Fiorello LaGuardia, George Norris, Robert Wagner, Woodrow Wilson, and Franklin D. Roosevelt. As labor grew in numbers and political influence, it became in many urban areas a major force for liberalism in American politics. Its growth in political and economic strength brought to the fore numerous problems that previously had not been cause for particular concern on the part of the government, such issues as hazardous working conditions, long work hours and low wages, workmen's compensation, social security and, primary to labor, the right to organize and bargain collectively.

When the Clayton Act was adopted in 1914, though it was primarily an antitrust measure, it was hailed by the head of the AFL, Samuel Gompers, as labor's Magna Charta. The object of Gomper's praise was the clause in the act that stated that "the labor of a human being is not a commodity or article of com-

## Major Labor Legislation

**Clayton Act of 1914.** Though an antitrust measure, this bill included a provision exempting labor unions from antitrust provisions.

**Railway Labor Act of 1926.** Provided railroad workers the right to organize unions and engage in collective bargaining activities.

**Davis-Bacon Act of 1931.** Provided that contractors on federal projects should pay at least the local prevailing wage in communities where projects were pursued.

**Norris-LaGuardia Anti-Injunction Act of 1932.** Proscribed the use of the federal courts in securing injunctions to enforce "yellow dog" contracts.

**National Labor Relations Act of 1935.** Also known as the Wagner Act, this measure created the National Labor Relations Board, guaranteed workers the right to organize and bargain collectively, and proscribed "unfair" labor practices by management.

**Byrnes Act of 1936.** Known as the "Anti-Strikebreaker Act," the measure prohibited employers from using strikebreakers against unions.

**Walsh-Healey Act of 1936.** Provided that contractors with federal government contracts in excess of $10,000 must meet certain minimum standards for wages and hours of employees.

**Fair-Labor Standards Act of 1938.** Known as the "wages and hours" or "minimum wage" law, this measure and its amendments through the years set minimum wages and hours requirements for employees of businesses operating in interstate commerce.

**Taft-Hartley Act of 1947.** Defined various union practices as "unfair" labor practices against employers and provided for state adoption of "right-to-work" laws.

**Labor-Management Reporting and Disclosure Act of 1959.** Also known as the Landrum-Griffin Bill, this measure outlined various provisions designed to protect rank-and-file union members from unfair union practices.

merce," thus exempting labor unions from application of the antitrust laws. Congress had not intended to include labor unions under the antitrust laws, but in the absence of a specific exemption, the courts had applied the Sherman Act to labor unions. While the Clayton Act failed to provide the great impetus for union growth the labor leaders had hoped for, it did mark a change in governmental policy that was encouraging to the unions.

While World War I stimulated the labor market and provided jobs for large numbers of workers, the labor movement did not really show any rapid and sustained growth during this period, and following the war, labor's organizational

> **Principal Departments and Agencies**
>
> **Department of Labor (DOL).** Cabinet-level department, created in 1913, which administers and enforces statutes seeking to promote the wage level, working conditions, and employment opportunities for workers.
>
> **Federal Mediation and Conciliation Service.** An independent agency that seeks to prevent, through mediation, strikes that would interfere with the flow of interstate commerce. Professional mediators assist in the settlement of labor-management disputes and try to promote better labor-management relations.
>
> **National Labor Relations Board (NLRB).** Created by the National Labor Relations Act, the NLRB has the responsibility for administering provisions of the Wagner and Taft-Hartley Acts relative to unfair labor practices.
>
> **National Mediation Board.** Created by the Railway Labor Act of 1926, the board mediates differences between management and labor in the rail and airline fields and determines bargaining representatives in an effort to prevent strikes and lockouts in the crucial areas of rail and air transport.

efforts again encountered strong opposition from management through the use of strikebreakers and court injunctions. The unions retained distinguished lawyer-politician Charles Evans Hughes to represent them, but even he could not turn the tide for them.

## EARLY FEDERAL ACTION

The first real political breakthrough by labor came in the railway industry with the adoption of the Railway Labor Act in 1926. Under this act employers were banned from interfering with the rail workers' right to organize, and the government became a third party in employer-employee relationships through the establishment of the National Mediation Board to help resolve labor disputes. It was during the Great Depression that the labor movement began to experience sustained growth and the foundations for modern labor-management policy were finally laid. With the passage of the Davis-Bacon Act in 1931, Congress took its first step in the regulation of wages. This act provided that those having government construction contracts of $2000 or more were required to pay no less than the prevailing wage for similar work in the community where work was being performed. In March 1932, Congress adopted the Norris-LaGuardia Act, a major breakthrough for organized labor. This act specifically prohibited the use of injunctions against such union activities as striking, joining or organizing a union, assembling for union purposes, and other peaceful activities by labor unions. While Norris-LaGuardia did not guarantee labor the right to organize, it did remove a number of obstacles from the path of the union organizational efforts.

## The Wagner Act

In 1933 labor received further encouragement with the adoption of the National Industrial Recovery Act (NIRA). Though the bill was shortlived, being struck down by the Supreme Court, it included several provisions that were pro-labor. In fact, several of the labor provisions of NIRA were incorporated into the National Labor Relations (Wagner) Act, which was adopted in 1935. The Wagner Act, passed three and one-half years after Roosevelt became president, was greeted by many as labor's "bill of rights." The act guaranteed the worker's right to organize and join unions and to bargain collectively with employers. Five types of employer labor practices were defined as being unfair, and the National Labor Relations Board was created to carry out the provisions of the act and to hear labor-management complaints of "unfair" practices. Defined as unfair on the part of the employer were: (1) interference with employees' right to bargain collectively, (2) domination or influencing of labor unions, (3) discrimination against union members in hiring and firing, (4) discrimination against an employee for taking advantage of his rights under the law, and (5) refusal to bargain collectively with the properly designated representatives of the employees. Management quickly complained that the act was too one-sided and challenged its provisions in the courts. To the surprise of many, the act was upheld by the Supreme Court in April 1937 in a 5 to 4 decision.[1]

The adoption of the Wagner Act marked the beginning of a period of vigorous union development and considerable legislative activity in the field of labor-management relations. At the time Wagner was adopted in 1935, union membership stood at about 3.6 million. During the next decade unions added over 10 million new members and by 1947 had 15 million members. Though they had become a rather powerful political factor, the unions still represented less than a majority of all workers and their influence was spotty; they were weak in the South and among farm laborers.

While Wagner was the centerpiece, several other pieces of legislation significant to the labor movement were also adopted in the 1930s. In 1936 Congress adopted two measures: the Byrnes Act and the Walsh-Healey Act. The Byrnes Act prohibited employers' use of strikebreakers, and under Walsh-Healey or the Public Contracts Act, suppliers of materials in contracts with the federal government in amounts of $10,000 or more had to observe the eight-hour workday and forty-hour week, pay the prevailing minimum wage for similar work, and meet certain other standards relative to working conditions. In 1938 Congress expanded on Davis-Bacon and Walsh-Healey with the adoption of the Fair Labor Standards (Black-Connery) Act. This act excluded from interstate commerce any goods produced by a firm not meeting certain minimum standards set by the federal government on wages and hours. The original legislation provided for a minimum wage of 25 cents per hour for 1938 and an increase to 30 cents per hour in 1939 and 40 cents per hour in 1945. The maximum work week was set at 44 hours for 1938, reduced to 42 in 1939 and to 40 hours in 1940 and after. This act laid the foundation for what is known today as the federal minimum wage law, which has been amended continuously through the years as wage scales have risen and coverage has been extended to more and more employees. Also adopted in the decade of the thirties was the Social Security Act (1935), which, though not exclusively for labor, was something the unions had been pushing for some time.

As the unions grew and their political influence became more obvious, some reaction began to develop among the more conservative political elements and the pendulum began to swing toward controls on unions and their growing power. This was first manifested in the Smith-Connally Act of 1943, which sanctioned federal seizure of vital industries to block strikes that might threaten national security and which temporarily barred union political contributions. During World War II, labor-management differences were subordinated to concerns with national security, but following the war the rivalry was quickly renewed. In an effort to "catch up" after wartime wage controls, the unions resorted to strikes in a number of major industries in 1945 and '46, contributing to a growing wave of anti-union sentiment. Strikes in the steel, coal, and auto industries caused public impatience with strikes and shortages, and in 1946 President Truman seized the railroads to block a strike, threatening in the process to draft all the strikers. The growing anti-union sentiment, coupled with the election of a Republican majority to Congress in 1946 for the first time since 1929, paved the way for the adoption of the first important post-war labor bill. Whereas labor had attained rather broad support in its earlier efforts to gain governmental protection against management abuses, many people had now come to feel the unions were abusing their collective power and it was time for some redress of an imbalance.

### Taft-Hartley

In June 1947, Congress adopted the Labor-Management Relations Act, better known simply as Taft-Hartley, after its sponsors, Senator Robert Taft (R-Ohio) and Representative Fred Hartley (R-N.J.). On June 20 President Truman vetoed the bill, informing the Congress that it was unworkable and manifestly unfair to labor. A strong alliance of Republicans and conservative Democrats proceeded to override the president's veto by votes of 331 to 83 in the House and 68 to 25 in the Senate. Backed strongly by business groups, especially the NAM and Chamber of Commerce, Taft-Hartley reflected the strong anti-union sentiment generated by the post-war strikes. While the act retained the basic guarantees to workers of their rights to join unions, bargain collectively, and strike, it reflected the growing fear of union influence by defining a number of union actions as unfair labor practices and reviving the injunction as a tool to be used against unfair union practices. Whereas the pro-labor Wagner Act had been designed primarily to protect unions and workers in their efforts to organize and bargain collectively, Taft-Hartley reflected a feeling that unions had become such a strong economic and political force that they, like business, must now be more closely supervised by government. Listed as unfair union practices were:

1. The restraint or coercion of employees in the right to join or assist a union or to refrain from joining or assisting a union.
2. The restraint or coercion of an employer in the selection of his representatives for collective bargaining or grievance procedures.
3. The influencing of an employer to discriminate against an employee in violation of the union-shop provisions of the act.
4. The requirement, under union shop arrangement, of an initiation fee for new members that the National Labor Relations Board finds "excessive or discriminatory under all circumstances."
5. The refusal to bargain collectively with an employer where the union involved is the certified bargaining agent.
6. The requiring of an employer to pay a sum "in the nature of an extraction," for services that are not performed or are not to be performed (featherbedding).
7. The engaging in, or encouragement of employees to engage in, a strike or concerted refusal to use or otherwise handle or work on any goods or to perform any services, where the object is to force or require:
    a. Any employer or self-employed person to join any labor or employer organization.
    b. Any employer or other person to cease using or dealing in the products of another person or to cease doing business with any other person (secondary boycott).
    c. Another employer to recognize an uncertified union.
    d. Any employer to violate an NLRB certification.
    e. Any employer to assign particular work to employees in a particular union or trade unless that employer is failing to conform to an order or certification of the NLRB (sympathy and jurisdictional strikes).

In addition to its enumeration of unfair union practices, Taft-Hartley also included a number of other provisions curbing the unions' power and influence. Anti-labor elements felt the Wagner Act had gone too far by making the NLRB both prosecutor and judge in complaint cases. Under Taft-Hartley, Congress made the NLRB's general counsel independent and gave that office supervision over all the attorneys and employees in the regional offices where cases are first handled. Another provision strongly resented by labor was the requirement that before unions could take advantage of federal laws for collective bargaining purposes, they must file with the secretary of labor extensive information on the union and its operations. Particularly offensive under this provision was the requirement that unions must file affidavits to the effect that none of their officers were members of the Communist Party or other organizations advocating the overthrow of the government by force or by illegal or unconstitutional means.

Long an issue between labor and management was the question of whether unions could compel membership as a condition for employment. Under the *closed shop* arrangement a prospective employee must join the union before being hired. Under the *union shop* an employee may be hired before joining the union, but must agree to join after a specified period of time, usually about one month. The Wagner Act had sanctioned both the closed and union shop arrangements. Taft-Hartley made the closed shop an unfair labor practice, and while it did not outlaw the union shop, it set up limitations under Section 14-b that the unions found distasteful. This provision authorizes union shops only when a union certified as a representative of the employees has been approved in a secret ballot by a majority of the employees eligible to vote, and when state laws do not prohibit it. This last clause is the basis for so-called "right-to-work" laws, which prohibit the requirement of union membership as a condition for employment. Under this provision, twenty states have adopted right-to-work laws in effect outlawing union shop agreements.

Another concern growing out of the union activities of the post-war period was that of work stoppages creating national emergencies. Resulting from this concern was the provision in Taft-Hartley of the much debated "eighty-day cooling-off period." This provision enables the president to delay the implementation of a strike for up to eighty days while a solution is being sought. When, in the opinion of the president, a strike or threatened strike poses a real danger to national health, safety, or security, he may convene a board of inquiry. This board determines the facts of the dispute and reports these without recommendations to the president. If the president feels the facts justify it, he may direct the attorney general to seek a court injunction to enjoin the strike or work stoppage. If an injunction is issued, then the board of inquiry is reconvened, and if the dispute is not resolved, it must report to the president again within sixty days, including in such report a statement of the employer's last offer of settlement. Within the next twenty days a secret ballot must be taken among the employees on the employer's last offer and the results of the election certified to the attorney general. If the offer at settlement is rejected, the injunction is dissolved and the strike becomes legal. The president then submits his report to Congress along with any recommendations he may desire to offer.

Feeling that the secretary of labor should not have control of a supposedly impartial mediation agency, Congress also provided in Taft-Hartley for the transfer of the mediation and conciliation functions of the former U. S. Conciliation Agency to the new, independent Federal Mediation and Conciliation Service. New procedures were also set up for handling disputes. The parties to a contract must give at least sixty days prior notice of a proposed termination or modification of an agreement, and within thirty days thereafter must notify the Federal Mediation and Conciliation Service and any appropriate state agencies. The Federal Mediation and Conciliation Service may enter a case at the request of either party involved or of its own initiative. Other provisions of the act make it illegal for any labor organization to make political contributions to candidates for president or Congress and prohibit federal employees from striking. Government employees are still permitted to join unions and bargain collectively but cannot use the strike.

Proponents of Taft-Hartley felt the act was an appropriate step in the direction of correcting the imbalance created by the Wagner Act, while labor complained that Taft-Hartley was a "slave labor law" drafted by the lawyers of the NAM. Proponents countered that this was only fair play since union lawyers had drafted the Wagner Act. Labor contended that Taft-Hartley would prevent further union organization, permit management to break many unions, and severely cripple labor's capacity to bargain effectively.

Many of the provisions in Taft-Hartley have proven controversial and their application has produced mixed results. The ban on closed shops has been relatively ineffective because in many industries and trades employers have been willing to hire only union members, since they know these workers will possess the desired skills. While the unions have tried for years to get the repeal of Section 14-b and fear the spread of state right-to-work laws, the movement seems to have reached its peak in spite of the efforts of the National Right-To-Work Committee. Currently twenty states have right-to-work laws and the voters in Missouri rejected a proposed right-to-work amendment in a 1978 referendum. The ban on union political contributions, while it may have complicated union fundraising, certainly has not prevented unions from being a major source of political campaign funds. To skirt the provisions of the law, the unions simply created semi-autonomous political action committees, such as the AFL-CIO's Committee on Political Education (COPE), to handle their political funds and activities. Probably one of the most debated provisions of Taft-Hartley has been the eighty-day cooling-off provision and its success or failure. This provision has been invoked by the president on about thirty occasions and several observers see it as an unwieldy procedure that causes about as many problems as it solves. Many feel the use of the provision may actually prolong a strike by simply delaying any really serious efforts at bargaining until after eighty days. President Carter did not choose to use the provision to seek an end to a rather lengthy coal strike in 1978 even though many counseled that he do so. If work stoppages are any measure, they now run about 3500 annually as compared to 2800 in the 1930s. On the whole, Taft-Hartley did not prove to be the blow to the unions that they had predicted. While its provisions may have hindered organizing efforts, especially in the South where union gains have been limited, the existing unions pretty well maintained their strength with membership growing from about 14 million in 1945 to over 16.5 million in 1962. Only in more recent years have they begun to decline.

Even after the adoption of Taft-Hartley, strong sentiment for further curbs on union power and activity continued and grew through the 1950s. Much of this sentiment was fed by the revelations and publicity attracted by the Senate Select Committee on Improper Activities in the Labor-Management Field headed by

Senator John McClellan (D-Ark.), which investigated corruption and labor racketeering from 1957 through 1960. While the evidence collected actually implicated only a few unions, the charges of corruption, labor-management collusion, theft and misuse of union funds, strongarm practices against members, and underworld ties contributed to growing sentiment for union reform. The McClellan Committee was especially critical of the Teamsters Union, which was expelled from the AFL-CIO in 1957, and its presidents Dave Beck and Jimmy Hoffa, charging that Hoffa ran a "hoodlum empire." Hoffa later served a prison term after being convicted of "jury tampering." Many labor leaders were fearful of new legislation growing out of the McClellan Committee investigations and resented the committee's painting the labor movement with such broad strokes. Senator Pat McNamara (D-Mich.), a former union leader, refused to sign the report of the committee. In March 1958, George Meany, president of the AFL-CIO, termed the report "a disgraceful example of the use of sensationalism in an attempt to smear the trade union movement." Meany went on to say, "There is great inherent danger in some of the legislation which is not and never will be justified."[2]

### Landrum-Griffin

Two new pieces of labor legislation were largely a result of the McClellan Committee's investigation: the Welfare and Pensions Disclosure Act of 1958 and the Labor-Management Reporting and Disclosure Act (Landrum-Griffin) of 1959. The Welfare and Pensions Act was aimed at protecting unions from the theft and misuse of their funds by union leaders. Landrum-Griffin, supported by President Eisenhower and various business groups, was a comprehensive labor reform bill aimed at insuring the proper handling of union finances by officials, preventing labor management collusion on contracts, racketeering, and extortion, and guaranteeing to union members the right to run their unions democratically. There was a growing feeling that many unions had come to be run primarily in the interest of union officials, and several provisions of Landrum-Griffin were aimed at protecting the rights of the rank-and-file union members. Title I of Landrum-Griffin is a sort of catch-all "bill of rights for labor" designed to insure the role of union members in union proceedings and to bring more democracy to union operations. Under its provisions unions are required to provide the secretary of labor with detailed reports on union finances and the operations of the union's constitution and bylaws; union members are guaranteed the right to sue the union for unfair practices and access to union records; ex-convicts, Communists and labor officials with conflicting business interests are barred from holding union offices; and periodic elections for union officials are required. The "bill of rights" section secures for members use of the secret ballot in union elections, freedom of speech in union meetings, and open hearings in disciplinary cases. The law makes the misuse of union funds a crime and requires the bonding of union officials. The act also broadens Taft-Hartley's restrictions on secondary boycotts and picketing as unfair labor practices.

Both Taft-Hartley and Landrum-Griffin reflect a substantial change from governmental policy as expressed in the Wagner Act of 1935. While Wagner was aimed primarily at protecting unions and their members from unfair labor practices by employers, both Taft-Hartley and Landrum-Griffin reflect a change from promotion of labor interest to a primary emphasis on the regulation of unions. Though Landrum-Griffin was designed to protect the integrity of law-abiding unions as well as to correct those guilty of improper procedures, many labor leaders disliked its negative tone and feared that its provisions would lead to increased governmental interference with organized labor. Since the act's adoption, thousands of unions have submitted reports to the Labor Department outlining their internal governing structures and operations and thousands of complaints by union members have been filed. While many investigations have been conducted, only a relatively small number of cases have required legal action. The main impact of Landrum-Griffin has been that its provisions stand as a warning to unions against corruption and abuse.

### Recent Legislative Efforts

Since 1960 there has been a standoff in the field of labor-management legislation. While both pro-labor and anti-labor groups have mounted major efforts to bring modification in certain provisions of existing laws, neither side has been successful. One area where the unions have sought a change in existing laws is that of the so-called "no-man's land" labor dispute. As a result of our federal system and gaps in the current laws, certain types of labor disputes presently fall under neither state nor federal jurisdiction. The National Labor Relations Board has declined to handle any cases involving less than specified dollar amounts, and the 1957 Supreme Court decision in *Guss* v *Utah* held that state agencies could not handle these cases excluded by the NLRB.[3] Although a bill to correct this situation was reported by the House Education and Labor Committee in 1960, it was bottled up in the Rules Committee, and further efforts to plug this loophole have failed thus far.

Throughout the 1960s a major issue with labor was its effort to secure "common-site picketing" legislation. Under a 1951 court ruling, common-site picketing (picketing by a union on a work site where several contractors or subcontractors are working that results in other unions on the same job stopping their work), was held to be a violation of the secondary boycott provisions of the Taft-Hartley Act.[4] Unions complained that this ruling denied them the right to strike any job site where more than one firm was working. Unions in the building trades were particularly concerned with this ruling and pushed for legislation to reduce its impact. Although several proposals have been introduced, none has been enacted.

In 1977, concerned with labor's declining success in its efforts to attract new union members, President George Meany and the AFL-CIO launched a massive campaign for amendments to the existing labor laws that would facilitate union recruitment efforts. While the labor effort touched off an extensive lobbying campaign generating millions of pieces of mail to congressmen and an intense debate on proposals for change in existing laws, nothing was enacted. The proposed Labor Reform Act would have made some changes in the National Labor Relations Act (Wagner Act) designed to expedite the handling of labor dispute cases by the NLRB and providing stiffer penalties for employers found guilty of unfair labor practices. The bill would have required the NLRB to conduct organizing elections within fifteen days after a petition was filed, thus speeding up elections and allowing management less time to mount a campaign against unionization. Because under existing laws some employers have resisted workers' organizing efforts with unfair practices, harassing and firing union organizers and ignoring NLRB orders with impunity, the reform bill also proposed stiffer penalties for violations. Employers found guilty of unfair practices could be required to make back-pay settlements up to 150 percent to employees fired for union activities, and employers who violated NLRB orders could be barred from receiving government contracts. The proposal also included an "equal access" provision opening places of work to union organizers if the employers campaigned against unionization on their own premises.

Proponents of the measure said it was simply a "fine tuning" of the National Labor Relations Act and would in no way lead to "push-button unionism" as its opponents charged. Secretary of Labor Ray Marshall said the bill "just punishes more severely, behavior that is already illegal." Some opponents on the other hand saw the proposal as a union powerplay. Columnist James Kilpatrick described it in these words: "A more brazen bid for union power could not have been contrived. The whole idea of the bill is to make life easier for the unions and harder for employers." Reflecting similar sentiments, Senator Malcolm Wallop (R-Wyo.) said, "I see this bill as nothing, nothing but a vehicle designed superbly" for "labor kings" to expand their influence. Senator Orrin G. Hatch (R-Utah) saw the bill as challenging "the very fiber of our system." Many employers contended that the proposed "reforms" would give the National Labor Relations Act a decided union slant discouraging employers from opposing unionization efforts and would intrude the federal government into the labor-management process to an unnecessary degree. In its opposition to the measure, the U. S. Chamber of Commerce singled out two provisions it felt were particularly dangerous: the provision allowing union organizers to speak for unionization in work places and the provision giving the government the authority to set wage rates for the employees of companies that refused to bargain in "good faith" with certified union representatives.[5] In the end, one of the most telling influences against the measure was a staff report of the Small Business Administration saying that the act would place a burden on small businesses. This and widespread opposition among the nation's small businesses were key elements in the measure's ultimate defeat.

The Labor Reform Bill was passed by the House in October 1977 by a vote of 257 to 163, but when brought up in the Senate in early 1978 it encountered determined opposition. Finally, after more than a half-dozen attempts to invoke cloture and end a nineteen-day filibuster by the bill's opponents, the measure was recommitted to the Senate Committee on Human Resources. Cloture required sixty votes and the closest supporters could come was fifty-eight, thus ending labor's hopes for the measure in the 95th Congress. Spokesmen for organized labor later indicated they would forego pushing for similar reform legislation in the 96th Congress and would focus their efforts on some piecemeal changes in labor laws.

More favorable to labor has been the blocking of efforts to repeal the forty-eight-year-old Davis-Bacon Act, which many see as inflationary. Known as the "prevailing wage law," the purpose of Davis-Bacon is to ensure that federal contractors pay their workers at least the minimum prevailing wage for similar work in the location where the work is being performed. With the Carter administration's growing concern with inflation, the General Accounting Office (GAO) investigated the act and concluded the measure was obsolete, clumsily and incorrectly administered, and possibly harmful to the best interest of those it was supposed to protect. GAO's report recommended repeal. In 1979 several efforts were made to amend or repeal the act by attaching amendments to various authorization bills. These efforts were turned back in committee but the votes were quite close. While organized labor generally supports Davis-Bacon, the business community and their supporters in Congress have pledged to continue their efforts at repeal. While the last decade has produced little in the way of federal legislation in the labor-management field, several efforts have been made for some changes. The two sides seem pretty evenly balanced in their ability to block the other's efforts.

## THE POLITICS OF LABOR-MANAGEMENT POLICY

During the early years of labor development in America its political influence was quite limited, both because of the relatively weak nature of the early unions and because the early unions did not view political action as a means for achieving labor's objectives. Since the turn of the century, organized labor has been more active politically and its influence spotty. One reason for this is that labor has not been totally successful in maximizing on its strength of numbers because of persistent internal differences.

During the 1930s and 1940s the labor movement was marked by competition between the AFL (American Federation of Labor) and the CIO (Congress of Industrial Organizations). The older AFL was made up largely of the smaller skills and craft-type unions and its leadership was very hesitant about organizing the large numbers of workers in the mass-production industries. This caused differences within the organization and in 1935 a dissident faction under the leadership of John L. Lewis of the United Mine Workers and Sidney Hillman of the Amalgamated Clothing Workers was expelled from the AFL. In 1938 they formed the competing Congress of Industrial Organizations. After competing with one another for two decades, the AFL and CIO merged in 1955, creating a confederation of 141 national unions with, at that time, over 12 million members.

Actually the AFL-CIO parent organization, aside from its powers to admit and expel members, has no control over member unions other than persuasion. Each member union retains a high degree of autonomy, collecting its own dues and carrying out its own political activities. Consequently, internal political differences are not unusual. In 1966 union leaders Walter Reuther, Joseph A. Beirne, and Albert E. Hayes charged that many unions were discriminating in their hiring and firing practices against minorities. A year later the United Auto Workers (UAW), the AFL-CIO's largest affiliate union, withdrew, at least partly in protest over AFL-CIO's failure to adopt and implement its own civil rights guidelines.

While labor traditionally has been considered an ally of the Democratic party and has helped to elect such Democratic presidents as Franklin Roosevelt, Harry Truman, and John F. Kennedy, the unions are not wedded to any one party. The guiding political philosophy of the AFL-CIO is still to "reward its friends and defeat its enemies" regardless of party affiliation. In fact, with the recent decline of political parties, Lane Kirkland, executive director of AFL-CIO, says of parties, "They have no policy function and just convene to nominate a presidential candidate, falling into disuse between conventions." While organized labor still is active in political campaigns and is a heavy financial contributor, much of the politics of labor policy is interest-group politics.

The AFL-CIO maintains its national headquarters just a few blocks up the street from the White House and is consistently among the top lobbying spenders on policy matters. It maintains extensive voting records of members of Congress and uses them in union lobbying and campaign efforts. In its efforts to influence public policy, organized labor frequently finds itself in conflict with business and management. On occasion, as in 1977 when the steelworkers unions aligned with management to push for government quotas on steel imports from Japan, unions and management may push for common objectives. More frequently than not, however, on such issues as labor law reforms, collective bargaining, minimum wages, the right to strike, etc., unions and management will be on different sides of the fence.

Of considerable concern to organized labor during the last decade has been the decline of unions' ability to attract new members and the accompanying erosion of union political influence. Though the workforce has grown considerably in recent years, from about 86 million in 1970 to over 100 million currently, the portion of the workforce that is affiliated with unions has declined from about 40 percent three decades ago to about 20 percent currently. For the last couple of decades, labor has not come close to matching the vast growth of the corporate sector. Union membership in the U.S. is the lowest in any industrial democracy—in Great Britain 60 percent of the workers are organized and in the Scandinavian countries 80 percent belong to unions.

A number of factors have contributed to organized labor's decline; in part it

Government and Labor-Management Policy  289

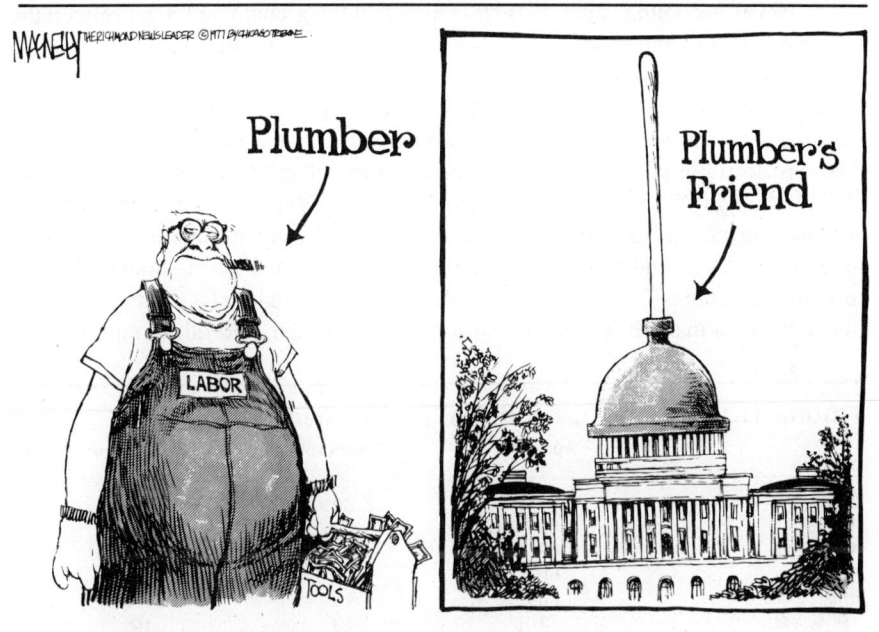

**Plumber**

**Plumber's Friend**

Reprinted by permission of Chicago Tribune-N.Y. News Syndicate, Inc.

is due to shifts of industry and employment to the South, where anti-union sentiment has traditionally been strong. Also, labor organizations, like other institutions, have suffered an erosion of public confidence. (See figure 11.1) In a 1973 survey, 55 percent of those polled felt organized labor had too much power; in 1977 this figure had grown to 65 percent. While the economy has changed from a largely manufacturing economy to a service economy and the major growth in the workforce has been in the service fields, union membership, with the exception of state and local government employees, has remained largely in the old-style, heavy-manufacturing industries. The traditional business unionism and conservative craft-union philosophy of the AFL-CIO have been major obstacles to union expansion into some of the new areas. For years the craft-dominated unions were the controlling force in the old AFL and even in the merged federation they remained the most cohesive force, exerting powerful influences that have tended to reduce the organization's drive to reach out for new members, a situation that brought new union organization to a virtual standstill in the late 1970s. At first George Meany and Lane Kirkland of the AFL-CIO strongly reflected the craft-union philosophy. In an interview with a *Washington Post* reporter, Kirkland said, "I've never been concerned about what proportion of the working force is organized." By 1977, however, in the light of labor's continued problems, Meany and the AFL-CIO executive council were voicing alarm at the decline in their membership and political influence.[6]

It was becoming apparent by this time that labor could no longer rely on the same approaches and arguments in its organizational efforts that had been effective in the past. NLRB records show that in 1977 union organizers won only 46 percent of all representation elections. In 1976 they won 48 percent; in 1972, 54 percent; and a decade earlier they were succeeding about 60 percent of the time. Unions also are losing a large number of decertification elections (about 80 percent in 1977). Along with their decline in organizational appeal, unions also are suffering an image problem. Various surveys have shown that many feel union leaders wield excessive power, and their confidence rating has declined among both union and non-union families. The AFL-CIO has developed a "middle-class" image and this has tended to make it less attractive to blacks, women, and other minorities.

**FIGURE 11.1 Rating of Labor Unions (43-year trend)**

|  | Approve | Disapprove | No Opinion |
| --- | --- | --- | --- |
| Latest | 55% | 33% | 12% |
| 1978 | 59 | 31 | 10 |
| 1973 | 59 | 26 | 10 |
| 1967 | 66 | 23 | 11 |
| 1965, June | 70 | 19 | 11 |
| 1965, Feb. | 71 | 19 | 10 |
| 1963 | 67 | 23 | 10 |
| 1962 | 64 | 24 | 12 |
| 1961, May | 63 | 22 | 15 |
| 1961, Feb. | 70 | 18 | 12 |
| 1959 | 68 | 19 | 13 |
| 1957, Sept. | 64 | 18 | 18 |
| 1957, Feb. | 76 | 14 | 10 |
| 1953 | 75 | 18 | 7 |
| 1949 | 62 | 22 | 16 |
| 1947 | 64 | 25 | 11 |
| 1941 | 61 | 30 | 9 |
| 1940 | 64 | 22 | 14 |
| 1939 | 68 | 24 | 8 |
| 1937 | 72 | 20 | 8 |
| 1936 | 72 | 20 | 8 |

Source: George Gallup Poll, Louisville, Ky. Courier-Journal, 6-17-79. Reprinted with permission of Gallup Poll.

# CONCLUSION

As labor tries to reverse the current trends and attract new union members, it must also build a new image for the labor movement. A major new target for union recruitment is the vast assortment of new service occupations, the retailing and finance fields, and government employees. One of the fastest-growing unions in recent years has been the American Federation of State, County and Municipal Employees, which has tripled its membership in a little over a decade and now has over 1 million members in its constituent unions. Still, fewer than half the eligible employees in state and local governments belong to unions. The union efforts on these fronts face some problem since many of the workers in these fields consider themselves technicians or professionals and are not very union oriented. Another area where the unions have lagged is among the large numbers of women entering the workforce. Women now make up 40 percent of the labor force but only 16 percent currently are union members.

The labor movement's loss of momentum and political power has also encouraged management to take much tougher positions in recent bargaining efforts and such terms as "regressive bargaining," "rollback," or "giveback" have been used to apply to the cancellation of some of labor's previous gains. In the 1978 coal miners' strike, the coal operators demanded a rollback in health-care benefits. Such developments as this, coupled with the fact that many non-union workers already profit from union benefits because many firms pass on union-attained benefits to their unorganized workers, sometimes make it difficult for the unions to convince workers of the advantages of union membership. New AFL-CIO Executive Director Lane Kirkland sees a tough struggle ahead in what he has referred to as a new "class war" in which corporations and the Business Roundtable will wage strong union-busting efforts.

As the unions carry their organizational efforts into the public sector, this will raise a whole host of new questions for policymakers. While Taft-Hartley outlaws strikes by federal employees, the question of strikes by other public employees is not yet resolved. In 1919 when faced by a strike of the Boston police, Calvin Coolidge, then governor of Massachusetts, said, "There is no right to strike against the public safety by anybody, anywhere, anytime." George Meany on the other hand, said, "Public employees have been told to feel free to strike any damn time they feel like going on strike." As more public employees join unions, this is a question that is bound to heat up.

Many observers feel that a strong and viable labor movement is important in our democratic system as a counterbalance to the power and influence of the business-management sector, as well as being a stabilizing force in our mixed economy and the protector of labor's share of national income.[7] Thus it is important as labor seeks to form new coalitions to help defend and promote its interests that these factors be considered. What is the role of the government in maintaining a proper balance of power between the forces of organized labor and management that will ensure our continued economic development and equal protection for all under the laws? Are the basic concepts and provisions of Wagner, Taft-Hartley, and Landrum-Griffin still appropriate for labor management relations in the 1980s, or are new approaches and new initiatives necessary to cope with the changing workforce and economic trends?

## Points to Ponder

Have labor unions outlived their usefulness to the American working class?

Is current labor-management legislation more favorable to unions or to management relations?

Should public employees—police, firemen, etc.—have the right to strike? Should federal employees?

What must unions do to recover from their recent decline?

Should labor unions be allowed to make political contributions from union dues?
Should Section 14-b of the Taft-Hartley Act be repealed?
Should the labor laws be amended to allow common-site picketing?

## Notes

1. *National Labor Relations Board* v *Jones and Laughlin Steel Corporation*, 301 U.S. 1 (1937).
2. George Meany as quoted in *Congress and the Nation, 1945-1964* (Washington, D.C.: Congressional Quarterly, 1965), p. 603.
3. *Guss* v *Utah Labor Relations Board*, 77 S.Ct. 609 (1957).
4. *National Labor Relations Board* v *Denver Building and Construction Trades Council*, 71 S.Ct. 943 (1951).
5. See Howard Fineman's "Senators face heavy labor-bill lobbying" in the Louisville, Ky. *Courier-Journal*, June 4, 1978; and "Senate showdown looms on the labor "reform" bill," Washington *Star* article reprinted in *Courier-Journal*, May 27, 1978.
6. See Irving Richter, "American Labor," *The Center Magazine* (May/June 1979), pp. 34–43.
7. *Ibid.*

## Suggestions for Further Reading

DAUGHERTY, C.A. and PARRISH, JOHN. *The Labor Problems of American Society*. Boston: Houghton-Mifflin, 1952.
DERBER, MILTON. *The American Idea of Industrial Democracy 1865-1965*. Champaign, Ill.: University of Illinois Press, 1970.
DULLES, FOSTER R. *Labor in America*, rev. ed. New York: Crowell, 1966.
DUNLOP, JOHN T. and GALANSON, WALTER, eds. *Labor in the Twentieth Century*. Academic Press, 1978.
GOLDBERG, ARTHUR. *AFL-CIO: Labor United*. New York: McGraw-Hill, 1956.
GREENSTONE, DAVID. *Labor in American Politics*. New York: Knopf, 1969.
HUTCHINSON, JOHN. *The Imperfect Union: A History of Corruption in American Trade Unions*. New York: Dutton, 1970.
LENS, SIDNEY. *The Labor Wars*. Garden City, N.Y.: Doubleday, 1973.
MCADAM, ALAN. *Power and Politics in Labor Legislation*. New York: Columbia University Press, 1964.
MCLAUGHLIN, DORIS and SCHOOMAKER, ANITA. *The Landrum-Griffin Act and Union Democracy*. Ann Arbor: University of Michigan Press, 1979.
NORTHRUP, HERBERT R. and BLOOM, GORDON. *Government and Labor*. Homewood, Ill.: Richard D. Irwin, 1963.
REHMUS, CHARLES; MCLAUGHLIN, DORIS; and NESBITT, FREDERICK, eds. *Labor and American Politics*. Ann Arbor: University of Michigan Press, 1974.
REYNOLDS, LLOYD. *Labor Economics and Labor Relations*, 4th ed. Englewood Cliffs, N.J.: Prentice-Hall, 1964.
TAFT, PHILIP. *The Structure and Government of Labor Unions*. Cambridge, Mass.: Harvard University Press, 1954.
TANNEBAUM, FRANK. *A Philosophy of Labor*. New York: Knopf, 1952.
WYKSTRA, RONALD and STEPHENS, ELEANOUR. *American Labor and Manpower Policy*. New York: Odyssey Press, 1970.
YELLEN, SAMUEL. *American Labor Struggles*. New York: Harcourt, Brace & Jovanovich, 1976.

# 12
# Governing the Environment and Natural Resources

Throughout most of the United States' early development, questions of natural resources and the environment were of little concern to government. The nation was blessed with an abundance of land, water, timber, and other natural resources; few citizens, including governmental policymakers, seriously contemplated any need for conservation or regulation of use. The general attitude was that the earth's natural resources were put there for man to exploit and most early policies, such as the land grants to railroads and the Homestead Act, were designed to encourage development, not regulate use. Only in this century have the conservation of natural resources and the preservation of a safe and healthful environment come to be considered major public responsibilities.

In more recent years, Americans have had to face the reality that our abundant resources are not inexhaustible, and the harsh reality of scarcity of certain resources has led to more political and governmental action in this field of policy. Because governmental involvement in this realm includes a broad variety of programs and interests, heated controversies concerning the development and use of our environment and natural resources have become a common element in American politics since the 1930s. Since a variety of interests compete for the use of available resources and because governmental policies can mean significant financial differences for the groups concerned, environmental and resources decisions have become an area of some of our most intense political conflicts. Because of the conflicting interests over such policies, it is next to impossible to please everyone. When President Carter sought to slow inflation and encourage home building by encouraging the harvesting of more timber from federal lands, environmentalists were mortified at his callous raping of our environment. On the

## Major Environmental and Natural Resources Statutes

**Forest Act of 1891.** Marked the beginning of the vast national forest system managed by the federal government. It authorized the president to set aside public lands with valuable timber resources as national forests.

**Reclamation Act of 1902.** Also known as the Newlands Act, this measure provided for federal assistance in irrigating arid lands and permitted withdrawals of public lands for use in federal reclamation projects.

**Antiquities Act of 1906.** Authorized the president to set aside certain lands as parks, historic sites, and national monuments.

**Pickett Act of 1910.** Provided the president authority to set aside public lands for various public purposes while retaining them under federal ownership.

**Weeks Act of 1911.** Authorized the purchase of lands to be added to the national forest system.

**Taylor Grazing Act of 1934.** Governs grazing on the public lands managed by the federal government.

**Flood Control Act of 1936.** Gave the federal government responsibility for nationwide flood control projects.

**Flood Control Act of 1944.** Firmly fixed into federal policy the principle of multiple-use water resources development and was the major statute on water policy for the immediate post-war era.

**Atomic Energy Act 1946.** Created the Atomic Energy Commission (now the NRC) and gave it responsibility over the use of atomic fuels and disposal of atomic wastes.

**Atomic Energy Act Amendment of 1954.** Extended to private industry the right to use atomic fuels commercially.

**Multiple Surface Use Act of 1955.** Tightened restrictions on private uses of public lands for mining and other purposes.

**Air Pollution Act of 1955.** Authorized a program of air pollution studies and research and experimentation in air pollution control.

**Price-Anderson Act of 1957.** Provided a federal insurance program for private firms in the atomic energy industry.

**Clean Air Act of 1963.** Provided for an expanded national program to control and prevent air pollution. It provided a matching grant program to advance pollution control programs.

**National Wilderness Act of 1964.** Established the National Wilderness Preservation System to maintain designated segments of publicly owned lands in a wild and undeveloped state.

**Motor Vehicle Air Pollution Control Act of 1965.** Authorized the secretary of HEW to set standards limiting the amounts of carbon monoxide, hydro-carbons, and other air pollutants that could be emitted by vehicles powered by internal combustion engines.

**Solid Waste Disposal Act of 1965.** The first major legislative action in this area; established a federal program of research for developing better methods of solid-waste disposal.

**Water Quality Act of 1965.** Required the states to establish water quality standards and authorized the secretary of HEW to establish standards when state standards were inadequate or nonexistent. The act also authorized the creation within HEW of a Federal Water Pollution Control Administration.

**Clean Waters Restoration Act of 1966.** Provided for federal grants to help states and communities pay the costs of meeting the water pollution standards established in the 1965 Water Quality Act.

**Air Quality Act of 1967.** Expanded federal grants to the states for implementing air quality standards, authorized the secretary of HEW to set air quality standards for various regions of the country if the states failed to do so, and established the President's Air Quality Advisory Board.

**National Wild and Scenic Rivers Act of 1968.** Designed to preserve outstanding scenic stretches of rivers and streams in a wilderness state of development.

**National Environmental Policy Act of 1969.** Made environmental protection a matter of national policy. The act required federal agencies to issue environmental impact statements before taking action or making recommendations having environmental consequences and created a Presidential Advisory Council on Environmental Quality.

**Water Quality Improvement Act of 1970.** Made petroleum companies liable for spill clean-ups, outlawed the flushing of raw sewage from boat toilets, tightened controls on thermal pollution, and created the Office of Environmental Quality.

**Clean Air Amendments of 1970.** Established specific deadlines for a 90 percent reduction in certain pollutants from new automobiles, set up new research programs, and established national air quality standards.

**Resource Recovery Act of 1970.** Expanded federal assistance for solid waste disposal programs and gave greater emphasis to the recycling and recovery of materials from solid wastes.

**Federal Water Pollution Control Act of 1972.** Provided a grants program to aid water clean-up and set a goal of clean waters by 1985. It established limits on effluent discharges and set basic water quality standards.

**Endangered Species Act of 1973.** Authorized the interior secretary to list and implement regulations designed to protect species of wildlife, fish, and plants threatened with extinction.

**Safe Drinking Water Act of 1974.** Directed EPA to establish national standards setting maximum allowable levels for certain chemical and bacteriological pollutants in water systems.

**Toxic Substances Control Act of 1976.** Provided for the screening of new substances to determine their safety before they are placed on the market.

**Federal Land Policy and Management Act of 1976.** Updated and consolidated about 3000 public laws dealing with the control, management, and use of public lands.

**Surface Mining Control and Reclamation Act of 1977.** Tightened regulations governing strip mining operations by providing that the states establish certain minimum standards. If the states failed to meet minimum standards, the Federal Office of Surface Mining (OSM) would set standards.

other hand, when he moved to put millions of acres of Alaskan wilderness "off limits" to developers, he was a hero to the environmentalists, but roundly criticized by the development interests for placing such vast resource potential beyond economic development. The heated battles that have taken place over many of these issues prompted Energy Secretary James Schlesinger to observe, "The art of legislative compromise has declined somewhat in recent years." While governmental involvement in the field is not new, the focus has shifted significantly in the last half century and the intensity of the issues confronted has mounted dramatically.

## LAND MANAGEMENT AND PRESERVATION

Through wars, treaties, and purchases the federal government quite early in our history became the owner of a vast public domain, at one time owning over three-fourths of the land area of the U. S. Today the federal government still owns over 700 million acres, with approximately 300 million set aside for special-purpose uses. Early federal management of the public domain was aimed primarily at encouraging the expansion and development of the emerging nation. Public lands were used for a variety of purposes in this respect: to encourage and help finance education (the Survey Ordinance of 1785, the Morrill Act); to encourage the westward expansion of the railroads (the land grants of the 1860s and '70s); and to encourage the westward expansion of the population (the Homestead Act and the Desert Land Act). Some of these early policies no doubt contributed to the exploitation of land resources that eventually turned governmental concern from one primarily of expansion and development to conservation.

In the 1870s Congress began to set aside some lands for special use; in 1875, 166 million acres were designated for Indian reservations and in 1872 Yellowstone became the first of more than 200 national parks eventually created. In 1881 the Division of Forestry was set up in the Department of Agriculture, and ten years later Congress authorized the president to withdraw public lands as "forest preserves," marking the beginning of the national forest system. The push for greater governmental involvement in resource management became stronger when the conservationists became a part of the Progressive movement. President Theodore Roosevelt, a dedicated outdoorsman, also provided leadership and momentum to the conservation movement. In 1906 the Antiquities Act was adopted, authorizing presidents to designate certain lands as historical sites and national monuments. The Pickett or General Withdrawal Act was passed in 1910, followed by the Weeks Act a year later which authorized the purchase of lands for national forests. The Clarke-McNary Act of 1924 further broadened the purchase provisions for acquiring national forest lands. Under this legislation the federal government has become the owner and manager of a vast national forest system of almost 200 million acres, making it the largest owner of timber resources in the country. The forest industry owns 16 percent of timber reserves, private owners control 20 percent, the states own 12 percent, and the federal government accounts for 52 percent.

## Principal Departments and Agencies

**Department of the Interior.** This department, particularly its Bureau of Land Management, discharges a number of responsibilities important in the resources and environmental fields.

**Department of Agriculture (USDA).** The Department of Agriculture includes the Forest Service and the Soil Conservation Service, both of which have conservation and environmental roles.

**Council on Environmental Quality (CEQ).** Established by the National Environmental Policy Act of 1969, CEQ has responsibility for formulating and recommending policies for the promotion and improvement of environmental quality.

**Environmental Protection Agency (EPA).** One of the largest of the federal regulatory agencies, the EPA has the responsibility for enforcing the environmental protection statutes.

**Occupational Safety and Health Administration (OSHA).** This agency is responsible for formulating and enforcing regulations to promote health and safety in the workplace.

**Food and Drug Administration (FDA).** One of the older regulatory agencies, the FDA is responsible for policing the food and drug industries to prevent the production and marketing of unsafe products.

**Nuclear Regulatory Commission (NRC).** The NRC is responsible for supervising the disposal of radioactive wastes produced by the use of atomic fuels.

**Office of Surface Mining and Reclamation Enforcement.** This agency is responsible for enforcing regulations governing strip mine operations and the effect of their activities on the environment.

**Office of Technology Assessment (OTA).** This office is responsible for advising Congress on the potential effect of technological applications and recommending alternative policies and programs.

Because the forests and other federally owned lands contain a variety of valuable resources, they have become more and more a subject of contention as other sources of available natural resources are depleted. At the same time interest in the valuable natural resources contained in these lands is growing, the emergence of an affluent urban society with growing recreational demands and a strong environmentalist movement have made federal policy in this area a volatile and controversial issue. Such commercial interests as the American Forestry Association, the American National Cattleman's Association, the American Mining Congress, the National Reclamation Association, the American Farm Bureau Federation, the Chamber of Commerce, the American Pulpwood Association, the National Lumber Manufacturers Association, the Rocky Mountain Oil and Gas Association, the National Association of Manufacturers, and the Independent

Retailers Association of America generally oppose efforts to close more public lands to use and development by private interest. The Taylor Grazing Act of 1934 provides for federal management of grazing and resources on federal lands, and in the 1950s conservationist groups began to push for further limits on access to public lands. Pushing the movement for establishment of a National Wilderness Preservation System were such groups as the Wilderness Society, Wildlife Management Institute, Citizens Committee on Natural Resources, Sierra Club, American Nature Association, AFL-CIO, Council of Conservationists, National Wildlife Federation, Izaak Walton League, National Audubon Society, Garden Clubs of America, American Planning and Civic Association, Trustees for Conservation, National Grange, American Youth Hostels, Defenders of Wildlife, and General Federation of Womens Clubs. After a vigorous campaign, a Wilderness Act was adopted by Congress in 1964 providing for the preservation of certain areas in a naturally wild state, thus placing these areas "off-limits" for the developmental interests.

Since 1964 there has been an ongoing struggle between the developmental interests who oppose the designation of more public lands as wilderness areas and the environmentalists who are constantly pushing to have more lands set aside. The latest confrontation between these elements has been over the vast public lands in Alaska, where in 1959 when the state joined the union, the federal government owned 99 percent of the land. The discovery of vast oil reserves and other valuable mineral resources have made Alaska's vast public domain of prime interest to developers. The environmentalists see Alaska as the one remaining area where a vast natural wilderness can be retained unexploited. They made an Alaska Lands Bill their top priority in the 95th Congress. The House passed an Alaska Lands Bill 277 to 31, but in the Senate last-minute maneuvering by Senator Mike Gravel (D-Alaska) to try to satisfy a host of special interests seeking to keep the lands open, blocked final action on the measure. To head-off an anticipated land rush into the area, Secretary of the Interior Cecil Andrus, acting under existing legislation, placed 100 million acres under limited protection; and President Carter, acting under the Antiquities Act of 1906, placed another 56 million acres under protection, a move prompting Senators Gravel and Ted Stevens (R-Alaska) to launch a move to rescind the 1906 legislation. The battle over Alaska lands was renewed in the 96th Congress when new legislation was introduced. The House Interior Committee reported a bill favored by developers, but on the floor a substitute bill was adopted 360 to 65. This measure, setting aside more than 100 million acres as wilderness, was a victory for a broad coalition of environmental groups. Senators Gravel and Stevens opposed the bill in the Senate. Stevens said the measure could deny access to "40 percent of all the oil and gas left in American soil." As a result of Stevens and Gravel's opposition the bill was not acted on in the Senate. Because of the delay Secretary of the Interior Cecil Andrus in February 1980 ordered 400 million acres in Alaska placed under long-term protection. Andrus's action allows development already underway to continue but precludes new claims and development of these lands.

In 1976 Congress adopted the Federal Land Policy and Management Act, which updated and consolidated about 3000 pieces of legislation dealing with the control, management, and use of public lands. Under these revisions the number of grazing permits has been reduced, additional areas are being considered for wilderness designation, and added emphasis has been given to uses for parks and recreation purposes. Developers and several western states have become alarmed with these trends. J. Allen Overton, Jr., president of the American Mining Congress, says, "It is a frightening fact that land areas equal in size to nearly all the states east of the Mississippi . . . have already been posted with federal signs that say, 'miners keep out.' "[1] The trend toward tighter controls has also alarmed the residents of several western states where federal holdings are substantial. In Nevada, where the federal government controls over 85 percent of the state's 71 million acres, the state legislature adopted a bill laying claim to 49 million acres now controlled by the federal government. In the latest states' rights movement, several western states have formed the Western Coalition on Public Lands and launched the "Sagebrush Rebellion," challenging federal lands control.

As the supplies of such resources as petroleum, natural gas, coal, and timber continue to be depleted, pressures from special economic interests seeking access to such resources on federal lands will also intensify. Already the environmental interests have been critical of President Carter over what they consider to be over-concern with economic considerations when viewing environmental questions. When Carter proposed to add 15.4 million acres to 15.3 million already designated as wilderness areas, the environmentalists were not pleased because they felt the action was too conservative. William A. Turnage, executive director of the Wilderness Society, said the president's action was "among the most negative decisions in the history of public land management."[2] A spokesman for the National Forest Products Association, on the other hand, expressed relief, stating, "We're relieved there was not a substantial move for more wilderness."[3] As scarcity, inflation, and other factors increase the pressures for new sources of raw materials, those pressing the causes of conservation and preservation will face even tougher battles.

## MANAGING WATER RESOURCES

Federal authority in the management of water resources was established with the Supreme Court's ruling in 1824 in *Gibbons* v *Ogden* that Congress should regulate interstate commerce on navigable streams.[4] That same year Congress passed the first rivers and harbors act, starting a long history of projects to improve the nation's waterways for shipping and commerce. In 1902 Congress adopted the Reclamation or Newlands Act, which provided assistance to those seeking to reclaim arid lands through irrigation, a program expanded through the Reclamation Project Act of 1939. Legislation creating the Tennessee Valley Authority in 1933 marked the beginning of the multi-purpose water project designed to improve navigation, flood control, irrigation, and water supplies, provide recreation, and generate hydroelectric power. The 1936 Flood Control Act assigned the federal government responsibility for flood control throughout the country. Thus, by the 1930s a pattern of extensive federal involvement in water resources management had been well-established.

As the government's role in water policy grew, so did the politics and competition surrounding such decisions. Today, water resources policy has come to be marked by intense bureaucratic rivalries, heated public versus private power disputes, myriad "pork barrel" projects, and White House–Congressional power struggles. Since most water projects involve construction, they are implemented by either the Army Corps of Engineers or the Bureau of Reclamation of the Department of Interior. Their mutual interest in the funding and construction of such projects has led to a strong political alliance among the congressional sponsors of various water projects and the federal agencies that design and build them. Thus, around the Capitol, it is said that old Corps of Engineer projects never die, they just remain under study. In 1936 Congress authorized construction of a dam on the Licking River in Kentucky to create Falmouth Lake. After forty-two years of study, the dam hasn't been built, but remains under study; and each year the "Battle of Falmouth" is a springtime ritual in the Public Works Committees as both sides repeat their arguments.

The creation of the TVA in 1933 touched off a long-running controversy between the public and private power interests. Since that time this dispute has surfaced on numerous occasions to complicate decisions on a variety of proposed projects. Proponents of the TVA–public power approach contended that such federal projects could provide power more economically and could serve as a yardstick for determining fair rates to be charged by private utilities. The private interests maintained the government should not be engaged in the production and sale of power in competition with private enterprise. The private interests did not object so much to the multi-purpose dams as to the preference clause in the TVA legislation, which gave public utilities first claim on the power produced and the construction of power lines by the government to transmit such power. The private companies contended this gave the public power companies an unfair advantage.

In more recent years, the public versus private dispute has been overshadowed by concerns with the environmental impact and economic value of proposed projects. Typifying these issues is the fifteen-year struggle surrounding the TVA's Tellico Dam project on the Little Tennessee River. Over the years as the Tennessee Valley Authority has grown steadily, building nuclear and steam power plants, taking more land, damaging more crops, and raising power rates, it has generated growing opposition. Its proposal for the Tellico Dam on the Little Tennesssee was opposed by farmers, sportsmen, environmentalists, the Cherokees, and some who questioned its economic feasibility. Nonetheless, plans proceeded and work on the project was begun.

In August 1973, a University of Tennessee professor discovered in the Little Tennessee River a rare, 3-inch fish that he named the *snail darter*. On December 28, 1973, Congress passed the Endangered Species Act, which bans projects that pose a threat to rare and endangered species of plants, animals, and other life forms. The 3-inch snail darter became a Trojan horse to the TVA and its Tellico

Dam and work on the project was halted. Supporters of the project then turned to the courts, challenging provisions of the Endangered Species Act, but on June 15, 1978, the U. S. Supreme Court ruled that the act required TVA abandonment of the Tellico project. Still refusing to drop the issue, proponents of the project including Senator Howard Baker (R-Tenn.) continued to seek ways to salvage the dam. In 1978 the Endangered Species Act was amended, providing for the creation of a special cabinet-level committee to review cases involving applications of the act and to allow exceptions if economic benefits outweighed other alternatives. The Tellico case was appealed to the special committee and the committee agreed with the Court and voted to kill the project, saying the cost of completing the dam was more than it was worth. Senator Baker then proposed legislation to abolish the special committee and allow completion of the dam. This failed, and at this point it appeared that after an investment of several million dollars, the project had become the victim of a 3-inch rare fish species. However, through legislative maneuvers in August and September 1978, Baker and other Tellico supporters succeeded in getting legislative approval for the completion of Tellico, and when President Carter declined to veto the legislation, fearing such action would jeopardize other pending legislation, TVA was ordered to complete work on the project.

In another ongoing dispute, economic factors are a major consideration though there are some environmental concerns as well. The Tennessee-Tombigbee Canal, a proposal for a 232-mile ditch to connect the Tennessee and Tombigbee Rivers, providing a shorter water route to the Gulf of Mexico for many southern shippers, was first authorized by Congress in 1946. (See figure 12.1) Soon after its

**FIGURE 12.1  Tennessee-Tombigbee Waterway**

*Reprinted courtesy of the Louisville, Ky. Courier-Journal.*

authorization, congressional staff studies rejected the project as an economic gamble and the project was shelved. Then President Nixon resurrected the proposal as a part of his "southern strategy," and funds to begin the project were provided in 1971. Though the Tenn-Tom, as it is called, is viewed by many as a threat to farms, forests, fisheries, and water quality (in the spring of 1979 many felt it contributed to a disastrous flood in the Tombigbee River Valley), the major concerns have been over its economics and the way the Army Corps of Engineers has handled the project. A 1975 GAO report charged that the corps had used "inaccurate" and "misleading" methods to calculate the cost-benefit ratio. Critics question that the Tenn-Tom can ever be a cost-effective operation. In 1977 Senator John Stennis (D-Miss.), one of the project's staunchest supporters, persuaded the GAO to withhold another report suggesting that the Army Corps of Engineers had misrepresented the costs and benefits of the waterway. The corps has also been accused of illegally enlarging the size of the canal, thereby increasing its cost, which is already 364 percent over the original budget. Senator Gaylord Nelson (D-Wis.), a leading critic, describes the project as "the biggest pork-barrel boondoggle of them all." At Nelson's urging, Senator Mike Gravel scheduled hearings on the Tennessee-Tombigbee project before his committee, then canceled them later, saying that Senator Stennis convinced him "a hearing was not necessary."

The first engineer to ever survey the Tennessee-Tombigbee idea reported in 1874, "I must confess that the merits of this enterprise are utterly beyond my comprehension.... No capitalist would accept it as a gift on condition that he should keep it in repair."[5] Despite persistent questions about its economic feasibility and its ever-increasing completion costs, Tenn-Tom seems to be an idea that won't be halted. The Louisville and Nashville Railroad and the Environmental Defense Fund, Inc. took a different route, filing a suit in federal court to block completion of the project. In April 1980 a U. S. Court of Appeals judge in New Orleans dismissed the suit; however the L&N and the EDF said they would appeal. In the meantime, President Carter, who had questioned numerous water projects, included a request of $165 million for construction on the Tenn-Tom in his proposed fiscal year 1980 budget.

For years water projects have been a major area of "pork barrel" legislation doled out by congressional committees among their colleagues. Traditionally all a project needed was the support of a few key senators and representatives from the state in which it would be built. Since assuming the presidency, Jimmy Carter engaged in a continuing battle with Congress in an effort to gain more executive control over water-project expenditures. Such water projects are a prime example of governmental policymaking by incrementalism. Traditionally Congress has paid for these projects on a piecemeal, year-by-year basis. Congress authorizes these projects, often starting with feasibility studies, and appropriates only a portion of the necessary funds for start-up costs, returning year after year to appropriate additional funds until projects are completed. Carter, in his effort to get a firmer grip on federal spending, wanted the full costs of projects included in the funding when construction is started. Many in Congress resist this full-funding approach because they fear this would take away Congress's power to control the pace of construction as they do under the present system. Furthermore, this would make the full costs of these pet projects much more obvious than is currently the case.

In an effort to gain more control over the spending on water projects, Carter created an Intergovernmental Task Force on Water Policy and asked the Water Resources Council to set new project standards and review construction decisions and administer grant programs. In 1979 he proposed, in addition to full-funding at the time construction begins, that the states share in the cost of projects and more funding for the Water Resources Council to carry out its review functions. When Carter's Water Resources Planning Act was reviewed by the House Public Works and Transportation Committee it was revised, neutralizing virtually every one of his proposals that would have strengthened executive control over water projects. While Carter was not highly successful in his efforts to gain more control, he focused attention on the need for more careful review of proposed projects, and some members of Congress are now introducing their own proposals to deauthorize certain projects and calling for hearings on questionable projects. As concern with inflation, spending, and budget deficits grows, a greater element of responsibility may be inserted into water-policy decisions than has characterized them in the past.

# THE MANAGEMENT AND REGULATION OF ENERGY RESOURCES

In an address to the nation on April 18, 1977, President Carter told his listeners, "With the exception of preventing war, this is the greatest challenge our country will face during our lifetimes. The energy crisis has not yet overwhelmed us, but it will if we do not act quickly...."[6] Thus, many Americans, if they had not already been made aware by tightening supplies and rising prices, were introduced to the "energy crisis." With its advanced technology, vast industrial capacity, and addiction to the automobile, America has become an energy hog. From 1945 to 1973, U.S. energy consumption increased at an annual rate of about 4.7 percent. In 1976 the rate was 5.3 percent, but since then has dropped below 4 percent to 2.5 percent for 1977 and 1.8 percent for 1978. While wood was the principal source of energy until 1850, the country now gets 90 percent of its energy from fossil fuels— petroleum, natural gas, and coal — sources which exist in finite supply. (See figures 12.2 and 12.3)

### Petroleum and Natural Gas

The steady growth in U.S. energy consumption coupled with a growing realization that available petroleum reserves are rapidly being depleted added to the concern about our energy future. In a 1978 study, the Petroleum Industry Research Foundation said an oil shortage before the late 1980s was unlikely and a shortage before the end of this century was a possibility but not a probability. On the other hand, a CIA report predicted a severe oil shortage that could occur as early as 1985, and the International Energy Agency predicted major shortages and higher prices by 1985. Many observers feel it is now clear that in the not-too-distant future, oil simply will not be available in sufficient quantities to meet our needs as demand continues to grow faster than production.

Already the United States imports petroleum to meet over 40 percent of its oil needs, a situation causing considerable concern to advocates of energy independence. (See figures 12.4 and 12.5) In an effort to reduce American dependence on foreign oil President Carter proposed to allow domestic prices of oil and natural gas to rise to world market levels. This move could have two beneficial effects—a reduction in demand and better conservation of available supplies. It would also mean substantially higher prices for consumers of petroleum and natural gas products and could contribute to the problem of inflation, adding to the squeeze on those with limited or fixed incomes.

Contributing to the increased dependence on foreign supplies also has been a decline in domestic production. Complicating efforts to find a means to stimulate domestic production has been strong disagreement over what approach will best accomplish this. The oil companies contend that a major factor discouraging more exploration and drilling has been governmental regulations. They argue that once the government deregulates the industry, companies will have more revenues to

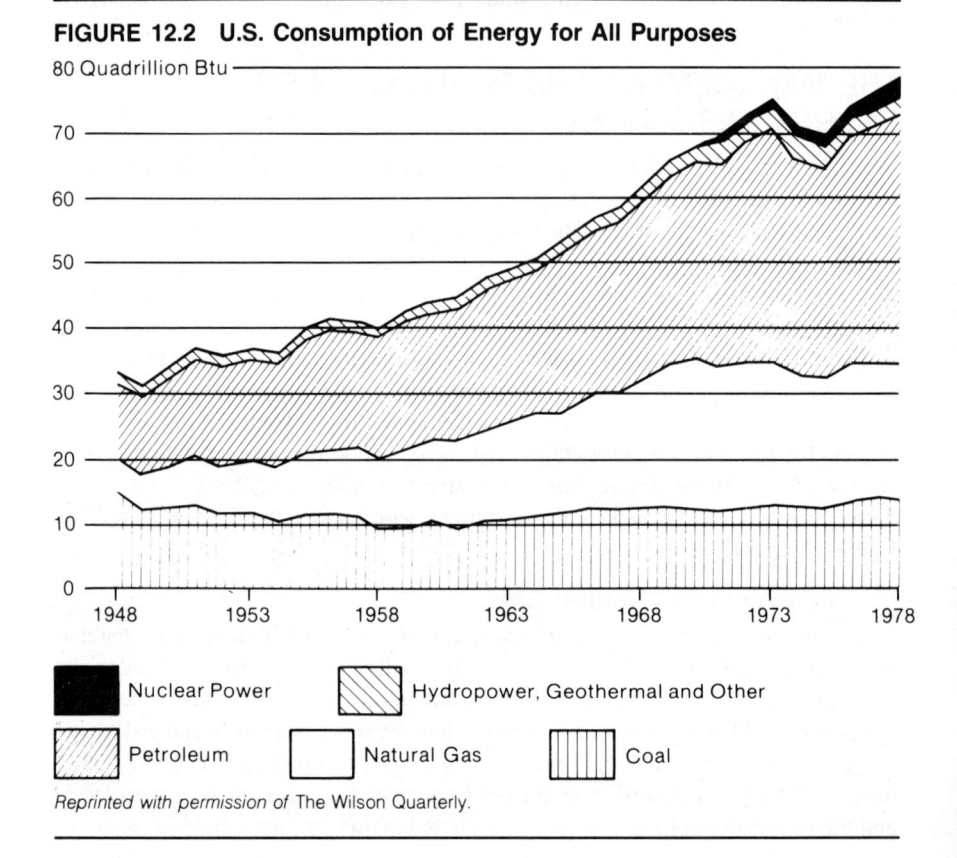

**FIGURE 12.2 U.S. Consumption of Energy for All Purposes**

*Reprinted with permission of* The Wilson Quarterly.

**FIGURE 12.3** Percentage of Types of Fuel Used by Power Plants

## Percentage of types of fuel used by power plants

| | COAL | NATURAL GAS | PETROLEUM | HYDRO | NUCLEAR | OTHER |
|---|---|---|---|---|---|---|
| 1973 | 43.6% | 18.9% | 17.3% | 15% | 4.6% | .02% |
| 1978 | 43.7% | 13.8% | 16.4% | 13% | 12.5% | .02% |

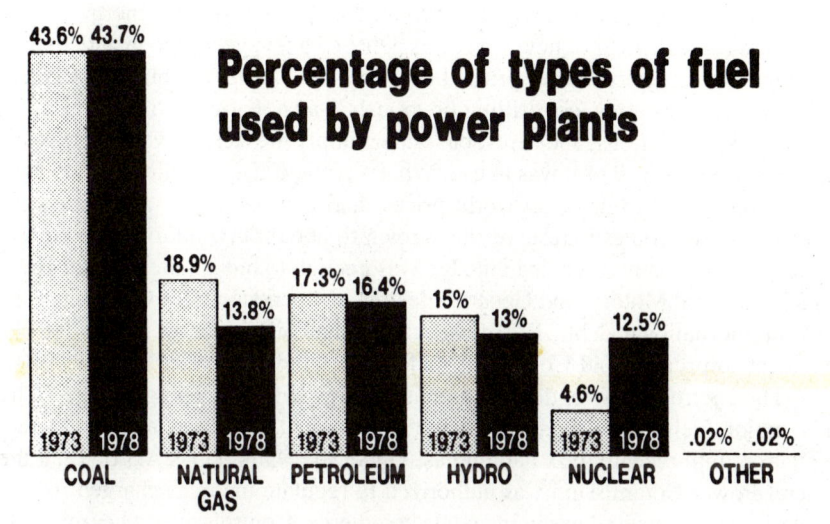

Because of rounding off, percentages do not add up to 100%.

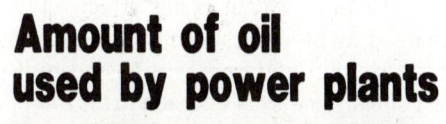

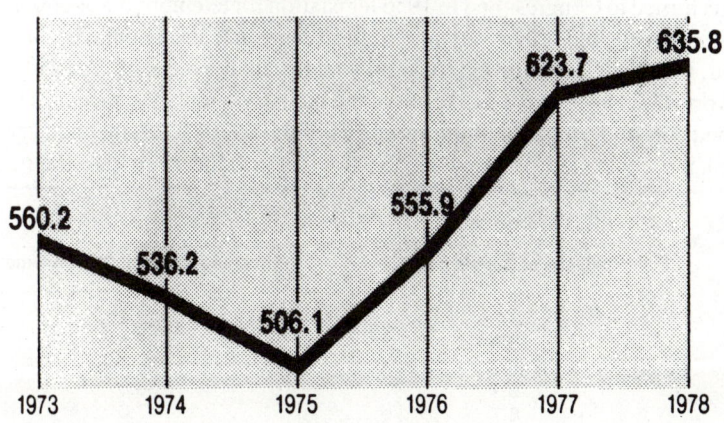

## Amount of oil used by power plants
### (in millions of barrels)

| Year | Barrels |
|---|---|
| 1973 | 560.2 |
| 1974 | 536.2 |
| 1975 | 506.1 |
| 1976 | 555.9 |
| 1977 | 623.7 |
| 1978 | 635.8 |

*Reprinted by permission of the Louisville, Ky. Courier-Journal.*

invest in exploration and drilling. Others feel this has not been the cause for lagging domestic production. Some observers feel that the major oil companies concentrated on foreign production, holding their domestic supplies in reserve until prices reached more favorable levels. James Flag of the Energy Action Committee says drilling of new wells was deferred a few years ago in anticipation of taking advantage of higher prices later. William Dudley, publisher of *World Oil*, says the reason for less drilling previously was not a result of federal rules, regulations, restrictions, and taxes, but rather simply the lack of available rigs and equipment because all of it was in use. Whatever the causes, declines in domestic production helped to drive up world prices, and because of these increases the value of known domestic reserves has grown to about $800 billion. The current value of oil company reserves in the U. S. is enough to buy all the stock of IBM, AT&T, General Motors, and General Electric, with enough left over to retire the bulk of the national debt. The prospect of huge oil company profits led the president to propose and Congress to adopt a "windfall profits" tax in 1980.

The controversy over deregulation is not new with the "energy crisis." The only major fuel source over which the government exercised any direct rate regulation until recently was natural gas. Under the Natural Gas Act of 1938 the Federal Power Commission was authorized to regulate the rates charged for the wholesale sale of natural gas in interstate commerce. Controls over other minerals were only indirect through production quotas, import controls, transportation rates, etc. The issue of FPC regulation of natural gas rates was the source of a protracted political struggle. Because the FPC could not regulate the rates charged by local distributors, the only way it could effectively control rates was by regulating prices charged by producers when selling to interstate pipeline companies. Legislation to exempt producers was passed by Congress in 1950 but vetoed by President Truman. In a 1954 decision in the *Phillips Petroleum* case the Supreme Court ruled that the FPC had the authority to regulate.[7] Again the gas interests turned to Congress and in 1956 legislation for exemption was adopted; but because of an alleged bribery attempt in the Senate and strong unfavorable public opinion, President Eisenhower felt compelled to veto the measure. A 1957 legislative effort was also defeated as a result of the industry's lobbying tactics. The issue remained sort of dormant until the shortages of the 1970s when the industry again claimed the controlled prices were too low for producers to risk their money

**FIGURE 12.4  U.S. Oil Imports**

|      | Millions of Barrels a Day | Percentage of Total Oil Consumption |
|------|---------------------------|-------------------------------------|
| 1969 | 3.2                       | 22.4%                               |
| 1971 | 3.9                       | 25.8                                |
| 1973 | 6.3                       | 36.1                                |
| 1975 | 6.1                       | 36.8                                |
| 1977 | 8.7                       | 47.0                                |
| 1978 | 6.4                       | 43.5                                |

Source: *Congressional Research Service,* Energy Information Digest, *p. 36;* Monthly Energy Review, *July 1978. Reprinted with permission from* The Wilson Quarterly.

searching for more gas. At first President Carter and a majority in the House felt that the amount of gas left to be found would not justify the higher prices resulting from deregulation. A deadlock developed over the issue of deregulation, holding up President Carter's energy package proposal for a year. A compromise was finally struck that provided for the lifting of oil controls in 1981 and gas controls in 1985.

While it is hoped deregulation will encourage increased domestic production and reduce dependence on foreign oil, there is also concern that the oil companies will reap huge profits. Congress debated at length and finally adopted modified versions of the president's tax proposal to limit such profits, as well as legislation to encourage the development and production of synthetic fuels to reduce our dependence on petroleum and natural gas as energy sources. However, there is no

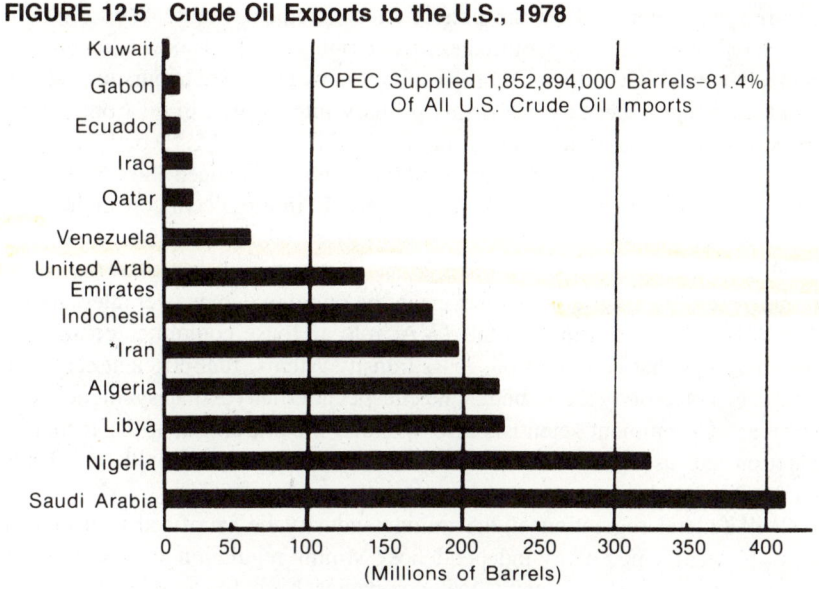

**FIGURE 12.5 Crude Oil Exports to the U.S., 1978**

OPEC Supplied 1,852,894,000 Barrels–81.4% Of All U.S. Crude Oil Imports

(Millions of Barrels)

*Iran Exports Curtailed After Shah's Overthrow

Source: U.S. Dept. of Energy & American Petroleum Institute

Reprinted with permission from the Louisville, Ky. Courier-Journal.

assurance the oil companies will use their increased profits for exploration and new production. For years the so-called "oil depletion allowance," a special tax deduction given petroleum companies, was supposed to have been used for exploration and development. Instead many companies used this allowance to move into other areas—Exxon owns extensive coal fields and uranium mines, as do other petroleum companies, and Texaco has patented a coal gasification technique. They, as well as the government, are moving to other energy alternatives, but will they really seek to develop such alternatives before their existing petroleum reserves are used up?

## Coal

Coal is the United States' most abundant source of fossil fuel, accounting for 87 percent of our total fossil-fuel reserve. Utilities are the nation's biggest consumers of energy, and coal is the major source of fuel for electric power plants. (See figure 12.1) In 1979, 713 million tons of coal were produced, with the electric utilities using 500 million tons. In a July 15, 1979 speech on energy, President Carter called for the use of more coal to help reduce the use of foreign oil. The administration's goal was to double consumption of coal by 1985. The Power Plant and Industrial Fuel Act of 1978 required electric power and industrial plants to burn coal rather than oil and natural gas. With the pressing need to become less dependent on foreign oil, both President Carter and Congress developed an increased interest in the development of synthetic fuels and a coal conversion process. Previous efforts at coal conversion lacked the current note of urgency and were vigorously opposed by the petroleum companies. Before World War II Standard Oil of New Jersey acquired exclusive rights to a coal conversion process developed by the I. G. Farben Company of Germany but failed to pursue development of the process because the firm's primary interest was in oil from natural sources. President Carter and Representative Carl Perkins (D-Ky.) both proposed the creation of a huge government corporation to be financed through federal bonds or loans to develop synthetic fuels primarily through coal conversion. All signs point to tremendous growth in coal production in the next decade, which will inevitably lead to more deaths and injuries in the mines, more damage from stripping, and more pollution. However, in the ongoing debate over alternatives, S. David Freeman, chairman of the TVA, told a House committee conducting energy hearings that conservation, mass transit systems, fuel-efficient cars, and greater use of electricity are all better and cheaper alternatives than synthetic fuels. A number of prominent scientists also sounded the warning that the increased production and use of synfuels could raise levels of carbon dioxide and bring possible climate changes.

Will federal regulation of the mining industry be sacrificed to a greater concern for achieving energy independence? Mining regulation has always been somewhat ineffective and many coal companies have found it economically advantageous to pay the small fines imposed for violations rather than take the necessary corrective action. Recent legislation has laid the groundwork, however, for more effective regulation, and the courts upheld the authority of the Office of Surface Mining Reclamation and Enforcement (OSMRE) to close mines for violations of regulations. Stronger regulations were adopted governing the environmental impact of mining operations with the passage, after a seven-year battle, of the Surface Mining Control and Reclamation Act of 1977. This legislation set standards governing strip mine operations and created the Office of Surface Mining to enforce the act. OSM has met numerous delays, however, having to wait from August 1977 to March 1978 before Congress finally got around to funding the agency. Still the agency encountered further delays. Under the law, coal states were to submit plans for the regulation of strip mines and OSM was to approve or reject them. Under the guidelines operators would restore land to the approximate original contour and were barred from pushing debris down hillsides. OSM was to approve state plans by June 3, 1980. In July the administration asked Congress for a delay until January 3, 1981 for full enforcement of the act. Subsequently, in a move pushed by a coalition of the coal industry, coal-state governors, and the coal-state representatives in Congress, the 1977 law was amended giving to the states rather than the federal government the primary responsibility for setting standards regulating strip mine operations. Environmental lobbyists, caught totally off-guard when Majority Leader Robert Byrd of coal-rich West Virginia scheduled the proposed changes for consideration with only one day's notice, fear the coal states will be much more lax in their regulation of mine operators. Changes in the 1977 act were pushed as a reduction in federal bureaucratic controls and a step toward energy security.

The mining industry had complained that federal regulations were too stringent and added unnecessarily to the cost of coal, thereby contributing to inflation. Testifying at a Coal Commission hearing in Charleston, West Virginia in October 1978, the president of Peabody Coal Company said:

> The surface mining act, black lung tax and federal mine health and safety amendments of 1977 have caused for Peabody, a 21 percent increase in our costs of 1978 over 1977.
>
> The industry is in urgent need of a period of quiet adjustment. We need time to develop new methods, new technologies, and systems for complying with the multitude of requirements which have been imposed upon us in just the last year or two.[8]

Such appeals were not totally ignored by an administration greatly concerned about inflation and rising costs. Many environmental groups expressed concern that President Carter's economic advisers were exerting undue and possibly illegal influence on regulatory agencies. The Natural Resources Defense Council, Inc., the National Wildlife Federation, and the Council of the Southern Mountains Inc. filed suit in federal court to prevent the Council of Economic Advisers from influencing OSM on federal strip mine regulations. They feared environmental considerations were being sacrificed to economic considerations.

## Nuclear Energy

The most regulated of all the energy sources is nuclear energy. The dropping of atomic bombs on Japan to end World War II brought rampant speculation about the potential uses of this powerful new energy source. Many predicted that in a matter of decades nuclear energy would provide power to light our cities, cook our food, even heat our sidewalks to melt the winter snow and ice. It was felt, however, that because of its implications for national security, atomic energy must be developed under strict governmental controls. In 1946, after considerable debate, the Atomic Energy (McMahon) Act was adopted, establishing a civilian agency, the Atomic Energy Commission, and giving it control over all sources of atomic fuels. Five years later the first electric power was generated using atomic energy in a government experiment at an installation in Idaho. Private power advocates became concerned that atomic energy might be developed as a governmental monopoly and set out to get legislation preventing this. In 1954 the Atomic Energy Act Amendments were adopted forbidding the federal government from engaging in the commercial production of electricity using nuclear energy and providing for the licensing of private commercial nuclear power plants. Still, private nuclear development lagged because other sources of power were cheaper and the initial investment and risks involved in nuclear power plants were high.

In an effort to encourage private commercial development and reduce the risk factor, Congress in 1957 adopted the Price-Anderson Act, which provided federally financed insurance for commercial nuclear plants. That year also was the first year for the sale of commercially produced nuclear power. During the 1960s the nuclear power industry grew slowly and its promoters became one of the country's most aggressive special interest groups, with the American Nuclear Energy Council and the Atomic Industrial Forum, Inc. heading their efforts. By 1979, seventy-two nuclear plants were operational across the country, providing about 12.5 percent of the nation's electric energy. Ninety-four additional plants were under construction and thirty-four more were in the planning stage. President Carter, Energy Secretary James Schlesinger, and many members of Congress viewed nuclear energy as a source with great potential for helping the country reduce its dependence on oil.

Then at the very time when nuclear energy seemed to be on the threshold of a period of rapid development, a series of events placed it under a cloud of fear and suspicion. The nuclear industry had been the target of environmental groups for some time, and a variety of events in the 1970s provided these groups substantial grist for their mills. The Union of Concerned Scientists, an antinuclear group, requested the Nuclear Regulatory Commission's (successor to the Atomic Energy Commission) files on nuclear plant accidents under the Freedom of Information Act and released details of a variety of mishaps in various nuclear plants. In January 1975 the NRC ordered twenty-three plants closed down for a check of their systems for cracked pipes that might leak radioactive water. Criticism of the industry continued to mount as more safety issues were raised, and in 1979 the roof fell on nuclear power.

In January 1979 the Nuclear Regulatory Commission disavowed its own three-year-old Reactor Safety Study or "Rasmussen Report," which had come under heavy criticism. The Rasmussen Report, a 2400-page, 11-volume study carried out by an industrial-academic-governmental team under the direction of Professor Norman C. Rasmussen, a professor of nuclear engineering at MIT, was commissioned by the AEC. From the time of its release in 1975, the report was highly controversial, being attacked by its critics as a "whitewash job." In spite of widespread criticism, the report, which said death from a nuclear reactor accident was about as likely as being struck by a meteor, was relied on by the NRC and the nuclear industry for a variety of policy decisions. Finally, under the prodding of critics and Representative Morris Udall (D-Ariz.), the NRC requested an independent panel of scientists to review the Rasmussen Report. A team headed by Dr. Harold W. Lewis, physics professor at the University of California at Santa

Barbara, evaluated the report and said they found it to be misleading and technically flawed. Dr. Lewis's team concluded the Rasmussen group "was driven to make numerical assessments for the sake of public policy." Faced with these findings, the NRC dropped the controversial report as a guide for policy decisions.

The Rasmussen Report projected the likelihood of a severe reactor breakdown as once in 20,000 reactor-years—such an incident happened in the first 500 reactor years and less than three months after the NRC disavowal of the Rasmussen Report. The movie "The China Syndrome," centered around a nuclear power plant disaster, had just been released and was playing across the country when the nuclear power plant on Three Mile Island in the Susquehanna River in Pennsylvania suffered a malfunction resulting in the release of radioactive steam and gases. What followed was a series of incidents very similar to the situation portrayed by the newly released film, a situation that left many grave concerns regarding the nuclear industry and its overseer, the Nuclear Regulatory Commission.

Nuclear energy, once regarded as the prime energy source of the future, was under a rising storm cloud. The Three Mile Island accident touched off an intensive review of the entire nuclear industry—its technology, its safety standards, its quality of performance, its public relations, its ability to deal with emergencies, and its future. No fewer than nine congressional inquiries were ordered and President Carter appointed an eleven-member commission to investigate the accident. While both Congress and the NRC have resisted pressures to close down all nuclear plants, the NRC in May 1979 announced a three-month moratorium on nuclear power plant construction permits and operating licenses, delaying as many as fifteen projects. In June 1979 the House voted overwhelmingly for a measure requiring federal safety inspectors at all nuclear power plants, and in July the Senate voted to shut down all nuclear plants for which the states had no emergency evacuation plans. This action could have affected as many as thirty-nine of seventy licensed plants unless the states submitted satisfactory evacuation plans to the NRC.

Daniel Yergin of the Harvard Business School said of Three Mile Island "This nuclear accident pretty much marks the closing down of a significant future nuclear energy option. America's energy choices are narrowing rapidly."[9] While the near disaster at Three Mile Island became a focusing point for all the forces building against nuclear energy, the industry was in deep trouble long before that accident. The utility companies, wary of rising costs, high risks, and regulatory problems, were already cancelling more nuclear plant orders than they were completing. In 1978, twelve orders were cancelled and only two were completed. Even with uranium production doubling since 1973, the price increased 500 percent in five years. Not only are there risks of malfunctions and melt-downs, but other liabilities as well. In May 1979, a federal district court awarded a $10.5 million judgment against the Kerr-McGee Corporation to the estate of Karen Silkwood, an employee allegedly contaminated by radioactive material from her employer's operation. Should this judgment stand, it would make nuclear facilities responsible for any radiation releases despite their compliance with federal regula-

312   REGULATORY POLICY

"Sure, that contraption scares hell outa me, but it's hooked up to my pacemaker!"

*Reprinted courtesy of Hugh Haynie and the Louisville, Ky. Courier-Journal.*

tions. Another drawback to rapid growth is the delay involved in getting a facility operational. The time between the decision to build a nuclear power plant and its actual operation is about ten to twelve years currently.

Even before the nuclear debate heated up with the series of incidents in 1979, President Carter appeared to be moving toward other options. His proposed budget for fiscal year 1980 reflected a rather obvious shift in priorities on energy policy. Nuclear energy was downplayed while solar energy was given more emphasis. Funds in the budget for nuclear energy were cut 12 percent while the solar budget was increased by 25 percent to $819 million, double what was proposed one year earlier. Whether Carter's renewed efforts to reduce the nation's dependence on foreign oil would bring a new shift in priorities and would help to revive the sagging nuclear power industry remained to be seen. Such a move would be certain to encounter strong opposition from those who feel there are safer alternatives.

### Other Energy Sources

Currently America produces about 75 percent of its energy from fossil fuels, another 12.5 percent comes from nuclear fuels. This leaves only 12.8 percent from other sources. Of this remainder, 12.6 percent comes from hydroelectric power and 0.2 percent from other sources, primarily geothermal. Most of the prime possibilities for hydroelectric power have been developed, or would encounter formidable issues of environmental and ecological impact should they be proposed for such areas as the Grand Canyon. About 40 percent of the nation's potential geothermal energy lies under federal lands and proposals to tap geothermal sources in Idaho have already raised questions as to their potential impact on Yellowstone Park and Old Faithful. Solar energy is coming more and more to be viewed as possibly our best potential energy source. Solar energy is clean and in almost inexhaustible supply and the sun is owned by no one, factors which would seem to remove many of the areas for dispute surrounding other energy sources. On May 3, 1979, "Sun Day" was held to raise public consciousness of the possibilities of solar energy. About sixty members of Congress have formed a "solar coalition." More and more people are beginning to share with David Roe, attorney for the Environmental Defense Fund, a feeling that, "We don't have to limit our choices to three forms of white elephants (oil, coal, and nuclear power plants)." What remains, however, is the tough task of coming up with a national energy policy that puts all the pieces together in a workable program.

### Developing a National Energy Policy

For years a number of people looking down the road ahead had predicted that unless it changed its fuel habits, America faced an energy crisis. In the winter of 1972-73 the seriousness of the situation was brought home to many Americans when fuel shortages left many homes without heat, schools and factories were shut down, and thousands of workers were laid off their jobs. In November 1973, President Nixon announced his "Project Independence" to free the U. S. from dependence on foreign oil and develop adequate domestic fuel sources. The succeeding Ford and Carter administrations proclaimed essentially the same goals; yet U. S. imports of oil continued to rise throughout the 1970s until by 1979, 40 percent of the oil consumed was imported. From 1973-77 U. S. imports of oil from the OPEC countries rose by 70 percent and in 1979 imported oil cost over ten times per barrel what it did in 1973. Eighty-one major studies of the energy situation and the adoption of four major bills and several lesser ones have failed to produce a long-awaited comprehensive national energy policy.

Carter entered the presidency determined to resolve the energy situation as quickly as possible, but he and his aides failed to fully understand and appreciate the complexities of the issue. Initially the president insisted that his energy program be ready for Congress three months after inauguration day. In its haste to get something to Congress quickly, the administration overlooked several difficult questions such as price controls versus deregulation, environmental implications, and alternative energy sources. As a result, the administration's waffling on issues and on-and-off pushing of various alternatives produced more confusion than action.

Finally in 1979, when U. S. imports of foreign oil exceeded 40 percent and Americans were sitting in lines for hours at the gasoline pumps, President Carter called a domestic summit at Camp David, Maryland, to seek advice on the energy situation. After ten days he appeared on national television to announce his plans for reducing American imports of foreign oil and increasing efforts to develop alternative sources of energy. Carter's plan called for the investment of $140 billion over the next ten years on the development of alternative energy sources, the improvement of mass transportation systems, stepped-up research on fuel-efficient automobiles, and the development of solar power. To carry out these programs, the president proposed the creation of an Energy Security Corporation to develop synthetic fuels with the objective of replacing 2.5 million barrels of oil a day by 1990, and a three-member Energy Mobilization Board to oversee major energy projects and to cut through federal red tape in carrying forward such projects. At the same time the president announced the removal of price controls on heavy crude oil and said utilities would be required to use more coal and less oil. Most of the president's energy proposals were to be paid for out of a "windfall profits" tax to be levied on the petroleum companies.

The president's new energy initiative encountered many of the same obstacles that have thus far prevented the development of an effective response to our energy woes. In many respects the debate over national energy policy involves some of the most basic divisions in our society—producers versus consumers, Republicans versus Democrats, White House versus Congress, regulators versus free marketers, national interest versus local and regional interests, the environmentalists versus the developers. Energy has become the testing ground for basic conflicts over much broader social and political issues. It involves disagreement over the kind of future people want, and the allocation of costs, benefits, and risks incurred in the acquisition and distribution of energy. Yale business professor Daniel Yergin says, "To frame an energy policy is to allocate large benefits and large costs and to distribute or redistribute income."[10] As a result, federal energy policy has been held hostage to a host of competing and unyielding special interests.

Contributing further to the standoff on energy policy have been the decentralization and parochialism of Congress. Congress's structure makes the handling of energy proposals both confusing and difficult. In the House, eighty-three committees and subcommittees have some jurisdiction over energy matters. The synfuels bill passed by the House in June 1979 came from the Banking, Finance and Urban Affairs Committee, not one of those with major energy responsibilities. In the Senate, which has a standing committee on Energy and Natural Resources, no fewer than six different committees considered President Carter's energy proposals. With so many committees getting into the act, proposals are laid open to cross-pressures from an extremely broad range of regional and special interests. The local constituency orientation of members of Congress has been most apparent in the energy debate as national interest has taken a backseat to regional interests. Representatives from the oil-dependent Northeast have fought to keep domestic oil prices low, while representatives from oil-producing states have pushed for removing present limits on oil prices and profits. Speaker of the House Tip O'Neill

(D-Mass.), after trying to get some action on energy legislation, lamented, "It is extremely difficult to write an energy bill. This, perhaps, has been the most parochial issue that could ever hit the floor."[11] To overcome such parochial and special interest pressures, strong leadership and insistence on compromise are essential; thus far on energy policy this has been lacking. The 96th Congress finally enacted watered-down versions of Carter's proposed windfall profits tax and synthetic fuels corporation, but his proposed Energy Mobilization Board was sidetracked, so he still ended up with only part of his energy package.

## REGULATING THE ENVIRONMENT

A hallmark of this century has been that our technological and industrial development have always seemed to outstrip our knowledge of the full human consequences of such progress. Our economic progress has frequently been marked by a failure to predict or anticipate the environmental and health-related consequences. Only in the last two decades has widespread concern developed over such manmade health problems as "black lung," asbestosis, and radiation and chemical poisoning. The automobile was identified as a source of pollution by Dr. Arie J. Haagen-Smit of Cal Tech nearly thirty years ago, yet strict standards on auto emissions are still an issue of policy debate. Each year over 300,000 Americans die of cancer and at current trends eventually one of every four Americans will develop cancer. Scientists now estimate that as much as 60 to 90 percent of cancer is related to environmental factors, and a National Cancer Institute study suggests that at least 20 percent of the nation's cancer can be traced to industrial poisons of one kind or another. Over the years our air, water, food, schools, and workplaces have been contaminated, and only in recent years has much attention been directed toward stopping pollution and reversing this trend.

The 1960s and '70s saw the emergence of a strong environmental movement, and a growing concern with protecting the environment led to the emergence of a new term, *ecology*. Such writers and environmentalists as Rachel Carson, Barry Commoner, and Jacques Cousteau began to attract public attention, and the older environmentalist groups were joined on the scene by a host of newcomers as the environmental lobby became a potent political force. In 1969 Congress responded to environmentalist pressure by passing the National Environmental Policy Act, creating a federal Environmental Protection Agency and requiring federal agencies to prepare "environmental impact" statements on how their actions would affect the environment. On April 22, 1970, Earth Day was held nationwide to focus attention on pollution problems, and millions of Americans attended environmental teach-ins, antipollution protests, and clean-up projects. This massive demonstration stimulated interest and provided the impetus for more stringent governmental efforts to control pollution. In 1970 Congress adopted the Clear Air Act, establishing deadlines for reductions in auto emissions and other pollutants. In his January 1971 State of the Union Address President Nixon endorsed the environmental effort, pledging to continue efforts, "to restore and

**The Thinker**
*Reprinted courtesy of Ray Osrin and the* Cleveland Plain Dealer.

enhance our natural environment.'' Congress has responded with a variety of acts aimed at cleaning up and protecting the environment. Among these are the Federal Water Pollution Control Act of 1972 and the Safe Drinking Water Act of 1974, which set the goal of clean water by 1985; the Endangered Species Act of 1973, which aims at protecting rare plant and animal life forms; the Toxic Substances Control Act of 1976, aimed at regulating the sale and use of hazardous chemical substances; the Federal Land Policy and Management Act of 1976; and the Clean Air Act Amendments of 1977. Other legislation has made petroleum companies responsible for oil spill clean-up costs, banned hunting from aircraft, and expanded wildlife conservation, reforestation, and lands reserved as national wilderness areas.

The agency with primary responsibility for enforcing environmental regulations is the Environmental Protection Agency (EPA). Among the largest of the federal regulatory agencies, EPA has a staff of approximately 9000 employees and spends about $2 million per day in its efforts to protect the environment. Just how effective the EPA is in its efforts is subject to debate. In September 1976 the

Council on Environmental Quality reported that "significant progress" was being made and the country would have relatively clean air and water by the 1980s. Just what this means is a bit more difficult to say. In 1969 the Cuyahoga River in Cleveland, Ohio caught fire; today the river is no longer a fire hazard and even has a few fish, but it is far from being pure. The General Accounting Office (GAO) has been less favorable in its assessments of the EPA's efforts. In 1975 the GAO reported that both the EPA and the FDA (Food and Drug Administration) were making inadequate efforts to protect the public. It charged that after years of warnings, the public still was poorly protected against the hazards of pesticides and their residues. In 1978 the EPA claimed that in the area of air pollution it had achieved 92 percent compliance with its regulations. However, the GAO reported that the EPA did a poor job of monitoring compliance and enforcing its standards, and claimed that as high as 70 percent of the sources of pollution failed to meet compliance standards. Not only is the EPA criticized on its enforcement, many critics feel the standards set frequently are unrealistic. Massachusetts Governor Michael Dukakis accused the EPA of "sewering cornfields." James H. Elliott of PPG Industries said, "If a trout dying of old age staggered up onto the shore, and if we were dumping water in that stream, it would automatically be PPG's fault."[12]

Following such episodes as Kepone in the James River; PCBs in livestock feed, milk, eggs, turkeys, and several streams and lakes; asbestos in the schools; the Love Canal in New York; and the "Valley of the Drums" in Kentucky, the latest focus of the environmentalists is on toxic substances and hazardous wastes.[13] To a certain extent this problem is a spinoff of the efforts to reduce air and water pollution which have in turn produced more residues for land disposal. Currently the United States generates 57 million metric tons of hazardous wastes per year. The chemical industry, which experienced tremendous growth following World War II, produces over 30,000 agents commercially, many of them hazardous. The problem with hazardous substances is twofold—how to safeguard the environment and the populace from the introduction of new and additional hazardous elements, and how to clean up the problems that already exist from hazardous wastes and residues.

In response to the first part of the problem, Congress adopted in 1976 the Toxic Substances Control Act, aimed at requiring industry to prove that its chemicals are safe before marketing them commercially. If the EPA believes a substance is hazardous, it may ban its use. Such decisions can be challenged in the courts, but the burden of proof is on the producer. The act also requires companies to report to the EPA any occurrences that could pose a substantial risk to public health, something they may not be eager to do. Officials of the Hooker Chemical Company apparently knew of the potential dangers of the Love Canal dump in Niagara Falls, New York twenty years before disaster struck, but chose to say nothing. Critics of the EPA feel the agency is sometimes too concerned with the economic impact of its decisions. PCBs were finally banned, for example, but only after a five-year delay to avoid severe economic impact on companies with large supplies on hand. Like much of the recent regulatory legislation, the Toxic

Substances Control Act (TOSCA) is caught up in controversy between environmentalists and industry; and the EPA finds it impossible to please both. Currently the EPA, the chemical industry, and the environmental groups are bogged down in a dispute over testing standards, with the result of few chemicals even being tested much less banned. Until this issue is resolved, chemical pollution will continue.

Widespread problems with waste dump sites in New York, Kentucky, Tennessee, Louisiana, Massachusetts, North Carolina, and New Jersey, among others, have caused growing concern over hazardous waste disposal. In 1979 consultant Fred C. Hart and Associates in a report to EPA estimated 32,000 to 51,000 dump sites containing hazardous materials. They estimated those posing serious problems at from 1200 to 34,000. Clean-up costs were projected at $44.2 billion, of which maybe one-half would be borne privately. The EPA, leaning toward the more conservative figures, estimates there are at least 1200 abandoned waste sites that pose health hazards and puts the clean-up cost at about $30 billion. The General Accounting Office reported in 1979 that the states generally did a poor job of regulating waste disposal, thus making the EPA's role more significant. In 1979 President Carter asked for the creation of a $1.6 billion "super fund" to be used for environmental clean-ups. The fund would be built over a four-year period, with about 80 percent coming from fees imposed on petroleum and chemical companies. Long range, however, the solution to the problems of toxic pollutants and hazardous wastes becomes much more complex than the establishment of a fund to clean up past mistakes. It would appear that if the environment and the public's health are to be protected, more effective regulation will be necessary. Having heard residents of Niagara Falls testify on the Love Canal debacle, Senator John H. Chaffee (R-R.I.) observed, "Here is a situation where we have allowed the free market to work. We have allowed people to dump where they please, and look what we have got."[14] The debate over stricter controls on toxic wastes disposal is heating up as environmental groups such as Environmental Action, the Sierra Club, the National Wildlife Federation, the League of Women Voters, and other citizen groups are pressing for requirements of more responsibility on the part of producers of toxic wastes. Tort liability has become a big issue with the chemical companies opposing strict liability legislation that would allow civil suits by those suffering damages from improper waste disposal. William M. Stover of the Chemical Manufacturers Association, principal spokesman for the industry, says, "We will not stand by and watch the lynching of the chemical industry." Thus the battle lines are forming on the issue of who will foot the bill for toxic wastes clean-up.

In the late 1970s the quest for a clean and healthful environment ran head-on into concerns with inflation and energy shortages. The environmentalists as a consequence frequently found themselves on the defensive rather than pressing the attack. While expenditures on pollution control efforts do not increase production, they do affect prices and profits by increasing the cost of production. As is frequently the case in public policy decisions, environmental policy decisions boil down to a trade-off between the amount of protection required and the economic impact on business, industry, and the consumer. In a 1975 address, President Ford put the choices this way: "I pursue the goal of clean air and pure water, but I must also pursue the objective of maximum jobs and continued economic progress. Unemployment is as real and sickening a blight as any pollutant that threatens the nation."[15]

The cost of complying with federal environmental regulations has become substantial. The Council on Environmental Quality estimated that for 1977 the U. S. spent $40.6 billion on pollution control, or about $187 per citizen. CEQ indicated that $18.1 billion of this was a result of environmental legislation. Thirty-eight percent was for water pollution control, 32 percent for air pollution control, and 23 percent for solid waste control. Of the total costs, 50 percent was paid by industry, 30 percent by government, and 20 percent by consumers. In an April 1977 report, General Motors listed regulatory related costs for 1974-75 at $2.2 billion; Dow Chemical in a February 1978 report indicated compliance costs of $268 million, an 82 percent increase over 1975; Caterpillar reported compliance costs for 1977 of $67.6 million; and R. J. Reynolds reported 1977 costs of $28.9 million. Pollution regulations add substantially to costs in other ways also.[16] Louisville Gas and Electric, a Kentucky utility company, projected capital construction costs of $259 million during 1979-80; of this amount $95 million would go for pollution control.

As prices continued to climb and inflation worsen, some members of Carter's administration began to feel that federal regulations might be causing more economic harm than environmental good. As the president sought means to curb inflation, pressures mounted to relax various environmental regulations. The president created the Regulatory Analysis Review Group to evaluate federal agency regulations and to try to insure that regulations were written to avoid unnecessary inflationary costs. When the EPA proposed in December 1978 a comprehensive "cradle to grave" regulatory scheme taking up eighty-three pages in the *Federal Register* and with an annual price tag of $800 million, the Regulatory Analysis Review Group immediately raised questions. Carter's chief economic advisors were also involved in raising questions about the cost of regulations on cotton dust control in the textile industry and strip mining of coal. Various environmental groups have become quite disturbed with this cost-analysis approach to environmental regulations and some turned to the courts to try to block what they viewed as illegal interference in the regulatory process by Carter's economic advisors. They charged that regulatory reviews by the U. S. Regulatory Council and the Regulatory Analysis Review Group had been used to "veto" environmental regulations. The environmentalists and their supporters charge that business and industry are using the economic argument as leverage to get a relaxation in governmental regulations. They also point out that there are tremendous costs attached to pollution in terms of lives lost, medical bills, lost worktime and environmental losses. Former Senator Ed Muskie (D-Maine), while chairman of the Environmental Pollution Subcommittee of the Senate Environment and Public Works Committee, said, "Pollution itself, however, has costs that can only be measured in lost jobs, lost health, lost recreation and fewer options for the future. How do we measure these in dollars and cents on an economist's graph?"[17]

In spite of such efforts by the environmentalists, the pendulum seems to be swinging against them currently. After some earlier successes, environmental interests have failed in their efforts to block the Grayrocks project in Wyoming, which was approved after measures were undertaken to protect the whooping crane, an endangered species. Even the Endangered Species Act, which breezed through Congress almost unopposed in 1973, came under fire and was amended in 1978 to allow a special cabinet-level committee to grant exceptions to the act and allow projects if they are determined to be in the national interest. Environmentalists vigorously oppose efforts to weaken the act further, but its supporters in Congress feel they may have to compromise to salvage any protective law at all. In spite of vigorous opposition by environmentalists and fishermen, the Interior Department, reflecting the nation's concern with energy, in 1979 gave approval for oil and gas exploration in the Georges Bank fishing grounds.

The developing energy crisis of the 1970s became another factor in the declining support for stricter environmental regulation, as the nation's heightened environmental consciousness began to run counter to its need for cheaper and more abundant sources of energy. The Arab oil embargo, for example, caused the public to be more receptive to less rigorous enforcement of the Clean Air Act provisions. Environmentalists were inclined to view President Carter's July 1979 energy proposals with a mixture of dread and anger. Tom Galloway, an attorney with the Center for Law and Social Policy, said, "Depending on how it's set up, this board [Carter's proposed Energy Mobilization Board] could gut the major environmental laws of the 1970s." Several environmentalists termed the president's synfuels plan "a tragic error." They saw the proposal as a step in the direction of waiving environmental requirements to clear the way for needed energy projects.

The president's call for the use of more coal caused the already lengthy debate over sulfur dioxide emission standards to become even more significant. Since the utility companies are the principal users of coal, they have been a prime target of EPA regulations under the Clean Air Act and its amendments. The debate has centered on what level of "scrubbing" or reduction in emissions should be required. If vigorous sulfur removal is required, it results in high-cost regulation that provides the greatest health protection in areas with the least population.[18] This debate also has other economic overtones. Eastern mining interests favor lower emission standards because much of their coal is high sulfur content. The western mining interests, which produce coal with lower sulfur content, favor a system of flexible standards that would set different levels for different types of coal, while the environmental interests are more in favor of a uniform requirement setting maximum pollution controls for all grades of coal.

Since federal emission standards were adopted, the record on air pollution has been mixed. The Council on Environmental Quality reported that a study by Data Resources, Inc. for the period 1973-1976 showed improvements in air quality. A survey of sixteen major cities showed a decline of 8 percent in the number of "unhealthful days" during this period. On the other hand, sulfur pollutants have actually increased in some areas rather than declined. The EPA reports that in Lexington, Kentucky, for example, visibility has declined sharply because of pollutants in the atmosphere. The city is enveloped in a yellow haze caused by microscopic sulfate and nitrate pollutants suspended in the atmosphere. The build-up of such a situation is so gradual as to be almost unnoticeable, but over a period of time can bring substantial changes that may affect the climate, growing seasons, and people's health.

Another effect of sulfate pollution has been the increased incidence of "acid rain." Scientists note that in some parts of the country rainfall has now become 40 times more acidic than normal, as acidic as tomato juice or vinegar. Such high levels of acid in rainfall retards crop and forest growth, kills fish, causes corrosion damage, increases the need for lime in the soil, and poses health problems. More than 300 lakes in the Adirondack Mountains of the Northeast have already become too acidic to support fish life. Michael Berry of the EPA says that acid rain is a subtle, slow-moving monster that has sneaked up on us. Like hypertension, he notes, you don't realize how serious it is until the damage has already been done. This incidence of acid rain has become much more widespread since the mid-1950s. Some feel a contributing factor has been current antipollution policies, which they think have transformed local soot problems into a regional acid-rain problem. The basis for this charge is the tall smokestacks built by coal users to disperse the pollutants into the upper atmosphere where they blow away to fall elsewhere as acid rain. Much of the pollution suffered in many areas is not created locally but is blown in. This is a problem the EPA has not come to grips with and one that could increase with increased dependence on coal as a fuel source. Many governmental officials thus far fail to appreciate the seriousness of this problem and because not too many states have suffered yet, Congress has not become too interested.

Much more interest was expressed when the EPA issued new emission standards in 1979. Environmental interests had pushed for higher standards on emission controls while industry had pushed for lower limits. The National Coal Association did a study on tighter limits on sulfur emissions and said raising the scrubber requirement to 85 percent efficiency would exclude from use 99.9 percent of Ohio's coal, 84.8 percent of northern West Virginia's, and all of western Kentucky's. As finally adopted, the new regulations require a minimum of 70 percent scrubber efficiency on all coals and 90 percent removal for those plants burning low surfur coals. EPA head Douglas Costle said the new rules would eliminate more pollution at less cost. In the end neither the utilities nor the environmentalists were pleased with the new regulations.

President Carter has called for more wilderness and less dependence on foreign oil. What many environmentalists fear is that when push comes to shove, energy will take precedence and many environmental regulations will be sacrificed. Some of the nation's richest reserves of coal, oil, and natural gas lie beneath the Overthrust Belt of Utah, Wyoming, Idaho, and Montana — national forest lands slated to be preserved as wilderness areas. According to the U. S. Geological Survey, 40 percent of the U. S.'s undiscovered oil, 47 percent of its undiscovered natural gas, and 40 percent of its known coal reserves are under federal lands. When the chips are down, does our interest in preserving our environment or our hunger for energy take priority? The tough but apparently inevitable choice is expressed by Charles Peters and Glen Allerhand in these words:

> In the long term, ... the world does face exhaustion of its fossil fuels—which is good enough reason for energy research and conservation but not good enough reason for wrecking the economy and the environment in a headlong rush for energy independence.[19]

The American public wants a clean environment, but it also wants cheap fuel and more automobiles. The policymaker's task is to find a solution to these contradictory goals.

## CONCLUSION

Governmental involvement in resources and environmental policy on a significant scale is a fairly recent development, but one with substantial implications for our society's future lifestyle and possibly even its survival. Since policy in this area frequently involves decisions with substantial economic impact, policymaking in this field has become highly political and charged with often intense controversy among a variety of competing interests. In the 1960s and 1970s a whole host of environmental action groups began pushing environmental issues (see figure 12.6) and with widespread media coverage developed broad acceptance and support among the general public. One of these groups, Environmental Action, developed a "hit list" of congressmen who had poor voting records on environmental issues and regularly campaigned against their "Dirty Dozen." In 1970, 1972, and 1974, thirty-one incumbents were included among the "Dirty Dozen" list and twenty-four of these are no longer in Congress. With this kind of political clout, the

**FIGURE 12.6  Environmental Interest Groups**

| | |
|---|---|
| National Audubon Society | Wilderness Society |
| National Wildlife Federation | Izaak Walton League |
| Coalition for Water Project Review | National Clean Air Coalition |
| Council of the Southern Mountains, Inc. | Wildlife Management Institute |
| Citizens for Clean Air | Citizens Committee on Natural Resources |
| Environmental Action | American Nature Association |
| Environmental Policy Center | Council of Conservationists |
| Sierra Club | Garden Clubs of America |
| Friends of the Earth | Trustees for Conservation |
| Natural Resources Defense Council | Defenders of Wildlife |

environmentalists began to be heard. Over the last decade the environmental movement has begun to undergo some changes and take on a new look. In its early stages, the movement was characterized by many who regarded pollution and saving the environment as moral issues that could be solved only if the public interest in a clean and healthful environment took precedence over private economic interests in policy decisions. The movement was a crusade for what was right and there was little willingness to compromise. In the 1970s a clean environment became a more immediate matter of economic self-interest for many Americans. With the spread of pollutants, more and more farmers, fishermen, sportsmen, crabbers, shrimpers, and others see their livelihood threatened by pollution. At the same time that more people see their economic well-being threatened, public enthusiasm for environmental controls is beginning to dim somewhat. As it becomes clearer to the general public that they as consumers must bear much of the costs of many environmental regulations, their enthusiasm declines quickly. More and more of the general public as well as the policymakers are becoming aware of the tough trade-offs that are a part of decision-making on matters of energy, the economy, and environmental regulation.

As EPA Director Douglas Costle says, environmental protection has become a permanent part of our political value system, but many questions remain unanswered as to how the often conflicting environmental and economic objectives are to be resolved.[20] How clean should our air and water be? What price should we pay for a clean environment? Who should make the decisions on these questions? Many industry spokesmen view pollution as a technical problem that can be solved if science and industry are given enough time. They feel the governmental approach is frequently to rigid in its requirements and drives up costs unnecessarily. Many critics of current regulatory efforts feel that less costly but just-as-effective alternative approaches are often not given consideration. Instead of setting rigid standards on emissions into the air and effluents into the streams, why not come at the problem from a different direction? In 1974 the Japanese imposed a tax on utilities based on the amount of sulfur pollutants emitted into the air. Income from the tax was used to pay for the medical costs of patients diagnosed as having pollution-induced illnesses. Very shortly, several companies decided it would be cheaper in the long run to clean up their operations than pay the emissions tax. In other words, there are various approaches to solving pollution problems. Responding to industry complaints of inflexibility in its approach, the EPA has adopted what it calls the "bubble policy" on pollution. This new approach allows a plant with more than one polluting source to monitor the total level of its emissions rather than having to monitor emissions from every source individually. Armco Steel said EPA's new approach would save that firm $50 million in 1980. With the growing concern over regulatory costs, more agencies are likely to become sensitive to alternative approaches for discharging their public duties.

Thus far Americans and their policymakers alike have failed, or refused, to face the harsh necessity of trade-offs in the pursuit of economic growth and stability and a clean, healthful environment. Like Lyndon Johnson, we have pursued both "guns and butter." Senator Henry Jackson, chairman of the Senate Energy and Natural Resources Committee, says, "Working together, we can find the answers and mount a program that will provide the nation with an adequate—and secure—energy supply while at the same time protecting our environment and strengthening our economy."[21]

Maybe so, but as the nation's policymakers continue to grapple with problems of inflation, declining productivity, unemployment, and energy shortages, it will become more and more difficult to avoid the necessity of painful political and economic trade-offs involving environmental regulation. Acceptance of the fact that improvements in the quality of life may come only at the expense of improvements in the quantity of material life appears inevitable, but it is something Americans will no doubt find difficult.

## Points to Ponder

How can we explain a national commitment to programs costing billions of dollars for sending men to the moon, sending probes to Mars and other planets, or building more and more antiballistic missiles and other weapons, while ignoring the very real possibility that we may be creating an environment that will no longer sustain life on our own planet?

How far do we go in relaxing environmental safeguards to produce more energy?

Does regulation cost too much?

Are synthetic fuels the answer to our energy problem, or are they a major hazard to the environment?

## Notes

1. J. Allen Overton, Jr. as quoted in the *National Journal* (November 17, 1979), p. 1931.
2. William Turnage as quoted in the *National Journal* (April 12, 1979), p. 658.
3. *Ibid.*
4. *Gibbons* v *Ogden*, 9 Wheaton 1 (1824).
5. Dick Kirschten, "Playing Water Politics," *National Journal* (April 7, 1979), p. 570.
6. Jimmy Carter, Presidential Address, April 18, 1977.
7. *Phillips Petroleum Co.* v *Federal Power Commission*, 227 F. 2nd 470 (1954).
8. Peabody Coal Co. president as quoted in Dick Kirschten, "The Coal Industry's Rude Awakening to the Realities of Regulation," *National Journal* (February 3, 1979), p. 182.
9. Daniel Yergin, et al., *Energy Future: Report of the Energy Project at the Harvard Business School* (New York: Random House, 1979).
10. Daniel Yergin, "U.S. Energy Policy: Transition to What?" *The World Today* (March 1979).
11. Thomas "Tip" O'Neill as quoted in *Congress and the Nation*, vol. IV, p. 202.
12. James H. Elliott as quoted by Timothy Clark, "How One Company Lives with Government Regulation," *National Journal* (May 12, 1979), p. 776.
13. Kepone is a deadly poison, and PCBs and asbestos are carcinogens known to cause cancer in test animals. Love Canal and Valley of the Drums are chemical waste dumps in New York and Kentucky found to have hazardous substances endangering the environment and health.
14. John H. Chaffee as quoted by Dick Kirschten, "The New War on Pollution Is Over the Land," *National Journal* (April 14, 1979), p. 603.
15. Gerald Ford as quoted in *Congress and the Nation*, vol. IV, p. 287.
16. Timothy Clark, "How One Company Lives with Government Regulation," *National Journal* (May 12, 1979), p. 775.

17. Edmund Muskie as quoted by Robert Shogan, "Regulation: Costs and Causes," Louisville, Ky. *Courier-Journal* (June 24, 1979), © 1979, Los Angeles Times. Reprinted by permission.
18. To comply with early air pollution standards, many utilities and factories built tall smokestacks designed to release pollutants in the upper air levels where they were dispersed by the winds. Since the particulates released may be carried hundreds of miles, one effect has been for pollutants released in relatively rural settings to be carried to larger urban centers of population.
19. Charles Peters and Glen Allerhand, "The Case Against Energy Independence," *The Washington Monthly* (September 1975), p. 20.
20. Douglas Costle, "New Environmentalists find ecology and economics mix," Louisville, Ky. *Courier-Journal* (March 11, 1979).
21. Henry Jackson as quoted by John M. Berry, "If synthetic fuels are our salvation, what's the final bill?" Louisville, Ky. *Courier-Journal* (June 24, 1979), Los Angeles Times-Washington Post story, © 1979 Washington Post Company.

## Suggestions for Further Reading

ACKERMAN, BRUCE, et al. *The Uncertain Search for Environmental Quality*. New York: The Free Press, 1974.

ANDERSON, FREDERICK, et al. *Environmental Improvement Through Economic Incentives*. Baltimore: Johns Hopkins University Press, 1978.

CALDWELL, L. K., et al. *Citizens and the Environment*. Bloomington, Ind.: Indiana University Press, 1978.

CLAWSON, MARION. *America's Land and Its Uses*. Baltimore: Johns Hopkins University Press, 1972.

COMMONER, BARRY. *The Politics of Energy*. New York: Knopf, 1979.

CONGRESSIONAL QUARTERLY. *Earth, Energy and Environment*. Editorial Research Report. Washington, D.C.: Congressional Quarterly, 1977.

CRENSEN, MATTHEW. *The Un-Politics of Air Pollution*. Baltimore: Johns Hopkins University Press, 1971.

DAVIES, J. CLARENCE III. *The Politics of Pollution*, 2nd ed. New York: Pegasus, 1975.

DAVIS, DAVID H. *Energy Politics*, 2nd ed. New York: St. Martins Press, 1978.

DONIGER, DAVID D. *The Law and Policy of Toxic Substances Control: A Case Study of Vinyl Chloride*. Baltimore: Johns Hopkins University Press, 1979.

FORD FOUNDATION. *Energy: The Next Twenty Years: Resources for the Future*. Cambridge, Mass.: Ballinger, 1979.

FRANKEL, GLENN. "The Tragedy of TOSCA: Chemical Poisoning the EPA Can't Control," *The Washington Monthly* (July/August 1979), pp. 42–45.

FREEMAN, A. M. III. *The Benefits of Environmental Improvement: Theory and Practice*. Baltimore: Johns Hopkins University Press, 1979.

FREEMAN, A. M. III, et al. *The Economics of Environmental Policy*. New York: Wiley, 1973.

FREEMAN, S. DAVID, et al. *A Time to Choose: America's Energy Future*. Cambridge, Mass.: Ballinger, 1974.

FRISKEN, WILLIAM. *The Atmospheric Environment*. Baltimore: Johns Hopkins University Press, 1974.

HERFINDAHL, O. C. and KNEESE, ALLEN. *Quality of the Environment: An Economic Approach to Some Problems in Using Land, Water, and Air*. Baltimore: Johns Hopkins University Press, 1965.

HYDE, WILLIAM F. "Implications of Economic Forest Management." *Policy Analysis* (Summer 1979).

JACOBY, HENRY, et al. *Cleaning the Air: Federal Policy on Automotive Emissions Control.* Cambridge, Mass.: Ballinger, 1973.
JONES, CHARLES O. *Clean Air.* Pittsburgh: University of Pittsburgh Press, 1975.
KATZMANN, ROGER. *Regulatory Bureaucracy.* Cambridge, Mass.: MIT Press, 1979.
KNEESE, ALLEN and SCHULTZE, CHARLES. *Pollution, Prices, and Public Policy.* Washington, D.C.: The Brookings Institution, 1975.
LIEBER, HARVEY. *Federalism and Clean Waters.* Lexington, Mass.: Lexington Books, 1975.
LIKENS, GENE, et al. "Acid Rain," *Scientific American* (October 1979).
LIPSCHUTZ, RONNIE. *Radioactive Waste: Politics, Technology, and Risk.* Cambridge, Mass.: Ballinger, 1980.
LIROFF, RICHARD. *A National Policy for the Environment: NEPA and Its Aftermath.* Bloomington, Ind.: Indiana University Press, 1976.
LYDAY, NOREEN. *The Law of the Land: Debating National Land Use Legislation 1970-1975.* Washington, D.C.: Urban Institute, 1976.
NAGEL, STUART, ed. *Environmental Politics.* New York: Praeger, 1979.
NOVICH, SHELDON. *The Electric War: The Fight Over Nuclear Power.* New York: Sierra Club/Scribner's, 1976.
OAK RIDGE ASSOCIATED UNIVERSITIES. *Future Strategies for Energy Development: A Question of Scale.* Oak Ridge, Tenn.: Institute for Energy Analysis, 1977.
OPHULS, WILLIAM. *Ecology and the Politics of Scarcity.* New York: Freeman, 1977.
PETERS, TERRY. *The Politics and Administration of Land Use Control.* Lexington, Mass.: Lexington Books, 1974.
ROLPH, ELIZABETH. *Nuclear Power and the Public Safety.* Lexington, Mass.: Lexington Books, 1979.
ROSEBAUM, WALTER A. *The Politics of Environmental Concern.* New York: Praeger, 1977.
SAFER, ARNOLD. *International Oil Policy.* Lexington, Mass.: Lexington Books, 1979.
SPROUT, HAROLD and MARGARET. *The Context of Environmental Politics.* Lexington, Ky.: The University Press of Kentucky, 1979.
STEINMAN, MICHAEL, ed. *Energy and Environmental Issues: The Making and Implementation of Public Policy.* Lexington, Mass.: Lexington Books, 1979.
TELLER, EDWARD. *Energy from Heaven and Earth.* New York: Freeman, 1979.
TOBIN, RICHARD J. *The Social Gamble: Determining Acceptable Levels of Air Quality.* Lexington, Mass.: Lexington Books, 1979.
UNITED STATES NUCLEAR REGULATORY COMMISSION, *Reactor Safety Study: An Assessment of Risks in the U.S. Commercial Nuclear Power Plants.* October 1975, Wash-1400 NUREG-75/014.
WENNER, LETTIE. *One Environment Under Law: A Public Policy Dilemma.* Pacific Palisades, Calif.: Goodyear, 1976.
YERGIN, DANIEL, et al. *Energy Future*, Report of the Energy Project at the Harvard Business School. New York: Random House, 1979.
Periodicals:
*Policy Studies Journal* (Summer 1973 issue)
*Natural Resources Journal* (April 1976 issue)
*Environmental Affairs*
*Environmental Reporter*

# Part Five

# Redistributive Policy

In his classic definition, Harold Lasswell characterized politics as "who gets what, when and how." In our system, the federal government has become a principal actor in this political process, and in this unit the focus will be on the government's role in the distribution or allocation of political benefits. Redistributive policies, as we will term these actions, involve a conscious effort on the part of the government to manipulate the allocation of wealth, property, taxes, expenditures, civil rights, or something of value among broad categories of individuals or groups in society. Because such policy decisions result in "winners" and "losers," determining who gets what and at the expense of whom, they frequently involve considerable controversy and intense political competition. Debates on policies of redistribution may involve strong ideological arguments along with substantial amounts of economic self-interest.

The different categories of policy we have explored—management, subsidy, regulatory, and redistributive—are each characterized by their own distinctive brand of politics. Of the various types of policy, redistributive policies are the most likely to develop along class lines and to stimulate alignments along class lines. While the coalitions formed will shift from issue to issue, there are really only two sides and these remain clear and consistent—those who benefit most and those who benefit least. Because their impact can be substantial in terms of both their costs and benefits, redistributive policies are significantly influenced by socio-economic considerations. Generally, the higher socio-economic elements of society are more influential and better represented on such decisions; thus, those who would stand to benefit most from such policies may frequently be those with the least economic and political influence. Because of their socio-economic implications, policies of redistribution produce some of the most intense partisan divisions in Congress. While certain managerial (foreign policy) and subsidy policies (oil depletion allowance) may generate strong bipartisan support, redistributive policies (medicare, health insurance) frequently touch off some of the most intense partisan debates.

Different types of policy also result in different involvement for the president, Congress, and the courts. Subsidy policies, for example, are usually determined largely by the Congress, with only limited involvement by the president and almost no involvement by the courts. In the realm of redistribution, on the other hand, the president usually plays a key role, with most of the initiative coming from the White House (a president's reputation is frequently tied to his successes or failures in promoting such policies). Jimmy Carter encountered heavy criticism for abandoning the poor and minorities when his 1980 and 1981 budget proposals held the line or reduced expenditures on several programs of redistribution. Some of the most significant decisions of the U. S. Supreme Court also have involved policies of redistribution—in the area of civil rights in particular. Redistributive policies may frequently involve deep philosophical issues and may simmer for years before breaking into the policy arena to bring substantial change to society. Such was the case with school desegregation and the whole field of minority rights.

Whereas subsidy policies may be quite limited in their scope, bestowing benefits on a rather narrow sector of society, redistributive policies are usually much broader in scope and the government's impact through such policies may be far-reaching. Because redistributive policies, like regulatory policies, are more likely to affect more citizens more directly than are subsidy or management policies, they frequently attract considerable attention among the electorate. The much narrower focus of subsidy policies frequently results in their being shaped primarily by relatively small elites or subgovernments of those most directly involved (interest groups, congressional committees, and executive agencies) while redistributive policies, which are most likely to impact such immediate citizen concerns as taxes, social security benefits, employment opportunities, interest rates, etc., generate broader debate and involvement.

Periodic dissatisfaction with taxes, inflation, and levels of government expenditures will slow programs of redistribution. However, there is substantial political pressure for such programs and, according to Meltzer and Richard, as long as the disincentive to work, save, and invest does not lower future income enough to turn expected gains into losses, support for policies of redistribution will continue.[1] However, periodic dissatisfaction with high taxes or increased demands for expenditures in other areas, such as for defense, may slow expenditures for redistributive purposes. While, as was noted earlier, debate over redistributive policies may frequently involve such basic philosophical issues as effect on the work ethic, free enterprise and the profit motive, minority versus majority rights, and other economic as well as moral issues, the very basic questions when such techniques are employed by policymakers are usually how much is to be spent, where will the funds come from, and who will benefit at the expense of whom.

On close analysis almost all policies are to a certain degree redistributive in nature in that they benefit some elements of society more than others. The price support program for farmers treated earlier as a subsidy policy, for example, has a redistributive effect as well in that consumers pay higher prices for farm products as a result of government price supports. Federal support for education is redistributive in that money from more affluent states goes for educating students in less affluent states and districts. In the next two chapters the focus will be on two areas, however, where the government has engaged in concerted and conscious efforts to bring about reallocations in resources and benefits. Chapter 13 will focus on the government's efforts in the civil rights field, and Chapter 14 will deal with a variety of governmental programs undertaken to accomplish a redistribution of economic resources and benefits to improve the lot of those at the lower end of the socio-economic scale.

## Note

1. Allan Meltzer and Scott Richard, "Why Government Grows (and Grows) in a Democracy," *The Public Interest*, no. 52 (Summer 1978), p. 117.

## Suggestions for Further Reading

APTER, DAVID. *Choice and the Politics of Allocation*. New Haven, Conn.: Yale University Press, 1971.

BEER, SAMUEL. "The Adoption of General Revenue Sharing: A Case Study in Public Sector Politics," *Public Policy* (Fall 1978) vol. 1, no. 2, p. 82.

BOOMS, BERNARD and HALLDORSON, JAMES. "The Politics of Redistribution: A Reformulation," *American Political Science Review* 67 (September 1973).

EGGER, ROWLAND, and HARRIS, JOSEPH P. *The President and Congress*. New York: McGraw-Hill, 1963.

FRY, BRIAN and WINTERS, RICHARD. "The Politics of Redistribution," *American Political Science Review* 64 (June 1970).

HENDERSON, GORDON. *American Democracy: People, Politics and Policies*. Cambridge, Mass.: Winthrop, 1979.

HOCKMAN, HAROLD and PETERSON, GEORGE, eds. *Redistribution Through Public Choice*. New York: Columbia University Press, 1974.

LOWI, THEODORE. "American Business, Public Policy, Case-Studies and Political Theory," *World Politics*, vol. XVI, no. 4 (July 1964).

PALAMOUNTAIN, JOSEPH C., Jr. *The Politics of Distribution*. Cambridge, Mass.: Harvard University Press, 1955.

PIOUS, RICHARD M. *The American Presidency,* ch. 5, 6. New York: Basic Books, 1979.

SPITZER, ROBERT J. "The Presidency and Public Policy: A Preliminary Inquiry," *Presidential Studies Quarterly* IX (Fall 1979), pp. 441–56.

SULLIVAN, JOHN L. "A Note on Redistributive Politics," *American Political Science Review* 66 (December 1972).

WILDAVSKY, AARON, ed. *The Presidency*. Boston: Little, Brown & Co., 1969.

# 13

# Equal Rights for All: Affirmative Action or Reverse Discrimination?

Americans have traditionally displayed considerable concern with the protection of individual freedom, as is illustrated in such documents as the Declaration of Independence, the Northwest Ordinance, and the Constitution. Nevertheless, public policymaking through the years has been characterized by almost continuous efforts to defend individual rights against either governmental or individual infringements.

The first ten amendments, called the Bill of Rights, added to the Constitution in 1790, were directed primarily at protecting the rights of individuals from encroachment by the federal government; and the Thirteenth, Fourteenth, and Fifteenth Amendments were intended to provide similar protection from state governments. Over the years the "due process" clauses of the Fifth and Fourteenth Amendments and the "equal protection" clause of the Fourteenth Amendement have been extended to protect individual rights from infringements by other individuals as well. With the role of the government growing in the allocation of rights and privileges among individuals and groups in society, the process has become more and more politicized and controversial.

Policymaking in this field illustrates quite dramatically the impact of both public opinion and organized groups on policy decisions. The sit-ins, demonstrations, rallies, and riots, the pictures of police dogs attacking demonstrators, the church bombings and the murders have all been significant factors in the drive toward public policies ensuring equal rights. As the government has sought to provide remedies for past injustices, difficult questions have arisen concerning majority versus minority rights and reverse discrimination. A central issue now plaguing policymakers relative to the government's role in civil rights is the

> **Major Civil Rights Legislation**
>
> **Civil Rights Acts of 1866, 1870, 1871, and 1875.** Adopted by Congress to guarantee the rights of blacks. While most of the provisions were later held unconstitutional, sections of the '66 and '71 acts, making it a federal crime for persons acting under authority of state law to deprive another person of constitutional rights and authorizing suits for civil damages against state and local officials by persons whose rights are abridged by their actions, remain in effect.
>
> **Civil Rights Act of 1957.** Designed primarily to secure blacks the right to vote, the act empowered the Department of Justice to seek injunctions against voting rights infractions. The act created a Civil Rights Division in the Justice Department and the Civil Rights Commission.
>
> **Civil Rights Act of 1960.** Authorized the federal courts to appoint referees to help blacks register to vote.
>
> **Civil Rights Act of 1964.** Provided for further federal protection of the voting rights of black citizens.
>
> **Civil Rights Act of 1965.** Also known as the Voting Rights Act, it provided for direct federal action to enable blacks to register to vote by suspending literacy tests and authorizing federal voting examiners for districts where minority voter participation was low.
>
> **Civil Rights Act or Fair Housing Act of 1968.** Prohibited discrimination in employment on the basis of race or sex and expanded the enforcement powers of the Equal Employment Opportunity Commission.

growing conflict between the rights of individuals and the demands being pressed by numerous racial, ethnic, and sex groups regarding minority rights.[1] These demands have their roots in a history of discrimination and the black civil rights movement of the last century.

## BLACK CIVIL RIGHTS

Despite American concern with individual freedom, black people who were not accorded any constitutional rights and safeguards until after the Civil War. The Dred Scott decision held that blacks, regarded more as property than as individual persons, were not meant to be included under the term "citizen" in the Constitution.[2] The struggle to accord blacks equality under the law has been a long, embittered, and politically entangled struggle, unfinished more than a century after the slaves were freed. Once the Civil War was over, it quickly became clear that additional steps would be necessary to ensure the freed slaves their rights protected under the Constitution.

> **Principal Departments and Agencies**
>
> **Department of Justice.** The department includes two divisions with major responsibilities in the civil rights field—the Civil Rights Division, created by the Civil Rights Act of 1957, and the FBI.
>
> **Commission on Civil Rights.** Created by the Civil Rights Act of 1957, the commission conducts investigations to uncover evidence of civil rights abuses.
>
> **Equal Employment Opportunity Commision (EEOC).** This agency has the responsibility for seeking to eliminate discrimination based on race, color, religion, sex, national origin, age, or handicap in hiring, promotion, firing, wages, testing, training, apprenticeship, or other conditions of employment.

Congress responded by proposing three additions to the Constitution: the Thirteenth, Fourteenth, and Fifteenth Amendments. These amendments, adopted in 1865, 1868, and 1870, were designed to secure to blacks their rights as citizens and to protect these rights from encroachment by both the national and state governments. The Fourteenth Amendment provided that "No state shall make or enforce any law which shall abridge the privileges or immunities of citizens of the United States," and black citizens were extended "due process" and "equal protection" under the laws. These amendments were accompanied by civil rights legislation adopted in 1866, 1867, and 1875, designed to carry out the intent of the Constitution. The Civil Rights Act of March 1875 extended the amendment's provisions to individual acts as well as governmental, prohibiting discrimination on the basis of race or color in inns, public conveyances, theatres, and other places of amusement.

The courts, however, began to chip away at the intent of the amendments and the implementing legislation. In 1873 in the *Slaughterhouse Cases*, the Supreme Court by a one-vote majority ruled that the Fourteenth Amendment protected only the privileges and immunities of national citizenship and did not prevent the states from abridging state citizenship privileges, thus substantially weakening the intent of the Fourteenth Amendment and opening the door for a variety of state-sanctioned racially discriminating policies.[3] In the *Civil Rights Cases* in 1883, the Court struck another blow when it held that Congress did not have the constitutional authority to regulate the behavior of individuals who denied blacks equal use of hotels, theatres, and other public facilities.[4] The Court interpreted the Thirteenth and Fourteenth Amendments as proscribing only state, not individual, interference with the exercise of civil rights. In *Plessy* v *Ferguson* in 1896, the Court ruled that state policies requiring "separate but equal" educational facilities for the races were not violations of black students' constitutional rights.[5] Thus, at the turn of the century, in spite of the adoption of three constitutional amendments and several statutes, blacks had achieved few civil rights and were far short of the constitutional objective of equality.

Black progress toward equal rights during the years prior to World War II was excruciatingly slow. In the absence of executive and legislative action, the blacks turned to the courts, through which they were gradually able to attain limited access to public accommodations, higher education, and the electoral process. In a 1941 decision the Supreme Court invalidated an Oklahoma statute that permitted a rail carrier to have separate, white-only dining and sleeping cars and ruled that a black person could not be ejected from Pullman accommodations.[6] In 1946 the Court ruled that a Virginia statute requiring segregation on interstate transportation vehicles violated the commerce clause of the Constitution and in 1950 the Court broadened this concept, holding that interstate carriers could not subject persons to "prejudice or disadvantage."[7]

In the areas of higher and professional education, the Supreme Court also began to chip away at the "separate but equal" concept. In 1938 the Court ruled that Missouri could not exclude a black student from the state university's law school because separate but equal training was not available in the state.[8] In 1949 the University of Texas was ordered to admit a black law student on similar grounds, and a year later the Court ruled that the University of Oklahoma could not require a black student to sit apart from other students.[9] Slowly the barriers were being pulled down.

A major factor limiting progress toward equal rights for blacks was their lack of political power and influence. While the Fifteenth Amendment prohibited denying citizens the right to vote on the basis of race, the states and political parties for years used such subterfuges as "grandfather clauses," white primaries, poll taxes, and literacy tests to block effective political participation by blacks.[10] Only gradually were the barriers brought down through repeated challenges in the courts. In 1915 the Supreme Court struck down grandfather clauses as a voting requirement, holding that they violated the Fifteenth Amendment.[11] The white primary in one form or another persisted until 1944 when the Court, after a series of decisions, finally held these exclusive primary devises in violation of the Fifteenth Amendment also.[12] The Court further ruled in a 1941 decision that Congress could regulate the conduct of congressional elections, a move primarily to protect black voters' participation in these elections.[13] As the barriers to black political involvement were gradually eliminated, black citizens' influence began to increase, paving the way for more active civil rights movements in the 1950s and 1960s.

## Civil Rights Groups

Playing a key role in the growth of black political influence and black people's successes in the federal courts were increased organization and more effective leadership. A leading group in the push for black civil rights was the National Association for the Advancement of Colored People (NAACP), founded in New

York in 1909 by W.E.B. DuBois. The NAACP Legal Defense and Educational Fund, founded in 1938, has also been in the forefront of the black civil rights effort. The Congress of Racial Equality (CORE), founded in 1941, is smaller than the NAACP but has been active in promoting equal rights for blacks. The Southern Regional Council, started in 1942, is confined largely to the South and devotes its efforts to improving blacks' economic status and educational opportunities. The National Urban League also directs its efforts primarily toward securing better housing, employment, and educational opportunities for blacks. The Southern Christian Leadership Conference, founded in 1957 by Dr. Martin Luther King, has been another significant group in the civil rights movement, especially in the South. The Student Non-Violent Coordinating Committee (SNCC) was active in the movement in the 1960s. The Negro American Labor Council has pushed especially for equal opportunity for blacks in the labor movement. A coalition of various civil rights groups, the Leadership Conference on Civil Rights formed in 1949, helped to mobilize support for civil rights legislative efforts. These groups have frequently been joined in their efforts by others interested in promoting civil rights, such as the AFL-CIO, the National Council of Churches, Americans for Democratic Action, the American Civil Liberties Union, and the American Veterans Committee, among others.

With such groups as these taking up the cause for civil rights, pressures for governmental action began to mount. In 1941 President Roosevelt, under pressure from black leaders, created by executive order a Committee on Fair Employment Practices. Roosevelt's successor, Harry Truman, became the first president to propose a comprehensive civil rights legislative package, including antilynching, antipoll tax, antisegregation in public transportation, and antidiscrimination in employment provisions. Truman's proposals brought a quick reaction in Congress. In the House a group of seventy-four southern Democrats organized quickly to "cooperate" with the governors of southern states to block the Truman program. Failing to get action on his legislative proposals, President Truman issued executive orders banning segregation in the armed forces and discrimination in federal employment and work being done under governmental contracts.

The post-World War II years brought significant changes in federal civil rights policy as the government's role shifted from one of relative noninterference to active involvement. With the Supreme Court leading the way this time, the federal government took action to eliminate discrimination and segregation in the schools, public facilities, housing, employment, and voting. President Eisenhower continued the cause of civil rights through executive actions but proposed no new legislation in his first term. As blacks and their supporters grew more aggressive, and as a result of the *Brown* decision in 1954, a backlash began to develop.[14] In 1955, White Citizens Councils appeared in Mississippi and spread to other southern states in opposition to integration efforts. In 1956, 101 senators and representatives signed the Southern Manifesto denouncing the *Brown* decision and recommending resistance to integration "by any lawful means."

## Civil Rights Acts of 1957 and 1960

Blacks, however, buoyed by their success in the *Brown* case, pressed their cause with renewed vigor using litigation, economic boycotts, passive resistance, and voter registration drives to further their efforts. A large black vote cast in the 1956 elections did not go unheeded, and in 1957 Congress finally got into the act with its first civil rights legislation since Reconstruction days. The Civil Rights Act of 1957 was primarily a voting rights bill empowering the attorney general to seek court injunctions against actions obstructing or depriving blacks of their legal voting rights. The act also created a Commission on Civil Rights and established a Civil Rights Division in the Department of Justice under an assistant attorney general to carry out the provisions of the law.

Still not satisfied with the relatively narrow 1957 legislation, civil rights advocates continued to press for broader legislative guarantees. New legislation was proposed in 1960 but a southern-Democrat–Republican coalition in Congress was able to revise the bill sufficiently to make it a victory for the "moderates." Again the Civil Rights Act of 1960 was primarily a voting rights act, authorizing judges to appoint referees to help blacks to register and to vote and providing legal penalties for bombings, bomb threats, and mob action designed to obstruct court orders.

The 1960 Democratic Party platform pledged support for far-reaching civil rights action, but once in office the Kennedy administration failed to push civil rights legislation immediately. The only action in 1961 was the extension of the Civil Rights Commission for two years. Kennedy did continue the practice of extending civil rights through executive orders, establishing a Presidential Committee on Equal Employment Opportunity in 1961 and barring discrimination in federally assisted housing in 1962. While using executive action in an effort to placate civil rights groups, the Kennedy administration side-stepped general civil rights legislation, fearing the proposal of such legislation would jeopardize other administration proposals in Congress. Finally, under mounting pressure new civil rights legislation was sought in 1962, but only a proposal to amend the Constitution to outlaw the poll tax passed the Congress.

## Civil Rights Act of 1964

In 1963 racial protests, many accompanied by violence, erupted across the nation, bringing a domestic crisis of major proportions. Displeased with the pace of governmental civil rights efforts and better organized than ever before, civil rights groups stepped up their demands for action. When black demonstrations and boycotts throughout the country were met with violence—a Mississippi NAACP leader was murdered and four little black girls killed in the bombing of a church where they were attending Sunday school—President Kennedy quickly broadened his civil rights proposals. On June 11 he appeared on nationwide television to appeal for support for his proposals.

Though civil rights legislation became a top priority item for the administration, it was delayed in Congress when a debate arose in the Senate over whether the public accommodations clause should be considered under the Fourteenth Amendment or the commerce clause. Pro-civil rights elements favored the commerce clause because this meant the bill would go to the Senate Interstate Commerce Committee chaired by Warren Magnuson (D-Wash.), rather than to the Judiciary Committee chaired by James Eastland (D-Miss.) if based on the Fourteenth Amendment. Eastland was a staunch opponent of civil rights legislation. The Senate delayed consideration until the House had passed a bill and 1963 ended with no legislation being adopted.

By the end of 1963, civil rights demonstrations had taken place in 800 cities and towns, concluding with an August 28 "March on Washington for Jobs and Freedom" with 200,000 participants. By this point millions of whites had joined the blacks in their drive for fairer treatment, and the momentum for new legislation was building.

Southern congressmen, realizing they lacked the votes to prevent the adoption of new civil rights legislation, set about seeking modifications that would make the proposal as palatable as possible. They voiced particular concerns with the provisions for the cut-off of federal funds to programs where discrimination occurred and the fair employment requirements. The southerners launched a "three-platoon" filibuster and Senator Strom Thurmond (D-S.C., but now a Republican) fought a last-ditch effort with a marathon speech, but the proponents were too well-organized. The Leadership Conference on Civil Rights (a coalition of numerous civil rights groups) was joined in a well-organized and well-coordinated campaign by the Democratic Study Group (DSG), the AFL-CIO, various other groups, and a number of church groups including the National Council of Churches of Christ, National Catholic Conference for Interracial Justice, National Community Relations Advisory Council (Jewish), National Student Christian Federation, six other Jewish and eight other Protestant groups. The church groups in particular worked on senators from rural states who normally were not as concerned about civil rights issues. On June 10, 1964, the Senate voted 71-29 for cloture, marking the first time in history cloture had been invoked on a civil rights measure. The bill was passed 73-27 and sent to President Johnson, who signed it into law July 2, 1964.

The 1964 Civil Rights Act was the most far-reaching legislation since Reconstruction days. The act included new provisions to guarantee voting rights, guarantee access to public accommodations, authorize federal suits to desegregate public facilities, cut off federal funds when programs were being administered discriminatorily, and guarantee equal employment opportunity.

Adoption of the 1964 Civil Rights Act did not, however, bring an end to racial tensions that had been building for decades. President Johnson called on the nation to "close the springs of racial poison," but the situation remained tense. The summer of 1964 brought riots in several northern cities including Harlem,

Rochester, Jersey City, Patterson, Elizabeth, Chicago, and Philadelphia; and in Mississippi three young civil rights workers were murdered.

## Voting Rights Act of 1965

Voting rights, supposedly guaranteed by the Fifteenth Amendment adopted in 1875, became the main focus of the civil rights activists in 1965, and Selma, Alabama was selected as the focal point for voter registration efforts in the South. A March 7 civil rights march from Selma to Montgomery, Alabama was broken up by state troopers using tear gas, nightsticks, and whips. On March 11 the Reverend James Reeb, a white Unitarian minister from Boston who was participating in the voting march, died of injuries received in a beating. Two weeks later Mrs. Viola Liuzzo, a marcher from Detroit, was killed in an ambush on the road between Selma and Montgomery. The following day four members of the Ku Klux Klan were arrested in connection with the murders. President Johnson responded quickly, asking the Congress for stronger voting rights legislation.

Although all the civil rights bills passed since 1957 included provisions on voting rights, black voters were still discriminated against and their participation remained low in several southern states. In 1965 the Senate once again invoked cloture to close off a filibuster and Congress passed the Voting Rights Act of 1965. The act gave the attorney general the authority to appoint federal examiners to supervise voter registration in states or districts where literacy or other qualifying tests were used and where fewer than 50 percent of the eligible voters had registered or voted in 1964. The act also set stiff criminal penalties for interference with a voter's rights and prohibited the states from imposing new voter qualification laws unless they were approved by the federal district court in the District of Columbia. Less than six weeks after adoption of the Voting Rights Act, rioting broke out in the Watts area of Los Angeles, lasting for six days, leaving 34 dead and 856 injured, and causing damage estimated at $200 million.

The civil rights acts of 1964 and 1965 were not sufficient to stem a rising tide of black frustration and resentment. Succeeding summers in the mid-sixties brought racial riots accompanied by widespread burnings, looting, and violence. This, along with more and more frequent references by black leaders to "Black Power," began to cause a backlash, and both public and congressional support for the civil rights movement began to erode. While past violence directed toward those seeking equal rights for blacks had generated support for their cause, the new violence involving blacks appeared to some to be pointless and wanton destruction and the result was a loss of public support, especially among whites.

## Fair Housing Act of 1968

In 1966 LBJ suffered his first congressional defeat on a civil rights proposal when his supporters in the Senate were unable to cut off a filibuster. The most controversial part of Johnson's proposal was a section dealing with discrimination in the sale and rental of housing, and a frequently heard phrase in the congressional debate was "a man's home is his castle," implying this was not a matter for governmental regulation. Johnson's bill was also lobbied against vigorously by the National Association of Real Estate Boards. The president resubmitted his proposals in 1967, including open housing, which had become the most sensitive of the civil rights issues, and was again rebuffed by Congress.

By 1968 race relations had become the central domestic issue and feelngs on both sides were intense as the summers of rioting, burning, and looting had worn nerves thin. In April 1968, Martin Luther King, the civil rights movement's apostle of nonviolence, was assassinated in Memphis, Tennessee. Riots and demonstrations again erupted across the country, including in the nation's capital as leaders on both sides called for understanding and restraint. Johnson again submitted to Congress legislation providing protection for persons in the exercise of their civil rights, protection against discrimination in the sale and rental of housing, reforms in the selection of federal and state juries, and provisions for criminal penalties for rioting. This time the proposals were approved as the Fair Housing Act of 1968.

More civil rights legislation had been passed during Lyndon Johnson's administration than in any previous period; yet, as Johnson himself realized, eliminating the legal barriers alone was not a total remedy for the problem of race relations. In his 1968 message to Congress, Johnson observed, "The more we grapple with the civil rights problem—the most difficult domestic issue we have ever faced—the more we realize that the position of minorities in American society is defined not merely by law, but by social, education and economic conditions."[15]

With Johnson's departure from the White House and two succeeding Republican administrations in office there was a marked change in civil rights efforts. Nixon's first term was marked by an almost total lack of effort on the civil rights front, and both the Nixon and Ford presidencies offered few initiatives in the civil rights field. The legislation adopted in their terms built on the base already established earlier. In 1970 the Voting Rights Act was extended for five years over Nixon's strong opposition and veto, and in 1972 Congress adopted the Equal Employment Opportunities Enforcement Act giving the Equal Employment Opportunity Commission (EEOC) power to enforce its findings of job bias. Under the 1964 legislation creating the EEOC, the commission was given no enforcement powers and had to use the courts to carry out its orders. In 1975 the Voting Rights Act was amended again to extend coverage to Spanish-speaking Americans.

Actually, by the 1970s there wasn't much left to legislate; what was lacking was vigorous implementation and enforcement of what was already on the books. Pressures from a variety of sources were mounting that made vigorous enforcement of various provisions in the civil rights measures controversial and difficult. In September 1974, Secretary of Health, Education and Welfare (HEW) Caspar Weinberger justified the administration's actions on civil rights, saying, "We are doing our job under very difficult circumstances where there is a very strong divergence of viewpoints between what the law says and what the public wants."[16] Pressures from southern congressmen, for example, had kept the provision for withholding federal funds from becoming an effective tool in enforcing compliance with the civil rights laws.

By this time there was also a growing awareness that more was necessary than legislation to remedy the civil rights problem. Civil rights legislation touched many of the underlying racial problems only indirectly. Improving the overall lot of the black citizen was a part of much broader issues such as urban decay, crime, drugs, unemployment, poverty, welfare, and education. Once the necessary legislation was on the books, the next phase was to improve the blacks' economic situation by raising their income, reducing their unemployment, and improving their education and skills levels. Only in this way could the nation head off the dire predictions of President Johnson's National Advisory Commission on Civil Disorders (the Kerner Commission), which warned in its 1968 report, "This is our basic conclusion: our nation is moving toward two societies, one black, one white — separate and unequal."[17]

## DESEGREGATING THE SCHOOLS

Realizing that better education was a key to improving their economic lot, blacks made desegregation of the nation's schools one of the first targets in their movement for equal rights. Some of their earliest successes came in court decisions requiring the admission of black students to white public schools, but these early successes were limited to graduate and professional schools where "separate but equal" facilities were not available. The "separate but equal" concept sanctioned by the 1896 Supreme Court decision in *Plessy* v *Ferguson* was maintained into the 1950s by more than twenty states and the District of Columbia. In Topeka, Kansas, a 1949 law forced Linda Brown, a black student, to walk six blocks and ride a bus twenty-four blocks to an all-black school, passing a white school on her way. The NAACP and other civil rights advocates made the Brown case the basis for a court suit challenging the longstanding "separate but equal" concept. The case was decided by the Supreme Court in 1954 when Earl Warren had been chief justice for just a few months. Warren, writing for a unanimous court, stated that segregated schools were "inherently unequal" and violated the equal protection clause of the Fourteenth Amendment. While *Brown* reinterpreted the Constitution so as to make separate but equal educational systems illegal, it failed to spell out how equality was to be attained. Thus, while the *Brown* decision is a tribute to the responsiveness of our judicial institutions at a time when other branches of government were reluctant to act, it failed to provide the necessary guidelines for effective implementation of the decision. This coupled with the strong opposition in many sectors greatly reduced the immediate impact of the Court's ruling.

In spite of the Court's dictum to local school boards to integrate their schools with "all deliberate speed" and widespread action by the NAACP and other civil rights groups, progress was slow. In 1956 the NAACP filed 118 suits in the courts in thirteen states charging non-compliance with the Brown decision. In a 1958 decision, the Court held that no scheme of racial discrimination against Negro students in which there was any state involvement could withstand the test of the Fourteenth Amendment. The Court called on local officials to move promptly in eliminating such discrimination but again failed to spell out any specifics.[18] Five years later in *Watson v City of Memphis* the court again expressed impatience with the pace of school desegregation, stating, "The basic guarantees of our Constitution are warrants for the here and now, and unless there is an overwhelmingly compelling reason, they are to be promptly fulfilled."[19]

In 1964, ten years after the Brown decision, many of the nation's schools were still segregated. Only 68,850 black pupils out of 2,988,264 were enrolled in public schools with whites in the eleven former Confederate states, about 2.1 percent. Six border states and the District of Columbia had 59.2 percent of blacks in biracial schools. Still the combined southern and border states had only 10.8 percent of black students in integrated schools. Opposition to integration remained strong. In 1964 the doors of the schools in Prince Edward County, Virginia were locked by school officials who chose to close down rather than integrate the schools. In *Griffin v Prince Edward County School Board* the Supreme Court ruled the board could not close down all public schools to avoid desegregation.[20] The Court added that there had been "entirely too much deliberation and not enough speed" on school desegregation. Title IV of the Civil Rights Act of 1964 included additional legislative provisions calling for desegregation of public education. Through the late-sixties the courts continued to push for desegregation of the schools with "deliberate speed."

In the 1970s the federal courts moved from the concept of "deliberate speed" to "desegregation now," and a prime tool in the movement to achieve integration became court-ordered busing. Under this new approach, segregation per se came to be seen as evil, and integration became a statistical goal. Influenced by a report by Professor James Coleman of the University of Chicago that contended that the achievement of black students was hindered when they attended all-black schools, the courts came to view racial quotas and busing as necessary remedies for past practices that had resulted in segregated schools. In the 1971 decision in *Swann v Charlotte-Mecklenburg Board of Education* the Supreme Court for the first time required busing to achieve a racial balance in the public schools. Justice Burger stated:

> The remedy for such segregation may be administratively awkward, inconvenient and even bizarre in some situations and may impose burdens on some; but all awkwardness and inconvenience cannot be avoided in the interim period when remedial adjustments are being made to eliminate the dual school systems....
>
> Clearly where injuries and injustices have been inflicted on the basis of race, race cannot be totally disregarded in compensating for or correcting them.[21]

Some felt the *Swann* decision was in effect a reversal of the Brown decision, placing the federal government in the position of enforcing racial discrimination in reverse. In Louisville, Kentucky, where a federal judge ordered busing to correct racial imbalance in the schools, an editorialist for the *Courier-Journal* wrote, "But until someone can devise a better way to eliminate racial isolation in the schools, educators and courts must be able to use this tool."[22]

For the next decade busing became the central issue in the debate over school desegregation. Proponents of busing for purposes of desegregation contended that (1) the close daily association of white and black students in some schools would in and of itself bring better interracial understanding and harmony, and (2) black students, once brought into closer contact with more highly motivated and better-prepared white students, would themselves become better students. Opponents of court-ordered busing contended such claims were unverifiable. In one of the most comprehensive reanalyses of the 1966 Coleman report, a 1972 study edited by Frederick Mosteller and Daniel Moynihan concluded that such factors as family background, economic status, number of children in the family, and parental attitudes and education levels were more important in determining educational attainment. In one of the articles in the study, David K. Cohen, Thomas F. Pettigrew, and Robert S. Riley offer this conclusion: "Our findings on the school racial composition issue, then, are mixed...the initial EEDS [Equality of Educational Opportunity Survey] analysis overstressed the impact of school social class.... When the issue is probed at grade 6, a small independent effect of schools' racial composition appeared, but its significance for educational policy seems slight."[23] Professor James Coleman, whose earlier study was cited by many judges in their desegregation decisions, after further study now feels that most segregation is the result of residential patterns and cannot be successfully remedied by court orders. He also feels that school integration has not brought the achievement gains predicted for black students, and that court-ordered busing has brought white flight to the suburbs. Coleman now urges more incentives toward "voluntary cooperation" to achieve integration.[24] Professor Lino Graglia of the University of Texas says that compulsory school busing may be "the most socially destructive and indefensible government policy of our time."[25]

In light of growing questions about court-ordered busing and a growing number of studies connecting busing with white flight and little evidence of improvements in student achievement, the courts have begun to moderate their demands. In 1973 in *Keyes* v *Denver School District #1*, the Supreme Court for the first time required a district to desegregate public schools where segregation had not been required by law, holding that school officials were constitutionally obligated to desegregate a system if segregation had resulted from intentional school board policies.[26] Not all the justices agreed, however, as Justice Powell in a dissenting opinion called court-ordered busing "the single most disruptive element in education today." Three years later with Justice Powell speaking for the majority in *Austin Independent School District* v *U.S.* the court ruled, "Large-scale busing is permissible only where the evidence supports a finding that the extent of integration sought to be achieved by busing would have existed had the school authorities fulfilled their constitutional obligation in the past...."[27]

More recently, when the Court declined to review a busing plan imposed on the Dallas School System by lower federal courts, Justices Powell, Stewart, and Rhenquist dissented from the majority decision, contending that busing was counter-productive because it caused "white flight" and actually denied students equal opportunity and quality schooling.

As the focus has shifted away from primarily *de jure* (legally sanctioned) to *de facto* (resulting from residential, economic, and population patterns) segregation, the issues have become much more complex and difficult to resolve. In previous cases the Court had generally held that for busing to be required, segregated schools had to be the result of officially sanctioned policies or practices; with the shift in focus to de facto segregation this is no longer the prime consideration. It has become more and more apparent that integration delays, especially in many northern urban centers, stem not so much from legal barriers as from even more pervasive underlying factors such as persistently low incomes and high unemployment rates for blacks, residential patterns, and population shifts from the core cities to the suburbs. As attention has shifted to de facto segregation involving more northern and western school districts, a rift has developed between Congress and the courts. On the busing issue Congress has listened to the public and as the issue has spread to more and more congressional districts, Congress has retreated on the school desegregation issue. Various amendments to legislation have been adopted placing limits on the use of funds for busing, and in 1975 legislation was approved preventing HEW from forcing a school district to transport a student beyond the school closest to his or her home for the purpose of racial balance in the schools. While this language applied only to HEW and not the courts, it reflected widespread anti-busing sentiment in Congress. The Eagleton-Biden Amendment adopted in 1977 prohibits HEW from cutting off federal funds to districts that refuse to comply with busing requirements. A proposed constitutional amendment to ban busing was forced out of committee on a discharge petition in 1979, but failed to attain the two-thirds majority necessary for passage. It is doubtful, however, that the issue is laid to rest finally.

In spite of the courts' tougher stance and the expenditure of several million dollars on busing attempts, segregation remains a major problem. A 1976 HEW study reported that in some school districts "equality of education is taking on real meaning." The same report indicated, however, that other districts had "employed a variety of devices to prevent, obstruct or slow down desegregation." The study found that 46 percent of all minority students still attend "moderately" or "highly" segregated schools. On the twenty-fifth anniversary of the landmark *Brown* decision, the U. S. Civil Rights Commission announced that nearly one-half of the country's minority children still attended segregated schools. While some real progress has been made, especially in the South, where most schools are now more racially mixed than in the North and West, some 35 to 45 million students still attend schools yet untouched by desegregation. In the South less than one-half of the black students remain in predominantly black schools, while in the North and West almost two-thirds of black students are in predominantly black schools.

In some areas, in spite of all efforts, ground is being lost rather than gained. In 1954, New Orleans schools were about 50-50 black and white; today they are over 80 percent black. Atlanta schools in 1954 were 49 percent all white, today they are 90 percent all black. In the District of Columbia 96 percent of all public school students are black; in Detroit 82 percent are black. In twenty-nine of the country's largest school systems, whites now constitute a smaller minority than ten years ago as a result of whites leaving the central cities in large numbers. New York City has virtually given up on desegregating its schools. Even in areas where on the surface there has been some desegregation there are other subtle types of discrimination. In Louisville, Kentucky, a survey by a *Louisville Times* reporter revealed very low numbers of black students in "advanced" programs in the city's schools. Two of the 200 students in "advanced" high school programs were blacks, and in the elementary grades only 7 percent of blacks were in "advanced" programs, while the system had a 20 percent black enrollment.

Other factors complicate the quest for equality as well. The black drop-out rate is double the rate for whites, and proportionally three times as many blacks as whites are behind grade level. Much of this may point to deeper underlying problems that must be addressed if blacks are to attain equal educational opportunity. But the fact remains that a quarter century after the *Brown* decision, educational equality has not touched those blacks who are poor, who lack the skills and training for jobs, and who are locked into a vicious cycle of poverty and economic and educational deprivation.

### Higher Education

Higher and professional education also has been an area where blacks have encountered considerable discrimination. For many years colleges were among the most deliberately racist institutions in American society. Prior to the Civil War, only twenty-eight black students had been awarded degrees by American colleges, and from the end of the war until the eve of World War I, higher education for blacks was confined largely to private (for blacks only) colleges. Even in the supposedly more racially tolerant North, college doors didn't open to blacks until the 1920s. In 1930 the University of Dayton was still announcing, "We do not admit Negroes into our day classes because of the considerable number of students we have from the Southern states."[28] A national survey in 1940 found not a single tenured black professor at any non-all-black American university. Finally, with the civil rights movement of the 1950s and '60s and black petitions, boycotts, demonstrations, and lawsuits, higher education began to open up somewhat, but very slowly.

At the time of the *Brown* decision in 1954 very few blacks could hope to become doctors or lawyers. From 1947 to 1969 blacks accounted for about 2.5 percent of the enrollment in medical schools. Of this number 171 (22 percent) were enrolled in predominatly white medical schools. Only in 1968 did the American Medical Association ban racial bars to membership in its local and state affiliates. In 1969 there were 1042 black medical students enrolled; by 1975-76 the number had reached 3456 black students or 6.2 percent of total medical school enrollment. In 1965 blacks made up about 11 percent of the U. S. population but accounted for only about 2 percent of the legal profession and 1.3 percent of law school enrollments. About one-half of the law students were enrolled in black schools. In American Bar Association-approved white law schools there was a total enrollment of 434 black students, about 3 per school.

In the 1960s and '70s black enrollments in higher education increased dramatically. In 1966 there were 282,000 blacks in higher education; within a decade the number had tripled to 1,062,000. In 1965 about 9 percent of blacks and 20 percent of whites ages twenty to twenty-four were enrolled in higher education; by 1974 the percentages were 17 and 22 respectively. By 1976 enrollments were higher among middle and lower-income blacks of college age than for whites in the same category—21.7 percent to 20 percent. Currently black students account for about 11 percent of college enrollments and about 6.5 percent of the baccalaureate degrees earned. Since 1966 black college enrollment has grown by 277 percent while white enrollment for the same period increased 51 percent. Much of this increase is a result of federal laws and court orders that have permitted and encouraged black enrollment in formerly predominantly white institutions.

While the protests of the 1960s and expanding financial aid brought substantial increases in black enrollment, inequities persisted in higher education. In the South, where substantial progress has been made in the desegregation of elementary and secondary school systems, the colleges and universities have lagged behind. In Virginia and North Carolina, where blacks constitute about 20 percent of the population, only about 1 percent of the students in public institutions of higher education were black in 1967 and only 4 percent in 1979. In the 1970s no fewer than ten states were involved in litigation over desegregation of their institutions of higher education and eight others were being monitored. The majority of black students still earn their degrees from predominantly black institutions and 41 percent of black students as opposed to 34 percent of whites are enrolled in two-year colleges. While the percentage of black students attending all-black schools in the fourteen-state area covered by the Southern Regional Education Board (SREB) has declined from 82 percent in 1965 to 43 percent in 1976, black schools still awarded 69 percent of the bachelor's degrees and 46 percent of the graduate degrees awarded to blacks. A further inequity appears in the distribution of degrees earned by blacks; most blacks earned degrees in education, business, and the social sciences, with few getting degrees in health, the physical sciences, or professional fields.

Under pressure from the civil rights movement and the government, many graduate and professional schools developed special admissions policies for minority students. With the adoption of these special policies, the enrollment of blacks and minorities in professional schools such as law, medicine, and engineering have improved substantially. In 1972, 2200 minority students enrolled in engineering as freshmen, 4.2 pecent of all engineering freshmen. By 1977 the figure was 7600 or 8.5 percent of all freshmen enrollees in engineering. In law minorities accounted for about 4.3 percent of the enrollment in ABA-approved law schools in 1969-70. By 1976-77 this percentage had improved to 8.2 percent. By 1975-76 over 90 percent of the nation's medical schools had also developed special recruiting and admissions programs for blacks and other minorities, resulting in increases in their numbers enrolled.

### Affirmative Action or Reverse Discrimination?

As more institutions developed policies of "affirmative action" providing special consideration for those members of minorities who were frequent victims of discrimination, questions of majority rights and "reverse discrimination" began to arise. Could equal opportunity for disadvantaged minorities be promoted through programs of affirmative action without resulting in reverse discrimination? Could the government and other institutions "discriminate" to end "discrimination"? Or, does the equal protection clause of the Fourteenth Amendment bar the government and public institutions from giving special preference to individual members of racial groups recognized to have been the victims of past discrimination? Does such positive action by government and institutions constitute justifiable "compensatory assistance" or illegal "reverse discrimination?" Do the "goals" set in special programs for minorities in fact become "quotas," and are these discriminatory? Those pushing such special programs contend they are essential if equality is ever to be attained. In an interview with the *New York Times* while he was secretary of HEW, Joseph Califano, Jr., asked, "How am I, as Secretary of HEW, ever going to find first-class black lawyers, first-class black scientists, first-class women scientists, if these people don't have a chance to get into the best places (schools) in the country?"[29] Voicing similar sentiments, Professor John H. Ely stated:

> If we are to have even a chance of curing our society of the sickness of racism we will need a lot more black professionals. And, whatever the complex reasons, it seems we will not get them in the forseeable future unless we take blackness into account and weigh it positively when we allocate opportunities."[30]

Just what is permissible as affirmative action under the Constitution is not at all clear. One perplexed college dean said, "We have no desire to break anybody's law, if we can figure out what the law is."[31] In 1973 the Washington State Supreme Court got into the issue when it held in *DeFunis* v *Odegaard* that consideration of racial and ethnic background as a factor in selecting students did not violate the equal protection clause of state and federal constitutions. The U. S. Supreme Court clouded the issue further when in reviewing the *DeFunis* case it declined to address the constitutional questions raised. Justice William Brennan quite accurately predicted:

> The constitutional issues which are avoided today concern vast numbers of people, organizations and colleges and universities, as evidenced by the filing of twenty-six amici curiae [friends of the court] briefs. Few constitutional questions in recent history have stirred as much debate, and they will not disappear. They must inevitably return to the federal courts and ultimately again to this court.[32]

Justice Brennan was right; the issue was back before the Supreme Court in three years in a case widely debated and viewed by many as possibly the most significant civil rights litigation since the *Brown* case. Allan Bakke, a 37-year-old white male applicant, was denied admission to the University of California at Davis medical school. Bakke challenged the decision in the courts, claiming he was a victim of reverse discrimination because under U. C. Davis's special admissions policy, minority students with poorer records were admitted. Bakke charged he was denied admission purely on the basis of race.

Like many other graduate and professional schools, the Davis medical school had adopted a special affirmative action policy to encourage minority enrollments. The medical school reserved 16 of the 100 spaces for entering students each year for members of "disadvantaged minorities." "Disadvantaged" was defined by the school exclusively in terms of race; whites were not considered for any of the sixteen reserved slots. Bakke applied for admission in 1973 when there were 2644 applicants and again in 1974 when there were 3737 applicants. He was denied admission both times while minority candidates with lower qualifications were admitted. Bakke filed suit, maintaining he had been denied admission solely because of race, a violation of his right to equal protection of the law under the Fourteenth Amendment.

The University of California at Davis maintained that its admission policy was aimed at expanding medical education opportunities for persons from economically or educationally disadvantaged backgrounds. In its brief filed on the case, the university asked:

> When only a small fraction of thousands of applicants can be admitted, does the Equal Protection Clause forbid a state university professional school from voluntarily seeking to counteract effects of generations of pervasive discrimination against ... [specific] minorities by establishing a limited special admissions program that increases opportunities for well-qualified members of such racial and ethnic minorities?[33]

The California court hearing the case ruled that the Davis policy discriminated against Bakke but declined to order his admission. Not satisfied with this, both Bakke and the university appealed the decision to the California Supreme Court. In reviewing the case, Justice Mosk put the issue in these terms: Does a special admissions program that benefits disadvantaged minority students who apply for admission to the medical school offend the constitutional rights of better qualified applicants who are denied admission because they are not identified with a minority? The court split on the issue, with the majority finding in favor of Bakke, but Justice Matthew Tobriner (dissenting) wrote, "By today's decision, the majority deliver a severe, hopefully not fatal, blow to these voluntary efforts to integrate our society's institutions and to ameliorate the continuing effects of past discriminations."[34]

Still the issue was not laid to rest, as the decision was appealed to the U. S. Supreme Court. Argument on the case was heard in October 1977. Few court cases have attracted more attention or been debated so widely as *Bakke*, and few cases in recent history have raised social issues generating more debate within policymaking circles about the government's role in allocating rights and privileges among individuals and groups in American society. A *Change* magazine writer commenting on the case observed, "Not since the assassination of Martin Luther King [1968], has this country engaged in as much soul searching about its race relations as has been triggered by Bakke."[35] Not only could this case affect the political status of minority groups for decades to come, it had much broader policy implications as well relative to the government's role in protecting individual rights and allocating rights and privileges among its citizens. The broader political questions posed by *Bakke* were among the most difficult judicial/political issues faced by policymakers during the last two decades.

When the Supreme Court finally ruled in the Bakke case in June 1978, it held that Bakke had been denied his constitutional rights and ordered his admission to the U. C. Davis medical school; however, the Court's decision left unanswered many of the questions raised regarding affirmative action programs and reverse discrimination. While the Court struck down the Davis quota system for admissions, it did not preclude the constitutionality of admissions programs giving special advantages to members of minorities and held that race could still be a factor in choosing applicants. While some felt the Bakke decision left the entire affirmative action program enshrouded in doubt and uncertainty, most lawyers regarded the decision as ambiguous and not the last word in the matter.

Predictions that *Bakke* would become an officially sanctioned signal to turn against blacks appear to have been premature. In 1978 blacks constituted 5.9 percent of freshmen medical students and in 1979 they accounted for 6.1 percent. While institutions have reviewed their affirmative action programs and changes have been made, they have not, for the most part, been abandoned. In April 1979, the Supreme Court declined to review the case of *DiLeo* v *Board of Regents* involving the claims of an Italian-American who contended that he had been discriminated against when the University of Colorado law school refused to consider his application under a special admissions program for blacks, Chicanos, and American Indians. This and other subsequent decisions by the Court seem to indicate that Bakke was not an abandonment of the concept of affirmative action efforts by institutions of higher education, but it is too early to assess the long-range impact on efforts to improve black enrollments in graduate and professional schools. Another factor that has contributed to the difficulty of successful integration of graduate and professional schools has been the elitist nature of these institutions, coupled with the intentional efforts by various professional organizations to limit the supply in their particular fields. These are barriers that must somehow be eliminated if blacks are to achieve not only educational equality, but economic and social equality as well. Policymakers have yet to seize upon the right tools for achieving these goals.

## ECONOMIC AND POLITICAL DISCRIMINATION

While efforts continue to bring greater equality on the educational and political fronts, growing emphasis in this decade has been placed on jobs and economic opportunity. Commenting on the status of blacks, attorney George McAlmon notes, "Poor people in poor surroundings, faced with unemployment do not raise readers, writers, mathematicians, scientists, young people who will excell in higher education, in government, and in business."[36] Gains on the political and educational fronts have not yet brought comparable gains on the economic front. Black educational progress has been substantial, as the median school years completed by blacks aged twenty-five to twenty-nine has risen from 7 in 1940 to 12.4 in 1972. In 1960 only 38 percent of young black males had completed four years of high school; by 1974 this figure was 64 percent. For young black women the figures were 43 percent and 66 percent. On the political front progress has been slower, but in 1978 there were 4503 blacks in elective posts, an increase of 192 (4 percent) over 1977. The southern political process has opened up substantially as 61 percent of these elective officials are in the South, which now has less than 30 percent of the nation's black population. From 1964 to 1976 the percentage of blacks registered to vote in those states covered by the Voting Rights Act increased from 29 to 56. Even with such gains, however, blacks still have a long way to go to attain equality; they still hold only 3 percent of elective offices in the South, where they comprise about 30 percent of the population.

On the economic front, in spite of what Ben Wattenberg has described as a remarkable "catching-up" during the 1960s, blacks are still far short of economic parity.[37] The 1970 census showed that during the 1960s, incomes of white families went up by 69 percent and income for black families went up 99.6 percent; still black incomes were only 64 percent of white incomes in 1970 and have declined

**FIGURE 13.1   Ratio of Median Income for Blacks to Whites**

| Years | Percentage |
|---|---|
| 1950-54 | 55 |
| 1955-59 | 53 |
| 1960-64 | 54 |
| 1965-69 | 61 |
| 1970 | 64 |
| 1971 | 63 |
| 1972 | 62 |
| 1973 | 62 |
| 1974 | 62 |
| 1975 | 62 |
| 1976 | 59 |

since then. (See figure 13.1) Also, while only 7 percent of white families were in poverty, 28 percent of black families were. Though black incomes improved in the 1960s with 30 percent of black families earning $15,000 or more per year and 7 percent earning $25,000 or more, the proportion of black families classified as "middle class" has remained unchanged at about 25 percent since 1972. In 1976, 25 million Americans had incomes below the official poverty level; 11 million (44 percent) of these were ethnic minorities. Thirty-one percent of blacks and 25 percent of Hispanics as compared to only 9 percent of whites were below poverty level. For 1976, 39 percent of black families earned only $1000 to $7000.

A major problem in the economic plight of blacks has been a high rate of chronic unemployment, which has persisted through more than a decade of civil rights enforcement and minority job programs. This persistent unemployment results partially from changes in the nation's economy and population trends. As the number of farms in the South diminished and those remaining became more mechanized, blacks by the millions moved to the cities just at the time that factory and laboring jobs were declining or moving out of the cities. Coupled with union and industry discrimination, this made jobs for blacks doubly difficult to secure. In 1954 the unemployment rates for 16 to 19-year-olds was 16.5 percent for blacks and 12.1 percent for whites. In the 1970s the situation for blacks worsened. In 1978 the unemployment rate for black males age sixteen to nineteen was 36.3 percent compared to 13.9 percent for whites. Among blacks twenty to twenty-four years old the unemployment rate was 20.7 percent compared to 9.5 percent for whites. Overall the unemployment rate for 1978 was about 12 percent for blacks and between 6 and 7 percent for all workers. (See figure 13.2)

Not only was the black unemployment rate more than twice that for whites, there were other inequities as well. In relation to their distribution in the population, blacks hold disproportionate numbers of jobs at the labor and managerial levels. In South Carolina, for example, blacks, who constitute about 30 percent of the state's population, hold 55 percent of laborer positions but only 5 percent of the managerial positions. Though blacks have made substantial gains, they have yet to overcome patterns of subtle but persistent discrimination. By 1975 black males twenty to twenty-four years old were still earning only 85 percent as much as their white counterparts, and 45 to 54-year-old blacks earned only 70 percent as much as their white peers. For black women the picture was better, as they were earning 99 percent as much as white women.

Those black workers with education and skills were able to close the gap on status and salaries in the 1970s. More black males entered professional and managerial positions and received comparable pay to their white counterparts. The more difficult problem facing policymakers is the remaining large black class not equipped to take advantage of this more open system. A rather large group described by Herbert Hill, former labor director of the NAACP, as "a permanent black underclass," remain destined for chronic unemployment, hopelessness, and despair. This is the group that, it is hoped, will benefit most from opening up the educational system and promoting programs of affirmative action.

A Rand Corporation study attributed gains made by blacks in their incomes

**FIGURE 13.2  Who Was Unemployed in 1978**

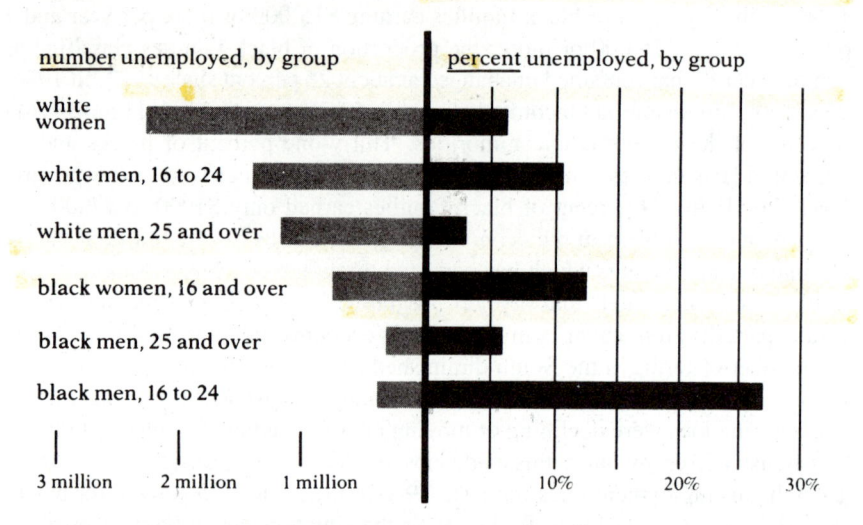

| group | number unemployed | percent unemployed |
|---|---|---|
| white women | ~2.3 million | ~8% |
| white men, 16 to 24 | ~1.3 million | ~11% |
| white men, 25 and over | ~1.5 million | ~3% |
| black women, 16 and over | ~0.7 million | ~14% |
| black men, 25 and over | ~0.3 million | ~7% |
| black men, 16 to 24 | ~0.4 million | ~31% |

Source: Employment and Unemployment During 1978: An Analysis, U.S. Department of Labor, Bureau of Labor Statistics. Reprinted by permission of The Wilson Quarterly.

to improved education. The study, while reporting that many blacks entering the job market were now earning 90–95 percent of what whites with similar qualifications earn, said it could still be thirty to forty years before parity is achieved. It was against this backdrop that many observers viewed the *Bakke* decision with so much misgiving. It was felt that without vigorous programs of affirmative action the move for equal opportunity for minorities would take even longer. More recent decisions have helped to alleviate some of this concern, as the Court has endorsed programs of affirmative action for hiring and promoting members of minorities. Shortly after *Bakke*, the Supreme Court supported AT&T and its federally sanctioned system of "numerical goals" for hiring and promoting women and members of minority groups. In 1979 in a case reminiscent of *Bakke*, an employee of the Kaiser Aluminum and Chemical Corporation of Louisiana sued his employers for reverse discrimination. Brian Weber, a white employee who had been passed over when the company selected blacks with less seniority for special job training, challenged the company's training program on the grounds that it violated the 1964 Civil Rights Act's protection against "discrimination." Again the case raised some difficult and far-reaching issues involving affirmative action and reverse discrimination. Employers were caught in the middle. If they admitted to past discrimination in hiring to justify current policies, they could be sued by minorities; on the other hand they faced suits by whites charging reverse discrimination. While admitting that such programs often operated at the expense of white males, civil rights advocates maintained that the abandonment of such "voluntary" affirmative action programs as Kaiser's would jeopardize efforts of the past fifteen years to improve job opportunities for minorities and women. The Kaiser

Company attorney contended that such suits as Weber's, if upheld by the Supreme Court, would end affirmative action programs. The Court held that Kaiser's program did not constitute reverse discrimination and that such efforts were justified to offset the injustices of past discrimination and attain equality of employment opportunity. The Court further confirmed its support of affirmative action with a decision in July 1980 upholding Congress's action guaranteeing minority businesses 10 percent of federal public works grants.

## CHANGING TRENDS IN CIVIL RIGHTS

As the emphasis has shifted in the civil rights movement, opposition has become more pronounced and internal stresses and strains have developed within the movement. As the movement came to focus more on economic and social discrimination, not just the schools, and as the efforts broadened to address de facto as well as de jure discrimination, more congressional districts and more constituencies outside the South began to feel the impact of desegregation policies. More congressional members began to hear from disgruntled constituents who objected to governmental interference in their lives. This, coupled with reaction to civil rights sit-ins, marches, and demonstrations and the violent racial rioting of the summers in the 1960s, began to cause a backlash. By the time of court-ordered busing and affirmative action, considerable opposition had developed on several fronts to slow down and redirect the efforts of the 1960s.

In the early stages of the black civil rights movement many believed that the elimination of racial barriers would be sufficient to bring equality of opportunity. As the focus shifted from constitutional rights to economic and social issues, internal cracks began to develop, however, because these economic and social issues affect blacks in different ways. On these issues the national black elite frequently do not reflect the views of the rank-and-file black citizens. On some issues blacks may be quite fragmented, and there are really very few issues on which a majority of whites line up on one side and a majority of blacks on the other. The deeper questions raised in the last decade by the issues of social and economic equality, affirmative action, and busing have tended to break down the earlier moral, political, and ideological consensus that led to much of the government's civil rights policy. It is not so much that the morality of the cause has gone away, but that the morality of the issue has come to be overshadowed by considerations of more immediate self-interest as civil rights policies through such practices as busing and affirmative action have come to affect more people directly. The unity of the 1960s movement has been replaced to a marked degree by divisiveness and uncertainty among both the civil rights groups themselves and their allies. Black groups are torn over the issue of black separatism, and allies such as labor have been opposed to affirmative action. Blacks themselves appear uncertain about recent governmental policies: polls show a majority of blacks opposed to busing and preferential treatment in hiring and college admissions. This is not so much uncertainty about objectives as it is about the methods of achieving racial equality.

In the last decade the civil rights movement has also become more fragmented in another way. The black movement of the 1960s did much to make other ethnic groups aware of their failure to share fully in the privileges and advantages of American society. This affected the black movement in two ways: some of these groups came to perceive affirmative action for blacks as one more obstacle in their own path to social, political, and economic equality; and as they began to pressure the government on their behalf it meant the policymakers had to respond to a broader constituency of competing elements. As the movement broadened to include, along with the blacks, Mexican-Americans, Spanish-Americans, Chinese-Americans, American Indians, women, and the young, the Office of Civil Rights, the Equal Employment Opportunity Commission, and other federal policymakers have had to direct more effort and attention to the rights of other minority groups.

## Women's Rights

One of the strongest movements among these other groups has been that of equal rights for women. Growing out of the so-called "Sexual Revolution" of the 1960s and '70s was a vigorous movement to eliminate discrimination on the basis of sex.

In 1934 Attorney General Homer Cummings issued an order giving federal agencies the right to limit certain federal jobs to one sex or the other. However, Titles 5 and 42 of the U. S. Code, the Fair Labor Standards Act of 1938, and Executive Orders 11498 and 11521 forbid discrimination on the basis of sex in federal employment. In July 1962, President Kennedy issued a memorandum barring discrimination against women in the federal service. The Equal Pay Act of 1963, Title VII of the 1964 Civil Rights Act, and Title IX of the 1972 Educational Act Amendments also make discrimination on the basis of sex illegal. The Supreme Court in 1971 in *Reed* v *Reed* confirmed that the constitutional guarantee of "equal protection of the law" prohibited discrimination on the basis of sex.[38]

In spite of these numerous legal efforts to assure equality for women, evidence of sex discrimination remained widespread. In 1969 women constituted only one-fourteenth of law school enrollments, and enrollments in other professions such as medicine and engineering were also disproportionately low. On the other hand, 60 percent of all working women were clerks, salespersons, waitresses, or hairdressers. The New York-based Council on Interracial Books for Children concluded in a 1978 study that white males still dominated business, government, the news media, education, and health institutions.[39] Working women earned only 73 percent as much as males, with a female college graduate averaging $10,861 to the male counterpart's $17,891. Even in the federal government, women professionals lagged behind their male counterparts. Of 1700 governmental microbiologists about one-third are women. The average male's salary in 1977 was $23,260 while his female colleagues averaged $18,550. Only a very few women make it to the top of their fields. In the media industry, where women hold 25-35 percent of all jobs, only 5 percent are in policymaking positions. Women account for only 2.3 percent of executives earning $25,000 or more annually; and though they constitute a majority in the population, fewer than 10 percent of elected officials are female. Like blacks, women also suffer higher unemployment rates than white males. (See figure 13.2) The unemployment rate for professionally trained women is two to five times higher than for men in the same fields with the same level of training.

It is this picture that has led to a strong push for vigorous affirmative action efforts and a constitutional amendment guaranteeing equal rights for women. Both of these issues have touched off considerable debate and policy disputes. In 1972 Congress adopted and sent to the states a proposed constitutional amendment stating that, "Equality of rights under the law shall not be denied or abridged by the United States or by any state on account of sex." ERA, as the proposed amendment came to be known, touched off a prolonged and heated debate in state legislatures as vigorous lobbying efforts were mounted by both proponents and opponents. Many opponents contended that such an amendment was unnecessary in light of all the legislation already on the books. In a statement to the North Carolina General Assembly on January 24, 1977, former U. S. Senator Sam Ervin said, "I do affirm... with absolute conviction that using the blunderbuss Equal Rights Amendment to nullify any such remaining laws would be even more foolish than exploding an atomic bomb to eradicate a few mice." On the other hand, proponents felt the extra efforts through ERA and affirmative action were necessary to eradicate the last vestiges of discrimination and achieve total equality. Dr. Robert B. Moore, director of the resource center on the Council of Interracial Books for Children, says his group's 1978 study provides "strong evidence of the need for decisive affirmative-action programs to alleviate the injustice suffered by those who happen to be born female or dark-skinned in the United States."[40]

After an initial flurry of ratifications, the Equal Rights Amendment has encountered stiff opposition in a number of state legislatures. Ratification by thirty-eight states is required, and after Indiana's approval as the thirty-fifth state in January 1977, the proposal reached a stalemate. With three more ratifications needed, the proponents were able to get Congress in October 1978 to extend the ratification deadline to June 30, 1982. However, proponents have been less successful in the state legislatures, suffering setbacks in Nevada and Florida shortly after Congress's extension of the deadline. In 1978 and 1979 ERA resolutions were defeated in nine states; and in 1979, despite efforts by the White House and the governor, the Florida legislature rejected ERA for the fourth time. Rejection by the Illinois legislature in 1978 was accompanied by allegations of attempted bribery by some women's group lobbyists, a further blow to the ratification effort. The issue has been further clouded by the action of five state legislatures (South Dakota, Kentucky, Tennessee, Idaho, and Nebraska) rescinding their earlier ratifications. Whether such changes of heart are legal has not been determined to date.

Though ERA ratifications have ground to a standstill, progress has been made on other fronts. While total equality is yet to be achieved, substantial gains have been made in employment, pay, availability of credit, and professional school admissions. (See figure 13.3) In 1970 there were only 636,000 women in the U. S. workforce; by 1978 the number had reached 38.6 million. In 1978 when the workforce grew by 3 million, 1.9 million of these newly employed were women. As their numbers increase, salaries, promotions, and status are also

**FIGURE 13.3  Graduate School Enrollments**

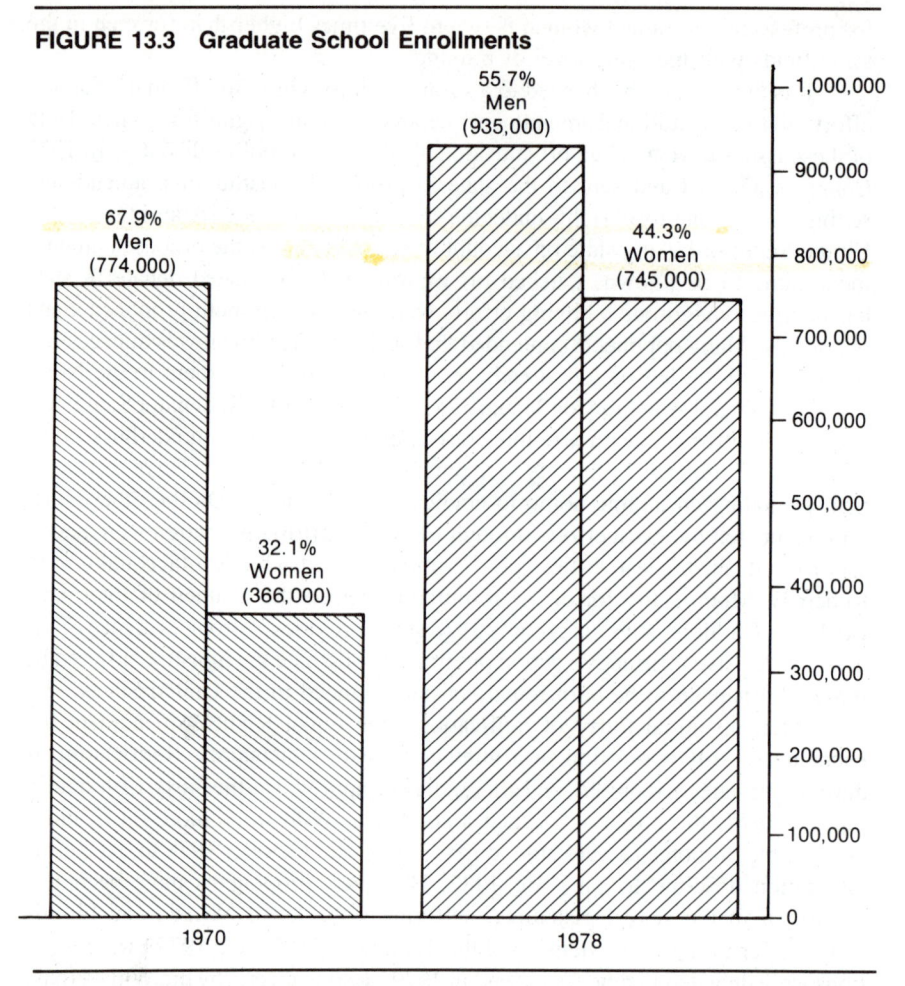

1970:
- 67.9% Men (774,000)
- 32.1% Women (366,000)

1978:
- 55.7% Men (935,000)
- 44.3% Women (745,000)

improving, but more slowly. A 1979 study by the Office of Personnel Management showed women and minorities were making progress in federal employment. They gained more higher-paying professional and technical jobs; and for 1977-78, one of five females was promoted while the ratio for males was one in eight. In 1969 women comprised only one-fourteenth of law school enrollments; by 1975 this figure was up to one-fourth. While gains in other professions have been slower, they also have shown improvement. While there was progress on equal rights, there were also disappointments. The 1978 reforms of the Civil Service did not eliminate the veterans preference clause, which discriminates against women, and in a court challenge the Massachusetts veterans preference law was held by the Supreme Court not to constitute sex discrimination because it favored all veterans regardless of sex. Forty-six states have similar laws. Congress withheld medicaid funds for abortions, making this a major losing cause for the women's movement.

While President Carter made a conscious effort to include women among his cabinet and judicial appointments, his administration encountered strong criticism on occasion. In April 1977, the president established a forty-member National Advisory Committee for Women and named outspoken former New York Congresswoman Bella Abzug as chairman. When Abzug was dismissed in January 1979, half the members of the committee resigned in protest. The women's movement still attracts attention and NOW (National Organization for Women) has grown to over 100,000 members since its 1978 Houston convention, which attracted national media coverage.

The debate over equal rights for women was given a sort of reverse twist early in 1980 when President Carter requested reinstatement of registration for the military draft. Carter's indication that females as well as males should be required to register touched off a debate on whether females should be drafted for combat duty. Congressional approval for the reinstitution of the draft registration system in 1980 did not include females.

As the equal rights picture becomes more complicated by the entry into the picture of more aliens, more blacks, more women and other minority elements, the fair distribution of rights and opportunities becomes more and more difficult for policymakers.

## CONCLUSION

With increased competition for rights and opportunities, the political pressures frequently become intense. As various groups seek to enhance their economic, political, and social status, even a matter such as the U. S. census may become a political issue. When the 1980 census survey included a number of items dealing with minorities, some sources charged that several items were designed mainly to enhance the political power of minority leaders. Mary Zitter, chief of the Census Bureau's Population Division, says the bureau is only "addressing legislative intent and the needs of government. . . . We are trying to balance the needs of many different interests."[44] No doubt some ethnic groups feel their political influence will be enhanced if they can point to census data when lobbying legislators. Vilma Martinez, head of the Mexican-American Legal Defense and Educational Fund, stated: "We are trying to get our just share of political influence and federal funds. There's nothing sinister about it."[42]

This dispute over the census illustrates a key point in the politics of the distribution of civil and constitutional rights. A major portion of minority group members remain among the poor and propertyless, and consequently, the least influential politically. In the black movement, for example, as things now stand, the interests and aspirations of the working and primarily middle-class blacks go largely unrepresented. What effect should limited resources have on the allocation of constitutional rights? Currently the Supreme Court has held that it is not a denial of equal protection of the law to deny medical benefits to indigent women for abortions. In *Gideon* v *Wainwright* the Supreme Court held that indigents who could not hire legal counsel for themselves would have it provided. This right has not been extended to many other areas, however. Does our system provide equal rights and protection only for those who can afford to pay? If so, how can those who lack political power and economic resources be assured the full exercise of their rights?

To a certain extent much of the move toward equality of opportunity over the last two decades has been illusory. While in many areas the legal barriers have been dismantled, other factors, much more diffficult to pinpoint and overcome, have remained. Though the *Brown* decision declared separate but equal school facilities unconstitutional, it has meant little to the masses of poor blacks remaining locked in a cycle of poverty and deprivation making it impossible to escape from their urban ghettos. Removal of the legal barriers alone does not address the roots of the minority discrimination problem. As one black leader put it, "What good is a seat at the front of the bus if you don't have the money for the fare?" The Reverend Jesse Jackson, founder of the Push to Excel movement, observes, "The door of opportunity is open for our people, but they are too drunk, too unconscious to walk through the door."[43]

Governmental policies thus far have not reached the real problem underlying minority discrimination. Numerous executive orders, several acts of Congress, and scores of court decisions have helped thousands of minority citizens, but thus far millions have been left out. As Lady Birk, Britain's under-secretary of state for environment, said, "Today's discrimination may be more polite than it was but it is still a barrier to full equality." In 1978 both the New York and Chicago Urban Leagues reported deterioration in black/white relations. The *New York Times*, in an analysis of race relations since the 1968 Kerner Report, said racial polarization still existed and "chances of healing the rift may be more dismal today than they were ten years ago."

In 1963 in a speech at the Lincoln Memorial to a group of civil rights marchers, Martin Luther King said:

> I have a dream that one day this nation will rise up and live out the true meaning of its creed: "We hold these truths to be self-evident, that all men are created equal."...I have a dream that my four little children will one day live in a nation where they will not be judged by the color of their skin but by the content of their character.[45]

In the late sixties and seventies the civil rights movement began to change from the largely racial crusade of the fifties and early sixties to a broader movement for equality for not only blacks, but women, Puerto Ricans, Chicanos, Indians, and other minorities. This broadened base, coupled with the advent of affirmative action programs, began to create more of a backlash as other groups in society came to see these minority demands as a challenge to their own political, social and economic positions. In her book *The Greek Way*, Edith Hamilton wrote, "It is not men's greed, nor their ambition, nor yet their machines; it is not even the removal of their ancient landmarks, that is filling our present world with turmoil and dissention, but our new vision of the individual's claim against the majority's claim."[46] A major issue in the government's effort to eliminate discrimination and provide equal rights for all has become the age-old question of majoirty rule versus minority rights. As special treatment is accorded minority elements to compensate for past injustices, the issues of reverse discrimination and minority rule are raised. Can our democratic system provide the means for eradicating discrimination and injustice while at the same time maintaining the basic concepts upon which our democracy is based? On the other hand, can our system really be characterized as truly democratic unless such inequities are eliminated? The future of our government and society rests heavily on the resolution of these issues because as long as substantial segments of our population are denied equal rights under the law, there is potential for instability and disruption of the democratic process.

## Points to Ponder

Can racial balance in the schools be achieved and individuals retain the freedom to live where they choose?

Should minority rights be honored regardless of their implications for other social values?

If policies such as busing and affirmative action cause changes in residential and business location patterns, are they really solving problems of discrimination?

Is reverse discrimination justified in redressing a history of social injustice?

Do voluntary affirmative action programs that set quotas based on race or sex violate constitutional guarantees of equal protection of the law?

## Notes

1. See Paul Seabury, "Advancement by Group Affiliation," *The Alternative; An American Spectator* (June/July 1976).
2. *Dred Scott v Sanford*, 19 Howard 393 (1857).
3. *Slaughterhouse Cases*, 16 Wallace 36 (1873).
4. *Civil Rights Cases*, 109 U.S. 3 (1883).
5. *Plessy v Ferguson*, 163 U.S. 537 (1896).
6. *Mitchell v U.S.*, 313 U.S. 80 (1941).
7. *Morgan v Virginia*. 328 U.S. 373 (1946); *Henderson v U.S.*, 339 U.S. 816 (1950).
8. *Missouri ex rel Gaines v Canada*, 305 U.S. 337 (1938).
9. *Sweatt v Painter*, 339 U.S. 629 (1949); *McLaurin v Oklahoma State Regents*, 339 U.S. 637 (1950).
10. Grandfather clauses were an early devise used by the states to block Negro voting by disqualifying those who were not descendants of qualified voters. Since most blacks were former slaves or descendants of slaves who had been ineligible to vote, they were disqualified under these provisions.
11. *Guinn v U.S.*, 238 U.S. 347 (1915).
12. *Smith v Allright*, 321 U.S. 649 (1944).
13. *U.S. v Classic*, 313 U.S. 299 (1941).
14. *Brown v Board of Education of Topeka*, 347 U.S. 483 (1954) was a high-water mark in the movement for equal rights. The Supreme Court ruled that "separate but equal" schools were "inherently unequal" and ordered desegregation of all public schools. This decision is explored more fully under education later in the chapter.
15. Lyndon Johnson, Message to Congress, 1968, as quoted in *Congress and the Nation*, vol. III, p. 345.

16. Caspar Weinberger as quoted in *Congress and the Nation*, vol. IV, p. 661.
17. Report of the President's National Advisory Commission on Civil Disorders, Washington, D.C., 1968.
18. *Aaron* v *Cooper*, 358 U.S. 1 (1958).
19. *Watson* v *City of Memphis*, 373 U.S. 526 (1962).
20. *Griffin* v *Prince Edward County School Board*, 377 U.S. 218 (1964).
21. *Swann* v *Charlotte-Mecklenburg Board of Education*, 402 U.S. 1 (1971).
22. "Busing: An UnAmerican Amendment," Louisville, Ky. *Courier- Journal* (July 21, 1979).
23. See David K. Cohen, Thomas F. Pettigrew and Robert S. Riley, "Race and the Outcomes of Schooling," in Frederick Mosteller and Daniel Moynihan, eds., *On Equality of Educational Opportunity*. New York: Random House, 1972, pp. 351-52.
24. See Lorenzo Middleton, "The Effects of School Desegregation: The Debate Goes On," and "Coleman's New Study Could Settle Some Questions," *The Chronicle of Higher Education* (November 6, 1978), pp. 1, 4-5.
25. Lino A. Graglia, *The Supreme Court's Busing Decisions: A Study of Government by the Judiciary*, (Los Angeles: International Institute for Economic Research, 1979).
26. *Keyes* v *Denver School District No. 1*, 413 U.S. 189 (1973).
27. *Austin Independent School District* v *U.S.*, 429 U.S. 990 (1976).
28. Meyer Weinberg, *A Chance to Learn: The History of Race and Education in the United States* (New York: Cambridge University Press, 1977).
29. Joseph Califano in interview with the *New York Times*, March 18, 1977.
30. John H. Ely as quoted in Kenneth Tollett, "What Led to Bakke?" *The Center Magazine* (January/Feburary 1978), p. 9.
31. As quoted by the *New York Times*, November 24, 1977.
32. *DeFunis* v *Odegaard*, 416 U.S. 312, 350 (1974).
33. University of California Bakke brief as quoted by Alan Sindler in *Bakke, DeFunis and Minority Admissions* (New York: Longman, 1978), p. 25.
34. Sup. 132 California Reporter 680 (1976).
35. *Change* (October 1977), editorial, p. 18.
36. George A. McAlmon, "A Critical Look at Affirmative Action," *The Center Magazine* (March/April 1978), pp. 43-47.
37. Ben Wattenberg, *The Real America* (New York: Doubleday, 1974).
38. *Reed* v *Reed*, 404 U.S. 71 (1971).
39. Richard T. Pienciak, "Sexual and racial discrimination is prevalent in business, study finds," Louisville, Ky. *Courier-Journal* (January 21, 1979), © 1979 Associated Press. Reprinted with permission.
40. *Ibid*.
41. Robert Reinhold, "Will racial questions clutter the census?" Louisville, Ky. *Courier-Journal* (May 21, 1978), New York Times News Service Story, © 1978 New York Times Company. Reprinted with permission.
42. *Ibid*.
43. Letter from Push to Excel organization, April 1978.
44. As quoted by Louis H. Bolce III and Susan H. Gray, "Blacks, Whites, and 'race politics'," *The Public Interest*, no. 54, (Winter 1979), p. 61.
45. Martin Luther King, speech at Lincoln Memorial in 1963 as quoted in *Congress and the Nation*, p. 356.
46. Edith Hamilton, *The Greek Way* (New York: Norton, 1958), p. 204.

## Suggestions for Further Reading

AMUNDSEN, KIRSTEN. *A New Look at the Silenced Majority: Women and American Democracy.* Englewood Cliffs, N.J.: Prentice-Hall, 1977.
BOLES, JANET K. *The Politics of the Equal Rights Amendment.* New York: Longman, 1979.
BULLOCK, CHARLES and RODGERS, HARRELL. *Racial Equality in America.* Pacific Palisades, Calif.: Goodyear, 1975.
CHAFE, WILLIAM H. *Women and Equality: Changing Patterns in American Culture.* New York: Oxford University Press, 1977.
CLARK, KENNETH B. *Dark Ghetto.* New York: Harper & Row, 1965.
COHEN, MARSHALL, et al. *Equality and Preferential Treatment.* Princeton, N.J.: Princeton University Press, 1977.
CONGRESSIONAL QUARTERLY. *The Women's Movement: Achievements and Effects.* Washington, D.C.: Congressional Quarterly, 1977.
DORN, EDWIN. *Rules and Racial Equality.* New Haven, Conn.: Yale University Press, 1979.
DYE, THOMAS. *The Politics of Equality.* New York: Bobbs-Merrill, 1971.
FISS, OWEN M. *The Civil Rights Injunction.* Bloomington, Ind.: Indiana University Press, 1978.
FREEMAN, JO. *The Politics of Women's Liberation.* New York: David McKay, 1975.
GARROW, DAVID. *Protest at Selma: Martin Luther King, Jr. and the Voting Rights Act of 1965.* New Haven, Conn.: Yale University Press, 1978.
GLAZER, NATHAN. *Affirmative Discrimination: Ethnic Inequality and Public Policy.* New York: Basic Books, 1979.
GOLDMAN, ALAN. *Justice and Reverse Discrimination.* Princeton, N.J.: Princeton University Press, 1979.
HENTOFF, NAT. *The New Equality.* New York: The Viking Press, 1964.
HOLE, JUDITH and LEVINE, ELLEN. *Rebirth of Feminism.* New York: Quadrangle, 1971.
JENCKS, CHRISTOPHER. *Who Gets Ahead?* New York: Basic Books, 1979.
JONES, LEON. *From Brown to Boston: Desegregation in Education.* Metuchen, N.J.: Scarecrow Press, 1979.
KEECH, WILLIAM. *The Impact of Negro Voting.* Chicago: Rand McNally, 1968.
MEIER, AUGUST and RUDWICK, ELLIOT. *Black Protest in the Sixties.* Chicago: Quadrangle, 1970.
MELTZER, BERNARD. "The Weber Case: Double Talk and Double Standards," *Regulation* (September/October 1979), pp. 34–43.
ORFIELD, GARY and TAYLOR, WILLIAM. *Racial Segregation: Two Policy Views.* Naugatuck, Conn.: Ford Foundation, 1979.
POLE, J. R. *The Pursuit of Equality in American History.* Berkeley: University of California Press, 1978.
RAINWATER, LEE, ed. *Social Problems and Public Policy: Inequality and Justice.* Chicago: Aldine-Atherton, 1974.
RATNER, RONNIE S. *Equal Employment Policy for Women.* Philadelphia: Temple University Press, 1979.
SINDLER, ALLAN P. *Bakke, DeFunis and Minority Admissions: The Quest for Equal Opportunity.* New York: Longman, 1978.
SOWELL, THOMAS."Affirmative Action Reconsidered," *The Public Interest* (Winter 1976).
URBAN INSTITUTE. *The Subtle Revolution: Women at Work.* Washington, D.C.: National Urban Institute, 1979.
WALTON, HANES, Jr. *Black Politics.* Philadelphia: Lippincott, 1972.
WERTHEIMER, BARBARA. *We Were There: The Story of Working Women in America.* New York: Pantheon, 1977.
WILKINSON, J. H. *From Brown to Bakke: The Supreme Court and School Integration, 1954-1978.* New York: Oxford University Press, 1979.

# 14

# Government and Human Services

This chapter addresses one of the most controversial and widely discussed areas of public policy—that broad category of governmental programs and activities most frequently referred to as "welfare." I have not used the term "welfare" in the chapter title because the term has taken on so many connotations that one must almost define it each time it is used. Also the term has become somewhat inappropriate because while many of the programs in this area of policy, in concept at least, have a positive thrust socially, the term "welfare" holds a negative connotation for many readers. The idea of extensive governmental involvement in efforts to provide economic security, medical care, housing, and other personal benefits is still viewed by many as going counter to the traditional American values of private initiative and rugged individualism. In the minds of many, such benefits provided by the government cannot help but dampen individual initiative to work and encourage the growth of a parasitic class supported by governmental programs.

Because of strong traditional attitudes against governmental programs in the human services field, federal involvement in this area of policy is a relatively recent development. Despite references in the Constitution's preamble and in Article I, Section 8 to the government's "promotion" or "providing for" the "general welfare," the general feeling among the nation's early leaders was that such charges did not extend to governmental efforts to aid individuals. Writing in *The Federalist*, Madison assured his readers that providing for the general welfare did not extend to providing for individual citizens.[1] Early presidents vetoed numerous bills because they felt the measures provided only localized or individual benefits rather than national benefits. Grover Cleveland, who during his two terms as president vetoed numerous veterans' pension bills, lamented, "The unhappy decadence among our people of genuine love and affection for our Government as the embodiment of the highest and best aspirations of humanity, and not as a giver of gifts."[2] Three decades later, reflecting the growing concern of some over the expanding federal role, Warren G. Harding observed, "Just government is merely the guarantee to the people of the right and opportunity to support themselves. The one outstanding danger of today is the tendency to turn to Washington for the things which are the tasks or the duties of the forty-eight commonwealths."[3] Harding's words pretty well reflect the prevailing attitude of the early decades of the twentieth century. While there was a growing acceptance in the twentieth century of governmental efforts in certain areas, such as the promotion of the health, welfare, and growth of children, it was still felt that most programs of this type were the responsibility under the Tenth Amendment of state and local governments.

In 1921, Congress approved the Sheppard-Towner Act providing federal grants for maternal and child welfare and hygiene, but the program was allowed to lapse in 1929. Other early programs provided for health care and other benefits for rather narrow groups considered to be wards of the government such as Indians, institutional inmates, etc. However, prior to 1930, general programs for protecting against old age, unemployment, poor health, and other economic hardships were considered primarily the function of the individual, the family, the state, or local and private charitable institutions. Federal involvement in such programs was very limited. For the bulk of the population, there were no programs.

Nevertheless, an optimistic Herbert Hoover assured the nation in 1928, "Given a chance to go forward with the policies of the last eight years, we shall soon with the help of God be within sight of the day when poverty will be banished from this nation." Instead, the financial crash of 1929 ushered in the worst depression the nation had ever experienced. Millions of Americans were without jobs and had no choice but to accept welfare benefits. Under the burden of the Great Depression, state and local programs broke down, and attitudes toward federal involvement in economic assistance programs underwent a drastic change. Movements such as Francis E. Townsend's Old Age Revolving Pension, Huey P. Long's Share-the-Wealth, and Father Charles E. Coughlin's National Union for Social Justice gained considerable strength during the 1930s. Townsend's plan called for payments of $200 per month to persons sixty years of age or older, to be financed by a national tax of 2 percent levied on all commercial transactions. Though the plan was impracticable, it generated considerable public appeal, with Townsend Clubs appearing across the country, and created an expectation on the part of older Americans for some form of federal help. Senator Long's proposal was that the federal government make "Every Man a King" by guaranteeing to every family a minimum annual incoem of $5000. Coughlin, who supported a program of social reform, was less specific on details but attracted a national audience with his radio broadcasts. Though such movements never united under a single, continuous leadership, they gained considerable support and added

### Significant Health and Welfare Statutes

**Social Security Act of 1935.** The most important piece of social legislation in U.S. history, this act laid the cornerstone for a variety of social service programs.

**Social Security Act Amendments of 1939.** Expanded the social security program to include dependents and survivors.

**Public Health Service Act of 1944.** Consolidated some of the federal programs in the health field and expanded the role and support for the Public Health Service.

**Hill-Burton Act of 1946.** Provided federal grants for hospital construction.

**Research Institutes Act of 1950.** Expanded federal research activities in the health field by paving the way for research institutes such as the Cancer Institute, Heart Institute, Mental Health Institute, and Dental Institute.

**Omnibus Social Security Amendments of 1956.** Added benefits for the permanently and totally disabled to the social security program.

**Health Research Facilities Act of 1956.** Provided federal funds for additional research facilities in the health field.

**Kerr-Mills Act of 1960.** Provided for federal grants to the states to help fund programs of medical assistance to the aged who do not qualify for such aid under the old-age assistance program.

**Social Security Act Amendments of 1965.** Provided for medicare medical care for those over sixty-five or disabled, under the social security program.

**Food Stamp Act of 1961.** Established the program enabling needy persons to purchase food stamps at reduced rates to supplement their food purchasing power.

**Social Security Act Amendments of 1974.** Provided for the program of Supplemental Security Income (SSI) under social security.

momentum to the movement toward more federal involvement in social assistance programs.

## SOCIAL SECURITY

In 1935, under the impact of the Great Depression, with its high unemployment and widespread privation and growing public support for assistance programs such as the Townsend plan, Congress launched the federal government on its biggest social experiment with the passage of the Social Security Act. Presented by President Roosevelt as a plan to protect citizens against those "misfortunes which cannot be wholly eliminated in this man-made world of ours," the Social Security

> **Important Agencies and Departments**
>
> **Department of Health and Human Services.** Successor to the Department of Health, Education and Welfare, this department has responsibility for a variety of social service programs and the largest budget in government.
>
> **Social Security Administration.** Created by the Social Security Act of 1935, the agency supervises the administration of grants-in-aid to the states for old-age assistance, aid to the blind, aid to dependent children, and aid to the disabled.
>
> **National Institutes of Health (NIH).** The National Institutes are responsible for conducting research programs in the health field.
>
> **Public Health Service.** The Public Health Service conducts research in the causes and cures of disease and seeks to prevent the spread of communicable diseases.

Act was one of the most significant innovations among the New Deal programs. While the United States lagged behind other industrial nations in adopting a general social security system — twenty-two European and six non-European nations already had such systems—enactment of this legislation marked a radical break with traditional American concepts in the area of social legislation. This act changed both the traditional concept of individual economic responsibility and the existing pattern of federal-state relationships in the welfare field. The adoption of the Social Security Act marked the federal government's assumption of responsibility for activities traditionally reserved to the states, local governments, and the family. The income replacement programs of social security provided the federal government a mechanism for insuring large numbers of American citizens against some of the major economic hardships of life. The programs also had as a secondary objective the stabilization of the economy through maintenance of the purchasing power of various groups in good and bad times economically.

The initial program adopted in 1935 was designed to provide a degree of economic security for those who suffered loss of income as a result of old age, blindness, unemployment, or loss of parental support. The heart of the act was five ''income replacement'' programs: old-age insurance, old-age assistance, aid to the blind, aid to dependent children, and unemployment insurance. The most significant program under the original Social Security Act was the old-age insurance plan, which called for a national retirement insurance program financed through a payroll tax paid by both employer and employee. Income from the payroll tax, originally set at 1 percent on the first $3000 earned, went into a specially ear-marked fund in the treasury. Compulsory for a majority of the nation's working population, the insurance plan made eligibility for benefits a matter of right, not need.

With the exception of the old-age retirement insurance program, which was administered directly by the federal government, the Social Security Act left the states with wide latitude to shape public assistance programs to suit their own desires. Participation in the old-age assistance, aid to the blind, and aid to dependent children programs was not compulsory and the states were given broad discretion in determining eligibility standards, benefit schedules, costs, etc. To participate, the states were required to submit a plan to the appropriate federal agency establishing their eligibility for federal grant funds by meeting certain minimum standards.

### Old Age Assistance

This portion of the act provided for matching federal grants to the states to help them support programs providing assistance for the indigent over age sixty-five. Unlike the insurance program, this was basically a charity program with the basis for assistance being *need* determined by the states through a "means" test. Eligibility thus varies from state to state as do benefits. Though states were not required to participate in this part of the program, all states had adopted old age assistance programs by 1938.

### Aid To The Blind

This program for providing income to those unable to support themselves and their families because of blindness works in essentially the same way as the old age assistance program.

### Aid For Dependent Children (AFDC)

This program also is funded through federal grants for needy children deprived of normal parental support as a result of the death, incapacity, or absence from the home of a parent or parents. While in recent years this program has come under considerable discussion because of a growing concern with support for the children of unwed mothers, the program is one most members of Congress find it difficult not to support. After all, its supporters point out, the children's plight is not their fault.

### Unemployment Insurance

Under this provision of the Social Security Act no program was really established directly; however, the states were induced to set up a system of unemployment compensation through a tax-offset provision. Employers were assessed a 3 percent payroll tax to cover unemployment benefits but receive credit for most of this if their states already had an unemployment insurance program in which the employer participated. By 1939 all states had established such programs, most of them being financed through state payroll taxes on employers.

Following the adoption of the original legislation, the federal social security programs have undergone tremendous change and have been a continuing issue for policy disagreement and debate. When the social insurance program went into effect in 1937, the payroll tax was 1 percent for both employer and employee and was scheduled to rise in steps to 3 percent in 1949. However, in spite of expanded coverage and increased benefits the tax rate was still only 1.5 percent in 1950. In 1952 Congress increased benefits by 14 percent and again in 1969 by 15 percent. For several years Congress was able to increase benefits and finance them from rising earnings and extensions in coverage, since many workers were not covered under the original plan. By the 1970s, however, approximately 90 percent of the workforce was covered and 93 percent of the nation's population over age sixty-five was drawing benefits. Congress then had to come to grips with the necessity for raising both the rate and the salary base for the payroll tax. In January 1980 the rate was raised from 6.13 percent for employers and employees to 6.65 percent. In 1986 the rate is scheduled to reach 7.15 percent and in 1990 will go to 7.65 percent. The salary base, which started at $3000 in 1935 is currently $29,700 and in 1982 will rise to $31,800.

Not only have the costs of the program risen as a result of increased benefits, but many other programs have been added through the years. Because of its popularity and growing political support, social security was seized as a means of getting other assistance programs passed. In 1939 the program was expanded to provide benefits for dependents and survivors, and in 1956 a disability benefits program was added. In 1965 medicare was enacted and made a part of the social security program. In 1974 the supplemental security income (SSI) program was added to provide income assistance for the aged poor. In 1950 the proram was opened to participation by self-employed persons and in 1954 to farmers. By 1961 about nine-tenths of the nation's workforce was covered by social security. (See Figure 14.1 for a summary of social security benefits.)

In the 1970s the social insurance program began to encounter severe criticism as it suffered fiscal difficulties stemming from significant demographic changes and somewhat irresponsible, or at least short-sighted, past decisions. The retirement insurance program under social security provided that a worker who had paid payroll taxes long enough to qualify, became eligible for a monthly pension based on his contributions during the years prior to retirement. Workers could retire at age sixty-five—or sixty-two with reduced benefits—and draw the pension for the rest of their lives. In 1940 there were nine active workers for every retired person, and in 1950 there were fourteen taxpayers for every beneficiary; however, by 1970 there were only four active contributors for each beneficiary. In 1940 only 17 percent of married women held jobs, in 1977 the figure was 47 percent and growing. Currently about 24 million or 11 percent of all Americans are over sixty-five, but HHS calculates that by the year 2030 there will be 55 million senior citizens or about 18 percent of the population. And, while living longer, Americans are retiring earlier. In 1979 only one male in five who was over sixty-five remained in the workforce, whereas twenty years earlier 37 percent remained beyond age sixty-five. More and more workers have been taking early retirement

### FIGURE 14.1 Social Security Benefits, 1950-1976

| Beneficiary or benefit | 1950 | 1960 | 1965 | 1970 | 1974 | 1975 | 1976 |
|---|---|---|---|---|---|---|---|
| Number of beneficiaries (millions)[1] | | | | | | | |
| Total | 3.5 | 14.8 | 20.9 | 26.2 | 30.9 | 31.9 | 33.0 |
| Retired workers, dependents and survivors | 3.5 | 14.2 | 19.1 | 23.6 | 26.9 | 27.6 | 28.1 |
| Retired workers only | 1.8 | 8.1 | 11.1 | 13.3 | 16.0 | 16.5 | 17.1 |
| Disabled workers and dependents | — | .7 | 1.7 | 2.7 | 3.9 | 4.3 | 4.6 |
| Annual cash benefits (billions of dollars) | 1.0 | 11.3 | 18.3 | 31.9 | 58.5 | 67.1 | 75.6 |
| Average monthly benefits (dollars) | | | | | | | |
| All retired workers[1] | 44 | 74 | 84 | 118 | 188 | 206 | 221[3] |
| Maximum to men retiring at age 65[2] | 45 | 119 | 132 | 190 | 305[3] | 342[3] | 413[3] |
| Maximum to women retiring at age 65[2] | 45 | 119 | 136 | 196 | 316[3] | 360[3] | 422[3] |
| Minimum to persons retiring at age 65[2] | 10 | 33 | 44 | 64 | 94[3] | 101[3] | 108[3] |

1. As of December of each year.
2. Assumes retirement at beginning of year.
3. As of June.

Source: Department of Health, Education and Welfare (now Health and Human Services). Reprinted by permission from Congressional Quarterly, Inc.

---

at age sixty-two under social security. This means that by year 2030 there will probably be only three active workers for every retired worker. Already in 1978 $112 billion or approximately 24 percent of the federal budget went to the elderly which, according to then HEW Secretary Joseph Califano, made payments to the elderly "the largest income redistribution in the history of this country."

These changes in population and retirement patterns, coupled with repeated expansions in programs, have produced economic strains in the social security system. In 1945 the fund paid out only $267 million in benefits, while in 1979 $101 billion was paid to 35 million Americans. Until the last decade, social security had been an outstanding success story, but the steadily rising costs and substantial increases in benefits without accompanying expansion in either the revenue base or the contribution rates produced difficulties in the mid-1970s. In 1975 social security had a 1.5 billion dollar deficit and continued to show a deficit for the next four years. In 1977 Congress adopted amendments raising social security taxes and the salary base on which they were collected. These increases, it was felt, would put the system on a sound financial footing again. Less than two years after this action, however, Alice Rivlin, director of the Congressional Budget Office, was again warning that the old-age trust fund was in trouble. She said that because inflation and cost-of-living increases had driven benefits up faster than expected, "There could be a significant deterioration in the financial soundness of the social security system during the next five years."

The financial difficulties of the social security system have resulted in extensive discussion of the program and some erosion of political support. Passage of the 1977 amendments designed to shore up the system was not a foregone conclusion as votes are becoming harder to get in the Congress after decades of

'DO YOU HAVE MEDICARE?'

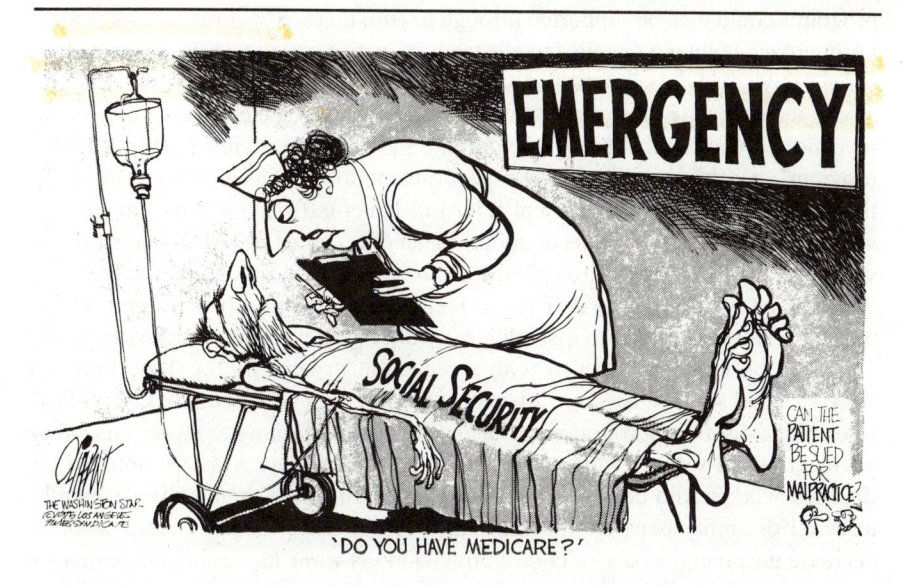

Copyright, 1975, Washington Star. Reprinted with permission of Universal Press Syndicate. All rights reserved.

strong bipartisan support. There is a growing feeling that the system needs careful scrutiny and debate with attention to some adaptations that could help it meet future needs on a sounder financial base. In 1978 the *New York Times* criticized social security for having evolved into a different program without public debate. Voicing a similar sentiment, Martha Derthick says social security has been dominated by a small group of specialists and has been insufficiently debated and understood by others. She says the program has evolved through a highly incremental approach, in which the policymakers have taken a small step or two and then assessed the efforts of what they have done. This is a safe technique, but she contends the program could be opened up and treated like other programs, with a reduction in benefits being a legitimate alterative for debate.[5]

Many feel that in the light of current trends, fairer means for keeping the social security system financially sound must be explored. The growing proportion of retirees relative to active workers have already produced financial strains, and the post-World War II "baby boom" workers won't retire until about 2015. If current trends continue, the country will be faced with a situation where a huge group of aged former workers draws benefits from a pension system supported by a shrinking base of active wage-earners. Some have suggested this burden could be alleviated somewhat by shifting some programs such as disability benefits and medicare to support from general tax revenues. The government's Advisory Council on Social Security has recommended removing medicare from social security and financing it with income taxes. The old-age and survivors insurance programs could then be supported through payroll taxes. Supporters of the general tax approach point out that the income tax is more progressive while the payroll tax is regressive, and therefore use of the income tax to generate the needed revenues would have a less depressing effect on the economy. Some oppose the general revenue approach as changing these programs from the social insurance concept to programs of outright assistance or a government dole. It has also been suggested that raising the age for retirement with full benefits from sixty-five to seventy would save the system billions of dollars in benefits payments. At the same time, it would increase the period for paying payroll taxes and reduce the period over which benefits would be paid. There is feeling that currently some programs have built-in features that tend to discourage continuing to work or returning to work. The limit on earnings allowed with a reduction in benefits for those between sixty-five and seventy-two may discourage working beyond retirement age. Features of the disability program may also discourage returning to work. Disability payments for a worker whose earnings were $16,000 are $11,000 untaxed. A disabled worker who does return to work and earns more than $280 per month, loses all disability benefits and medicare. All of these features could work to decrease the potential base of contributing workers while increasing the burden of benefits payments. These are factors the policymakers must give some attention as they seek to develop a system to provide the economic redistribution that will insure both a strong and stable economy and promote a more democratic society.

## MEDICAL AND HEALTH PROGRAMS

The health field is an area of the government's earliest involvement in social services type programs. The Marine Hospital Service was established in 1798 to provide health services for merchant seamen and its research arm, the Hygienic Laboratory, was started in 1887 and changed to the National Institutes of Health (NIH) in 1930. In 1912 the name of the Marine Hospital Service was changed to the Public Health Service. Under this early legislation, the federal government provided medical services for certain groups for whom the government has assumed responsibility, such as merchant seamen, coast guardsmen, and federal prisoners; conducted research into causes and cures of disease and other health problems; and joined in efforts to control and eradicate mass diseases. Most of these early efforts were confined to research activities and provision of health and medical services for a very limited clientele for whom it was felt the federal government had some direct responsibility. The Committee on Economic Security, which prepared the Social Security Act proposal for President Franklin Roosevelt, also submitted a plan of national health insurance. FDR, however, chose not to include it in his proposal to Congress. In 1943 the Wagner-Murray-Dingell Bill was introduced in Congress proposing a system of compulsory national health insurance. No action was taken on this proposal. The following year in his State of the Union Address, President Roosevelt included in his "economic bill of rights" the "right to adequate medical care and the opportunity to achieve and enjoy good health." However, no specific legislative proposal followed.

Harry Truman became the first president to strongly advocate a comprehensive plan of medical insurance. In 1945 he proposed a plan of pre-paid medical insurance to be financed through an increase in social security contributions, stressing that his proposal was not "socialized medicine." Senate Republican leader Robert Taft of Ohio immediately attacked the proposal as "the most socialistic measure that this Congress has ever had before it." Truman's proposal was not acted on by the Congress.

Following World War II, medical care became a major policy issue at the national level. In 1946 Congress adopted the Hill-Burton Act, which provided federal funds for the construction of community hospitals, but support for general health insurance was still only spotty. Senator Lister Hill (D-Al.) and Representative John E. Fogarty (D-R.I.) were both ardent advocates of expanded federal activity in the health field and as chairmen of the Senate and House appropriations subcommittees handling health programs they usually increased appropriations even above amounts requested by the president. Opposition to health insurance was persistent, however. In 1949 President Truman again presented a comprehensive health and welfare program to Congress. Massive lobbying efforts were launched on both sides of the insurance issue with the AFL, CIO, Americans for Democratic Action, Committee for the Nation's Health, Physicians Forum, National Farmers Union, American Veterans Committee, and Consumers Union lining up in support; while the AMA, American Dental Association, American Pharmaceutical Association, Blue Cross, U.S. Chamber of Commerce, American Legion, American Farm Bureau Federation, Grange, and National Catholic Welfare Conference lined up in opposition. The president's health care plan was attacked as "socialized medicine," and opponents contended that only a small portion of the population could not afford adequate medical care and wanted or needed a federal program. They charged that the president's proposal if enacted would result in increased bureaucratic interference in medicine and would move the nation further in the direction of a welfare state. The president's plan was soundly defeated in Congress.

While Congress refused to adopt a plan of national health insurance, federal involvement in the health field continued to grow. In 1950 Congress approved the Research Institutes Act, and over the next decade the government's role in medical research grew rapidly with the founding of the National Cancer Institute, the Mental Health Institute, the Heart Institute, the Dental Institute, and others. The tendency to look to the national government for the solution of problems not being adequately handled otherwise, and the growing public awareness of the lack of knowledge and understanding of disease and cures, made Congress more receptive to expenditures in the health field. In 1956 the Health Research Facilities Act was passed, and in 1960 Congress approved the Kerr-Mills Act. Kerr-Mills provided funds to the states to help pay medical bills for aged persons who did not qualify for old-age assistance but were classified as "medically needy." In 1962 Kerr-Mills aid was expanded to include the aged blind, partially and totally disabled, and dependent children. In 1961, 1963, and 1964 Congress passed legislation to help expand training and research facilities in the medical field. Thus the Public Health Services budget which was $65.6 million in 1945 had grown to $1.9 billion in 1965. While shying away from a comprehensive national health insurance program, Congress was gradually expanding its services in the health care field.

In 1965 Congress took another step in the direction of national health insurance with the adoption of medicare, providing health insurance for Americans over age sixty-five and those who are disabled. The program provides hospital insurance that pays for in-patient hospital care and follow-up treatment, and medical insurance that covers doctors fees and out-patient services. The latter program is available for an additional monthly fee.

Impetus for a national health-insurance program, which has now been on the agenda for thirty years, has been increased by the tremendous growth in health care costs over the last decade. Hospital costs have increased 194 percent over the last ten years, with the average cost of a hospital stay rising from $533 to $1634. Annual increases for health care costs have been running about 14 to 17 percent and the Congressional Budget Office estimates that, left unchecked, hospital costs will rise at a rate of 14.2 percent per year over the next five years. When HEW Secretary Califano issued voluntary guidelines in 1979 calling for hospitals to limit their cost increases to 9.7 percent, he elicited howls of protest. A spokesman for the Federation of American Hospitals said this request was "totally unrealistic" and the American Hospital Association representative said meeting the guideline was "simply impossible." With hospital costs growing rampantly, federal spending on hospital care has risen 330 percent since 1969. In 1963 about 4 percent of the federal budget went for health costs; by 1973 this had risen to 10 percent. Currently about 9.6 percent of the GNP is spent on health care as compared to 5 percent in Great Britain and 7 percent in Canada. This means Americans work almost twice as long to pay for their health care as their British or Canadian counterparts. As matters currently stand, the cost of health care is doubling every five years, prompting more and more people to look with favor on some form of national health insurance.

While there is still considerable disagreement on the health insurance issue, the focus has shifted to less emphasis on philosophical arguments and more concern with economic considerations. The American Medical Association maintains there is no need for national health insurance, since 90 to 95 percent of Americans already have health insurance. Spokesmen for the Department of Health and Human Services say this is a misrepresentation. They say that 24 million Americans have no coverage at all: 9 million who are below the poverty level and 15 million who are above the poverty level. Another 19 million, they say,

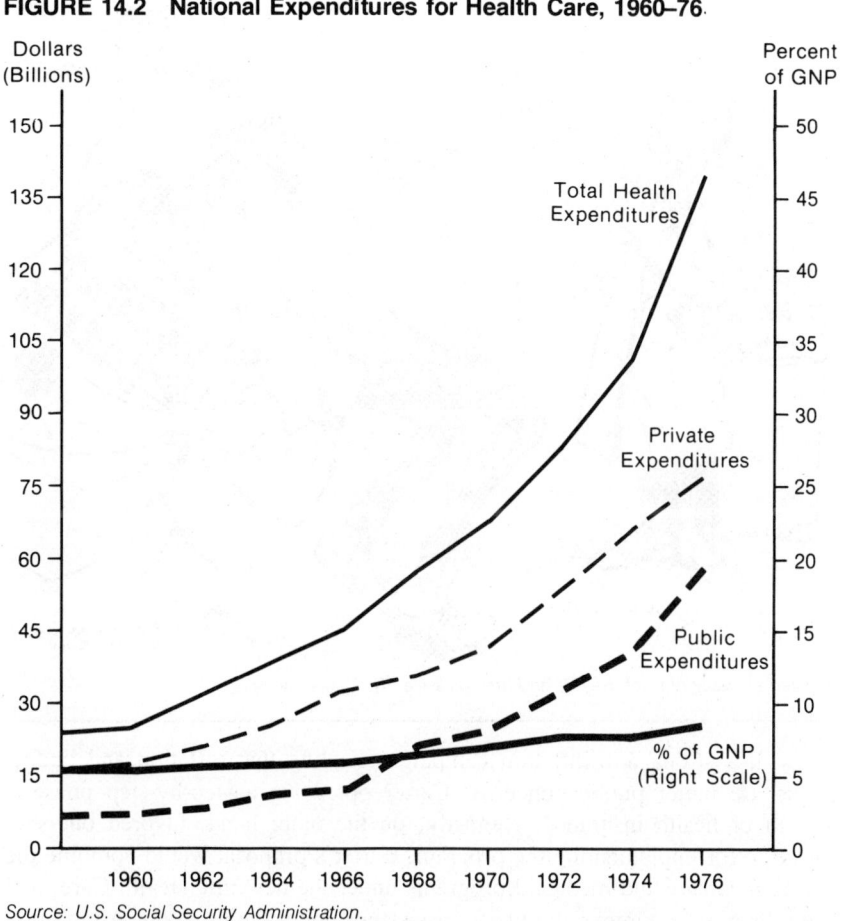

**FIGURE 14.2  National Expenditures for Health Care, 1960–76.**

Source: U.S. Social Security Administration.

have inadequate insurance coverage. As many as 88 million, HHS says, would suffer bankruptcy if hit with a catastrophic, long-term illness.

In 1979 the health care insurance program became an issue between Senator Ted Kennedy (D-Mass.) and President Carter. Senator Kennedy said that only a national health insurance program with stringent cost-containment requirements could stop runaway health care costs and also provide the care that is the right, not the privilege, of all Americans. Kennedy proposed a plan that would guarantee complete health care for every American with a price tag of $28.6 billion. Under his proposal, 75 percent of health insurance premiums would be paid by employers. President Carter, while he favored a comprehensive, mandatory system of health insurance, had to wrestle with reconciling a costly health insurance

"Okay, old timer... I'd better give you a li'l shot in the arm."

Reprinted courtesy of Hugh Haynie and the Louisville, Ky. Courier-Journal.

plan with a strong anti-inflation campaign. Feeling that inflation and budget deficits are major public concerns, Carter opted for a step-by-step phase-in program of health insurance. Kennedy, on the other hand, favored one-shot legislation for implementing the program. Carter's proposal would combine the existing medicare and medicaid programs under the new title Health Care, and would double the number eligible for assistance under the program. Any family whose income falls below 55 percent of the offficial poverty line would be eligible, and a family's out-of-pocket health care costs would be limited to a maximum of $2500 per year. Cost of Carter's plan was projected to reach $23–25 billion by 1983.

Health care insurance is a prime example of how American governmental institutions move quite slowly toward new ideas and new policies. On liberal social issues, the public is generally ahead of both the president and Congress, especially the latter. A majority of the public now favors health care insurance, but it remains for the president and Congress to come up with a mutually acceptable plan and to adopt it as public policy. While rising health-care costs increase support for such a program, inflation and concerns over methods of funding and the total price tag complicate the formulation of a progam.

## HUNGER AND NUTRITION

Though the federal government has had programs for the nutrition of mothers and children and school lunches for decades, widespread concern with wiping out hunger in a land of abundance is a rather recent public concern. In the 1960s the Southern Christian Leadership Conference and the Field Foundation did much to focus attention on the incidence of widespread hunger in the United States. Michael Harrington's *The Other America*, the "Hunger in America" television program, and the Citizens Board of Inquiry into Hunger and Malnutrition in the United States' report "Hunger USA" all served to promote awareness of the problems of hunger and malnutrition. Many citizens and legislators were shocked to learn that 20 to 30 million Americans faced hunger.

In 1961 the federal food stamp program was adopted on an experimental basis to provide assistance to needy families by allowing them to purchase at a reduced price stamps that could be redeemed for food at their higher face value. By 1968, when the White House Conference on Food, Nutrition and Health was convened, 2.8 million poor were being aided under the food stamp program, 3 million children were receiving free or reduced-price school lunches, and food programs for needy mothers, children, and the elderly were serving 4 million. Though the Field Foundation reported less hunger in 1968 than ten years earlier, many still felt such programs were falling short of the mark. A spokesman for the Senate Select Committee on Nutrition and Human Needs said that in spite of the government's efforts "... the sad and tragic truth is that, over the past several years, we have moved backwards in our struggle to end hunger, poverty, and malnutrition."[6] Because of inflation, the impact of federal programs was reduced and some people were discovered using dog and cat food in their diets.

Because it was felt that the very poor most in need of assistance were the ones who didn't have the money to purchase food stamps, the law was amended in 1977. The purchase requirement was removed and more stringent eligibility standards were adopted at the higher end of the income scale. The new amendments made it easier for more low income and elderly persons to get stamps while making it more difficult for those with higher incomes to qualify. The changes added about 3 million recipients to the 15 million already receiving stamps and cut about 1 million from the program. Participation in the program grew from 15.9 million in December 1978 to 19.1 million in April 1979. Another 8 to 10 million Americans were eligible if they applied under the program. Under the new law a family of four can have an income of $2000 and qualify for $154 per month in food stamps, an income of $4000 for $105 per month, and $6000 for $54 per month. The upper limit to qualify for food stamps is a net income of $7152. While federally funded, the food stamp program is administered through state public assistance agencies.

While the food and nutrition programs come in for their share of criticism, they have generated a rather strong base of political support. A recent Field

### FIGURE 14.3 Federal Food Programs, 1950-75 (fiscal years)

| Program | 1950 | 1960 | 1965 | 1970 | 1974 | 1975 | 1976[1] |
|---|---|---|---|---|---|---|---|
| **Food distribution program for needy families:** | | | | | | | |
| Number of participants (millions)[2] | 0.2 | 4.3 | 5.8 | 4.1 | 2.4 | .8 | .1 |
| Federal cost: | | | | | | | |
| Total (in millions) | 6 | 59 | 227 | 289 | 189 | 37 | 11 |
| Per participant (dollars) | 24 | 14 | 39 | 70 | 80 | 46 | 110 |
| **Food stamp program:** | | | | | | | |
| Number of participants (millions)[2] | — | — | .4 | 4.3 | 12.9 | 17.1 | 18.5 |
| Federal cost: | | | | | | | |
| Total (in millions) | — | — | 35 | 550 | 2,728 | 4,386 | 5,320 |
| Per participant (dollars) | — | — | 76 | 127 | 212 | 257 | 287 |
| **National school lunch program:** | | | | | | | |
| Number of children participating (millions)[3] | 8.6 | 14.1 | 18.7 | 23.1 | 25.0 | 24.9 | 25.5 |
| Percent of enrolled children: | | | | | | | |
| Total number of participants (percent) | 34.1 | 35.0 | 39.2 | 44.4 | 48.8 | 49.5 | 51.2 |
| Participants receiving free lunches or lunches at reduced prices (percent) | 16.6 | 10.1 | 9.9 | 20.7 | 37.1 | 40.3 | 42.4 |
| Federal cost (in millions) | 120 | 226 | 403 | 566 | 1,377 | 1,713 | 1,936 |
| **Special milk program:** | | | | | | | |
| Federal cost (in millions) | — | 80.3 | 97.2 | 101.5 | 61.4 | 122.9 | 144.1 |
| **School breakfast program:** | | | | | | | |
| Number of children participating (thousands)[3] | — | — | — | 536 | 1,550 | 1,800 | 2,200 |
| Federal cost (in millions) | — | — | — | 10.9 | 70.1 | 86.1 | 113.0 |
| **Special preschool food service program:** | | | | | | | |
| Number of children participating (thousands)[3] | — | — | — | 93.4 | 346.4 | 375.0 | 401.0 |
| Federal cost (in millions) | — | — | — | 6.3 | 28.2 | 48.8 | 76.8 |
| **Special summer food service program:** | | | | | | | |
| Number of children participating (thousands)[3] | — | — | — | 461.9 | 1,415.2 | 1,400.0 | 2,000.0 |
| Federal cost (in millions) | — | — | — | 6.5 | 36.1 | 50.3 | 72.4 |

1. Preliminary estimate.
2. Monthly average.
3. Daily average.

Note — Federal cost excludes administrative expenses.
Source: Department of Agriculture. Reprinted by permission of Congressional Quarterly, Inc.

Foundation study reported that the federal food stamp, school lunch, and related programs were a huge success. Food-aid programs may represent one of the unsung, yet most effective, anti-poverty efforts of the last fifteen years, the report concluded. The Louisville, Ky. *Courier-Journal* observed, "By helping all who really are in need, not just the old or very young, this program [food stamps] is the keystone of any reasonable welfare system."[7] With its media and public support growing, the food/nutrition lobby — a loose coalition of labor, consumer, religious, poverty, and health and nutrition groups — is gaining influence in the policymaking arena.

## POVERTY

One of the most controversial areas in federal social programs has been that directed toward eliminating or reducing poverty. While even conservative Republican presidents such as Herbert Hoover have seen the eradication of poverty as a legitimate governmental objective, there has been considerable disagreement over method. Taking from some segments of society and giving to others is always a matter of controversy, and it is the maldistribution of resources—jobs, opportunities, commodities, wealth—that must be remedied to eradicate poverty. While the United States is indeed one of the world's most affluent societies, this affluence is far from equally distributed. Two percent of American families have gross incomes which equal the total incomes of 45 percent of the other families. Six-tenths of 1 percent of U. S. families have incomes that equal the total incomes of 30 percent of the other families. In this group of higher-income families, one family's income is equal to that of fifty low-income families combined. In 1978 about one-fourth of all families in the U. S. had incomes of less than $10,000.

Faced with inflation and continued rising prices, more and more families fall into the cost of living–income squeeze. From 1977 to 1978, the number falling below the government's poverty level declined by only 200,000. More than 20 million, 11 percent of the population, remained below the poverty level. In 1978 the Department of Labor said an urban family of four needed to earn $17,106 for a "moderate" standard of living and $10,481 for a "lower level" standard of living. This was a 5.4 percent increase in requirements since 1976. In 1979 the Department of Labor set the official poverty level at $67000 for a non-farm family of four, $8900 for a non-farm family of six, and $5700 for a farm family of four. Can government provide programs that will help citizens maintain a standard of living that enables them to escape poverty and deprivation?

Many see such programs as essential to the maintenance of stable government because they fear continued unemployment and poverty will lead to growing frustration and loss of confidence in the ability of the system to provide any improvement. There is a danger that a substantial class of such frustrated and hopeless citizens may ultimately resort to violent and illegal acts in an effort to remedy their situation. It is this concern that has prompted government to undertake various redistribution policies in an effort to reduce the incidence and impact of poverty in our society.

In his State of the Union address of March 16, 1964, President Johnson proclaimed:

> We have never lost sight of our goal: an America in which every citizen shares all the opportunities of his society.... To finish that work, I have called for a national war on poverty.... This administration today, here and now, declares an unconditional war on poverty in America.... We shall not rest until the war is won.

The Economic Opportunity Act of 1964 wrote President Johnson's War on Poverty into law, establishing the Office of Economic Opportunity (OEO) and creating a host of programs including Community Action, Headstart, Job Corps, Legal Services, Neighborhood Youth Corps, VISTA, Upward Bound, Foster Grandparents, Green Thumb, Indian Opportunities, and the Migrant Program. An ambitious undertaking, the War on Poverty has left considerable contention, conflict, and disagreement. Some charge that the war simply expanded the welfare state and made the poor more dependent upon the federal government, rather than really promoting self-help and improvement. Some even suggest the poor would have been better off had a war never been declared, because for many the result was only raised expectations and disillusionment.[8] The program evidently did produce some changes in the poverty picture. Before the program was undertaken, over one half the poor resided in rural America, with nearly one-half living in the South. The last two decades have seen reduction in poverty, especially in rural areas and the South, and about one-half of the remaining poor now live in the urban North.

With Richard Nixon's election, many of the War on Poverty programs were dropped or redirected. In recent years more emphasis has been given to "income transfers" or "income maintenance" programs under which the government makes payments to individuals whose incomes are determined to be deficient. While a guaranteed annual income is seen by many as being fundamentally inconsistent with traditional American attitudes toward work and individual self-support, minimum-income maintenance programs have come to be advocated by both conservative and liberal economists as a way to make aid to the poor fairer, simpler, and more dignified than it is currently under the patchwork of federal welfare programs.

With program being added on top of program for forty years, the Institute for Socioeconomic Studies in a 1977 study identified 182 federal programs for income maintenance and the reduction of poverty with a total price tag of $248.1 billion. Both Nixon's Family Assistance Plan and Carter's Better Jobs and Income Program were modified versions of the guaranteed minimum-income approach. The concept encountered some disfavor in Congress when a 1979 study of experiments with income maintenance programs on a limited scale in Seattle and Denver reported that such payments had resulted in slight reductions in work effort and increased dissolution of marriages in families receiving such payments.

Concern has been mounting that with growing demands for increased defense spending and continuing problems with inflation, efforts to benefit the poor will get low priority. Richard Bolling (D-Mo.), chairman of the House Rules Committee, says:

> There's a great feeling up here now that we just ought to abandon the poor, because inflation is the only issue that counts anyway.
> That's okay unless you have a feeling for social justice. And we don't have a party that has that today.... I think a lot of the newer members are from upper-middle-class families themselves. They have an entirely different reaction to these issues than those of us who grew up in the Depression.

Nowhere is the gap between the younger and older generations in Congress referred to by Bolling more clearly reflected than in the area of welfare programs. The older generation, grounded in the 1930s and shaped by the Great Depression, tends to have greater confidence in the government's ability to improve people's lives, and they ask, How can we help more people in need? The new generation, skeptical of the government's ability to solve society's problems, asks, How can we limit the spending of the federal government and make it more effective as well? The new generation is made up of relative newcomers. In the House, in the 96th Congress, 320 members were first elected in the 1970s, and over 230 (53 percent) were elected since Richard Nixon resigned as president. Unlike older members and many in leadership, they do not feel obligated to past policies and programs.[9] Carl Perkins (D-Ky.), chairman of the House Education and Labor Committee, urges, "We have to hold fast to programs we've enacted in the past, and make sure they're not hamstrung because of lack of funds."[10] Reflecting the attitude of the new generation, Representative James J. Blanchard (D-Miss.) says:

> Clearly we don't think of ourselves as New Dealers — at all — or proponents of the Great Society either. The question is, how can we best deliver services, and limit our objectives to what we do best? We don't assume that what was enacted in 1939 should set the priorities for 1979.[11]

These differences in views stem from deep-seated differences in backgrounds, experience, and constituencies, and they hold significant implications for future policy decisions, especially those involving the expenditure and allocation of government resources. The new generation of congressmen is highly constituent oriented and their decisions will be shaped by what they read as their constituents' wishes. Commenting on federal spending programs, Representative Norman Y. Mineta (D-Calif.) said, "There's a feeling among middle-income Americans that they are packing the weight for these programs but not getting the benefits. And they're tired of paying."[12]

These changing attitudes do not augur well for programs designed to aid the poor, because those living in poverty are largely inarticulate and lack most of the means for exerting much social and political influence. It is much easier for policymakers to ignore the needs of the voiceless poor than those of other, better organized, better financed, and more vociferous segments of society. In the escalating competition for dwindling resources, the wealthy have the political advantages.

With considerable concern being expressed by traditional Democratic constituencies who favor spending programs—mayors, minorities, teachers, labor unions, and the elderly—Carter and his budget-makers stressed that everything possible was done to assure that the poor and elderly would not be hurt by the 1980 and 1981 budgets. The 1980 budget proposed about $20 billion in additional funds for income-security and welfare programs, accounting for about 34 percent of the budget total. The question is, with the changing attitudes in Congress, will congressmen continue to support programs for the poor? Representative Parren J. Mitchell (D-Md.) takes a rather pessimistic viewpoint, saying, "It's really very sad. Despite everything we talk about, I feel we have just about abandoned the poor for now."

## REFORMING THE WELFARE SYSTEM

Like bureaucratic reform, welfare reform has been an objective of virtually every administration for the last two decades. The House Ways and Means Committee even created a separate subcommittee to consider welfare reform. The widespread demands for reform in the welfare system stem from many factors, one of which is the piecemeal fashion in which the programs have been put together, along with their sheer size and the proportion of the budget they have come to account for. The agency responsible for administering most of the federal welfare programs is the Department of Health and Human Services, created in 1953 as the Department of Health, Education and Welfare. Starting with a budget of about $7 billion and 35,000 employees, the department has grown to over 140,000 employees with a budget approaching $200 billion, or about 34 percent of the total federal budget. The department spends more than all fifty states combined and only the total budgets of the U. S. government and the Soviet Union are larger. In fiscal year 1977, the Department of Health, Education and Welfare misspent $6.3 to $7.4 billion due to waste, fraud, and abuse, approximately 5 cents of each dollar appropriated. This discovery led to increased demands for reform in the vast welfare system.

Currently, too much money is being spent with too little impact. The total expenditures—federal, state, and local—for social welfare programs increased from $77.2 billion in 1965 to $286.5 billion in 1975; yet there was no appreciable decrease in the number of poor. (See figure 14.4) Thomas Sowell, professor of economics at UCLA, says that the total amount of money needed to lift every man, woman, and child out of poverty by simply mailing out checks is only one-third of the costs of the numerous programs that are vainly trying to do the same thing through various bureaucratic undertakings. Other critics point out that if the more than $100 billion now being spent in the name of poverty were evenly distributed, this would be approximately $32,000 for each poor family in the country. No doubt but that too much of current appropriations goes for running these programs, but the distribution suggestion overlooks the fact that hardcore poverty may have underlying causes that require more than a monthly government check to solve. Root causes such as lack of education and training, unemployment, discrimination, and other factors must be considered. Bishop Robert Colletti of the Archdiocese of Los Angeles has said, "The only cure for poverty and social exclusion is self-respect gained through self-improvement." Welfare reform must address not only the necessity for making sure the dollars appropriated go further, but also that programs be designed that address the root causes of our social problems as well. Another element of reform sorely needed is considerable streamlining and integration of many existing programs.

Many of those calling for welfare reform do so out of gross misconceptions about current programs, their impact, and their misuse. Many Americans are convinced that welfare has become a way of life for many, yet evidence does not

### FIGURE 14.4 The Steady Growth of the Welfare State (beneficiaries in thousands)

|  | 1945 | 1950 | 1960 | 1970 | 1979 | Projected 1985 | 1990 |
|---|---|---|---|---|---|---|---|
| Social security |  |  |  |  |  |  |  |
|   retirement | 691 | 2,326 | 10,599 | 17,076 | 22,496 | 25,977 | 28,702 |
|   disability | — | — | 687 | 2,665 | 4,792 | 6,356 | 7,311 |
|   survivors | 579 | 1,152 | 3,558 | 6,468 | 7,595 | 10,209 | 7,149 |
| Medicare | — | — | — | 19,312 | 26,317 | 30,572 | NA |
| Medicaid | — | — | — | 14,507 | 21,378 | NA | NA |
| Supplementary security |  |  |  |  |  |  |  |
|   income | 2,100 | 3,000 | 2,800 | 3,100 | 4,200 | NA | NA |
| Veterans retirement* | 2,232 | 3,376 | 4,457 | 5,511 | 5,164 | 4,911 | 4,792 |
| Civil service |  |  |  |  |  |  |  |
|   retirement* | 85 | 172 | 512 | 959 | 1,617 | 1,932 | 2,099 |
| Military retirement | NA | 138 | 243 | 750 | 1,287 | 1,373 | 1,464 |
| Railroad retirement | 177 | 398 | 809 | 979 | 1,026 | NA | NA |
| Aid to families with |  |  |  |  |  |  |  |
|   dependent children** | 1,450 | 3,099 | 4,317 | 10,715 | 11,203 | NA | NA |
| Food stamps | — | — | — | 4,340 | 17,700 | 19,000 | NA |
| School lunch | — | 8,600 | 14,100 | 23,100 | 27,000 | NA | NA |
| Housing*** | — | — | 426 | 932 | 3,007 | 3,800 | NA |
| Unemployment aid | — | 1,600 | 2,100 | 2,100 | 2,400 | NA | NA |

*includes disability and survivors' benefits
**includes general assistance
***number of housing units

Source: Federal agencies. Printed with permission of The National Journal.

---

tend to bear this out. In fact, several studies indicate that from one-half to three-fourths of those who are needy never receive public assistance. Some are unaware they are eligible, and many simply will not apply. Martin Rein and Lee Rainwater concluded in their study that the so-called "welfare class" was quite small.[13] A Rand Corporation study in 1978 of New York welfare recipients found that 40 to 50 percent of all families who turned to welfare stayed on the rolls a year or less and that less than one-third of their income came from welfare over a five-year period. Fewer than 8 percent of recipients were on the rolls for longer than ten years. A two-and-one-half-year study of aid for dependent children in Indiana revealed similar evidence regarding that program. This study showed that recipient families were not large; 60 percent were on the rolls for less than three years; many who left the rolls did so to go to work; having babies to make money was not profitable; and the number of families receiving aid was decreasing rather than increasing. Rein and Rainwater also found from their study that the idea of "disincentive" to work from welfare programs had been "considerably exaggerated." Richard Nathan, while acknowledging the need for improving present programs, concluded that the "welfare mess" had been exaggerated.[14]

President Carter, who had made the "welfare mess" one of his prime targets for reform, scaled down his 1979 proposal considerably and it contained relatively little that was really new. Reflecting the concern that welfare programs have reduced the inclination of recipients to seek work, Carter's plan provided that all able-bodied persons who apply for welfare or who are currently receiving it would have to look for private jobs for at least eight weeks as a condition for receiving benefits. The program would also provide 700,000 jobs for the able-bodied poor, half in the public sector and half in the private sector. This was scaled down from a proposed 1.4 million public jobs in Carter's 1977 proposal. The other basic element in Carter's plan was a guaranteed minimum income provision that would provide cash income supplements based on the aid for dependent children and food stamp programs. Benefits under this portion were set at 65 percent of the poverty level, or approximately $4700 for a family of four. Again this portion was scaled down from 1977 and would not provide coverage for single individuals or childless couples. The total package was reduced from the $17 billion proposed in 1977 to $5.7 billion for 1979. With the administration's continuing concerns with inflation and energy, many feared welfare programs would be given relatively low priority on the policy agenda.

## CONCLUSION

After more than three decades of federal programs aimed at reducing economic inequality and maldistribution of resources, the United States still suffers in the words of distinguished French social observer Raymond Aron, "the social failure of economic success." In the world's most affluent society persistent pockets of poverty, hunger, deprivation, and inequality show little response to governmental efforts at solution. In "Who Rules America? Power and Politics in the Democratic Era, 1825-1975," Edward Pessen observes that for the past 150 years the myth of the self-made man has proclaimed America a land of plenty, where every ambitious and hardworking person can achieve material success. Yet, he says, the growth of democracy has really done very little to improve prevailing conditions of pervasive social and economic inequality.[15] For many Americans the major challenge remaining in the so-called affluent society is not that of finding some spiritual meaning in a life of material ease and growing leisure, but how to find the means to live at a level of minimum decency.

While attitudes have changed substantially over the last few decades, and both Republicans and Democrats now embrace the need to reduce poverty, improve health, eliminate hunger, and provide a variety of social services, there is still considerable discussion over how much should be done and what methods should be used. Some economists now believe it is no longer possible to take care of all the unmet needs of the poor and sick while still improving the standard of living for society generally. The American masses have never actively sought a political solution to the problems of economic inequality. As we move into the era of increasing scarcity of certain desirable resources—jobs, commodities, opportunities, income—will the masses continue to accept the current maldistribution? Can our policymakers reconcile rising demands for social and economic equality with the apparent emerging revolt of the taxpayer? Can our policymaking process provide the necessary policies of economic reallocation that will ensure the survival of democratic government? The very future of our system as we know it may well hang in the balance on this issue.

## Points to Ponder

Are social welfare programs a damper on individual initiative and the incentive to work?

Should programs such as medicare and disability insurance be financed out of general tax revenues?

Since our political system responds most readily to those with money, organizational skills, expertise in political involvement and higher socio-economic status, does it respond sufficiently to the needs of those lacking in political and economic skills and influence?

Are good health and a sound and financially accessible health-care system responsibilities of the government?

## Notes

1. James Madison, *The Federalist*, No. 41 (New York: Modern Library, 1937), pp. 268–69.
2. As quoted by Thomas James Norton in *The Constitution of the United States: Its Sources and Its Application* (New York: World Publishing, 1940, Committee for Constitutional Government, 1943), p. 46.
3. *Ibid.*, p. 46.
4. Health, safety, and general welfare were regarded as falling under the "police powers" retained by the states under the Tenth Amendment. The federal government was not considered to have these general police powers under this narrow interpretation.
5. Martha Derthick, "How easy votes on social security came to an end," *The Public Interest*, no. 54, pp. 94–105.
6. William Robbins, "U.S. Needy Found Poorer, Hungrier Than Four Years Ago," *New York Times* (June 20, 1974).
7. "Food stamp changes provide more help for the neediest," Louisville, Ky. *Courier-Journal* (November 29, 1978).
8. See Henry J. Aaron, *Politics and the Professors: The Great Society in Perspective* (Washington, D.C.: The Brookings Institution, 1978).
9. Steven Roberts, "The generation gap in Congress," Louisville, Ky. *Courier-Journal* (April 8, 1979), © 1979 by The New York Times Company. Reprinted by permission.
10. *Ibid.*
11. *Ibid.*
12. *Ibid.*
13. Martin Rein and Lee Rainwater, "How Large Is the Welfare Class?" *Challenge* (September/October 1977), pp. 20–23.
14. Richard P. Nathan, "Approaches to Welfare Reform: The Case for Incrementalism," *City Almanac* (December 1976).
15. Edward Pessen, "Who Rules America: Power and Politics in the Democratic Era, 1825-1975," *Prologue* (Spring 1977), pp. 5–26.

## Suggestions for Further Reading

ADAY, LUANN, et al. *Health Care in the United States: Equity for Whom?* Beverly Hills: Sage, 1980.

AMERICAN ENTERPRISE INSTITUTE FOR PUBLIC POLICY RESEARCH. *Financing Social Security*. Washington, D.C., 1978.
BARTH, MICHAEL, et al. *Toward An Effective Income Support System: Problems, Prospects, Choices*. Madison, Wis.: Institute for Research on Poverty, 1974.
BOULDING, KENNETH and M. PFAFF, eds. *Redistribution to the Rich and the Poor*. Belmont, Calif.: Wadsworth, 1972.
BURKE, VEE. *Welfare Reform*. Congressional Research Service. Washington, D.C.: Government Printing Office, 1976.
BROWNING, EDGAR K. *Redistribution and the Welfare System*. Washington, D.C.: American Enterprise Institute, 1975.
CLARKSON, KENNETH. *Food Stamps and Nutrition*. Washington, D.C.: American Enterprise Institute, 1975.
CONGRESSIONAL QUARTERLY. *Future of Social Programs*. Washington, D.C.: Congressional Quarterly, 1973.
CONGRESSIONAL QUARTERLY. *National Health Issues*. Editorial Research Report. Washington, D.C.: Congressional Quarterly, 1977.
COOK, FAY L. *Who Should Be Helped? Public Support for Social Services*. Beverly Hills: Sage, 1979.
DANZIGER, SHELDON and PLOTNICK, ROBERT. "Can Welfare Reform Eliminate Poverty?" *Social Service Review* (June 1979), pp. 244–60.
DANZIGER, SHELDON and PLOTNICK, ROBERT. *Has the War on Income Poverty Been Won?* New York: Academic Press, 1980.
DERTHICK, MARTHA. *Policymaking for Social Security*. Washington, D.C.: The Brookings Institution, 1979.
DONOVAN, JOHN C. *The Politics of Poverty*, 2nd ed. Indianapolis: Pegasus, 1973.
FORD FOUNDATION and DUKE UNIVERSITY. *Welfare: The Elusive Consensus*. New York: Praeger, 1978.
FURNISS, NORMAN and TILTON, TIMOTHY. *The Case for the Welfare State: From Social Security to Social Equality*. Bloomington, Ind.: Indiana University Press, 1979.
GALBRAITH, JOHN K. *The Nature of Mass Poverty*. Cambridge, Mass.: Harvard University Press, 1979.
HARRINGTON, MICHAEL. *The Other America*. Baltimore: Penguin Books, 1963.
KRAUSE, ELLIOTT. *Power and Illness: The Political Sociology of Health and Medical Care*. New York: Elsevier, 1979.
MARMOR, THEODORE, ed. *Poverty Policy*. Chicago: Aldine-Atherton, 1971.
PIVEN, FRANCES F. and CLOWARD, RICHARD. *Regulating the Poor: The Functions of Public Welfare*. New York: Vintage Books, 1971.
PLOTNICK, ROBERT and SKIDMORE, FELICITY. *Progress Against Poverty*. Institute for Research on Poverty Series. New York: Academic Press, 1975.
PRESIDENT'S COMMISSION ON INCOME MAINTENANCE PROGRAMS. *Poverty Amid Plenty*. Washington, D.C.: Government Printing Office, 1969.
REIN, MARTIN and RAINWATER, LEE. "How Large Is the Welfare Class?" *Challenge* (September/October 1977), pp. 20–23.
SOMERS, HERMAN and RAMSAY, ANNE. *Workmen's Compensation*. New York: Wiley & Sons, 1954.
STEINER, GILBERT. *The State of Welfare*. Washington, D.C.: The Brookings Institution, 1971.
STREET, DAVID, et al. *The Welfare Industry: Functionaries and Recipients in Public Aid*. Beverly Hills: Sage, 1979.
THUROW, LESTER. *Generating Inequality: Mechanism of Distribution in the U.S. Economy*. New York: Basic Books, 1975.
VAN GORKOM, J. W. *Social Security Revisited*. Washington, D.C.: American Enterprise Institute, 1979.

# Conclusion

# The Role of Policy Analysis and Evaluation in Policymaking

One of the fastest-growing fields in the social sciences during the last decade has been policy analysis and evaluation. Much of the focus of the social sciences has shifted from traditional concerns with the institutions, structure, and philosophy of government to what governments do. As the traditional American faith in the ability of government to solve a multitude of social problems through public policies has steadily eroded, it is quite natural that interest has grown in methods for assessing more effectively the policies our government undertakes, why it undertakes those it does, and what the impact of such policies is. A better understanding of the factors shaping public policy decisions and the consequences of these decisions is socially relevant and concerns many citizens. In an era when available resources and finances become more and more limited relative to growing demands, formulating and implementing successful public policies becomes critical.

It is this growing concern with effective policymaking on the part of both professionals and interested citizens that has given rise to the rapid growth of policy analysis in recent years. Broadly defined, policy analysis is the study of the formation, causes, content, and effects of different public policies. It undertakes to provide answers to what governments do, why they do it, and what difference their actions make. Policy analysis is concerned with the examination and description of the causes and consequences of governmental policy actions. Analysis that has as its primary focus the extent to which particular policies or programs are implemented according to established guidelines is called *process evaluation*. Analysis that has as its principal concern an examination of the extent to which a policy or program results in change in an intended direction is called *impact evaluation.* While policy analysts do not discount the formulation and implementation of policies, current policy analysis focuses rather heavily on impact analysis. Recent policy analysis has tended to be more concerned with policy results than with formulation and agenda setting.

Because many policy issues involve matters that are highly controversial and often emotion-filled, careful distinction must be maintained between policy advocacy and policy analysis. There is a significant difference between *condemning* governmental action and *explaining* it. In his work on policy analysis, Thomas Dye lists three basic considerations for policy analysts:

1. A primary concern with explanation rather than prescription.
2. A rigorous search for the causes and consequences of public policies [through] the use of scientific standards of inference.
3. An effort to develop and test general propositions about the causes and consequences of public policy and to accumulate reliable research findings of general significance.[1]

Effective policy analysis and evaluation is complicated considerably by the nature of the policymaking process. Were all policy decisions made on the rational comprehensive basis, then evaluation would be simplified, as goals and objectives could be readily identified. This factor, no doubt, is one reason for the rational comprehensive model's appeal to professional social scientists. In reality most public policy is closer to the incremental mode than the rational mode of policymaking, and this makes analysis and evaluation much more difficult. With the incremental approach, goals and objectives are less clearly identified and may change over time, as policies often evolve rather than being carefully planned. Other characteristics of the process are also difficult to assess. Is a policy developed through the democratic-pluralist process a better policy than one developed in an elitist setting? Is impact the prime consideration in evaluating policy effectiveness, or is participation in the process an important factor? Are actual results from a policy the only factors to be weighed, or should the symbolic and intangible aspects be weighed as well? These are difficult questions that make policy analysis and evaluation less than an exact science with all the answers. Because many of our difficult social issues have at best only partial solutions, policy analysis cannot provide all the answers to our policy problems. However, students and citizens cannot become constructive critics until they learn to think clearly about public policies. Policy analysis can help because it encourages scholars and students to approach difficult policy issues on the basis of systematic inquiry. The concluding chapter explores the role of policy analysis and evaluation in policymaking and its possibilities for the future.

## Note

1. Thomas Dye, *Understanding Public Policy*, 3rd ed., (Englewood Cliffs, N.J.: Prentice-Hall, 1978), p. 7.

# 15
# Policy Analysis and the Utility of Evaluation in Policymaking

Though polls in recent years show considerable erosion of confidence, Americans traditionally have displayed a strong faith in the possibility for solving society's problems through governmental action. One need only look at the U. S. Code for ample testimony to the belief that everything from good health (cigarette labeling act) to good morals (the Eighteenth Amendment) can be legislated. Citizens and policymakers alike have manifested a persistent belief that most any problem can be solved by passing a law and spending enough money. In numerous instances this approach to policymaking has proven to be quite naive. Many of the problems faced in modern-day society have proved quite intractable and there is no assurance that some of society's problems will respond to *any* amount of governmental action or money.

With much of the government's action having seemingly little impact upon the problems toward which it is directed, demands for more effective policymaking are frequent. To improve on current policies and procedures, it is necessary to determine their effect and assess the extent of their success or failure. Simple logic would dictate that the most effective governmental programs be retained and that those least effective be terminated or altered. The big question is how to measure program effectiveness. This is the task of policy analysis and evaluation in the policymaking process.

## SOCIAL SCIENTISTS AND POLICYMAKING

While the social sciences in the last two decades have become considerably more policy oriented, considerable disagreement still exists as to the appropriate role for social scientists in the policy process. The Policy Studies Organization, founded by social scientists in 1971, states as its purpose the promotion of "the application of political science to important public policy problems." Noted sociologist Amitai Etzioni has proposed a Congressional Office of Social Science to help the Congress evaluate and assess the impact of its programs, and a growing number of social scientists view participation in and research and writing about public policy as mutually supportive. Others, however, feel that social scientists should not become involved in the policymaking process but should confine their efforts to research and empirical analysis. Though accompanied by misgivings in some circles, the last decade has witnessed a decided shift in the social sciences. Professor of education and social structure at Harvard, Nathan Glazer, says that while earlier social scientists were interested primarily in contributing to the development of role theory or other theories of social structure, the social sciences are now shifting from purely theoretical studies to those focusing more on social institutions and policies.[1]

Currently there is a growing commitment both inside and outside government to more systematic efforts to improve the basis on which policymakers make their decisions. In announcing a forthcoming volume in its policy evaluation series, Sage Publications said the work was in keeping with a vision of evaluation as a methodological enterprise with outcomes at both the policymaking and services delivery levels and was designed to present state-of-the-art volumes for instructors and students of evaluation, researchers, practitioners, policymakers, and program administrators. Another Sage publication in the field, *Evaluation* magazine is billed as an experimental publication designed to further the adoption of program evaluation and knowledge utilization as a means of stimulating, facilitating, and guiding organizational change, at both the policy and practice levels.[2] Senator Daniel Moynihan (D-N.Y.) observes that currently there is very little in the way of human behavior that the social sciences do not *in theory* undertake to explain.[3]

The shifting focus in the social sciences does not mean that policymakers will automatically begin to seek and use such data in their decision-making, however. The subtle and indirect influences may be considerable, as expressed by Lord John M. Keynes in these words:

> The ideas of economists and political philosophers, both when they are right and when they are wrong, are more powerful than is commonly understood.... Practical men, who believe themselves to be quite exempt from any intellectual influences, are usually the slaves of some defunct economist. Madmen in authority, who hear voices in the air, are distilling their frenzy from some academic scribbler of a few years back.[4]

In a more direct sense, many decision-makers still tend to share Bismarck's admonition to the Prussian Chamber that "politics is not an exact science." Bismarck's remarks were prompted by the claims of German academics who proposed that they had systematized most fields of knowledge and were treating history and politics as though they too could be explained with a set of formulae. It is this tendency toward quantification and scientific certainty that today still frequently divides the academic social scientists and the practitioners of policymaking.

From the times of Plato and Aristotle to the present, there has been recognition of the relationship between scholars and governors. Shortly later Henry VIII assumed the English throne in 1509, Erasmus observed that the king had created "not a court but a temple of the muses." Centuries later, as Britain's prime minister, Winston Churchill observed that noted physicist R. V. Jones "did more to save us from disaster than many who are glittering with trinkets." Despite substantial contributions from the scholarly "experts," there has not been any systematic effort on the part of federal policymakers to incorporate policy analysis and research into the decision-making process. A study by the Department of Housing and Urban Development concluded that the most impressive finding on the evaluation of social programs in the federal government was that substantial work in the field was almost nonexistent. Few significant studies had been undertaken, reported HUD, and most of those carried out were poorly conceived. The various small studies carried out over the country lacked the uniformity of design and objectives that would have made results comparable and therefore useful to those making policy.[5] While the last decade has brought a more widespread attempt among social scientists to apply their concepts, methods, and findings to public policymaking, this has not been accompanied by any rush by decision-makers to use such analysis and research in their decisions. Probably the courts have been more inclined to rely on social research than the other branches of government, and their use has been sporadic. In the *Brown* decision, the Warren court drew heavily on a broad range of social inquiry, and in more recent decisions on busing the courts cited Professor James Coleman's data on pupil achievement as a basis for their findings. Of the courts' use of social science research, Senator Moynihan writes:

> If it is quite clear that the courts employ social science with considerable deftness on some occasions, then it must be allowed that on other occasions the courts have got themselves into difficult situations by being too casual, even trusting, about the "truths" presented to them by ways of research on individual and group behavior.[6]

For a variety of reasons, Congress has been less inclined than the courts to use social science research in its decision-making. Because of its stronger political and constituent orientation, members of the legislative branch seldom seek information for its own sake as an aid to policymaking. The member usually knows his position on many issues in advance, and if information is sought, it is usually not objective information, but information to promote the predetermined position or to fend off perceived threats to this position. Halperin says that ". . . most of the time, members (and their staffs) are not in abstract search of better information on which to base a policy to be formulated at some indefinite point in the future." He concludes that the prevailing value preferences of the policymakers are most important in molding their decisions.[7] The impact of evaluation evidence may be further reduced in the decision-making process by other factors as well. As Nachmias notes, "such evidence will... have to compete with a host of other factors that decision makers take into consideration in the process of making public policy decisions."[8] Decisions on public programs may be substantially influenced by considerations of political and social values, partisan preferences, constituent views, personal philosophies and biases, vested interests, and a host of other factors. Thus evaluation and research information must compete with numerous other factors for the attention of the policymakers.

Current evidence indicates that on the whole policymakers do not rely heavily on social science research and in many instances regard it as having only limited application in their efforts. In an interview with a staff member of the *Educational Record*, former U. S. Commissioner of Education Ernest L. Boyer observed:

> In my recollection on my several years in government, only rarely did I hear someone say, "Well, the universities have experts on that subject" — whether the topic was energy, the economy, education, or the environment. Rather, government increasingly is turning to special-interest groups, not to academic specialists.[9]

Even in the courts, where the most use has been made, there are frequent questions as to applicability. In *Witherspoon* v *Illinois* (1968), Justice Stewart, commenting on social surveys being cited, observed, "We can only speculate... as to the precise meaning of the terms used in those studies, the accuracy of the techniques employed, and the validity of the generalizations made."[10] Such skepticism on the part of policymakers is not confined just to academic research. Over the last two decades the institutionalized structure within the federal bureaucracy for policy analysis and evaluation has grown substantially with such agencies as OMB, the Congressional Budget Office, the Office of Technology Assessment, and the General Accounting Office undertaking more and more program evaluation. As pressures for program accountability build, as reflected in proposals for "sunset legislation," the need for effective program evaluation will grow.[11] However, in spite of such trends, current efforts at evaluation are frequently met with considerable skepticism. GAO's expanded role in program assessment and evaluation has generated considerable criticism for the agency, and such efforts are frequently largely discounted by policymakers if they don't like the results. In the recent debate on federal assistance for the financially ailing Chrysler Corporation, the Treasury Department discounted the results of studies conducted by the research arm of the Department of Transportation and by Data Resources Inc. on the economic implications of Chrysler's failure and chose to do its own study. This is not unusual. A recent GAO survey reported that only 4 percent of high-level federal officials think social research has a "substantial effect" on policy decisions, while 54 percent feel such research is less than "moderately" effective. The OMB appears to regard federally funded social science research as a subsidy to academicians rather than a source of information for federal policymakers. The uncertain connection between academic research and governmental policymaking is reflected in the National Academy of Sciences' title for its study: *Knowledge and Policy: The Uncertain Connection.*

## Analysts versus Policymakers

One of the major reasons why policy analysis and policy research is not used more widely in policymaking is a lack of understanding and communication between the policymakers and the social scientists. This lack of understanding and communication stems from a variety of factors ranging from differences in objectives to mutual suspicion and professional snobbishness.

Policymakers and policy analysts often operate from quite different perspectives and reach decisions on issues in basically different ways. The social scientist is interested in determining what society is like and what made it the way it is, frequently seeking to explain societal conditions that may or may not be relevant to public policy. The policymaker, on the other hand, is concerned primarily with questions dealing with alternative approaches to policy issues and their probable consequences. While the scholars generally seek scientific objectivity in their research, policymakers are usually interested in determining what ought to be, and their decisions, while guided by objective data, may be based on considerations of moral and value judgments as well. A major criticism sometimes lodged against the value-free quantitative policy analysis efforts of many academics has been that they are too capable of being used to promote socially undesirable goals as well as socially desirable ones. While policymakers are more problem oriented, seeking practical solutions to social issues that are real rather than theoretical, the policy analyst's efforts are frequently more theory-directed, with the ultimate objective being a contribution to existing scientific knowledge. The policymakers are usually looking for information and predictions that chart alternative courses of action in addressing real problems and are little concerned with the methodological sophistication and purity of the research. A primary concern of the analyst, on the other hand, may well be the methodological techniques and scientific purity of the research. Typical of this concern with methodology is the dispute that developed between the Office of the Assistant Secretary for Policy, Evaluation and Research and the Manpower Administration in the Department of Labor over the evaluation of CETA (Comprehensive Employment Training Act) programs. While the Manpower Administration favored a relatively straightforward process analysis of the program, ASPER's view was, "Let's not worry about how it works; let's analyze it correctly." After months of wrangling, ASPER contended, "We still have the basic problem that until we develop a working model of the CETA system, it will not be possible to determine the appropriate methodology and inputs and outputs."[12] A similar concern is reflected in this comment in a review of the literature on environmental policy: "Much of the literature on environmental policymaking continues to be descriptive case studies of specific decisions or agencies, with very little attention to theory construction or to methodological issues."[13]

This concern with theory and analytical methods has been a major factor contributing to the gulf between policy analysts and policymakers, who are more concerned with results and applicability of research findings. Many practitioners in the field of policymaking are already inclined to view policy analysis as an analytical trap, and as the questions and techniques employed become more theoretical and employ complex statistical procedures, models, and simulations, the uneasiness is likely to increase. As the procedures and analyses used by the researchers become more sophisticated and abstract, the practitioners' fear of being locked into conclusions that become politically unacceptable increases. They fear they are being sold a package of theoretical concepts that will have no practical application in the real political world in which they must function. As Wolanin observes, the analysts may "... leave the legislators with a warm glow of high ideals, but frequently without the words of legislative art that could transform noble sentiments into legislative realities."[14]

Several factors contributing to differences between analysts and policymakers stem from the system itself. Our policymaking system is basically an adversary system involving considerable political points of difference for the scholar and the practitioner. The system does not lend itself readily to the ideal models of disinterested research and rational, objective decision-making. In the policy process there are no established criteria for deciding what is desirable public policy. Each policy decision-maker weighs arguments and data against his own policy objectives and philosophies and determines whether these objectives will be promoted by a particular course of action. Most policymakers are truly "open" and objective in their approach only a small portion of the time. This makes effective analysis difficult because the political realities of the process are messy, unquantifiable things that get in the way of rigorous analysis and methodological purity.

Because of their different perspectives and frequently differing objectives, academic policy analysts and practicing policymakers are often inclined to view one another with some suspicion and misunderstanding. To the policymakers the academic analysts are seen as sanctimonious, olympian, fuzzy, abstract, unaware, and lacking in appreciation of political realities and the legitimacy of the political process, always demanding more but unwilling to be held accountable. The academics, on the other hand, are inclined to see the policymakers as unprincipled, overly pragmatic, unethical, dominated by special interests, uninformed, and arrogant.[15] These attitudes tend to complicate effective communication between the two and reduce the potential for more effective use of policy analysis and research in the policymaking process.

### Shortcomings of Current Policy Analysis

In 1664 Leibnitz offered "mathematical proof" that the Count Palatine would ascend the Polish throne. In succeeding decades social scientists have continued their efforts to apply scientific methods in analyzing and predicting social and political events. In their pursuits, the social scientists seek to establish a fixity of relationships enabling them to predict behavior in advance, or at least to narrow possibilities to a manageable number. In their efforts to emulate the methodologies and laboratory techniques of the natural sciences, social scientists have made theirs largely a quantitative discipline dealing in statistical probabilities.

Theory development and model building have become key elements in most modern social science studies of policymaking. Social scientist E. S. Quade says, "There is no such thing as not using a model in analyzing a decision," and David Nachmias contends, "Models in general are fundamental to public policy research." Nachmias generally reflects the prevailing philosophy of the policy analysts in his book *Public Policy Evaluation*. In the preface he states as his objective, "attempts to analyze and compare various conceptual models on which evaluations can be based and to explain the statistical techniques most useful in evaluation research." He defines the primary function of the still-emerging discipline of policy analysis as the "construction of theoretical models of cause-and-effect relationships and the development of research designs to test such models." He says, "Obviously, if there are no solid theoretical grounds for expecting that a particular policy will accomplish its goals, one should not be too surprised if in fact the policy does not accomplish them."[16]

The preoccupation of many social scientists with theory building and scientific methodology creates two problems in policy analysis. The first problem stems from the attempt to impose an element of certainty on an area where certitude is unattainable. Even in the natural sciences certainty is rare, and the history of science is a graveyard of discarded, disproven, inadequate, and outdated theories. Arthur C. Clarke, in "Clarke's Law" says, "The next great scientific advance will be the one which the most eminent scientist has most recently declared impossible," and Joseph J. Schwab notes that scientific knowledge is at best incomplete, uncertain, and fluid.[17] In the final analysis there is no such thing as "the scientific method"; no one method or technique which assures the right answers. Old theories are frequently no longer appropriate for explaining new facts that crop up. This is particularly true in the social sciences, which are labile in the extreme. What was thought to be explained and settled in one decade may become the major unsettled social question of the next decade.

The love affair between social scientists and the scientific method has sometimes led to premature judgments and generalizations that have damaged the credibility of policy analysis with policymakers. Robert Conquest, one of the harshest critics of social scientists' infatuation with models and statistical analysis, charges that in a variety of fields lending themselves less readily to the scientific rigors of testing and experimentation than the natural sciences, highly inflated theorizings have been treated as established doctrine. He charges that much of the work of current social research occupies ground somewhere between misapplied scientism and worthless generalization. He says that while the academic mind cannot be kept from premature theory, "The academic urge to premature and inadequately supported generalities, . . . is a sure sign of primitivism. . . . We are plainly in the presence not of an intellectual but of a psychological phenomenon: an astonishing tribute to the power and persistence of the human desire for tidiness and certitude, even when these are totally inappropriate."[18] Robert Hutchins, the noted American scholar, remarked on this penchant when he observed, "He [the American] is not at home with anything he cannot count, because he is not sure of any other measure. He cannot estimate or appraise quality. This leaves him with quantity."[19] Columnist William Greider, commenting on sociological studies on equality, observes:

> Thus do the great universities and think tanks and government agencies spend small fortunes in computer and time to discover what ordinary people already know. For some reason sociologists seem to believe they have discovered something new when they have assigned a specific percentage to an ancient influence in life.[20]

The policy analysts' efforts to employ models and scientific methods in explaining policymaking are an attempt to simplify reality and make an extremely complex system manageable. In the effort to fit the highly complex process into the analytical framework, however, the analyst may render the results virtually meaningless. Conquest contends that use of the term "model" is inappropriate because the workings of the original have not been mastered. Because the number of variables affecting a policy are really infinite and will differ from policy to policy, models inevitably simplify and frequently modify reality. Thus, since policy analysis requires that the methodology be adapted to a particular set of circumstances, the results become difficult to generalize about and may have only a very limited applicability. Because a variety of methodologies are used in evaluation research, with very little consideration of their suitability and more general application, different evaluations quite frequently are not comparable. Consequently, policy studies currently have failed to provide an accumulative and comparative body of research and analysis for the policymakers' use.

The policy analysts' role is further complicated by other characteristics of the policy process. Many policies and programs are not readily amenable to experimentation and scientific analysis. For analysis to be quantifiable, a policy's goals must be expressed in measurable terms. According to Nachmias, "If a policy's objectives cannot be stated clearly, specifically, and in measurable terms, there is no point in pursuing a scientific impact evaluation study."[21] While this may appear rather simple, for many policies it is not. Policy goals may vary from one branch of government to another—Congress, president, courts—or from participant to participant. Congress's goals for revenue sharing may differ considerably from those of local governments. Also, objectives are frequently altered after a program is underway. Similar problems may arise when trying to assess program impact. Nationwide a program's impact will vary substantially—in some areas a program may be highly successful while in another locale the same program can be a dismal failure. What is the overall impact? No one instrument or measure of results is good for every policy. While cost-benefit analysis may be appropriate for some policies, it may have only limited applicability for others.

Effective policy evaluation has been hindered by the cold, hard fact that most of society's problems are influenced by such a multitude of variables—available resources, technology, population changes, class structure, political values and ideology, religion, race, sex, regional interests—that no simple explanation or solution is possible. In fact, even a full understanding of our complex, fast-changing society may be beyond the social scientist's present capabilities. Today it may be difficult even to achieve agreement on what the problems are, much less on their solutions. Our social and political problems have become so complex that policy analysts are unable to make accurate predictions about the relative impact of alternative policies. Social scientists simply have not reached the point where they know enough to be able to give reliable advice to policymakers. Economists were once thought to have made the most progress among social scientists toward the mastery of their field. Only a few years ago, Stuart Nagel wrote:

> Of all the social sciences, the field of economics has clearly developed the most sophisticated mathematical models for synthesizing normative and empirical premises in order to deduce means-ends policy recommendations. These mathematical models relate to the optimum allocation of scarce resources, the optimum level at which to pursue a given policy which has a curvilinear relation with net benefits achieved, and the optimum strategy to follow when the net benefits achievable are dependent on the occurrence of a contingent event.[22]

In the decade of the 1970s economics lost much of its lustre, however, as it was unable to provide workable solutions to the nation's economic problems, especially the persistent spiral of inflation. As the government wrestled with continuing economic problems and economists spoke with as many tongues as the people of ancient Babel, their mathematical models came to be viewed with growing skepticism. Generally social scientists are still faced with the task of proving the applicability of their research and evaluation efforts to the real world of policymaking. In the words of one real-world decision-maker, Senator Daniel Moynihan, "It is a melancholy fact that, recurrently, even the most rigorous efforts in social science come up with devastatingly imprecise stuff." He goes on to add, "The profession, in a word, has a way to go."[23] George W. Bonham, editor of *Change* magazine, observes that, "There is a growing sense of unease, even among the most thoughtful observers, that social science research has in fact often failed to give us the necessary wisdom to convert social theory into effective public practice."[24] And Charles Lindblom of Yale's Institute for Social and Policy Studies and David Cohen of Harvard's Graduate School of Education have concluded that professional social scientists greatly overestimate the amount and distinctiveness of the information and analysis they offer.[25]

A second problem growing out of many policy analysts' preoccupation with theory and methodological technique is that it complicates their communication with policymakers and reduces the acceptance of their efforts by those involved in the decision-making process. Much of what is currently produced as policy analysis is directed primarily toward professional colleagues rather than toward policymakers. What policymaker, for example, will find extremely useful and interesting such topics as "The Contributions of Analytic Theory to Normative Theory" or "Appalachian Praxis in the Politics of Advance Capitalism"? Should they decide to explore some of the current policy analysis efforts, however, the policymakers would undoubtedly need an interpreter to translate such professional jargon as "statistical inference," "cross-tabulation," "multivariate analysis," "multiple regressions," "cognitive constructs," "learning modules," "synergy at the interface," "linear and curvilinear regression," and "recursive and non-recursive structural equation models," for starters. Then, with the interpreter showing the way, they might be able to glean some meaning from such well-turned statements as the following:

> By social problem solving, we mean processes that are thought to eventuate in outcomes that by some standard are an improvement on the previously existing situation, or are presumed to so eventuate, or are conceived of as offering some possibility to so eventuate.[26]

> Since the high-crime jurisdictions that are most likely to be looking to incapacitation to relieve their crime problems also tend to have relatively lower rates of time served per crime, they can expect to have the largest percentage increases in prison populations to achieve a given percentage of reduction in crime.[27]

It is not too difficult to see why policymakers may fail to seek out policy analysts for assistance or use their information once they get it. They simply cannot understand it. For policy analysis to be really effective, researcher and policymaker must understand each other. To date, political scholars have not generally addressed themselves to the question of translating their research efforts into public policy. Many have shown little concern with the communications gap between researcher and practitioner because their efforts have been directed primarily at professional colleagues rather than practical application. For policy evaluation to play an effective part in the policy process this lack of communication and understanding must be eliminated. In *Speaking Truth to Power*, Aaron Wildavsky of the University of California at Berkeley writes: "Evaluation must lead to programs that connect the interests of political leaders to the outcomes of governmental actions; otherwise, they will reject evaluation and the people who do it."[28]

To bring down the barriers between policy analysts and policymakers, the analysts must overcome several real or perceived shortcomings of their efforts to date: Analysts must be less concerned with broad theoretical concepts and methodological elegance and more concerned with the political realities of the process and the practical application of their findings. The policymakers are looking for some alternative approaches for action on real social issues, and in the past many analytic studies were rejected because they were unrealistic politically. In the words of Grover Starling, "These analytical studies—festooned with the latest mathematical and economic techniques but performed with little application for the political realities of the policymaking process they are supposed to support—become little more than a series of glassbead games."[29] Analysts must guard against allowing analytical methods to become ends in themselves and must develop a broader appreciation of the political implications involved in the analysis of governmental policies and the recommendation of alternative courses of action.

Analysts must appreciate that policymakers function in a world of a variety of social and political constraints and that in making policy decisions some of the most logical alternatives may be socially and politically out of the question. In this regard, policymakers, who are frequently much more sensitive to "psychic" factors or the symbolic impact of certain policies than scholars, may regard analysts as being "politically" insensitive or unrealistic. News columnist Edwin A. Roberts charges, "The trouble with many of the nation's most articulate professors and writers is that they really don't know what's going on. They don't know what are the primary concerns of the American people...."[30]

Scholars must appreciate that in the final analysis policymaking is a political process and their research and analytical efforts must take this into consideration; otherwise, their efforts will be rejected to collect dust on the library shelves. As a general rule analysts achieving the most acceptance by policymakers have been those displaying "sensitivity to political reality" and the ability to move comfortably in both the worlds of research and policymaking.

Lest all this emphasis on realism create a wrong impression, this is in no way a suggestion that policy analysts compromise their objectivity to political expediency or water down the quality and standards of their research and evaluation efforts. In fact, if their efforts are to have more impact, policy analysts must work to improve both their objectivity and the applicability and quality of their research. As George Bonham notes, a growing number of well-recognized scholars have already begun to ask serious questions about both the quality and scientific reliability of much that research claims to produce in the way of practical social solutions.[31] In spite of their claims of scientific objectivity and value-free research, policy analysts can be biased and incompetent, and they can be wrong. In his book *Politics and the Professors*, Henry Aaron writes,

> The intellectual standards of the social sciences may camouflage distortions, selective reporting of results, or more subtle violations of objectivity. Outsiders may be lulled into thinking that issues are being debated with scholarly impartiality, when in fact more basic passions are parading before the reader clad in the jargon of academic debate.[32]

Because social scientists are human and since the issues with which they deal are rarely dispassionate, policy analysts are frequently caught up in the politics that their work quite naturally involves. On many issues there is neither technical nor political agreement. In 1979 when Dr. Gio B. Gori, a researcher with the National Cancer Institute, announced that his studies showed that new, low-tar cigarettes presented little "apparent risk" to smokers, he touched off a furor. The ensuing battle between antismoking forces and pro-tobacco interests was anything but "a reasoned scientific discussion." This has been equally true in other areas as well, and social scientists, says Daniel Moynihan, are never more revealing of themselves than when challenging the objectivity of one another's work. In the area of race relations and desegregation the scholars and educational experts have been divided on even the most basic questions, and many of the participants have been interested in promoting particular social objectives. Scholarly disagreement is one thing, but policy advocacy is another. Too many social scientists have allowed their personal preferences and political biases to influence the outcome of their work. In the words of Senator Moynihan, much of the research and analysis has been characterized by "a somewhat-too-ardent searching for evidence that will help sustain a hoped-for conclusion."[33]

Several factors have contributed to this lack of objectivity and acceptance on the part of policy analysts. Many social scientists by their nature are activist oriented and are inclined to merge social research and social involvement. Consequently, their studies may almost inevitably reflect their hope that their findings will guide public policy toward positive social change. The nature of the issues, professional visibility, and the availability of research funds may attract researchers to certain areas and these factors can sometimes color the results of studies conducted. Healthy disagreement and scholarly debate on public issues are good for our democracy, but policy analysts must guard against political biases that lead to misapplied statistics, inappropriate methodologies, and conceptual sloppiness. Unscholarly disagreements resulting from politically biased and poorly executed analyses can only serve to discredit policy analysis as a useful tool for the policymaker. While they should certainly exercise their rights as citizens, policy analysts must maintain a clear distinction between advocacy and analysis.

There remains a real need for policy analysts to upgrade the quality of their work in some other respects also. If policymakers are going to rely on the analysts for expertise, they must be able to provide a product of high quality and utility. Policymakers are not looking for highly theoretical scientific research reports, which they are unable to use in the practical formulation of policy. They are looking for helpful information that is readily available at the time a decision must be reached. To be helpful to policymakers, policy analysts must be prepared to provide partial results at various points in time rather than full-blown, time-consuming research studies. As former Oregon governor Tom McCall noted, if you "spend two years studying something, by the time you conclude it's a good thing to do, the best time for doing it has passed." Frequently policy decisions must be made with quick, instinctual, and pragmatic judgments that preclude time-consuming efforts at objective and rational analysis. Consequently, simple projections of past trends and a judicious application of past experiences may be better predictors and more usable than scientifically derived, more-elaborate predictions. Since policymaking includes no allowances for self-correction, wrong answers can be costly or disastrous for policymakers and constituents. Therefore, it is important for policy analysts to develop the capability not only to produce timely information, but also information that is accurate. In this respect, current efforts leave considerable room for improvement. Robert Reinhold, commenting on a social science analysis of a federal experiment with a guaranteed minimum income, noted, "These findings illustrate the frequent tendency of social research to produce homogenized, distilled and summarized data that often mask subtle and less easily measured human effects of government programs."[34]

In their analysis of professional social inquiry efforts, Lindblom and Cohen charged that social science research knowledge often was less conclusive than ordinary knowledge. They went on to say that sometimes, as in the area of race in education, social science research is not only "overblown, pretentious and meddling" but "a positive obstruction to social problem-solving" because of the amount of worthless "noise or distraction" it introduces into the discussion.[35] Policy analysis definitely has a way to go to improve its track record, not only with policymakers, but with other social scientists as well.

## FUTURE DIRECTIONS IN POLICY ANALYSIS

For the last several years pollsters and political observers have reported evidence of growing dissatisfaction with governmental performance and policies. Complaints of inefficiency, waste, ineffectiveness, and maladministration have become more and more widespread. Responding effectively to such manifestations of dissatisfaction is not easy in our system for at least a couple of reasons. First of all, the government has no systematic means for determining whether many of the things it does are worth doing, and it has no systematic plan for carrying out a program that is capable of attaining the results it seeks. Second, while many citizens are dissatisfied and frustrated with the government's performance, they don't know where to turn for help in remedying the situation. Theoretically, in our democratic system policy decisions ultimately rest with the citizens. But in such a complex system where public policy is so saturated with competing, often contradictory claims, the citizen is free to decide among these only if he or she is able to compare and look critically at the alternatives and interpret what they mean. In performing this task the average citizen desperately needs the assistance of trained observers. In *Capitalism, Socialism, and Democracy*, Joseph Schumpeter says, "The typical citizen drops down to a lower level of mental performance as soon as he enters the political field.... He becomes a primitive again."[36]

While Schumpeter's assessment may be overly pessimistic, in today's complex society, the average citizen certainly needs help in interpreting political reality and determining the potential impact of alternative policies on his/her life. As Robert Dahl has observed, "If it were possible for experts to predict with reasonable certainty the outcome of a policy measure, and if the experts agreed, the citizen might substitute for the conflicting assertions of politicians the predictions of the expert."[37] However, in today's complex world the experts in almost every field are themselves in such wild disagreement as to be of little help to anyone, and the erosion of faith in political institutions is also reflected in a loss of faith in the experts to whom these institutions look for advice. Many citizens no longer feel so sure that even the experts know what is happening.

In this setting, policy analysts face an extremely challenging task and their response can have significant impact on the future of policymaking. The government needs a more systematic approach to policymaking and better means for assessing the impact of its policies once they are implemented. It needs facts and reliable judgments about the outcomes of particular policies because effective policy planning and policy analysis are keys to improving the efficiency and effectiveness of governmental performance. In the absence of these, policy decisions will be made on the basis of incomplete data that are likely to be biased toward objectives that are tangible, quantifiable, and possibly irrelevant. This can be bad because many policy outcomes—possibly some of the most significant ones — are intangible and not easily measurable.

Thomas R. Wolanin of the University of Wisconsin says a good decision-making process is one that brings to bear the available information and analysis in a fairly systematic and orderly fashion.[38] Good decicision-making, on national policy issues, is complicated by several factors:

1. Many of the difficult social issues faced have, by their very nature, only partial and incomplete solutions.
2. The issues frequently involve questions of values and preferences that cannot be resolved readily through rational analysis.
3. The internal dynamics and organizational structure of government frequently work against good decision-making.
4. The sources and availability of necessary information are often limited.
5. On many issues the policymakers have to rely on their judgment and values rather than rational analysis.
6. The policymaker's range of discretion in making policy choices is frequently quite limited.
7. In weighing alternative approaches, valid comparisons are sometimes difficult to make. For example, how many jobs or how many kilowatts of additional power are equivalent to the preservation of a scenic wilderness area or an endangered specie?

In this setting, what can policy analysis contribute? What do the policy analysts have to say to an audience that it doesn't already know? What use does evaluation hold for the policy-making process? In seeking to respond to such questions, policy analysts need to appreciate the need for something more than mere narrow technical competence. Sophisticated quantitative tools and elaborate theoretical concepts alone do not make for effective policy analysis. Neither quantitative methodology nor mastery of the "political realities" constitutes the best approach to policy evaluation. The idea is to focus on the concepts of analysis without getting bogged down in the details of particular methodologies and scholarly biases. Sound policy analysis with some prospect of being used by policymakers must include substantial amounts of common-sense judgment and be based on hard work, persistent intellectual curiosity, and reasonable analytical ability. Experience and the evidence of one's senses may sometimes contribute more to this process than elegant social theories and complex methodologies.

While it is doubtful that policy analysis can ever provide "solutions" or predict with any degree of scientific precision the impact of future policies, it can nonetheless contribute to the improvement of the policymaking process. Policy analysis can encourage social analysts to approach policy issues with the tools of systematic inquiry, and analysts can at least attempt to systematically measure the impact of existing policies and make such information available to the policymakers. With information from systematic, objective, analytical assessments of policy impacts, better decisions can be made, ineffective programs can be dropped or changed, and programs that are working can be expanded. Policymakers do not simply have to rely on "muddling through," but can approach decisions on difficult issues in a systematic fashion and armed with useful information. Halperin says information that is cogent and concise, that is expressed in de-jargonized terms, and that is stated compellingly in its claim to a hearing, *will* tend to have an impact.[39] This is a need policy analysis can fill in the policymaking process. By taking rigorous looks at existing policies and providing pertinent information to those making the decisions, analysts can help the government develop programs that work better. The problem with policy analysis thus far has been, to paraphrase Josh Billings, not so much that we are ignorant, but that we know so much that is irrelevant. The result has been an unbridged gulf between the analysts and those making the policy decisions.

## Points to Ponder

What is a *good* policy?

What can policy analysis and evaluation do for the policymakers?

Should policy evaluation measure only impact, or should how policies are made also be an important consideration in evaluation?

What factors tend to complicate effective evaluation of public policies?

Would the incorporation of more policy analysis and evaluation into policymaking decisions result in improved quality?

## Notes

1. As quoted by Malcolm Scully in "Striking Change Seen Reshaping Social Sciences," *The Chronicle of Higher Education*, (May 15, 1978).
2. From publications announcements, Sage Publications, Beverly Hills, CA, 1979.
3. Daniel P. Moynihan, "Social Science and the Courts," *The Public Interest*, No. 54, (Winter 1979), p. 22.
4. Quoted by Theodore Lowi in *The End of Liberalism* (New York: Norton, 1979), p. 1.
5. Joseph S. Wholey, et al., *Federal Evaluation Policy* (Washington, D.C.: Urban Institute, 1975).
6. Moynihan, "Social Science and the Courts," p. 15.
7. Samuel Halperin, "Politicians and Educators: Two World Views," *Phi Delta Kappan* (November 1974), p. 398.
8. David Nachmias. *Public Policy Evaluation: Approaches and Methods* (New York: St. Martins, 1979), p. 18.
9. Interview with Ernest L. Boyer, president, Carnegie Foundation, in *Educational Record* (Winter 1980), p. 5.
10. *Witherspoon v Illinois*, 391 U.S. 510 (1968).
11. "Sunset legislation" is legislation for periodic review and justification of programs; if not justified, they are automatically terminated.
12. Michael Nelson, "What's Wrong with Policy Analysis?" *The Washington Monthly* (September 1979), p. 55.
13. Paul Sabatier and Geoffrey Wandesforde-Smith, "Major Sources on Environmental Politics, 1944-77: The Maturing of a Literature," *Policy Studies Journal* (Spring 1979), p. 599.

14. Thomas R. Wolanin, "Congress, Information and Policy Making for Postsecondary Education: 'Don't Trouble Me With the Facts'," *Policy Studies Journal* (Summer 1976), p. 391.
15. Halperin, "Politicians and Educators," p. 398.
16. Nachmias, *op. cit.*, p. 6.
17. Joseph J. Schwab, "The Social Sciences," *The Center Magazine* (January/February 1980), p. 36.
18. Robert Conquest, "Some Notes on Political Science," *The Wilson Quarterly* (Spring 1977), p. 157.
19. As quoted by Grady Boque in "The Hazards of Mediocrity," *Vital Speeches* (December 15, 1979), p. 148.
20. William Greider, "Equality in the world of the sociologists: What of inheritance?" Louisville, Ky. *Courier-Journal* (September 30, 1979), © The Washington Post, 1979.
21. Nachmias, *op. cit.*, p. 14.
22. Stuart Nagel, "Policy Studies Across the Social Sciences: A Bibliographic Memo," *Policy Studies Journal* (Spring 1979), p. 622.
23. Moynihan, *op. cit.*, p. 19.
24. George W. Bohmam, "Social Science and Social Practice," *Change* (Jan. 1980), p. 12.
25. Charles E. Lindblom and David Cohen, *Usable Knowledge: Social Science and Social Problem Solving* (New Haven: Yale University Press, 1979), p. 12.
26. *Ibid.*, p. 4.
27. National Academy of Sciences, Study on Capital Punishment, as quoted by Moynihan, *op. cit.*, p. 18.
28. Aaron Wildavsky, *Speaking Truth to Power: The Art and Craft of Policy Analysis* (Boston: Little, Brown and Co., 1979), p. 231.
29. Grover Starling, *The Politics and Economics of Public Policy* (Homewood, Ill.: Dorsey Press, 1979), p. ix.
30. Edwin A. Roberts, "What the 'New Class' Doesn't Know," *The National Observer* (February 10, 1973).
31. Bonham, *op. cit.*, p. 12.
32. Henry J. Aaron, *Politics and the Professors: The Great Society in Perspective* (Washington, D.C.: The Brookings Institution, 1978), p. 156.
33. Moynihan, *op. cit.*, p. 21.
34. Robert Reinhold, "Guaranteed income? It's no warranty of happiness," Louisville, Ky., *Courier-Journal* (February 11, 1979), © 1979 The New York Times Company. Reprinted by permission.
35. Lindblom and Cohen, *op. cit.*, pp. 86–88.
36. Joseph Schumpeter, *Capitalism, Socialism and Democracy*, 3rd ed. (New York: Harper & Row, 1950), p. 262.
37. Robert A. Dahl, *Congress and Foreign Policy* (New York: Norton, 1950), p. 82.
38. Wolanin, *op. cit.*, p. 382.
39. Halperin, *op. cit.*, p. 399.

## Suggestions for Further Reading

ABT, CLARK C., ed. *The Evaluation of Social Programs.* Beverly Hills: Sage, 1976.
ARCHIBALD, K. A. "Three Views on the Expert's Role in Policymaking: Systems Analysis,

Incrementalism, and the Clinical Approach,'' *Policy Sciences* 1 (Spring 1970), pp. 73–86.
BATEMAN, WORTH. "Assessing Program Effectiveness: A Rating System for Identifying Relative Project Success," *Welfare in Review* 6 (January/February 1968), pp. 1–10.
COHEN, DAVID. "Politics and Research: Evaluation of Social Action Programs in Education," *Review of Educational Research* 40 (April 1970), pp. 213–38.
COOK, THOMAS J. and SCIOLI, FRANK P. *Methodologies for Analyzing Public Policies.* Lexington, Mass.: Lexington Books, 1975.
DOLBEARE, KENNETH, ed. *Public Policy Evaluation.* Beverly Hills: Sage, 1975.
FERMAN, LOUIS A., ed. "Evaluating the War on Poverty," *Annals of the American Academy of Political and Social Science* 385 (September 1969), entire issue.
FRANKLIN, JACK L. and THRASHER, JEAN H. *An Introduction to Program Evaluation.* New York: Wiley-Interscience, 1976.
FREEMAN, HOWARD E. and SHERWOOD, CLARENCE C. *Social Research and Social Policy.* Englewood Cliffs, N.J.: Prentice-Hall, 1970.
GLASER, DANIEL. *Routinizing Evaluation: Getting Feedback on Effectiveness of Crime and Delinquency Programs.* Washington, D. C.: Center for Studies of Crime and Delinquency, National Institute of Mental Health, 1974.
HATRY, HARRY; WINNIE, RICHARD E.; and FISH, DONALD M. *Practical Program Evaluation for State and Local Government Officials.* Washington, D.C.: Urban Institute, 1973.
HAVEMAN, ROBERT H., and MARGOLIS, JULIUS, eds. *Public Expenditure and Policy Analysis*, 2nd ed., Chicago: Rand McNally, 1977.
HINRICHS, HARLEY and TAYLOR, GRAEME M. *Systematic Analysis: A Primer on Benefit-Cost Analysis and Program Evaluation.* Pacific Palisades, Calif.: Goodyear, 1972.
HOLZER, MARC, ed. *Productivity in Public Organizations.* Port Washington, N. Y.: Kennikat, 1976.
LEWIS, FRANK L. and ZARB, FRANK G. "Federal Program Evaluation from the OMB Perspective," *Public Administration Review* 34 (July/August 1974), pp. 308–17.
LYONS, GENE M., ed. *Social Research and Public Policies.* Hanover, N.H.: University Press of New England, 1975.
MACRAE, DUNCAN, JR. "Policy Analysis as an Applied Social Science Discipline," *Administration and Society* 6 (February 1975), pp. 363–88.
MARVIN, KEITH E. and HEDRICK, JAMES L. "GAO Helps Congress Evaluate Programs," *Public Administration Review* 34 (July/August), 327–33.
MOREHOUSE, THOMAS A. "Program Evaluation: Social Research Versus Public Policy," *Public Administration Review* 32 (November/December 1972), pp. 868–74.
PRESSMAN, JEFFREY L. and WILDAVSKY, AARON. *Implementation: How Great Expectations in Washington Are Dashed in Oakland, or, Why It's Amazing that Federal Programs Work at All.* Berkeley: University of California Press, 1973.
RIVLIN, ALICE M. *Systematic Thinking for Social Action.* Washington, D. C.: The Brookings Institution, 1971.
SCHUMACHER, E. F. *Small Is Beautiful: Economics As If People Mattered.* New York: Harper & Row, 1973. (Particularly part II, chap. 2.)
STAATS, ELMER. "The Challenge of Evaluating Federal Social Programs," *Evaluation* 1, no. 3 (1973), pp. 50–54.
WALKER, ROBERT A. "The Ninth Panacea: Program Evaluation," *Evaluation* 1, no. 1 (1972), pp. 45–53.
WHOLEY, JOSEPH and WHILE, BAYLA. "Evaluation's Impact on Title I Elementary and Secondary Education Program Management," *Evaluation* 1, no. 3 (1973), pp. 73–76.
WILDAVSKY, AARON. *Speaking Truth to Power: The Art and Craft of Policy Analysis.* Boston: Little, Brown and Co., 1979.

# Index

Aaron, Henry, 395
Acid rain, 321
Adams, Brock, 173, 182
*Addyston Pipe Co.* v. *U.S.*, 254
Afghanistan, 145, 148, 152, 156, 222
AFL-CIO, 38, 204, 205, 275, 276, 285, 287-91, 298, 334, 336, 369
Agency for International Development (AID), 71, 107, 118-19, 136
Agricultural Adjustment Act, 214, 217
Agriculture, Committees on, 230-31
Agriculture, Department of, 8, 213, 215, 218, 220, 222-23, 229-30, 297
Aid for Dependent Children (AFDC), 364
Airlines, 178-79
Air Transport Association, 181
Alaska Lands Bill, 298
American Agricultural Movement, 212, 213, 221-22, 228, 229
American Enterprise Institute, 4, 38
American Farm Bureau Federation, 38, 204, 216, 227, 229, 369
American Federation of Teachers, 203, 205, 207
American Medical Association, 38, 369, 370
American Trucking Association, 181, 183, 265
American Waterways Operators, 181
Americans for Democratic Action, 38, 204, 334, 369
Amtrak, 168, 172-74
Andrus, Cecil, 298
Antiquities Act (1906), 294, 296, 298
Anti-trust Division, 180, 244, 252, 265
Anti-trust Improvements Act, 251, 257
Apportionments, 59
Appropriations bill, 67
Appropriations, Committee on, 59, 64-66
Armed Forces Policy Council, 135
Armed Services, Committees on, 139, 153
Army Corps of Engineers, 8, 179, 184, 300, 302
Arnold, Thurman, 265
Articles of Confederation, 47, 132
Aspin, Les, 144, 154
Association of American Railroads, 181, 183
Atomic Energy Act (1946), 294, 309
*Austin Independent School District* v. *U.S.*, 341-42
Authorization bill, 67

Backdoor spending, 71
Baker, Howard, 122, 301
*Bakke* case, 346-47, 350
Barden, Graham, 196
Bauer, Raymond A., 14
Benson, Ezra Taft, 218
Bentson, Lloyd, 156
Berger, Warren, 340
Bergland, Bob, 221-22, 230
Berle, A.A., Jr., 265
Bicameralism, 26
Bingham, Eula, 261
Black Caucus, 28
Black, Hugo, 250
Blanchard, James, 377

Bok, Derek, 39
Bolling, Richard, 376
Bonham, George, 393, 395
Boyer, Ernest, 388
Brademas, John, 65
Brennan, William, 346
Brookings Institution, 4, 38
Brown, Clarence, 206
Brown, Harold, 145, 149
Brown, Sam, 66
*Brown Shoe Co.* v. *U.S.*, 257
*Brown* v. *Board of Education*, 197-98, 334, 339, 342, 344, 356, 387
Brzezinski, Zbigniew, 115
Budget and Accounting Act, 51, 54, 69
Budget reform, 73-75
Bumpers, Dale, 68
Bureaucracy, 33-37
Business Roundtable, the, 259, 291
Busing, 199-200, 340-43
Byrd, Robert, 309

Calhoun, John C., 164
Califano, Joseph, 200, 205, 206, 345, 366, 370
Cambodia, 22
Cappiello, Frank, 22
Carter, Jimmy, 15, 29, 30-31, 32, 36-37, 52, 57, 68, 95, 97, 99, 105, 110, 111, 127, 128, 145, 146, 147, 151, 154-55, 156-57, 173, 178, 182, 200, 204-5, 220, 226, 229, 235, 243, 246, 263, 268-69, 293, 298, 299, 302-3, 304, 306-7, 308, 310, 312, 313, 321, 328, 354-55, 371, 377, 379
Carter, Rosalyn, 58
Celler-Kefauver Act, 251, 256-57
Central Intelligence Agency (CIA), 22, 36, 71, 107, 115-17, 136
Chaffee, John, 318
Chamber of Commerce, U.S., 38, 204, 260, 280, 286, 369
Checks and balances, 23, 24-25, 48, 51, 110
Chiefs of Staff, Joint, 135, 136, 141, 152
Civil Aeronautics Board, 168, 178, 242, 264
Civil Rights Act (1957), 331, 335; (1960), 331, 335; (1964), 198, 201, 331, 335-36, 340, 352; (1965), 331, 337; (1968), 3, 331, 338
*Civil Rights Cases*, 332
Civil Rights, Commission on, 332, 335, 342
Clay, Henry, 164
Claybrook, Joan, 261
Clayton Act, 251, 255-56, 276, 277
Clean Air Act, 242, 294, 315, 320
Cleveland, Grover, 275, 360
Closed shop, 282, 283
*Cochran* v. *Board of Educ.*, 195
Cohen, David, 393, 396
Cold War, 131, 133, 145, 147, 148
Coleman, James, 200, 206, 340, 341, 387
Commerce Clause, 32, 333, 336
Commerce, Dept. of, 15, 33, 252
Common Cause, 38, 264
Comptroller general, 69
Conglomerates, 266, 267-69

Congress of Racial Equality, 334
Congress Watch, 38, 231, 246
Congressional Budget Committees, 64
Congressional Budget and Impoundment Control Act, 51, 59, 64, 70-71
Congressional Budget Office, 52, 64, 366, 370, 388
Congressional oversight, 69-73
Conquest, Robert, 391-92
ConRail, 168, 174-75
Consumer Product Safety Commission, 242, 244, 252
Consumers Union, 38
Containment, 125
Cooley Doctrine, 252, 273n
Coolidge, Calvin, 216, 291
COPE, 283
Costle, Douglas, 321, 323
Council of Economic Advisors, 52, 81, 85, 244, 309
Council on Environmental Quality, 246, 297, 317, 319, 320
Courts, role in policymaking, 22, 32-33
Cranston, Alan, 27
Cruise missile, 146

Dahl, Robert, 108, 119, 397
Davis-Bacon Act, 277, 278, 287
Dawson, Richard, 20
Defense, Dept. of, 135, 154
Defense Intelligence Agency (DIA), 115-16, 135
Deferral, 70
*DeFunis* v. *Odegaard,* 345-46
de Gaulle, Charles, 43
Democratic Study Group (DGS), 259, 336
Depletion allowance, 160, 307
Deregulation, 182-83, 244, 263-65, 306-7
Derthick, Martha, 367
Desegregation, 197-200, 328, 339-45
Deterrence, 143-44, 145
de Tocqueville, Alexis, 32, 38, 120
*DiLeo* v. *Board of Regents*, 347
*Dred Scott* decision, 331
Dulles, John Foster, 103, 114
Dye, Thomas, vii, 2, 23, 92, 384

Eagleton, Thomas, 152
Eastland, James, 336
*E.C. Knight* case, 254
Economic Opportunity Act, 34, 375
Education, Dept. of, 188, 189, 190, 204, 206
Eighty-day-cooling-off period, 282, 283
Eisenhower, Dwight, 25, 82, 114, 140, 144, 150, 151, 192, 218, 260, 284, 306, 334
Eizenstat, Stuart, 15
Elementary and Secondary Education Act of 1965 (ESEA), 189, 198, 201-203, 207
Elite theory, 7
Ellender, Allen, 71
Employment Act of 1946, 80, 81-82
Endangered Species Act (1973), 295, 300-1, 316, 320
Energy, 178, 304-15
*Engle* v. *Vitale*, 195
Engman, Lewis, 243
Environmental Protection Agency (EPA), 17, 75, 240, 242, 245, 297, 315, 316-18, 319, 320-21, 323

Equal Employment Opportunity Commission (EEOC), 242, 332, 338
Equal Rights Amendment (ERA), 3, 21, 353-54
Ervin, Sam, 353
Etzioni, Amitai, 386
Eulau, Heinz, 4
*Everson* v. *Board of Education*, 195
Eyestone, Robert, 2

Fair Labor Standards Act, 277, 279, 352
Fairlie, Henry, 42-43
Farm bloc, 213, 216
Farm Bureau. *See* American Farm Bureau Federation
Farmers Home Administration, 215, 226-27
Federal Aviation Administration (FAA), 161
Federal Bureau of Investigation (FBI), 22, 36, 66, 115, 135
Federal Communications Commission (FCC), 242, 267
Federal Election Commission (FEC), 258-59
Federal Farm Board, 216
Federal Mediation and Conciliation Service, 278, 282
Federal Power Commission (FPC), 306
Federal Reserve Act, 80
Federal Reserve Board, 81, 85, 86-88
Federal Trade Commission (FTC), 17, 244, 252, 255-57, 266-68, 270-71
Federalism, 23-24
Federalist, the, 23, 38, 68, 360
Federation of Independent Businessmen, 258
Fenno, Richard, 65
Fenwick, Millicent, 264
Field Foundation, 373
Finance, Committee on, 48, 89-90
First Amendment, 155, 194-96
Fiscal policy, 85, 88-89
Fisher, Louis, 73
Fogarty, John E., 369
Food and Drug Administration, 17, 242, 297, 317
Food Stamp program, 231, 362, 373-74
Ford, Gerald, 10, 25, 70, 105, 126, 220, 319
Ford, Henry, II, 261
Foreign aid, 118-19
Foreign Relations, Committee on, 109
Foreign Service, the, 107, 117-18
Fourteenth Amendment, 32, 194, 330, 332, 336, 339-40, 345, 346
Freedman, Leonard, 67
Freeman, S. David, 308
Friedman, Milton, 97
Fulbright, William, 109

Galbraith, John K., 268
Gans, Curtis, 42
"Garrison state," 142-43
Gaus, John M., 80
General Accounting Office, 52, 69-70, 152, 185, 229, 287, 302, 317, 318, 388
Gergen, Kenneth, 14
Giaimo, Robert, 97
*Gibbons* v. *Ogden*, 164-65, 299
GI Bill, 189, 190, 191, 197
*Gideon* v. *Wainright*, 355
Glazer, Nathan, 386
Goldschmidt, Neil, 182

## 404  INDEX

Gompers, Samuel, 276
Grange, the National, 216, 227, 298, 369
Grassley, Charles, 223
Gravel, Mike, 298, 302
Gray power, 21
Great Depression, 27, 48, 80, 216, 278, 361, 362, 376
Greenbackers, 213
Greider, William, 392
*Griffin* v. *Prince Edward County*, 340
Griffith, Ernest, 8
Gross National Product, 52, 84, 100, 150-51, 370
Group theory, 5
*Guss* v. *Utah*, 285

Haig, Alexander, 141
Halperin, Samuel, 387-88, 399
Hamilton, Alexander, 47-48
Hamilton, Edith, 356
Harding, Warren G., 80, 114, 361
Harrington, Michael, 373
Harris, Patricia, 15, 58, 206
Hart, Phillip, 269, 271
Hartley, Fred, 280
Harvey, Paul, 262, 267
Hatfield, Mark, 139
Hatch Act (1887), 214
Hatch, Orrin, 286
Hays, Wayne, 22
Health and Human Services, Dept. of, 53, 58, 191, 204, 363, 370
Health insurance, 369, 370-72
Hebert, Edward, 154
Heclo, Hugh, 3
HEW. *See* Health and Human Services.
Higher Education Act (1965), 189
Highway Trust Fund, 167, 174, 177, 178, 181, 183
Hill-Burton Act, 362, 369
Hill, Lister, 369
Hillman, Sidney, 287
Hoffa, Jimmy, 284
Homestead Act, 213, 293, 296
Hoover, Herbert, 216, 361, 375
Hoover, J. Edgar, 66
Howard, James J., 184
Housing and Urban Development, Dept. of, 15, 58, 387
Hubbard, Carroll, 260
Hufstedler, Shirley, 206
Hughes, Charles Evans, 253, 278
Hughes-Ryan Amendment, 117
Human Resources, Committee on, 287
Hutchins, Robert, 392

Impacted areas aid, 68
Impoundment, 70-71
Income tax, 90-91
Incremental theory, 10-11
Inflation, 82-83
Institutional theory, 12
Integration. *See* Desegregation
Interest groups, 38-40, 123-24, 227-30, 248, 258-60, 297-98, 310, 322-23, 333-34
Interior, Dept. of, 66-67, 297, 320
Internal Revenue Service, 81
International Communications Agency (ICA), 107, 119, 136

Interstate Commerce Act, 14, 32, 169, 241, 252
Interstate Commerce Commission, 168, 169, 182, 183, 241, 242, 243-44, 253, 264, 265
Isolationism, 102-03

Jackson, Andrew, 165
Jackson, Henry, 323
Jackson, Jesse, 356
Jackson, Robert, 241
Jefferson, Thomas, 69, 112, 187, 195, 212
Johnson, James, 71, 161
Johnson, Lyndon, 31, 35, 55, 98, 114, 147, 179-80, 201, 323, 336, 337, 338, 375
Johnson, Nicholas, 180
Johnston, Bennett, Jr., 29
Jones, David C., 142
Justice, Dept. of, 332, 335

Kahn, Alfred, 264
Katzenbach, Nicholas, 133
Kemp-Roth, 96-97
Kennan, George, 125
Kennedy, John F., 16, 114, 144, 156-57, 179, 184, 197, 219, 263, 335, 352
Kennedy, Ted, 183, 244, 264, 371-72
Kerner Commission, 339, 356
Kerr-Mills Act, 362, 370
*Keyes* v. *School District #1*, 199, 341
Keynes, John M., 48, 81, 386
Kilpatrick, James J., 239, 247, 262, 286
King, Martin Luther, 334, 338, 356
King, Susan B., 272
Kirkland, Lane, 288, 289, 291
Kissinger, Henry, 103, 105, 111, 114, 115, 126, 127, 147
Knights of Labor, 275
Kosygin, Alexei, 156

Labor, Dept. of, 75, 278, 285, 375
Laffer curve, the, 96
LaGuardia, Fiorello, 276
Land grant colleges. *See* Morrill Act
Landrum-Griffin Act, 277, 284-85, 291
Lanham Act, 189-90
Lasswell, Harold, 50, 142, 327
Leadership Conference on Civil Rights, 334, 336
Leath, Marvin, 221
Legislative Reorganization Act (1946), 51
Legislative veto, 29, 110, 134
Lewis, John L., 287
Lind, William, 153
Lindblom, Charles E., 10, 394, 396
Long, Russell, 180
Lowi, Theodore, 13, 47, 213

MacArthur, Douglas, 141
Madison, James, 23, 38, 68, 164, 360
Magnuson, Warren, 336
Mahon, George, 57, 70, 140
Management policy, 13, 47-49
Mann, Horace, 188
Marshall, John, 164-65
Marshall, Ray, 286
Mass transit, 167, 177-78, 183-84, 314
McClellan, John, 284
McCormick, Cyrus, 212
*McCullom* v. *Board of Education*, 195
McGovern, George, 147
McIntyre, James, 15, 58, 73

McNamara, Pat, 284
McNamara, Robert, 74, 147, 154
McNary-Haugen bills, 216
Meany, George, 284, 285, 289, 291
Medicare, 365, 367, 370, 372
Mergers, 265-69
Meyers, John, 221
Michel, Robert, 66
Mikoyan, Vladimir, 147
Miles, Jerome, 77
Miller-Tydings Act, 251, 257
Mills, C. Wright, 7
Mills, Wilbur, 22
Mineta, Norman, 377
Mining Enforcement and Safety Administration, 269
Mitchell, John, 200
Mitchell, Parren, 377
Mondale, Walter, 30, 150
Monetary policy, 86-88
Monroe, James, 164
Morrill Act, 188, 189, 214, 296
Moynihan, Daniel, 200, 386, 387, 393, 395
Multinational corporations, 38, 123
*Munn* v. *Illinois*, 241, 248n, 252
Muskie, Edmund, 64, 72, 319
MX Missile, 149

NAACP, 197, 204, 333-34, 339
Nachmias, David, 388, 391, 392
Nader, Ralph, 179
Nagel, Stuart, 393
NASA, 135
Natcher, William, 66, 161, 231
National Association of Broadcasters (NAB), 17, 270, 271
National Association of Manufacturers (NAM), 38, 204, 258, 280, 283
National Defense Education Act, 189, 191, 197, 207
National Education Association (NEA), 196, 203, 205, 207
National Environmental Policy Act, 295, 315
National Farmers Organization, 228, 229
National Farmers Union, 204, 227, 229, 369
National Institutes of Health, 363, 368
National Labor Relations Act. *See* Wagner Act
National Labor Relations Board, 278, 279, 281, 285, 286, 290
National Mediation Board, 278
National Rivers and Harbors Congress, 8
National Science Foundation, 190, 191
National Security Act (1947), 106, 134, 136, 141
National Security Agency (NSA), 107, 115-16
National Security Council, 107, 114-15, 134, 136, 141
National Urban League, 334
National Wilderness Act, 294, 298
National Gas Act (1938), 306
Nedzi, Lucien, 71
Nelson, Gaylord, 223, 302
Neutron bomb, 139, 145, 146
New Deal, 16, 80, 216, 240, 363
New economics, 81, 95
Nixon, Richard, 57, 64, 70, 103, 114, 127-28, 147, 200, 202, 302, 313, 315, 338, 376
Norris, George, 276

Norris-LaGuardia Act, 227, 278
Northwest Ordinance, 187
*Northern Securities* Case, 254
Nuclear power, 309-12
Nuclear Regulatory Commission, 135, 136, 297, 310, 311

Obey, David, 259
Occupational Safety and Health Administration (OSHA), 17, 242, 246, 297
Office of Economic Opportunity, 34-36, 375
Office of Management and Budget, 15, 52, 57-59, 244, 388, 389
Office of Surface Mining and Reclamation Enforcement, 297, 308
Office of Technology Assessment, 297, 388
Okun, Arthur, 246
Old Age Assistance, 363, 364
O'Neill, Thomas "Tip," 26, 260, 314-15
Open Market Committee, 87

Paarlberg, Don, 225, 231
PACs, 258
Panama Canal Treaty, 42, 122, 124
Parity, 212, 217-18, 237n
PCBs, 262, 318
Peace Corps, 106, 107, 119
Penn Central Railroad, 170-72
Perkins, Carl, 308, 377
Pertshuk, Michael, 270
Peyser, Peter, 221
Pincus, Walter, 143
*Plessy* v. *Ferguson*, 197, 332, 339ff
Pluralist theory, 5-7
Poage, Bob, 224, 229-30, 231
Policy analysis, 383-99
Policy committees, 37
Policy Studies Organization, 385
Political parties, 22, 36-37, 41, 44, 121-23
Populists, 213, 240, 251
Powell, Adam Clayton, 198
Powell, Lewis, 341-42
PPBS, 74
Progressives, 240, 251, 296
Proxmire, William, 69, 71
Public Health Service, 363, 370

Quade, E.S., 391

Railsback, Thomas, 259
Railway Labor Act (1926), 277, 278
Rangel, Charles, 206
Rasmussen Report, 310-11
Rational-Comprehensive theory, 9-10
Redford, Emmette, 50, 80-81, 263
Redistributive policy, 14, 327-29
Reed-Bullwinkel Act, 167, 183, 264
*Reed* v. *Reed,* 352
Regulatory Analysis Review Group, 319
Regulatory policy, 14, 239-48
Rescission, 70
Reserve requirement, 86-87
Reston, James, 31
Ribicoff, Abraham, 156
Richmond, Frederick, 271
Right-to-work laws, 282, 283
Rivlin, Alice, 366
Roberts, Edwin, 395
Robinson-Patman Act, 251, 257

# 406 INDEX

Rockefeller, Nelson, 126
*Roemer* v. *Maryland*, 196
Rogers Act, 106
Roosevelt, Franklin D., 43, 276, 334, 362, 368
Roosevelt, Theodore, 30, 103, 296
Rose, Charles, 247
Russell, Bertrand, 143

Sagebrush Rebellion, 299
SALT I, 148; SALT II, 42, 148, 156-57
*San Antonio* v. *Rodriguez*, 194
Schick, Allen, 74
Schelling, Thomas, 150
Schlesinger, James, 143, 148, 151, 296, 310
Schuck, Peter, 243
Schultze, Charles, 96, 99, 141, 247
Schumpeter, Joseph, 397
Secretary of state, 112-14
Securities and Exchange Commission, 244
Segregation. *See* Desegregation
Separation of powers, 23, 24, 33, 48, 51, 110
*Serrano* v. *Priest*, 193-94
Sharkansky, Ira, 76
Sherman Act, 14, 32, 241, 251, 253-55, 277
Sierra Club, 38, 298, 318
Singlaub, John, 142
Sixteenth Amendment, 80
*Slaughterhouse* Cases, 332
Small Business Administration, 226, 286
Smith, Adam, 48, 49n, 100n, 239
Smith-Connally Act, 280
Smith-Hughes Act, 188-189
Smith-Lever Act, 214
Snail darter, 300
Social Darwinism. *See* Spencer, Herbert
Social Security Act, 280, 362-63, 364-68
Soil bank, 214, 218-19
Soil Conservation Service, 214, 217
Solar energy, 313, 314
Southern Christian Leadership Conference, 334, 373
Soviet Union, 143, 144, 145, 147, 156-57
Spellman, Francis Cardinal, 196
Spencer, Herbert, 48, 49n
Spitzer, Robert, 31
Stagflation, 83, 84
Staggers, Harley, 173
*Standard Oil* case, 254
Starling, Grover, 394
State, Dept. of, 107, 112-14
Stennis, John, 302
Stevens, Ted, 298
Stewart, Potter, 388
Sub-government theory, 8-9
Subsidy policy, 13, 159-62, 328
Sumner, William G., 48, 49n
*Sun Oil* case, 258-59
Supplemental security income, 365
Supreme Court, 141, 194-96, 197-99, 217, 230, 241, 252, 254, 279, 301, 328, 333, 334, 339-41, 346-47
Surface Mining Control and Reclamation Act, 296, 308-9
Survey Ordinance, 187, 189, 296
*Swann* v. *Board of Education*, 199, 340
Symington, Stuart, 153
Synfuels, 308, 314, 315, 320
Systems theory, 12

Taft, Robert H., 190, 280, 369
Taft-Hartley Act, 231, 277, 280-85, 291
Taney, Roger, 250
Tax reform, 93-97
Taylor Grazing Act, 294, 298
Teamsters Union, 163, 181, 183, 204, 265, 284
Tellico Dam, 300-1
Tennessee-Tombigbee Waterway, 69, 301-2
Tennessee Valley Authority (TVA), 299, 300-1
Thomas, Norman, 33
Three Mile Island, 311
Thurmond, Strom, 336
Tonkin, Gulf of, 132, 134
Townsend Plan, 361
Toxic Substances Control Act (1976), 296, 316, 317
Transportation, Dept. of, 168, 180, 185-86
Treasury, Dept. of, 81, 85, 86
Truman, Harry, 25, 114, 141, 184, 191, 280, 306, 334, 369

Udall, Morris, 28, 310
Unemployment, 80, 82, 349-50
Unemployment insurance, 364
Union shop, 282
Ustinov, Dmitry, 147

Vance, Cyrus, 115
Vietnam, 22, 32, 55, 104, 109, 110, 122, 126, 144
Volunteer army, 151

*Wabash, St. Louis and Pacific Railway* v. *Illinois*, 241, 248n, 252
Wagner Act, 277, 279-90, 285, 286, 291
Wagner, Robert, 276
Wallop, Malcolm, 286
Walsh-Healey Act, 277, 279
War on Poverty, 34, 55, 375-76
War Powers Act, 110, 133, 134
Warnke, Paul, 149, 150
Warren, Earl, 339
Washington, George, 47, 143, 275
Water carriers, 179-80
Watergate, 22, 31, 110, 114
*Watson* v. *City of Memphis*, 340
Wattenberg, Ben, 44, 348
Ways and Means, Committee on, 48, 89-90, 378
*Weber* case, 351
Weidenbaum, Murray, 246
Weinberger, Caspar, 338
Weston, J. Fred, 268
Whitten, Jamie, 66, 161, 230, 231
Will, George, 159
Wildavsky, Aaron, 31, 76, 394-95
Wilson, Woodrow, 25, 27, 30, 103, 106, 107-8, 131, 169, 255, 276
Windfall Profits Tax, 306, 314, 315
*Witherspoon* v. *Illinois*, 388
Wolanin, Thomas, 398
Women's Movement. *See* ERA
World War II, 103, 136, 138, 155

Yellow dog contract, 276
Yellowstone National Park, 296, 313
Yergin, Daniel, 311, 314

Zero-based budgeting, 74
*Zorach* v. *Clauson*, 195
Zwick, Charles, 153